COBOL

Jean Longhurst

Harper College, Palatine, IL

Audrey Longhurst

Motorola, Inc.

PRENTICE HALL Englewood Cliffs, New Jersey 07632

Library of Congress Cataloging-in-Publication Data

Longhurst, Jean.
COBOL.

Includes index.
1. COBOL (Computer program language) I. Longhurst, Audrey. II. Title.
QA76.73.C25L66 1988 005.13'3 87-35683
ISBN 0-13-139387-1

Editorial/production supervision: Allison DeFren and Arthur Maisel
Interior design: Jayne Conte and Maureen Eide
Cover design: Maureen Eide
Manufacturing buyers: Barbara Kittle and Lorraine Fumoso
Page layout: Karen Noferi

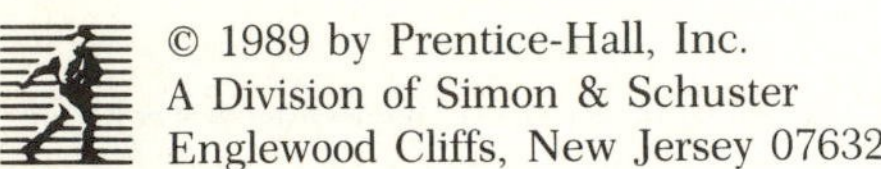

A Division of Simon & Schuster
Englewood Cliffs, New Jersey 07632

Printed in the United States of America

10 9 8 7 6 5 4 3 2 1

ISBN 0-13-139387-1 01

Prentice-Hall International (UK) Limited, *London*
Prentice-Hall of Australia Pty. Limited, *Sydney*
Prentice-Hall Canada Inc., *Toronto*
Prentice-Hall Hispanoamericano, S.A., *Mexico*
Prentice-Hall of India Private Limited, *New Delhi*
Prentice-Hall of Japan, Inc., *Tokyo*
Prentice-Hall of Southeast Asia Pte. Ltd., *Singapore*
Editora Prentice-Hall do Brasil, Ltda., *Rio de Janeiro*

BRIEF CONTENTS

Contents

Preface

Three of the most troublesome topics for beginning COBOL students are programming logic, debugging, and tables. This text attempts to deal more fully with these topics.

The text is built around one business system, an order system. Our objective is to allow the student to become so familiar with the files used they can concentrate on the COBOL instead of a variety of record descriptions. Using a variety of program design tools, the system builds from simple listings through extracts, control breaks, table handling, edits, updates, and sorts.

Debugging is emphasized from diagnostics to data exceptions. For the more common diagnostics a list of items the student should check is provided. For data exceptions and usage emphasis on IBM storage types is used. The use of trace and display are encouraged for solving logic problems.

There never seems to be enough material in a text about tables to satisfy a beginning student. We have tried to include more information about structure, loading, accessing, and printing tables with the hope the student will be able to find an example that fits the current problem they are trying to program.

Material on the 1985 standard is included as the associated topic is covered. It is, however, differentiated so it can be used or not based on its availability.

We wish to thank the following, who reviewed the manuscript of this book: Gail L. Kroepel, DeVry Institute of Technology (Chicago); J. Patrick Fenton, West Valley College (Saratoga, California); Henry J. Walker, State University of New York at Farmingdale; Rose M. Laird, Northern Virginia Community College (Annandale); Barbara Harris, DeVry Institute of Technology (Chicago); Ron Teemley, DeVry Institute of Technology (Irving, Texas); Beverly Bilshausen, College of DuPage (Glen Ellyn, Illinois); Lou R. Goodman, University of Wisconsin-Madison; and E. Gladys Norman, Linn-Benton Community College (Albany, Oregon). We also want to thank members of the staff at Prentice Hall: Dennis Hogan, editor; Jayne Conte and Maureen Eide, designers; and Allison DeFren and Arthur Maisel, production editors.

Jean Longhurst
Audrey Longhurst

CHAPTER

1 Introduction to Programming in COBOL

This chapter presents introductory material which is necessary to begin learning the COBOL programming language. It includes an introduction to COBOL, program development, data organization, and COBOL topics.

The introduction to COBOL covers the history and characteristics of COBOL.

Program development is the process by which programs are created. Coverage of program development includes the development process, analysis tools and techniques, structured programming, and design tools.

Data organization involves the storage of data on files, including a description of the files, access methods, storage media, physical considerations, and file description techniques.

Included among COBOL topics are basic information about COBOL, the compilation process, and an overview of the COBOL language.

INTRODUCTION TO COBOL

The History of COBOL

The development of COBOL began in 1959 with the creation of the Conference on Data System Languages (CODASYL). CODASYL was created because of a need for a common programming language for use in business applications. CODASYL's objective was to create a language which would not be the property of any particular computer manufacturer, yet could be adopted by a wide range of manufacturers. In 1960 CODASYL published a document which described its newly developed language, COBOL. (COBOL is an acronym for Common Business Oriented Language.)

In 1968 the first standard version of COBOL was approved (USA Standard COBOL 1968). The 1968 standard was revised and updated, and in 1974 a new standard was approved (American National Standard COBOL 1974). In 1985 there was another revision, and a new standard was approved (American National Standard COBOL 1985). It is this revision process which keeps the COBOL language current.

Characteristics of COBOL

COBOL is an English-like programming language. It uses English words and relatively few symbols. Because of this, it is a very readable language. To an extent, nonprogrammers can read and understand a COBOL program. This also allows a COBOL program to be self-documenting. It is usually a simple matter to determine the function of a COBOL program from an examination of the program itself. Therefore, a COBOL program requires little additional documentation.

COBOL is a business-oriented language and has extensive data and file-handling capabilities. COBOL's ability to manipulate data makes it a good language for dealing with the vast amounts of data which businesses process. COBOL's ability to handle numbers is not as strong. Where extensive and complex calculations are required, as in scientific applications, there are other languages which are better suited to the task.

PROGRAM DEVELOPMENT

The Development Process

In creating a computer program, the development process is the same regardless of which programming language is used. The development process may be divided into the phases of (1) analysis, (2) design, (3) coding, and (4) testing. Depending on the size and complexity of the programming project, a different person (or group of people) might be responsible for each of the phases, or one person might complete the entire process alone.

Analysis

The development process begins with a problem to be solved. The analyst meets with the people who have requested a computerized solution to their problem to determine their requirements. He or she then analyzes the current existing and computerized systems that relate to the problem. With this information, the analyst determines the input, output, and processing requirements for the program. In general, the analyst will produce documents which describe these requirements. These documents usually include program specifications, input layouts, output layouts, and system flowcharts. These documents are described later in this chapter.

Design

The designer begins with the information gathered during the analysis phase and develops the logic which will be used to solve the problem. The processing requirements are divided into smaller and smaller pieces until the logical flow is described for the entire program.

Several design tools are available which are useful for describing program logic. These tools include flowcharts, pseudocode, Warnier-Orr diagrams, Nassi-Schneiderman charts, Chapin charts, hierarchy charts, and IPO diagrams. The tool used for design may be mandated by the institution; if not, it will depend upon the preferences of the designer.

Coding

Coding is the process of translating the logic design into programming language code. Each step of the logic must be converted into code which conforms to the rules of the language. In many programming languages, including COBOL, each piece of data used by the program must also be described. If the logic design is complete and comprehensive, coding will consist only of translating the design to fit the syntax of the programming language.

Testing

After a program is coded, it must be tested in order to discover and correct any errors that might have occurred during the analysis, design, and coding phases. Testing involves converting the program into machine language. In COBOL, a commercially available program (a COBOL compiler) is used to convert the program into machine language. A computer cannot run a program unless it is in machine language. Two types of errors may be uncovered during testing: syntax errors and errors causing incorrect output.

Syntax Errors

Syntax errors occur when the program code violates a rule of the programming language. A syntax error might be caused by a typographical error, a misspelling, or a misunderstanding of the rules of the language. For example, a syntax error would occur if the word MVOE were used instead of the word MOVE. It may not be possible to run a program that has syntax errors.

Errors Causing Incorrect Output

Once syntax errors have been removed from the program, the program is executed to determine whether it produces correct output. Test data must be carefully prepared to assure thorough testing of the program. All possible combinations of data, correct and incorrect, should be tested, and the output must be carefully examined to locate any errors which might be present. If the output is incorrect, the program is debugged. Debugging is the process of locating and removing program errors. Incorrect output may be caused by coding errors or by errors in the logic of the program.

Analysis Tools and Techniques

Analysis begins when a user group (such as the accounting or marketing department) approaches the data processing department and asks for assistance in obtaining information necessary to solve a business problem. The analyst then meets with the user group to determine its requirements and analyzes the systems (both manual and computerized) the group is currently working with. Then the analyst explores the options available to solve the problem and determines which option should be used. The analyst will usually put this solution into writing using program specifications, input/output layouts, and system flowcharts.

Program Specifications

A program specification is a document which is produced during the analysis phase. It describes the requirements of the program to be written and is used as the basis for designing, coding, and testing the program.

The contents of a program specification will vary greatly from installation to installation. Usually, a program specification will include the program name, program function, input and output file descriptions, processing requirements, and output requirements. For example, the order processing department might approach the data processing department with a request for a printed report which will list all orders. The analyst then determines the requirements for the report, determines that the needed data is available on an existing file, and produces the program specification shown in Figure 1–1.

The program specification consists of the following elements:

Program Name The program is given a name by which it will be recognized by the computer system. The program name is usually created using a set of naming standards which are in place at the installation.

Program Function The function and purpose of the program are described, in order to give an overview of the program.

File Descriptions Often, a program must use or create data which exists outside of the program. This data is stored in files. (Files are discussed in greater detail later in the chapter.) Each file which will be used in the program is described in the file description section. The description provides basic information about the file, including the name of the file and whether the file is used as input to the program or as output from the program.

Processing Requirements There are no processing requirements in the example of Figure 1–1. When included, however, processing requirements provide an overview of the logic needed in the program, including whatever manipulation of the data and mathematical formulas are necessary.

Output Requirements The content and format required for the output are described.

PROGRAM SPECIFICATION

Program Name: LISTING

Program Function:

The program will produce a printed listing of all orders from the ORDER FILE.

Input Files:

I. ORDER-FILE

INPUT DEVICE:	DISK
FILE ORGANIZATION:	SEQUENTIAL
RECORD LENGTH:	70 BYTES
FILE SEQUENCE:	ASCENDING ON BRANCH / SALES REP

Output Files:

I. PRINT-FILE

OUTPUT DEVICE:	PRINTER
RECORD LENGTH:	133 BYTES

Output Requirements:

Each record read from the order file should be printed on one line of the output report. All fields from the input record are to be included on the output.

The following are formatting requirements for the report:

1. The first page of the report should contain:
   (a) a main heading which includes the company name and report name.
   (b) column headings which describe the items which are printed underneath.
2. The detail lines should include all fields from the input.
3. The detail lines should be double spaced.
4. Do not include provisions for page overflow.

FIGURE 1–1

Input/Output Layouts

Input and output layouts are usually included with the program specification. They describe the data items which are or will be stored on the files. Layouts for the ORDER-FILE and PRINT-FILE of Figure 1–1 are shown in Figures 1–2 and 1–3. Input/output layouts are discussed in greater detail later in the chapter.

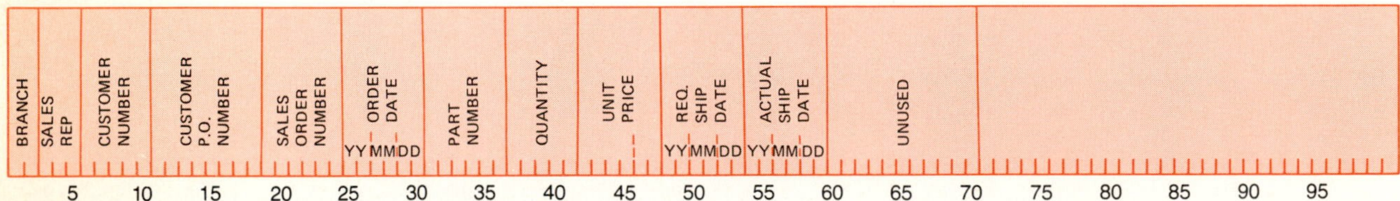

FIGURE 1–2

System Flowcharts

A system flowchart describing the flow of data through the system may be included with the program specification. Each symbol on the flowchart represents a file or

```
                                              PRODUCT DISTRIBUTION INC. - CURRENT ORDERS

             SALES   CUSTOMER     PURCHASE      SALES     ORDER         PART              UNIT      REQUESTED      ACTUAL
     BRANCH   REP     NUMBER       ORDER        ORDER     DATE         NUMBER  QUANTITY   PRICE     SHIP DATE     SHIP DATE

       99     999     99999     XXXXXXXX      XXXXXX     99-99-99     XXXXXX    99999    9999.99     99-99-99      99-99-99

       99     999     99999     XXXXXXXX      XXXXXX     99-99-99     XXXXXX    99999    9999.99     99-99-99      99-99-99
```

FIGURE 1–3

a program. Flowlines and arrows are used to show the relationships between the files and the programs. The following symbols are used in system flowcharting.

Process Symbol

This symbol indicates an entire program. In a system flowchart, the name of the program is written inside the box.

Magnetic Disk Symbol

This symbol is used to indicate a file which is or will be stored on magnetic disk. The name of the file is written inside the symbol.

Magnetic Tape Symbol

This symbol is used to indicate a file which is or will be stored on magnetic tape. The name of the file is written inside the symbol.

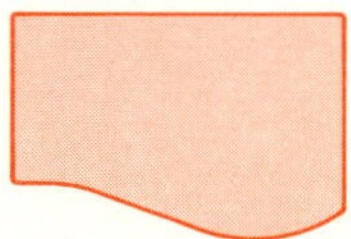

Document Symbol

This symbol indicates an output file which is a document (i.e., a printed report) or an input function where the input is obtained from a source document. The name of the document is written inside the symbol.

Flowlines

Flowlines are used to connect the symbols used in a system flowchart. The arrowhead indicates the direction of data flow.

Figure 1–4 shows the system flowchart for the LISTING program of Figure 1–1. A process symbol is used to represent the program. The program name, LISTING, is written inside this symbol. Flowlines are used to connect the input and output files to the program. The input file is stored on magnetic disk and is called the ORDER FILE. The document symbol is used for the output and indicates that the output is in printed form. The output file is called the CURRENT ORDER REPORT.

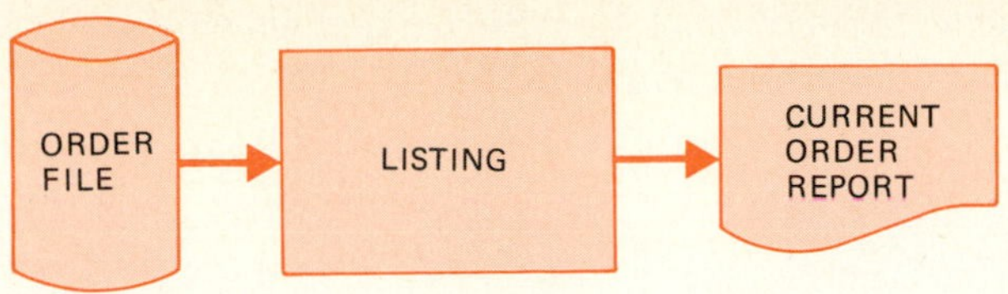

FIGURE 1–4

Structured Programming

Until the early 1970s, programming techniques were relatively unsophisticated. Programs written before then were generally not written using structured methodology. In an unstructured program, the flow of program logic is unrestricted. Consequently, the program logic of an unstructured program can become quite confusing and cumbersome. The larger an unstructured program is, the more difficult it is to decipher the logic. It may be exceedingly difficult to modify such a program or even to make it work correctly in the first place.

Structured programming places restrictions on the flow of logic. A structured program uses only three basic logic structures, each of which has only one entry point and one exit point. These structures are as follows.

Sequence A sequence structure consists of one or more instructions which are to be executed in sequence, one after another.

Selection A selection structure allows for a choice between two paths of logic. It is also called an IF-THEN-ELSE structure or a decision structure.

Iteration An iteration structure allows for the repetition of some set of instructions repeatedly until a condition tests out true. This looping structure is also called a DO-WHILE structure.

Any problem which can be solved using a computer can be solved using only these three logic structures. These structures will be discussed further in the section on design tools.

Structured programming increases program modularity and reduces program complexity. Because of this, a structured program is easier to write, read, understand, test, and maintain. Structured programs are also less prone to errors than are unstructured programs. All these factors together lead to increased programmer productivity, which provides a cost saving for institutions which employ programmers. It was this cost saving which won acceptance of structured programming throughout the computer industry as well as the business community.

Design Tools

After analysis has been completed, the programmer begins the task of creating a COBOL program. However, before beginning to code the program, the programmer should design the logic necessary to solve the problem. While it is possible to code a program without a logic design, it would be a mistake to do so. A program which is coded without the benefit of a logic design will take longer to code and to test, and is also more likely to contain errors.

There are a number of tools available for logic design. The choice of a design tool is generally a matter of preference. Some of the more popular design tools are flowcharts, pseudocode, hierarchy charts, IPO diagrams, Warnier-Orr diagrams, Nassi-Schneiderman diagrams, and Chapin charts. Flowcharts, pseudocode, and hierarchy charts will be used to show logic design in this text.

Flowcharts

A flowchart may be used for both logic planning and final documentation. A flowchart is made up of symbols whose shape conveys a general meaning, words which indicate a more specific meaning, and flowlines which connect the symbols and indicate a direction of logic flow. The following are descriptions of the symbols and their general meanings.

The *terminal symbol* is used to begin or end a section of the flowchart. When used with the main or controlling section of the flowchart, the terminal symbol contains words like START and STOP. If the section of flowchart represents a subroutine, the name of the subroutine is placed in a terminal symbol at the beginning of the routine, and a word like EXIT or RETURN is used in a terminal symbol at the end of the routine.

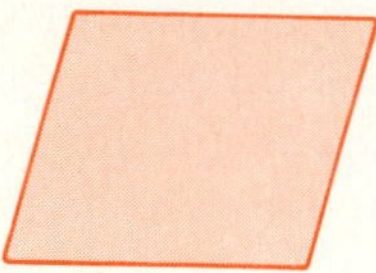

The *input/output symbol* indicates the transfer of data from a device into computer memory or from computer memory out to a device. In COBOL, words like READ and WRITE are associated with this symbol.

The *process symbol* is used to indicate operations like opening or closing files, calculations, and transfers of data within computer memory. Some COBOL words associated with this symbol are OPEN, CLOSE, COMPUTE, ADD, SUBTRACT, MULTIPLY, DIVIDE, and MOVE.

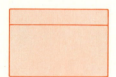

The *predefined process symbol* indicates that a subroutine is to be performed. The horizontal bar in the process symbol indicates that a detailed description of the subroutine can be found in another part of the same set of flowcharts. In COBOL these subroutines are PERFORMED.

A second type of predefined process symbol is used when the subroutine to be executed is not a part of the same set of flowcharts. This type has vertical rather than horizontal bars. It indicates that the logic was developed separately, programmed, and stored in the computer system so that it is available to this and other programs. COBOL uses CALL rather than PERFORM for this type of subroutine.

The *decision symbol* indicates that a condition is to be tested. One of two paths leading from the symbol will be taken depending on the outcome of the test. COBOL words associated with this decision symbol are IF and AT END.

Flowlines are used to connect the symbols of a flowchart. Flow is assumed to be from top to bottom and from left to right. If this is the case, arrowheads may be omitted; if the flow is to be from right to left or from bottom to top, arrowheads are required.

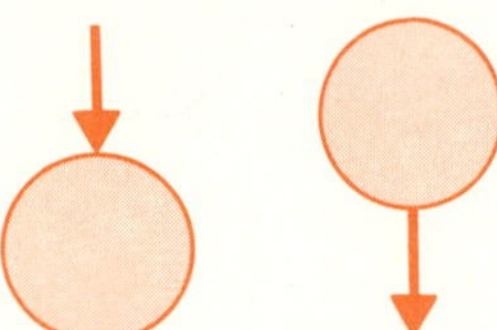

Connectors are used to indicate a movement from one point in the flowchart to another where flowlines would be awkward to draw. We shall use connectors only when the drawing has reached the edge of the paper and it is necessary to move either to a new position on the same page or to a new page.

This figure is a connector which is *not* an ANSI standard. However, it is in common use as an off-page connector in many installations.

Flowcharts and Logic Structures

The following are examples of the three basic logic structures as they are depicted in flowcharts.

Sequence Structures

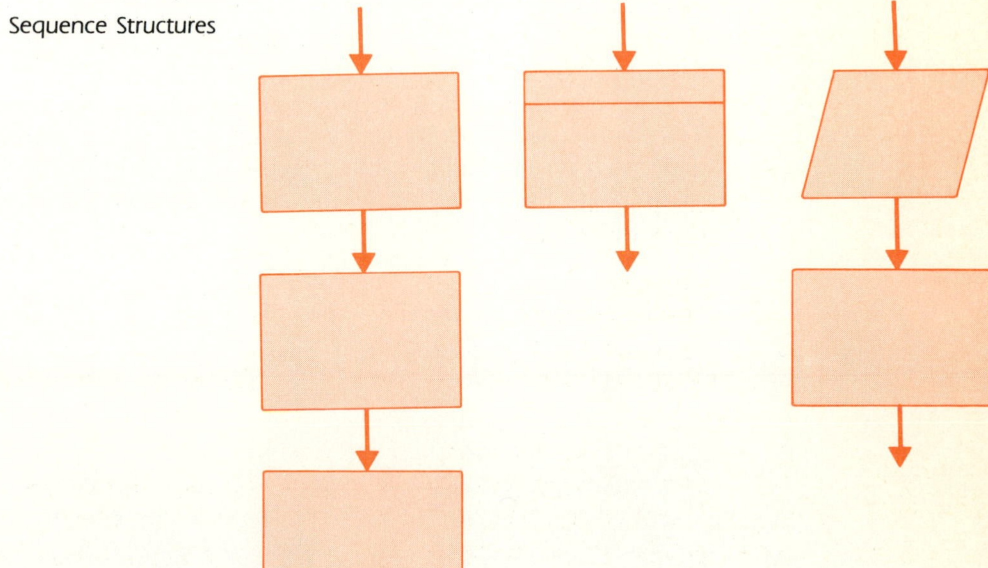

In a flowchart, a sequence structure is shown by one or more processes, predefined processes, and input/output symbols joined by flowlines. In a sequential structure there is only one path of logic, from top to bottom. There is no branching of flowlines.

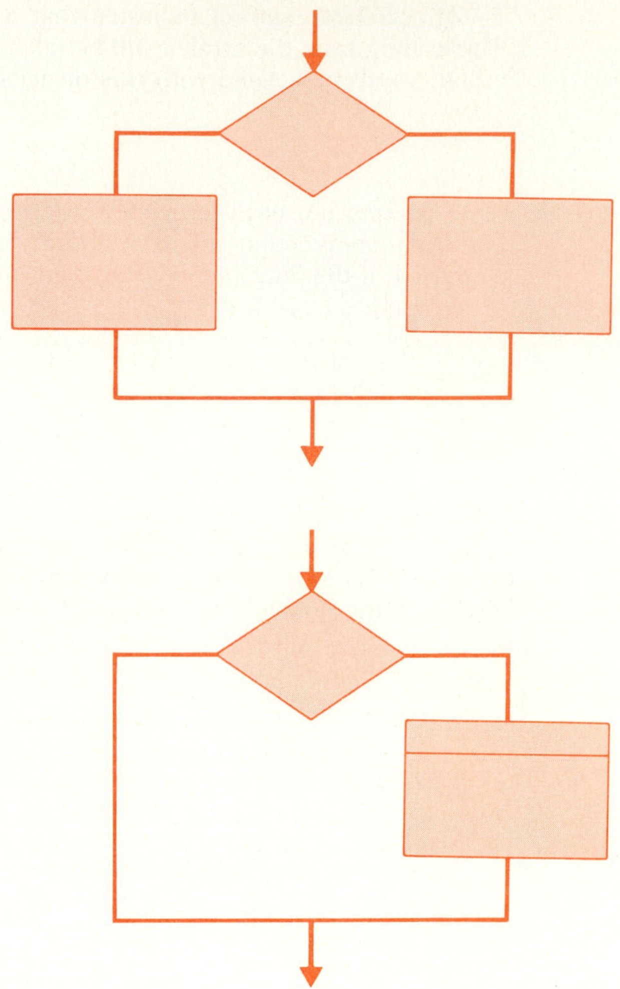

A selection structure begins with a single flowline entering a decision symbol. The decision symbol represents a test. Based on the results of the test, either the logic path on the right is taken or the logic path on the left is taken. Both logic paths come back together at the bottom of the structure, and a single flowline exits the structure.

Iteration Structure (Do While)

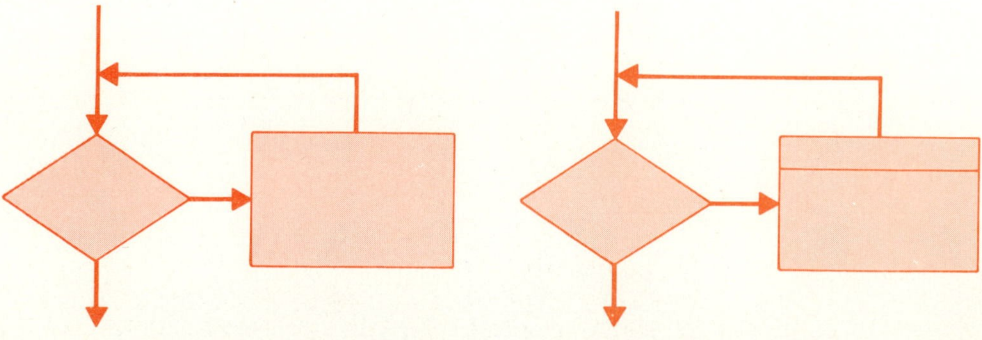

Like a selection structure, an iteration structure also begins with a single flowline entering a decision symbol. However, in an iteration structure there is a potential looping. Based on the result of the test shown in the decision symbol, either the structure will be exited or some logic step(s) will be performed and then the test will be made again. This creates a looping process with a provision for halting the looping process. The logic step(s) inside the loop will be performed repeatedly while the condition is true. When the condition becomes false, the loop is exited. If the condition is false initially, the logic step(s) inside the loop will not be executed at all.

EXAMPLE

The flowchart in Figure 1–5 depicts the logic necessary to print a listing of orders. A COBOL program which uses this logic will be developed in Chapters 2 and 3.

All three logic structures are present in this flowchart. Sequence structures are used throughout; a selection structure is used in the READ AN ORDER routine to determine whether there are any more orders to be processed; an iteration structure is used in the main routine so that the PROCESS routine is repeated, once for each order, until there are no more orders.

Pseudocode

Pseudocode is similar to flowcharting, except that it does away with the drawn symbols and uses words to express the basic structures. There are many different schemes in use for writing pseudocode. What follows describes the pseudocode conventions used throughout this text.

Routine Name

Each routine (including the main routine) is begun with its name, written in all capital letters. The pseudocode for the routine is written below the name and is indented.

Predefined Processes

Performance of a subroutine is indicated by the word DO followed by the subroutine name. DO is written in capital letters, and the subroutine name is written in lowercase letters, e.g., DO initialization.

Other Processes and Input/Output

All other processes and input/output functions are indicated by the function name, written in capital letters, followed by a description written in lowercase letters.

```
Examples:  OPEN files
           WRITE main heading line
```

Pseudocode and Logic Structures

Sequence Structure A sequence structure is depicted by listing some combination of predefined processes, processes, and input/output functions, thus:

```
WRITE ———————
DO ———————
MOVE ———————
```

Selection Structure A selection structure is depicted by using the words IF, ELSE, and ENDIF. The word IF is followed by the condition to be tested. If the condition tests out true, the logic written under the IF is done. If the condition

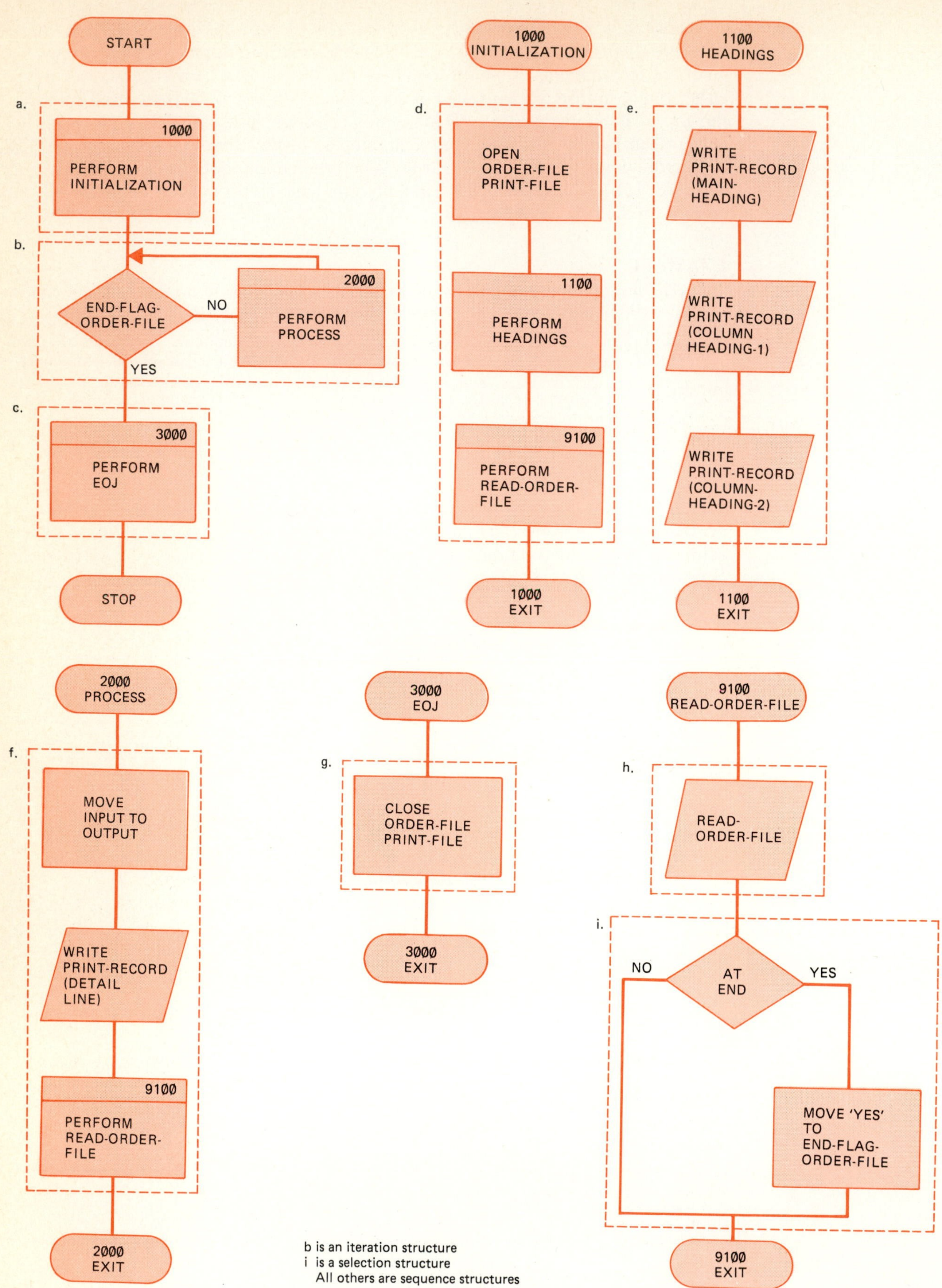

b is an iteration structure
i is a selection structure
All others are sequence structures

FIGURE 1–5

tests out false, and if an ELSE is present, the logic under the ELSE is done. ENDIF marks the completion of the IF. Each IF must have an ENDIF in pseudocode.

```
IF condition
     _______________                logic to be done when the condi-
     _______________                tion tests out true
     _______________
ELSE
     _______________                logic to be done when the condi-
     _______________                tion tests out false
ENDIF
IF condition
     _______________                logic to be done when the condi-
     _______________                tion tests out true
ENDIF
```

Iteration Structure (DO WHILE) An iteration structure is depicted by means of the words DO WHILE and ENDDO. The iteration structure begins with the words DO WHILE followed by a condition. If the condition tests out true, the logic under the DO WHILE is executed. Then the test of the condition is repeated. The logic beneath the DO WHILE will be repeated as long as the condition remains true. The ENDDO marks the end of the logic which is contained within the loop. When the condition tests out false, execution continues with the logic which follows the ENDDO.

```
DO WHILE condition
     _______________
     _______________                logic to be repeated while the
     _______________                condition remains true
     _______________
ENDDO
```

Figure 1–6 shows pseudocode that depicts the logic necessary for the LISTING program.

Hierarchy Chart

A hierarchy chart is usually used in combination with some other design tool. A hierarchy chart shows the relationships between the various routines in a program.

Each routine is depicted by a box with the routine name written inside it. The top box in the hierarchy chart represents the main routine, and all subroutines which are called from the main routine are shown below it. Similarly, all subroutines called from those subroutines are shown below them. If a subroutine is called from

```
MAIN LINE
  DO initialization
  DO WHILE more order records
    DO process
  ENDDO
  DO end of job

INITIALIZATION
  OPEN files
  DO headings
  DO read an order

HEADINGS
  WRITE main heading line
  WRITE column heading line one
  WRITE column heading line two

PROCESS
  MOVE input to output
  WRITE detail line
  DO read an order

END OF JOB
  CLOSE files

READ AN ORDER
  READ order file
```

FIGURE 1–6

more than one place, the corner of the box is blackened to indicate this. Figure 1–7 shows a hierarchy chart for the LISTING program.

DATA ORGANIZATION

Programs are written in order to manipulate data and produce information. COBOL is a programming language that is well suited for handling large amounts of data. There are two types of data which may be manipulated by a COBOL program, internal data and external data. Internal data is held in primary storage, the storage within the computer itself. Internal data is data which is created by the execution of the program and which ceases to exist once the program finishes executing. External data is data which is stored on some auxiliary storage medium such as disk, tape, or paper. External data is organized into units called files. Files may exist before, during, and after program execution.

File Structure

A file is a set of related data. A file might contain a business' current orders, last month's payroll data, or names and birthdates of employees. The units of data which make up a file are as follows.

Characters

A character is the smallest unit of data which makes up a file. A character is a single symbol—a letter (A through Z), a number (0 through 9), or a special character (e.g., $, #, :, &, =, /). Normally, a character occupies one byte of storage.

B

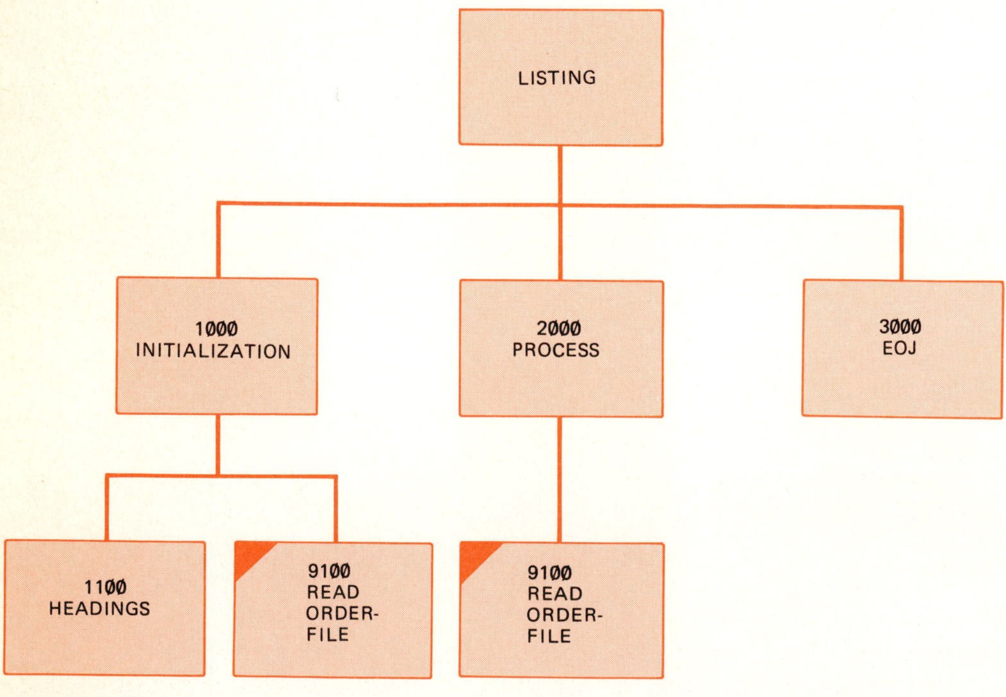

FIGURE 1–7

Field

A field consists of one or more characters of related data. A field is an individual item of data such as order number, a payroll period, or a last name.

BOGATZ

Record

A record consists of one or more related fields which refer to a particular person, place, or thing. A record could contain the data for one order or for one employee. The following record is made up of four fields: last name, first name, middle initial, and date of birth.

BOGATZ	JANE	E	590412

File

A file consists of one or more related records. The following file contains seven employee records.

BOGATZ	JANE	E	590412
TERRY	GENE		361219
HUMPHREYS	OLIVER	K	340928
GAUGER	JAMES	J	580612
EBNER	MICHAEL	R	540414
LEIB	JO		461130
BABCOCK	PEGGY	M	480204

Access Methods

Basically, there are three ways by means of which one may access files: sequentially, nonsequentially, and via a database.

Sequential Access

In sequential access each record of the file is read, starting with the first record. It is not possible to read only a few selected records. If a particular record is needed, each record in the file which is physically before the desired record must also be read. Sequential access is very useful if we wish to perform some action on all (or most) of the records in a file, as, for example, listing all of the records in the file.

Nonsequential Access

A nonsequential (or random) access method allows the processing of selected records. If a particular record is desired, it is possible to read just that record. To do this, all the records in the file must be keyed. A key is a field which is used to identify an individual record. In an order file, the key might be the order number. To retrieve an order using a nonsequential access method, we would need to know its order number.

Database

A database is a special type of file used to store large collections of data. Databases are accessed using a type of software called a database management system. The details concerning database access vary, each database system using its own method.

Storage Media

Every file must be stored on a storage medium. Storage media include disks, tapes, paper, and cards.

Disk Storage

Disk storage is a magnetic storage medium which consists of one or more disks which are coated with iron oxide. A disk drive spins the disk while a read/write head is moved over the surface to perform data transfer. The material the disk is made of may be hard (hard disks) or soft (diskettes or floppy disks). On large systems, disks are often organized into disk packs, which contain many recording surfaces.

Disk access is high speed. Disk storage can support sequential, nonsequential, and database processing, and disks may be used for both input and output files. Within the limits set by the computer system, a disk record may be any length.

Tape Storage

Like disk storage, tape storage is a magnetic storage medium. A tape is a reel (or cartridge) of magnetic tape. On a tape drive, the tape is moved past a read/write head. Tapes may be used only for sequential processing, for both input and output files. As with disk records, tape records may be any length within the limits set by the computer system.

Paper

Paper is most often used as an output medium. Printers are used to transfer data to paper. For paper output, the record length is restricted by the size of the paper. Standard computer paper is 14 inches wide and can hold 132 printed characters.

Cards

In the past, the 80-column punched card was a very popular input and output storage medium. With the advent of faster, smaller, and more flexible storage media such as tape and disk, however, cards have become almost obsolete. Nonetheless, the 80-column punched card has had an effect on current programming practices: many programming languages (including COBOL) use an 80-column format, and most video display screens are 80 columns wide.

Physical Organization

Label Records

Files which are stored on magnetic media (disk and tape) will be preceded and followed by label records. Label records are blocks of information, written on the disk or tape, which describe the file. They usually contain the name, date of creation, and size of the file (number of records). Figure 1–8 depicts label records on a file.

LABEL RECORDS (HEADER)	DATA PORTION OF THE FILE	LABEL RECORDS (TRAILER)

FIGURE 1–8

Blocking

For purposes of efficiency, records stored on magnetic media are usually grouped into units called blocks. A block is a number of records which are physically stored together. An individual record is called a logical record, and a block of records is called a physical record. The computer system inserts extra space (called an interblock gap, or IBG) between each block. If a file is not blocked (that is, if one logical record is the same as one physical record), there will be an interblock gap between each logical record. (See Figure 1–9.) Unblocked files result in both a great deal of wasted space and slower input and output operations. Contrast this with blocked files, where a number of logical records are combined to create one physical record and interblock gaps are present only between the physical records. (See Figure 1–10.)

IBG	LOGICAL RECORD	IBG	LOGICAL RECORD	IBG	LOGICAL RECORD	IBG	LOGICAL RECORD	IBG	LOGICAL RECORD	IBG

FIGURE 1–9

IBG	LOGICAL RECORD	LOGICAL RECORD	LOGICAL RECORD	LOGICAL RECORD	IBG	LOGICAL RECORD	LOGICAL RECORD	LOGICAL RECORD	LOGICAL RECORD	IBG

FIGURE 1–10

File Description Techniques

Input/Output Record Layouts

Input/output record layouts are used to describe the format of a record on disk, tape, or cards. An input/output record layout form is used, and vertical bars are drawn to delimit the various fields on a record. If a field is further divided into subfields, or if a field contains a decimal, this is shown with a short dashed line. An example of an input/output record layout is shown in Figure 1–11.

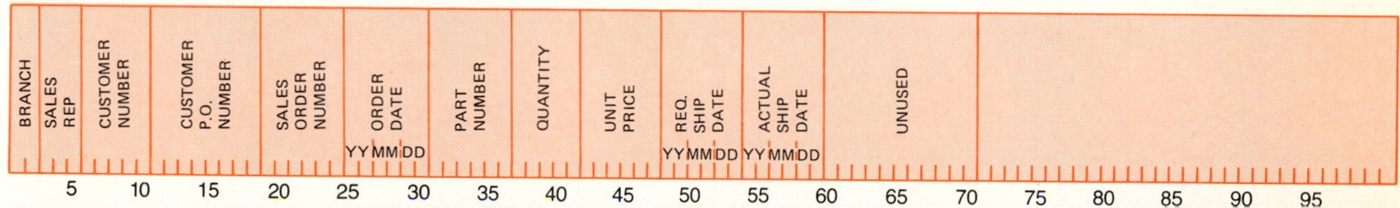

FIGURE 1–11

Printer Layout

The format of printed output is described using a printer layout. A printed report is designed using a printer layout form, on which each type of line of the report to be printed is shown. The amount of space between fields on a line, as well as the amount of space between two lines, is shown on a printer layout. (See Figure 1–12.)

```
                                                PRODUCT DISTRIBUTION INC. - CURRENT ORDERS

                  SALES    CUSTOMER      PURCHASE        SALES         ORDER        PART                      UNIT          REQUESTED          ACTUAL
     BRANCH        REP      NUMBER         ORDER         ORDER          DATE       NUMBER      QUANTITY       PRICE         SHIP DATE       SHIP DATE

         99        999       99999       XXXXXXXXX      XXXXXX       99-99-99      XXXXXX        99999       9999.99         99-99-99         99-99-99

         99        999       99999       XXXXXXXXX      XXXXXX       99-99-99      XXXXXX        99999       9999.99         99-99-99         99-99-99
```

FIGURE 1–12

COBOL TOPICS

The Compilation Process

COBOL is a high-level language. That is, a COBOL program (a source program) must be converted to machine language (an object module) before it can be executed by the computer. This conversion is done by a piece of software called a compiler. Figure 1–13 illustrates the compilation process.

Once a COBOL program is written, it must be transferred to a storage medium so that it may be accessed by the computer. Most often, COBOL programs are stored on disk and are entered into the computer system at a video display terminal using a piece of software called a text editor.

After the COBOL program (source program) has been entered, it is compiled. The compiler will produce a listing of the COBOL program (source listing) which will identify any syntax errors which are present. If there are no serious syntax errors, an object module in machine language will be produced. In executing the program, it is the object module which is used.

If syntax errors are present, the text editor is used to correct the errors and the program is compiled again.

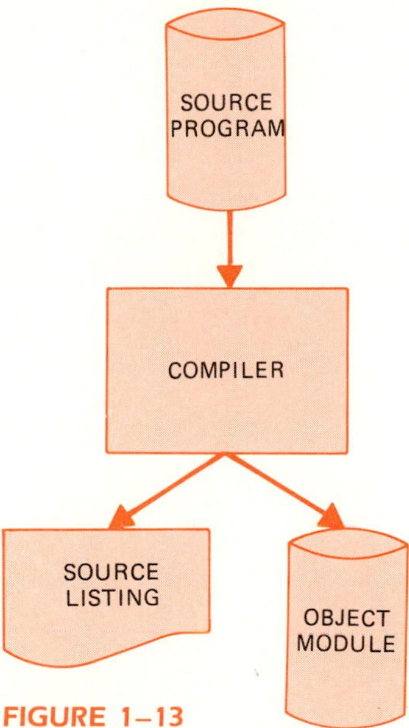

FIGURE 1–13

Overview of COBOL

The Four Divisions

A COBOL program is made up of four divisions, the IDENTIFICATION DIVISION, the ENVIRONMENT DIVISION, the DATA DIVISION, and the PROCEDURE DIVISION.

The IDENTIFICATION DIVISION provides a name for the program.

The ENVIRONMENT DIVISION specifies the computer(s) on which the program will be compiled and executed, and the files which will be used by the program.

The DATA DIVISION describes all data which will be used by the program.

The PROCEDURE DIVISION contains the logic steps necessary to solve the programming problem.

COBOL Elements

The following elements are used to construct a COBOL program.

Character Set The following are the characters which may be used in a COBOL program.

Characters used for COBOL words:

```
numerals    0 through 9
```

```
letters    A through Z
hyphen     -
```

Characters used for punctuation:

```
. ' ( ) = space , ;
```

Characters used in arithmetic operations:

```
+ - * / **
```

Characters used in relations:

```
= > <
```

Characters used in editing:

```
B 0 + - CR DB Z * $ , . /
```

COBOL Words There are three categories of words in a COBOL program: user-defined words, system names, and reserved words.

User-Defined Words A user-defined word is a word which is created by the programmer. User-defined words are used, for example, to name data items.

System Names System names are used to tie into the computer's operating system, e.g., to assign data files to input/output devices. They are determined by the COBOL compiler which is used.

Reserved Words Reserved words are words which have a special meaning to the COBOL compiler. These words may not be used in instances where a programmer must supply a name. A list of COBOL reserved words is found in Appendix A.

Literals A literal is a numeric or nonnumeric constant.

COBOL Coding Forms

COBOL programs are normally written in 80-character format, various areas of which are used for different purposes. Figure 1–14 shows a blank COBOL coding form.

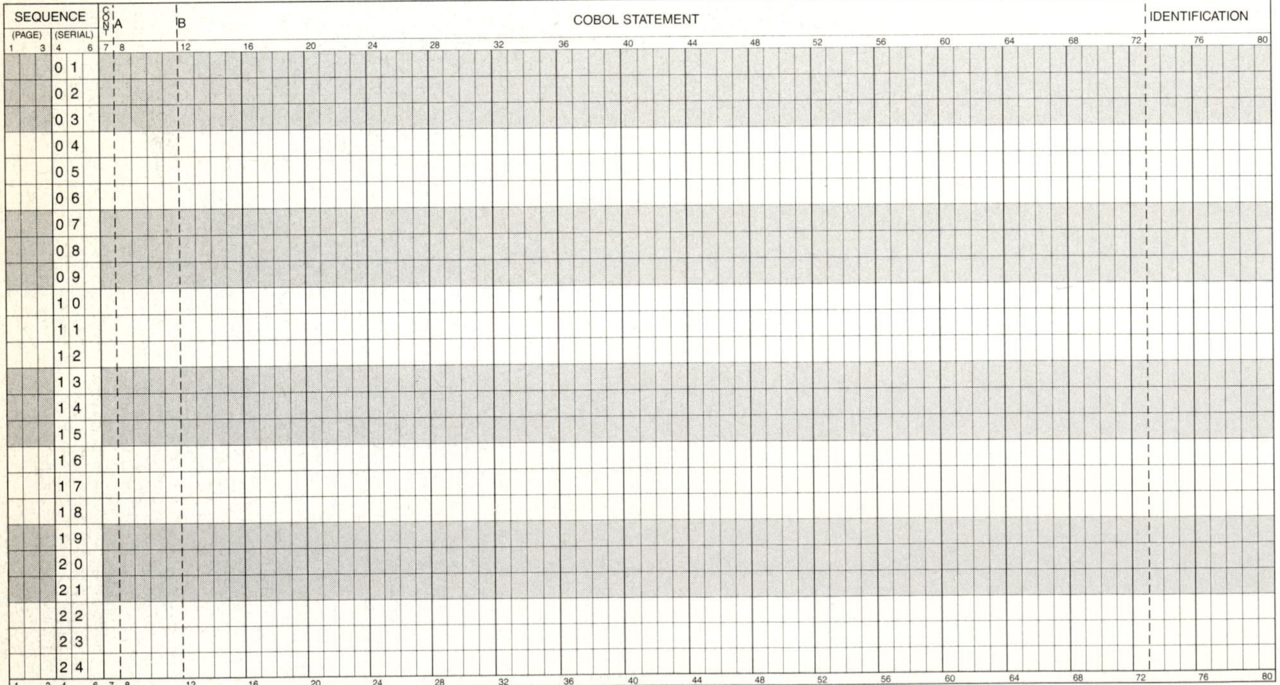

FIGURE 1–14

Columns	Description
1 through 6	Sequence
7	Comments and continuations
8 through 11	Area A
12 through 72	Area B
73 through 80	Can be used by the text editor or for identification

Sequence (1–6) The sequence area is used to number the source records in a COBOL program. These numbers are not required, but are often convenient. Most text editors provide automatic numbering.

Comments and Continuations (7) This column is left blank unless a line is intended to be a comment line or is a continuation of a previous line.

Area A (8–11) Some elements of COBOL (e.g. division headers, paragraph names) are coded beginning in Area A.

Area B (12–72) Other elements of COBOL (e.g. COBOL verbs) may not begin before column 12. COBOL statements must not extend beyond column 72.

Identification (73–80) Columns 73 through 80 are often used by the text editor, or they may be used for purposes of identification.

SUMMARY

Program Development

Program development involves the analysis, design, coding, and testing of a program. The products of analysis are program specifications, input/output layouts, and systems flowcharts. Structured programming is a programming method which produces better programs by placing restrictions on the flow of logic. Design tools like flowcharts, pseudocode, and hierarchy charts are used to design the logic of a program.

Data Organization

Data is organized into units called files. There are three methods used to access files: sequential access, nonsequential access, and databases. Files may be stored on disks, tapes, paper, or cards. Tape and disk files have label records and may be blocked. Input/output record layouts and printer layouts are used to describe files.

COBOL Topics

COBOL was first developed in 1959–60. COBOL standards were approved in 1968 and revised in 1974 and 1985. COBOL is an English-like, business-oriented language capable of handling large amounts of data. A COBOL source program requires compilation before it may be executed. A COBOL program is made up of four divisions, the IDENTIFICATION, ENVIRONMENT, DATA, and PROCEDURE divisions. Reserved words are words which have special meaning for the COBOL compiler. A list of these words is found in Appendix A.

EXERCISES

I. Match the following items with the data structure that is most likely to represent them.

a. FILE
b. RECORD
c. FIELD
d. CHARACTER

_____ **1.** a size
_____ **2.** information pertaining to the employees of a company
_____ **3.** a social security number
_____ **4.** a period (.)
_____ **5.** information pertaining to an order
_____ **6.** a name
_____ **7.** information pertaining to the accounts receivable for a company
_____ **8.** information pertaining to a student
_____ **9.** a zip code
_____ **10.** a B

II. Indicate whether each of the following is a system flowcharting symbol (S), a program flowcharting symbol (P), or both (B).

_____ **1.** Document
_____ **2.** Process
_____ **3.** Input/output
_____ **4.** Magnetic tape
_____ **5.** Terminal
_____ **6.** Decision
_____ **7.** Magnetic disk
_____ **8.** Connector
_____ **9.** Flowlines
_____ **10.** Predefined process

III. Indicate whether each of the following actions is most likely to take place in the analysis (A), design (D), coding (C), or testing (T) phase of program development.

_____ **1.** Correcting a misspelling in a program source listing.
_____ **2.** Adjusting the spacing on a report.
_____ **3.** Writing COBOL statements.
_____ **4.** Choosing a style for a report.
_____ **5.** Meeting with representatives of the accounting department to discuss a problem with accounts receivable reporting.
_____ **6.** Selecting tape or disk as the choice on which to store a file.
_____ **7.** Reviewing reports currently produced for the accounts receivable department.
_____ **8.** Doing a calculation with a hand-held calculator in order to compare the results of the calculation with the output from a program.

CHAPTER 2

The IDENTIFICATION, ENVIRONMENT, and DATA Divisions

This chapter presents the specifications for a program which will produce a printed listing of an input file. It covers the first three of four divisions which make up a COBOL program.

The IDENTIFICATION DIVISION supplies a name for the program. It may also contain some documentary information about the program. The PROGRAM-ID paragraph, as well as all optional paragraphs are covered.

The ENVIRONMENT DIVISION describes the hardware "environment," including input and output files in which the program will be compiled and executed. Coverage of the ENVIRONMENT DIVISION includes the CONFIGURATION and INPUT-OUTPUT sections.

The DATA DIVISION describes all data elements which are processed by the program. Coverage of the DATA DIVISION includes the FILE and WORKING-STORAGE sections. File description entries, record description entries, and data description entries are examined, as well as data formats (numeric, alphanumeric, alphabetic, numeric edited, and alphanumeric edited).

INTRODUCTION

This chapter begins a programming project that continues through Chapter 3. Each chapter in this text will have programming projects. The specification for each project will be presented, along with design tools to assist in the solution, and then the COBOL solution will be given, including the COBOL code, the test data, and the output produced. Chapter 2 and Chapter 3 together present a complete project; each chapter thereafter contains one or more complete projects. Chapter 2 covers the material needed for the first three divisions of the COBOL program.

The IDENTIFICATION DIVISION provides a name and some documentation for the program. The ENVIRONMENT DIVISION identifies the equipment used, the source of the input data, and the destination of the output data. To accomplish this, file names are associated with equipment from which the data will be read or to which the data will be written. The DATA DIVISION describes in detail each data item that will be needed in the solution of the problem. The fourth division, the PROCEDURE DIVISION, is examined in Chapter 3.

PROGRAM SPECIFICATION: LISTING

The program specification for the project in this and the next chapter is shown in Figure 2–1.

PROGRAM SPECIFICATION

Program Name: LISTING

Program Function:

The program will produce a printed listing of all orders from an order file.

Input Files:

I. ORDER-FILE

INPUT DEVICE:	DISK
FILE ORGANIZATION:	SEQUENTIAL
RECORD LENGTH:	70 BYTES
FILE SEQUENCE:	ASCENDING ON BRANCH / SALES REP

Output Files:

I. PRINT-FILE

OUTPUT DEVICE:	PRINTER
RECORD LENGTH:	133 BYTES

Output Requirements:

Each record read from the order file should be printed on one line of the output report. All fields from the input record are to be included on the output.

The following are formatting requirements for the report:

1. The first page of the report should contain:
   (a) a main heading which includes the company name and report name.
   (b) column headings which describe the items printed underneath them.
2. The detail lines should include all fields from the input.
3. The detail lines should be double spaced.
4. Do not include provisions for page overflow.

FIGURE 2–1

Input Record Layout

The input for the project is an order file. Each record in the file contains the data that describes one order and is 70 bytes long. The input record layout is shown in Figure 2–2. This layout represents the arrangement of data items in each record of a disk file. The input record can also be defined using a written record description. This description is also shown in Figure 2–2. The written record description includes information about the class of each field of data (numeric or alphanumeric).

Print Chart

The output of the program for the project is a printed report which is a listing of the input records from the ORDER FILE. The print chart showing the design of the output is given in Figure 2–3. The project requires the transfer of the data from each input record to a print line and the writing of the line.

THE COBOL PROGRAM (FIRST THREE DIVISIONS)

The first three divisions of the COBOL program are shown in Figure 2–4. They are presented here as an overview; sections of the code will be repeated as the explanation for each division is given.

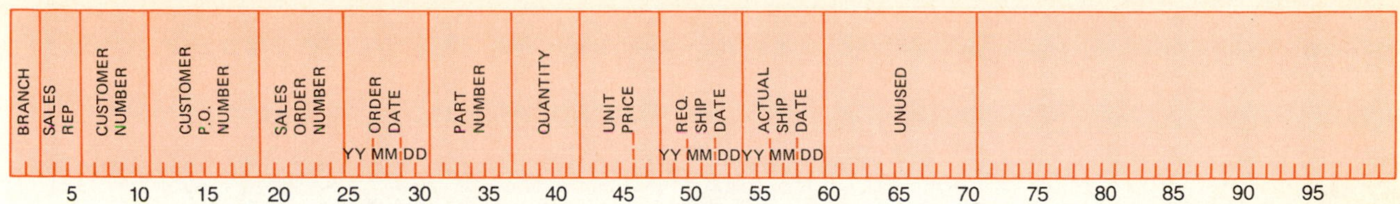

DATA ITEM	COLUMN LOCATION	CLASS
Branch	1–2	Numeric
Sales representative	3–5	Numeric
Customer number	6–10	Numeric
Customer P. O. number	11–18	Alphanumeric
Sales order number	19–24	Alphanumeric
Order date		
Order year	25–26	Numeric
Order month	27–28	Numeric
Order day	29–30	Numeric
Part number	31–36	Alphanumeric
Quantity	37–41	Numeric
Unit Price	42–47	Numeric (6.2)*
Requested shipping date		
Requested shipping year	48–49	Numeric
Requested shipping month	50–51	Numeric
Requested shipping day	52–53	Numeric
Actual shipping date		
Actual shipping year	54–55	Numeric
Actual shipping month	56–57	Numeric
Actual shipping day	58–59	Numeric
Unused	60–70	Alphanumeric

* 6.2 indicates that this data item has six numeric positions, two of which are to the right of the decimal point.

FIGURE 2–2

IDENTIFICATION DIVISION

The IDENTIFICATION DIVISION is the first of the four divisions of a COBOL program. It gives a name to the program and may also include other general information about the program.

Format

```
 IDENTIFICATION DIVISION.
 PROGRAM-ID.          program-name.
[AUTHOR.              [comment-entry] . . .]
[INSTALLATION.        [comment-entry] . . .]
[DATE-WRITTEN.        [comment-entry] . . .]
[DATE-COMPILED.       [comment-entry] . . .]
[SECURITY.            [comment-entry] . . .]
```

Each time new COBOL elements are introduced in this text, a format for the elements will be shown. There are generally accepted conventions for writing these formats. Each time a new convention is shown in a format, it will be explained.

Uppercase COBOL reserved words are always shown in uppercase in a format. Reserved words are words which have a special meaning to the compiler. Some examples in the preceding format are IDENTIFICATION, DIVISION, PROGRAM-ID, and AUTHOR.

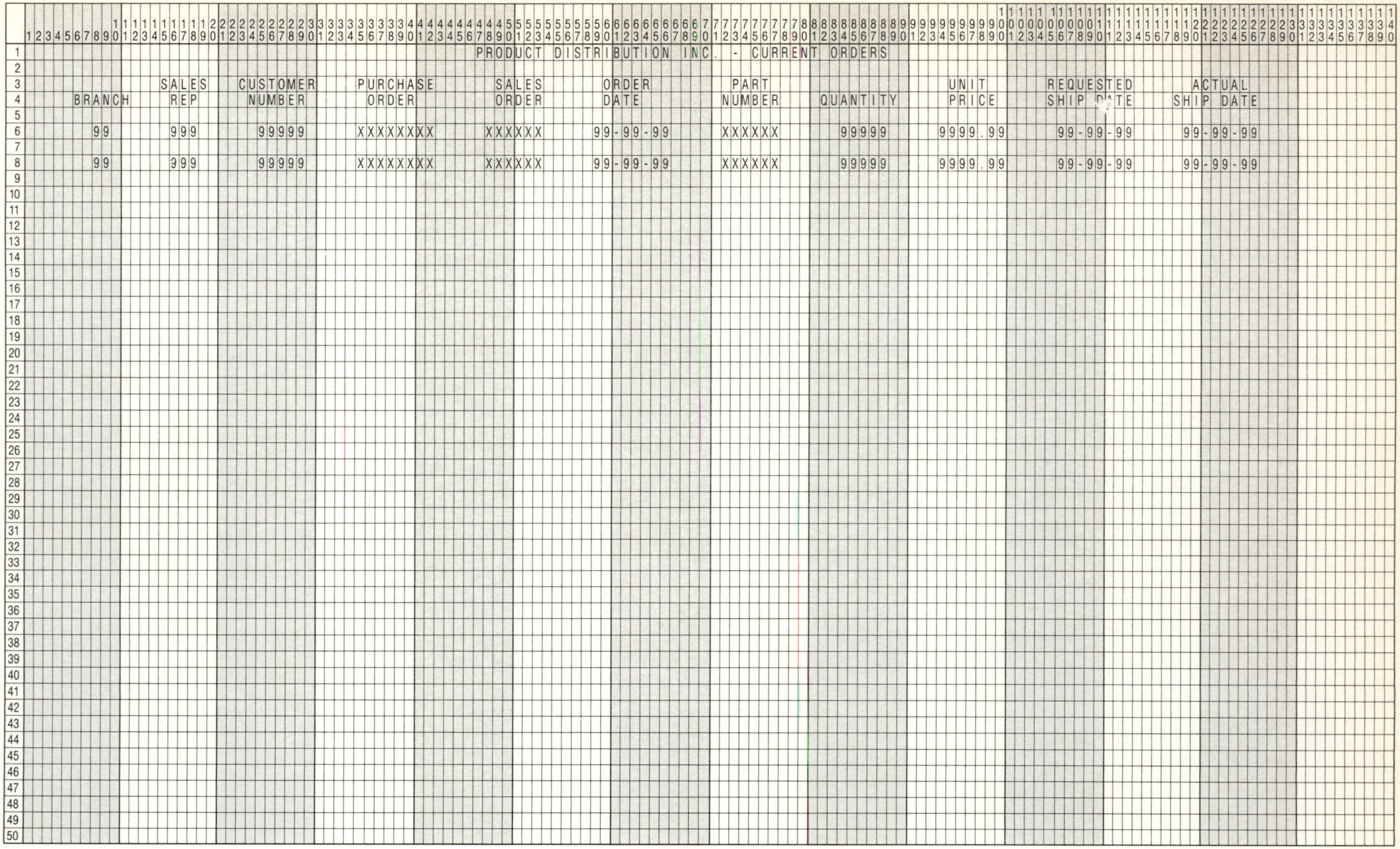

```
                                              PRODUCT DISTRIBUTION INC. - CURRENT ORDERS

              SALES   CUSTOMER    PURCHASE      SALES      ORDER        PART                  UNIT      REQUESTED      ACTUAL
     BRANCH    REP     NUMBER      ORDER        ORDER      DATE        NUMBER    QUANTITY     PRICE     SHIP DATE    SHIP DATE

       99      999      99999     XXXXXXXXX    XXXXXX     99-99-99    XXXXXX      99999     9999.99     99-99-99     99-99-99

       99      999      99999     XXXXXXXXX    XXXXXX     99-99-99    XXXXXX      99999     9999.99     99-99-99     99-99-99
```

FIGURE 2–3

```
       IDENTIFICATION DIVISION.

       PROGRAM-ID.    LISTING.

       AUTHOR.        HELEN HUMPHREYS.

       INSTALLATION.  PRODUCT DISTRIBUTION INC.

       DATE-WRITTEN.  Ø3/15/87.

       DATE-COMPILED. Ø3/22/87.

      *****************************************************************
      *                                                               *
      *    THIS PROGRAM PRODUCES A PRINTED LISTING OF ALL ORDERS      *
      *    FROM THE ORDER FILE.                                       *
      *                                                               *
      *****************************************************************

       ENVIRONMENT DIVISION.

       CONFIGURATION SECTION.

       SOURCE-COMPUTER.
              IBM-37Ø.
       OBJECT-COMPUTER.
              IBM-37Ø.

       INPUT-OUTPUT SECTION.
       FILE-CONTROL.
           SELECT ORDER-FILE ASSIGN TO DISK.
           SELECT PRINT-FILE ASSIGN TO PRINTER.

       DATA DIVISION.
       FILE SECTION.

       FD  ORDER-FILE
           LABEL RECORDS ARE STANDARD
           RECORD CONTAINS 7Ø CHARACTERS
           DATA RECORD IS ORDER-RECORD.

       Ø1  ORDER-RECORD.
           Ø5  ORD-BRANCH                PIC 9(2).
           Ø5  ORD-SALES-REP             PIC 9(3).
           Ø5  ORD-CUSTOMER-NBR          PIC 9(5).
           Ø5  ORD-CUST-PO-NBR           PIC X(8).
           Ø5  ORD-SALES-ORD-NBR         PIC X(6).
           Ø5  ORD-DATE.
               1Ø  ORD-YY                PIC 9(2).
               1Ø  ORD-MM                PIC 9(2).
               1Ø  ORD-DD                PIC 9(2).
           Ø5  ORD-PART-NBR              PIC X(6).
           Ø5  ORD-QUANTITY              PIC 9(5).
           Ø5  ORD-UNIT-PRICE            PIC 9(4)V9(2).
           Ø5  ORD-REQ-SHIP-DATE.
               1Ø  ORD-REQ-SHIP-YY       PIC 9(2).
               1Ø  ORD-REQ-SHIP-MM       PIC 9(2).
               1Ø  ORD-REQ-SHIP-DD       PIC 9(2).
           Ø5  ORD-ACT-SHIP-DATE.
               1Ø  ORD-ACT-SHIP-YY       PIC 9(2).
               1Ø  ORD-ACT-SHIP-MM       PIC 9(2).
               1Ø  ORD-ACT-SHIP-DD       PIC 9(2).
           Ø5  FILLER                    PIC X(11).

       FD  PRINT-FILE
           LABEL RECORDS ARE OMITTED
           RECORD CONTAINS 133 CHARACTERS
           DATA RECORD IS PRINT-RECORD.

       Ø1  PRINT-RECORD                  PIC X(133).

       WORKING-STORAGE SECTION.

       Ø1  HOLDS-COUNTERS-SWITCHES.
           Ø5  END-FLAG-ORDER-FILE       PIC X(3)       VALUE 'NO'.

       Ø1  MAIN-HEADING.
           Ø5  FILLER                    PIC X(46)      VALUE SPACES.
           Ø5  FILLER                    PIC X(42)
               VALUE 'PRODUCT DISTRIBUTION INC. - CURRENT ORDERS'.
           Ø5  FILLER                    PIC X(45)      VALUE SPACES.
```

FIGURE 2–4

FIGURE 2-4 cont.

```
       Ø1  COLUMN-HEADING-1.
           Ø5  FILLER               PIC X(14)      VALUE SPACES.
           Ø5  FILLER               PIC X(5)       VALUE 'SALES'.
           Ø5  FILLER               PIC X(3)       VALUE SPACES.
           Ø5  FILLER               PIC X(8)       VALUE 'CUSTOMER'.
           Ø5  FILLER               PIC X(4)       VALUE SPACES.
           Ø5  FILLER               PIC X(8)       VALUE 'PURCHASE'.
           Ø5  FILLER               PIC X(6)       VALUE SPACES.
           Ø5  FILLER               PIC X(5)       VALUE 'SALES'.
           Ø5  FILLER               PIC X(6)       VALUE SPACES.
           Ø5  FILLER               PIC X(5)       VALUE 'ORDER'.
           Ø5  FILLER               PIC X(8)       VALUE SPACES.
           Ø5  FILLER               PIC X(4)       VALUE 'PART'.
           Ø5  FILLER               PIC X(18)      VALUE SPACES.
           Ø5  FILLER               PIC X(4)       VALUE 'UNIT'.
           Ø5  FILLER               PIC X(6)       VALUE SPACES.
           Ø5  FILLER               PIC X(9)       VALUE
                                                   'REQUESTED'.
           Ø5  FILLER               PIC X(6)       VALUE SPACES.
           Ø5  FILLER               PIC X(6)       VALUE 'ACTUAL'.
           Ø5  FILLER               PIC X(8)       VALUE SPACES.

       Ø1  COLUMN-HEADING-2.
           Ø5  FILLER               PIC X(5)       VALUE SPACES.
           Ø5  FILLER               PIC X(6)       VALUE 'BRANCH'.
           Ø5  FILLER               PIC X(4)       VALUE SPACES.
           Ø5  FILLER               PIC X(3)       VALUE 'REP'.
           Ø5  FILLER               PIC X(5)       VALUE SPACES.
           Ø5  FILLER               PIC X(6)       VALUE 'NUMBER'.
           Ø5  FILLER               PIC X(6)       VALUE SPACES.
           Ø5  FILLER               PIC X(5)       VALUE 'ORDER'.
           Ø5  FILLER               PIC X(8)       VALUE SPACES.
           Ø5  FILLER               PIC X(5)       VALUE 'ORDER'.
           Ø5  FILLER               PIC X(6)       VALUE SPACES.
           Ø5  FILLER               PIC X(4)       VALUE 'DATE'.
           Ø5  FILLER               PIC X(8)       VALUE SPACES.
           Ø5  FILLER               PIC X(6)       VALUE 'NUMBER'.
           Ø5  FILLER               PIC X(4)       VALUE SPACES.
           Ø5  FILLER               PIC X(8)       VALUE 'QUANTITY'.
           Ø5  FILLER               PIC X(5)       VALUE SPACES.
           Ø5  FILLER               PIC X(5)       VALUE 'PRICE'.
           Ø5  FILLER               PIC X(5)       VALUE SPACES.
           Ø5  FILLER               PIC X(9)       VALUE
                                                   'SHIP DATE'.
           Ø5  FILLER               PIC X(4)       VALUE SPACES.
           Ø5  FILLER               PIC X(9)       VALUE
                                                   'SHIP DATE'.
           Ø5  FILLER               PIC X(7)       VALUE SPACES.

       Ø1  DETAIL-LINE.
           Ø5  FILLER               PIC X(7)       VALUE SPACES.
           Ø5  DET-BRANCH           PIC 9(2).
           Ø5  FILLER               PIC X(6)       VALUE SPACES.
           Ø5  DET-SALES-REP        PIC 9(3).
           Ø5  FILLER               PIC X(6)       VALUE SPACES.
           Ø5  DET-CUSTOMER-NBR     PIC 9(5).
           Ø5  FILLER               PIC X(5)       VALUE SPACES.
           Ø5  DET-CUST-PO-NBR      PIC X(8).
           Ø5  FILLER               PIC X(5)       VALUE SPACES.
           Ø5  DET-SALES-ORD-NBR    PIC X(6).
           Ø5  FILLER               PIC X(5)       VALUE SPACES.
           Ø5  DET-ORDER-MM         PIC 9(2).
           Ø5  FILLER               PIC X(1)       VALUE '-'.
           Ø5  DET-ORDER-DD         PIC 9(2).
           Ø5  FILLER               PIC X(1)       VALUE '-'.
           Ø5  DET-ORDER-YY         PIC 9(2).
           Ø5  FILLER               PIC X(5)       VALUE SPACES.
           Ø5  DET-PART-NBR         PIC X(6).
           Ø5  FILLER               PIC X(6)       VALUE SPACES.
           Ø5  DET-QUANTITY         PIC 9(5).
           Ø5  FILLER               PIC X(5)       VALUE SPACES.
           Ø5  DET-UNIT-PRICE       PIC 9(4).9(2).
           Ø5  FILLER               PIC X(5)       VALUE SPACES.
           Ø5  DET-REQ-SHIP-MM      PIC 9(2).
           Ø5  FILLER               PIC X(1)       VALUE '-'.
           Ø5  DET-REQ-SHIP-DD      PIC 9(2).
           Ø5  FILLER               PIC X(1)       VALUE '-'.
           Ø5  DET-REQ-SHIP-YY      PIC 9(2).
           Ø5  FILLER               PIC X(5)       VALUE SPACES.
           Ø5  DET-ACT-SHIP-MM      PIC 9(2).
           Ø5  FILLER               PIC X(1)       VALUE '-'.
           Ø5  DET-ACT-SHIP-DD      PIC 9(2).
           Ø5  FILLER               PIC X(1)       VALUE '-'.
           Ø5  DET-ACT-SHIP-YY      PIC 9(2).
           Ø5  FILLER               PIC X(7)       VALUE SPACES.
```

Underline When a reserved word is required in an entry, it is underlined. All of the reserved words in the format for the IDENTIFICATION DIVISION are required. They must be used if the entry they are part of is used.

Lowercase The items specified in lowercase are to be provided by the programmer. In the preceding format, these are the program-name and any comment-entries. The programmer may choose the characters which make up the program-name, as well as the comments he or she thinks are appropriate.

Brackets [ ] Those portions of the format enclosed in brackets are optional. Thus, for the IDENTIFICATION DIVISION, the last five lines are optional.

Ellipsis . . . The ellipsis indicates that the item preceding it may be repeated an arbitrary number of times. Accordingly, in the IDENTIFICATION DIVISION format, there may be any number of comments for each of the last five lines.

The first statement in a COBOL program must be the IDENTIFICATION DIVISION header, which consists of the words IDENTIFICATION DIVISION and a period. The IDENTIFICATION DIVISION header must begin in Area A (column 8). The remaining entries in the IDENTIFICATION DIVISION are called paragraphs. The PROGRAM-ID paragraph is required; all of the other paragraphs are optional. However, if any of the other paragraphs are supplied, they must be in the order shown in the format.

PROGRAM-ID

Format

```
PROGRAM-ID.   program-name.
```

The PROGRAM-ID paragraph provides a name by which the compiled version of the COBOL program (the object program) is identified to the computer system. COBOL allows the program-name to be 1 to 30 characters in length and to contain letters, digits, and hyphens. However, many computer systems cannot use the full 30 characters. These systems ignore characters in excess of the number that they can use. The user must find out the number and type of characters his or her computer system can accommodate and name programs accordingly. The PROGRAM-ID paragraph is required and must immediately follow the IDENTIFICATION DIVISION header. The reserved word PROGRAM-ID must begin in Area A, the program-name in Area B.

AUTHOR

Format

```
[AUTHOR.   [comment-entry] . . .]
```

The AUTHOR paragraph is used to indicate the programmer or programmers who coded the program. The programmer name or names are written in the comment-entry position of this paragraph.

The reserved word AUTHOR must begin in Area A. The comment-entry, and all comment-entries in the IDENTIFICATION division, may be written in columns 12–72 (Area B) and may continue over any number of lines. Comment-entries are used only to document the source program, and do not affect compilation.

INSTALLATION

Format

```
[INSTALLATION.   [comment-entry] . . .]
```

The INSTALLATION paragraph is used to indicate the name of the company at which the program is written. The reserved word INSTALLATION must begin in Area A.

DATE-WRITTEN

Format

```
[DATE-WRITTEN.   [comment-entry] . . .]
```

The DATE-WRITTEN paragraph is used to show the calendar date on which the program was written. The reserved word DATE-WRITTEN must begin in Area A.

DATE-COMPILED

Format

```
[DATE-COMPILED.   [comment-entry] . . .]
```

When the DATE-COMPILED paragraph is specified, the compiler will insert into the source listing the actual date on which the program was compiled. If a comment-entry is written by the programmer, it will be replaced by the compilation date provided by the computer. The reserved word DATE-COMPILED must begin in Area A.

SECURITY

Format

```
[SECURITY.   [comment-entry] . . .]
```

The SECURITY paragraph would be used in a security-sensitive installation to indicate the level of security clearance which would be required to have access to the program. The reserved word SECURITY must begin in Area A.

The 1985 standard places AUTHOR, INSTALLATION, DATE-WRITTEN, DATE-COMPILED, and SECURITY on the obsolete list. This means that they are still a part of the 1985 standard, but will be eliminated in the next standard.

The Sample Program

The IDENTIFICATION DIVISION for the sample program segment of Figure 2–4, as it would be coded by the programmer, appears in Figure 2–5. The PROGRAM-ID paragraph assigns the name LISTING to the program. The AUTHOR, INSTALLATION, DATE-WRITTEN, and DATE-COMPILED paragraphs are all optional. They are included to provide reference information. Note that no comment entry has been written for the DATE-COMPILED paragraph; the compiler will insert the date on which the program is compiled.

COMMENT LINES

Comment lines may be placed in a COBOL program to clarify or explain some part of the program. To indicate a comment line, an asterisk is placed in column 7. The asterisk may be followed by any combination of characters in columns 8 through 72. Note that every line of a comment must have an asterisk in column 7. Comment lines will appear in the compiled listing of the program, but are ignored by the compiler and therefore have no effect on the execution of the program.

```
 IDENTIFICATION DIVISION.

 PROGRAM-ID.     LISTING.

 AUTHOR.         HELEN HUMPHREYS.

 INSTALLATION.   PRODUCT DISTRIBUTION INC.

 DATE-WRITTEN.   Ø3/15/87.

 DATE-COMPILED.

******************************************************************
*                                                                *
*    THIS PROGRAM PRODUCES A PRINTED LISTING OF ALL ORDERS      *
*    FROM THE ORDER FILE.                                        *
*                                                                *
******************************************************************
```

FIGURE 2–5

EXAMPLE OF COMMENT LINES

Comments are often enclosed in a box of asterisks because, when so enclosed, they stand out from the rest of the program and are easily distinguished from the actual code.

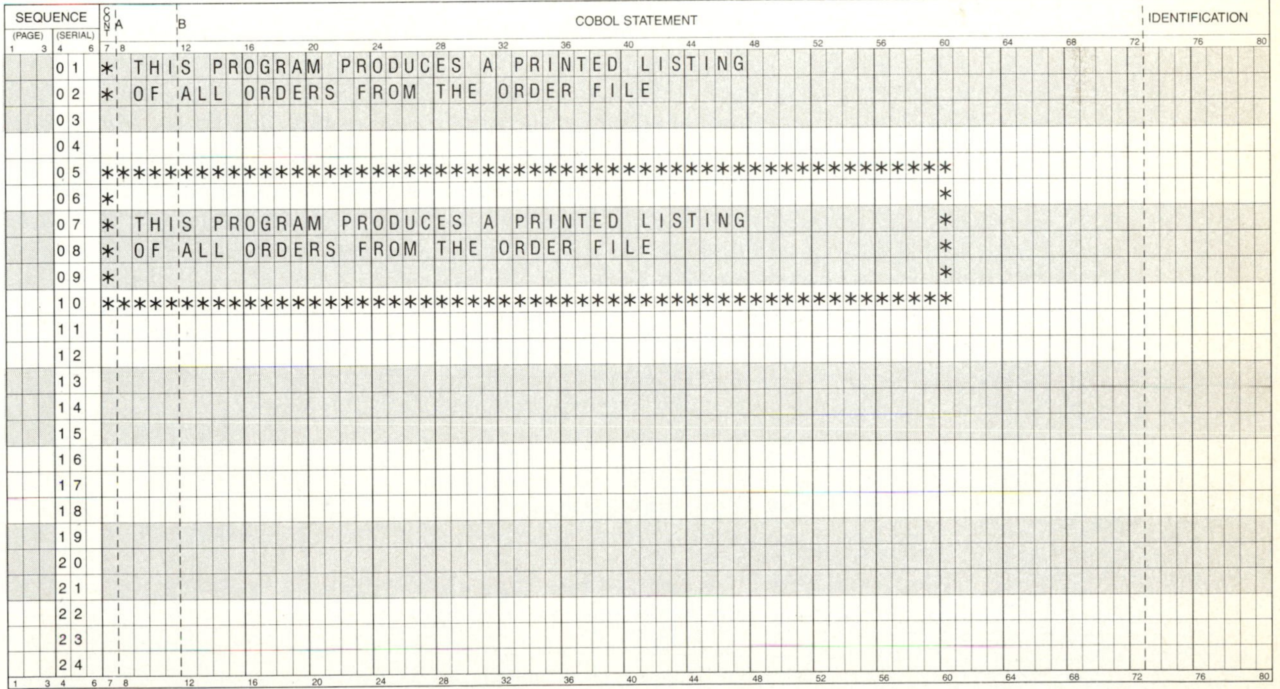

```
* THIS PROGRAM PRODUCES A PRINTED LISTING
* OF ALL ORDERS FROM THE ORDER FILE


******************************************************
*                                                    *
* THIS PROGRAM PRODUCES A PRINTED LISTING            *
* OF ALL ORDERS FROM THE ORDER FILE                  *
*                                                    *
******************************************************
```

ENVIRONMENT DIVISION

The ENVIRONMENT DIVISION provides information about the computer(s) on which the program will be compiled and executed and about the files the program will access.

Format

```
ENVIRONMENT DIVISION.
CONFIGURATION SECTION.
SOURCE-COMPUTER.  source-computer-entry
OBJECT-COMPUTER.  object-computer-entry
[INPUT-OUTPUT SECTION.
FILE-CONTROL. {file-control-entry} . . .]
```

The first statement in the ENVIRONMENT DIVISION is the ENVIRONMENT DIVISION header, which consists of the words ENVIRONMENT DIVISION followed by a period. The ENVIRONMENT DIVISION header must begin in Area A. The two sections of the ENVIRONMENT DIVISION are the CONFIGURATION SECTION and the INPUT-OUTPUT SECTION.

CONFIGURATION SECTION

Format

```
CONFIGURATION SECTION.
SOURCE-COMPUTER.   computer-name.
OBJECT-COMPUTER.   computer-name.
```

The CONFIGURATION SECTION is the first of the two sections which make up the ENVIRONMENT DIVISION. It is required and consists of two required paragraphs, the SOURCE-COMPUTER paragraph and the OBJECT-COMPUTER paragraph. In the SOURCE-COMPUTER paragraph, the programmer replaces the computer-name with the name of the computer on which the program (source module) will be compiled. In the OBJECT-COMPUTER paragraph, the programmer replaces the computer-name with the name of the computer on which the compiled program (object module) will be executed. The rules for forming computer-names will vary from compiler to compiler. Each programmer must learn the correct name for his or her installation, usually from an instructor or the computer information center. The reserved words CONFIGURATION, SOURCE-COMPUTER, and OBJECT-COMPUTER must all begin in Area A. The computer-names must be coded in Area B.

INPUT-OUTPUT SECTION

Format

```
[INPUT-OUTPUT SECTION.
FILE-CONTROL.
    SELECT  file-name ASSIGN TO  system-name ...]
```

The INPUT-OUTPUT SECTION is used to give names to all files accessed by the program. It also identifies the input or output device to be used for each file. This section must be present if the program requires any input or output files.

In the preceding format, there is a reserved word TO which is not underlined. This means that the reserved word is not required and may or may not be used, depending on the programmer's preference.

The FILE-CONTROL paragraph associates each file with an input or output device. For every file used in a program, there must be a SELECT clause followed by an ASSIGN clause. Together, the SELECT and ASSIGN clauses assign an input or output device to a file. In the SELECT clause, the file-name is the name given to the file by the programmer, and it must match the file-name used in the file description (FD) entry, which is described shortly. In the ASSIGN clause, the system-name specifies the input or output device. The method for specifying the system-name varies from system to system, so again, the programmer must learn the appropriate entry from the instructor or the information center. The section header consisting of the words INPUT-OUTPUT SECTION followed by a period must begin in Area A; SELECT and ASSIGN clauses are coded in Area B.

The Sample Program

Figure 2–6 shows the ENVIRONMENT DIVISION for the sample program segment of Figure 2–4 as it would be coded on a coding form. In the CONFIGURATION SECTION, the source-computer and object-computer clauses indicate that this program will be compiled and executed on an IBM-370 computer.

In the INPUT-OUTPUT SECTION, two files are assigned to I/O devices. The ORDER-FILE is an output file which resides on disk storage, and it is assigned a system-name which indicates this. The PRINT-FILE is an output file that is to be written to a printer. It is assigned a system-name which identifies the printer.

```
ENVIRONMENT DIVISION.

CONFIGURATION SECTION.
SOURCE-COMPUTER.
    IBM-370.
OBJECT-COMPUTER.
    IBM-370.

INPUT-OUTPUT SECTION.
FILE-CONTROL.
    SELECT ORDER-FILE ASSIGN TO DISK.
    SELECT PRINT-FILE ASSIGN TO PRINTER.
```

FIGURE 2–6

DATA DIVISION

Format

```
 DATA DIVISION.
[FILE SECTION.
 [file description entry
 [record description entry]...]...]
[WORKING-STORAGE SECTION.
 [data item description entry]...
 [record description entry]...]
```

The DATA DIVISION describes the data that will be processed by the program. Every item of data used by the program must be described in this division, including data that is read from or written to files, as well as data that is only used internally by the program.

The DATA DIVISION begins with the division header, which consists of the words DATA DIVISION followed by a period. The DATA DIVISION is divided into sections. The FILE SECTION describes each of the input and output files and the data in those files. The WORKING-STORAGE SECTION describes all other data used by the program. The DATA DIVISION header, the FILE SECTION header, and the WORKING-STORAGE SECTION header must all begin in Area A.

FILE SECTION

For each file used in a COBOL program, the FILE SECTION must contain a file description entry followed by a record description entry.

File Description Entry

Format

```
FD  file-name
    LABEL RECORDS clause
    [RECORD CONTAINS clause]
    [DATA RECORDS clause].
```

A file description entry begins with the letters FD in Area A, followed by a file name which begins in Area B. The file-name must match the file-name in the SELECT clause in the ENVIRONMENT DIVISION. The file-name is followed by one or more clauses. (The formats for these clauses will be shown later.) The LABEL RECORDS clause is required for each FD, the other clauses being optional. A period is placed after the last clause.

LABEL RECORDS Clause

Format

```
LABEL  {RECORD IS  }  {OMITTED                          }
       {RECORDS ARE}  {STANDARD                         }
                      {data-name-1 [data-name-2]...     }
```

The preceding format contains braces { }. The braces indicate that a choice is to be made: the programmer may choose the RECORD IS or RECORDS ARE option. The programmer must also choose either OMITTED, STANDARD, or a data-name.

The words RECORD IS and RECORDS ARE are interchangeable; either may be used. The OMITTED option is used when the file has no label records. This is always the case when the input/output device is a device such as a printer, card reader, or card punch. When label records are present on a disk or tape, they may be standard labels or user labels. Standard labels are label records which conform to the standards of the computer system. They are commonly used and are indicated by using the STANDARD option of the LABEL RECORDS clause. User labels are nonstandard labels which are formatted and processed by the program. They are indicated by using the data-name-1 option of the clause.

RECORD CONTAINS Clause

Format

```
RECORD CONTAINS [integer-1 TO] integer-2 CHARACTERS
```

The RECORD CONTAINS clause indicates the size of the data record in the file. If all the records in the file are the same size, only integer-2 is coded. If the records in the file vary in length, both integer-1 and integer-2 are coded to show the range of record sizes possible for the file. The RECORD CONTAINS clause is not required; if it is not supplied, the record size will be determined from the record description entry that follows the FD.

DATA RECORDS Clause

Format

```
DATA  {RECORD IS  }  data-name-1 [data-name-2]...
      {RECORDS ARE}
```

The DATA RECORDS clause provides the names of the records in the file. The words RECORD IS and RECORDS ARE are interchangeable. If only one record will be described for the file, only data-name-1 is coded. If multiple types of records will be described for the file, more data names are coded. The DATA RECORDS clause is optional; if it is not supplied, all records described in the record description entry, which follows the FD, will be considered data records associated with the file. In the file description entry, the letters FD must begin in Area A. The file-name and all clauses are coded in Area B.

The Sample Program

The FILE SECTION for the sample program segment of Figure 2–4, as it would be coded by the programmer, is shown in Figure 2–7. Two file description entries are coded, one for each file the program uses. The file-names ORDER-FILE and PRINT-FILE match the file-names that were coded in the SELECT clauses of the ENVIRONMENT DIVISION. The FD for the ORDER-FILE indicates that label records are present on the disk file and that they are standard. Each record in the file is 70 bytes long, and the record-name associated with the file is ORDER-RECORD. For the PRINT-FILE, there are no label records. This is because the output device is a printer. Each record in the print file is 133 bytes long, and the record-name associated with the file is PRINT-RECORD. In the completed program, each file description entry will be followed by a record description entry.

```
       DATA DIVISION.
       FILE SECTION.

       FD  ORDER-FILE
           LABEL RECORDS ARE STANDARD
           RECORD CONTAINS 70 CHARACTERS
           DATA RECORD IS ORDER-RECORD.

       (record description entry goes here)


       FD  PRINT-FILE
           LABEL RECORDS ARE OMITTED
           RECORD CONTAINS 133 CHARACTERS
           DATA RECORD IS PRINT-RECORD.

       (record description entry goes here)
```

FIGURE 2–7

Record Description Entry

Format

```
level number {data-name}  [PICTURE clause]
             {FILLER   }
```

The record description entry describes the format of the data on the record and it provides names for the various data elements in the record.

Each record description entry consists of one or a series of data description entries, the format of which is as shown in the preceding box. The record description entry for the ORDER-FILE is shown in Figure 2–8. It is made up of 22 data description entries, each on one line in this example. Each data description entry has two or three parts:

1. A level number
2. A data-name or the word FILLER
3. A PICTURE clause (not used on items which have been subdivided)

Each data description entry begins with a two-digit level number. The level number of a data description entry describes the relationship of that data item to the other data items in the record description entry. That is, it shows which data items are divided into smaller pieces and which are not.

The second part of each data description entry is the data-name. This assigns a name to the data item which will be used to reference that item in the logic portion (PROCEDURE DIVISION) of the program.

The third piece of the data description entry, the PICTURE clause, may not be present on every data description entry. The PICTURE clause describes the size and the type of the data item. When a data item is subdivided, as are the dates in Figure 2–8, only the subdivisions, and not the item that is subdivided, have a PICTURE clause associated with them.

```
       01  ORDER-RECORD.
           05  ORD-BRANCH              PIC 9(2).
           05  ORD-SALES-REP           PIC 9(3).
           05  ORD-CUSTOMER-NBR        PIC 9(5).
           05  ORD-CUST-PO-NBR         PIC X(8).
           05  ORD-SALES-ORD-NBR       PIC X(6).
           05  ORD-DATE.
               10  ORD-YY              PIC 9(2).
               10  ORD-MM              PIC 9(2).
               10  ORD-DD              PIC 9(2).
           05  ORD-PART-NBR            PIC X(6).
           05  ORD-QUANTITY            PIC 9(5).
           05  ORD-UNIT-PRICE          PIC 9(4)V9(2).
           05  ORD-REQ-SHIP-DATE.
               10  ORD-REQ-SHIP-YY     PIC 9(2).
               10  ORD-REQ-SHIP-MM     PIC 9(2).
               10  ORD-REQ-SHIP-DD     PIC 9(2).
           05  ORD-ACT-SHIP-DATE.
               10  ORD-ACT-SHIP-YY     PIC 9(2).
               10  ORD-ACT-SHIP-MM     PIC 9(2).
               10  ORD-ACT-SHIP-DD     PIC 9(2).
           05  FILLER                  PIC X(11).
```

FIGURE 2–8

Level Numbers

Level numbers used for subdividing data items range from 01 to 49. COBOL also has level numbers 66, 77, and 88, which are used for special purposes.

01 Level

The first data description entry in a record description entry is always a 01 level. The 01 is coded in Area A, and the data-name is coded in Area B.

02–49 Levels

If the data item named in the 01 level is to be divided into smaller data items, the smaller data items are described using level numbers which range from 02 through 49. Any data item which is divided into component parts is called a group item. A group item is composed of all of the data items listed below it, up until a data description entry is encountered which has a level number lower than or equal to the level number of the group item. For example, in Figure 2–8, the 01 level data item ORDER-RECORD is composed of all of the 05 and 10 level items listed below it. The 05 level data item ORD-DATE is composed of the three 10 level items which are listed below it.

In coding record description entries, it is good practice to increment level numbers consistently. In the examples in this text, level numbers 01, 05, 10, 15, 20, . . . are used. The gap between these level numbers allows for new data items to be inserted between them if the need arises.

Also, the record description entries will be easier to read and understand if each level is indented consistently. In our examples, each lower level is indented four spaces. Consequently, all 10 levels begin in column 16, all 15 levels begin in column 20, and so on. In addition, data-names are started two spaces after the second digit of the level numbers associated with them so that they will line up in the same columns as the level numbers of the items they are subdivided into.

Level numbers 02–49 must be coded in Area B.

Data-Names

Following the level number, a data-name or the reserved word FILLER is coded. A data-name provides a name for the data item which is used to reference the item. The word FILLER is used when the data item will not be referenced by the program. For example, in Figure 2–8, FILLER is used for the 11 unused bytes at the end of the input record. Since these bytes are unused, they will never be referenced by the program and they are not given a meaningful data-name. The remaining data items on the input record are given data-names.

In the 1985 standard the use of the word FILLER for unreferenced data items is optional. Instead of the word FILLER, the area may be left blank.

Forming Data-Names

A data-name may be 1 to 30 characters in length and may contain the following characters:

digits 0 through 9
letters A through Z
hyphen -.

Data-names must begin with a letter and must not begin or end with a hyphen. Reserved words may not be used as data-names. However, reserved words may be combined with other words to form data-names. Figure 2–9 shows examples of valid and invalid data-names.

Since data-names may be up to 30 characters in length, they should be as descriptive as possible. The more accurately a data-name describes the actual contents of the data item, the more readable the COBOL program will be.

Valid Data Names

DIVISION-NBR
INTEREST-RATE
JANUARY-SALES
PRINCIPAL
MONTH-1-SALES

Invalid Data Names

1ST-MONTH-SALES	Data-names must not begin with a number.
PRINCIPAL-	Data-names must not end with a hyphen.
INTEREST RATE	Data-names must not contain spaces.
SALES$	Data-names must not contain special characters other than the hyphen.
DEPARTMENT-FIVE-SALES-FOR-SEPTEMBER	Data-names must be 30 characters or less.
DIVISION	Reserved words must not be used as data-names.

FIGURE 2–9

PICTURE Clause

Format

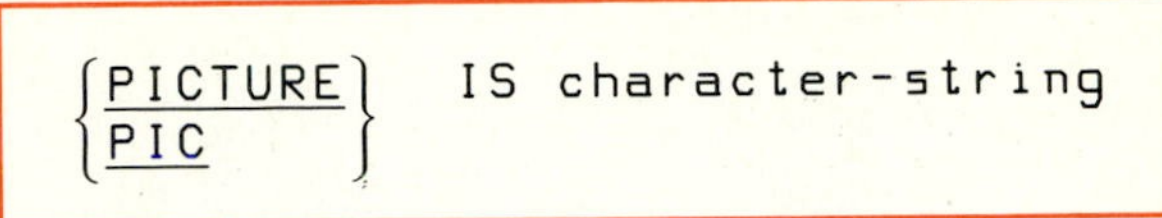

The PICTURE clause is the portion of the data description entry which describes the size and format of an elementary data item. Each data item which is not divided into smaller pieces must have a PICTURE clause. Group items must not have PICTURE clauses. When coding a PICTURE clause, the words PIC and PICTURE may be used interchangeably. The word IS is an optional reserved word and may be coded or omitted without affecting the meaning of the clause.

The character-string is a combination of symbols, each of which describes an aspect of the data item. The combination determines the format of and the amount of memory needed to store the data item.

The following are some of the symbols which may be used in character-strings.

9 — A 9 in the character-string indicates that the character position referenced may contain a numeral (0 through 9).

A — An A in the character-string indicates that the character position referenced may contain a letter (A through Z) or a space.

X — An X in the character-string indicates that the character position referenced may contain a numeral (0 through 9), a letter (A through Z), a space, or a special character (e.g., $ # & .).

V — A V in the character-string is an assumed decimal point. The assumed decimal point indicates the position in the data item where the decimal point belongs. (The V is used in describing input data items or other data items which are used in calculations. In these fields, the decimal is not actually present in the data item.) A character-string may contain only one V.

. — A period in the character-string is an editing character which indicates the position at which a decimal point will be inserted. (The period is used in describing output data in which a decimal point needs to be inserted to make the output readable.) A character-string may contain only one period.

When a symbol in a character-string needs to be repeated a number of times, the symbol may be coded repeatedly, or it may be coded once and followed by the number of repetitions desired enclosed in parentheses. Thus, the character-string XXXXX is equivalent to the character-string X(5). Figure 2–10 shows examples of PICTURE clauses.

```
PIC 9(4)          or    PIC 9999
PIC X(6)          or    PIC XXXXXX
PIC 9(2)V9(2)     or    PIC 99V99
PIC 9(4).9(2)     or    PIC 9999.99
```

FIGURE 2–10

The symbols B S Z 0 , + − CR DB * and $ may also be used in the character-string of a PICTURE clause. They are discussed in Chapter 5.

Data Formats

Each elementary data item is placed into one of five categories of data, based on the symbols used in its PICTURE clause. The five categories of data are as follows:

NUMERIC	A character-string which contains only 9's or only 9's and a V describes a numeric data item. Character-strings for numeric data items may not contain more than 18 digits (9's).
ALPHABETIC	A character-string which contains only A's describes an alphabetic data item.
ALPHANUMERIC	A character-string which contains all X's or which contains some combination of X's, A's, and 9's describes an alphanumeric data item.
ALPHANUMERIC EDITED	A character-string which contains X's combined with B's and/or 0's, or which contains A's combined with 0's, describes an alphanumeric-edited data item.
NUMERIC EDITED	A character-string which contains allowable combinations of the symbols B P V Z 0 9 , . * + − CR DB and $ describes a numeric-edited data item.

All group items are considered alphanumeric regardless of the category of the elementary items which make them up. A more complete description of alphanumeric-edited and numeric-edited data items is found in Chapter 5.

The Sample Program

The complete coding for the FILE SECTION of the sample program segment of Figure 2–4 is shown in Figure 2–11. The record description entry for the ORDER-FILE describes the input record in detail. The 01 level ORDER-RECORD is made up of all the 05 and 10 level entries listed below it. A reference to ORDER-RECORD references all 70 bytes of the record. The fields within the record are described using 05 and 10 level entries. All data items within the ORDER-RECORD are either numeric or alphanumeric. The record description entry for the PRINT-FILE describes the PRINT-RECORD as an alphanumeric data item 133 bytes in length. Describing the PRINT-RECORD in this way allows the printing of any number of differently formatted print lines (i.e., heading lines, detail lines, total lines).

Notice that one record, ORDER-RECORD, is described in detail while PRINT-RECORD is shown as a single data-item. The programmer may elect to describe a record in detail in either the FILE SECTION or the WORKING-STORAGE SECTION which follows it. In some cases where the record is to be transferred from one location to another as a single unit, it is never described in detail.

WORKING-STORAGE SECTION

The WORKING-STORAGE SECTION of a program describes all data items used by the program except for those described in the FILE SECTION. Data items described in the WORKING-STORAGE SECTION may include both record descriptions and data items which are used internally by the program.

Entries in the WORKING-STORAGE section are created using the same rules for forming record description entries in the FILE section, with one addition:

```
       FILE SECTION.

       FD  ORDER-FILE
           LABEL RECORDS ARE STANDARD
           RECORD CONTAINS 70 CHARACTERS
           DATA RECORD IS ORDER-RECORD.

       01  ORDER-RECORD.
           05  ORD-BRANCH                      PIC 9(2).
           05  ORD-SALES-REP                   PIC 9(3).
           05  ORD-CUSTOMER-NBR                PIC 9(5).
           05  ORD-CUST-PO-NBR                 PIC X(8).
           05  ORD-SALES-ORD-NBR               PIC X(6).
           05  ORD-DATE.
               10  ORD-YY                      PIC 9(2).
               10  ORD-MM                      PIC 9(2).
               10  ORD-DD                      PIC 9(2).
           05  ORD-PART-NBR                    PIC X(6).
           05  ORD-QUANTITY                    PIC 9(5).
           05  ORD-UNIT-PRICE                  PIC 9(4)V9(2).
           05  ORD-REQ-SHIP-DATE.
               10  ORD-REQ-SHIP-YY             PIC 9(2).
               10  ORD-REQ-SHIP-MM             PIC 9(2).
               10  ORD-REQ-SHIP-DD             PIC 9(2).
```

```
           05  ORD-ACT-SHIP-DATE.
               10  ORD-ACT-SHIP-YY             PIC 9(2).
               10  ORD-ACT-SHIP-MM             PIC 9(2).
               10  ORD-ACT-SHIP-DD             PIC 9(2).
           05  FILLER                          PIC X(11).

       FD  PRINT-FILE
           LABEL RECORDS ARE OMITTED
           RECORD CONTAINS 133 CHARACTERS
           DATA RECORD IS PRINT-RECORD.

       01  PRINT-RECORD.                       PIC X(133).
```

FIGURE 2–11

in the WORKING-STORAGE section, elementary items may also have a VALUE clause.

Format

```
level number  { data name }     [PICTURE clause]  [VALUE clause]
              { FILLER    }
```

VALUE Clause

Format

```
VALUE IS literal
```

A VALUE clause is used to give a data item an initial value. When the program begins execution, the data item will contain the value specified. The contents of the data item may be changed by instructions in the PROCEDURE DIVISION as the program executes. Areas of memory that are reserved but have no VALUE clause contain whatever was left there by the previous program.

Literals

A literal is a string of characters which make up a constant. There are two types of literals, numeric and nonnumeric. The type of literal used in a VALUE clause should be consistent with the category of data described in the PICTURE clause. If the PICTURE clause describes a numeric data item, a numeric literal should be used in the VALUE clause; otherwise, a nonnumeric literal should be used in the VALUE clause.

Numeric Literals A numeric literal is a numeric constant. Numeric literals are composed of the digits 0 through 9. There may be 1 to 18 such digits in a numeric literal. A sign character (+ or −) may be included to the left of the digits. A decimal point may also be included, but it may not be the rightmost character in the literal. No other characters are permitted in a numeric literal. Figure 2–12 shows examples of valid and invalid numeric literals.

Numeric literals may be used in VALUE clauses when the PICTURE clause describes a numeric data item. Numeric literals may also be used in the PROCEDURE DIVISION for calculations and comparisons.

Nonnumeric Literals A nonnumeric literal is a constant that may contain any valid characters except the quotation mark. Nonnumeric literals must be enclosed in quotation marks. Whether a single or double quote is used depends on a choice made by the operations staff at the computer facility. A nonnumeric literal may

Valid Numeric Literals

600.000
−5
+1.15
80
.075

Invalid Numeric Literals

9.5−	Sign characters are only allowed as the leftmost character of a numeric literal.
24.	A decimal point may not be the rightmost character of a numeric literal.
5,000	Commas are not allowed in numeric literals.
9218610085402361810	A maximum of 18 digits is allowed in numeric literals.

FIGURE 2–12

have a maximum of 120 characters, including spaces. The quotation marks which surround the literal are not counted as being among the 120 characters.

The 1985 standard allows a nonnumeric literal to have a maximum length of 160 characters.

Figure 2–13 shows examples of valid and invalid nonnumeric literals.

When placed in a VALUE clause, nonnumeric literals are used when the PICTURE clause describes an alphabetic, alphanumeric, numeric-edited, or alphanumeric-edited data item. Nonnumeric literals may also be used in PROCEDURE DIVISION instructions.

Some examples of literals as they might be placed on a coding sheet are shown in Figure 2–14. Notice how the literal may be placed on a new line if there is not room for it on the line where the entry began. Sometimes one line is not sufficient for a nonnumeric literal. If this is the case, the literal may be continued to one or more additional lines. When a nonnumeric literal is to be continued, follow the steps listed below. Refer to Figure 2–14 for examples.

1. Start the literal with a quote, and code the literal through column 72. Any spaces left before column 72 will be included in the literal. Do not end this line with a quote.
2. Place a hyphen in column 7 of the next line. This is the continuation character.
3. Start in the B margin on the continuation line. Begin with a quote, then continue coding the literal. If the literal is completed on this line, place a quote and then a period at the end of the literal. If the literal cannot be completed on this line, simply code to column 72.
4. If a third line is required, repeat step 3.

Figurative Constants

A figurative constant is a constant which has a reserved word associated with it. A figurative constant may be used wherever a literal is allowed. The figurative constants and their meanings are shown in Figure 2–15.

For each of the figurative constants, the singular and plural versions are interchangeable. Figurative constants may be used in place of the literal in the VALUE clause. However, when the PICTURE clause describes a numeric data item, the only figurative constants which may be used are ZERO, ZEROS, or ZEROES.

Valid Nonnumeric Literals

'ORDER LISTING'

'***'

'$10,000'

'B'

'123'

Invalid Nonnumeric Literals

'C	Nonnumeric literals must be completely enclosed in quotes.
'JOE'S GARAGE'	Nonnumeric literals may not contain quotes.

FIGURE 2–13

```
       01  NUMERIC-LITERALS.
           05  LITERAL-1                PIC 9V9(3)      VALUE 1.645.
           05  LITERAL-2                PIC 9(5)        VALUE 462.
           05  LITERAL-3                PIC V9(2)       VALUE .55.
           05  LITERAL-4                PIC 9(9)        VALUE 440618350.
```

```
       01  ALPHANUMERIC-LITERALS.
           05  LITERAL-ONE              PIC X(6)        VALUE 'ORDERS'.
           05  LITERAL-TWO              PIC X(10)       VALUE 'INCOME TAX
      -        ''.
           05  LITERAL-THREE            PIC X(25)       VALUE 'PRODUCT DI
      -        'STRIBUTION INC.'.
           05  LITERAL-FOUR             PIC X(102)      VALUE 'THIS IS AN
      -        '  EXTRAORDINARILY LONG ALPHANUMERIC LITERAL -- IT EXTENDS
      -        'OVER THREE LINES OF THE CODING SHEET'.
```

FIGURE 2–14

The Sample Program

For the program segment shown in Figure 2–4, only two types of data items appear in the WORKING-STORAGE section. The first entry in the WORKING-STORAGE section is a switch which will be used to determine when all input records have been read. The switch is given the data-name END-FLAG-ORDER-FILE. It is described as a three-byte alphanumeric item and is given an initial value of NO. Notice that NO is an alphanumeric literal and is enclosed in quotes in the COBOL code. The remaining entries all describe print lines. The WORKING-STORAGE section, as it would be coded by the programmer, is shown in Figure 2–16. The

FIGURE 2–15

FIGURATIVE CONSTANTS	MEANING
ZERO ZEROES ZEROS	The value 0, or one or more 0 characters.
SPACE SPACES	One or more spaces (blanks).
HIGH-VALUE HIGH-VALUES	One or more characters of the highest possible binary value (1111 1111).
LOW-VALUE LOW-VALUES	One or more characters of the lowest possible binary value (0000 0000).
QUOTE QUOTES	One or more quotation marks.
ALL literal	One or more occurrences of a nonnumeric literal.

print chart is repeated in Figure 2–17 so that you can compare it with the code for the heading lines.

Each different type of line from the print chart is described in the WORKING-STORAGE section. For the sample program, there are four print lines: a main heading, two column headings, and a detail line. For each of these, the layout shown on the print chart is transferred to an entry in the WORKING-STORAGE section. Notice that when a programmer codes the COBOL for a line from the print chart, the entire line is represented by a 01 level. Then, moving from left to right, each area on the line is described using a 05 level to indicate that it is part of the line.

All three of the heading lines for the sample program contain only constant fields. There is no information in these heading lines which would change from page to page or from run to run. Because of this, the individual items on the heading lines will never be referenced by the logic portion of the program, and each elementary item uses the word FILLER instead of a data-name. Each area from the print chart is described with an alphanumeric PICTURE clause and

```
    05  DET-ORDER-MM            PIC 9(2).
    05  FILLER                  PIC X(1)        VALUE '-'.
    05  DET-ORDER-DD            PIC 9(2).
    05  FILLER                  PIC X(1)        VALUE '-'.
    05  DET-ORDER-YY            PIC 9(2).
    05  FILLER                  PIC X(5)        VALUE SPACES.
    05  DET-PART-NBR            PIC X(6).
    05  FILLER                  PIC X(6)        VALUE SPACES.
    05  DET-QUANTITY            PIC 9(5).
    05  FILLER                  PIC X(5)        VALUE SPACES.
    05  DET-UNIT-PRICE          PIC 9(4).9(2).
    05  FILLER                  PIC X(5)        VALUE SPACES.
    05  DET-REQ-SHIP-MM         PIC 9(2).
    05  FILLER                  PIC X(1)        VALUE '-'.
    05  DET-REQ-SHIP-DD         PIC 9(2).
    05  FILLER                  PIC X(1)        VALUE '-'.
    05  DET-REQ-SHIP-YY         PIC 9(2).
    05  FILLER                  PIC X(5)        VALUE SPACES.
    05  DET-ACT-SHIP-MM         PIC 9(2).
    05  FILLER                  PIC X(1)        VALUE '-'.
    05  DET-ACT-SHIP-DD         PIC 9(2).
    05  FILLER                  PIC X(1)        VALUE '-'.
    05  DET-ACT-SHIP-YY         PIC 9(2).
    05  FILLER                  PIC X(7)        VALUE SPACES.
```

FIGURE 2–16

```
       WORKING-STORAGE SECTION.

       01  HOLDS-COUNTERS-SWITCHES.
           05  END-FLAG-ORDER-FILE     PIC X(3)        VALUE 'NO'.

       01  MAIN-HEADING.
           05  FILLER                  PIC X(45)       VALUE SPACES.
           05  FILLER                  PIC X(42)
               VALUE 'PRODUCT DISTRIBUTION INC. - CURRENT ORDERS'.
           05  FILLER                  PIC X(45)       VALUE SPACES.

       01  COLUMN-HEADING-1.
           05  FILLER                  PIC X(14)       VALUE SPACES.
           05  FILLER                  PIC X(5)        VALUE 'SALES'.
           05  FILLER                  PIC X(3)        VALUE SPACES.
           05  FILLER                  PIC X(8)        VALUE 'CUSTOMER'.
           05  FILLER                  PIC X(4)        VALUE SPACES.
           05  FILLER                  PIC X(8)        VALUE 'PURCHASE'.
           05  FILLER                  PIC X(6)        VALUE SPACES.
           05  FILLER                  PIC X(5)        VALUE 'SALES'.
           05  FILLER                  PIC X(6)        VALUE SPACES.
           05  FILLER                  PIC X(5)        VALUE 'ORDER'.
           05  FILLER                  PIC X(8)        VALUE SPACES.
           05  FILLER                  PIC X(4)        VALUE 'PART'.
```

```
           05  FILLER                  PIC X(18)       VALUE SPACES.
           05  FILLER                  PIC X(4)        VALUE 'UNIT'.
           05  FILLER                  PIC X(6)        VALUE SPACES.
           05  FILLER                  PIC X(9)        VALUE
                                                       'REQUESTED'.
           05  FILLER                  PIC X(6)        VALUE SPACES.
           05  FILLER                  PIC X(6)        VALUE 'ACTUAL'.
           05  FILLER                  PIC X(8)        VALUE SPACES.

       01  COLUMN-HEADING-2.
           05  FILLER                  PIC X(5)        VALUE SPACES.
           05  FILLER                  PIC X(6)        VALUE 'BRANCH'.
           05  FILLER                  PIC X(4)        VALUE SPACES.
           05  FILLER                  PIC X(3)        VALUE 'REP'.
           05  FILLER                  PIC X(5)        VALUE SPACES.
           05  FILLER                  PIC X(6)        VALUE 'NUMBER'.
           05  FILLER                  PIC X(6)        VALUE SPACES.
           05  FILLER                  PIC X(5)        VALUE 'ORDER'.
           05  FILLER                  PIC X(8)        VALUE SPACES.
           05  FILLER                  PIC X(5)        VALUE 'ORDER'.
           05  FILLER                  PIC X(6)        VALUE SPACES.
           05  FILLER                  PIC X(4)        VALUE 'DATE'.
           05  FILLER                  PIC X(8)        VALUE SPACES.
           05  FILLER                  PIC X(6)        VALUE 'NUMBER'.
```

FIGURE 2-16 cont.

```
   01      05  FILLER                      PIC X(4)        VALUE SPACES.
   02      05  FILLER                      PIC X(8)        VALUE 'QUANTITY'.
   03      05  FILLER                      PIC X(5)        VALUE SPACES.
   04      05  FILLER                      PIC X(5)        VALUE 'PRICE'.
   05      05  FILLER                      PIC X(5)        VALUE SPACES.
   06      05  FILLER                      PIC X(9)        VALUE
   07                                                      'SHIP DATE'.
   08      05  FILLER                      PIC X(4)        VALUE SPACES.
   09      05  FILLER                      PIC X(9)        VALUE
   10                                                      'SHIP DATE'.
   11      05  FILLER                      PIC X(7)        VALUE SPACES.
   12
   13  01  DETAIL-LINE.
   14      05  FILLER                      PIC X(7)        VALUE SPACES.
   15      05  DET-BRANCH                  PIC 9(2).
   16      05  FILLER                      PIC X(6)        VALUE SPACES.
   17      05  DET-SALES-REP               PIC 9(3).
   18      05  FILLER                      PIC X(6)        VALUE SPACES.
   19      05  DET-CUSTOMER-NBR            PIC 9(5).
   20      05  FILLER                      PIC X(5)        VALUE SPACES.
   21      05  DET-CUST-PO-NBR             PIC X(8).
   22      05  FILLER                      PIC X(6)        VALUE SPACES.
   23      05  DET-SALES-ORD-NBR           PIC X(6).
   24      05  FILLER                      PIC X(5)        VALUE SPACES.
```

FIGURE 2-16 cont.

VALUE clause. Where an area should be blank, the figurative constant SPACES is used in the VALUE clause. Where words are to be placed in the heading lines, alphanumeric literals are used.

The detail line consists of constant fields (spaces or hyphens) and variable fields (the output information). The variable fields will be referenced by the logic portion of the program and are given data-names. All these data-names are prefixed with the letters DET to indicate that they are a part of the detail line. Most of the fields on the detail line are numeric or alphanumeric; one field (DET-UNIT-PRICE) is numeric edited.

COBOL requires that each data item be moved from the input record to the corresponding data-name in the detail line. This is done in the PROCEDURE DIVISION. For example, ORD-BRANCH will be moved to DET-BRANCH, ORD-SALES-REP will be moved to DET-SALES-REP, and so on.

DEBUGGING

Each chapter in this text includes a section on debugging. These sections are designed to provide additional help with, and understanding of, both programs read and programs written.

Spaces and Hyphens

One of the things that bothers a beginning programmer is when to use spaces and when to use hyphens. Let us take the following line from the WORKING-STORAGE SECTION in Figure 2–16 and examine the spaces and hyphens in it:

```
05  DET-BRANCH   PIC 9(2).
```

When the COBOL compiler examines a line in its search for syntax errors, it moves from space to space to locate the individual COBOL elements. The compiler does not make a distinction between one space and multiple spaces.

```
05  DET-BRANCH   PIC 9(2).
```

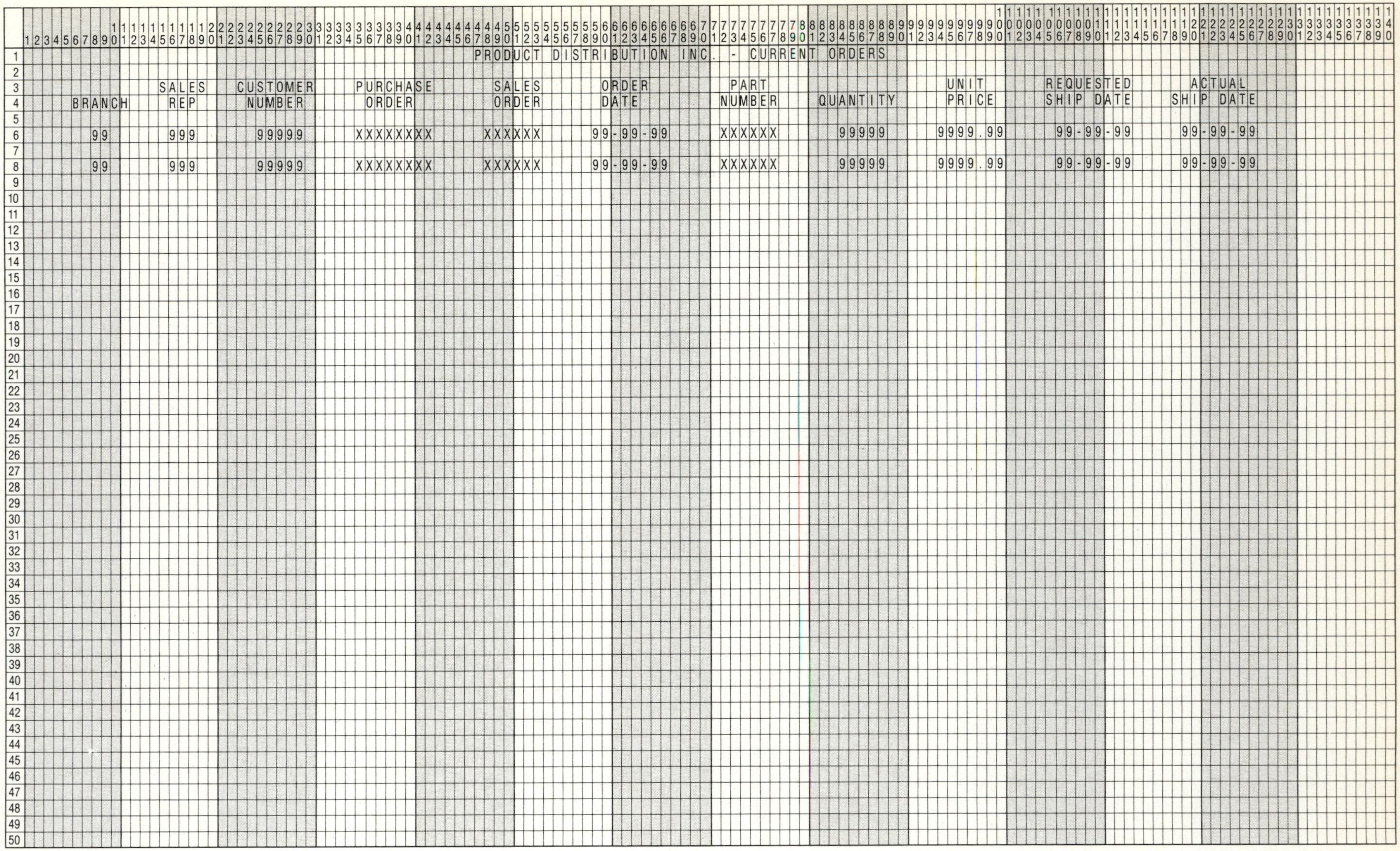

```
1                                               PRODUCT DISTRIBUTION INC. - CURRENT ORDERS
2
3                 SALES    CUSTOMER      PURCHASE      SALES      ORDER           PART                   UNIT      REQUESTED       ACTUAL
4       BRANCH     REP      NUMBER          ORDER      ORDER      DATE           NUMBER    QUANTITY      PRICE     SHIP DATE    SHIP DATE
5
6           99     999       99999       XXXXXXXX      XXXXXX  99-99-99         XXXXXX      99999      9999.99      99-99-99     99-99-99
7
8           99     999       99999       XXXXXXXX      XXXXXX  99-99-99         XXXXXX      99999      9999.99      99-99-99     99-99-99
```

FIGURE 2–17

As indicated by the arrows, there are four elements on this line that are surrounded by spaces:

05	a level number
DET-BRANCH	a data-name
PIC	reserved word for PICTURE
9(2)	a character string describing the format of the data item

All of these are valid COBOL elements in a proper order. Let us see what happens if the hyphen is removed.

```
05  DET BRANCH  PIC 9(2).
```

Again as the arrows indicate, now there are five COBOL elements on the line:

05	a level number
DET	a data-name
BRANCH	an error—not one of the acceptable elements on this type of line since we already have a data-name on it
PIC	this item is disregarded, since it follows an error
9(2)	this item is disregarded, since it follows an error

From the preceding discussion, it is plain that hyphens are used in COBOL data-names to avoid leaving spaces when words are combined to form data-names. If a space is left in a data-name, the compiler considers it to be a data-name and an extra unidentifiable element. We leave spaces in COBOL coding to separate each new COBOL element so that the compiler can recognize it.

The 1985 standard makes the comma, semicolon, and space interchangeable as separators.

SUMMARY

This chapter has presented the specifications for a program to produce a printed listing. The COBOL code for the first three divisions of the program, the IDENTIFICATION DIVISION, the ENVIRONMENT DIVISION and the DATA DIVISION, were examined. Formats for those divisions are summarized as follows:

Format

```
 IDENTIFICATION DIVISION.
 PROGRAM-ID.          program-name.
[AUTHOR.              [comment-entry] . . .]
[INSTALLATION.        [comment-entry] . . .]
[DATE-WRITTEN.        [comment-entry] . . .]
[DATE-COMPILED.       [comment-entry] . . .]
[SECURITY.            [comment-entry] . . .]
```

Format

```
ENVIRONMENT DIVISION.
CONFIGURATION SECTION.
SOURCE-COMPUTER.    computer-name.
OBJECT-COMPUTER.    computer-name.
[INPUT-OUTPUT SECTION.
FILE-CONTROL.
  {SELECT  file-name
   ASSIGN TO  system-name}...]
```

Format

```
DATA DIVISION.
FILE SECTION.
FD  file-name.
    LABEL  {RECORD IS  }  {OMITTED                      }
           {RECORDS ARE}  {STANDARD                     }
                          {data-name-1 [data-name-2]... }
    RECORD CONTAINS [integer-1 TO] integer-2 CHARACTERS
    DATA   {RECORD IS  }  data-name-1 [data-name-2]...
           {RECORDS ARE}

level number {data-name}  [PICTURE clause]
             {FILLER   }

WORKING-STORAGE SECTION.
level number {data-name}  [PICTURE clause] [VALUE clause]
             {FILLER   }
```

Level Numbers

01	Record description
02-49	For subdividing

Data Names

Formed using 0–9, A–Z, and the hyphen -
Must begin with a letter
Must not begin or end with a hyphen
Must be 30 characters or less

PICTURE Character-Strings

9	Numeric
X	Alphanumeric
A	Alphabetic
V	Assumed decimal position
.	Decimal point

Categories of Data

Numeric
Alphabetic
Alphanumeric
Alphanumeric edited
Numeric edited

Value

VALUE clauses are used to initialize data items

Literals

- Numeric
  - May contain 1–18 digits
  - May have + or – to the left
  - May contain a decimal point
- Nonnumeric
  - Enclosed in quotes
  - May contain 1–120 characters

Figurative Constants

- ZERO, ZEROS, ZEROES
- SPACE, SPACES
- HIGH-VALUE, HIGH-VALUES
- LOW-VALUE, LOW-VALUES
- QUOTE, QUOTES
- ALL literal

EXERCISES

I. For each of the following PICTUREs, indicate whether it represents a numeric (N), alphabetic (AL), or alphanumeric (AN) data item.

_____ **1.** PIC 9(5)
_____ **2.** PIC X(9)
_____ **3.** PIC 99
_____ **4.** PIC A(6)
_____ **5.** PIC XXX
_____ **6.** PIC A
_____ **7.** PIC 9(2)V9(2)
_____ **8.** PIC 99V99
_____ **9.** PIC X(120)
_____ **10.** PIC V99

II. Indicate which of the following PICTURE clauses are valid (V) and which are invalid (I).

_____ **1.** PIC 9(4)
_____ **2.** PIC X(6)
_____ **3.** PIC 5(9)
_____ **4.** PIC A(3)
_____ **5.** PIC 2(X)
_____ **6.** PIC 9VX
_____ **7.** PIC XXX
_____ **8.** PIC 9V9
_____ **9.** PIC 92
_____ **10.** PIC X(133)

III. Using the following record description entry, indicate which data items are group items (G) and which are elementary items (E).

```
_____  1.   01  PAYROLL-RECORD.
_____  2.       05  PAY-GROUP.
_____  3.           10  PAY-DIVISION     PIC 9(2).
_____  4.           10  PAY-DEPARTMENT   PIC 9(3).
_____  5.       05  PAY-NAME             PIC X(25).
_____  6.       05  PAY-ADDRESS.
_____  7.           10  PAY-STREET       PIC X(20).
_____  8.           10  PAY-CITY         PIC X(15).
_____  9.           10  PAY-STATE        PIC X(2).
_____ 10.           10  PAY-ZIP          PIC X(9).
```

```
_____ 11.      05  PAY-RATE                 PIC 9(4)V9(2).
_____ 12.      05  PAY-HIRE-DATE.
_____ 13.          10  PAY-HIRE-YEAR        PIC 9(2).
_____ 14.          10  PAY-HIRE-MONTH       PIC 9(2).
_____ 15.          10  PAY-HIRE-DAY         PIC 9(2).
```

IV. Using the following record description, indicate which data items are numeric (N) and which data items are alphanumeric (AN).

```
_____ 1.   01  PAYROLL-RECORD.
_____ 2.       05  PAY-GROUP.
_____ 3.           10  PAY-DIVISION         PIC 9(2).
_____ 4.           10  PAY-DEPARTMENT       PIC 9(3).
_____ 5.       05  PAY-NAME                 PIC X(25).
_____ 6.       05  PAY-ADDRESS.
_____ 7.           10  PAY-STREET           PIC X(20).
_____ 8.           10  PAY-CITY             PIC X(15).
_____ 9.           10  PAY-STATE            PIC X(2).
_____ 10.          10  PAY-ZIP              PIC X(9).
_____ 11.      05  PAY-RATE                 PIC 9(4)V9(2).
_____ 12.      05  PAY-HIRE-DATE.
_____ 13.          10  PAY-HIRE-YEAR        PIC 9(2).
_____ 14.          10  PAY-HIRE-MONTH       PIC 9(2).
_____ 15.          10  PAY-HIRE-DAY         PIC 9(2).
```

V. Indicate which of the following data-names are valid (V) and which are invalid (I).

_____ **1.** NET-PAY
_____ **2.** DIVISION
_____ **3.** OUT-OF-POCKET EXPENSE
_____ **4.** $-VALUE
_____ **5.** STREET-ADDRESS
_____ **6.** SECTION-4
_____ **7.** DIVISION-NBR
_____ **8.** VALID-REIMBURSEMENT-FOR-PETTY-CASH
_____ **9.** DIVISION#
_____ **10.** GROSS PAY

VI. Indicate which of the following value clauses describe numeric data (N), which describe alphanumeric data (AN), and which are invalid (I).

_____ **1.** VALUE '2'.
_____ **2.** VALUE 'ZERO'.
_____ **3.** VALUE BALANCE
_____ **4.** VALUE 98.00.
_____ **5.** VALUE 10,000.
_____ **6.** VALUE 2.
_____ **7.** VALUE −18.
_____ **8.** VALUE .1.
_____ **9.** VALUE SPACES.
_____ **10.** VALUE '10,000'.

PROJECTS

For each of the following program specifications and input record layouts, design a print chart and code the first three divisions of a COBOL program that satisfies the specification.

PROJECT 2–1 Payroll

PROGRAM SPECIFICATION

Program Name: PAY2

Program Function:

The program will produce a listing of a payroll file.

Input Files:

I. PAYROLL-FILE

INPUT DEVICE:	DISK
FILE ORGANIZATION:	SEQUENTIAL
RECORD LENGTH:	80 BYTES
FILE SEQUENCE:	ASCENDING ON DIVISION / DEPARTMENT

Output Files:

I. PRINT-FILE

OUTPUT DEVICE:	PRINTER
RECORD LENGTH:	133 BYTES

Output Requirements:

Each record read from the payroll file should be printed on one line of the report. All fields from the input record are to be included on the output. Design your own output using a print chart.

The following are formatting requirements for the report:

1. The first page of the report should contain:
   (a) a heading which includes the company name and report name.
   (b) column headings which describe the items printed underneath them.
2. The detail lines should include all fields from the input.
3. The detail lines should be double spaced.
4. Do not include provisions for page overflow.

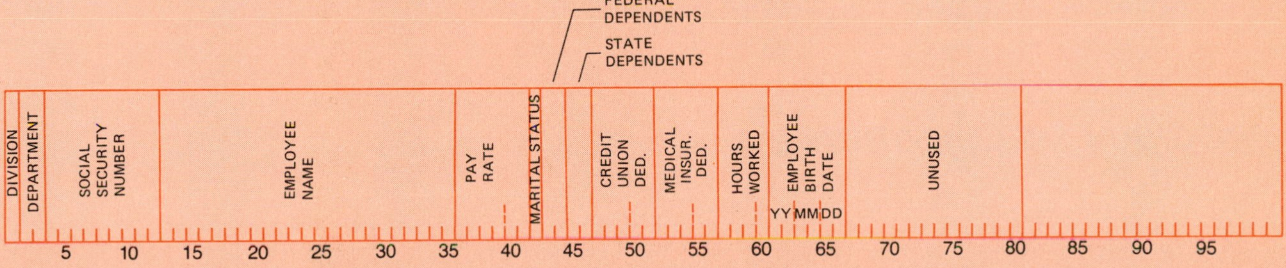

PROJECT 2–2 Inventory

PROGRAM SPECIFICATION

Program Name: INV2

Program Function:

The program will produce a listing of an inventory file.

Input Files:

I. INVENTORY-FILE

INPUT DEVICE:	DISK
FILE ORGANIZATION:	SEQUENTIAL
RECORD LENGTH:	80 BYTES
FILE SEQUENCE:	ASCENDING ON INVENTORY STOCK NUMBER

Output Files:

I. PRINT-FILE

OUTPUT DEVICE:	PRINTER
RECORD LENGTH:	133 BYTES

Output Requirements:

Each record read from the inventory file should be printed on one line of the report. All fields from the input record are to be included on the output. Design your own output using a print chart.

The following are formatting requirements for the report:

1. The first page of the report should contain:
   (a) a heading which includes the company name and report name.
   (b) column headings which describe the items printed underneath them.
2. The detail lines should include all fields from the input.
3. The detail lines should be double spaced.
4. Do not include provisions for page overflow.

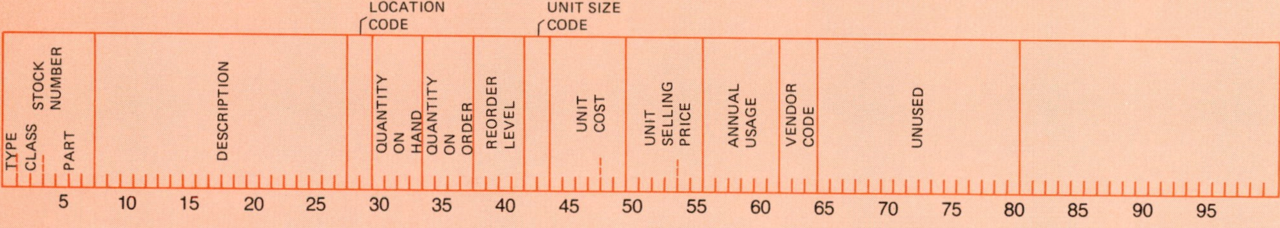

PROJECT 2–3 Accounts Payable

PROGRAM SPECIFICATION

Program Name: AP2

Program Function:

The program will produce a listing of an accounts payable file.

Input Files:

I. ACCOUNTS-PAYABLE-FILE

INPUT DEVICE:	DISK
FILE ORGANIZATION:	SEQUENTIAL
RECORD LENGTH:	80 BYTES
FILE SEQUENCE:	ASCENDING ON DIVISION / CONTROL NBR

Output Files:

I. PRINT-FILE

OUTPUT DEVICE:	PRINTER
RECORD LENGTH:	133 BYTES

Output Requirements:

Each record read from the accounts payable file should be printed on one line of the report. All fields from the input record are to be included on the output. Design your own output using a print chart.

The following are formatting requirements for the report:

1. The first page of the report should contain:
   (a) a heading which includes the company name and report name.
   (b) column headings which describe the items printed underneath them.
2. The detail lines should include all fields from the input.
3. The detail lines should be double spaced.
4. Do not include provisions for page overflow.

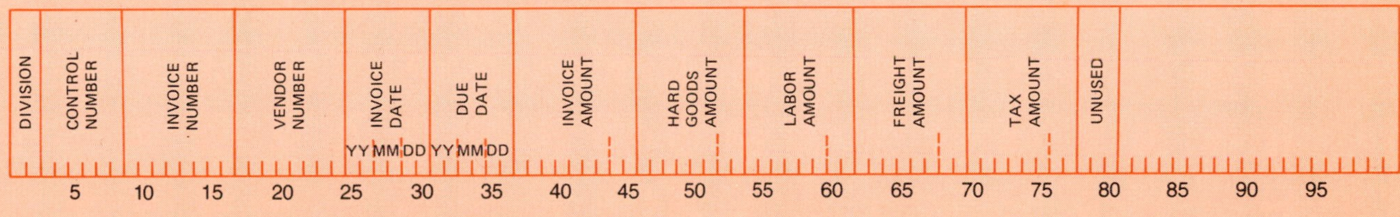

PROJECT 2–4 Pension

PROGRAM SPECIFICATION

Program Name: PEN2

Program Function:

The program will produce a listing of a pension file.

Input Files:

I. PENSION-FILE

INPUT DEVICE:	DISK
FILE ORGANIZATION:	SEQUENTIAL
RECORD LENGTH:	80 BYTES
FILE SEQUENCE:	ASCENDING ON DIVISION / DEPARTMENT

Output Files:

I. PRINT-FILE

OUTPUT DEVICE:	PRINTER
RECORD LENGTH:	133 BYTES

Output Requirements:

Each record read from the pension file should be printed on one line of the report. All fields from the input record are to be included on the output. Design your own output using a print chart.

The following are formatting requirements for the report:

1. The first page of the report should contain:
   (a) a heading which includes the company name and report name.
   (b) column headings which describe the items printed underneath them.
2. The detail lines should include all fields from the input.
3. The detail lines should be double spaced.
4. Do not include provisions for page overflow.

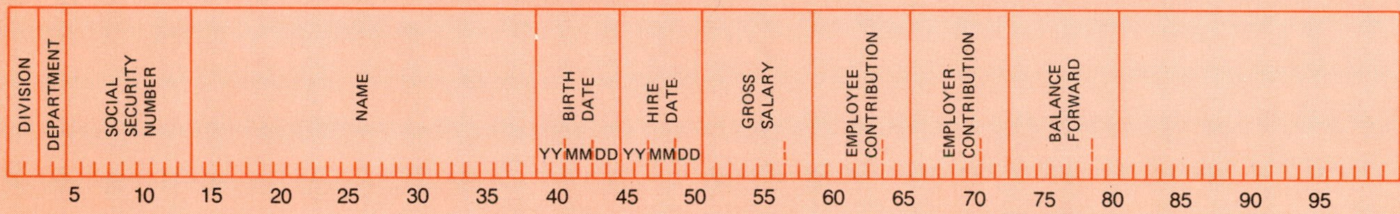

PROJECT 2–5 Bill of Materials

PROGRAM SPECIFICATION

Program Name: BOM2

Program Function:

The program will produce a listing of a bill-of-materials file.

Input Files:

I. BILL-OF-MATERIAL-FILE

INPUT DEVICE:	DISK
FILE ORGANIZATION:	SEQUENTIAL
RECORD LENGTH:	55 BYTES
FILE SEQUENCE:	ASCENDING ON DIVISION / PRODUCT LINE

Output Files:

I. PRINT-FILE

OUTPUT DEVICE:	PRINTER
RECORD LENGTH:	133 BYTES

Output Requirements:

Each record read from the bill-of-materials file should be printed on one line of the report. All fields from the input record are to be included on the output. Design your own output using a print chart.

The following are formatting requirements for the report:

1. The first page of the report should contain:
   (a) a heading which includes the company name and report name.
   (b) column headings which describe the items printed underneath them.
2. The detail lines should include all fields from the input.
3. The detail lines should be double spaced.
4. Do not include provisions for page overflow.

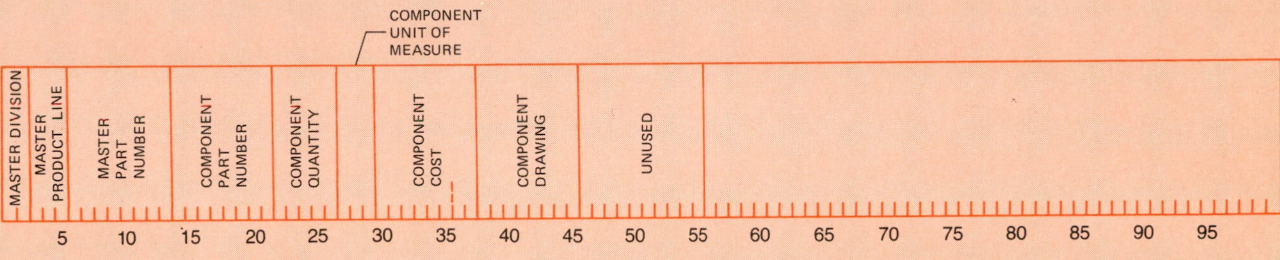

PROJECT 2–6 Cost

PROGRAM SPECIFICATION

Program Name: COST2

Program Function:

The program will produce a listing of a cost file.

Input Files:

I. COST-FILE

INPUT DEVICE:	DISK
FILE ORGANIZATION:	SEQUENTIAL
RECORD LENGTH:	75 BYTES
FILE SEQUENCE:	ASCENDING ON DIVISION / PRODUCT LINE

Output Files:

I. PRINT-FILE

OUTPUT DEVICE:	PRINTER
RECORD LENGTH:	133 BYTES

Output Requirements:

Each record read from the cost file should be printed on one line of the report. All fields from the input record are to be included on the output. Design your own output using a print chart.

The following are formatting requirements for the report:

1. The first page of the report should contain:
   (a) a heading which includes the company name and report name.
   (b) column headings which describe the items printed underneath them.
2. The detail lines should include all fields from the input.
3. The detail lines should be double spaced.
4. Do not include provisions for page overflow.

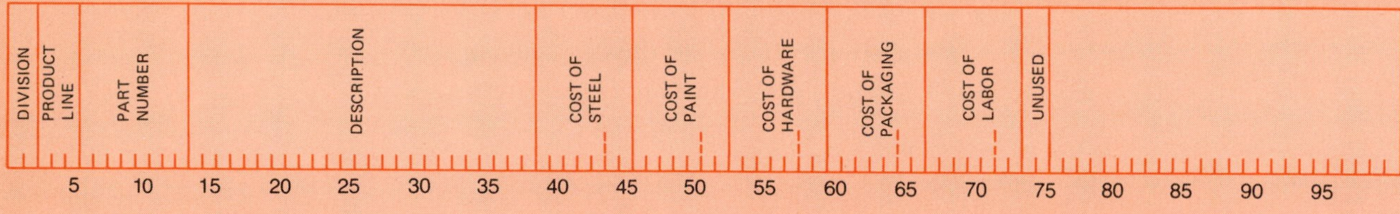

CHAPTER

3 The PROCEDURE Division

The programming project begun in Chapter 2 is completed in this chapter. In Chapter 2 we named the program, specified the environment in which it would run, and reserved storage for data. Here, we present the logic necessary to produce the desired output, a simple listing of the data from an input file.

There are seven COBOL verbs used to implement programming logic. PERFORM is used to control the flow of the logic. OPEN, CLOSE, READ, and WRITE are used to obtain data from one file (disk) and write it to another file (printer). MOVE transfers data internally, and STOP terminates execution of the program.

The debugging section includes diagnostic messages which might be generated by a program of this type. Suggestions are included on finding the causes of the diagnostics and correcting the errors.

PROGRAM SPECIFICATION: LISTING

The programming project for this chapter is a continuation of the project in Chapter 2. The program specification is repeated in Figure 3–1 for convenience.

Input Record Layout

The input is an order file in which each record contains the data for one order and is 70 bytes long. The input record layout is shown in Figure 3–2. This layout represents the arrangement of data items in each record of a disk file.

Print Chart

The output is a printed report which is a listing of the input records from the order file. The print chart showing the design of the output is given in Figure 3–3. The project requires the transfer of each input record to a print line and the writing of each line. The printed output will not exceed one page; therefore, we do not need logic for producing multiple pages.

LOGIC FOR SIMPLE LISTING

The logic development of the program will be shown using three techniques: a hierarchy chart, pseudocode, and a flowchart. An explanation of the logic steps will be given following the flowchart.

Hierarchy Chart

The top box of the hierarchy chart shown in Figure 3–4 indicates the main line of the program. The routines which are performed from the main line are drawn below it. In this hierarchy chart, the routines performed from the main line are 1000-INITIALIZATION, 2000-PROCESS, and 3000-EOJ. The routines that are performed from these routines are drawn underneath them. Note that 9100-READ-ORDER-FILE is drawn below both the 1000-INITIALIZATION and the 2000-

PROGRAM SPECIFICATION

Program Name: LISTING

Program Function:

The program will produce a printed listing of all orders from an order file.

Input Files:

I. ORDER-FILE

INPUT DEVICE:	DISK
FILE ORGANIZATION:	SEQUENTIAL
RECORD LENGTH:	70 BYTES
FILE SEQUENCE:	ASCENDING ON BRANCH / SALES REP

Output Files:

I. PRINT-FILE

OUTPUT DEVICE:	PRINTER
RECORD LENGTH:	133 BYTES

Output Requirements:

Each record read from the order file should be printed on one line of the output report. All fields from the input record are to be included on the output.

The following are formatting requirements for the report:

1. The first page of the report should contain:
   (a) a main heading which includes the company name and report name.
   (b) column headings which describe the items printed underneath them.
2. The detail lines should include all fields from the input.
3. The detail lines should be double spaced.
4. Do not include provisions for page overflow.

FIGURE 3–1

PROCESS routines. The darkened corner indicates that the routine is used more than once.

Pseudocode

Pseudocode for this project is shown in Figure 3–5. The rules for its formation were covered in Chapter 1 in the section on program development.

Flowchart

A flowchart for the project is shown in Figure 3–6.

Explanation of Logic

We shall use the appropriate segments of the hierarchy chart, pseudocode, an flowchart to step through the logic in general terms before introducing the COBO statements needed to express the logic.

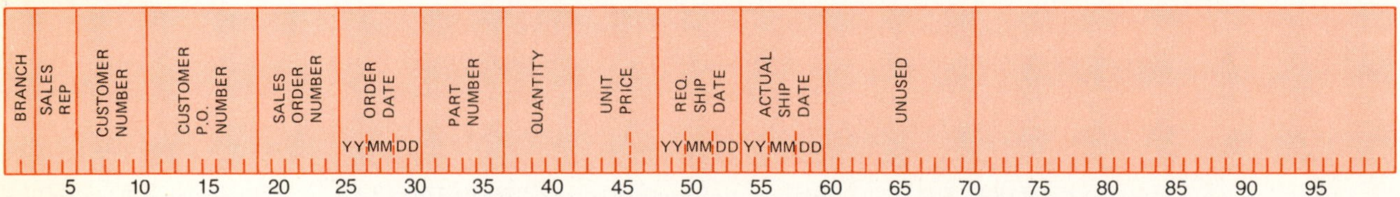

FIGURE 3–2

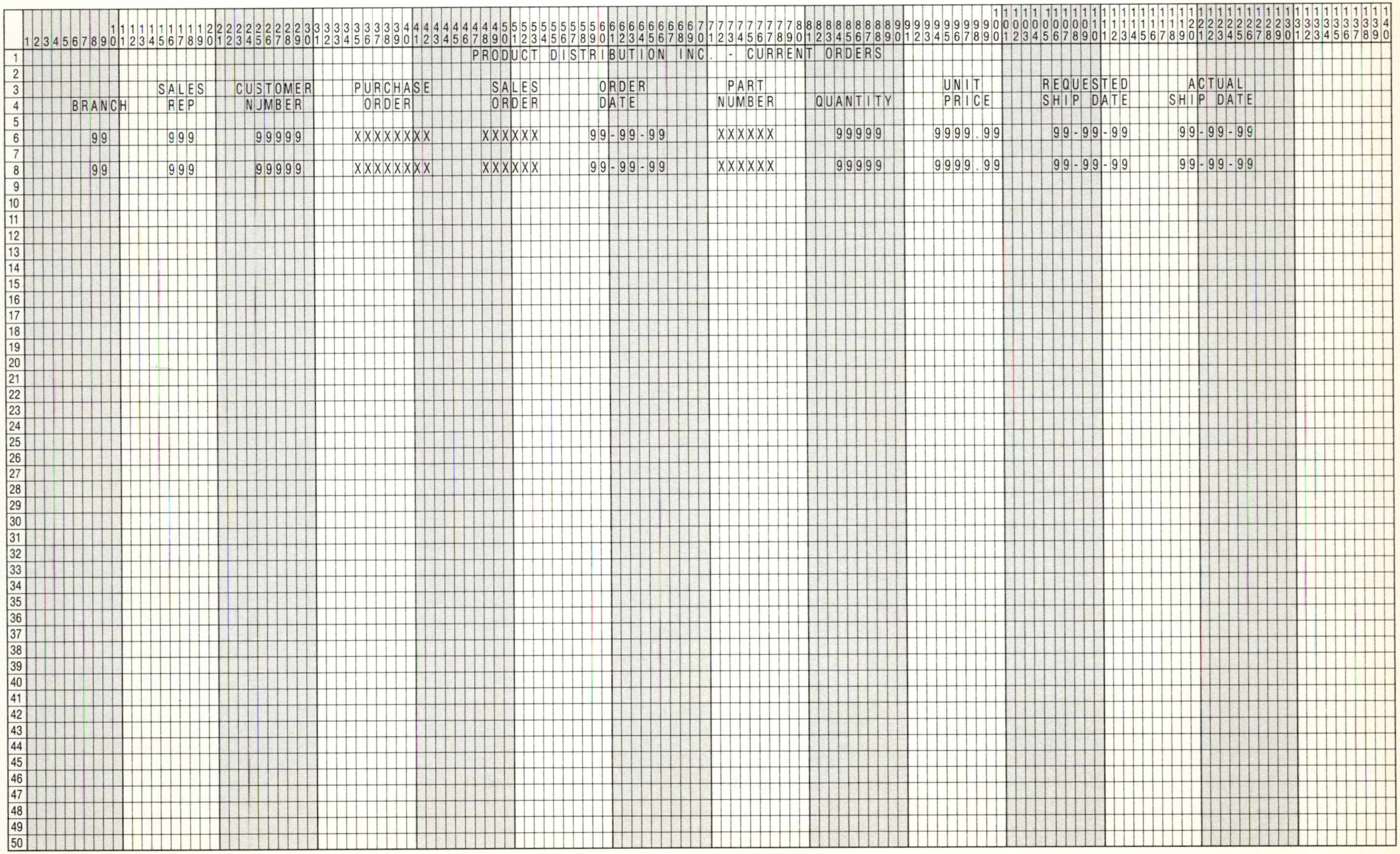

```
                                              PRODUCT DISTRIBUTION INC. - CURRENT ORDERS

              SALES   CUSTOMER    PURCHASE      SALES      ORDER        PART                  UNIT      REQUESTED      ACTUAL
     BRANCH    REP     NJMBER      ORDER        ORDER      DATE       NUMBER    QUANTITY      PRICE     SHIP DATE    SHIP DATE

       99      999      99999    XXXXXXXX     XXXXXX    99-99-99    XXXXXX       99999     9999.99     99-99-99    99-99-99

       99      999      99999    XXXXXXXX     XXXXXX    99-99-99    XXXXXX       99999     9999.99     99-99-99    99-99-99
```

FIGURE 3–3

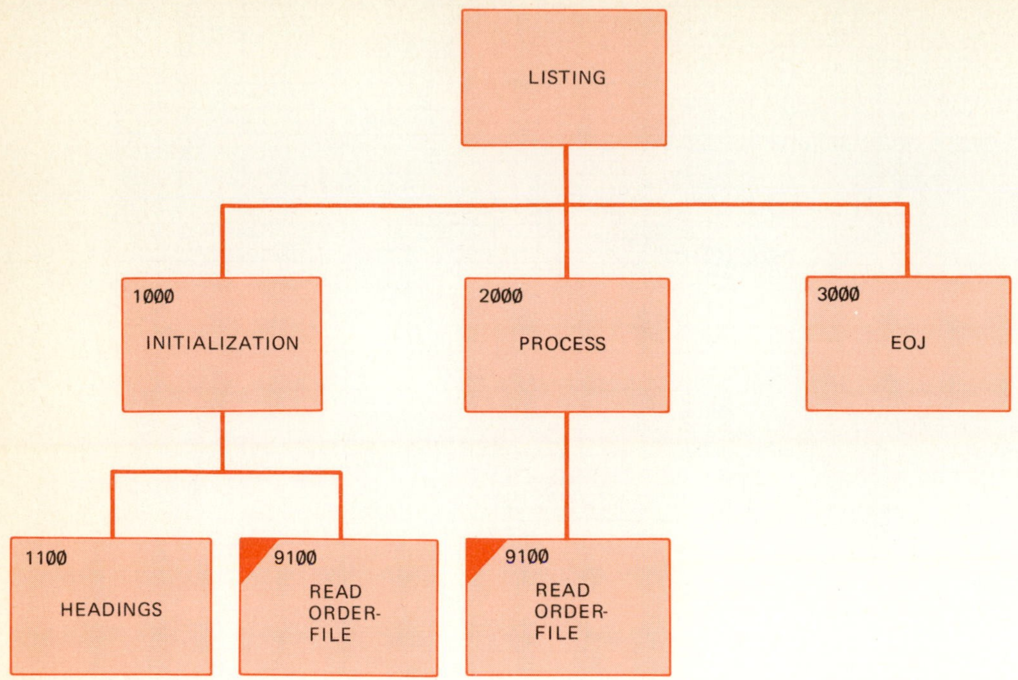

FIGURE 3–4

```
MAIN LINE
     DO initialization
     DO WHILE more order records
          DO process
     ENDDO
     DO end of job

INITIALIZATION
     OPEN files
     DO headings
     DO read an order

HEADINGS
     WRITE main heading line
     WRITE column heading line one
     WRITE column heading line two

PROCESS
     MOVE input to output
     WRITE detail line
     DO read an order

END OF JOB
     CLOSE files

READ AN ORDER
     READ order file
```

FIGURE 3–5

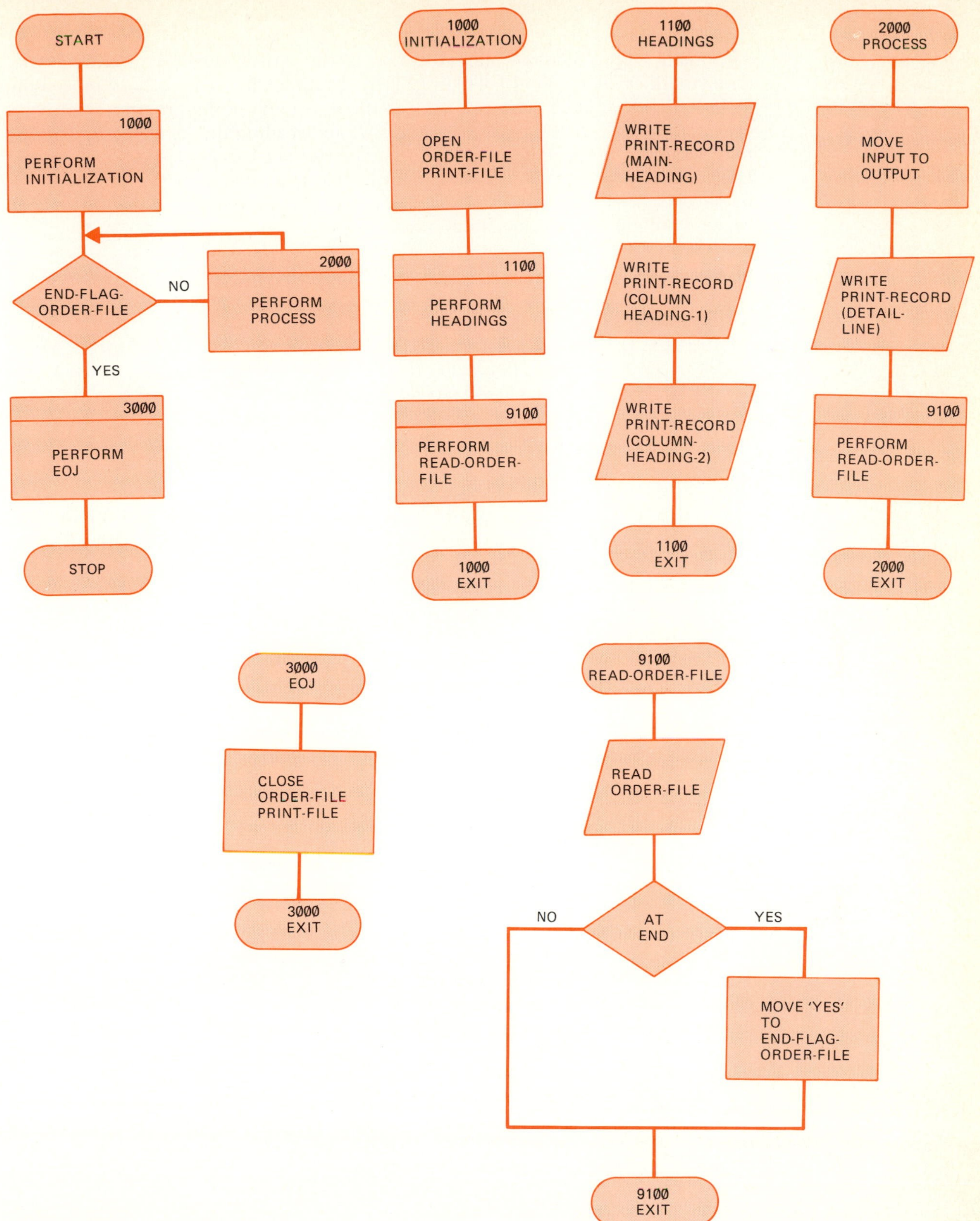

START
1000
PERFORM INITIALIZATION
END-FLAG-ORDER-FILE
NO
YES
2000
PERFORM PROCESS
3000
PERFORM EOJ
STOP
1000 INITIALIZATION
OPEN ORDER-FILE PRINT-FILE
1100
PERFORM HEADINGS
9100
PERFORM READ-ORDER-FILE
1000 EXIT
1100 HEADINGS
WRITE PRINT-RECORD (MAIN-HEADING)
WRITE PRINT-RECORD (COLUMN HEADING-1)
WRITE PRINT-RECORD (COLUMN-HEADING-2)
1100 EXIT
2000 PROCESS
MOVE INPUT TO OUTPUT
WRITE PRINT-RECORD (DETAIL-LINE)
9100
PERFORM READ-ORDER-FILE
2000 EXIT
3000 EOJ
CLOSE ORDER-FILE PRINT-FILE
3000 EXIT
9100 READ-ORDER-FILE
READ ORDER-FILE
AT END
NO
YES
MOVE 'YES' TO END-FLAG-ORDER-FILE
9100 EXIT

FIGURE 3–6

MAIN LINE

The main routine controls the execution of the entire program, invoking three other routines. The 1000-INITIALIZATION routine will contain those processing steps which should be done only once at the beginning of the program. Examples are opening files, accessing the system date, and reading the first record. Reading may seem out of place here, as the program will need to read additional records later on. However, the READ statement is placed here so that the program may be developed without using GO TO statements, which are viewed as obstructions to good programming in most circumstances.

2000-PROCESS is a routine which will be repeated once for each record to be processed. The decision END-FLAG-ORDER-FILE = 'YES' is a test made to determine whether 2000-PROCESS should be executed or whether it is time to perform 3000-EOJ (end of job) instead. The program begins with END-FLAG-ORDER-FILE having a value of 'NO'. This value was established when END-FLAG-ORDER-FILE was defined in the WORKING-STORAGE SECTION. A read is performed in 1000-INITIALIZATION. If the read is successful, END-FLAG-ORDER-FILE will retain the value 'NO'. If, on the other hand, the read finds an end-of-file indicator instead of a data record, END-FLAG-ORDER-FILE will be changed to 'YES'. Thus, either 2000-PROCESS or 3000-EOJ will be performed depending on the outcome of the read.

There is a read at the end of 2000-PROCESS. Each time 2000-PROCESS, and hence the read, is performed, if it is successful, END-FLAG-ORDER-FILE will retain the value 'NO'. If it is not successful, END-FLAG-ORDER-FILE will be changed to 'YES'. 2000-PROCESS is repeated until there are no more records in the input file and END-FLAG-ORDER-FILE is changed to 'YES'. At that time, 3000-EOJ is performed.

3000-EOJ will contain those processing steps which should be done only once after all the records have been processed. Examples are printing totals and closing files.

The MAIN LINE section of the flowchart is repeated in Figure 3–7 with appropriate portions of the hierarchy chart and pseudocode.

1000-INITIALIZATION

The routine 1000-INITIALIZATION contains three steps. The first step is to OPEN the files. This must be done before any reading from input files or writing to output files can be performed.

The second step is to PERFORM the heading routine. Since the program produces less than one full page of output, only one set of headings is needed. This makes 1000-INITIALIZATION a suitable place to perform the heading routine. If multiple pages of output were required, headings would have to be printed many times, and the routine would be performed from 2000-PROCESS, where there is an opportunity to determine whether new headings are needed each time a record is processed.

The third step is to PERFORM the read routine. This routine is performed once, from 1000-INITIALIZATION. It causes the first record to be read. If the file is empty, END-FLAG-ORDER-FILE will be changed to 'YES'. If a record is available, END-FLAG-ORDER-FILE will retain the value 'NO'. (See Figure 3–8.)

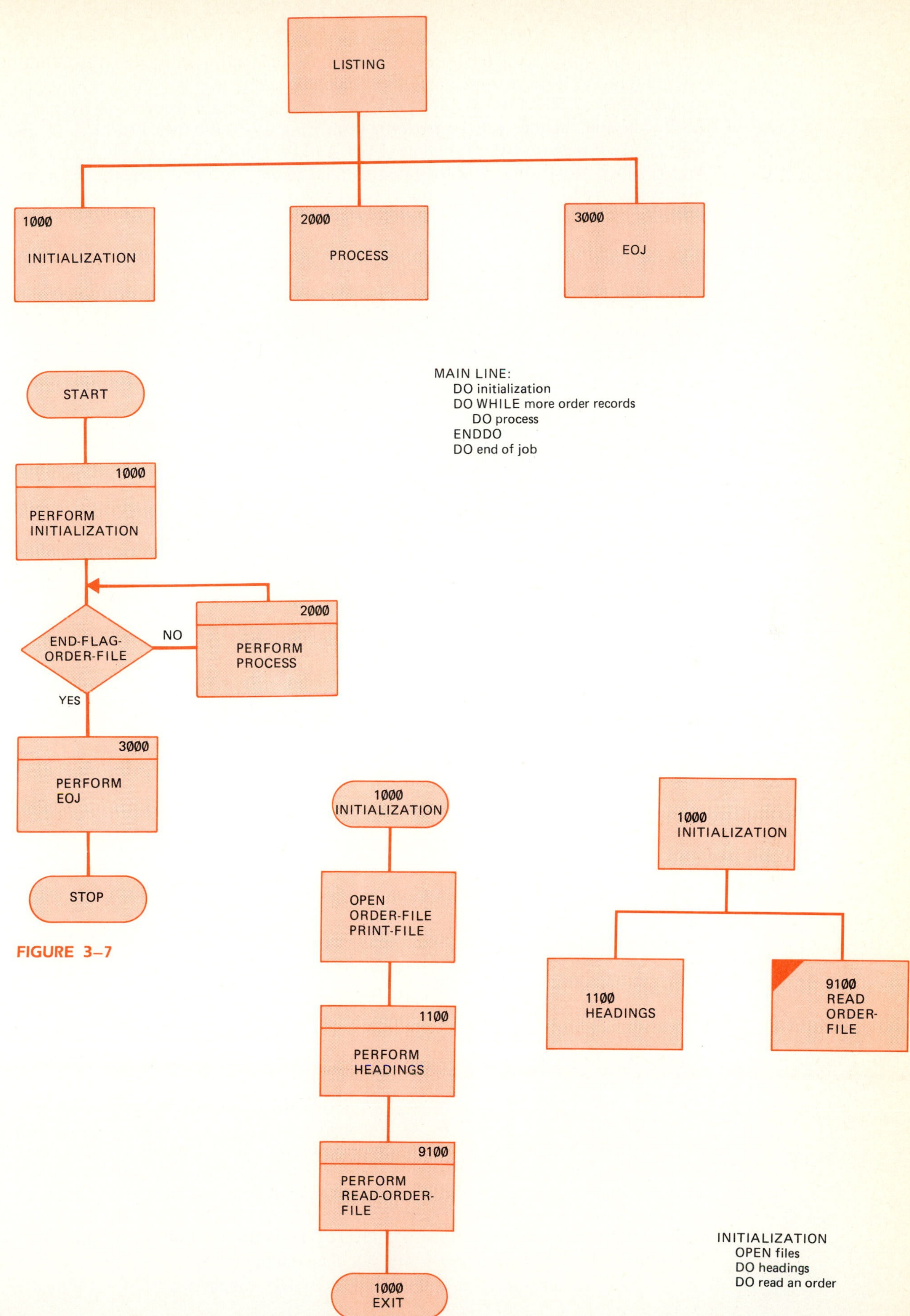

FIGURE 3–7

FIGURE 3–8

1100-HEADINGS

The routine 1100-HEADINGS writes three lines of headings. Each input/output symbol represents the writing of one line. The type of line that is written is indicated in parentheses. The 1100-HEADINGS routine is performed from 1000-INITIALIZATION and, hence, will be performed only once. Positioning headings at the top of a page is part of the function of the WRITE statement in COBOL and will be explained when the COBOL statements necessary to implement this logic are discussed. (See Figure 3–9 for the HEADINGS routine.)

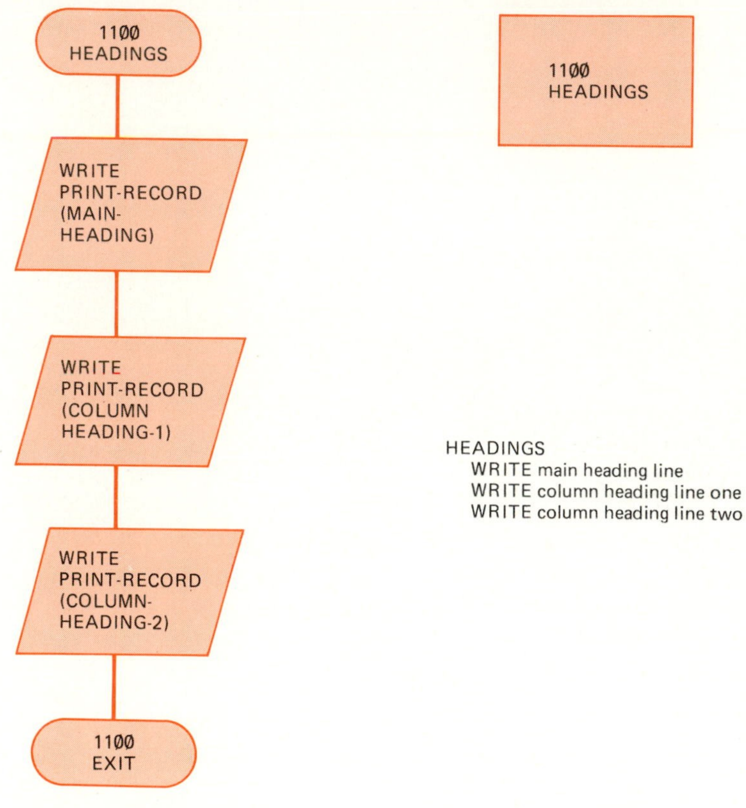

FIGURE 3–9

2000-PROCESS

Since the first record was read in 1000-INITIALIZATION, 2000-PROCESS is started by moving the data from the input area where it was placed by the read to an area which describes how it will look when output as a detail line. If spaces between the columns of data are required (as is usually the case), the data items from the input record must be moved to the detail line one at a time. Each of these moves could be shown separately, but we have elected to consolidate them in the flowchart as MOVE INPUT TO OUTPUT. In the COBOL code, there will be multiple MOVE statements for this one logic step.

After each data item from the input record has been moved to the detail line, the detail line will contain all of the data needed for printing one line. The program then WRITEs that line, transferring the data from computer memory, through a printer, and onto paper. The COBOL language incorporates instructions for the movement of paper between printed lines in the WRITE statement.

Now the 9100-READ-ORDER-FILE routine is performed. This will cause the next record to be read. As with all sequential reads, a test will be made to see whether the end of the file has been reached. If it is, the value of END-FLAG-ORDER-FILE will be changed to 'YES', and 3000-EOJ will be performed rather than 2000-PROCESS again.

Notice the general order of the logic of 2000-PROCESS:

MOVE
WRITE
READ

This is probably not what would be expected. The 2000-PROCESS routine starts with MOVE because the first record was read in 1000-INITIALIZATION; therefore, as the routine is entered, there is a record ready to be moved and written. READ is at the end of the routine so that immediately after reading, the test to see whether the value of END-FLAG-ORDER-FILE has been changed to 'YES' can be made. If the value is 'YES', 3000-EOJ will be performed.

What if the arrangement were as follows, with no READ in 1000-INITIALIZATION?

READ
MOVE
WRITE

With this arrangement, a logic error would occur when the attempt to read would find the end-of-file condition raised. The value of END-FLAG-ORDER-FILE would be changed to 'YES', but we would not be in a position to test it! The next step would be to MOVE and WRITE the data, but there would be no data to MOVE or WRITE. (See Figure 3–10 for the PROCESS routine.)

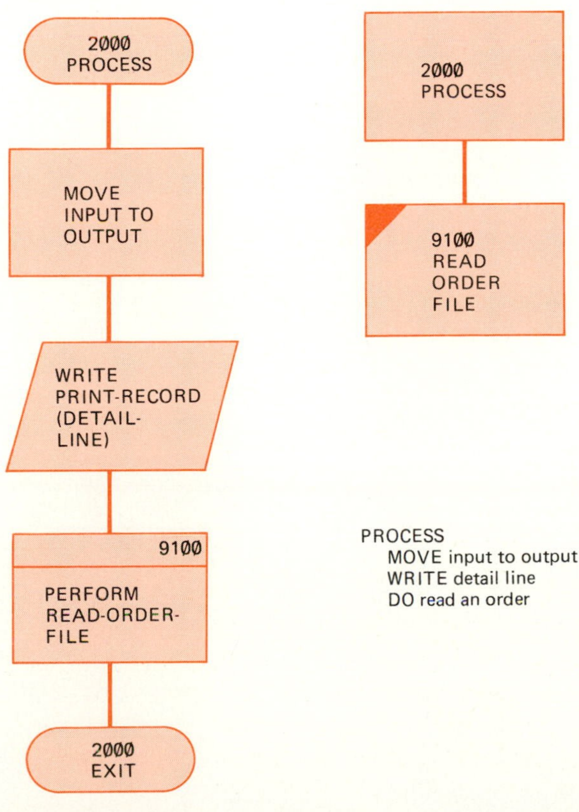

FIGURE 3–10

3000-EOJ

The program has no totals or other special processing to be completed after all the records are printed. Hence, CLOSEing the files is all that is necessary. (See Figure 3–11.)

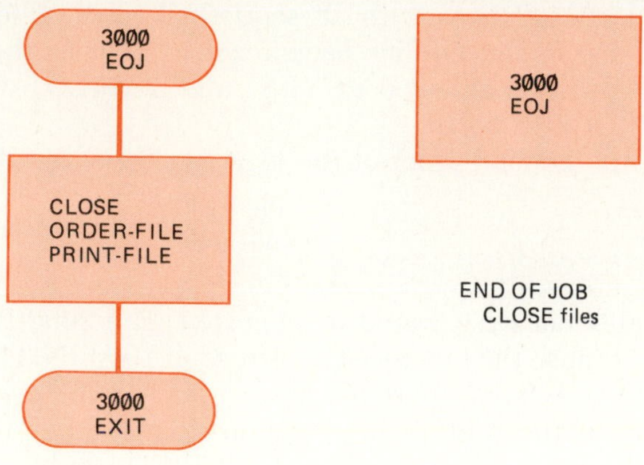

FIGURE 3–11

9100-READ-ORDER-FILE

The READ routine reads one record from the file. Each time an attempt to read is made, an AT END test is performed wherein the computer looks for an end-of-file indicator. If that indicator is present, AT END is true, the YES path is taken, and 'YES' is moved to END-FLAG-ORDER-FILE. If, instead, a data record is present, the AT END condition is false and the NO path is taken, i.e., END-FLAG-ORDER-FILE retains the value 'NO'. (See Figure 3–12.)

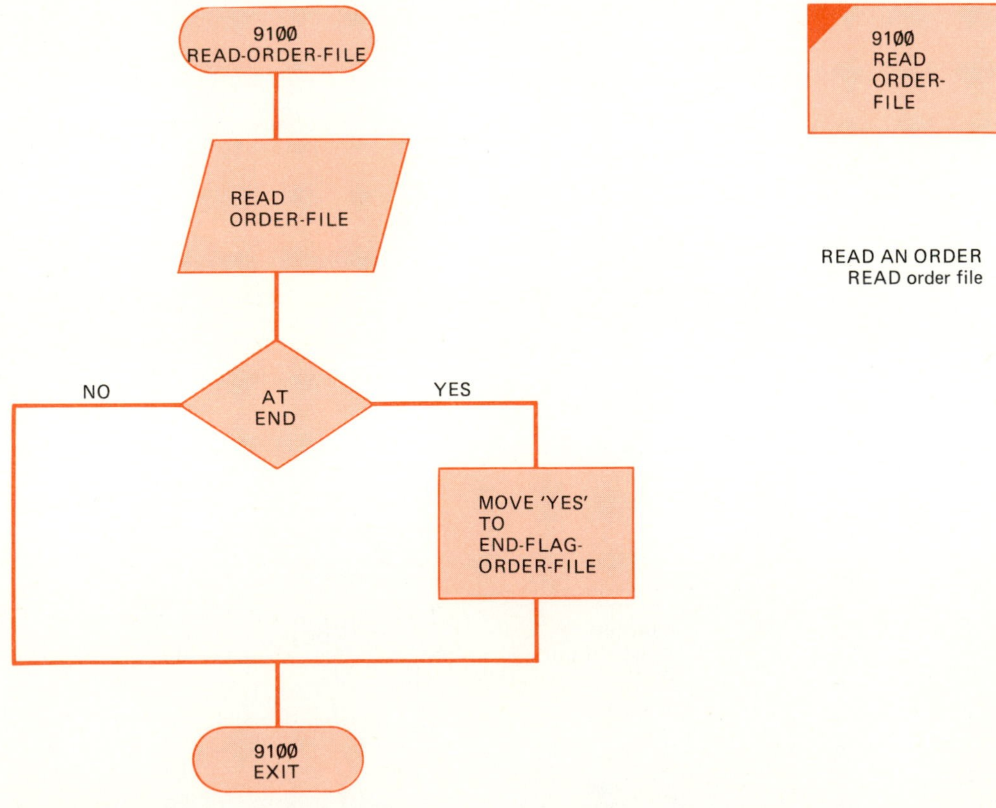

FIGURE 3–12

THE COBOL PROGRAM

Test Data

Test data for the LISTING program is shown in Figure 3–13.

Sample Output

Sample output from the LISTING program is shown in Figure 3–14.

The Program

The complete COBOL program is shown in Figure 3–15. Boxes are used to indicate recommended stylistic techniques.

```
Ø12Ø1ØØ3ØØPO173   B12383871Ø25GN4Ø2AØØØØ1Ø45ØØØ871116ØØØØØØ
Ø12Ø1Ø47278372    G4838887Ø913WB7Ø2XØØØ9ØØ115ØØ8711Ø1ØØØØØØ
Ø12Ø1ØØ3ØØE1Ø12   B123358711Ø5WB493EØØØØ2Ø54ØØØ871122ØØØØØØ
Ø3ØØ7473ØØ        H8477787Ø223MF4Ø3TØØØØ5Ø4ØØØØ87Ø5Ø2ØØØØØØ
Ø3ØØ7ØØ378EBNER   H8457987Ø811VX922PØØ8ØØØØ127589112ØØØØØØØ
Ø3ØØ7739897747    B892888711Ø6MF848JØØØØ5Ø2145Ø88Ø13ØØØØØØØ
Ø3ØØ7ØØ28334567X  B34237871Ø3ØHL834EØØØ16Ø19ØØØ871121ØØØØØØ
Ø3ØØ7473ØØ        Y289Ø387Ø811VXØØ1LØØ2ØØØØ622Ø8712Ø3ØØØØØØ
Ø344Ø6948187Ø341  GØ418Ø87Ø2Ø9JGØ4ØXØØØØ1Ø525ØØ88Ø619ØØØØØØ
Ø361182888P2783733B8433Ø871Ø25HL289BØØØ1ØØ234ØØ871113ØØØØØØ
Ø361128375T7838   T7829987Ø323JG563WØØØØ6Ø43ØØØ871Ø18ØØØØØØ
Ø36115Ø912        H6915Ø87Ø2Ø6MF848TØØØØ3Ø36ØØØ8712Ø1ØØØØØØ
Ø817431408Ø65     H4189187Ø412TK61ØLØØØ18ØØ78ØØ87Ø63ØØØØØØØ
Ø8174Ø18Ø5R7278   T2164287Ø81ØTK497XØØØ1ØØ118ØØ87113ØØØØØØØ
Ø8174Ø18Ø5R8322   Y211Ø587Ø6Ø1TN116TØØØØ1Ø3ØØØØ871221ØØØØØØ
Ø891562Ø54SCHUH   L5Ø6818711Ø8TK812EØØØØ6Ø573ØØ88Ø1Ø5ØØØØØØ
Ø891521Ø78        B71Ø45871ØØ1FV782TØØØØ3ØØ28ØØ871115ØØØØØØ
```

FIGURE 3–13

PRODUCT DISTRIBUTION INC. - CURRENT ORDERS

BRANCH	SALES REP	CUSTOMER NUMBER	PURCHASE ORDER	SALES ORDER	ORDER DATE	PART NUMBER	QUANTITY	UNIT PRICE	REQUESTED SHIP DATE	ACTUAL SHIP DATE
01	201	00300	PO173	B12383	10-25-87	GN402A	00001	0450.00	11-16-87	00-00-00
01	201	04727	8372	G48388	09-13-87	WB702X	00090	0115.00	11-01-87	00-00-00
01	201	00300	E1012	B12335	11-05-87	WB493E	00002	0540.00	11-22-87	00-00-00
03	007	47300		H84777	02-23-87	MF403T	00005	0400.00	05-02-87	00-00-00
03	007	00378	EBNER	H84579	08-11-87	VX922P	00800	0012.75	11-20-89	00-00-00
03	007	73989	7747	B89288	11-06-87	MF848J	00005	0214.50	01-30-88	00-00-00
03	007	00283	34567X	B34237	10-30-87	HL834E	00016	0190.00	11-21-87	00-00-00
03	007	47300		Y28903	08-11-87	VX001L	00200	0062.20	12-03-87	00-00-00
03	440	69481	870341	G04180	02-09-87	JG040X	00001	0525.00	06-19-88	00-00-00
03	611	82888	P2783733	B84330	10-25-87	HL289B	00010	0234.00	11-13-87	00-00-00
03	611	28375	T7838	T78299	03-23-87	JG563W	00006	0430.00	10-18-87	00-00-00
03	611	50912		H69150	02-06-87	MF848T	00003	0360.00	12-01-87	00-00-00
08	174	31408	65	H41891	04-12-87	TK610L	00018	0078.00	06-30-87	00-00-00
08	174	01805	R7278	T21642	08-10-87	TK497X	00010	0118.00	11-30-87	00-00-00
08	174	01805	R8322	Y21105	06-01-87	TN116T	00001	0300.00	12-21-87	00-00-00
08	915	62054	SCHUH	L50681	11-08-87	TK812E	00006	0573.00	01-05-88	00-00-00
08	915	21078		B71045	10-01-87	FV782T	00003	0028.00	11-15-87	00-00-00

FIGURE 3–14

```
       IDENTIFICATION DIVISION.

       PROGRAM-ID.    LISTING.

       AUTHOR.        HELEN HUMPHREYS.

       INSTALLATION.  PRODUCT DISTRIBUTION INC.

       DATE-WRITTEN.  Ø3/15/87.

       DATE-COMPILED. Ø3/22/87.

      ******************************************************************
      *                                                                *
      *    THIS PROGRAM PRODUCES A PRINTED LISTING OF ALL ORDERS       *
      *    FROM THE ORDER FILE.                                        *
      *                                                                *
      ******************************************************************

       ENVIRONMENT DIVISION.

       CONFIGURATION SECTION.

       SOURCE-COMPUTER.
              IBM-37Ø.
       OBJECT-COMPUTER.
              IBM-37Ø.

       INPUT-OUTPUT SECTION.
       FILE-CONTROL.
           SELECT ORDER-FILE ASSIGN TO DISK.
           SELECT PRINT-FILE ASSIGN TO PRINTER.

       DATA DIVISION.
       FILE SECTION.

       FD  ORDER-FILE
           LABEL RECORDS ARE STANDARD
           RECORD CONTAINS 7Ø CHARACTERS
           DATA RECORD IS ORDER-RECORD.

       Ø1  ORDER-RECORD.
           Ø5  ORD-BRANCH                PIC 9(2).
           Ø5  ORD-SALES-REP             PIC 9(3).
           Ø5  ORD-CUSTOMER-NBR          PIC 9(5).
           Ø5  ORD-CUST-PO-NBR           PIC X(8).
           Ø5  ORD-SALES-ORD-NBR         PIC X(6).
           Ø5  ORD-DATE.
               1Ø  ORD-YY                PIC 9(2).
               1Ø  ORD-MM                PIC 9(2).
               1Ø  ORD-DD                PIC 9(2).
           Ø5  ORD-PART-NBR              PIC X(6).
           Ø5  ORD-QUANTITY              PIC 9(5).
           Ø5  ORD-UNIT-PRICE            PIC 9(4)V9(2).
           Ø5  ORD-REQ-SHIP-DATE.
               1Ø  ORD-REQ-SHIP-YY       PIC 9(2).
               1Ø  ORD-REQ-SHIP-MM       PIC 9(2).
               1Ø  ORD-REQ-SHIP-DD       PIC 9(2).
           Ø5  ORD-ACT-SHIP-DATE.
               1Ø  ORD-ACT-SHIP-YY       PIC 9(2).
               1Ø  ORD-ACT-SHIP-MM       PIC 9(2).
               1Ø  ORD-ACT-SHIP-DD       PIC 9(2).
           Ø5  FILLER                    PIC X(11).

       FD  PRINT-FILE
           LABEL RECORDS ARE OMITTED
           RECORD CONTAINS 133 CHARACTERS
           DATA RECORD IS PRINT-RECORD.

       Ø1  PRINT-RECORD                  PIC X(133).

       WORKING-STORAGE SECTION.

       Ø1  HOLDS-COUNTERS-SWITCHES.
           Ø5  END-FLAG-ORDER-FILE       PIC X(3)        VALUE 'NO'.

       Ø1  MAIN-HEADING.
           Ø5  FILLER                    PIC X(46)       VALUE SPACES.
           Ø5  FILLER                    PIC X(42)
               VALUE 'PRODUCT DISTRIBUTION INC. - CURRENT ORDERS'.
           Ø5  FILLER                    PIC X(45)       VALUE SPACES.
```

USE 01, 05, 10, ETC. FOR LEVEL NUMBERS

FIGURE 3–15

FIGURE 3-15
continued

```
       Ø1  COLUMN-HEADING-1.
           Ø5  FILLER              PIC X(14)       VALUE SPACES.
           Ø5  FILLER              PIC X(5)        VALUE 'SALES'.
           Ø5  FILLER              PIC X(3)        VALUE SPACES.
           Ø5  FILLER              PIC X(8)        VALUE 'CUSTOMER'.
           Ø5  FILLER              PIC X(4)        VALUE SPACES.
           Ø5  FILLER              PIC X(8)        VALUE 'PURCHASE'.
           Ø5  FILLER              PIC X(6)        VALUE SPACES.
           Ø5  FILLER              PIC X(5)        VALUE 'SALES'.
           Ø5  FILLER              PIC X(6)        VALUE SPACES.
           Ø5  FILLER              PIC X(5)        VALUE 'ORDER'.
           Ø5  FILLER              PIC X(8)        VALUE SPACES.
           Ø5  FILLER              PIC X(4)        VALUE 'PART'.
           Ø5  FILLER              PIC X(18)       VALUE SPACES.
           Ø5  FILLER              PIC X(4)        VALUE 'UNIT'.
           Ø5  FILLER              PIC X(6)        VALUE SPACES.
           Ø5  FILLER              PIC X(9)        VALUE
                                                    'REQUESTED'.
           Ø5  FILLER              PIC X(6)        VALUE SPACES.
           Ø5  FILLER              PIC X(6)        VALUE 'ACTUAL'.
           Ø5  FILLER              PIC X(8)        VALUE SPACES.

       Ø1  COLUMN-HEADING-2.
           Ø5  FILLER              PIC X(5)        VALUE SPACES.
           Ø5  FILLER              PIC X(6)        VALUE 'BRANCH'.
           Ø5  FILLER              PIC X(4)        VALUE SPACES.
           Ø5  FILLER              PIC X(3)        VALUE 'REP'.
           Ø5  FILLER              PIC X(5)        VALUE SPACES.
           Ø5  FILLER              PIC X(6)        VALUE 'NUMBER'.
           Ø5  FILLER              PIC X(6)        VALUE SPACES.
           Ø5  FILLER              PIC X(5)        VALUE 'ORDER'.
           Ø5  FILLER              PIC X(8)        VALUE SPACES.
           Ø5  FILLER              PIC X(5)        VALUE 'ORDER'.
           Ø5  FILLER              PIC X(6)        VALUE SPACES.
           Ø5  FILLER              PIC X(4)        VALUE 'DATE'.
           Ø5  FILLER              PIC X(8)        VALUE SPACES.
           Ø5  FILLER              PIC X(6)        VALUE 'NUMBER'.
           Ø5  FILLER              PIC X(4)        VALUE SPACES.
           Ø5  FILLER              PIC X(8)        VALUE 'QUANTITY'.
           Ø5  FILLER              PIC X(5)        VALUE SPACES.
           Ø5  FILLER              PIC X(5)        VALUE 'PRICE'.
           Ø5  FILLER              PIC X(5)        VALUE SPACES.
           Ø5  FILLER              PIC X(9)        VALUE
                                                    'SHIP DATE'.
           Ø5  FILLER              PIC X(4)        VALUE SPACES.
           Ø5  FILLER              PIC X(9)        VALUE
                                                    'SHIP DATE'.
           Ø5  FILLER              PIC X(7)        VALUE SPACES.

       Ø1  DETAIL-LINE.
           Ø5  FILLER              PIC X(7)        VALUE SPACES.
           Ø5  DET-BRANCH          PIC 9(2).
           Ø5  FILLER              PIC X(6)        VALUE SPACES.
           Ø5  DET-SALES-REP       PIC 9(3).
           Ø5  FILLER              PIC X(6)        VALUE SPACES.
           Ø5  DET-CUSTOMER-NBR    PIC 9(5).
           Ø5  FILLER              PIC X(5)        VALUE SPACES.
           Ø5  DET-CUST-PO-NBR     PIC X(8).
           Ø5  FILLER              PIC X(5)        VALUE SPACES.
           Ø5  DET-SALES-ORD-NBR   PIC X(6).
           Ø5  FILLER              PIC X(5)        VALUE SPACES.
           Ø5  DET-ORDER-MM        PIC 9(2).
           Ø5  FILLER              PIC X(1)        VALUE '-'.
           Ø5  DET-ORDER-DD        PIC 9(2).
           Ø5  FILLER              PIC X(1)        VALUE '-'.
           Ø5  DET-ORDER-YY        PIC 9(2).
           Ø5  FILLER              PIC X(5)        VALUE SPACES.
           Ø5  DET-PART-NBR        PIC X(6).
           Ø5  FILLER              PIC X(6)        VALUE SPACES.
           Ø5  DET-QUANTITY        PIC 9(5).
           Ø5  FILLER              PIC X(5)        VALUE SPACES.
           Ø5  DET-UNIT-PRICE      PIC 9(4).9(2).
           Ø5  FILLER              PIC X(5)        VALUE SPACES.
           Ø5  DET-REQ-SHIP-MM     PIC 9(2).
           Ø5  FILLER              PIC X(1)        VALUE '-'.
           Ø5  DET-REQ-SHIP-DD     PIC 9(2).
           Ø5  FILLER              PIC X(1)        VALUE '-'.
           Ø5  DET-REQ-SHIP-YY     PIC 9(2).
           Ø5  FILLER              PIC X(5)        VALUE SPACES.
           Ø5  DET-ACT-SHIP-MM     PIC 9(2).
           Ø5  FILLER              PIC X(1)        VALUE '-'.
           Ø5  DET-ACT-SHIP-DD     PIC 9(2).
           Ø5  FILLER              PIC X(1)        VALUE '-'.
           Ø5  DET-ACT-SHIP-YY     PIC 9(2).
           Ø5  FILLER              PIC X(7)        VALUE SPACES.
```

```
       PROCEDURE DIVISION.

           PERFORM 1000-INITIALIZATION.
           PERFORM 2000-PROCESS
               UNTIL END-FLAG-ORDER-FILE = 'YES'.
           PERFORM 3000-EOJ.
           STOP RUN.

       1000-INITIALIZATION.
           OPEN INPUT  ORDER-FILE
                OUTPUT PRINT-FILE.
           PERFORM 1100-HEADINGS.
           PERFORM 9100-READ-ORDER-FILE.

       1100-HEADINGS.
           WRITE PRINT-RECORD FROM MAIN-HEADING
               AFTER ADVANCING PAGE.
           WRITE PRINT-RECORD FROM COLUMN-HEADING-1
               AFTER ADVANCING 2 LINES.
           WRITE PRINT-RECORD FROM COLUMN-HEADING-2
               AFTER ADVANCING 1 LINE.

       2000-PROCESS.
           MOVE ORD-BRANCH             TO DET-BRANCH.
           MOVE ORD-SALES-REP          TO DET-SALES-REP.
           MOVE ORD-CUSTOMER-NBR       TO DET-CUSTOMER-NBR.
           MOVE ORD-CUST-PO-NBR        TO DET-CUST-PO-NBR.
           MOVE ORD-SALES-ORD-NBR      TO DET-SALES-ORD-NBR.
           MOVE ORD-YY                 TO DET-ORDER-YY.
           MOVE ORD-MM                 TO DET-ORDER-MM.
           MOVE ORD-DD                 TO DET-ORDER-DD.
           MOVE ORD-PART-NBR           TO DET-PART-NBR.
           MOVE ORD-QUANTITY           TO DET-QUANTITY.
           MOVE ORD-UNIT-PRICE         TO DET-UNIT-PRICE.
           MOVE ORD-REQ-SHIP-YY        TO DET-REQ-SHIP-YY.
           MOVE ORD-REQ-SHIP-MM        TO DET-REQ-SHIP-MM.
           MOVE ORD-REQ-SHIP-DD        TO DET-REQ-SHIP-DD.
           MOVE ORD-ACT-SHIP-YY        TO DET-ACT-SHIP-YY.
           MOVE ORD-ACT-SHIP-MM        TO DET-ACT-SHIP-MM.
           MOVE ORD-ACT-SHIP-DD        TO DET-ACT-SHIP-DD.
           WRITE PRINT-RECORD FROM DETAIL-LINE
               AFTER ADVANCING 2 LINES.
           PERFORM 9100-READ-ORDER-FILE.

       3000-EOJ.
           CLOSE ORDER-FILE
                 PRINT-FILE.

       9100-READ-ORDER-FILE.
           READ ORDER-FILE
               AT END
                   MOVE 'YES' TO END-FLAG-ORDER-FILE.
```

INDENT BY 4 OR ALIGN SIMILAR ITEMS

INDENT SECOND AND SUCCESSIVE LINES OF A STATEMENT

NUMBER PARAGRAPHS TO MATCH HIERARCHY CHART AND ARRANGE IN NUMERICAL ORDER

LINE UP TO IN MOVE STATEMENTS

FIGURE 3-15
continued

PROCEDURE DIVISION

The PROCEDURE DIVISION of a COBOL program contains the instructions necessary to produce a desired result. In the IDENTIFICATION DIVISION, the program was given a name to be used by the computer for purposes of locating the program. The ENVIRONMENT DIVISION specified the equipment to be used and the names of the files associated with that equipment. In the DATA DIVISION, the files were described and each element of data was defined. These included data to be input and output as well as data items (END-FLAG-ORDER-FILE) needed to control the processing steps. Now we shall utilize the data items which were defined in the DATA DIVISION as we specify the processing steps in the PROCEDURE DIVISION. If a data item has not been defined in the DATA DIVISION, it must not be referred to in the PROCEDURE DIVISION.

Organization

Before we create a PROCEDURE DIVISION, we need to know its general organization. The PROCEDURE DIVISION is composed of a header (the words PROCEDURE DIVISION followed by a period), sections, paragraphs, sentences, and statements. Let us start with the smaller item, statements, and group things together until we have an entire PROCEDURE DIVISION.

A statement is made up of COBOL elements such as reserved words, identifiers, literals, figurative constants, and symbols. A COBOL statement must begin with a COBOL verb (a special type of reserved word). Examples of COBOL verbs are ADD, SUBTRACT, MOVE, IF, and PERFORM. In the following example, there is a reserved word that is a verb (IF), an identifier (FIELD-A), a symbol (<), and a literal (6). There is no figurative constant. (Recall that figurative constants are words like ZEROS and SPACES.)

```
IF FIELD-A < 6
```

A COBOL sentence is one or more statements ending with a period and followed by a space. In the following example, two statements make up one sentence. The first statement could not be used alone as a sentence, whereas the second statement could.

```
IF FIELD-A < 6
    ADD 1 TO FIELD-A.
```

A paragraph starts with a paragraph-name. Paragraph-names are created by the programmer and are coded beginning in AREA A. The naming of a paragraph follows the same rules as the formation of a data-name except that a paragraph-name may be composed entirely of digits. If a data-name were made entirely of digits, it could not be distinguished from a numeric literal. A paragraph-name is followed by a period and a space. A paragraph is composed of one or more COBOL sentences.

```
2000-PROCESS.
    IF FIELD-A < 6
        ADD 1 TO FIELD-A.
    MOVE FIELD-A TO FIELD-A-OUT.
```

A paragraph ends when another paragraph-name, a section-name, or the end of the program is encountered. There are two paragraphs in the following example.

```
2000-PROCESS.
    IF FIELD-A < 6
        ADD 1 TO FIELD-A.
    MOVE FIELD-A TO FIELD-A-OUT.
                                   <---------END OF 2000-PROCESS
3000-EOJ.
    MOVE 'END OF JOB' TO MESSAGE-AREA.
    WRITE PRINT-RECORD FROM EOJ-LINE
        AFTER ADVANCING 2 LINES.
    CLOSE INPUT-FILE
          OUTPUT-FILE.
                                   <---------END OF 3000-EOJ
```

A section consists of a section-name (the rules are the same as those for forming a paragraph-name) followed by the word SECTION and a period, followed by the paragraphs of which it is composed. A section ends when the next section-name or the end of the program is encountered.

```
A-FIRST SECTION.

2000-PROCESS.
    IF FIELD-A < 6
        ADD 1 TO FIELD-A.
    MOVE FIELD-A TO FIELD-A-OUT.

3000-EOJ.
    MOVE 'END OF JOB'  TO MESSAGE-AREA.
    WRITE PRINT-RECORD FROM EOJ-LINE
        AFTER ADVANCING 2 LINES.
    CLOSE INPUT-FILE
          OUTPUT-FILE.
                                 <------------- END OF A-FIRST SECTION
B-SECOND SECTION.
     .
     .
     .
```

Execution of a COBOL program begins with the first instruction in the PROCEDURE DIVISION and continues with the execution of each instruction as it is physically encountered. Some instructions (PERFORM, GO TO) cause branching to an instruction other than the next physical instruction. This will be more fully explained shortly in the section on the PERFORM statement.

Notation

Each COBOL statement to be introduced in subsequent sections will be presented in a box labeled FORMAT in which a consistent style of notation will be used to identify the various elements of the statement. An example of this notation is as follows:

Format

```
MOVE  {identifier-1}    TO identifier-2 [identifier-3]...
      {literal     }
```

Reserved words are printed in capital letters, thus:

```
MOVE
TO
```

Keywords are required reserved words. To indicate that they are required, they are underlined:

<u>MOVE</u>
<u>TO</u>

Optional words are reserved words that are not required. They are capitalized, but not underlined.

Words printed in lowercase letters represent programmer-supplied information. The programmer provides his or her own data name or literal to replace any of the following:

```
identifier-1
literal
identifier-2
identifier-3
```

If there is more than one programmer-supplied item of the same kind, a suffix is added to identify which item is being referred to (e.g., identifier-1, identifier-2, or identifier-3). At this point, the word 'identifier' may be used interchangeably with 'data-name'; the difference between the two will be explained later.

Braces are used to indicate that the programmer is to choose exactly one of the enclosed items. Thus, in the preceding FORMAT box, the programmer may choose to MOVE either an identifier or a literal.

```
{identifier-1}
{literal     }
```

Square brackets indicate that the enclosed item is optional. It is left to the programmer to decide whether the option is necessary to the program. In the preceding FORMAT box, either an identifier or a literal may be moved to a receiving field (say, identifier-2). There is also the option of moving it to one or more additional receiving fields.

```
[identifier-3]
```

Ellipses (. . .) mean that the preceding item in the format may be repeated a number of times. Thus, in the FORMAT box, an identifier or a literal may be MOVEd to one (identifier-2), two (identifier-3), or more (. . .) receiving fields.

Any *arithmetic or relational operators* appearing in formats are required. They are not underlined in order to avoid confusing them with other kinds of symbols. There are no arithmetic or relational operators in the MOVE format presented. Figure 3–16 shows the common arithmetic and relational operators used in COBOL.

The 1985 standard includes two new relational operators:

>=	**is greater than or equal to**
<=	**is less than or equal to**

COBOL Verbs

Each PROCEDURE DIVISION statement begins with a COBOL verb. The verb indicates the action to be taken. COBOL verbs covered in this chapter are PERFORM, OPEN, READ, MOVE, WRITE, CLOSE, STOP, and GO TO.

The PERFORM Statement

Format

```
                                  {THROUGH}
PERFORM procedure-name-1  [ {THRU   }  procedure-name-2]
[UNTIL condition-1]
```

PERFORM transfers control to the procedure (paragraph or section) named after the word PERFORM. After that procedure or routine is executed, control is

FIGURE 3–16

ARITHMETIC OPERATORS		RELATIONAL OPERATORS	
+	addition	=	is equal to
−	subtraction	<	is less than
*	multiplication	>	is greater than
/	division		
**	exponentiation		

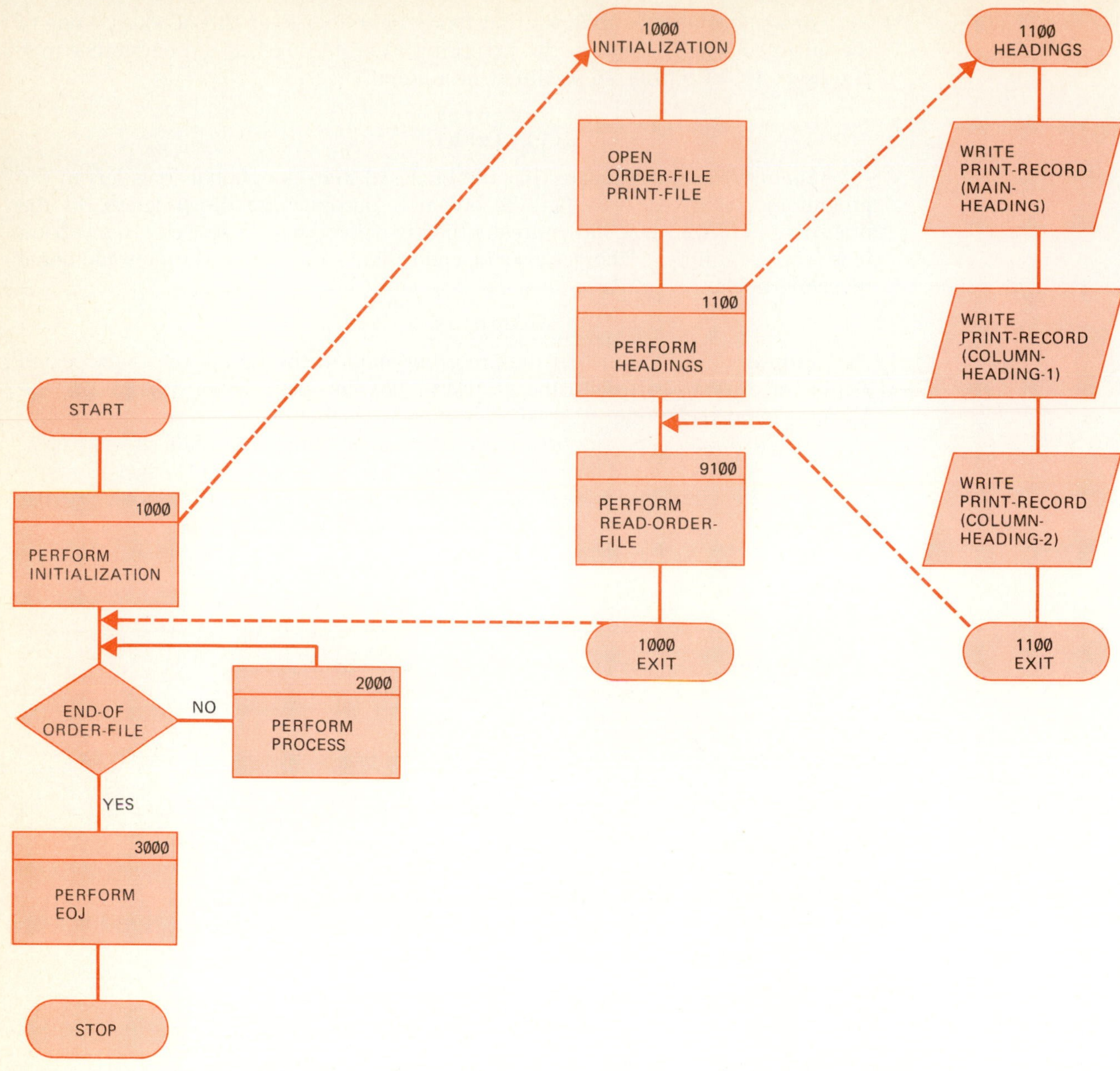

FIGURE 3–17

returned to the statement following the PERFORM statement. If the THRU option is used, then two or more procedures can be included in the group to be executed before control is returned. (See Figure 3–17 for a flowchart indicating passing of control from PERFORM statements to various routines and back to the main logic flow.)

The UNTIL option allows us to PERFORM a routine many times over until a condition is true. The condition is tested before each performance of the routine, including the first. As long as the condition is false, the routine will be executed. As soon as it becomes true, control drops to the next statement. A PERFORM/UNTIL represents an iterative (or DO WHILE) structure.

```
PERFORM 2000-PROCESS
     UNTIL END-FLAG-ORDER-FILE = 'YES'.
```

The 1985 standard for the PERFORM verb has been amended to include (1) a TEST AFTER and (2) in-line PERFORMs.

Format

```
                                 [ {THROUGH}                    ]]
PERFORM [procedure-name-1        [ {THRU   }  procedure-name-2  ]]

                   {BEFORE}
[WITH TEST         {AFTER }] UNTIL condition-1

[imperative-statement-1 END-PERFORM]
```

The TEST AFTER is used to implement a DO UNTIL structure. The routine is performed first and then the condition is tested. When the TEST AFTER option is used the routine will always be performed at least once.

DO UNTIL STRUCTURE

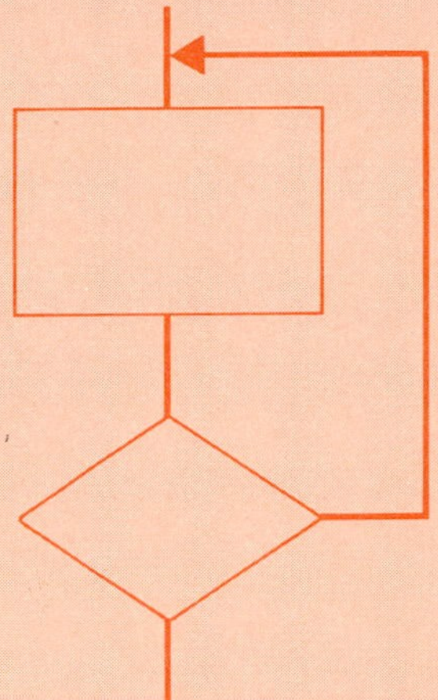

By leaving out the procedure-name and using an END-PERFORM, a routine may be performed in-line as in:

```
PERFORM UNTIL ROW > 30
        ADD. . .
        MOVE. . .
        WRITE. . .
END-PERFORM.
```

In this example the three statements between PERFORM and END-PERFORM will be repeated until ROW is greater than 30.

The OPEN Statement

Format

```
OPEN  {INPUT   file-name-1                   }
      {        [file-name-2] . . .           }
      {OUTPUT  file-name-3                   }
      {        [file-name-4] . . .           } . . .
```

The OPEN statement initiates processing that will make a file (or files) accessible to a program. Each file used in a program must be opened before any READ or WRITE statements may be issued for that file. The OPEN statement indicates how the file is to be opened (as INPUT or as OUTPUT) and the file-name.

A file that is opened as input must already exist. When the OPEN statement is used, a pointer is positioned before the first data record in the file. The OPEN statement does not itself result in any retrieval of data from the file.

A file that is opened as output must not already exist. Opening a file as output indicates that the program is creating a new file. The OPEN statement does not itself result in any placement of data into the file.

Examples

```
OPEN INPUT  ORDER-FILE
     OUTPUT PRINT-FILE.
```

The LISTING program of Chapters 1 and 2 uses only two files: the ORDER-FILE, which exists before the program is run; and the PRINT-FILE, which is a printed report created by the program. Both files are opened in the 1000-INITIALIZATION routine. The ORDER-FILE is opened as INPUT and the PRINT-FILE is opened as OUTPUT.

In the following examples, the OPEN statements on the right are equivalent to the ones on the left. The right-hand statements, with fewer occurrences of the verb OPEN, are generally more machine efficient. Pay special attention to the placement of periods and the use of the reserved words INPUT and OUTPUT.

```
OPEN INPUT  ORDER-FILE.        OPEN INPUT  ORDER-FILE
OPEN OUTPUT PRINT-FILE.             OUTPUT PRINT-FILE.

OPEN INPUT  ORDER-FILE         OPEN INPUT  ORDER-FILE
            INVOICE-FILE.                  INVOICE-FILE
OPEN OUTPUT PRINT-FILE              OUTPUT PRINT-FILE
            DISK-FILE.                     DISK-FILE.
```

The READ Statement

Format

```
READ file-name [INTO identifier] [AT END imperative statement]
```

READ makes a record available to the COBOL program. The record is retrieved from the file specified in the READ statement. The record is placed in the area of memory reserved by the PICTURE clause(s) in the FD for that file. The FD is part of the FILE SECTION, and the area reserved by the PICTURE clause(s) in the FD is referred to as the input area. Before the READ statement is executed, the file must have been opened as INPUT. (See Figure 3–18.)

```
READ ORDER-FILE
     AT END
          MOVE 'YES' TO END-FLAG-ORDER-FILE.
```

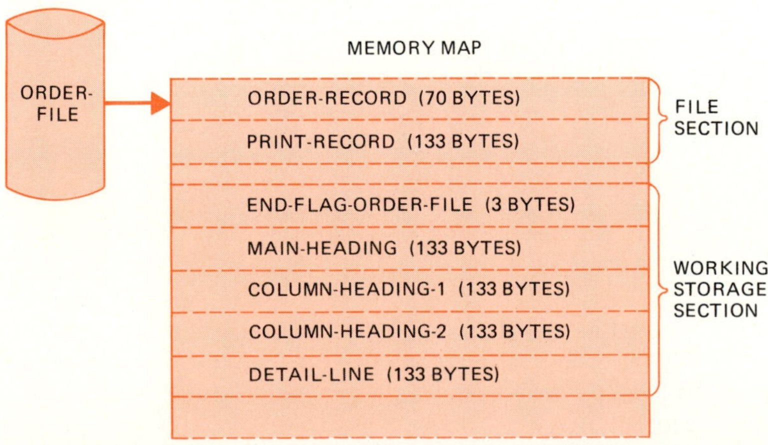

FIGURE 3–18

If we want the record to be placed in an additional area of memory, we can use the INTO option. The record remains in the input area, and a copy of it is moved to the area of memory named by the identifier. Since the description of storage did not provide a second area in which to put the incoming record, in order to use the INTO option a new data item must be added to the WORKING-STORAGE section and the READ statement must be revised as in Figure 3–19. The format of the record may be described in detail in either or neither location, or in both locations. The choice will depend on what processing needs to be done with the record. (See Figure 3–19.)

```
READ ORDER-FILE INTO WS-ORDER-RECORD
    AT END
        MOVE 'YES' TO END-FLAG-ORDER-FILE.
```

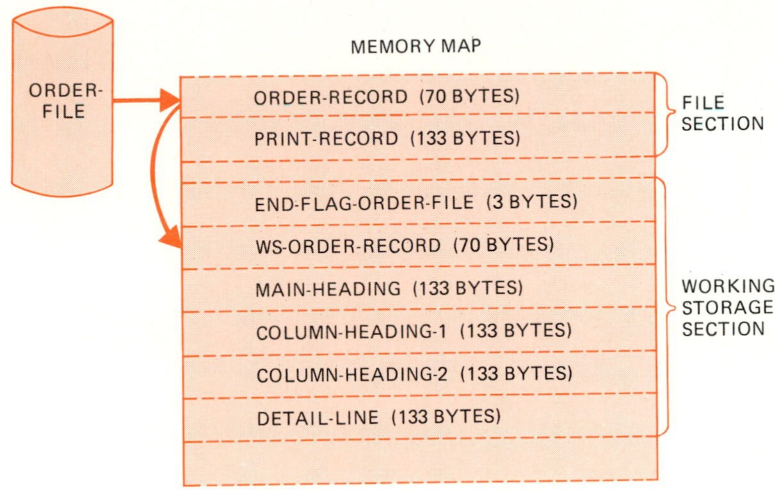

FIGURE 3-19

The AT END option is used to test for an end-of-file condition on sequential files. When a sequential file is created, an end-of-file indicator (usually a /*) is placed after the last record. When a READ instruction is executed, a test is made for the end-of-file indicator. If it is present, the AT END condition is true and any statement following the words AT END up to the first period will be executed. We can have a single statement as in

```
READ ORDER-FILE
    AT END
        MOVE 'YES' TO END-FLAG-ORDER-FILE.
```

or multiple statements as in

```
READ ORDER-FILE
    AT END
        MOVE 'YES' TO END-FLAG-ORDER-FILE
        MOVE 'END OF JOB' TO MESSAGE-AREA
        WRITE PRINT-RECORD FROM MESSAGE-LINE
            AFTER ADVANCING 3 LINES.
```

Note the alignment of the statements under the words AT END and the placement of the period. This alignment is not required by COBOL syntax, but is used to improve the readability of the program. It readily shows anyone who reads the program which statements are dependent on the AT END condition's being true. The period indicates to the COBOL compiler the end of the series of statements that should be executed only when the AT END condition is true.

With READ and READ INTO, the data in the record is transferred as a group and the program makes no decisions as to whether each individual data item is in the correct position or of the correct type (numeric or alphanumeric). Any such errors will be discovered during testing, when the data is used in calculations, comparisons, or printing.

Figure 3–20 shows a COBOL record description, the record layout, and a diagram associating data with data-names. Notice that EMPLOYEE-NAME is 24 characters in length in the record layout. An error has been made in the COBOL code, where EMPLOYEE-NAME is described as 23 characters. Accordingly, when the data is referenced in the program, each data item will be set forward one character starting with PAY-RATE. Thus, the last character of EMPLOYEE-NAME will become a part of PAY-RATE, the last character of PAY-RATE will become part of NBR-DEPENDENTS, and so on.

COBOL RECORD DESCRIPTION

```
05 SOCIAL-SECURITY-NUMBER     PIC 9(9).
05 EMPLOYEE-NAME              PIC X(23).
05 PAY-RATE                   PIC 9(4)V9(2).
05 NBR-DEPENDENTS             PIC 9(2).
05 HOURS-WORKED               PIC 9(3)V9(1).
```

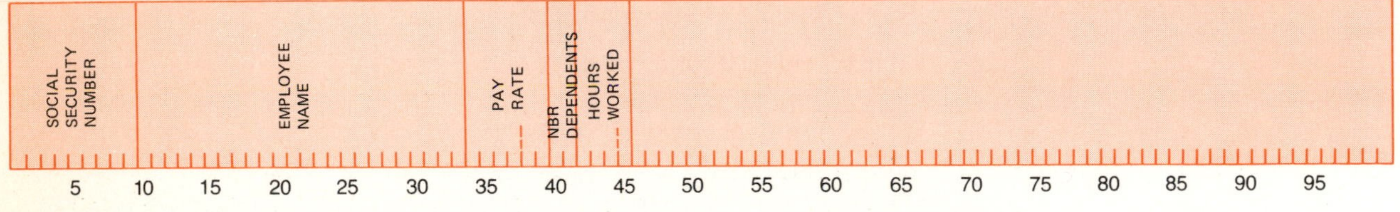

THE ORIGINAL RECORD LAYOUT

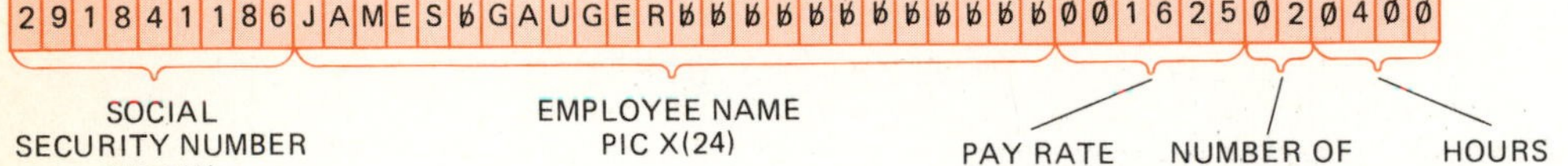

THE RECORD LAYOUT AS DESCRIBED TO THE COBOL PROGRAM

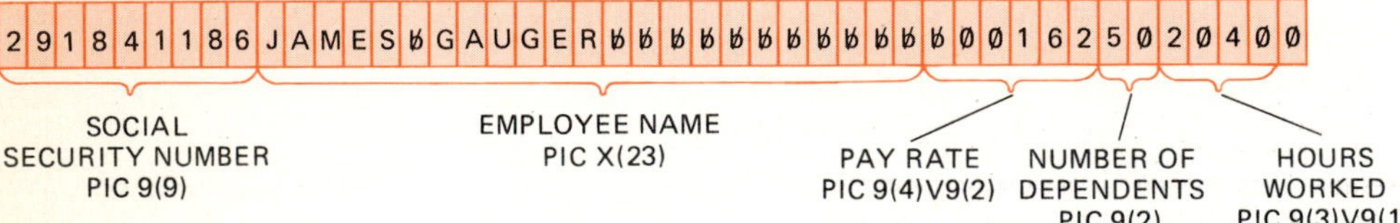

FIGURE 3-20

Since PAY-RATE will have picked up a space or an alphabetic character from EMPLOYEE-NAME, it will no longer be usable in calculations. NBR-DEPENDENTS will contain the last digit of PAY-RATE and the first digit of NBR-DEPENDENTS. It will still be numeric and usable in calculations, but will produce a incorrect answer. HOURS-WORKED will contain the last digit of NBR-DEPENDENTS and the first three digits of HOURS-WORKED.

READ Examples

In the sample program, READ file-name was used as opposed to the READ file-name INTO identifier option. The READ file-name INTO identifier option will be discussed in a later chapter. In the meantime, consider

```
READ ORDER-FILE
     AT END
          MOVE 'YES' TO END-FLAG-ORDER-FILE.
```

This routine is performed at the end of 1000-INITIALIZATION and 2000-PROCESS, so that the first record is read in 1000-INITIALIZATION and subsequent records are read in 2000-PROCESS. The AT END condition is tested each time. Although we do not expect this condition to occur on the first read in 1000-INITIALIZATION, it should be tested anyway in case the file is empty.

The ORDER-FILE was defined in an FD in the FILE SECTION of the DATA DIVISION. The area of memory where the record will be stored was called ORDER-

RECORD. The record was described in detail using 05 and 10 levels for the individual data items. The record is repeated in Figure 3–21. Later, we shall move the individual data items from their place in ORDER-RECORD to a position in DETAIL-LINE. The file was opened as INPUT in 1000-INITIALIZATION prior to the first READ.

```
01  ORDER-RECORD.
    05  ORD-BRANCH                  PIC 9(2).
    05  ORD-SALES-REP               PIC 9(3).
    05  ORD-CUSTOMER-NBR            PIC 9(5).
    05  ORD-CUST-PO-NBR             PIC X(8).
    05  ORD-SALES-ORD-NBR           PIC X(6).
    05  ORD-DATE.                   PIC 9(2).
        10  ORD-YY                  PIC 9(2).
        10  ORD-MM                  PIC 9(2).
        10  ORD-DD                  PIC 9(2).
    05  ORD-PART-NBR                PIC X(6).
    05  ORD-QUANTITY                PIC 9(5).
    05  ORD-UNIT-PRICE              PIC 9(4)V9(2).
    05  ORD-REQ-SHIP-DATE.
        10  ORD-REQ-SHIP-YY         PIC 9(2).
        10  ORD-REQ-SHIP-MM         PIC 9(2).
        10  ORD-REQ-SHIP-DD         PIC 9(2).
    05  ORD-ACT-SHIP-DATE.
        10  ORD-ACT-SHIP-YY         PIC 9(2).
        10  ORD-ACT-SHIP-MM         PIC 9(2).
        10  ORD-ACT-SHIP-DD         PIC 9(2).
    05  FILLER                      PIC X(11).
```

FIGURE 3-21

The MOVE Statement

Format

```
      {identifier-1}
MOVE  {literal     }  TO identifier-2 [identifier-3]...
```

MOVE transfers data from one location in memory to another. The data remains in the original location, and a copy of it is put in the new location(s). In the preceding format, identifier-1 or literal represents the *sending* field. Identifier-2, identifier-3, and so on represent the *receiving* fields. How the data is aligned and "padded" (i.e., filled in with spaces or zeros) in the receiving field depends upon the type of move (numeric or alphanumeric), which is in turn determined by the data class of the sending and receiving fields. (See Figure 3–22.)

Alphanumeric Moves

In an alphanumeric move, the data movement is from left to right. If the receiving field is shorter than the sending field, the rightmost characters of the sending field will be truncated. If the receiving field is longer than the sending field, the receiving field will be padded with spaces on the right. Figure 3–23 shows several alphanumeric moves.

FIGURE 3–22

SENDING FIELD	RECEIVING FIELD	TYPE OF MOVE
Alphanumeric	Alphanumeric	Alphanumeric
Alphanumeric	Numeric	Alphanumeric
Numeric	Alphanumeric	Alphanumeric
Numeric	Numeric	Numeric

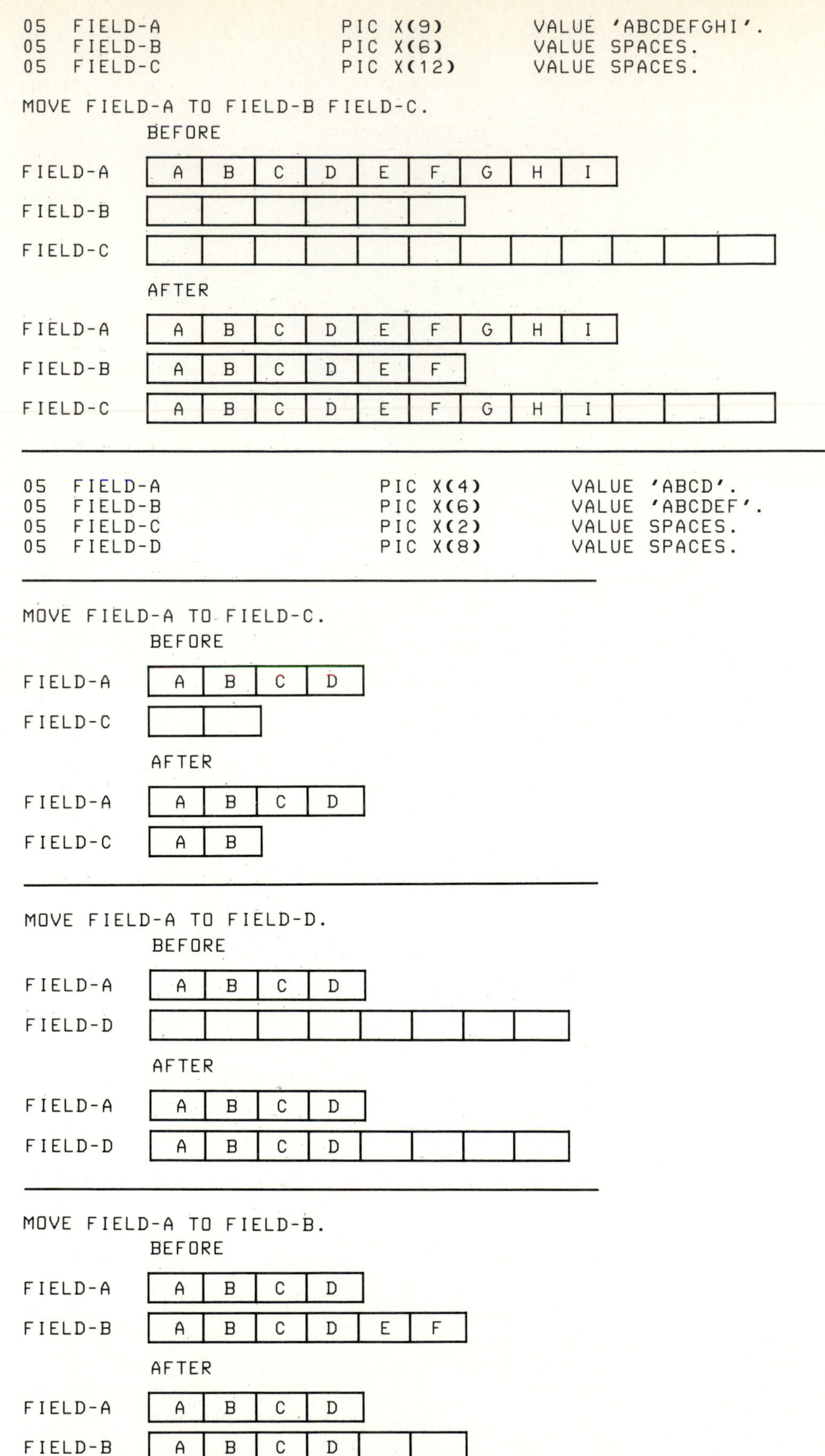
05 FIELD-A PIC X(9) VALUE 'ABCDEFGHI'.
05 FIELD-B PIC X(6) VALUE SPACES.
05 FIELD-C PIC X(12) VALUE SPACES.
MOVE FIELD-A TO FIELD-B FIELD-C.
BEFORE
FIELD-A A B C D E F G H I
FIELD-B
FIELD-C
AFTER
FIELD-A A B C D E F G H I
FIELD-B A B C D E F
FIELD-C A B C D E F G H I
05 FIELD-A PIC X(4) VALUE 'ABCD'.
05 FIELD-B PIC X(6) VALUE 'ABCDEF'.
05 FIELD-C PIC X(2) VALUE SPACES.
05 FIELD-D PIC X(8) VALUE SPACES.
MOVE FIELD-A TO FIELD-C.
BEFORE
FIELD-A A B C D
FIELD-C
AFTER
FIELD-A A B C D
FIELD-C A B
MOVE FIELD-A TO FIELD-D.
BEFORE
FIELD-A A B C D
FIELD-D
AFTER
FIELD-A A B C D
FIELD-D A B C D
MOVE FIELD-A TO FIELD-B.
BEFORE
FIELD-A A B C D
FIELD-B A B C D E F
AFTER
FIELD-A A B C D
FIELD-B A B C D

FIGURE 3-23

FIGURE 3–23 cont.

```
MOVE FIELD-B TO FIELD-D.
MOVE FIELD-A TO FIELD-D.

          BEFORE

FIELD-B   | A | B | C | D | E | F |
FIELD-A   | A | B | C | D |
FIELD-D   |   |   |   |   |   |   |   |   |

          AFTER

FIELD-B   | A | B | C | D | E | F |
FIELD-A   | A | B | C | D |
FIELD-D   | A | B | C | D |   |   |   |   |
```

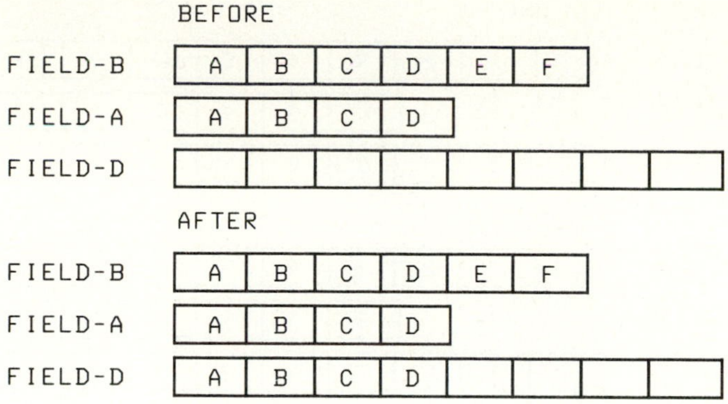

```
MOVE FIELD-C TO FIELD-A.

          BEFORE

FIELD-C   |   |   |
FIELD-A   | A | B | C | D |

          AFTER

FIELD-C   |   |   |
FIELD-A   |   |   |   |   |
```

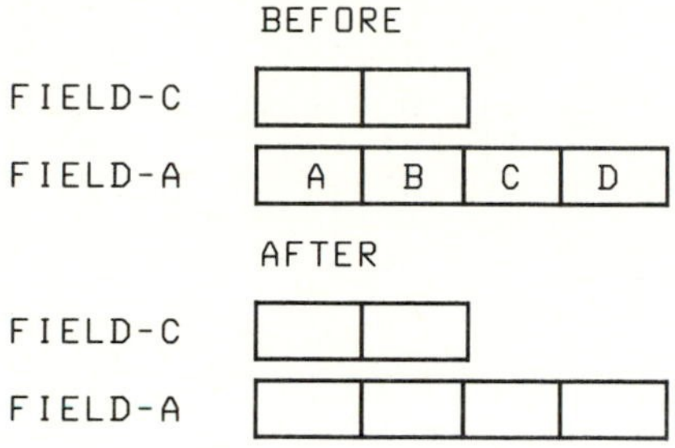

An important point to remember is that all group fields are considered to be alphanumeric. Thus, in the following example, A-DATE is alphanumeric, while A-MONTH, A-DAY, and A-YEAR are numeric. As a result, movement from A-DATE would be from left to right while movement of A-MONTH, A-DAY, and A-YEAR would follow the rules for numeric moves to be explained next.

```
01  A-DATE.
    05  A-MONTH    PIC 9(2).
    05  A-DAY      PIC 9(2).
    05  A-YEAR     PIC 9(2).
```

Numeric and Numeric-Edited Moves

In numeric and numeric-edited moves, data items are aligned on the assumed (99V99) or actual (99.99) decimal point. If neither a V nor a decimal point is present in the PICTURE clause, the decimal point is assumed to be at the right of the item. After the decimal alignment, movement takes place as follows:

Right to left for the integer portion of the number
Left to right for the decimal portion of the number

```
     (integer)             (decimal)
                     V
<-------------- . --------------->
```

If the receiving field is too short on either end, digits will be truncated from the sending field. If the receiving field is too long on either end, zeros will be used for padding. Figure 3–24 shows several examples of numeric and numeric-edited moves.

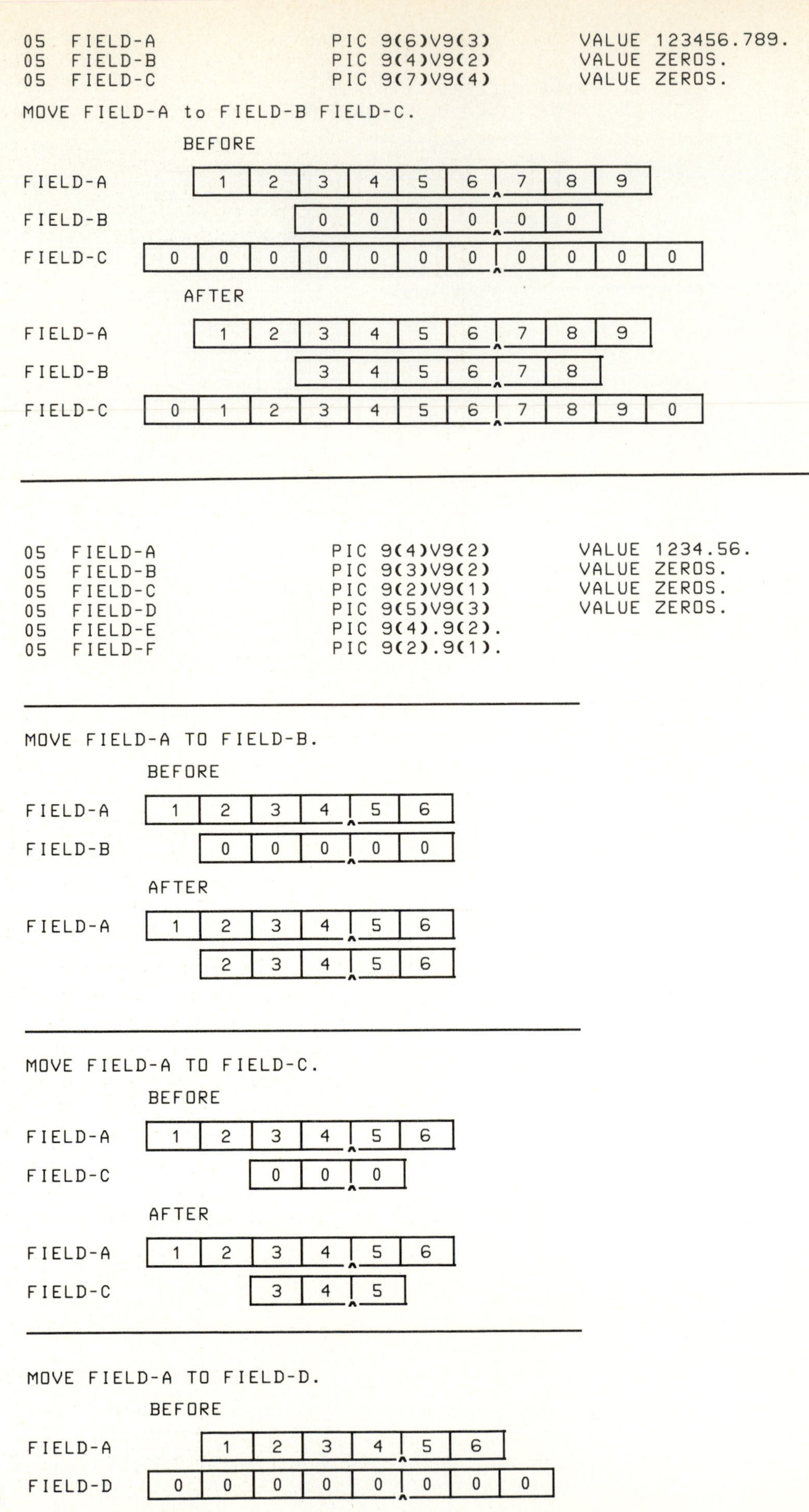
05 FIELD-A PIC 9(6)V9(3) VALUE 123456.789.
05 FIELD-B PIC 9(4)V9(2) VALUE ZEROS.
05 FIELD-C PIC 9(7)V9(4) VALUE ZEROS.
MOVE FIELD-A to FIELD-B FIELD-C.
BEFORE
FIELD-A 1 2 3 4 5 6 7 8 9
FIELD-B 0 0 0 0 0 0
FIELD-C 0 0 0 0 0 0 0 0 0 0 0
AFTER
FIELD-A 1 2 3 4 5 6 7 8 9
FIELD-B 3 4 5 6 7 8
FIELD-C 0 1 2 3 4 5 6 7 8 9 0
05 FIELD-A PIC 9(4)V9(2) VALUE 1234.56.
05 FIELD-B PIC 9(3)V9(2) VALUE ZEROS.
05 FIELD-C PIC 9(2)V9(1) VALUE ZEROS.
05 FIELD-D PIC 9(5)V9(3) VALUE ZEROS.
05 FIELD-E PIC 9(4).9(2).
05 FIELD-F PIC 9(2).9(1).
MOVE FIELD-A TO FIELD-B.
BEFORE
FIELD-A 1 2 3 4 5 6
FIELD-B 0 0 0 0 0
AFTER
FIELD-A 1 2 3 4 5 6
2 3 4 5 6
MOVE FIELD-A TO FIELD-C.
BEFORE
FIELD-A 1 2 3 4 5 6
FIELD-C 0 0 0
AFTER
FIELD-A 1 2 3 4 5 6
FIELD-C 3 4 5
MOVE FIELD-A TO FIELD-D.
BEFORE
FIELD-A 1 2 3 4 5 6
FIELD-D 0 0 0 0 0 0 0 0

FIGURE 3–24

FIGURE 3-24

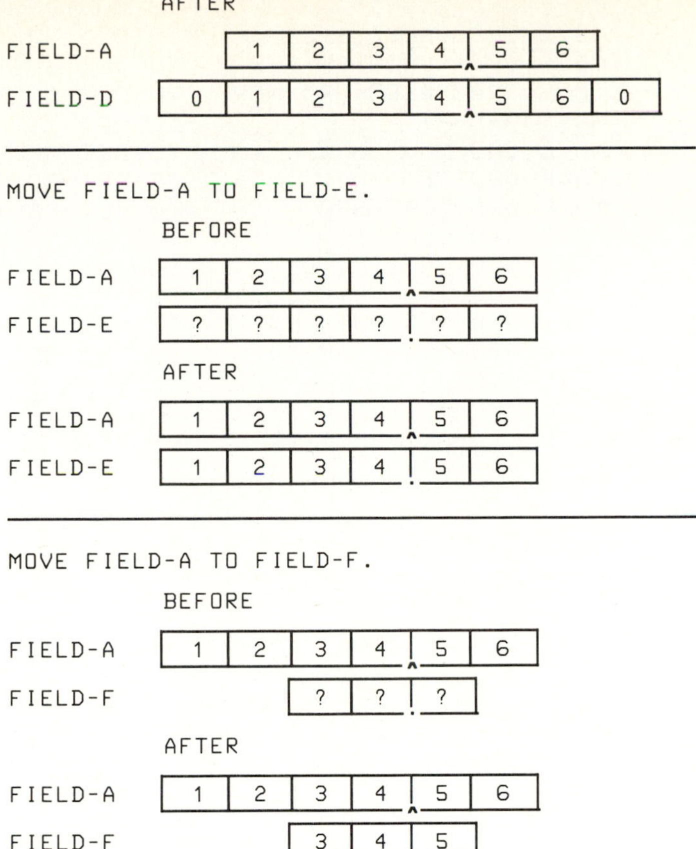

The Sample Program

There are two types of moves in the sample program. The first,

```
MOVE 'YES' TO END-FLAG-ORDER-FILE.
```

is the movement of an alphanumeric literal to an identifier. The literal (YES) is stored in memory by COBOL in an area called the literal pool. When this MOVE statement is executed, the literal is transferred from the literal pool to the area of memory identified as END-FLAG-ORDER-FILE.

The second type of move transfers data from the input area (ORDER-RECORD) to the area of memory reserved for DETAIL-LINE. This transfer is shown in Figure 3–25. The data items in ORDER-RECORD have no spaces between them, making it difficult to read them if they were printed in this manner. To provide spaces between the items, a detail line was designed on the print chart which includes such spaces. The layout of this detail line is described in the WORKING-STORAGE SECTION of the DATA DIVISION and is given the name DETAIL-LINE.

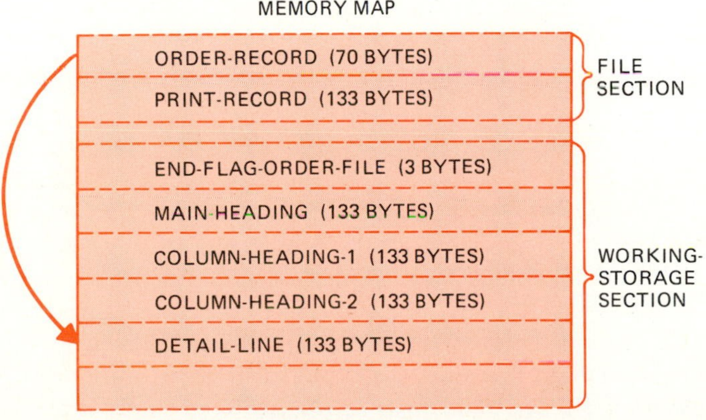

FIGURE 3–25

```
MOVE ORD-BRANCH          TO DET-BRANCH.
MOVE ORD-SALES-REP       TO DET-SALES-REP.
MOVE ORD-CUSTOMER-NBR    TO DET-CUSTOMER-NBR.
MOVE ORD-SALES-ORD-NBR   TO DET-SALES-ORD-NBR.
MOVE ORD-YY              TO DET-YY.
MOVE ORD-MM              TO DET-MM.
MOVE ORD-DD              TO DET-DD.
MOVE ORD-PART-NBR        TO DET-PART-NBR.
MOVE ORD-QUANTITY        TO DET-QUANTITY.
MOVE ORD-UNIT-PRICE      TO DET-UNIT-PRICE.
MOVE ORD-REQ-SHIP-YY     TO DET-REQ-SHIP-YY.
MOVE ORD-REQ-SHIP-MM     TO DET-REQ-SHIP-MM.
MOVE ORD-REQ-SHIP-DD     TO DET-REQ-SHIP-DD.
MOVE ORD-ACT-SHIP-YY     TO DET-ACT-SHIP-YY.
MOVE ORD-ACT-SHIP-MM     TO DET-ACT-SHIP-MM.
MOVE ORD-ACT-SHIP-DD     TO DET-ACT-SHIP-DD.
```

Each item needed in the DETAIL-LINE is moved separately. Alignment will subsequently take place according to the rules of alignment for each type of data. The movement of the fields is shown in Figure 3–26.

The 1985 standard allows reference modification for accessing a portion of a field. The data-name is followed by a set of parentheses which includes two numbers separated by a colon. The first indicates a starting position within the field and the second indicates the number of characters required.

```
WORKING-STORAGE SECTION.
    .
    .
    05  ORD-PART-NBR          PIC X(5).

PROCEDURE DIVISION.
    .
    .
    .
```

MOVE ORD-PART-NBR (1:2) TO FIRST-TWO-DIGITS-OF-PART-NBR.
MOVE ORD-PART-NBR (3:3) TO LAST-THREE-DIGITS-OF-PART-NBR.

The first MOVE starts at position 1 in ORD-PART-NBR and moves two characters. The second MOVE starts at position 3 and moves three characters.

The WRITE Statement

Format

```
WRITE record-name [FROM identifier-1]
 [                          { { identifier-2 } [LINE ] } ]
 [ {BEFORE}                 { { integer      } [LINES] } ]
 [ {AFTER } ADVANCING       {                          } ]
 [                          { {mnemonic-name}          } ]
 [                          { {PAGE         }          } ]
```

The WRITE statement releases a record to an output file. The file must have been described in an FD in the DATA DIVISION and opened as OUTPUT in the PROCEDURE DIVISION. Notice that the record-name (not the file-name) is used in a WRITE statement. This will be the record-name of the file which was opened as output. The record is transferred from the output area to the output device associated with the file. The effect of the statement WRITE PRINT-RECORD is shown on the memory map of Figure 3–27.

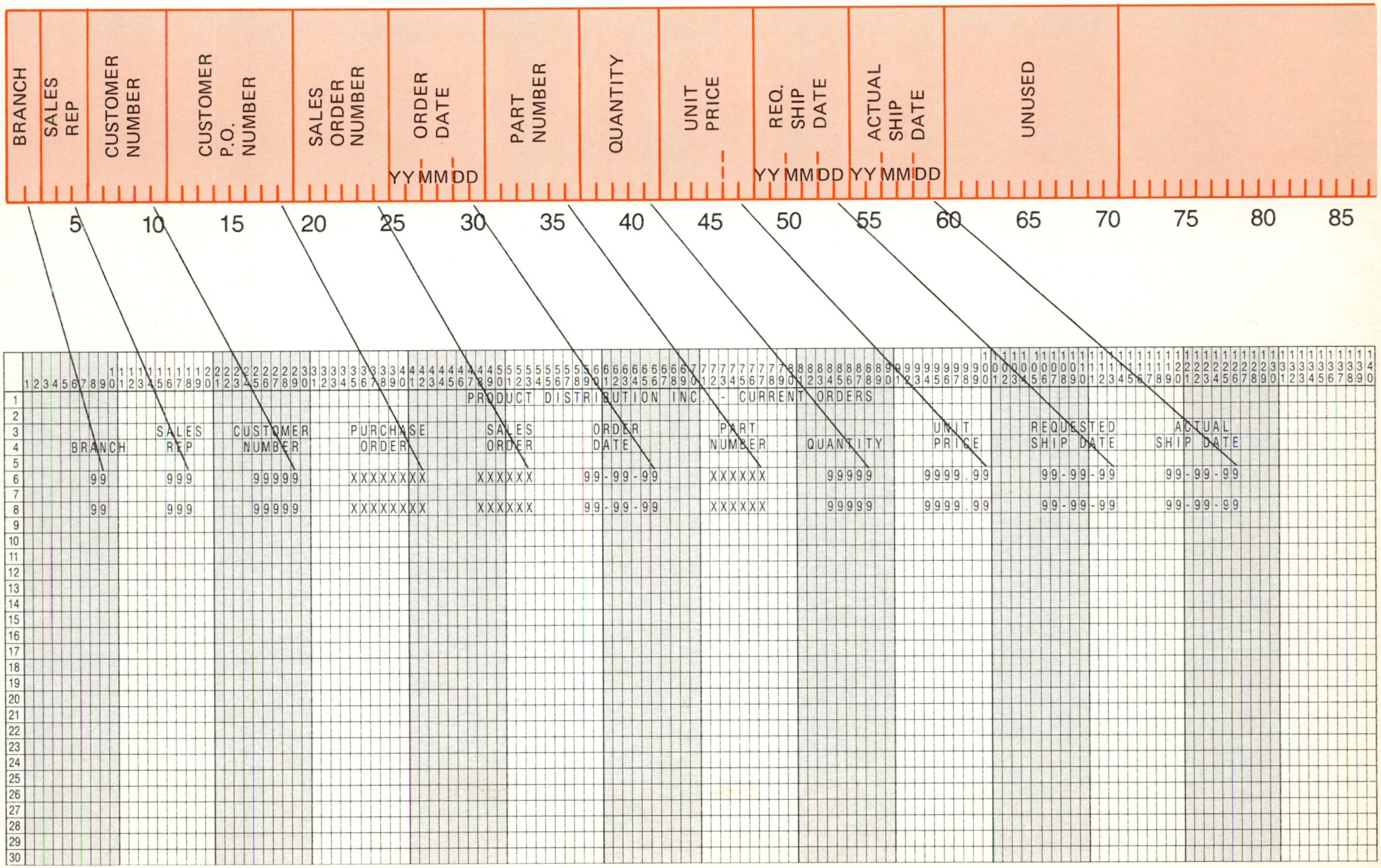

BRANCH
SALES REP
CUSTOMER NUMBER
CUSTOMER P.O. NUMBER
SALES ORDER NUMBER
ORDER DATE
YY MM DD
PART NUMBER
QUANTITY
UNIT PRICE
REQ. SHIP DATE
YY MM DD
ACTUAL SHIP DATE
YY MM DD
UNUSED
5 10 15 20 25 30 35 40 45 50 55 60 65 70 75 80 85
PRODUCT DISTRIBUTION INC. - CURRENT ORDERS
SALES CUSTOMER PURCHASE SALES ORDER PART UNIT REQUESTED ACTUAL
BRANCH REP NUMBER ORDER ORDER DATE NUMBER QUANTITY PRICE SHIP DATE SHIP DATE
99 999 99999 XXXXXXXX XXXXXX 99-99-99 XXXXXX 99999 9999.99 99-99-99 99-99-99
99 999 99999 XXXXXXXX XXXXXX 99-99-99 XXXXXX 99999 9999.99 99-99-99 99-99-99

FIGURE 3–26

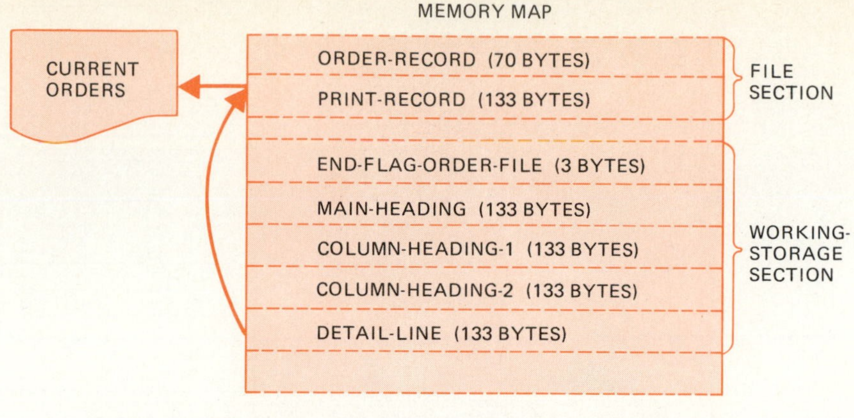


```
MOVE DETAIL-LINE TO PRINT-RECORD.
WRITE PRINT-RECORD AFTER ADVANCING 2 LINES.
```

FIGURE 3–27

The FROM option allows the transfer of data from another area of memory to the output area and then to the appropriate device. WRITE PRINT-RECORD FROM DETAIL-LINE moves DETAIL-LINE to PRINT-RECORD and then releases it to the printer. This movement is shown in Figure 3–28.

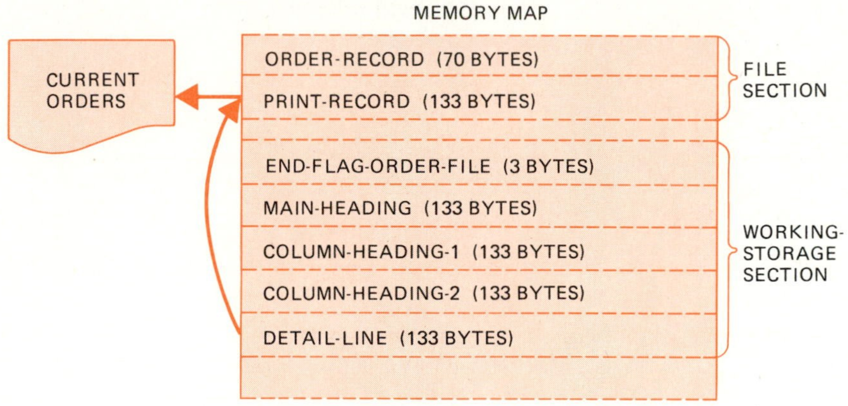


```
WRITE PRINT-RECORD FROM DETAIL-LINE
    AFTER ADVANCING 2 LINES.
```

FIGURE 3–28

The ADVANCING option controls the vertical positioning of a line on paper. This option is used when the printer is the output device. In using the option, the programmer must select either BEFORE ADVANCING or AFTER ADVANCING. BEFORE ADVANCING prints the line and then advances the paper. AFTER ADVANCING advances the paper and then prints the line. (See Figure 3–29.)

After the word ADVANCING, there are two general options: either advance a number of lines, or advance the paper to the top of a new page. Within each of these actions, there are further options.

In advancing a number of lines, there are two choices: an identifier or an integer. In order to specify an identifier, the identifier must have been defined in the DATA DIVISION as an elementary numeric item with no decimal positions. It must also have a zero or positive value up to 99 at the time the WRITE statement is executed. The following example specifies triple spacing. The advantage of using an identifier is that it can be changed during execution of the program, whereas an integer cannot.

WRITE PRINT-RECORD AFTER ADVANCING 2 LINES.

XXXX

WRITE PRINT-RECORD BEFORE ADVANCING 2 LINES.

XXXX

FIGURE 3–29

```
DATA DIVISION.

    05  VARIABLE-SPACE        PIC 9(2)        VALUE 3.

PROCEDURE DIVISION.

    WRITE PRINT-RECORD FROM DETAIL-LINE
        AFTER ADVANCING VARIABLE-SPACE LINES.
```

The choice of an integer requires only an entry in the PROCEDURE DIVISION. The integer is included as a literal in the WRITE statement and, as with an identifier, ranges from zero to 99. An integer is used where the vertical spacing produced by the WRITE statement does not need to be changed during execution of the program. The following example specifies double spacing:

```
WRITE PRINT-RECORD FROM DETAIL-LINE
    AFTER ADVANCING 2 LINES.
```

To advance the paper to the top of a new page, there are two options: PAGE or mnemonic-name. The PAGE option, which is simpler to code and understand, is shown in the following example:

```
WRITE PRINT-RECORD FROM HEADING-LINE
    AFTER ADVANCING PAGE.
```

The mnemonic-name option requires the establishment of a mnemonic-name in the SPECIAL-NAMES paragraph of the ENVIRONMENT DIVISION. In that paragraph, we equate C01 (which the system understands to mean the top of the form) with a name we associate with the top of the form. In the following example, TOP-OF-PAGE is the mnemonic-name.

```
ENVIRONMENT DIVISION.
.
.

SPECIAL-NAMES.
    C01 IS TOP-OF-PAGE.

PROCEDURE DIVISION.
.
.

    WRITE PRINT-RECORD FROM HEADING-LINE
        AFTER ADVANCING TOP-OF-PAGE.
```

WRITE Examples

The sample program uses the FROM option with each WRITE statement. In each case, data is transferred from WORKING-STORAGE to the output area and then printed.

```
WRITE PRINT-RECORD FROM MAIN-HEADING
    AFTER ADVANCING PAGE.

WRITE PRINT-RECORD FROM COLUMN-HEADING-1
    AFTER ADVANCING 2 LINES.

WRITE PRINT-RECORD FROM COLUMN-HEADING-2
    AFTER ADVANCING 1 LINE.

WRITE PRINT-RECORD FROM DETAIL-LINE
    AFTER ADVANCING 2 LINES.
```

In all cases, the ADVANCING clause was used since the output device was the printer. AFTER ADVANCING rather than BEFORE ADVANCING was selected, as it is more machine efficient. To advance the paper to the top of a new page, the PAGE option was used rather than the mnemonic-name. To advance lines, the integer option was used rather than the identifier option, because there was no need to change the spacing during execution of the program.

The CLOSE Statement

Format

```
CLOSE file-name-1
     [file-name-2] . . .
```

The CLOSE statement terminates processing of a file or files. Every file which was opened with an OPEN statement must be closed before the program ends. After the CLOSE statement is issued, the file is no longer accessible to the program, and READ or WRITE statements will have no effect on the closed files. Unlike the OPEN statement, the type of file (INPUT or OUTPUT) is not specified in the CLOSE statement.

EXAMPLE

```
CLOSE ORDER-FILE
      PRINT-FILE.
```

Both files used in the LISTING program are closed in the 3000-EOJ routine. All READ and WRITE statements that the program has issued have been completed at that time.

The STOP Statement

Format

```
STOP RUN
```

STOP RUN terminates execution of the program. It is placed at the logical end of the program.

In the LISTING program, the STOP statement is placed directly after the main logic routine of the program. It will halt execution of the program after the main routine is completed.

The GO TO Statement

Format

```
GO TO procedure-name
```

COBOL executes each statement in the PROCEDURE DIVISION in a sequential manner. If we wish to change this order, a GO TO statement is available. GO TO transfers control to the paragraph-name or section-name following the words GO TO. Starting at the paragraph or section designated, each statement is executed sequentially. Unlike PERFORM, GO TO is not designed to return to the next statement after it; rather, it simply keeps on going. GO TO statements can be executed unconditionally or conditionally, as shown in the following example.

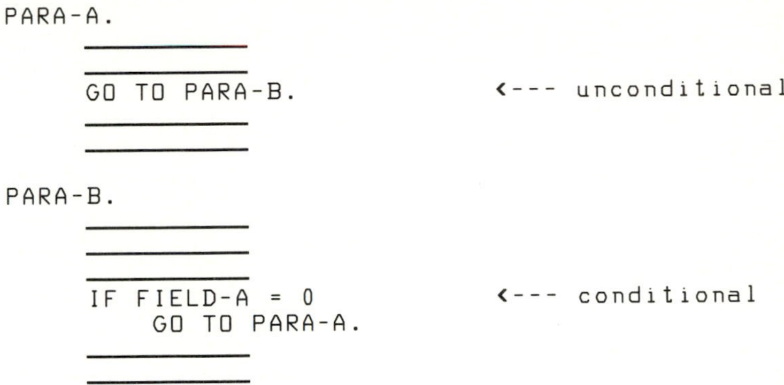

```
PARA-A.
        ____________
        ____________
        GO TO PARA-B.            <--- unconditional
        ____________
        ____________

PARA-B.
        ____________
        ____________
        ____________
        IF FIELD-A = 0           <--- conditional
            GO TO PARA-A.
        ____________
        ____________
```

The use of GO TO statements is not recommended. Structured programming techniques eliminate the need for GO TO statements.

DEBUGGING

Diagnostics

Diagnostic messages are generated upon violations of the coding rules of the COBOL language. The messages are printed either by the line of code that generated them or as a group near the end of the listing. If they are all grouped together, each diagnostic message will be prefaced with a statement number for easy location of the statement in question in the source listing.

IBM assigns four levels to diagnostics depending on their severity:

`W--Warning`

This is the least serious level of diagnostic message. The program may still be executed when W-level diagnostics are present. However, the output may be incorrect. One of the more common W-level diagnostics indicates the possibility of losing significant leading digits from a number.

`C--Conditional`

A program may still be allowed to execute with C-level diagnostics. In this case, the compiler makes an assumption about the action to be taken. However, this action may or may not agree with the action the programmer intended.

`E--Error`

The presence of E-level diagnostics will suppress the creation of an object module. Therefore, the program cannot execute. It is very disappointing to correct a group of diagnostics and recompile, only to find that there is still one E-level diagnostic remaining.

D--Disaster

A D-level diagnostic causes the compiler to terminate compilation. D-level diagnostics are rare. Forgetting to write any program at all and then attempting to compile can produce a D-level diagnostic.

The following diagnostics are typical of the type of diagnostics that a simple listing program might produce. The wording of diagnostics varies from compiler to compiler, so these may not agree exactly with the ones generated by a user's particular compiler. However, key terms are common to most compilers.

DATA-NAME IS NOT UNIQUE

This diagnostic points to a statement in the PROCEDURE DIVISION which uses the data-name mentioned in the diagnostic. The diagnostic occurred because, when the COBOL compiler looked for the data-name in the DATA DIVISION, it discovered that there was more than one data item with that name. The compiler does not know which one is to be used.

To solve the problem, the programmer should

1. Look through the DATA DIVISION until he or she finds at least two data items with the data-name specified in the diagnostic.
2. Change one of them in the DATA DIVISION.
3. Change any references to the revised one in the PROCEDURE DIVISION.

DATA-NAME IS NOT DEFINED

This diagnostic points to a statement in the PROCEDURE DIVISION which contains the data-name mentioned in the diagnostic. The diagnostic occurred because, when the COBOL compiler looked for the data-name in the DATA DIVISION, it discovered that there was no data-name with that exact spelling.

To solve the problem, the programmer should

1. Check the spelling of the word in the PROCEDURE DIVISION to determine whether it is spelled as intended.
2. Try to locate the word in the DATA DIVISION.
3. Check whether there is a spelling variation.
4. Check whether there is a missing hyphen.
5. Check whether there is an extra hyphen.
6. Check whether there are any numeric zeros (0) which should be alphabetic O's or the other way around.
7. Check whether there is another error on the DATA DIVISION line where the data-name is defined. If so, this may have caused the data-name to be ignored.
8. Check whether the name was included in the DATA DIVISION.

SHOULD NOT BEGIN IN AREA A

This diagnostic can point to statements in any division. It informs the progammer that the word mentioned in the diagnostic should not begin in Area A.

To solve the problem, the programmer should not move the word out of Area A until he or she has checked the following:

1. Is the word spelled correctly?
2. Should it be connected to another word with a hyphen?
3. Does it belong in Area B?

END OF SENTENCE SHOULD PRECEDE 05

This diagnostic points to statements in the DATA DIVISION and says that the error in question occurred on the line previous to the one mentioned.

To solve the problem, the programmer should

1. Look at the statement prior to the one specified.
2. Place a period at the end of that line.

SYNTAX REQUIRES RECORD-NAME

This diagnostic points to a WRITE statement in the PROCEDURE DIVISION. Recall that only a record-name can follow the word WRITE.

There can be a variety of causes of the problem. To solve it, the programmer should check each of the following:

1. Is the word spelled correctly?
2. Is it the name of a record defined in an output file?
3. Is it hyphenated correctly?
4. Are there any previous diagnostics which may have invalidated the file-name? (This can cause the record-name to be discarded.)
5. Are there any previous diagnostics which invalidated the record-name?

HIGH-ORDER TRUNCATION

This diagnostic generally points to a MOVE statement. It means that if the move is made with the field sizes specified, digits can be lost on the left side because the receiving field is not large enough to hold them all. This may be because either the sending field is too large or the receiving field is too small.

To solve the problem, the programmer should

1. Determine which field is the correct size.
2. Change the size of the incorrect field by either reducing the size of the sending field or increasing the size of the receiving field.

In so doing, the programmer must remember that the option of changing the size of an input field is probably not available, since the programmer usually is not the one who created the file. Also, if the programmer changes an output field, he or she needs to consider the effect the change has on the print chart.

SUMMARY

This chapter has presented the COBOL code for the fourth (PROCEDURE) division of the program begun in Chapter 2. Formats for the COBOL verbs used in the chapter are summarized as follows, along with a brief explanation of the use of each verb.

The PERFORM Statement

Format

```
                                  {THROUGH}
PERFORM procedure-name-1  [       {THRU   }  procedure-name-2]
[UNTIL condition-1]
```

The PERFORM statement transfers control to the beginning of a procedure and then returns control to the statement following the PERFORM statement after the procedure has been executed.

The OPEN Statement

Format

```
OPEN { INPUT  file-name-1                }
     {         [file-name-2] . . .       }
     { OUTPUT file-name-3                }
     {         [file-name-4] . . .       } . . .
```

The OPEN statement makes files available for processing. It checks the labels on input files and write labels on output files.

The READ Statement

Format

```
READ file-name [INTO identifier] [AT END imperative statement]
```

The READ statement transfers records from external storage to an input area for the file named.

The MOVE Statement

Format

```
     {identifier-1}
MOVE {literal     } TO identifier-2 [identifier-3]...
```

The MOVE statement transfers data from one memory location to another.

The WRITE Statement

Format

```
WRITE record-name [FROM identifier-1]
[                        { {identifier-2 } [LINE ] } ]
[                        { {integer      } [LINES] } ]
[ {BEFORE}               {                         } ]
[ {AFTER } ADVANCING     { {mnemonic-name}         } ]
[                        { {PAGE         }         } ]
```

The WRITE statement transfers data from an output area in memory to external storage (including printed reports).

The CLOSE Statement

Format

```
CLOSE file-name-1
        [file-name-2] . . .
```

The CLOSE statement terminates processing of the file named.

The STOP Statement

Format

```
STOP RUN
```

The STOP statement terminates execution of the program.

The GO TO Statement

Format

```
GO TO procedure-name
```

The GO TO statement transfers control to a new procedure.

EXERCISES

I. For each box in the following hierarchy chart, choose the paragraph number which belongs in the box.

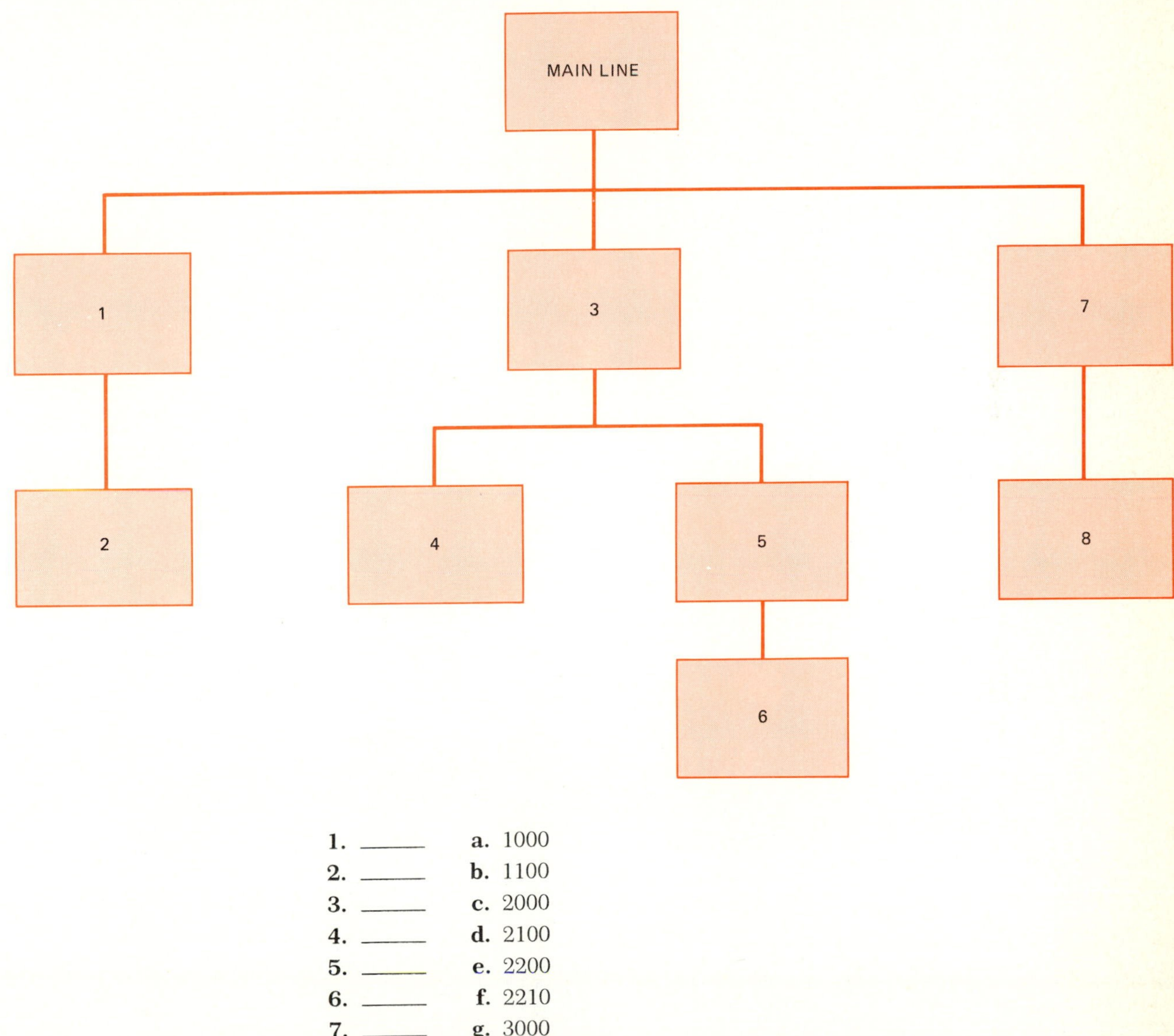

1. ______	**a.** 1000
2. ______	**b.** 1100
3. ______	**c.** 2000
4. ______	**d.** 2100
5. ______	**e.** 2200
6. ______	**f.** 2210
7. ______	**g.** 3000
8. ______	**h.** 3100

II. For each COBOL statement listed below, determine whether it is valid or invalid. Assume that PAYROLL-FILE and PRINT-FILE are file-names and PAYROLL-RECORD is a record-name.

______ **1.** READ PAYROLL-RECORD AT END . . .

______ **2.** OPEN PAYROLL-FILE.

_____ 3. MOVE FIELD-A TO 10.
_____ 4. CLOSE INPUT PAYROLL-FILE.
_____ 5. PERFORM 2000-PROCESS.
_____ 6. MOVE 10 TO FIELD-A.
_____ 7. WRITE PRINT-RECORD AFTER PAGE.
_____ 8. WRITE PRINT-FILE AFTER ADVANCING 2 LINES.
_____ 9. WRITE PRINT-RECORD FROM DETAIL-LINE AFTER 2.
_____ 10. WRITE PRINT RECORD AFTER ADVANCING 2.
_____ 11. READ PAYROLL-FILE AT END . . .
_____ 12. OPEN OUTPUT PRINT-FILE.

III. For each COBOL verb listed, choose the symbol which would be used to represent it in a flowchart.

_____ 1. PERFORM
_____ 2. OPEN
_____ 3. READ
_____ 4. MOVE
_____ 5. WRITE
_____ 6. AT END
_____ 7. EXIT
_____ 8. CLOSE

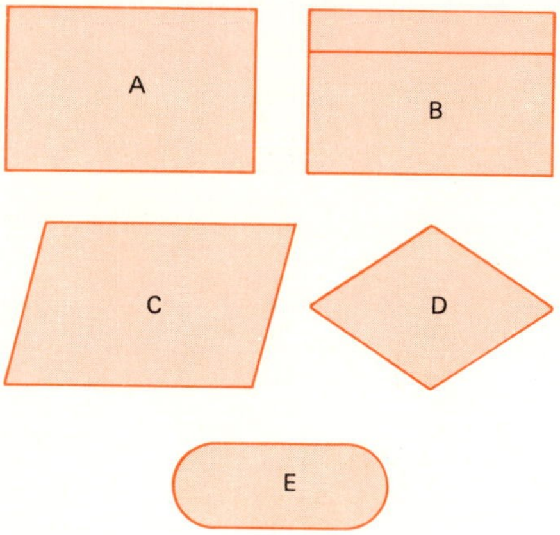

A

B

C

D

E

IV. MULTIPLE CHOICE

Select the most appropriate COBOL element to fill in the blank.

1. READ _____ AT END . . .
   - **a.** file-name
   - **b.** record-name
   - **c.** identifier
   - **d.** literal
   - **e.** reserved word
2. WRITE _____ AFTER 2.
   - **a.** file-name
   - **b.** record-name
   - **c.** identifier
   - **d.** literal
   - **e.** reserved word
3. WRITE PRINT-RECORD BEFORE ADVANCING _____.
   - **a.** identifier
   - **b.** literal
   - **c.** reserved word
   - **d.** A or B
   - **e.** none of the above

4. MOVE _____ TO FIELD-A.
   a. identifier
   b. literal
   c. reserved word
   d. A or B
   e. A or C
5. MOVE FIELD-A TO _____.
   a. identifier
   b. literal
   c. reserved word
   d. A or B
   e. A or C
6. OPEN _____ PRINT-FILE.
   a. identifier
   b. literal
   c. reserved word
   d. A or B
   e. A or C
7. CLOSE _____.
   a. file-name
   b. record-name
   c. identifier
   d. literal
   e. reserved word
8. WRITE PRINT-RECORD FROM _____ AFTER 2.
   a. identifier
   b. literal
   c. reserved word
   d. A or B
   e. A or C
9. WRITE PRINT-RECORD FROM PRINT-REC AFTER 2 _____.
   a. identifier
   b. literal
   c. reserved word
   d. A or B
   e. A or C
10. _____ PAYROLL AT END . . .
   a. identifier
   b. literal
   c. reserved word
   d. A or B
   e. A or C

PROJECTS

For each of the following specifications and input record layouts, design a print chart and a code a COBOL program that satisfies the specification.

PROJECT 3–1 Payroll

PROGRAM SPECIFICATION

Program Name: PAY3

Program Function:

The program will produce a listing of a payroll file.

Input Files:

I. PAYROLL-FILE

INPUT DEVICE:	DISK
FILE ORGANIZATION:	SEQUENTIAL
RECORD LENGTH:	80 BYTES
FILE SEQUENCE:	ASCENDING ON DIVISION / DEPARTMENT

Output Files:

I. PRINT-FILE

OUTPUT DEVICE:	PRINTER
RECORD LENGTH:	133 BYTES

Output Requirements:

Each record read from the payroll file should be printed on one line of the report. All fields from the input record are to be included on the output. Design your own output using a print chart.

The following are formatting requirements for the report:

1. The first page of the report should contain:
   (a) a heading which includes the company name and report name.
   (b) column headings which describe the items printed underneath them.
2. The detail lines should include all fields from the input.
3. The detail lines should be double spaced.
4. Do not include provisions for page overflow.

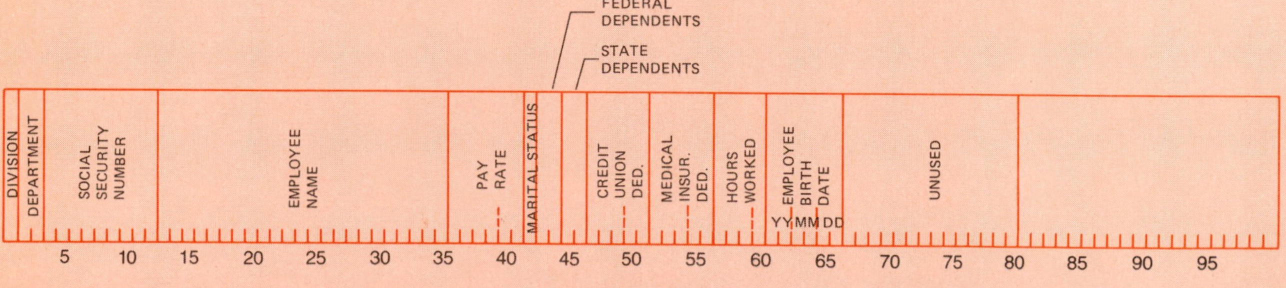

PROJECT 3–2 Inventory

PROGRAM SPECIFICATION

Program Name: INV3

Program Function:

The program will produce a listing of an inventory file.

Input Files:

I. INVENTORY-FILE

INPUT DEVICE:	DISK
FILE ORGANIZATION:	SEQUENTIAL
RECORD LENGTH:	80 BYTES
FILE SEQUENCE:	ASCENDING ON INVENTORY STOCK NUMBER

Output Files:

I. PRINT-FILE

OUTPUT DEVICE:	PRINTER
RECORD LENGTH:	133 BYTES

Output Requirements:

Each record read from the inventory file should be printed on one line of the report. All fields from the input record are to be included on the output. Design your own output using a print chart.

The following are formatting requirements for the report:

1. The first page of the report should contain:
   (a) a heading which includes the company name and report name.
   (b) column headings which describe the items printed underneath them.
2. The detail lines should include all fields from the input.
3. The detail lines should be double spaced.
4. Do not include provisions for page overflow.

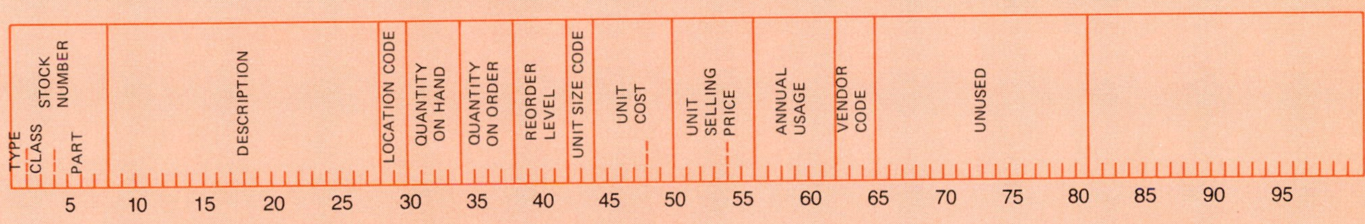

PROJECT 3–3 Accounts Payable

PROGRAM SPECIFICATION

Program Name: AP3

Program Function:

The program will produce a listing of an accounts payable file.

Input Files:

I. ACCOUNTS-PAYABLE-FILE

INPUT DEVICE:	DISK
FILE ORGANIZATION:	SEQUENTIAL
RECORD LENGTH:	80 BYTES
FILE SEQUENCE:	ASCENDING ON DIVISION / CONTROL NBR

Output Files:

I. PRINT-FILE

OUTPUT DEVICE:	PRINTER
RECORD LENGTH:	133 BYTES

Output Requirements:

Each record read from the accounts payable file should be printed on one line of the report. All fields from the input record are to be included on the output. Design your own output using a print chart.

The following are formatting requirements for the report:

1. The first page of the report should contain:
   (a) a heading which includes the company name and report name.
   (b) column headings which describe the items printed underneath them.
2. The detail lines should include all fields from the input.
3. The detail lines should be double spaced.
4. Do not include provisions for page overflow.

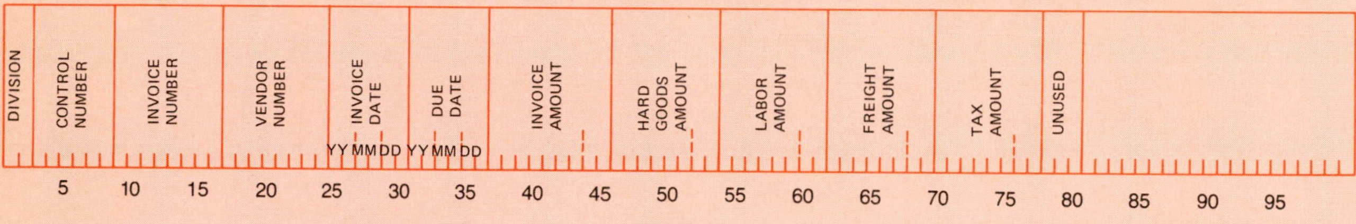

PROJECT 3–4 Pension

PROGRAM SPECIFICATION

Program Name: PEN3

Program Function:

The program will produce a listing of a pension file.

Input Files:

I. PENSION-FILE

INPUT DEVICE:	DISK
FILE ORGANIZATION:	SEQUENTIAL
RECORD LENGTH:	80 BYTES
FILE SEQUENCE:	ASCENDING ON SOCIAL SECURITY NUMBER

Output Files:

I. PRINT-FILE

OUTPUT DEVICE:	PRINTER
RECORD LENGTH:	133 BYTES

Output Requirements:

Each record read from the pension file should be printed on one line of the report. All fields from the input record are to be included on the output. Design your own output using a print chart.

The following are formatting requirements for the report:

1. The first page of the report should contain:
   (a) a heading which includes the company name and report name.
   (b) column headings which describe the items printed underneath them.
2. The detail lines should include all fields from the input.
3. The detail lines should be double spaced.
4. Do not include provisions for page overflow.

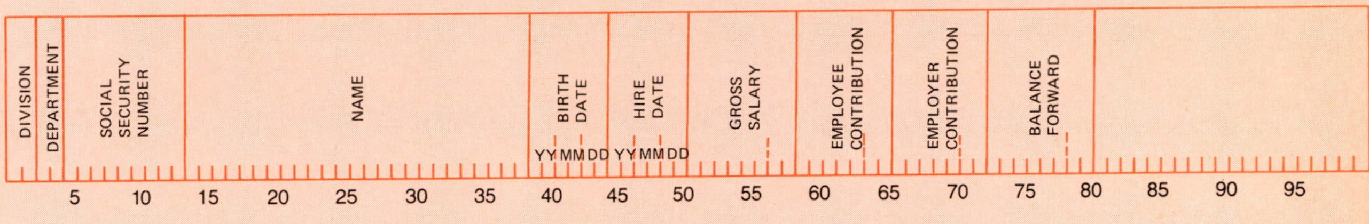

PROJECT 3–5 Bill of Materials

PROGRAM SPECIFICATION

Program Name: BOM3

Program Function:

The program will produce a listing of a bill-of-materials file.

Input Files:

I. BILL-OF-MATERIALS-FILE

INPUT DEVICE:	DISK
FILE ORGANIZATION:	SEQUENTIAL
RECORD LENGTH:	55 BYTES
FILE SEQUENCE:	ASCENDING ON PRODUCT-LINE / PART NUMBER

Output Files:

I. PRINT-FILE

OUTPUT DEVICE:	PRINTER
RECORD LENGTH:	133 BYTES

Output Requirements:

Each record read from the bill-of-materials file should be printed on one line of the report. All fields from the input record are to be included on the output. Design your own output using a print chart.

The following are formatting requirements for the report:

1. The first page of the report should contain:
   (a) a heading which includes the company name and report name.
   (b) column headings which describe the items printed underneath them.
2. The detail lines should include all fields from the input.
3. The detail lines should be double spaced.
4. Do not include provisions for page overflow.

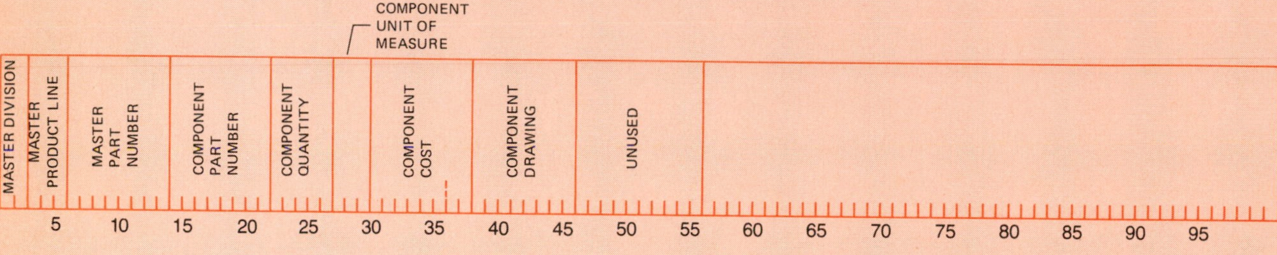

PROJECT 3–6 Manufacturing Cost

PROGRAM SPECIFICATION

Program Name: COST3

Program Function:

The program will produce a listing of a cost file.

Input Files:

I. COST-FILE

INPUT DEVICE:	DISK
FILE ORGANIZATION:	SEQUENTIAL
RECORD LENGTH:	75 BYTES
FILE SEQUENCE:	ASCENDING ON PRODUCT-LINE / PART NUMBER

Output Files:

I. PRINT-FILE

OUTPUT DEVICE:	PRINTER
RECORD LENGTH:	133 BYTES

Output Requirements:

Each record read from the cost file should be printed on one line of the report. All fields from the input record are to be included on the output. Design your own output using a print chart.

The following are formatting requirements for the report:

1. The first page of the report should contain:
   (a) a heading which includes the company name and report name.
   (b) column headings which describe the items printed underneath them.

2. The detail lines should include all fields from the input.
3. The detail lines should be double spaced.
4. Do not include provisions for page overflow.

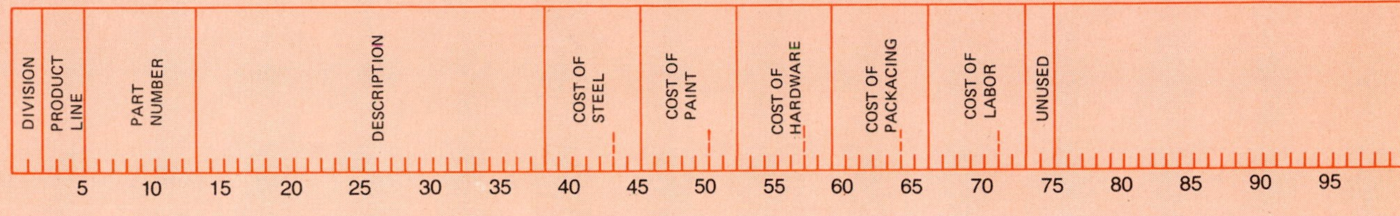

CHAPTER

4 Extraction

In this chapter, two new programming projects, as well as the following new logical concepts, are presented:

1. Producing multiple pages of output.
2. Selecting certain records to be printed (extracting).
3. Producing final totals.

The COBOL language emphasis here is on decision making (IF/ELSE) and calculations (COMPUTE, ADD, SUBTRACT, MULTIPLY, and DIVIDE). Output editing is expanded to include suppression of zeros.

A section on debugging covers diagnostics that are likely to be generated when using the new COBOL language elements discussed. Also, coverage of the internal data representation scheme EBCDIC is begun, and USAGE clauses are introduced beginning with USAGE IS DISPLAY.

PROGRAM SPECIFICATION: EXTRACT

In this chapter, there are two programming projects. The first program includes the printing of multiple pages of output with page numbers, the selection of certain records for printing, and the accumulation and printing of final totals. The specification for this program is given in Figure 4–1.

Input Record Layout

The input record layout of the EXTRACT program is shown in Figure 4–2. This is the same input file used in Chapters 2 and 3. The layout is repeated here for convenience.

Print Chart

The print chart for the project is shown in Figure 4–3. It includes the current date, page number, extended price, and final totals, none of which was included in the print chart for the program in Chapters 2 and 3.

LOGIC FOR EXTRACT PROGRAM

The logic design for the EXTRACT program is shown in Figure 4–4 in a hierarchy chart, in Figure 4–5 in pseudocode, and in Figure 4–6 in a flowchart.

PROGRAM SPECIFICATION

Program Name: EXTRACT

Program Function:

The program will produce a printed report of all orders wherein the extended price is greater than $2,000.00.

Input Files:

I. ORDER-FILE

INPUT DEVICE:	DISK
FILE ORGANIZATION:	SEQUENTIAL
RECORD LENGTH:	70 BYTES
FILE SEQUENCE:	ASCENDING ON BRANCH / SALES REP

Output Files:

I. PRINT-FILE

OUTPUT DEVICE:	PRINTER
RECORD LENGTH:	133 BYTES

Processing Requirements:

For each record from the order file, the extended price for the order should be calculated. (Extended price = quantity × unit price.) An order record should be included in the output listing only if the extended price is greater than $2,000.00. Totals for quantity and extended price should be accumulated and printed at the end of the report.

Output Requirements:

The following are formatting requirements for the report:

1. Each page of the report should contain:
   (a) a main heading which contains the company name, the report name, the current date, and a page number.
   (b) column headings which describe the items printed underneath them.
2. Detail lines should include all fields from the input record and the extended price.
3. Detail lines should be double spaced.
4. Total lines should be double spaced.

FIGURE 4–1

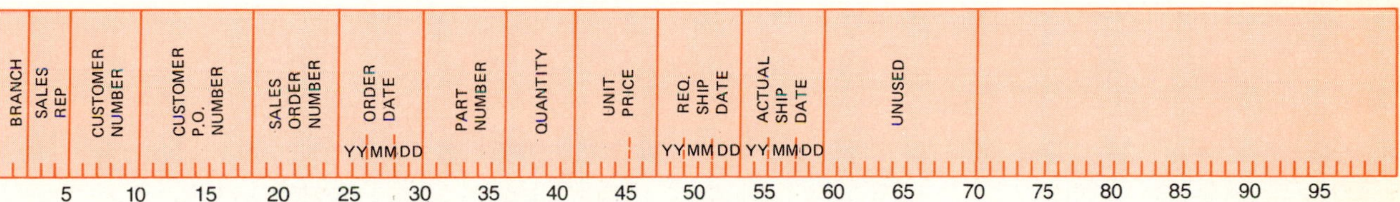

FIGURE 4–2

```
       DATE: XX-XX-XX                        PRODUCT DISTRIBUTION INC. - EXTRACTED ORDERS                               PAGE: ZZ9

             SALES    CUSTOMER    SALES       ORDER      REQUESTED     ACTUAL       PART               UNIT        EXTENDED
     BRANCH   REP      NUMBER     ORDER        DATE     SHIP DATE    SHIP DATE     NUMBER   QUANTITY    PRICE          PRICE

        99    999       99999    XXXXXX     99-99-99     99-99-99     99-99-99     XXXXXX      ZZZZ9   ZZZ9.99     ZZZZZZ9.99

        99    999       99999    XXXXXX     99-99-99     99-99-99     99-99-99     XXXXXX      ZZZZ9   ZZZ9.99     ZZZZZZ9.99


                                                                                              ZZZZZ9              ZZZZZZZ9.99
```

FIGURE 4–3

Hierarchy Chart

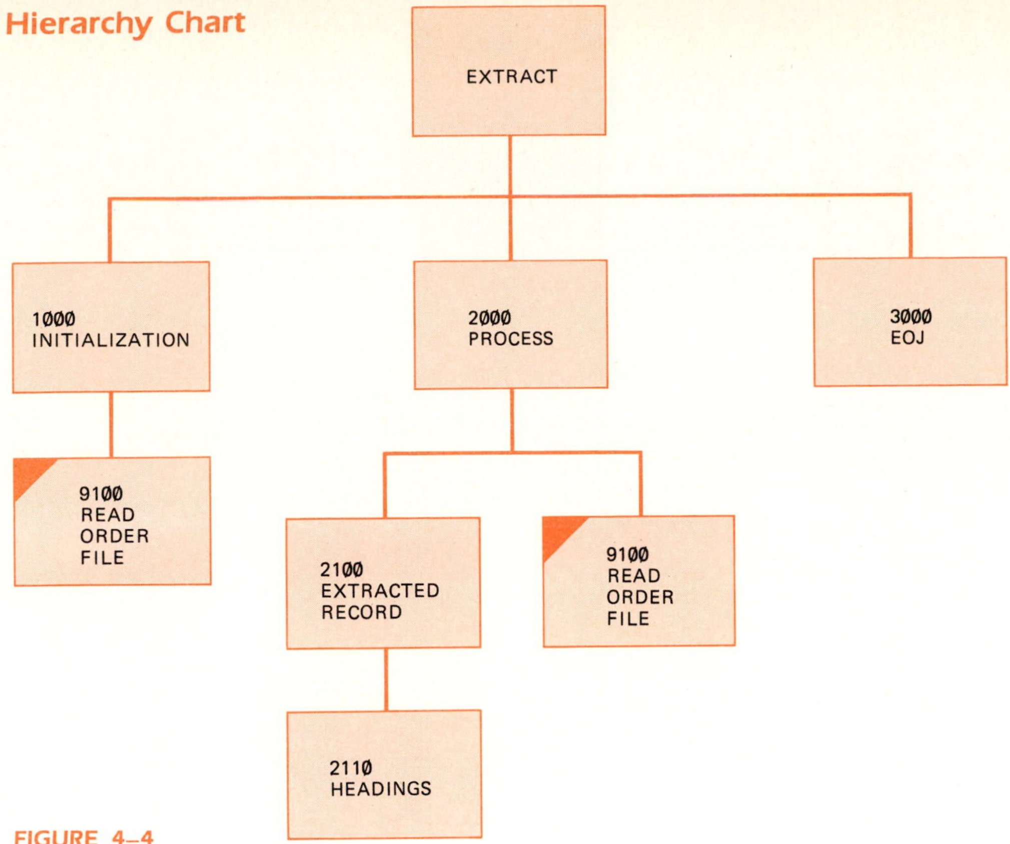

FIGURE 4–4

Pseudocode

```
MAIN LINE
     DO initialization
     DO WHILE more order records
          DO process
     ENDDO
     DO end of job

INITIALIZATION
     OPEN files
     MOVE date to heading
     DO read an order

PROCESS
     CALCULATE extended price
     IF extended price > 2,000.00
          DO extracted record
     ENDIF
     DO read an order


EXTRACTED RECORD
     IF line count > 50
          DO headings
     ENDIF
     MOVE input to output
     MOVE extended price to output
     ADD quantity to final total quantity
```

FIGURE 4–5

```
        ADD extended price to final total extended
          price
        WRITE detail line

HEADINGS
        ADD 1 to page count
        MOVE page count to output
        WRITE main heading line
        WRITE column heading line one
        WRITE column heading line two
        MOVE 4 to line count

END OF JOB
        MOVE final total quantity to output
        MOVE final total extended price to output
        WRITE final total line
        CLOSE files

READ AN ORDER
        READ order file
```

FIG. 4-5
cont.

Flowchart

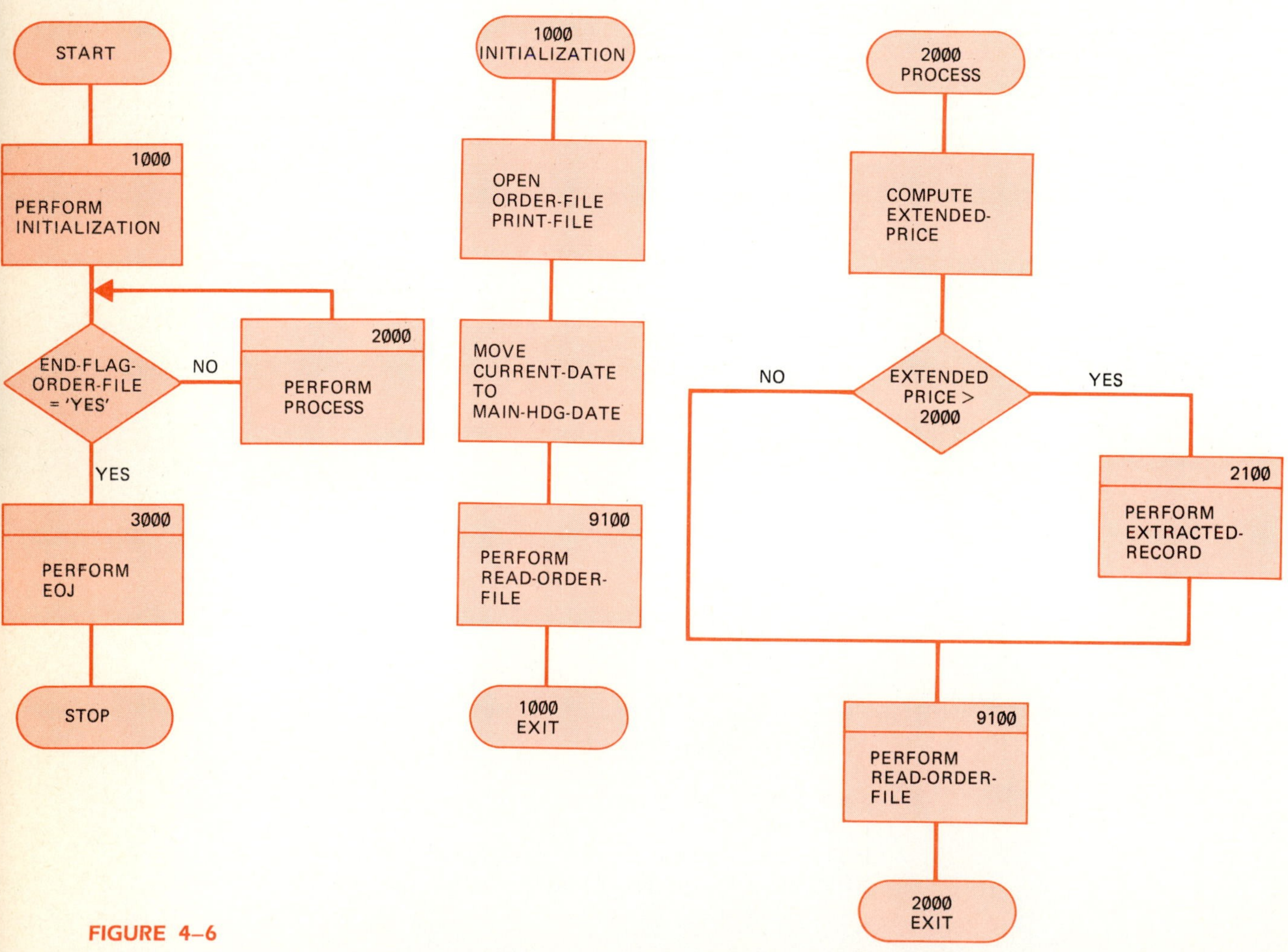

FIGURE 4–6

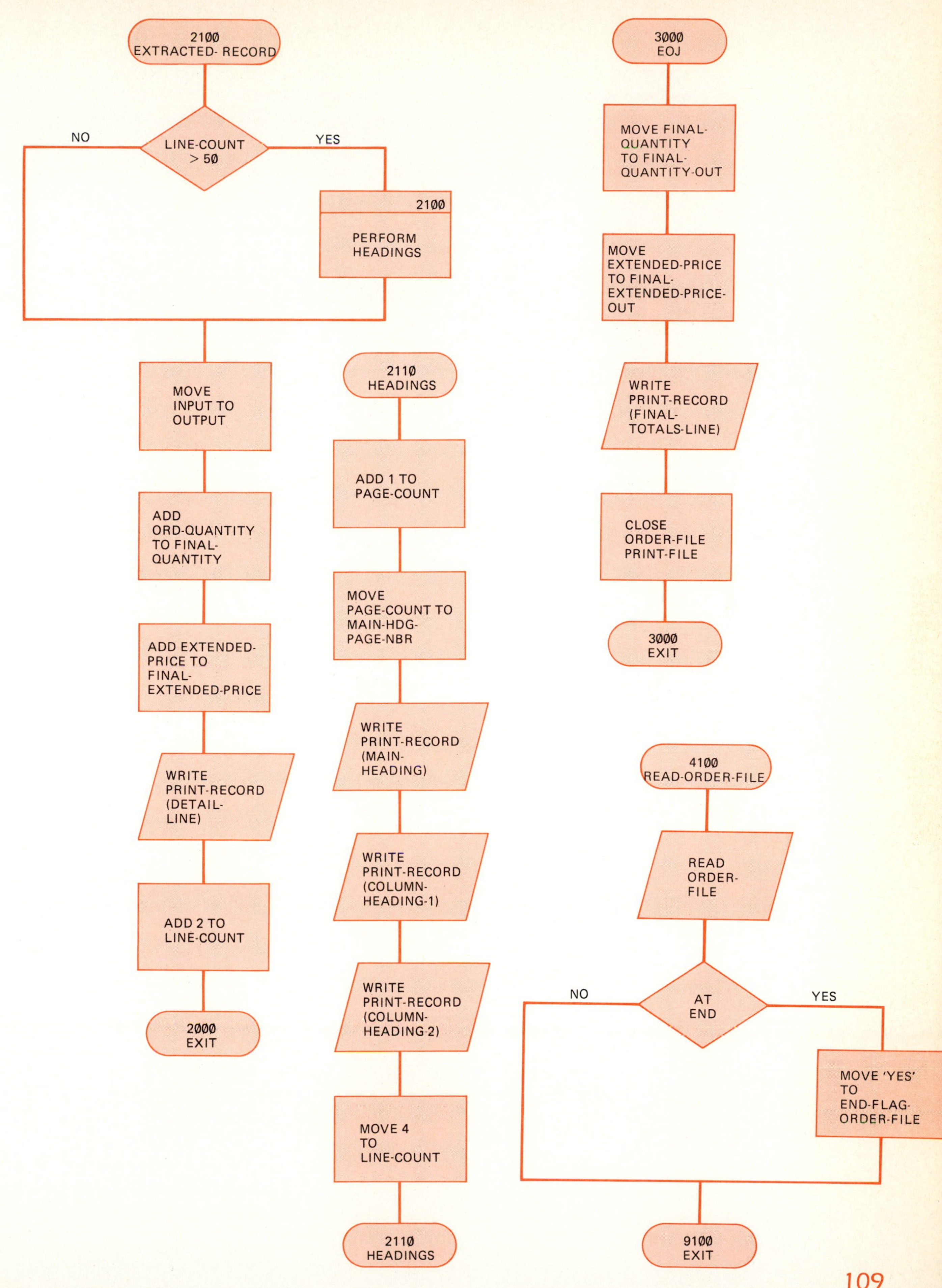

2100
EXTRACTED- RECORD
LINE-COUNT
> 50
NO
YES
2100
PERFORM
HEADINGS
MOVE
INPUT TO
OUTPUT
ADD
ORD-QUANTITY
TO FINAL-
QUANTITY
ADD EXTENDED-
PRICE TO
FINAL-
EXTENDED-PRICE
WRITE
PRINT-RECORD
(DETAIL-
LINE)
ADD 2 TO
LINE-COUNT
2000
EXIT
2110
HEADINGS
ADD 1 TO
PAGE-COUNT
MOVE
PAGE-COUNT TO
MAIN-HDG-
PAGE-NBR
WRITE
PRINT-RECORD
(MAIN-
HEADING)
WRITE
PRINT-RECORD
(COLUMN-
HEADING-1)
WRITE
PRINT-RECORD
(COLUMN-
HEADING-2)
MOVE 4
TO
LINE-COUNT
2110
HEADINGS
3000
EOJ
MOVE FINAL-
QUANTITY
TO FINAL-
QUANTITY-OUT
MOVE
EXTENDED-PRICE
TO FINAL-
EXTENDED-PRICE-
OUT
WRITE
PRINT-RECORD
(FINAL-
TOTALS-LINE)
CLOSE
ORDER-FILE
PRINT-FILE
3000
EXIT
4100
READ-ORDER-FILE
READ
ORDER-
FILE
AT
END
NO
YES
MOVE 'YES'
TO
END-FLAG-
ORDER-FILE
9100
EXIT

Explanation of Logic

A new routine, 2100-EXTRACTED-RECORD, is added to the program. This routine will do the processing for each record selected for extraction. The heading routine is performed from 2100-EXTRACTED-RECORD rather than 1000-INITIALIZATION as was the case in the previous programming project.

MAIN LINE

The EXTRACT program uses the same main logic as the previous program did. Again, the logic is divided into three major steps:

1. 1000-INITIALIZATION includes those logic steps which are done once at the beginning of the program.
2. 2000-PROCESS includes those logic steps which are repeated for every record. It is this routine which is repeated over and over until there are no more records to process. In the previous program, 2000-PROCESS contained most of the logic steps in the program. In this program, we shall separate some of those steps out and PERFORM them in a separate routine.
3. 3000-EOJ includes the logic steps required only once at the end of the program. In this program, 3000-EOJ will include the printing of the final totals.

See Figure 4–7 for the main-line routine.

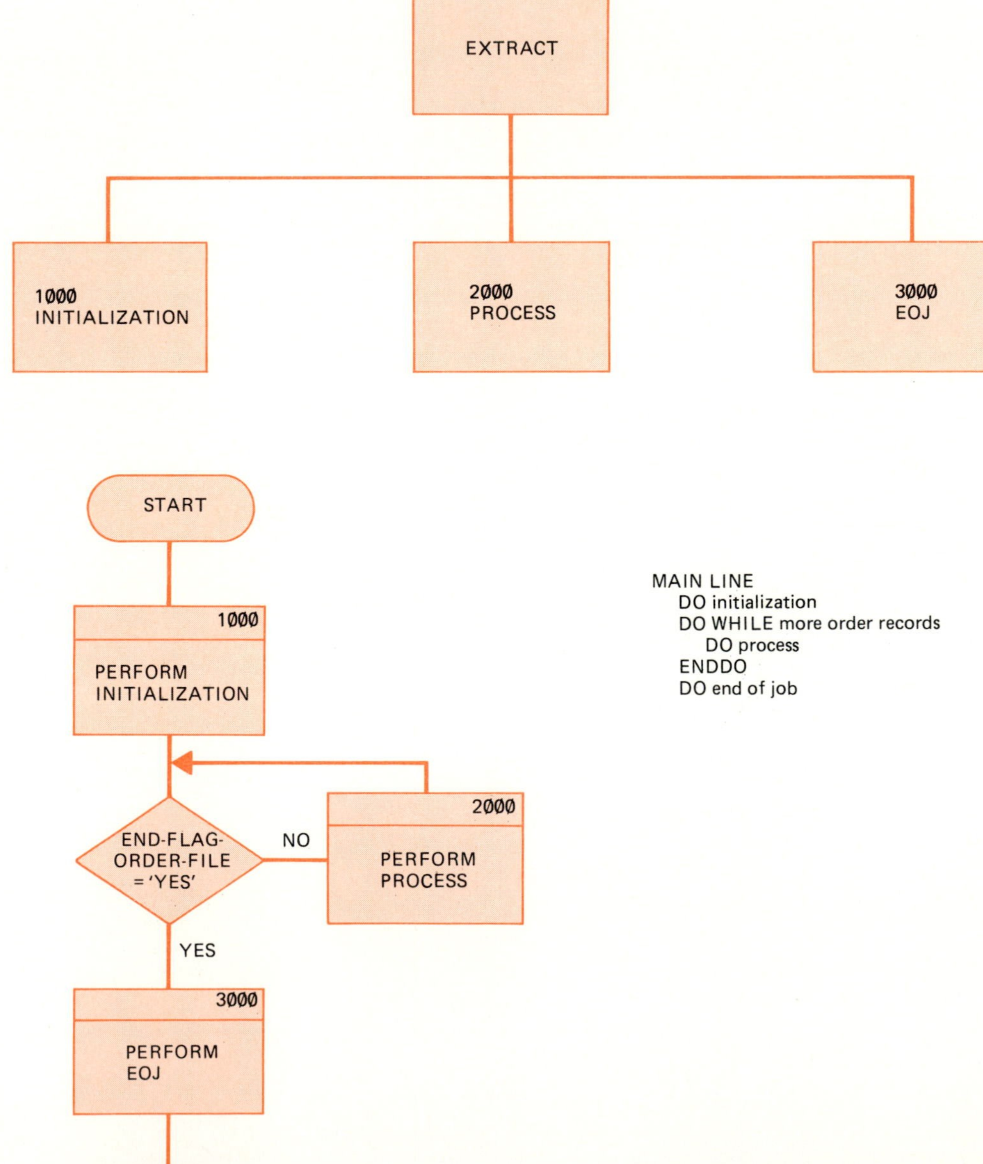

FIGURE 4–7

1000-INITIALIZATION

First the input and output files that are to be used in the program are opened. They will remain open for the entire program until they are closed in the last step in 3000-EOJ. Next, the date is retrieved from the computer system and placed in a part of the storage reserved for the main-heading line. The date is accessed from the system only once, even though the main-heading may be printed many times. This is possible because once the date is placed in the storage location for the main-heading line, it remains there and will be printed each time we print the main-heading.

9100-READ-ORDER-FILE is performed to read the first record before leaving 1000-INITIALIZATION. Control then returns to the main routine, and END-FLAG-ORDER-FILE is tested to see whether 2000-PROCESS or 3000-EOJ should be performed. (See Figure 4–8.)

2000-PROCESS

There are three major steps in 2000-PROCESS. First, the extended price is computed as the quantity multiplied by the price. This calculation is done first because the amount of the extended price is needed to determine whether or not to print the record.

After the extended price is computed, a test is made to determine whether it is greater than $2,000. If it is, 2100-EXTRACTED-RECORD is performed. This routine produces a line of printed output for each record and adds the order quantity and extended price for each record into the final totals for those items. If, on the other hand, extended price is equal to or less than $2,000, 2100-EXTRACTED-RECORD is not performed. In either case, 9100-READ-ORDER-FILE is performed so that the next record is read.

Remember, after leaving 2000-PROCESS, the program returns to the main routine where a test is made to see whether END-FLAG-ORDER-FILE contains

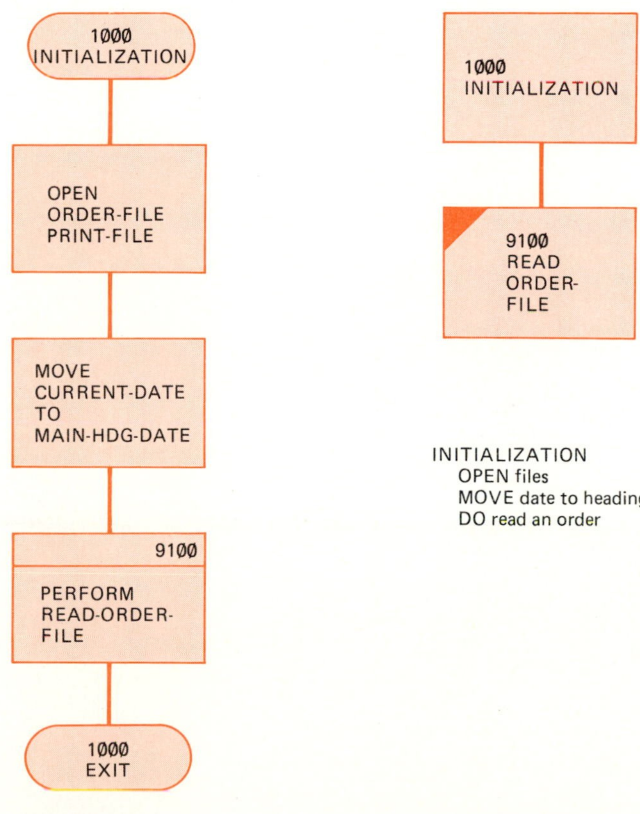

FIGURE 4–8

YES. If it does not, 2000-PROCESS is repeated until an end-of-file condition is encountered by the READ. At that point, END-FLAG-ORDER-FILE is changed to YES, and the test of END-FLAG-ORDER-FILE in the main routine transfers control to 3000-EOJ. (See Figure 4–9 for 2000-PROCESS.)

2100-EXTRACTED-RECORD

The routine 2100-EXTRACTED-RECORD will be performed only if the extended price of the order exceeds $2,000. In the previous program only one set of headings was printed, from 1000-INITIALIZATION. Here and in future programs, multiple pages of printed output, each with its own set of headings, will be allowed. Therefore, a new approach for printing headings is required.

LINE-COUNT is used to determine when headings are needed. LINE-COUNT is a numeric variable used to indicate the number of lines on the page which have already been used for output. Each time a line of output is printed, LINE-COUNT is incremented by two. It can then be determined whether or not a new set of headings is needed by testing this variable. A standard 11-inch piece of paper has room for 66 lines (6 per inch). Some of these lines should be reserved for top and bottom margins. Fifty, then, is a reasonable number of lines to expect to print on an 11-inch page. The variable LINE-COUNT is compared to see whether it is greater than 50. If it is, 2110-HEADINGS is performed.

The comparison will produce headings as soon as LINE-COUNT exceeds 50. In order to produce the first set of headings, LINE-COUNT is initially set to 99 when storage is reserved for it in the WORKING-STORAGE section. Because

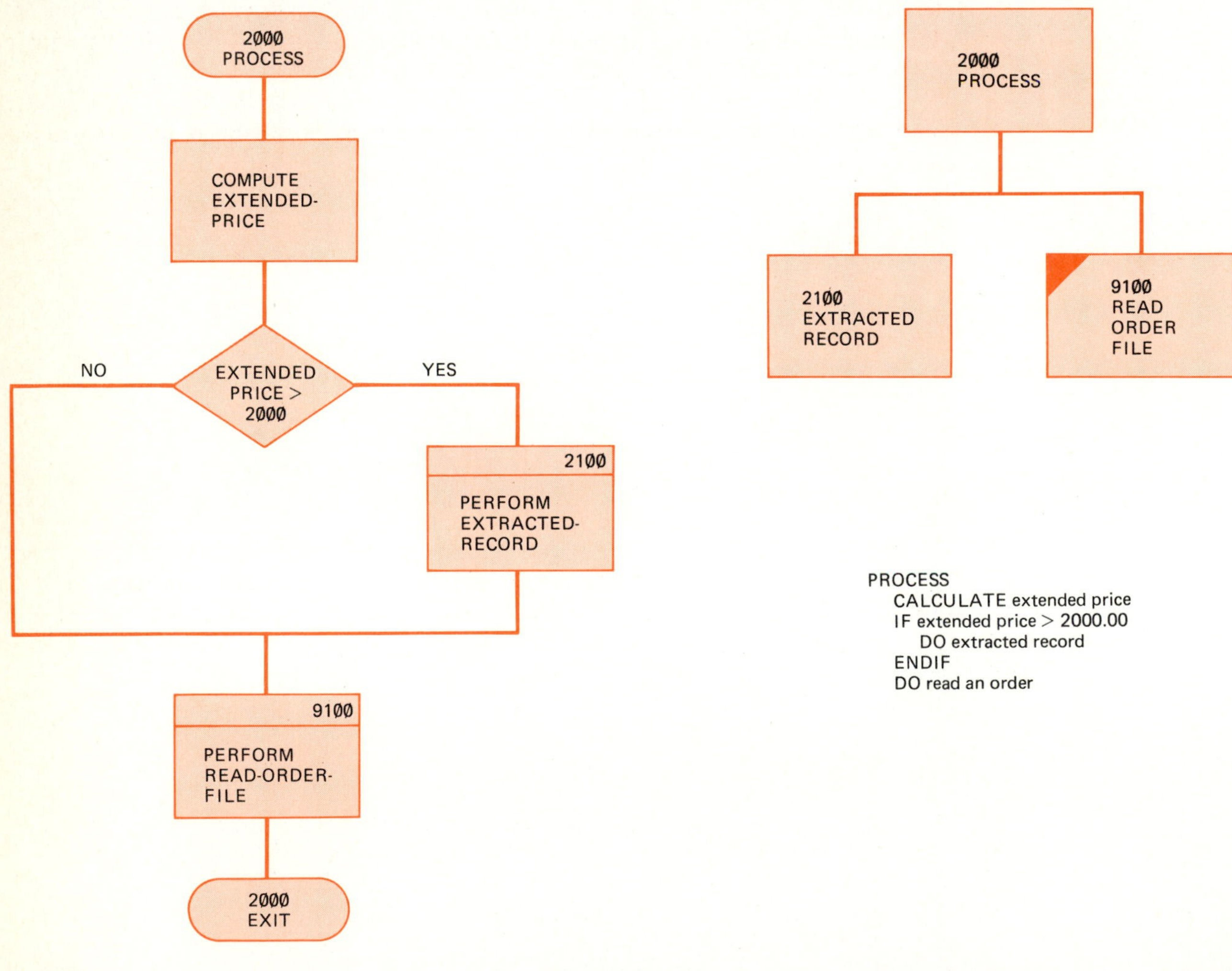

FIGURE 4–9

99 is greater than 50, headings will be produced the first time LINE-COUNT is checked. After the comparison with LINE-COUNT is made, data from the input record is moved to output. All input fields, as well as the extended price, are moved. (Recall that the extended price is calculated for all records at the beginning of 2000-PROCESS.)

Two final totals for the extracted records are to be produced. In order to do this, ORDER-QUANTITY and EXTENDED-PRICE are added to FINAL-ORDER-QUANTITY and FINAL-EXTENDED-PRICE, respectively. It is necessary to perform the addition each time a record is extracted so that after all input records have been processed the totals are available to print. We cannot wait until the end of the job to do the adding, for at that point all input records have come and gone.

It is not important whether the MOVEs precede the ADDs or vice versa; the program will work either way. When data is moved, it remains in the sending field and is still available to be used in other instructions, such as an ADD. The next step, however, is to WRITE a line. This must be done after the MOVEs, since it is the MOVE statements which place the data in the output line. The ADDs could be performed after, rather than before, the WRITEs. After finishing the 2100-EXTRACTED-RECORD routine, control returns to 2000-PROCESS in order to read the next record. (See Figure 4–10.)

2110-HEADINGS

PAGE-COUNT is a numeric variable which will be used in numbering pages of output. It is set to zero when it is reserved in WORKING-STORAGE. Consequently, so that the first page will be numbered 1, we ADD 1 TO PAGE-COUNT. This is done before PAGE-COUNT is moved to an area in the heading, and before the heading line which contains it is written. If PAGE-COUNT were initialized to 1 instead of zero, it would be necessary to wait until after PAGE-COUNT was moved to a heading area to add 1 to it.

The date is already in one of the heading lines, having been put there in 1000-INITIALIZATION so that it would only have to be accessed from the computer system and moved one item.

Three headings lines are written, the first at the top of a new page. After the lines are written, 4 is MOVEd to LINE-COUNT. Since LINE-COUNT had to exceed 50 for 2110-HEADINGS to be performed, the MOVE will both reduce LINE-COUNT and account for the lines taken up by the headings. (See Figure 4–11.) The same thing could have been accomplished using the following two steps.

```
MOVE ZERO TO LINE-COUNT.
ADD 4 TO LINE-COUNT.
```

3000-EOJ

The routine 3000-EOJ is executed after all records have been read and either printed or bypassed. For each extracted record, amounts have been added to the pair of final totals, FINAL-QUANTITY and FINAL-EXTENDED-PRICE. These totals are now moved to an output line and the line is written. Next, the files are closed and control is returned to the main routine where the program ends. (See Figure 4–12 for 3000-EOJ.)

9100-READ-ORDER-FILE

The 9100-READ-ORDER-FILE routine is performed once from 1000-INITIALIZATION and repeatedly from 2000-PROCESS. Each time the routine is performed, a test is made for an end-of-file indicator. When this indicator is encountered, AT END is true and YES is moved to END-FLAG-ORDER-FILE. The two places where 9100-READ-ORDER-FILE is performed are both just prior to a return to the main routine to test END-FLAG-ORDER-FILE. (See Figure 4–13.)

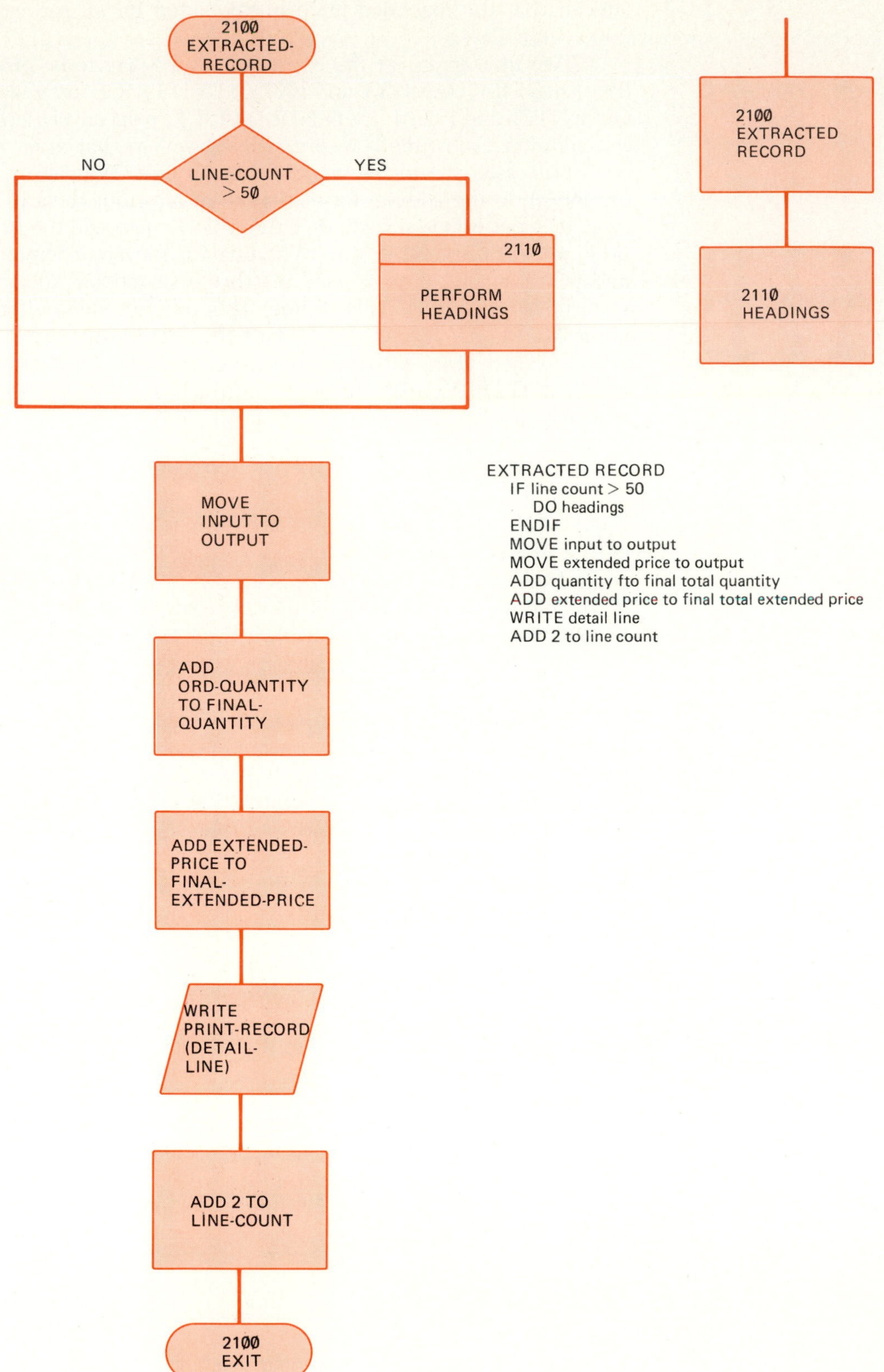
2100
EXTRACTED-
RECORD
NO
LINE-COUNT
> 50
YES
2110
PERFORM
HEADINGS
MOVE
INPUT TO
OUTPUT
ADD
ORD-QUANTITY
TO FINAL-
QUANTITY
ADD EXTENDED-
PRICE TO
FINAL-
EXTENDED-PRICE
WRITE
PRINT-RECORD
(DETAIL-
LINE)
ADD 2 TO
LINE-COUNT
2100
EXIT
2100
EXTRACTED
RECORD
2110
HEADINGS
EXTRACTED RECORD
IF line count > 50
DO headings
ENDIF
MOVE input to output
MOVE extended price to output
ADD quantity fto final total quantity
ADD extended price to final total extended price
WRITE detail line
ADD 2 to line count

FIGURE 4–10

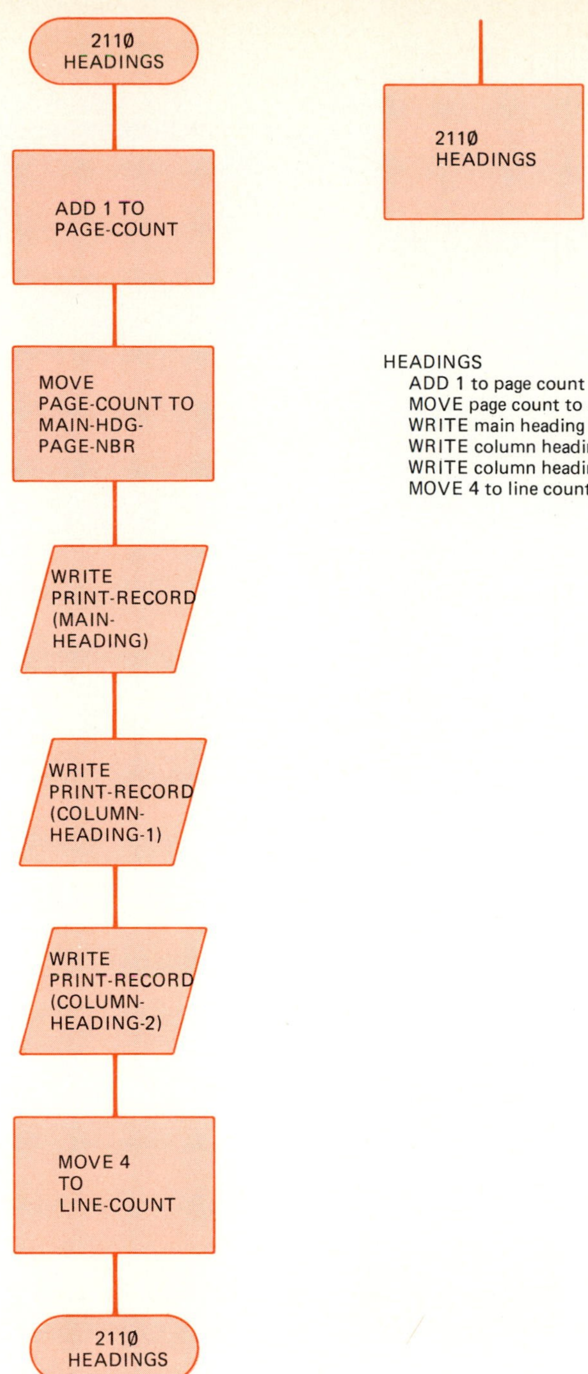

HEADINGS
  ADD 1 to page count
  MOVE page count to output
  WRITE main heading line
  WRITE column heading, line one
  WRITE column heading, line two
  MOVE 4 to line count

FIGURE 4–11

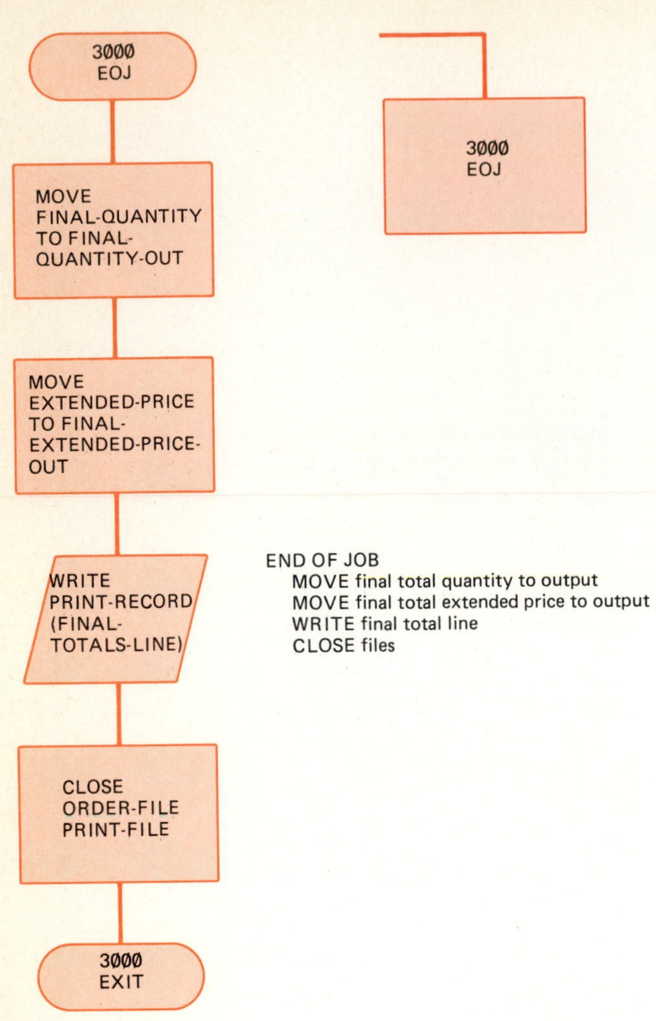

END OF JOB
    MOVE final total quantity to output
    MOVE final total extended price to output
    WRITE final total line
    CLOSE files

FIGURE 4–12

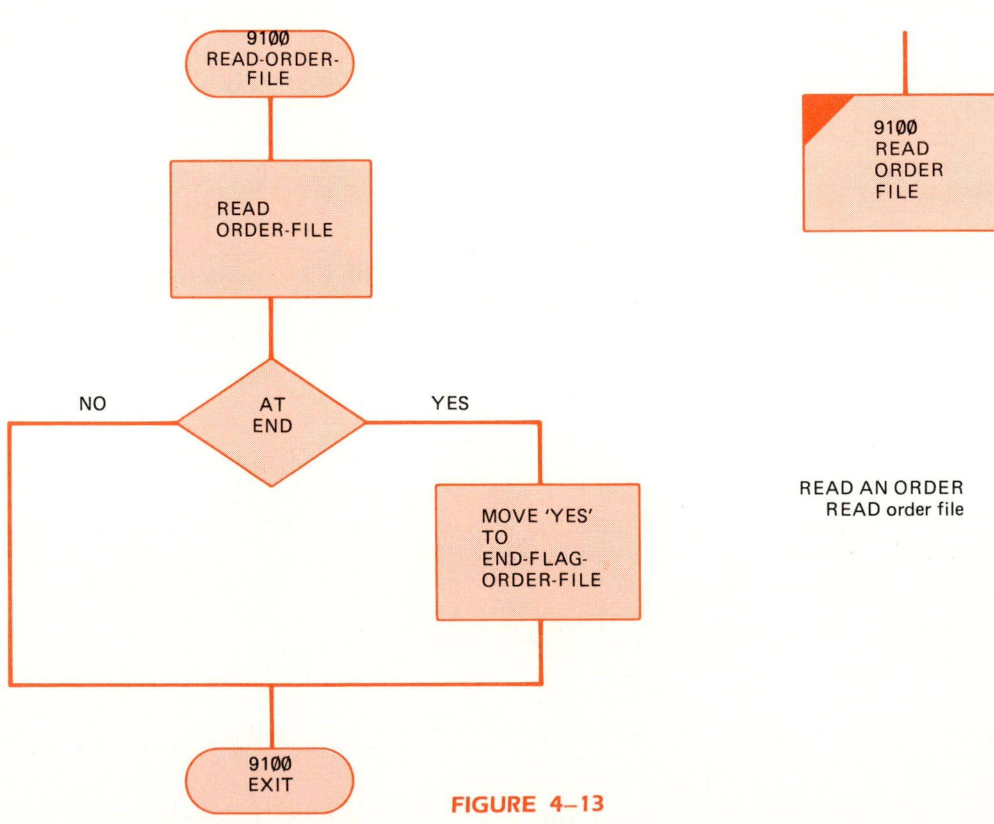

READ AN ORDER
    READ order file

FIGURE 4–13

THE COBOL PROGRAM

Test Data

Test data for the EXTRACT program is shown in FIGURE 4–14.

Sample Output

Sample output from the EXTRACT program is shown in FIGURE 4–15.

The Program

The complete COBOL EXTRACT program is shown in FIGURE 4–16. Boxes are used to indicate coding style that warrants attention.

```
Ø12Ø1ØØ3ØØPO173    B12383871Ø25GN4Ø2AØØØØ1Ø45ØØØ871116ØØØØØØ
Ø12Ø1Ø47278372     G4838887Ø913WB7Ø2XØØØ9ØØ115ØØ8711Ø1ØØØØØØ
Ø12Ø1ØØ3ØØE1Ø12    B12335871105WB493EØØØØ2Ø54ØØØ871122ØØØØØØ
Ø3ØØ747300         H8477787Ø223MF4Ø3TØØØØ5Ø4ØØØØ87Ø5Ø2ØØØØØØ
Ø3ØØ7ØØ378EBNER    H8457987Ø811VX922PØØ8ØØØØ127589112ØØØØØØØ
Ø3ØØ7739897747     B89288871106MF848JØØØØ5Ø2145Ø88Ø13ØØØØØØØ
Ø3ØØ7ØØ28334567X   B34237871Ø3ØHL834EØØØ16Ø19ØØØ871121ØØØØØØ
Ø3ØØ747300         Y2890387Ø811VXØØ1LØØ2ØØØØ622Ø8712Ø3ØØØØØØ
Ø344Ø6948187Ø341   GØ418Ø87Ø2Ø9JGØ4ØXØØØØ1Ø525ØØ88Ø619ØØØØØØ
Ø361182888P2783733B8433Ø871Ø25HL289BØØØ1ØØ234ØØ871113ØØØØØØ
Ø361128375T7838    T7829987Ø323JG563WØØØØ6Ø43ØØØ871Ø18ØØØØØØ
Ø36115Ø912         H6915Ø87Ø2Ø6MF848TØØØØ3Ø36ØØØ8712Ø1ØØØØØØ
Ø817431408 65      H4189187Ø412TK61ØLØØØ18ØØ78ØØ87Ø63ØØØØØØØ
Ø8174Ø18Ø5R7278    T2164287Ø81ØTK497XØØØ1ØØ118ØØ87113ØØØØØØØ
Ø8174Ø18Ø5R8322    Y211Ø587Ø6Ø1TN116TØØØØ1Ø3ØØØØ871221ØØØØØØ
Ø891562Ø54SCHUH    L5Ø6818711Ø8TK812EØØØØ6Ø573ØØ88Ø1Ø5ØØØØØØ
Ø891521Ø78         B71Ø45871ØØ1FV782TØØØØ3ØØ28ØØ871115ØØØØØØ
```

FIGURE 4–14

DATE: 11/09/87 PRODUCT DISTRIBUTION INC. - EXTRACTED ORDERS PAGE: 1

BRANCH	SALES REP	CUSTOMER NUMBER	SALES ORDER	ORDER DATE	REQUESTED SHIP DATE	ACTUAL SHIP DATE	PART NUMBER	QUANTITY	UNIT PRICE	EXTENDED PRICE
01	201	04727	G48388	09-13-87	11-01-87	00-00-00	WB702X	90	115.00	10350.00
03	007	00378	H84579	08-11-87	11-20-89	00-00-00	VX922P	800	12.75	10200.00
03	007	00283	B34237	10-30-87	11-21-87	00-00-00	HL834E	16	190.00	3040.00
03	007	47300	Y28903	08-11-87	12-03-87	00-00-00	VX001L	200	62.20	12440.00
03	611	82888	B84330	10-25-87	11-13-87	00-00-00	HL289B	10	234.00	2340.00
03	611	28375	T78299	03-23-87	10-18-87	00-00-00	JG563W	6	430.00	2580.00
08	915	62054	L50681	11-08-87	01-05-88	00-00-00	TK812E	6	573.00	3438.00
								1128		44388.00

FIGURE 4–15

```
       IDENTIFICATION DIVISION.

       PROGRAM-ID.     EXTRACT.

       AUTHOR.         HELEN HUMPHREYS.

       INSTALLATION.   PRODUCT DISTRIBUTION INC.

       DATE-WRITTEN.   Ø4/Ø2/87.

       DATE-COMPILED.  Ø4/1Ø/87.

```

FIGURE 4–16

```
      ******************************************************************
      *                                                                *
      *    THIS PROGRAM PRODUCES A PRINTED REPORT OF ALL ORDERS        *
      *    WHERE THE EXTENDED PRICE IS GREATER THAN $2ØØØ.ØØ.          *
      *                                                                *
      ******************************************************************

       ENVIRONMENT DIVISION.

       CONFIGURATION SECTION.

       SOURCE-COMPUTER.
              IBM-37Ø.
       OBJECT-COMPUTER.
              IBM-37Ø.

       INPUT-OUTPUT SECTION.
       FILE-CONTROL.
           SELECT ORDER-FILE ASSIGN TO DISK.
           SELECT PRINT-FILE ASSIGN TO PRINTER.

       DATA DIVISION.
       FILE SECTION.

       FD  ORDER-FILE
           LABEL RECORDS ARE STANDARD
           RECORD CONTAINS 7Ø CHARACTERS
           DATA RECORD IS ORDER-RECORD.

       Ø1  ORDER-RECORD.
           Ø5  ORD-BRANCH              PIC 9(2).
           Ø5  ORD-SALES-REP           PIC 9(3).
           Ø5  ORD-CUSTOMER-NBR        PIC 9(5).
           Ø5  ORD-CUST-PO-NBR         PIC X(8).
           Ø5  ORD-SALES-ORD-NBR       PIC X(6).
           Ø5  ORD-DATE.
               1Ø  ORD-YY              PIC 9(2).
               1Ø  ORD-MM              PIC 9(2).
               1Ø  ORD-DD              PIC 9(2).
           Ø5  ORD-PART-NBR            PIC X(6).
           Ø5  ORD-QUANTITY            PIC 9(5).
           Ø5  ORD-UNIT-PRICE          PIC 9(4)V9(2).
           Ø5  ORD-REQ-SHIP-DATE.
               1Ø  ORD-REQ-SHIP-YY     PIC 9(2).
               1Ø  ORD-REQ-SHIP-MM     PIC 9(2).
               1Ø  ORD-REQ-SHIP-DD     PIC 9(2).
           Ø5  ORD-ACT-SHIP-DATE.
               1Ø  ORD-ACT-SHIP-YY     PIC 9(2).
               1Ø  ORD-ACT-SHIP-MM     PIC 9(2).
               1Ø  ORD-ACT-SHIP-DD     PIC 9(2).
           Ø5  FILLER                  PIC X(11).

       FD  PRINT-FILE
           LABEL RECORDS ARE OMITTED
           RECORD CONTAINS 133 CHARACTERS
           DATA RECORD IS PRINT-RECORD.

       Ø1  PRINT-RECORD                PIC X(133).

       WORKING-STORAGE SECTION.

       Ø1  HOLDS-COUNTERS-SWITCHES.
           Ø5  END-FLAG-ORDER-FILE     PIC X(3)        VALUE 'NO'.
           Ø5  LINE-COUNT              PIC 9(2)        VALUE 99.
           Ø5  PAGE-COUNT              PIC 9(3)        VALUE ZEROS.

       Ø1  CALCULATED-FIELDS.
           Ø5  EXTENDED-PRICE          PIC 9(7)V9(2).

       Ø1  FINAL-TOTALS.
           Ø5  FINAL-QUANTITY          PIC 9(6)        VALUE ZEROS.
           Ø5  FINAL-EXTENDED-PRICE    PIC 9(8)V9(2)   VALUE ZEROS.

       Ø1  MAIN-HEADING.
           Ø5  FILLER                  PIC X(6)        VALUE SPACES.
           Ø5  FILLER                  PIC X(6)        VALUE 'DATE:'.
           Ø5  MAIN-HDG-DATE           PIC X(8).
           Ø5  FILLER                  PIC X(25)       VALUE SPACES.
           Ø5  FILLER                  PIC X(44)
               VALUE 'PRODUCT DISTRIBUTION INC. - EXTRACTED ORDERS'.
           Ø5  FILLER                  PIC X(28)       VALUE SPACES.
           Ø5  FILLER                  PIC X(6)        VALUE 'PAGE:'.
```

AREAS FOR CALCULATING TOTALS ARE GROUPED UNDER A 01 LEVEL

FIGURE 4-16 continued

```
           Ø5  MAIN-HDG-PAGE-NBR        PIC ZZ9.
           Ø5  FILLER                   PIC X(7)        VALUE SPACES.

       Ø1  COLUMN-HEADING-1.
           Ø5  FILLER                   PIC X(14)       VALUE SPACES.
           Ø5  FILLER                   PIC X(5)        VALUE 'SALES'.
           Ø5  FILLER                   PIC X(2)        VALUE SPACES.
           Ø5  FILLER                   PIC X(8)        VALUE 'CUSTOMER'.
           Ø5  FILLER                   PIC X(5)        VALUE SPACES.
           Ø5  FILLER                   PIC X(5)        VALUE 'SALES'.
           Ø5  FILLER                   PIC X(7)        VALUE SPACES.
           Ø5  FILLER                   PIC X(5)        VALUE 'ORDER'.
           Ø5  FILLER                   PIC X(6)        VALUE SPACES.
           Ø5  FILLER                   PIC X(9)        VALUE
                                                        'REQUESTED'.
           Ø5  FILLER                   PIC X(5)        VALUE SPACES.
           Ø5  FILLER                   PIC X(6)        VALUE 'ACTUAL'.
           Ø5  FILLER                   PIC X(7)        VALUE SPACES.
           Ø5  FILLER                   PIC X(4)        VALUE 'PART'.
           Ø5  FILLER                   PIC X(18)       VALUE SPACES.
           Ø5  FILLER                   PIC X(4)        VALUE 'UNIT'.
           Ø5  FILLER                   PIC X(7)        VALUE SPACES.
           Ø5  FILLER                   PIC X(8)        VALUE 'EXTENDED'.
           Ø5  FILLER                   PIC X(8)        VALUE SPACES.

       Ø1  COLUMN-HEADING-2.
           Ø5  FILLER                   PIC X(6)        VALUE SPACES.
           Ø5  FILLER                   PIC X(6)        VALUE 'BRANCH'.
           Ø5  FILLER                   PIC X(3)        VALUE SPACES.
           Ø5  FILLER                   PIC X(3)        VALUE 'REP'.
           Ø5  FILLER                   PIC X(4)        VALUE SPACES.
           Ø5  FILLER                   PIC X(6)        VALUE 'NUMBER'.
           Ø5  FILLER                   PIC X(6)        VALUE SPACES.
           Ø5  FILLER                   PIC X(5)        VALUE 'ORDER'.
           Ø5  FILLER                   PIC X(7)        VALUE SPACES.
           Ø5  FILLER                   PIC X(4)        VALUE 'DATE'.
           Ø5  FILLER                   PIC X(7)        VALUE SPACES.
           Ø5  FILLER                   PIC X(9)        VALUE
                                                        'SHIP DATE'.
           Ø5  FILLER                   PIC X(4)        VALUE SPACES.
           Ø5  FILLER                   PIC X(9)        VALUE
                                                        'SHIP DATE'.
           Ø5  FILLER                   PIC X(4)        VALUE SPACES.
           Ø5  FILLER                   PIC X(6)        VALUE 'NUMBER'.
           Ø5  FILLER                   PIC X(3)        VALUE SPACES.
           Ø5  FILLER                   PIC X(8)        VALUE 'QUANTITY'.
           Ø5  FILLER                   PIC X(5)        VALUE SPACES.
           Ø5  FILLER                   PIC X(5)        VALUE 'PRICE'.
           Ø5  FILLER                   PIC X(8)        VALUE SPACES.
           Ø5  FILLER                   PIC X(5)        VALUE 'PRICE'.
           Ø5  FILLER                   PIC X(1Ø)       VALUE SPACES.

       Ø1  DETAIL-LINE.
           Ø5  FILLER                   PIC X(8)        VALUE SPACES.
           Ø5  DET-BRANCH               PIC 9(2).
           Ø5  FILLER                   PIC X(5)        VALUE SPACES.
           Ø5  DET-SALES-REP            PIC 9(3).
           Ø5  FILLER                   PIC X(5)        VALUE SPACES.
           Ø5  DET-CUSTOMER-NBR         PIC 9(5).
           Ø5  FILLER                   PIC X(5)        VALUE SPACES.
           Ø5  DET-SALES-ORD-NBR        PIC X(6).
           Ø5  FILLER                   PIC X(5)        VALUE SPACES.
           Ø5  DET-ORDER-MM             PIC 9(2).
           Ø5  FILLER                   PIC X(1)        VALUE '-'.
           Ø5  DET-ORDER-DD             PIC 9(2).
           Ø5  FILLER                   PIC X(1)        VALUE '-'.
           Ø5  DET-ORDER-YY             PIC 9(2).
           Ø5  FILLER                   PIC X(5)        VALUE SPACES.
           Ø5  DET-REQ-SHIP-MM          PIC 9(2).
           Ø5  FILLER                   PIC X(1)        VALUE '-'.
           Ø5  DET-REQ-SHIP-DD          PIC 9(2).
           Ø5  FILLER                   PIC X(1)        VALUE '-'.
           Ø5  DET-REQ-SHIP-YY          PIC 9(2).
           Ø5  FILLER                   PIC X(5)        VALUE SPACES.
           Ø5  DET-ACT-SHIP-MM          PIC 9(2).
           Ø5  FILLER                   PIC X(1)        VALUE '-'.
           Ø5  DET-ACT-SHIP-DD          PIC 9(2).
           Ø5  FILLER                   PIC X(1)        VALUE '-'.
           Ø5  DET-ACT-SHIP-YY          PIC 9(2).
           Ø5  FILLER                   PIC X(5)        VALUE SPACES.
```

FIGURE 4-16 continued

```
           Ø5  DET-PART-NBR               PIC X(6).
           Ø5  FILLER                     PIC X(5)         VALUE SPACES.
           Ø5  DET-QUANTITY               PIC ZZZZ9.
           Ø5  FILLER                     PIC X(5)         VALUE SPACES.
           Ø5  DET-UNIT-PRICE             PIC ZZZ9.99.
           Ø5  FILLER                     PIC X(5)         VALUE SPACES.
           Ø5  DET-EXTENDED-PRICE         PIC ZZZZZZ9.99.
           Ø5  FILLER                     PIC X(7).

       Ø1  FINAL-TOTALS-LINE.
           Ø5  FILLER                     PIC X(93)        VALUE SPACES.
           Ø5  FINAL-QUANTITY-OUT         PIC ZZZZZ9.
           Ø5  FILLER                     PIC X(16)        VALUE SPACES.
           Ø5  FINAL-EXTENDED-PRICE-OUT      PIC ZZZZZZZ9.99.
           Ø5  FILLER                     PIC X(7)         VALUE SPACES.

       PROCEDURE DIVISION.

           PERFORM 1ØØØ-INITIALIZATION.
           PERFORM 2ØØØ-PROCESS
               UNTIL END-FLAG-ORDER-FILE = 'YES'.
           PERFORM 3ØØØ-EOJ.
           STOP RUN.

       1ØØØ-INITIALIZATION.
           OPEN INPUT  ORDER-FILE
                OUTPUT PRINT-FILE.
           MOVE CURRENT-DATE TO MAIN-HDG-DATE.
           PERFORM 91ØØ-READ-ORDER-FILE.

       2ØØØ-PROCESS.
           COMPUTE EXTENDED-PRICE = ORD-UNIT-PRICE * ORD-QUANTITY.
           IF EXTENDED-PRICE > 2ØØØ.ØØ
               PERFORM 21ØØ-EXTRACTED-RECORD.
           PERFORM 91ØØ-READ-ORDER-FILE.

       21ØØ-EXTRACTED-RECORD.
           IF LINE-COUNT > 5Ø
              PERFORM 211Ø-HEADINGS.
           MOVE ORD-BRANCH                TO DET-BRANCH.
           MOVE ORD-SALES-REP             TO DET-SALES-REP.
           MOVE ORD-CUSTOMER-NBR          TO DET-CUSTOMER-NBR.
           MOVE ORD-SALES-ORD-NBR         TO DET-SALES-ORD-NBR.
           MOVE ORD-YY                    TO DET-ORDER-YY.
           MOVE ORD-MM                    TO DET-ORDER-MM.
           MOVE ORD-DD                    TO DET-ORDER-DD.
           MOVE ORD-PART-NBR              TO DET-PART-NBR.
           MOVE ORD-QUANTITY              TO DET-QUANTITY.
           MOVE ORD-UNIT-PRICE            TO DET-UNIT-PRICE.
           MOVE ORD-REQ-SHIP-YY           TO DET-REQ-SHIP-YY.
           MOVE ORD-REQ-SHIP-MM           TO DET-REQ-SHIP-MM.
           MOVE ORD-REQ-SHIP-DD           TO DET-REQ-SHIP-DD.
           MOVE ORD-ACT-SHIP-YY           TO DET-ACT-SHIP-YY.
           MOVE ORD-ACT-SHIP-MM           TO DET-ACT-SHIP-MM.
           MOVE ORD-ACT-SHIP-DD           TO DET-ACT-SHIP-DD.
           MOVE EXTENDED-PRICE            TO DET-EXTENDED-PRICE.
           ADD ORD-QUANTITY               TO FINAL-QUANTITY.
           ADD EXTENDED-PRICE             TO FINAL-EXTENDED-PRICE.
           WRITE PRINT-RECORD FROM DETAIL-LINE
               AFTER ADVANCING 2 LINES.
           ADD 2 TO LINE-COUNT.

       211Ø-HEADINGS.
           ADD 1 TO PAGE-COUNT.
           MOVE PAGE-COUNT TO MAIN-HDG-PAGE-NBR.
           WRITE PRINT-RECORD FROM MAIN-HEADING
               AFTER ADVANCING PAGE.
           WRITE PRINT-RECORD FROM COLUMN-HEADING-1
               AFTER ADVANCING 2 LINES.
           WRITE PRINT-RECORD FROM COLUMN-HEADING-2
               AFTER ADVANCING 1 LINE.
           MOVE 4 TO LINE-COUNT.

       3ØØØ-EOJ.
           MOVE FINAL-QUANTITY TO FINAL-QUANTITY-OUT.
           MOVE FINAL-EXTENDED-PRICE TO FINAL-EXTENDED-PRICE-OUT.
           WRITE PRINT-RECORD FROM FINAL-TOTALS-LINE
              AFTER ADVANCING 3 LINES.
           CLOSE ORDER-FILE
                 PRINT-FILE.

       91ØØ-READ-ORDER-FILE.
           READ ORDER-FILE
               AT END
                   MOVE 'YES' TO END-FLAG-ORDER-FILE.
```

ZZZZ9 IS USED INSTEAD OF Z(4)9(1) BECAUSE IT CAN BE TRANSFERRED DIRECTLY FROM THE PRINT CHART

FIGURE 4-16 continued

NEW COBOL ELEMENTS

New WORKING-STORAGE Fields

To produce the output required from the extract program, several new data fields have been added to WORKING-STORAGE.

LINE-COUNT

LINE-COUNT is a two-digit *numeric* data item that is used to control the number of output lines written to a page. It is incremented when output lines are written. Before each detail line is written, LINE-COUNT is checked to determine whether or not the page is full. If the page is full, new page headings are written and LINE-COUNT is reset. LINE-COUNT is given an initial value of 99, which will force the first set of headings to be printed. In the heading routine it is reset to 4, which has the effect of reinitializing it to zero and incrementing it the number of lines used by the headings.

PAGE-COUNT and MAIN-HDG-PAGE-NBR

PAGE-COUNT and MAIN-HDG-PAGE-NBR are used to place a page number at the top of each page of printed output. PAGE-COUNT is a three-digit *numeric* data item that is used to count the pages as each set of headings is printed. PAGE-COUNT is given an initial value of zero and is incremented by 1 before each set of headings is printed. MAIN-HDG-PAGE-NBR is the area on the MAIN-HEADING output line where the page number will print. PAGE-COUNT is moved to MAIN-HDG-PAGE-NBR after it is incremented, but before the main heading line is printed.

EXTENDED-PRICE and DET-EXTENDED-PRICE

The EXTRACT program requires the calculation of the extended price of an order. This data item does not exist in the input to the program, but rather is created by the calculation. Any data item which is so created must be defined in the WORKING-STORAGE SECTION. EXTENDED-PRICE is a nine-digit *numeric* data item (seven digits before the assumed decimal and two after) that is not given any initial value (i.e., it has no VALUE clause). Each time EXTENDED-PRICE is calculated, the new value will overlay any previous data in the field. DET-EXTENDED-PRICE is the area on the detail line where extended price will be printed. It can hold up to nine digits (again, seven digits before the actual decimal and two after). The first six of these can be suppressed if they are zeros. (See next section.) Because of the Z's and decimal point included in its PICTURE, DET-EXTENDED-PRICE is a *numeric-edited* field.

FINAL-QUANTITY and FINAL-EXTENDED-PRICE

The EXTRACT program also creates final totals for quantity and extended price. In order to do so, the fields FINAL-QUANTITY and FINAL-EXTENDED-PRICE are initialized to zero in WORKING-STORAGE, and then the values of the individual items ORD-QUANTITY and EXTENDED-PRICE from each extracted record are added to whatever value already exists in FINAL-QUANTITY and FINAL-EXTENDED-PRICE, respectively. In this manner, the totals accumulate from the initial values of zero.

FINAL-TOTAL-LINE

A new output line is created in the program to print the final totals. This output line is 133 bytes in length and contains the two fields FINAL-QUANTITY-OUT and FINAL-EXTENDED-PRICE-OUT to hold the final totals.

Output Editing: Suppression of Zeros

In the previous chapter, the decimal point (.) and the hyphen (-) were discussed in connection with output editing. Here, we consider the technique for suppression of zeros. Suppression of zeros causes spaces (blanks) to be printed in place of leading zeros. The sending field must be a *numeric* field, the receiving field a *numeric-edited* field. The receiving field must be the same size as the sending field, and as many leading 9's as desired are replaced with Z's. The V in the sending field is replaced with a decimal point in the receiving field, as it was in the program of the previous chapter. If there is a Z in a given position of the receiving field, the data from the sending field is tested to see whether it is a zero. If it is, a space is placed in the receiving field. This is repeated until the first nonzero digit of the sending field is encountered, after which every digit is moved to the receiving field whether it is zero or not. Figure 4–17 shows several examples; Chapter 5 covers output editing more fully.

IF/ELSE

COBOL uses the IF/ELSE statement to allow a programmer to test a relation and define alternative courses of action depending on the outcome of the test. We shall first deal with the relationships tested by the IF and then concentrate on how IFs and ELSEs are combined to solve a problem.

Format

```
IF {identifier-1       }  IS [NOT]  {GREATER THAN}  {identifier-2       }
   {literal-1          }            {>           }  {literal-2          }
   {arithmetic-exp-1   }            {LESS THAN   }  {arithmetic-exp-2   }
                                    {<           }
                                    {EQUAL   TO  }
                                    {=           }
```

The preceding format indicates the types of operands that may be compared and how the relation may be expressed. At least one of the operands must be an identifier, and then the other may be either an identifier, a literal, or an arithmetic expression. The following relations are not valid because they contain only literals:

```
IF 7 = 14 . . .
IF 'OFF' = 'ON' . . .
```

The first can be made valid by changing one operand into an arithmetic expression which includes an identifier; the second can be made valid by changing one operand into an identifier. Two possibilities are:

```
IF 7 + FIELD-A = 17 . . .
IF FIELD-B = 'ON' . . .
```

FIGURE 4–17

SENDING FIELD		RECEIVING FIELD	
Picture	Data	Picture	Data
999V99	016‸42	ZZZ.99	16.42
	000‸15		.15
	483‸67		483.67
	000‸00		.00
999V99	106‸40	ZZ9.99	106.40
	048‸33		48.33
	007‸41		7.41
	000‸66		0.66
9999	0024	ZZZ9	24
	0186		186
	0000		0

Figure 4–18 shows the relations that can be formed from the general format, together with the meaning of each. Note that =, >, and < can replace EQUAL TO, GREATER THAN, and LESS THAN, respectively. Also, the reserved word IS can be included in any of the relations if desired.

The 1985 standard includes the following two new relational operators:

>=	**IS GREATER THAN OR EQUAL TO (the equivalent of IS NOT LESS THAN)**
<=	**IS LESS THAN OR EQUAL TO (the equivalent of IS NOT GREATER THAN)**

Comparisons can be made between numeric and alphanumeric operands. However, there are restrictions on such comparisons. These will be examined in Chapter 5; in the meantime, we shall suppose simply that both operands must be numeric or both operands must be alphanumeric.

In nonnumeric comparisons, the comparison is based on the character set being used for internal data representation (EBCDIC or ASCII). Some of the more commonly used characters in these two sets are shown in Figure 4–19.

A nonnumeric comparison is made from left to right one character at a time. If a difference is encountered between two characters, the relation (> or <) between the operands is determined by the relative position of those characters in the collating sequence.

If one operand is shorter than the other, the shorter one is padded on the right with spaces to make the two of equal length. In the following example, FIELD-A and FIELD-B are not of equal length, so FIELD-B is padded with a space. Then the T in FIELD-A is compared with the space in FIELD-B according to the appropriate collating sequence.

```
05 FIELD-A           PIC X(3)         VALUE 'NOT'.
05 FIELD-B           PIC X(2)         VALUE 'NO'.
IF FIELD-A = FIELD-B . . .
```

FIELD-A	N	O	T
FIELD-B	N	O	

FIGURE 4–18

```
IF FIELD-A EQUAL TO FIELD-B          }  IS EQUAL TO
IF FIELD-A = FIELD-B                 }

IF FIELD-A NOT EQUAL TO FIELD-B      }  IS NOT EQUAL TO
IF FIELD-A NOT = FIELD-B             }
-------------------------------------------------------
IF FIELD-A GREATER THAN FIELD-B           }  IS GREATER THAN
IF FIELD-A > FIELD-B                      }

IF FIELD-A NOT GREATER THAN FIELD-B       }  IS LESS THAN
IF FIELD-A NOT > FIELD-B                  }    OR EQUAL TO
-------------------------------------------------------
IF FIELD-A LESS THAN FIELD-B         }  IS LESS THAN
IF FIELD-A < FIELD-B                 }

IF FIELD-A NOT LESS THAN FIELD-B     }  IS GREATER THAN
IF FIELD-A NOT < FIELD-B             }    OR EQUAL TO
```

DEC	HEX	BINARY	ASCII	EBCDIC	DEC	HEX	BINARY	ASCII	EBCDIC
32	20	0010 0000	SP		91	5B	0101 1011		$
33	21	0010 0001	!		92	5C	0101 1100		*
34	22	0010 0010	"		93	5D	0101 1101		)
35	23	0010 0011	#		94	5E	0101 1110		;
36	24	0010 0100	$		95	5F	0101 1111		
37	25	0010 0101	%		96	60	0110 0000		–
38	26	0010 0110	&		97	61	0110 0001		/
39	27	0010 0111	'						
40	28	0010 1000	(		108	6C	0110 1100		%
41	29	0010 1001	)		109	6D	0110 1101		–
42	2A	0010 1010	*		110	6E	0110 1110		>
43	2B	0010 1011	+		111	6F	0110 1111		?
44	2C	0010 1100	,						
45	2D	0010 1101	–		122	7A	0111 1010		:
46	2E	0010 1110	.		123	7B	0111 1011		#
47	2F	0010 1111	/		124	7C	0111 1100		@
48	30	0011 0000	0		125	7D	0111 1101		'
49	31	0011 0001	1		126	7E	0111 1110		=
50	32	0011 0010	2		127	7F	0111 1111		"
51	33	0011 0011	3						
52	34	0011 0100	4		193	C1	1100 0001		A
53	35	0011 0101	5		194	C2	1100 0010		B
54	36	0011 0110	6		195	C3	1100 0011		C
55	37	0011 0111	7		196	C4	1100 0100		D
56	38	0011 1000	8		197	C5	1100 0101		E
57	39	0011 1001	9		198	C6	1100 0110		F
58	3A	0011 1010	:		199	C7	1100 0111		G
59	3B	0011 1011	;		200	C8	1100 1000		H
60	3C	0011 1100	<		201	C9	1100 1001		I
61	3D	0011 1101	=						
62	3E	0011 1110	>		209	D1	1101 0001		J
63	3F	0011 1111	?		210	D2	1101 0010		K
64	40	0100 0000	@	SP	211	D3	1101 0011		L
65	41	0100 0001	A		212	D4	1101 0100		M
66	42	0100 0010	B		213	D5	1101 0101		N
67	43	0100 0011	C		214	D6	1101 0110		O
68	44	0100 0100	D		215	D7	1101 0111		P
69	45	0100 0101	E		216	D8	1101 1000		Q
70	46	0100 0110	F		217	D9	1101 1001		R
71	47	0100 0111	G						
72	48	0100 1000	H		226	E2	1110 0010		S
73	49	0100 1001	I		227	E3	1110 0011		T
74	4A	0100 1010	J		228	E4	1110 0100		U
75	4B	0100 1011	K	.	229	E5	1110 0101		V
76	4C	0100 1100	L	<	230	E6	1110 0110		W
77	4D	0100 1101	M	(	231	E7	1110 0111		X
78	4E	0100 1110	N	+	232	E8	1110 1000		Y
79	4F	0100 1111	O		233	E9	1110 1001		Z
80	50	0101 0000	P	&					
81	51	0101 0001	Q		240	F0	1111 0000		0
82	52	0101 0010	R		241	F1	1111 0001		1
83	53	0101 0011	S		242	F2	1111 0010		2
84	54	0101 0100	T		243	F3	1111 0011		3
85	55	0101 0101	U		244	F4	1111 0100		4
86	56	0101 0110	V		245	F5	1111 0101		5
87	57	0101 0111	W		246	F6	1111 0110		6
88	58	0101 1000	X		247	F7	1111 0111		7
89	59	0101 1001	Y		248	F8	1111 1000		8
90	5A	0101 1010	Z		249	F9	1111 1001		9

FIGURE 4–19 Partial List of ASCII and EBCDIC

Decision Structures

We test relations because we want to choose between alternative courses of action. The decision structure in Figure 4–20 illustrates this. If FIELD-A = 0, routine 2100-A-ZERO is performed; if FIELD-A ≠ 0, routine 2200-A-NOT-ZERO is performed. The structure is implemented in COBOL as

```
IF FIELD-A = ZERO
     PERFORM 2100-A-ZERO
ELSE
     PERFORM 2200-A-NOT-ZERO.
```

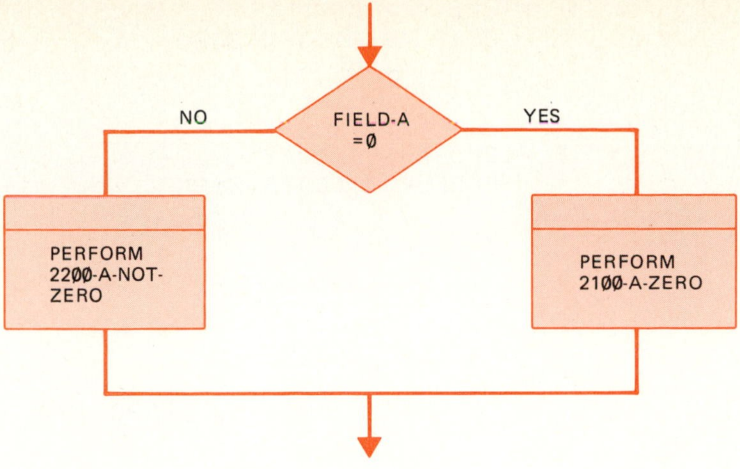

FIGURE 4–20

The 1985 standard allows the optional word THEN in the format of an IF statement:

```
IF FIELD-A = ZERO THEN
    PERFORM 2100-A-ZERO
ELSE
    PERFORM 2200-A-NOT-ZERO.
```

Flowcharting is one of the best planning tools for constructing IF statements. We shall use flowchart segments to illustrate combinations of decisions and the corresponding COBOL code.

When one outcome of a decision requires no action to be taken, COBOL uses the expression NEXT SENTENCE to indicate this. With NEXT SENTENCE, control is transferred to the sentence following the IF statement. With a single IF statement, ELSE NEXT SENTENCE is not required when there is no action that would follow the ELSE. It is required, however, when there is no action that follows the IF. Figure 4–21 illustrates these situations.

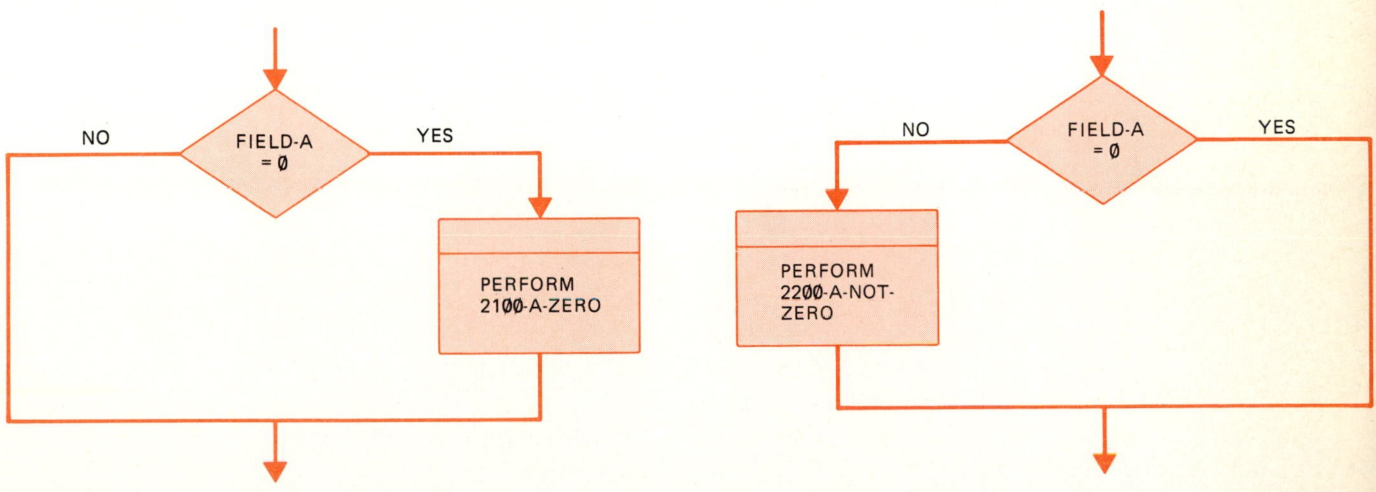

FIGURE 4–21

```
IF FIELD-A = ZERO
     PERFORM 2100-A-ZERO.

               or

IF FIELD-A = ZERO
     PERFORM 2100-A-ZERO
ELSE
     NEXT SENTENCE.
```

```
IF FIELD-A = ZERO
     NEXT SENTENCE
ELSE
     PERFORM 2200-A-NOT-ZERO THRU 2200-EXIT.
```

FIGURE 4-21 cont.

One IF statement may be nested inside another. Notice in Figure 4–22 where the period goes in the COBOL code in such a case. We can use a flowchart to help in the placement of the period. Look at where the flow line leaves the decision structure directly under the point where it entered the structure. This is the equivalent of where the period goes in the COBOL code.

Notice how the COBOL code is indented so that it is apparent to the reader which ELSE goes with which IF. COBOL does not require indenting of IFs and ELSEs, but good programming style does. COBOL matches each ELSE with the closest unpaired IF regardless of indenting.

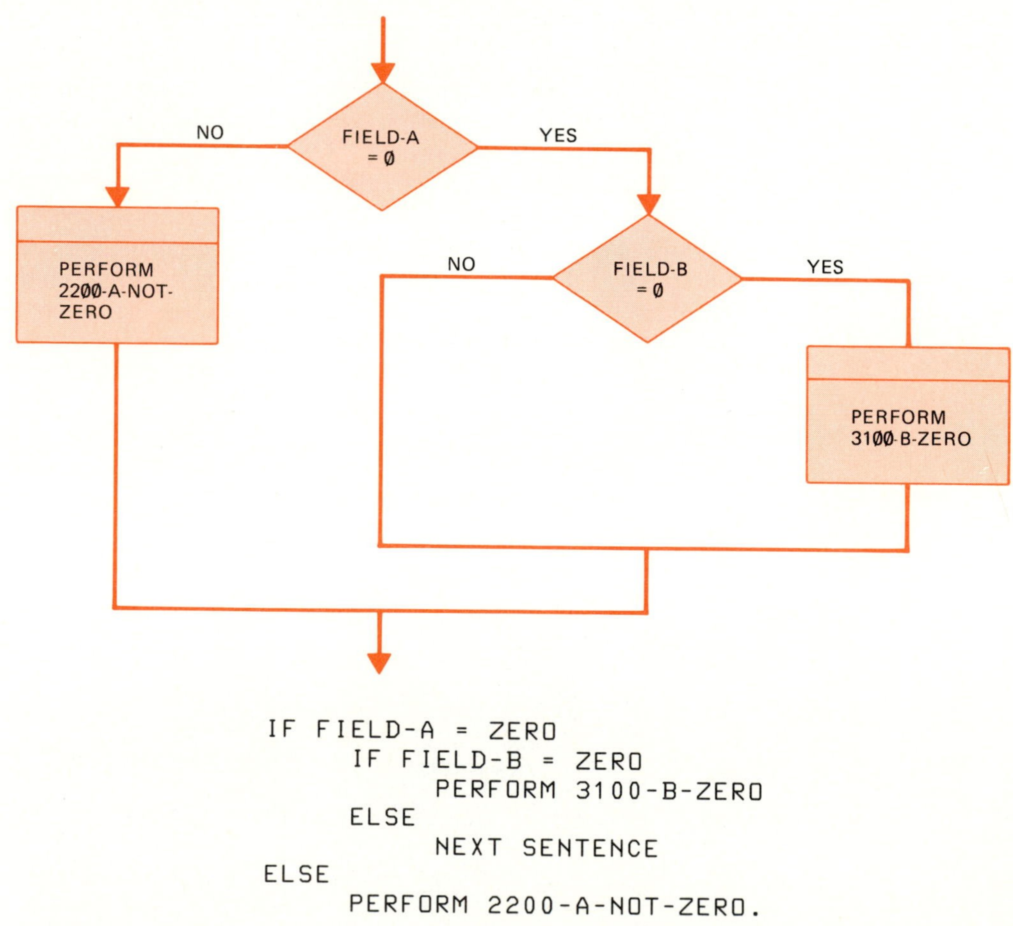


```
IF FIELD-A = ZERO
     IF FIELD-B = ZERO
          PERFORM 3100-B-ZERO
     ELSE
          NEXT SENTENCE
ELSE
     PERFORM 2200-A-NOT-ZERO.
```

FIGURE 4–22

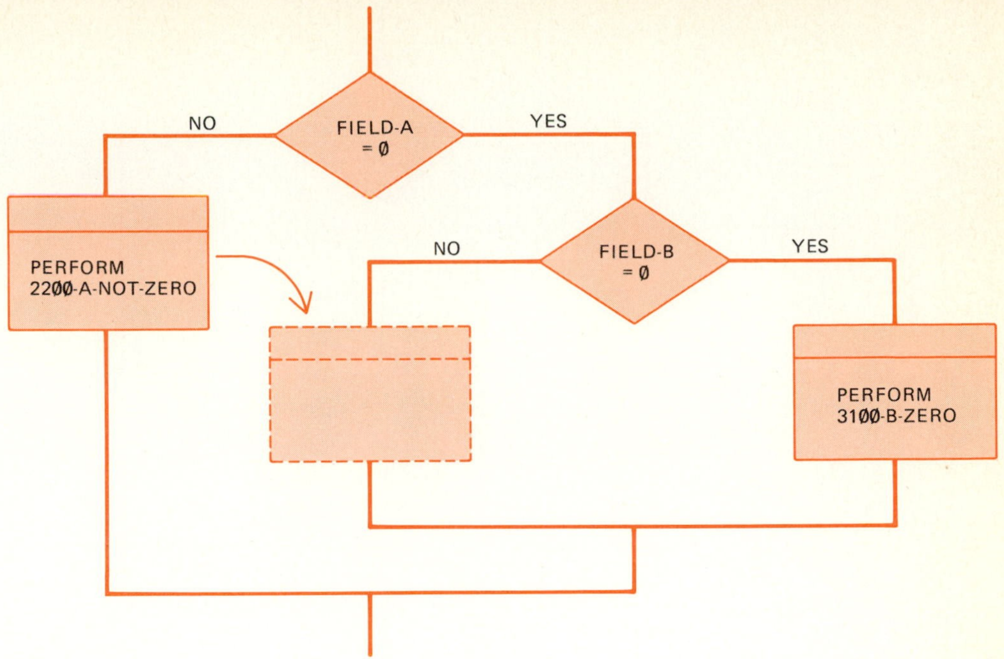

FIGURE 4–23

In Figure 4–22, ELSE NEXT SENTENCE is required to express the logic in the flowchart shown. The effect on the flowchart of leaving this expression out is shown in Figure 4–23. Since the ELSE is paired with the closest unmatched IF, the routine 2200-A-NOT-ZERO is inadvertently transferred to the NO side of FIELD-B = ZERO.

```
IF FIELD-A = ZERO
      IF FIELD-B = ZERO
            PERFORM 3100-B-ZERO

ELSE
      PERFORM 2200-A-NOT-ZERO.
```

An IF statement may be nested on either the YES, the NO, or both sides of another IF statement. Figure 4–24 illustrates the last two of these situations.

```
IF FIELD-A = ZERO
      NEXT SENTENCE
ELSE
      IF FIELD-B = ZERO
            PERFORM 3100-B-ZERO
      ELSE
            PERFORM 3200-B-NOT-ZERO.
```

```
IF FIELD-A = ZERO
      IF FIELD-B = ZERO
            PERFORM 3100-B-ZERO
      ELSE
            PERFORM 3200-B-NOT-ZERO
ELSE
      IF FIELD-C = ZERO
            PERFORM 4100-C-ZERO
      ELSE
            PERFORM 4200-C-NOT-ZERO.
```

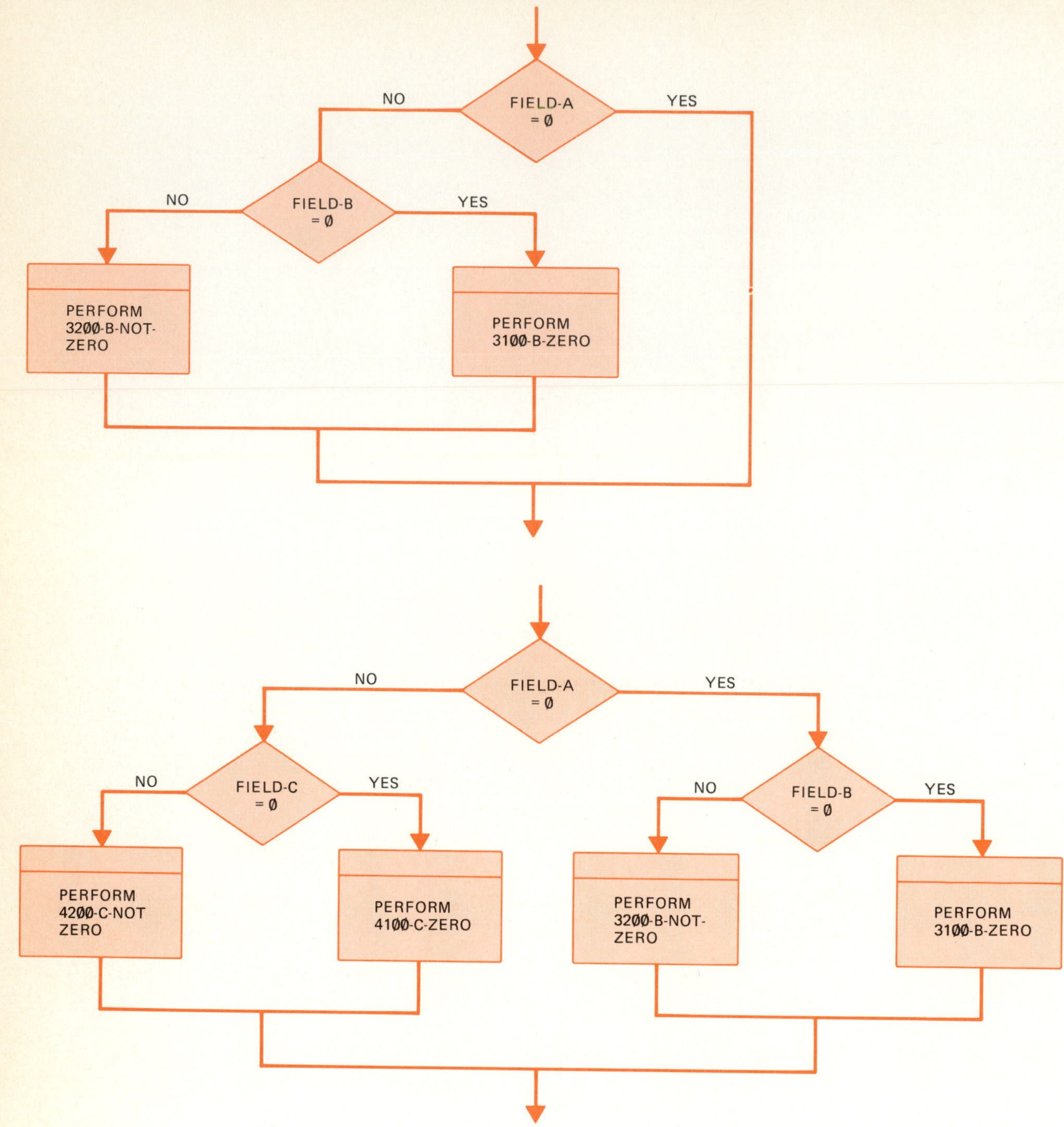

FIGURE 4–24

The 1985 standard includes the optional word THEN in the IF format. It also includes an END-IF. The scope terminator, END-IF, can be used to improve some awkward code necessary under the 1974 standard. Examples 1 and 2 represent two solutions to the same problem using the 1974 standard. Note the repetitive code in Example 1 and the need to PERFORM a subroutine in Example 2. Example 3 eliminates this awkward code by using the END-IF available in the 1985 standard.

Example 1

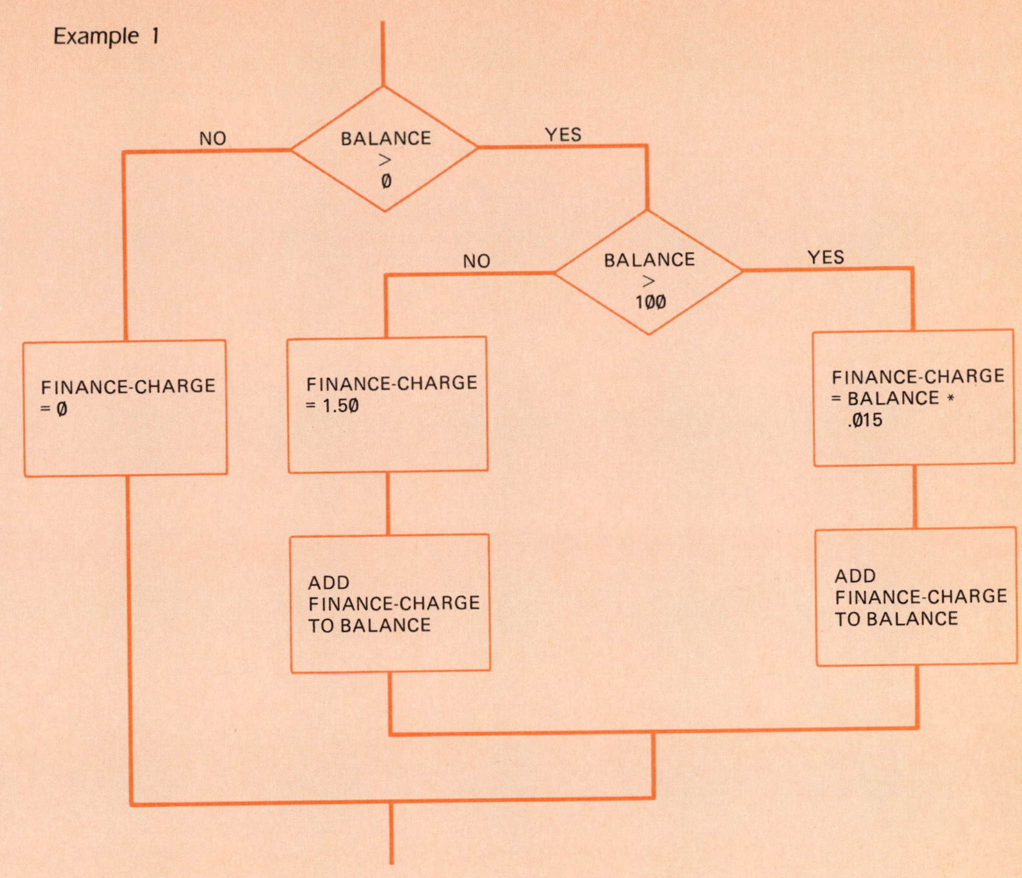


```
IF BALANCE > ZERO
    IF BALANCE > 100
         COMPUTE FINANCE-CHARGE = BALANCE * .015
         ADD FINANCE-CHARGE TO BALANCE
    ELSE
         MOVE 1.50 TO FINANCE-CHARGE
         ADD FINANCE-CHARGE TO BALANCE
ELSE
    MOVE ZERO TO FINANCE-CHARGE.
```

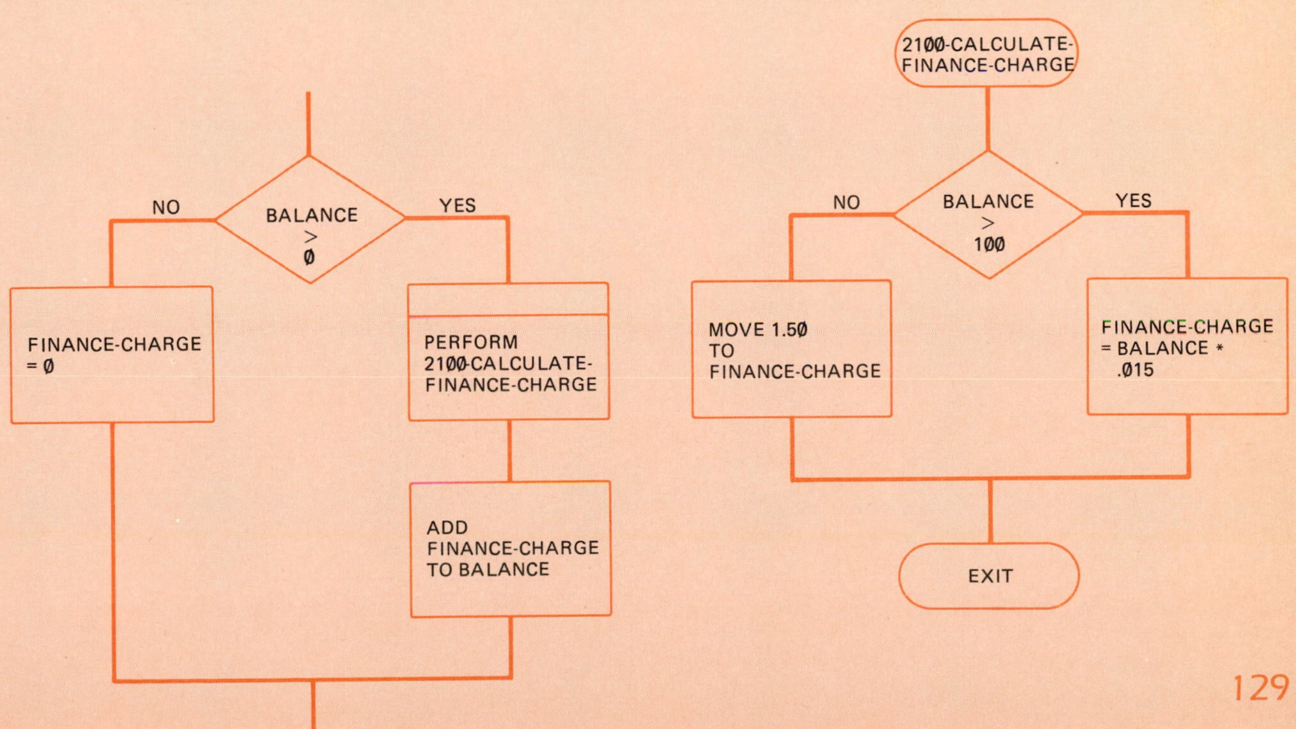

```
IF BALANCE > ZERO
    PERFORM 2100-CALCULATE-FINANCE-CHARGE
    ADD FINANCE-CHARGE TO BALANCE
ELSE
    MOVE ZERO TO FINANCE-CHARGE.

2100-CALCULATE-FINANCE-CHARGE.
    IF BALANCE > 100
        COMPUTE FINANCE-CHARGE = BALANCE * .015
    ELSE
        MOVE 1.50 TO FINANCE-CHARGE.
```

Example 3

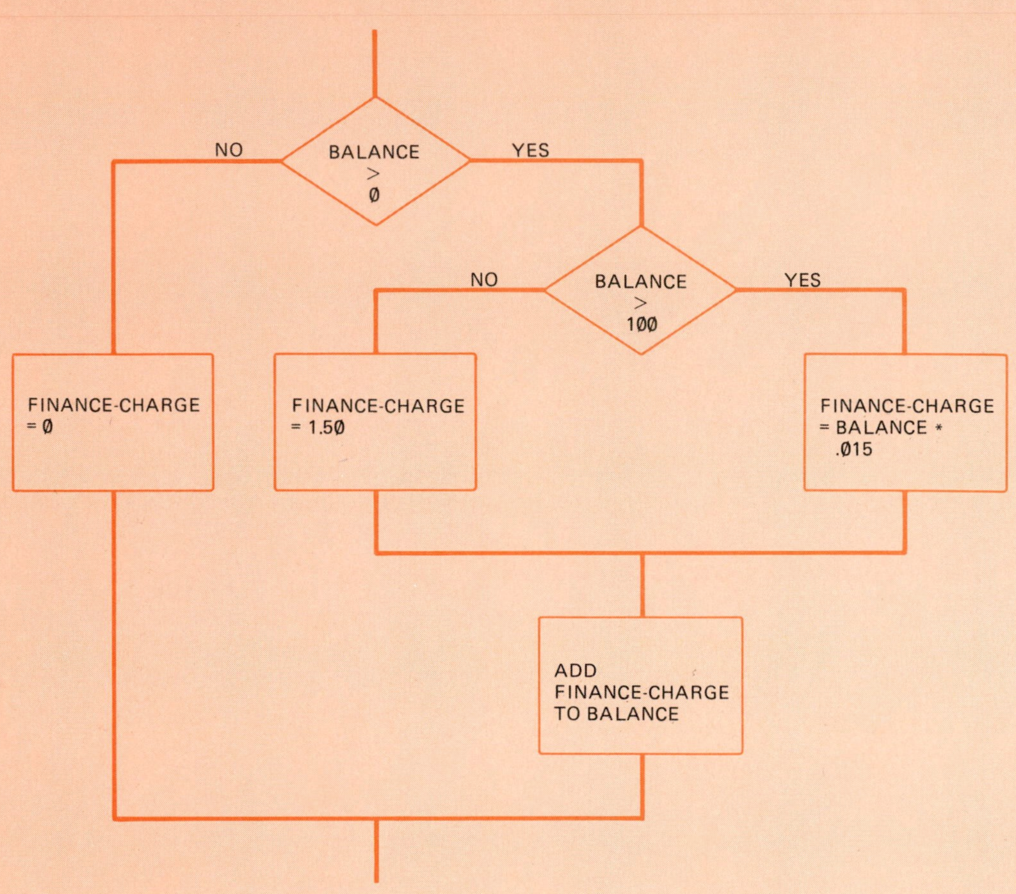


```
IF BALANCE > ZERO
    IF BALANCE > 100
        COMPUTE FINANCE-CHARGE = BALANCE * .015
    ELSE
        MOVE 1.50 TO FINANCE-CHARGE
    END-IF
    ADD FINANCE-CHARGE TO BALANCE
ELSE
    MOVE ZERO TO FINANCE-CHARGE
END-IF.
```

The COMPUTE Statement

Format

```
COMPUTE identifier-1 [ROUNDED] [identifier-2 [ROUNDED]] . . . =
{identifier-n          }
{literal-1             }
{arithmetic expression }
```

COMPUTE allows a programmer to

1. Set one or more identifiers equal to another identifier.
2. Set one or more identifiers equal to a numeric literal.
3. Evaluate arithmetic expressions, combining them into one result and placing that result in one or more identifiers.

Arithmetic Expressions

An arithmetic expression may contain the following items:

1. One or more numeric elementary items.
2. One or more numeric literals.
3. Binary arithmetic operators used to join the numeric elementary item(s) and/or numeric literal(s).
4. Parentheses to clarify or change the priority of an expression containing an arithmetic operator.
5. The unary operators + and/or −.

Arithmetic Operators

Figure 4–25 shows the seven arithmetic operators that can be used to form arithmetic expressions in a COMPUTE statement. The unary operators are used to indicate positive or negative value.

FIGURE 4–25

SYMBOL	MEANING
Binary Arithmetic Operators	
+	Addition
−	Subtraction
*	Multiplication
/	Division
**	Exponentiation
Unary Arithmetic Operators	
+	Multiplication by +1
−	Multiplication by −1

Priority of Operations

The order in which an arithmetic expression is evaluated depends on the presence or absence of parentheses in the expression and the priority of the arithmetic operators. Taking parentheses into account, the priority is as follows:

1. Expressions within parentheses are evaluated first. If one set of parentheses is nested inside another, the expression in the inside set is evaluated first.
2. Unary operators (i.e., whether a field is positive or negative) are evaluated.

3. Exponentiation is performed.
4. Multiplication and division (from left to right) are performed.
5. Addition and subtraction (from left to right) are performed.

Figure 4–26 shows the step-by-step evaluation of five COMPUTE statements. The steps demonstrate the priority of operations.

```
COMPUTE FIELD-A = 10 - 2 * 4 + 1
                  10 -   8   + 1
                         3
```

```
COMPUTE FIELD-B = (4 - 2) * (6 - 3)
                     2    *    3
                          6
```

```
COMPUTE FIELD-C = 4 * 2 ** 2
                  4 *   4
                   16
```

```
COMPUTE FIELD-D = 4 + 12 / 2 ** 2
                  4 + 12 /   4
                  4 +    3
                     7
```

```
COMPUTE FIELD-E = 4 * -6 + 2 * -8
                   -24   +  -16
                        -40
```

FIGURE 4–26

In a COMPUTE statement, the identifier(s) to the left of the equals sign (the result field) may be numeric or numeric edited. Identifiers and literals on the right of the equals sign must be numeric. If a result field is to be used in future calculations, it must be numeric also. The following show the contents of two fields before and after execution of the given COMPUTE statements.

```
05  FIELD-A          PIC 9(3)     VALUE ZEROS.
05  FIELD-B          PIC 9(3)     VALUE 643.
```

```
COMPUTE FIELD-A = FIELD-B.
           BEFORE

FIELD-A   | 0 | 0 | 0 |

FIELD-B   | 6 | 4 | 3 |

           AFTER

FIELD-A   | 6 | 4 | 3 |

FIELD-B   | 6 | 4 | 3 |
```

```
COMPUTE FIELD-A = 7
           BEFORE

FIELD-A   | 0 | 0 | 0 |
```

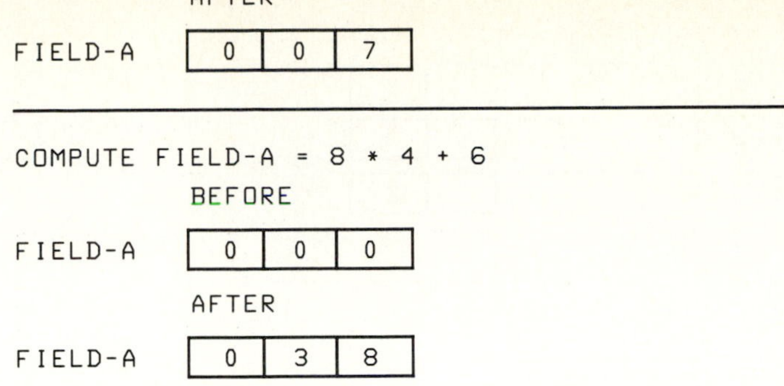

In the following example, FIELD-A is numeric edited. After a COMPUTE is performed on it, it may not be used to the right of the equals sign in any subsequent calculations.

```
05  FIELD-A          PIC ZZ9.
05  FIELD-B          PIC 9(2)          VALUE 15.
```

```
COMPUTE FIELD-A = FIELD-B * 10 - 80
```

BEFORE

FIELD-A	?	?	?
FIELD-B		1	5

AFTER

FIELD-A		7	0
FIELD-B		1	5

The ROUNDED option causes the result field(s) to be rounded. The position at which rounding takes place is controlled by the PICTURE of the result field. The results of the calculation are stored in a work area with more decimal positions than the PICTURE of the result field. A five is added to the work area one position to the right of the size of the result field. If there is a carry, the last position of the result field is rounded up by one.

```
05  FIELD-A          PIC 99V99.
05  FIELD-B          PIC  9V99          VALUE 1.63.
05  FIELD-C          PIC  9V9           VALUE 1.5.
05  FIELD-D          PIC 99V99          VALUE 1.82.
05  FIELD-E          PIC 99.
```

```
COMPUTE FIELD-A ROUNDED = FIELD-B * FIELD-C
```

BEFORE

FIELD-A	?	? ^	?	?
FIELD-B		1 ^	6	3
FIELD-C		1 ^	5	

AFTER

FIELD-A WORK AREA	0	2 ^	4	4	5 (+5)
FIELD-A ROUNDED	0	2 ^	4	5	
FIELD-B		1 ^	6	3	
FIELD-C		1 ^	5		

```
COMPUTE FIELD-A ROUNDED = FIELD-B * FIELD-D
             BEFORE

FIELD-A      [ ? | ? ^ ? | ? ]

FIELD-B          [ 1 ^ 6 | 3 ]

FIELD-D      [ 0 | 1 ^ 8 | 2 ]

             AFTER
FIELD-A
WORK         [ 0 | 2 ^ 9 | 6 | 6 | 6 ]
AREA                        +5

FIELD-A      [ 0 | 2 ^ 9 | 7 ]
ROUNDED

FIELD-B          [ 1 ^ 6 | 3 ]

FIELD-D      [ 0 | 1 ^ 8 | 2 ]
```

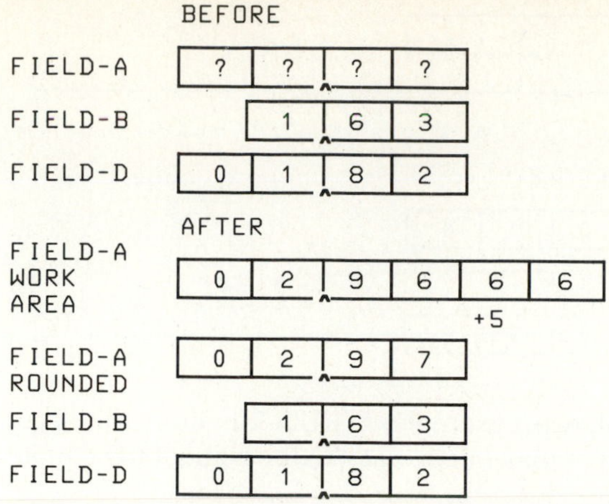

```
COMPUTE FIELD-E ROUNDED = FIELD-C * FIELD-D
             BEFORE

FIELD-E      [ ? | ? ]

FIELD-C          [ 1 ^ 5 ]

FIELD-D      [ 0 | 1 ^ 8 | 2 ]

             AFTER
FIELD-E
WORK         [ 0 | 2 ^ 7 | 3 ]
AREA                +5

FIELD-E      [ 0 | 3 ]
ROUNDED

FIELD-C          [ 1 ^ 5 ]

FIELD-D      [ 0 | 1 ^ 8 | 2 ]
```

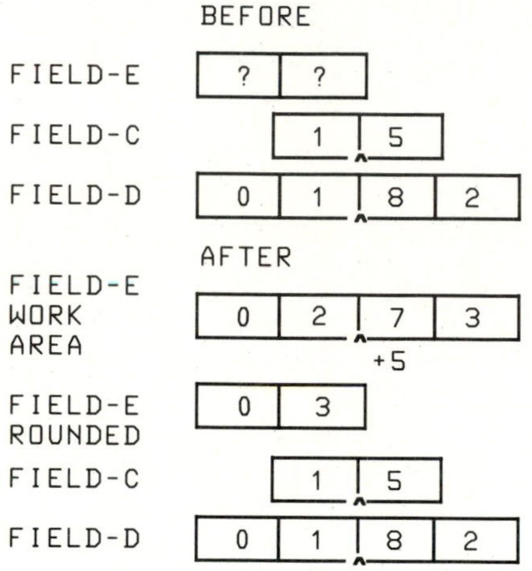

The ADD Statement

Format 1

```
    {identifier-1}  [identifier-2]
ADD {literal-1   }  [literal-2   ]  . . .TO identifier-m
[ROUNDED] [identifier-n [ROUNDED]] . . .
```

There are two commonly used formats for the ADD statement. In the first format, there may be one, two, or more data items added to one, two, or more result fields.

Any data items to the left of the word TO (identifier-1, identifier-2, . . .) are added together. This sum is then added to the contents of any result fields (identifier-n, identifier-m, . . .). All identifiers and literals in Format 1 must be numeric. An important thing to note here is that the original contents of the result field will affect the final result. Several result fields, then, may have a different value from each other based on their original contents.

```
05  FIELD-A          PIC 99V99        VALUE 68.42.
05  FIELD-B          PIC 999V99       VALUE 31.54.
05  FIELD-C          PIC 999V99       VALUE 15.48.
05  FIELD-D          PIC 999V9        VALUE 108.4.
```

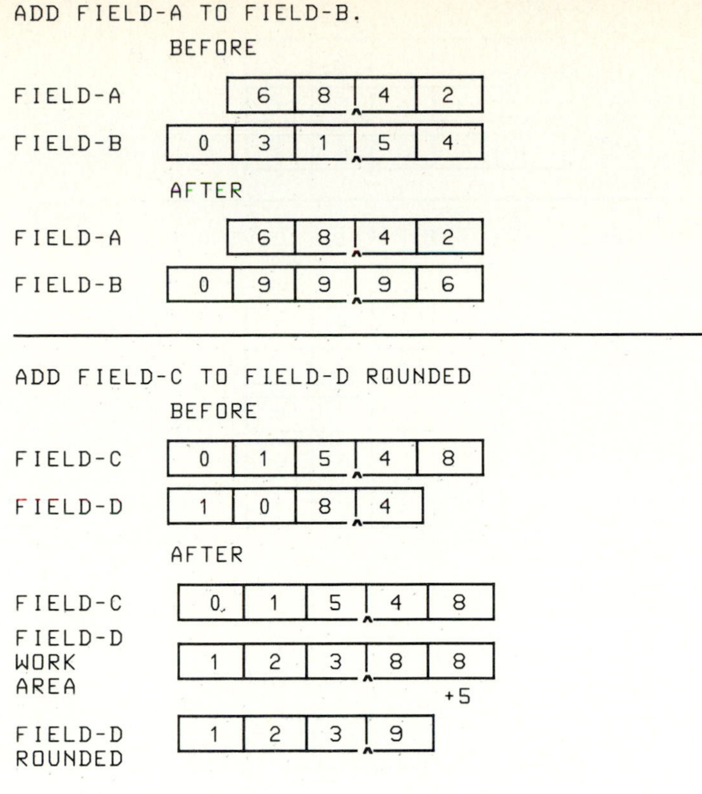

Format 2

```
ADD {identifier-1} {identifier-2} [identifier-3] . . . GIVING
    {literal-1   } {literal-2   } [literal-3   ]
identifier-m [ROUNDED] [identifier-n [ROUNDED]] . . .
```

The second ADD format requires at least two data items to the left of the word GIVING, and the original contents of the result field are not used in the calculation. The data items to the left of GIVING are added together, and the result is placed in the result field(s) coded following GIVING. The result field(s) may be numeric or numeric edited. The original contents of the result field are replaced with the sum of any data items to the left of the word GIVING. The contents of multiple result fields will vary only as to PICTURE size, type, and rounding.

```
05  FIELD-A        PIC 999V99     VALUE 421.86.
05  FIELD-B        PIC 99V99      VALUE 34.57.
05  FIELD-C        PIC 999V99     VALUE 786.42.
05  FIELD-D        PIC 99V99      VALUE 41.35.
05  FIELD-E        PIC 9V99       VALUE 9.24.
05  FIELD-F        PIC 9V99       VALUE 28.30.
```

ADD FIELD-A FIELD-B GIVING FIELD-C.

BEFORE

FIELD-A	4	2	1	8	6
FIELD-B		3	4	5	7
FIELD-C	7	8	6	4	2

```
        AFTER
FIELD-A  | 4 | 2 | 1 ^ 8 | 6 |
FIELD-B      | 3 | 4 ^ 5 | 7 |
FIELD-C  | 4 | 5 | 6 ^ 4 | 3 |
```

```
ADD FIELD-D FIELD-E FIELD-F GIVING FIELD-A FIELD-B.
        BEFORE
FIELD-D      | 4 | 1 ^ 3 | 5 |
FIELD-E          | 9 ^ 2 | 4 |
FIELD-F      | 2 | 8 ^ 3 | 0 |
FIELD-A  | 4 | 2 | 1 ^ 8 | 6 |
FIELD-B      | 3 | 4 ^ 5 | 7 |
        AFTER
FIELD-D      | 4 | 1 ^ 3 | 5 |
FIELD-E          | 9 ^ 2 | 4 |
FIELD-F      | 2 | 8 ^ 3 | 0 |
FIELD-A  | 0 | 7 | 8 ^ 8 | 9 |
FIELD-B      | 7 | 8 ^ 8 | 9 |
```

In both formats of the ADD statement, the data items representing the result fields are on the right and must be identifiers. Thus, ADD 10 TO FIELD-A is valid, but ADD FIELD-A TO 10 is not since no identifier is specified to the right of the word TO in which to store the result.

The 1985 standard will allow the optional word TO in Format 2 of the ADD statement:

Format 2

```
    {identifier-1}      {identifier-2}
ADD {literal-2   }  TO  {literal-2   }  . . . GIVING
identifier-m [ROUNDED] [identifier-n [ROUNDED]] . . .
```

The SUBTRACT Statement

Format 1

```
         {identifier-1} [identifier-2]
SUBTRACT {literal-1   } [literal-2   ]  . . . FROM identifier-m
[ROUNDED] [identifier-n [ROUNDED]] . . .
```

In Format 1 of the SUBTRACT statement, the identifiers or literals before the word FROM are added together, and this sum is subtracted from any identifier(s) to the right of the word FROM. The original contents of the result fields are used in the calculation and are changed by the calculation. All identifiers and literals in Format 1 must be numeric.

```
05  FIELD-A          PIC 99V99        VALUE 14.60.
05  FIELD-B          PIC 99V99        VALUE 87.86.
05  FIELD-C          PIC  9V99        VALUE  2.43.
05  FIELD-D          PIC  9V99        VALUE  6.75.
```

```
SUBTRACT FIELD-A FROM FIELD-B.
          BEFORE
FIELD-A   | 1 | 4 ^ 6 | 0 |
FIELD-B   | 8 | 7 ^ 8 | 6 |
          AFTER
FIELD-A   | 1 | 4 ^ 6 | 0 |
FIELD-B   | 7 | 3 ^ 2 | 6 |
```

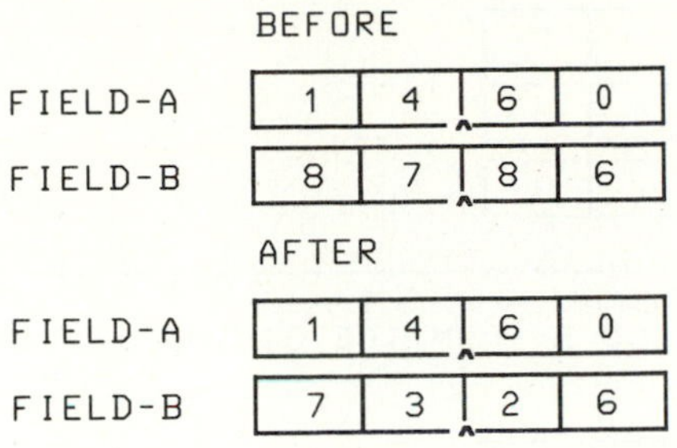

```
SUBTRACT FIELD-C FIELD-D FROM FIELD-A
          BEFORE
FIELD-C       | 2 ^ 4 | 3 |
FIELD-D       | 6 ^ 7 | 5 |
FIELD-A   | 1 | 4 ^ 6 | 0 |
          AFTER
FIELD-C       | 2 ^ 4 | 3 |
FIELD-D       | 6 ^ 7 | 5 |
FIELD-A   | 0 | 5 ^ 4 | 2 |
```

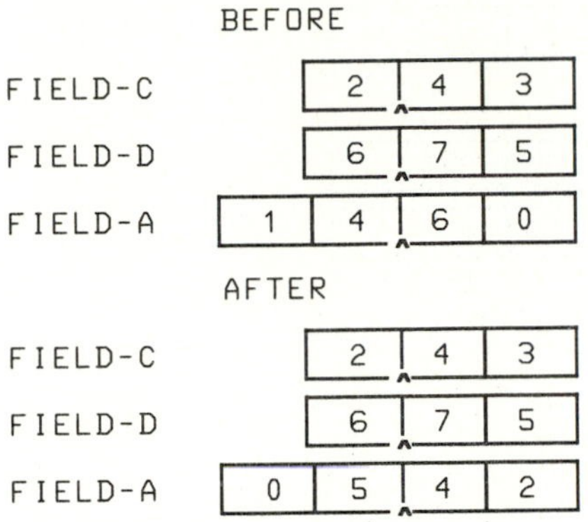

Care should be exercised in using Format 1: it is easy to lose or misname data, as in the statement

```
SUBTRACT TOTAL-DEDUCTIONS FROM GROSS-PAY.
```

Assuming the data-names are accurate representations of the contents of the fields, this calculation will cause the loss of the original contents of GROSS-PAY. The new contents will represent net pay, but the field will still be named GROSS-PAY.

Format 2

```
         {identifier-1}  [identifier-2]               {identifier-m}
SUBTRACT {literal-1   }  [literal-2   ]  . . .  FROM  {literal-m   }

GIVING identifier-n [ROUNDED] [identifier-o [ROUNDED]] . . .
```

In Format 2, data items to the left of FROM are added together, and this sum is then subtracted from the value in identifier-m or literal-m. The result is placed in the identifier(s) to the right of the word GIVING, and identifier-m remains unchanged. All identifiers and literals except those to the right of GIVING must be numeric. The result field(s) to the right of GIVING may be numeric or numeric edited.

```
05  FIELD-A          PIC 99V99        VALUE 25.30.
05  FIELD-B          PIC 99V99        VALUE 36.49.
05  FIELD-C          PIC 99V99        VALUE 67.40.
05  FIELD-D          PIC 999V99       VALUE 500.20.
```

```
SUBTRACT FIELD-A FROM FIELD-B GIVING FIELD-C.
                BEFORE
FIELD-A         | 2 | 5 ^ 3 | 0 |
FIELD-B         | 3 | 6 ^ 4 | 9 |
FIELD-C         | 6 | 7 ^ 4 | 0 |
                AFTER
FIELD-A         | 2 | 5 ^ 3 | 0 |
FIELD-B         | 3 | 6 ^ 4 | 9 |
FIELD-C         | 1 | 1 ^ 1 | 9 |
```

```
SUBTRACT FIELD-A FIELD-B FROM 100 GIVING FIELD-D.
                BEFORE
FIELD-A             | 2 | 5 ^ 3 | 0 |
FIELD-B             | 3 | 6 ^ 4 | 9 |
FIELD-D         | 5 | 0 | 0 ^ 2 | 0 |
                AFTER
FIELD-A             | 2 | 5 ^ 3 | 0 |
FIELD-B             | 3 | 6 ^ 4 | 9 |
FIELD-D         | 0 | 3 | 8 ^ 2 | 1 |
```

Format 2 has an advantage over Format 1 in that it leaves the identifier or literal immediately to the right of the word FROM unchanged. Thus, using Format 2, both TOTAL-DEDUCTIONS and GROSS-PAY remain unchanged in the payroll calculation SUBTRACT TOTAL-DEDUCTIONS FROM GROSS-PAY GIVING NET-PAY. The result of the subtraction is placed in a result field with an appropriate name.

The MULTIPLY Statement

Format 1

```
         {identifier-1}
MULTIPLY {literal-1   } BY identifier-2 [ROUNDED] [identifier-3
[ROUNDED]] . . .
```

In Format 1 of the MULTIPLY statement, the first identifier or literal is multiplied by each data item to the right of the word BY, and the products are then placed in these result fields. Notice that all identifiers and literals are involved in the calculation and must, therefore, be numeric. The original values of any data items to the right of the word BY are lost.

```
05  FIELD-A        PIC 99V99      VALUE 5.00.
05  FIELD-B        PIC 999V99     VALUE 50.00.
05  FIELD-C        PIC 99V99      VALUE 18.64.
05  FIELD-D        PIC 99V99      VALUE 12.21.
```

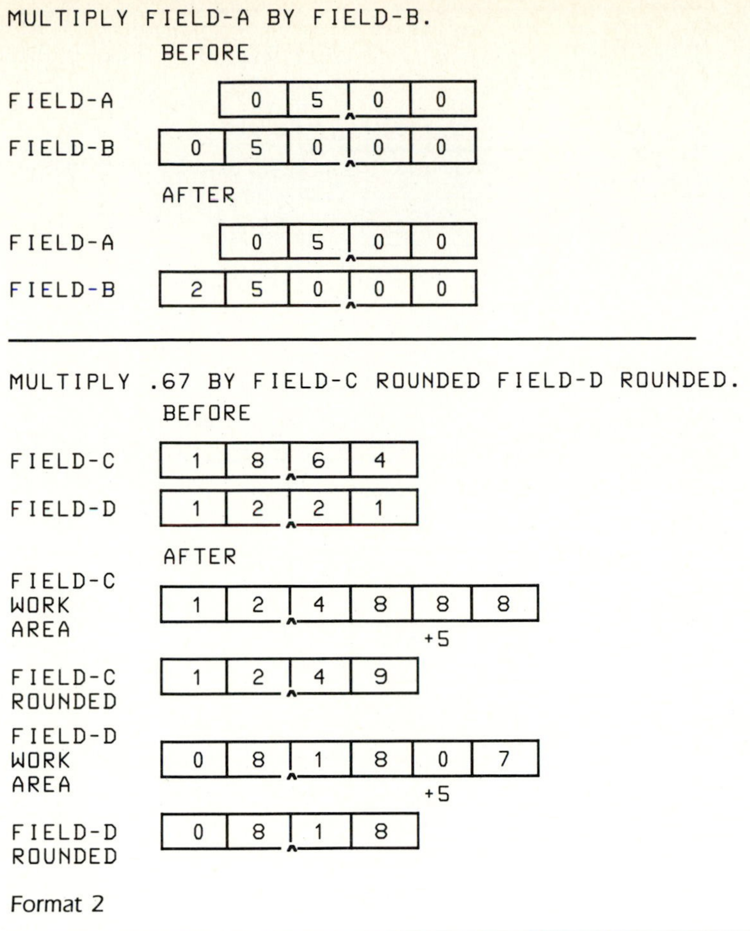

Format 2

```
MULTIPLY {identifier-1} BY {identifier-2} GIVING identifier-3
         {literal-1   }    {literal-2   }
[ROUNDED] [identifier-4 [ROUNDED]] . . .
```

In Format 2, identifier-1 or literal-1 is multiplied by identifier-2 or literal-2. Both of these items must be numeric and remain unchanged by the calculation. The product is placed in any identifier(s) to the right of the word GIVING. Identifiers to the right of GIVING are used to store the result and may be either numeric or numeric edited.

```
05  FIELD-A      PIC 99V99     VALUE 24.30.
05  FIELD-B      PIC  9V99     VALUE  2.65.
05  FIELD-C      PIC 99V99     VALUE 88.88.
05  FIELD-D      PIC 99V9      VALUE ZEROS.
```

```
MULTIPLY FIELD-A BY FIELD-B GIVING FIELD-C.
            BEFORE

FIELD-A     | 2 | 4 ^ 3 | 0 |
FIELD-B         | 2 ^ 6 | 5 |
FIELD-C     | 8 | 8 ^ 8 | 8 |

            AFTER

FIELD-A     | 2 | 4 ^ 3 | 0 |
FIELD-B         | 2 ^ 6 | 5 |
FIELD-C     | 6 | 4 ^ 3 | 9 |
```

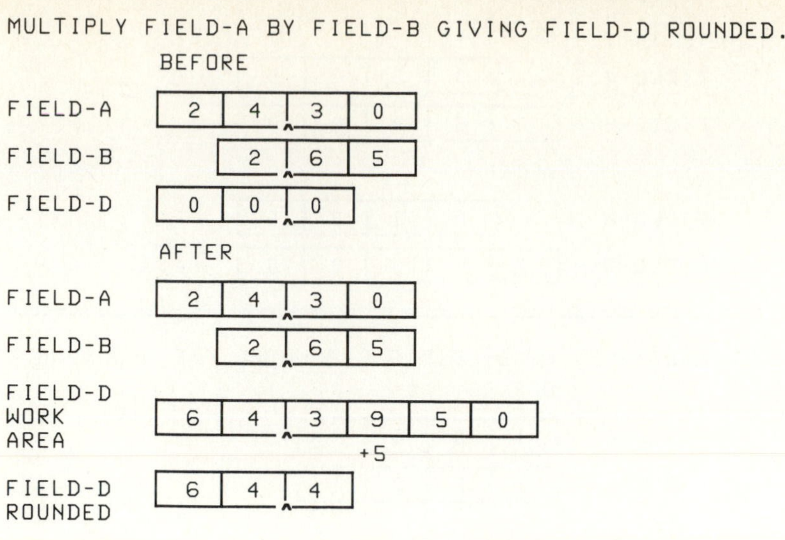

The DIVIDE Statement

Format 1

```
DIVIDE {identifier-1} INTO identifier-2 [ROUNDED] [identifier-3
       {literal-1   }
    [ROUNDED]] . . .
```

In Format 1 of the DIVIDE statement, identifier-1 or literal-1 is divided into the value(s) of any identifier(s) to the right of the word INTO. The result (quotient) is then placed in those identifiers. All data items in this format are involved in the calculation and must, therefore, be numeric.

```
05  FIELD-A          PIC 9V99         VALUE  4.18.
05  FIELD-B          PIC 99V99        VALUE 30.62.
05  FIELD-C          PIC 99V9         VALUE 42.5.
05  FIELD-D          PIC 99           VALUE 46.
```

```
DIVIDE FIELD-A INTO FIELD-B.
            BEFORE
FIELD-A          | 4 ^ 1 | 8 |
FIELD-B     | 3 | 0 ^ 6 | 2 |
            AFTER
FIELD-A          | 4 ^ 1 | 8 |
FIELD-B     | 0 | 7 ^ 3 | 2 |
```

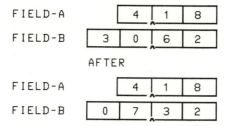

```
DIVIDE 8 INTO FIELD-C ROUNDED FIELD-D ROUNDED.
            BEFORE
FIELD-C     | 4 | 2 ^ 5 |
FIELD-D     | 4 | 6 |
            AFTER
FIELD-C
WORK        | 0 | 5 ^ 3 | 1 | 2 | 5 |
AREA                  +5
```

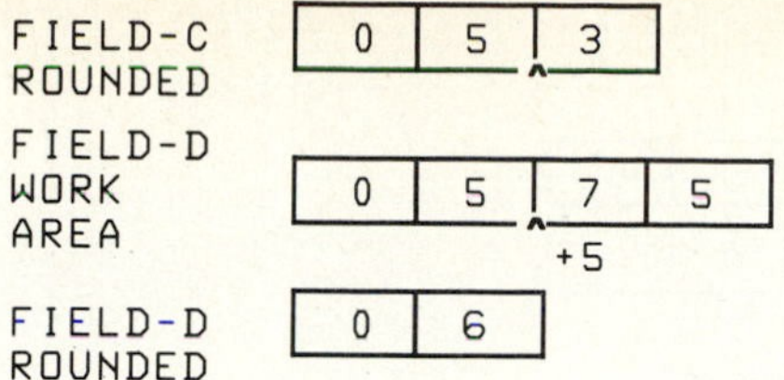

Format 2

```
DIVIDE {identifier-1} {INTO} {identifier-2} GIVING
       {literal-1   } {BY  } {literal-2   }
identifier-3 [ROUNDED] [identifier-4 [ROUNDED]] . . .
```

In Format 2, identifier-1 or literal-1 is divided either INTO or BY the value of identifier-2 or literal-2. The result is placed in any identifier(s) to the right of the word GIVING. Data items to the left of GIVING are involved in the calculation; hence, they must be numeric. Identifiers to the right of GIVING are not a part of the calculation. They are only used to store the result and may be numeric or numeric edited.

```
FIELD-A    PIC 99V99    VALUE 12.00.
FIELD-B    PIC 99V99    VALUE 48.00.
FIELD-C    PIC 99V99    VALUE ZEROS.
FIELD-D    PIC 99V99    VALUE 57.00.
FIELD-E    PIC 99V9     VALUE ZEROS.
FIELD-F    PIC 99V99    VALUE ZEROS.
```

DIVIDE FIELD-A INTO FIELD-B GIVING FIELD-C.

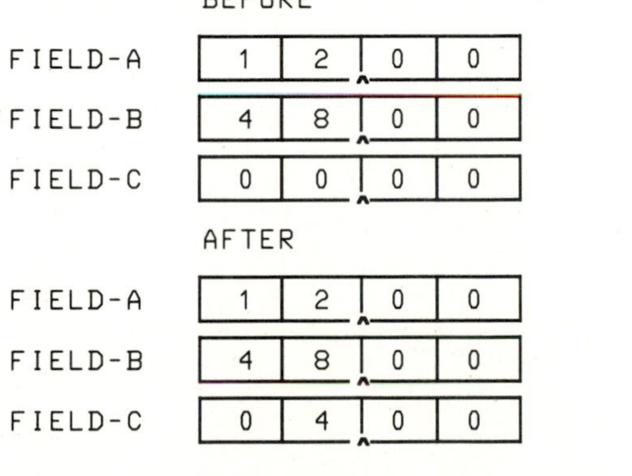

DIVIDE FIELD-A BY FIELD-B GIVING FIELD-C.

BEFORE

FIELD-A	1	2	0	0
FIELD-B	4	8	0	0
FIELD-C	0	0	0	0

AFTER

FIELD-A	1	2	0	0
FIELD-B	4	8	0	0
FIELD-C	0	0	2	5

```
DIVIDE FIELD-A INTO FIELD-D GIVING FIELD-E ROUNDED FIELD-F.
```

BEFORE

FIELD-A	1	2	0	0
FIELD-D	5	7	0	0
FIELD-E	0	0	0	
FIELD-F	0	0	0	0

AFTER

FIELD-A	1	2	0	0
FIELD-D	5	7	0	0
FIELD-E WORK AREA	0	4	7	5 (+5)
FIELD-E ROUNDED	0	4	8	
FIELD-F	0	4	7	5

Format 3

```
DIVIDE {identifier-1} {INTO} {identifier-2} GIVING
       {literal-1   } {BY  } {literal-2   }
identifier-3 [ROUNDED] [REMAINDER identifier-4]
```

The calculation in Format 3 is identical to that in Format 2, only one result field for the quotient is allowed and a remainder can be saved. The remainder is the result of subtracting the product of the quotient and the divisor from the dividend. All data items to the left of the word GIVING must be numeric. Identifiers to the right of GIVING may be numeric or numeric edited.

```
DIVIDE 8 INTO 50 GIVING FIELD-A REMAINDER FIELD-B
```

AFTER	
DIVISOR	8
DIVIDEND	50
QUOTIENT (FIELD-A)	6
DIVISOR TIMES QUOTIENT	48
REMAINDER (FIELD-B)	2

```
05  FIELD-A          PIC 9(3)      VALUE 20.
05  FIELD-B          PIC 9(3)      VALUE 145.
05  FIELD-C          PIC 9(3).
05  FIELD-D          PIC 9(3).
```

```
DIVIDE FIELD-A INTO FIELD-B GIVING FIELD-C REMAINDER FIELD-D
```

BEFORE

FIELD-A	0	2	0
FIELD-B	1	4	5
FIELD-C	?	?	?
FIELD-D	?	?	?

AFTER

FIELD-A	0	2	0
FIELD-B	1	4	5
FIELD-C	0	0	7
FIELD-D	0	0	5

CURRENT-DATE

In many instances, it is necessary for a program to have access to the current calendar date. For example, in producing a printed report, the date is usually placed in the headings. This allows the user of the report to determine how recent the information is and to differentiate between listings of the same report which were created on different dates.

The current date is accessible to a COBOL program through the use of the reserved word CURRENT-DATE. CURRENT-DATE is an eight-character alphanumeric field in the format MM/DD/YY. It may only be used as the sending field in a MOVE statement. The programmer does not reserve any storage for CURRENT-DATE. However, storage must be reserved for the receiving field of the MOVE statement.

The Sample Program

In the EXTRACT program, the current date is placed in the headings in the 1000-INITIALIZATION routine:

```
MOVE CURRENT-DATE TO MAIN-HDG-DATE.
```

The move is made in this routine rather than the heading routine so that it will only be executed once. Note that storage is defined for MAIN-HDG-DATE, but no storage is defined for CURRENT-DATE.

PROGRAM SPECIFICATION: LEAD-TIME

The second programming project of this chapter demonstrates additional extraction possibilities. It uses AND/OR logic in the selection of records to be printed. The same input file as in the first project is used. The specification for this program is given in Figure 4–27.

Input Record Layout

The input record layout of the LEAD-TIME program is shown in Figure 4–28. This is the same file used in the EXTRACT programming project. The layout is repeated here for convenience.

Print Chart

The print chart for the project is shown in Figure 4–29. It includes the number of days of lead time and a count of the extracted records.

LOGIC FOR EXTRACT WITH CALCULATIONS

A hierarchy chart for the LEAD-TIME program is shown in Figure 4–30. Pseudocode and flowcharts are shown in Figures 4–31 and 4–32 for the three routines which are changed from the previous EXTRACT program. These routines are PROCESS, EXTRACTED-RECORD, and EOJ.

PROGRAM SPECIFICATION

Program Name: LEAD-TIME

Program Function:

The program will produce a printed report of all orders for Branch 3 wherein the lead time for an order is less than 30 days or greater than 365 days.

Input Files:

I. ORDER-FILE

INPUT DEVICE:	DISK
FILE ORGANIZATION:	SEQUENTIAL
RECORD LENGTH:	70 BYTES
FILE SEQUENCE:	ASCENDING ON BRANCH / SALES REP

Output Files:

I. PRINT-FILE

OUTPUT DEVICE:	PRINTER
RECORD LENGTH:	133 BYTES

Processing Requirements:

An order record should be included in the output listing only if it is from Branch 3 and its lead time is less than 30 days or greater than 365 days. A count should be made of the records extracted and should be printed at the end of the report.

Output Requirements:

The following are formatting requirements for the report:

1. Each page of the report should contain:
   (a) a main heading which contains the company name, the report name, the current date, and a page number.
   (b) column headings which describe the items printed underneath them.
2. Detail lines should include all fields from the input record and the number of days of lead time.
3. Detail lines should be double spaced.
4. The count of extracted records should be double spaced.

FIGURE 4–27

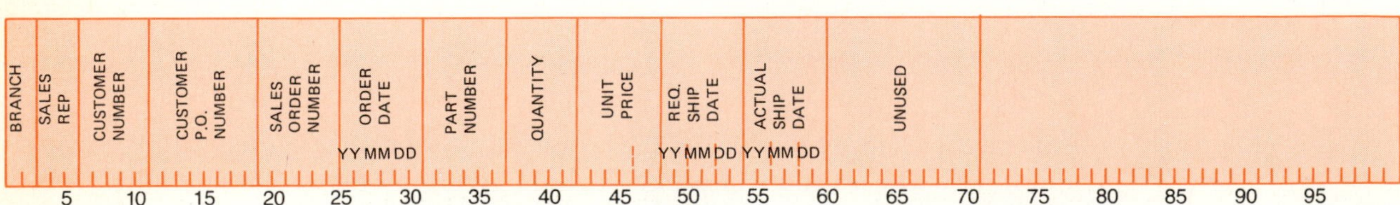

FIGURE 4–28

```
        DATE: XX-XX-XX                      PRODUCT DISTRIBUTION INC. - LEAD-TIME ERRORS                           PAGE: ZZ9

                SALES    SALES    CUSTOMER    CUSTOMER      PART                 UNIT        ORDER       REQUESTED     LEAD
        BRANCH   REP     ORDER      NUMBER         PO        NUMBER     QUANTITY    PRICE        DATE       SHIP DATE     TIME

          99     999     XXXXXX     99999     XXXXXXXX     XXXXXX     ZZZZ9     ZZZ9.99     99-99-99     99-99-99     ZZZZ9

          99     999     XXXXXX     99999     XXXXXXXX     XXXXXX     ZZZZ9     ZZZ9.99     99-99-99     99-99-99     ZZZZ9


        NUMBER OF LEAD-TIME ERRORS: ZZZ9
```

FIGURE 4–29

Hierarchy Chart

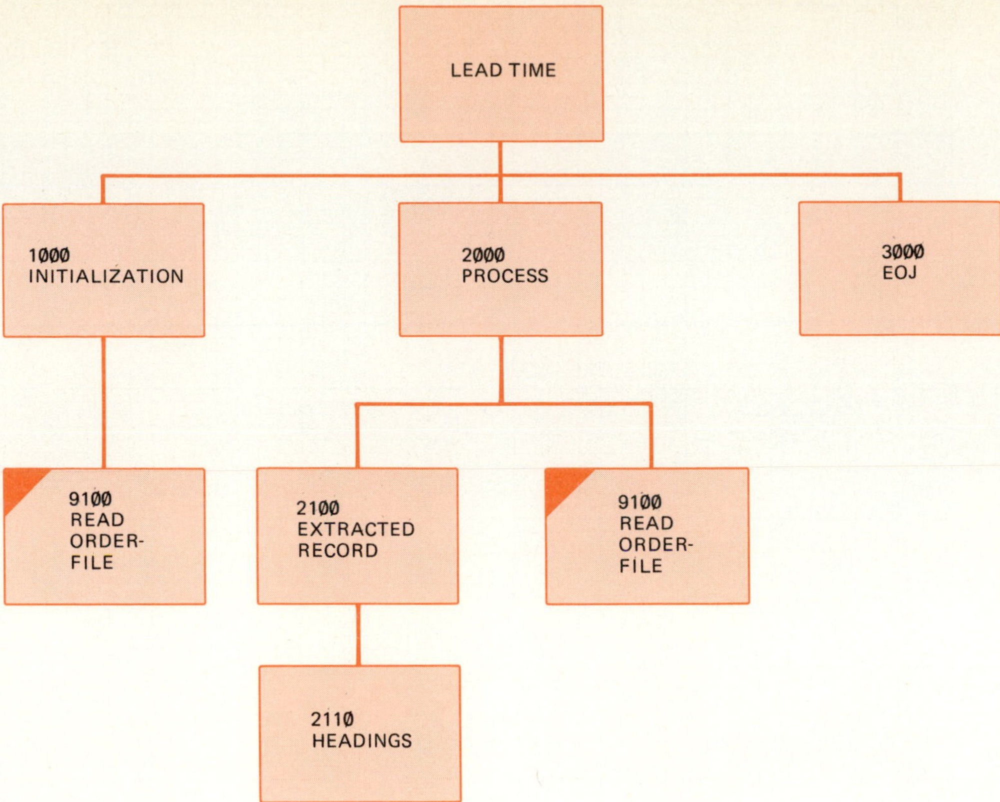

FIGURE 4–30

Pseudocode

```
PROCESS
     CALCULATE number of days for order date
     CALCULATE number of days for requested shipping
       date
     CALCULATE number of days lead time
       (number of days for requested shipping
       date - number of days for order date)
     IF order branch = 3 (and number of lead days <
       30 or number of lead days is > 365)
          DO extracted record
     ENDIF
     DO read an order

EXTRACTED RECORD
     IF line count > 50
          DO headings
     ENDIF
     MOVE input to output
     MOVE number of days lead time to output
     ADD 1 to number of lead-time errors
     WRITE detail line
     ADD 2 to line count


END OF JOB
     MOVE number of lead-time errors to output
     WRITE lead-time error line
     CLOSE files
```

FIGURE 4–31

Flowchart

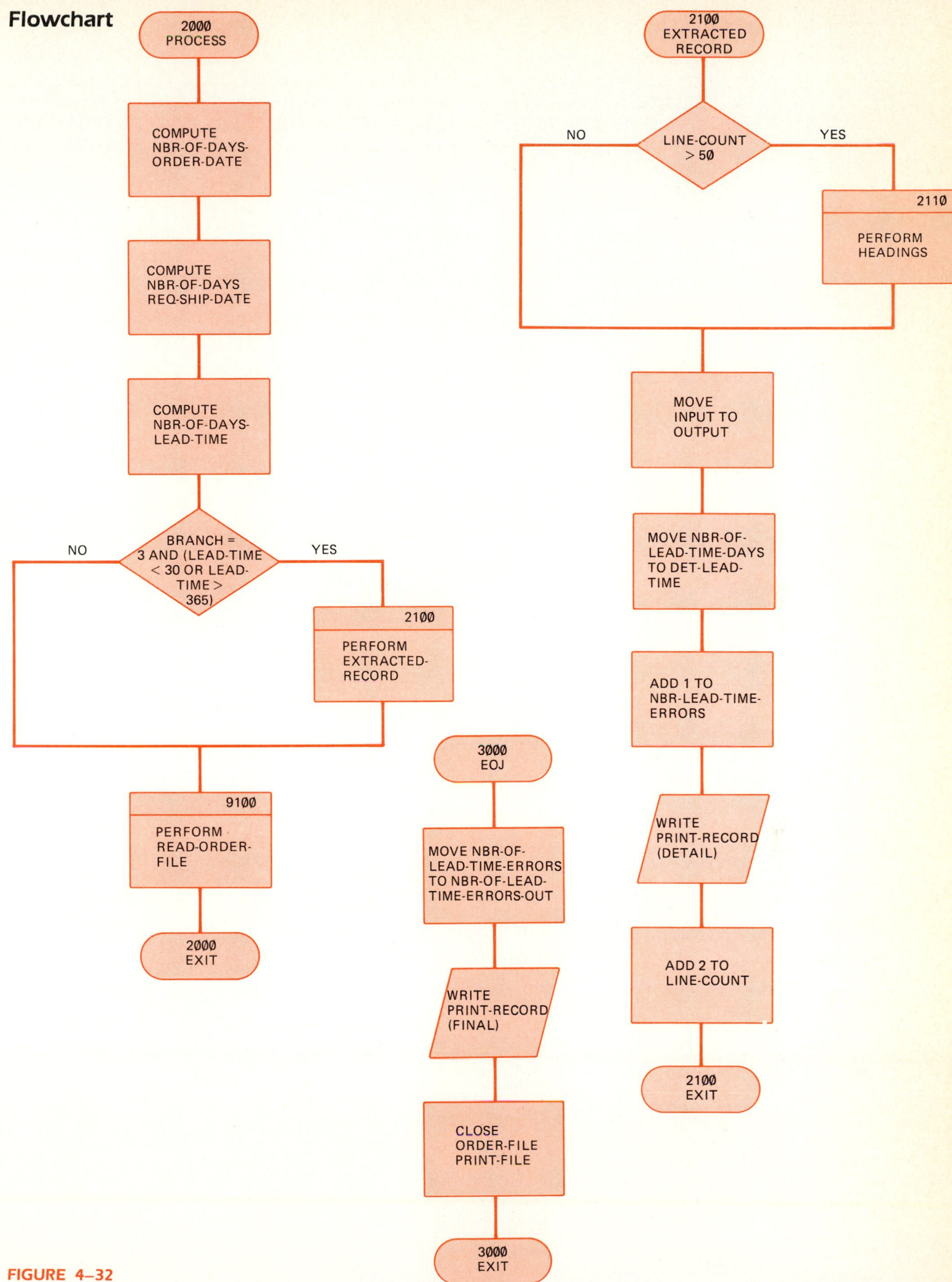

FIGURE 4–32

Explanation of Logic

2000-PROCESS

The report is to include all records from Branch 3 whose lead time is less than 30 days or greater than 365 days. The input record has a field named ORD-BRANCH which can be used to determine whether the record is of the selected branch. In order to determine the number of days of lead time, the ORD-DATE and ORD-REQ-SHIP-DATE fields are used to calculate numbers whose difference will be the number of days of lead time. This figure will be approximate, since 30 days is used for the length of a month and 365 days is used for the length of a year.

The tests for branch number and number of days of lead time were combined into one IF statement in order to demonstrate AND/OR logic. The tests could have been performed separately by a nested IF. Figure 4–33 shows the AND/OR logic.

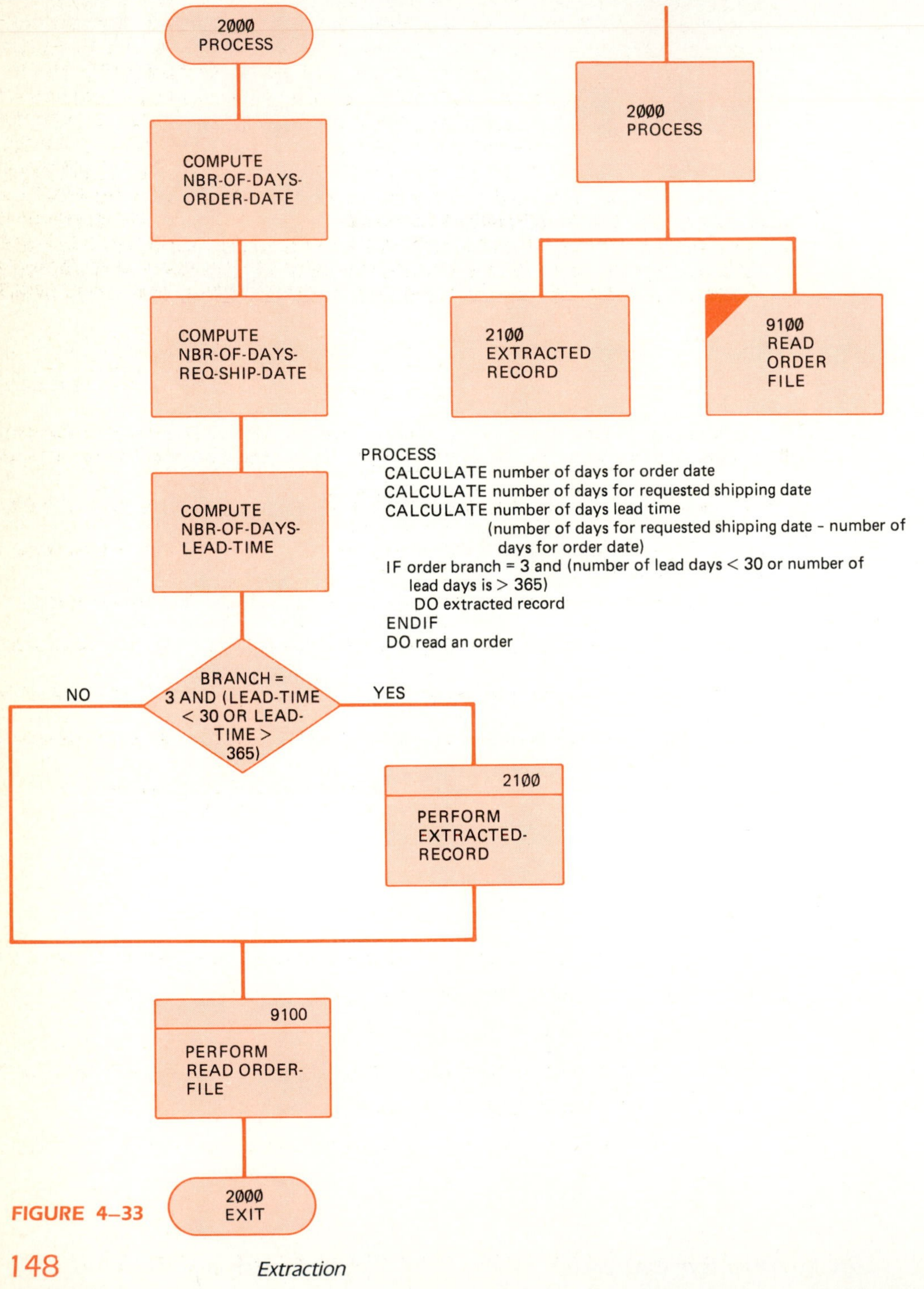

2000
PROCESS
COMPUTE
NBR-OF-DAYS-
ORDER-DATE
COMPUTE
NBR-OF-DAYS-
REQ-SHIP-DATE
COMPUTE
NBR-OF-DAYS-
LEAD-TIME
BRANCH =
3 AND (LEAD-TIME
< 30 OR LEAD-
TIME >
365)
NO
YES
2100
PERFORM
EXTRACTED-
RECORD
9100
PERFORM
READ ORDER-
FILE
2000
EXIT
2000
PROCESS
2100
EXTRACTED
RECORD
9100
READ
ORDER
FILE
PROCESS
CALCULATE number of days for order date
CALCULATE number of days for requested shipping date
CALCULATE number of days lead time
(number of days for requested shipping date - number of
days for order date)
IF order branch = 3 and (number of lead days < 30 or number of
lead days is > 365)
DO extracted record
ENDIF
DO read an order

FIGURE 4–33

2100-EXTRACTED-RECORD

There are two changes to 2100-EXTRACTED-RECORD routine of the previous program: the field being moved to output is now NBR-OF-LEAD-TIME-DAYS, and the number of extracted records is being tallied. This tally provides the number of records with a lead time considered to be in error. (See Figure 4–34.)

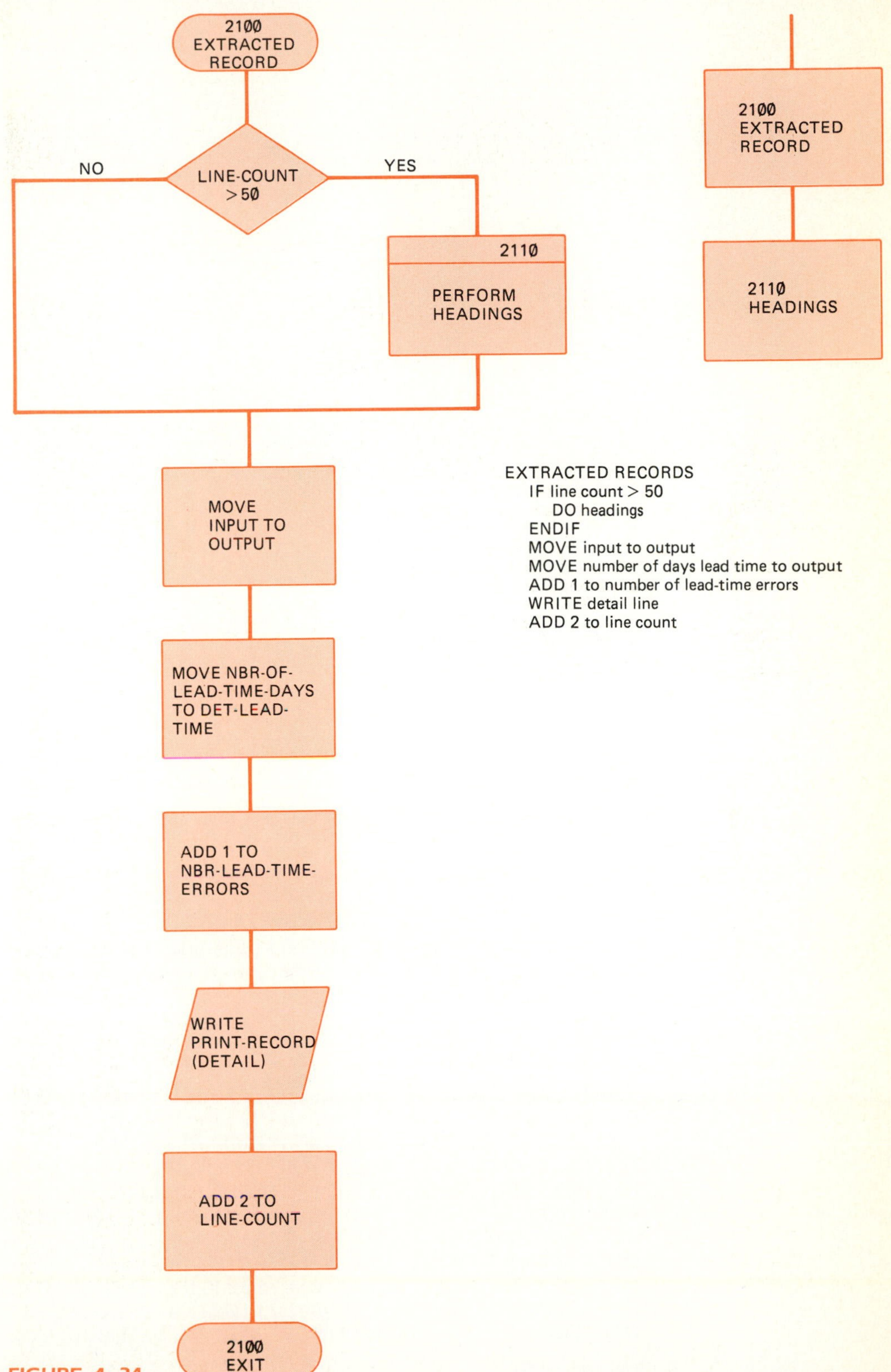

FIGURE 4–34

3000-EOJ

The only change in EOJ is to the field being moved to output. Instead of totals, the count of lead-time errors is printed. (See Figure 4–35.)

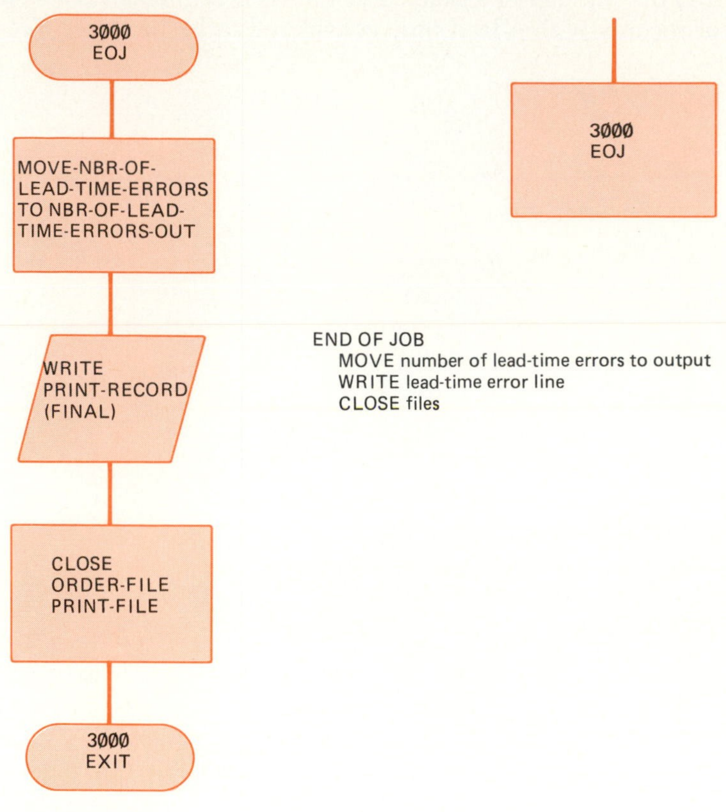
3000
EOJ
MOVE-NBR-OF-LEAD-TIME-ERRORS TO NBR-OF-LEAD-TIME-ERRORS-OUT
WRITE PRINT-RECORD (FINAL)
CLOSE ORDER-FILE PRINT-FILE
3000
EXIT
3000
EOJ
END OF JOB
MOVE number of lead-time errors to output
WRITE lead-time error line
CLOSE files

FIGURE 4–35

THE COBOL PROGRAM

Test Data Test data for the LEAD-TIME program is shown in Figure 4–36.

Sample Output Sample output from the LEAD-TIME program is shown in Figure 4–37.

```
Ø12Ø1ØØ3ØØPO173      B12383871Ø25GN4Ø2AØØØØ1Ø45ØØØ871116ØØØØØØ
Ø12Ø1Ø47278372       G4838887Ø913WB7Ø2XØØØ9ØØ115ØØ8711Ø1ØØØØØØ
Ø12Ø1ØØ3ØØE1Ø12      B123358711Ø5WB493EØØØØ2Ø54ØØØ871122ØØØØØØ
Ø3ØØ7473ØØ           H8477787Ø223MF4Ø3TØØØØ5Ø4ØØØØ87Ø5Ø2ØØØØØØ
Ø3ØØ7ØØ378EBNER      H8457987Ø811VX922PØØ8ØØØØ127589112ØØØØØØØ
Ø3ØØ7739897747       B892888711Ø6MF848JØØØØ5Ø2145Ø88Ø13ØØØØØØØ
Ø3ØØ7ØØ28334567X     B34237871Ø3ØHL834EØØØ16Ø19ØØØ871121ØØØØØØ
Ø3ØØ7473ØØ           Y289Ø387Ø811VXØØ1LØØ2ØØØØ622Ø8712Ø3ØØØØØØ
Ø344Ø6948187Ø341     GØ418Ø87Ø2Ø9JGØ4ØXØØØØ1Ø525ØØ88Ø619ØØØØØØ
Ø361182888P2783733B8433Ø871Ø25HL289BØØØ1ØØ234ØØ871113ØØØØØØ
Ø361128375T7838      T7829987Ø323JG563WØØØØ6Ø43ØØØ871Ø18ØØØØØØ
Ø36115Ø912           H6915Ø87Ø2Ø6MF848TØØØØ3Ø36ØØØ8712Ø1ØØØØØØ
Ø8174314Ø865         H4189187Ø412TK61ØLØØØ18ØØ78ØØ87Ø63ØØØØØØØ
Ø8174Ø18Ø5R7278      T2164287Ø81ØTK497XØØØ1ØØ118ØØ87113ØØØØØØØ
Ø8174Ø18Ø5R8322      Y211Ø587Ø6Ø1TN116TØØØØ1Ø3ØØØØ871221ØØØØØØ
Ø891562Ø54SCHUH      L5Ø6818711Ø8TK812EØØØØ6Ø573ØØ88Ø1Ø5ØØØØØØ
Ø891521Ø78           B71Ø45871ØØ1FV782TØØØØ3ØØ28ØØ871115ØØØØØØ
```

FIGURE 4–36

DATE: 11/09/87 PRODUCT DISTRIBUTION INC. - LEAD-TIME ERRORS PAGE: 1

BRANCH	SALES REP	SALES ORDER	CUSTOMER NUMBER	CUSTOMER PO	PART NUMBER	QUANTITY	UNIT PRICE	ORDER DATE	REQUESTED SHIP DATE	LEAD TIME
03	007	H84579	00378	EBNER	VX922P	800	12.75	08-11-87	11-20-89	829
03	007	B34237	00283	34567X	HL834E	16	190.00	10-30-87	11-21-87	21
03	440	G04180	69481	870341	JG040X	1	525.00	02-09-87	06-19-88	495
03	611	B84330	82888	P2783733	HL289B	10	234.00	10-25-87	11-13-87	18

NUMBER OF LEAD-TIME ERRORS: 4

FIGURE 4–37

The Program

The complete COBOL LEAD-TIME program is shown in Figure 4–38.

```
       IDENTIFICATION DIVISION.

       PROGRAM-ID.     LEAD-TIME.

       AUTHOR.         HELEN HUMPHREYS.

       INSTALLATION.   PRODUCT DISTRIBUTION INC.

       DATE-WRITTEN.   Ø4/14/87.

       DATE-COMPILED.  Ø4/18/87.

      *****************************************************************
      *                                                               *
      *    THIS PROGRAM PRODUCES A PRINTED REPORT OF ALL ORDERS FOR   *
      *    BRANCH 3 WHERE THE LEAD TIME FOR AN ORDER IS LESS THAN     *
      *    3Ø DAYS OR GREATER THAN 365 DAYS.                          *
      *                                                               *
      *****************************************************************

       ENVIRONMENT DIVISION.

       CONFIGURATION SECTION.

       SOURCE-COMPUTER.
               IBM-37Ø.
       OBJECT-COMPUTER.
               IBM-37Ø.

       INPUT-OUTPUT SECTION.
       FILE-CONTROL.
           SELECT ORDER-FILE ASSIGN TO DISK.
           SELECT PRINT-FILE ASSIGN TO PRINTER.

       DATA DIVISION.
       FILE SECTION.

       FD  ORDER-FILE
           LABEL RECORDS ARE STANDARD
           RECORD CONTAINS 7Ø CHARACTERS
           DATA RECORD IS ORDER-RECORD.

       Ø1  ORDER-RECORD.
           Ø5  ORD-BRANCH                 PIC 9(2).
           Ø5  ORD-SALES-REP              PIC 9(3).
           Ø5  ORD-CUSTOMER-NBR           PIC 9(5).
           Ø5  ORD-CUST-PO-NBR            PIC X(8).
           Ø5  ORD-SALES-ORD-NBR          PIC X(6).
           Ø5  ORD-DATE.
               1Ø  ORD-YY                 PIC 9(2).
               1Ø  ORD-MM                 PIC 9(2).
               1Ø  ORD-DD                 PIC 9(2).
           Ø5  ORD-PART-NBR               PIC X(6).
           Ø5  ORD-QUANTITY               PIC 9(5).
           Ø5  ORD-UNIT-PRICE             PIC 9(4)V9(2).
           Ø5  ORD-REQ-SHIP-DATE.
               1Ø  ORD-REQ-SHIP-YY        PIC 9(2).
```

FIGURE 4–38

FIG. 4-38 cont.

```
                10  ORD-REQ-SHIP-MM       PIC 9(2).
                10  ORD-REQ-SHIP-DD       PIC 9(2).
            Ø5  ORD-ACT-SHIP-DATE.
                1Ø  ORD-ACT-SHIP-YY       PIC 9(2).
                1Ø  ORD-ACT-SHIP-MM       PIC 9(2).
                1Ø  ORD-ACT-SHIP-DD       PIC 9(2).
            Ø5  FILLER                    PIC X(11).

        FD  PRINT-FILE
            LABEL RECORDS ARE OMITTED
            RECORD CONTAINS 133 CHARACTERS
            DATA RECORD IS PRINT-RECORD.

        Ø1  PRINT-RECORD                  PIC X(133).

        WORKING-STORAGE SECTION.

        Ø1  HOLDS-COUNTERS-SWITCHES.
            Ø5  END-FLAG-ORDER-FILE       PIC X(3)        VALUE 'NO'.
            Ø5  LINE-COUNT                PIC 9(2)        VALUE 99.
            Ø5  PAGE-COUNT                PIC 9(3)        VALUE ZEROS.
            Ø5  NBR-OF-LEAD-TIME-ERRORS PIC 9(4)          VALUE ZEROS.

        Ø1  CALCULATED-FIELDS.
            Ø5  NBR-OF-DAYS-ORDER-DATE  PIC 9(5).
            Ø5  NBR-OF-DAYS-REQ-SHIP-DATE   PIC 9(5).
            Ø5  NBR-OF-DAYS-LEAD-TIME    PIC 9(5).

        Ø1  MAIN-HEADING.
            Ø5  FILLER                    PIC X(8)        VALUE SPACES.
            Ø5  FILLER                    PIC X(6)        VALUE 'DATE:'.
            Ø5  MAIN-HDG-DATE             PIC X(8).
            Ø5  FILLER                    PIC X(21)       VALUE SPACES.
            Ø5  FILLER                    PIC X(44)
                VALUE 'PRODUCT DISTRIBUTION INC. - LEAD-TIME ERRORS'.
            Ø5  FILLER                    PIC X(26)       VALUE SPACES.
            Ø5  FILLER                    PIC X(6)        VALUE 'PAGE:'.
            Ø5  MAIN-HDG-PAGE-NBR         PIC ZZ9.
            Ø5  FILLER                    PIC X(1Ø)       VALUE SPACES.

        Ø1  COLUMN-HEADING-1.
            Ø5  FILLER                    PIC X(16)       VALUE SPACES.
            Ø5  FILLER                    PIC X(5)        VALUE 'SALES'.
            Ø5  FILLER                    PIC X(4)        VALUE SPACES.
            Ø5  FILLER                    PIC X(5)        VALUE 'SALES'.
            Ø5  FILLER                    PIC X(4)        VALUE SPACES.
            Ø5  FILLER                    PIC X(8)        VALUE 'CUSTOMER'.
            Ø5  FILLER                    PIC X(4)        VALUE SPACES.
            Ø5  FILLER                    PIC X(8)        VALUE 'CUSTOMER'.
            Ø5  FILLER                    PIC X(6)        VALUE SPACES.
            Ø5  FILLER                    PIC X(4)        VALUE 'PART'.
            Ø5  FILLER                    PIC X(17)       VALUE SPACES.
            Ø5  FILLER                    PIC X(4)        VALUE 'UNIT'.
            Ø5  FILLER                    PIC X(8)        VALUE SPACES.
            Ø5  FILLER                    PIC X(5)        VALUE 'ORDER'.
            Ø5  FILLER                    PIC X(7)        VALUE SPACES.
            Ø5  FILLER                    PIC X(9)        VALUE
                                                          'REQUESTED'.
            Ø5  FILLER                    PIC X(5)        VALUE SPACES.
            Ø5  FILLER                    PIC X(4)        VALUE 'LEAD'.
            Ø5  FILLER                    PIC X(1Ø)       VALUE SPACES.

        Ø1  COLUMN-HEADING-2.
            Ø5  FILLER                    PIC X(8)        VALUE SPACES.
            Ø5  FILLER                    PIC X(6)        VALUE 'BRANCH'.
            Ø5  FILLER                    PIC X(3)        VALUE SPACES.
            Ø5  FILLER                    PIC X(3)        VALUE 'REP'.
            Ø5  FILLER                    PIC X(5)        VALUE SPACES.
            Ø5  FILLER                    PIC X(5)        VALUE 'ORDER'.
            Ø5  FILLER                    PIC X(5)        VALUE SPACES.
            Ø5  FILLER                    PIC X(6)        VALUE 'NUMBER'.
            Ø5  FILLER                    PIC X(8)        VALUE SPACES.
            Ø5  FILLER                    PIC X(2)        VALUE 'PO'.
            Ø5  FILLER                    PIC X(8)        VALUE SPACES.
            Ø5  FILLER                    PIC X(6)        VALUE 'NUMBER'.
            Ø5  FILLER                    PIC X(4)        VALUE SPACES.
            Ø5  FILLER                    PIC X(8)        VALUE 'QUANTITY'.
            Ø5  FILLER                    PIC X(4)        VALUE SPACES.
            Ø5  FILLER                    PIC X(5)        VALUE 'PRICE'.
            Ø5  FILLER                    PIC X(8)        VALUE SPACES.
            Ø5  FILLER                    PIC X(4)        VALUE 'DATE'.
            Ø5  FILLER                    PIC X(7)        VALUE SPACES.
            Ø5  FILLER                    PIC X(9)        VALUE
                                                          'SHIP DATE'.
```

FIG. 4-38 cont.

```
           Ø5  FILLER                   PIC X(5)         VALUE SPACES.
           Ø5  FILLER                   PIC X(4)         VALUE 'TIME'.
           Ø5  FILLER                   PIC X(1Ø)        VALUE SPACES.

       Ø1  DETAIL-LINE.
           Ø5  FILLER                   PIC X(1Ø)        VALUE SPACES.
           Ø5  DET-BRANCH               PIC 9(2).
           Ø5  FILLER                   PIC X(5)         VALUE SPACES.
           Ø5  DET-SALES-REP            PIC 9(3).
           Ø5  FILLER                   PIC X(5)         VALUE SPACES.
           Ø5  DET-SALES-ORD-NBR        PIC X(6).
           Ø5  FILLER                   PIC X(5)         VALUE SPACES.
           Ø5  DET-CUSTOMER-NBR         PIC 9(5).
           Ø5  FILLER                   PIC X(5)         VALUE SPACES.
           Ø5  DET-CUST-PO-NBR          PIC X(8).
           Ø5  FILLER                   PIC X(5)         VALUE SPACES.
           Ø5  DET-PART-NBR             PIC X(6).
           Ø5  FILLER                   PIC X(5)         VALUE SPACES.
           Ø5  DET-QUANTITY             PIC ZZZZ9.
           Ø5  FILLER                   PIC X(5)         VALUE SPACES.
           Ø5  DET-UNIT-PRICE           PIC ZZZ9.99.
           Ø5  FILLER                   PIC X(5)         VALUE SPACES.
           Ø5  DET-ORDER-MM             PIC 9(2).
           Ø5  FILLER                   PIC X(1)         VALUE '-'.
           Ø5  DET-ORDER-DD             PIC 9(2).
           Ø5  FILLER                   PIC X(1)         VALUE '-'.
           Ø5  DET-ORDER-YY             PIC 9(2).
           Ø5  FILLER                   PIC X(5)         VALUE SPACES.
           Ø5  DET-REQ-SHIP-MM          PIC 9(2).
           Ø5  FILLER                   PIC X(1)         VALUE '-'.
           Ø5  DET-REQ-SHIP-DD          PIC 9(2).
           Ø5  FILLER                   PIC X(1)         VALUE '-'.
           Ø5  DET-REQ-SHIP-YY          PIC 9(2).
           Ø5  FILLER                   PIC X(5)         VALUE SPACES.
           Ø5  DET-LEAD-TIME            PIC ZZZZ9.
           Ø5  FILLER                   PIC X(1Ø)        VALUE SPACES.

       Ø1  FINAL-TOTALS-LINE.
           Ø5  FILLER                   PIC X(8)         VALUE SPACES.
           Ø5  FILLER                   PIC X(28)
               VALUE 'NUMBER OF LEAD-TIME ERRORS:'.
           Ø5  NBR-OF-LEAD-TIME-ERRORS-OUT PIC ZZZ9.
           Ø5  FILLER                   PIC X(93)        VALUE SPACES.

       PROCEDURE DIVISION.

           PERFORM 1ØØØ-INITIALIZATION.
           PERFORM 2ØØØ-PROCESS
               UNTIL END-FLAG-ORDER-FILE = 'YES'.
           PERFORM 3ØØØ-EOJ.
           STOP RUN.

       1ØØØ-INITIALIZATION.
           OPEN INPUT  ORDER-FILE
                OUTPUT PRINT-FILE.
           MOVE CURRENT-DATE TO MAIN-HDG-DATE.
           PERFORM 91ØØ-READ-ORDER-FILE.

       2ØØØ-PROCESS.
           COMPUTE NBR-OF-DAYS-ORDER-DATE =
               ORD-YY * 365 + ORD-MM * 3Ø + ORD-DD.
           COMPUTE NBR-OF-DAYS-REQ-SHIP-DATE =
               ORD-REQ-SHIP-YY * 365 + ORD-REQ-SHIP-MM * 3Ø +
                   ORD-REQ-SHIP-DD.
           SUBTRACT NBR-OF-DAYS-ORDER-DATE FROM
               NBR-OF-DAYS-REQ-SHIP-DATE GIVING NBR-OF-DAYS-LEAD-TIME.
           IF ORD-BRANCH = 3 AND
               (NBR-OF-DAYS-LEAD-TIME < 3Ø OR
                NBR-OF-DAYS-LEAD-TIME > 365)
               PERFORM 21ØØ-EXTRACTED-RECORD.
           PERFORM 91ØØ-READ-ORDER-FILE.

       21ØØ-EXTRACTED-RECORD.
           IF LINE-COUNT > 5Ø
              PERFORM 211Ø-HEADINGS.
           MOVE ORD-BRANCH              TO DET-BRANCH.
           MOVE ORD-SALES-REP           TO DET-SALES-REP.
           MOVE ORD-SALES-ORD-NBR       TO DET-SALES-ORD-NBR.
           MOVE ORD-CUSTOMER-NBR        TO DET-CUSTOMER-NBR.
           MOVE ORD-CUST-PO-NBR         TO DET-CUST-PO-NBR.
           MOVE ORD-PART-NBR            TO DET-PART-NBR.
           MOVE ORD-QUANTITY            TO DET-QUANTITY.
           MOVE ORD-UNIT-PRICE          TO DET-UNIT-PRICE.
           MOVE ORD-YY                  TO DET-ORDER-YY.
```

FIG. 4-38 cont.

```
           MOVE ORD-MM                   TO DET-ORDER-MM.
           MOVE ORD-DD                   TO DET-ORDER-DD.
           MOVE ORD-REQ-SHIP-YY          TO DET-REQ-SHIP-YY.
           MOVE ORD-REQ-SHIP-MM          TO DET-REQ-SHIP-MM.
           MOVE ORD-REQ-SHIP-DD          TO DET-REQ-SHIP-DD.
           MOVE NBR-OF-DAYS-LEAD-TIME    TO DET-LEAD-TIME.
           ADD 1 TO NBR-OF-LEAD-TIME-ERRORS.
           WRITE PRINT-RECORD FROM DETAIL-LINE
               AFTER ADVANCING 2 LINES.
           ADD 2 TO LINE-COUNT.

       211Ø-HEADINGS.
           ADD 1 TO PAGE-COUNT.
           MOVE PAGE-COUNT TO MAIN-HDG-PAGE-NBR.
           WRITE PRINT-RECORD FROM MAIN-HEADING
               AFTER ADVANCING PAGE.
           WRITE PRINT-RECORD FROM COLUMN-HEADING-1
               AFTER ADVANCING 2 LINES.
           WRITE PRINT-RECORD FROM COLUMN-HEADING-2
               AFTER ADVANCING 1 LINE.
           MOVE 4 TO LINE-COUNT.

       3ØØØ-EOJ.
           MOVE NBR-OF-LEAD-TIME-ERRORS TO NBR-OF-LEAD-TIME-ERRORS-OUT.
           WRITE PRINT-RECORD FROM FINAL-TOTALS-LINE
              AFTER ADVANCING 3 LINES.
           CLOSE ORDER-FILE
                 PRINT-FILE.

       91ØØ-READ-ORDER-FILE.
           READ ORDER-FILE
               AT END
                   MOVE 'YES' TO END-FLAG-ORDER-FILE.
```

NEW COBOL ELEMENTS

AND/OR Logic

A single IF statement may contain several conditions, combined using the words AND or OR. When conditions are combined with the word AND in an IF statement, each condition must be true for the IF statement to be true. When conditions are combined with the word OR, at least one condition must be true for the IF statement to be true. When AND and OR are included in an IF statement, there is a definite order in which the conditions will be evaluated. This order is shown in Figure 4–39.

FIGURE 4–39

1. Parentheses
2. Arithmetic expressions
3. Relational operators
4. NOT
5. AND
6. OR

In the examples in Figure 4–40, values are provided so that a determination can be made whether the IF statement is true or false.

Notice the change in meaning when parentheses are used to change the order of evaluation.

The AND operator can be used in place of a nested IF in some cases. However, when a compound condition is placed in a single IF, we limit the number of alternative actions. (See Figure 4–41.)

DEBUGGING

Diagnostics

The following are a few of the more common diagnostics that are likely to be encountered in working with the material from this chapter.

```
⎧ALPHABETIC     ⎫
⎨NUMERIC-EDITED ⎬ DATA ITEM MAY NOT BE USED AS AN
⎩ALPHANUMERIC   ⎭   ARITHMETIC OPERAND
```

```
FIELD-A = 75
FIELD-B = 68

IF FIELD-A > FIELD-B + 6 AND FIELD-A < 100 . . .
               68    +6
      75   >     74         75    < 100
         TRUE         AND      TRUE
                     TRUE

IF FIELD-A > 100 OR FIELD-B < 100 . .
      75   > 100       68   < 100
        FALSE      OR     TRUE
                  TRUE

* IF FIELD-A NOT = 70 OR FIELD-A NOT = 75 . . .
        75    NOT = 70       75   NOT = 75
          TRUE          OR       FALSE
                       TRUE

IF FIELD-A = 70 AND FIELD-B = 65 OR FIELD-B > 65 . . .
      75   = 70        68   = 65       68   > 65
       FALSE     AND    FALSE            TRUE
               FALSE               OR    TRUE
                          TRUE

IF FIELD-A = 70 AND (FIELD-B = 65 OR FIELD-B > 65) . . .
                       68   = 65        68   > 65
                         FALSE     OR     TRUE
                                  TRUE
     75    = 70
      FALSE      AND              TRUE
                FALSE
```

FIGURE 4–40

```
     ⎧ADD      ⎫
     ⎪SUBTRACT ⎪
IN   ⎨MULTIPLY ⎬ STATEMENT
     ⎪DIVIDE   ⎪
     ⎩COMPUTE  ⎭
```

COBOL requires that all operands used in calculations be numeric. To correct the problem, the programmer should

1. Check the PICTURE clause for the data item in the DATA DIVISION. The PICTURE clause for a numeric item must not contain any A's, X's, Z's, or .'s.
2. Check whether the correct data item is in fact being used in the calculation. Be careful not to confuse the data item used in the calculation with the similarly named data item used when printing the value.

ELSE UNMATCHED BY CONDITION

COBOL attempts to match each ELSE with the closest unmatched IF. It issues this diagnotic when no IF is available to match an ELSE.

* Beware of combining NOTs and ORs when testing a single field; an IF statement will always be true if it tests a single field against two different values.

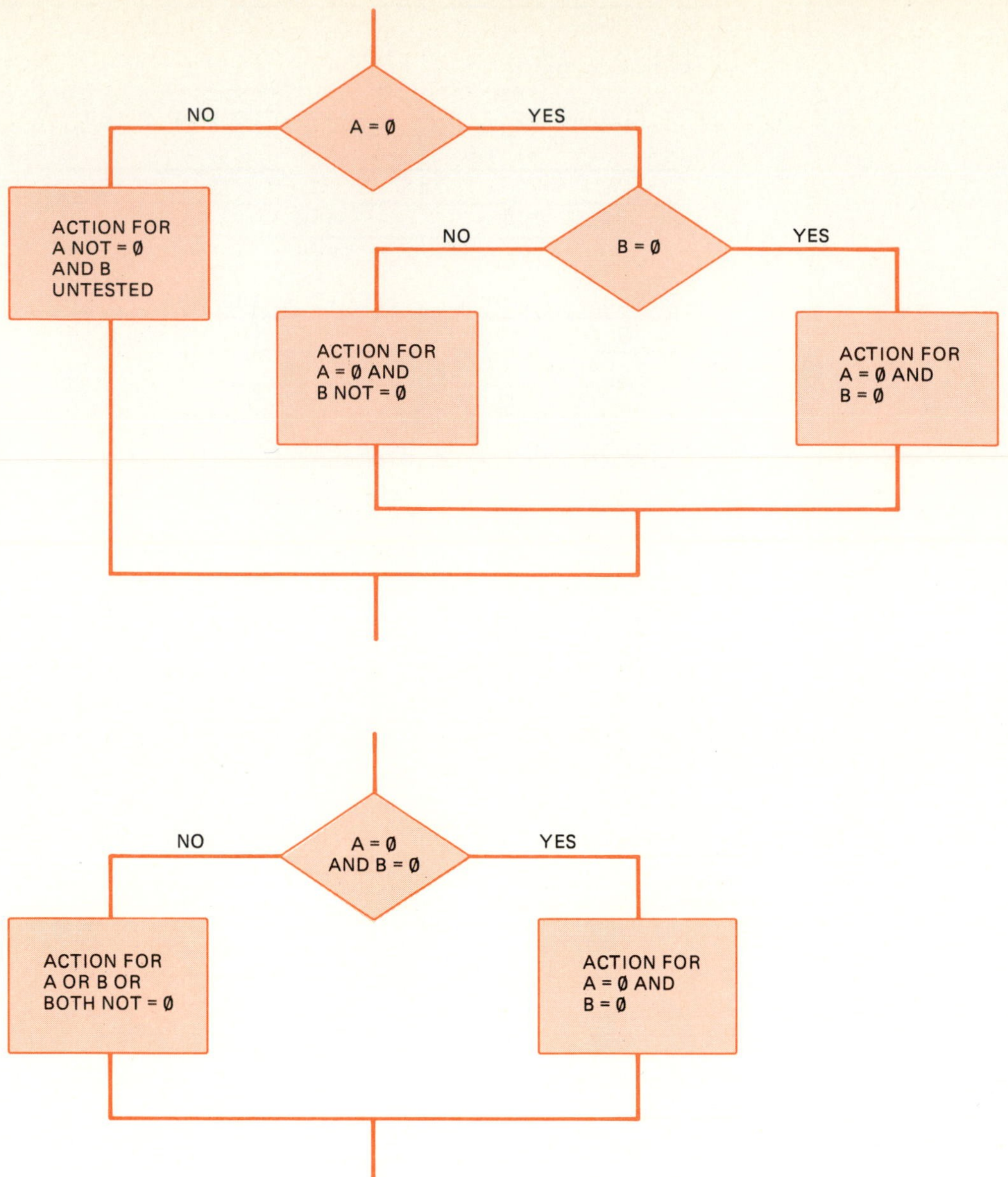

FIGURE 4–41

To correct the problem, the programmer should

1. Check for an unintended period in the IF/ELSE structure.
2. Draw brackets to connect each IF/ELSE pair. If an extra ELSE exists, check the code against a flowchart of the program or pseudocode.

```
NO ACTION INDICATED IF PRECEDING CONDITION IS TRUE
```

There is an IF statement with no action(s) following it.
To correct the problem, the programmer should

1. Look for a stray period in the IF statement.
2. Check the code against a flowchart or pseudocode. If there is a discrepancy, make the correction. If there is no discrepancy, use NEXT SENTENCE following the IF statement.

EBCDIC

Coding schemes have been developed to represent our alphabet, digits, and special characters when they are stored in a computer's memory. A commonly used coding scheme for internal data representation on mainframe computers is called the

Extended Binary Coded Decimal Interchange Code (EBCDIC). EBCDIC uses an eight-bit byte; given that each bit may be either a 0 or a 1, there are 256 possible combinations. We need 26 of these combinations to represent the letters A–Z and 10 more of these combinations to represent the digits 0–9. The remaining 220 combinations are available to represent lower-case letters and special characters such as $, #, and (.

An EBCDIC byte is separated into two parts, a zone portion and a digit portion. In the following chart we show the EBCDIC for the uppercase alphabet and digits. Both the binary and its hexadecimal equivalent are shown for each half-byte in Figure 4–42.

FIGURE 4–42

	ZONE		DIGIT	
	Binary	Hex	Binary	Hex
A–I	1100	C	0001 through 1001	1 through 9
J–R	1101	D	0001 through 1001	1 through 9
S–Z	1110	E	0010 through 1001	2 through 9
0–9	1111	F	0000 through 1001	0 through 9

From the figure, the letter A would be stored in memory as 1100 0001 (C1 in hexadecimal), while the letter I would be stored as 1100 1001 (C9). We often express the binary contents of memory in hexadecimal when printing them, since it takes only one-quarter the space on paper. Thus, memory dumps are often in hexadecimal. The relationship between the binary, decimal, and hexadecimal digits is shown in Figure 4–43.

FIGURE 4–43

BINARY	DECIMAL	HEXADECIMAL
0001	1	1
0010	2	2
0011	3	3
0100	4	4
0101	5	5
0110	6	6
0111	7	7
1000	8	8
1001	9	9
1010	10	A
1011	11	B
1100	12	C
1101	13	D
1110	14	E
1111	15	F

USAGE IS DISPLAY

Each time we define an area of storage, it has a USAGE. USAGE indicates the form for the internal representation of the data in computer memory. The format for the USAGE clause is as follows.

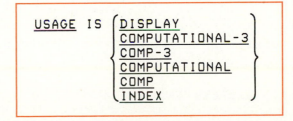

Format

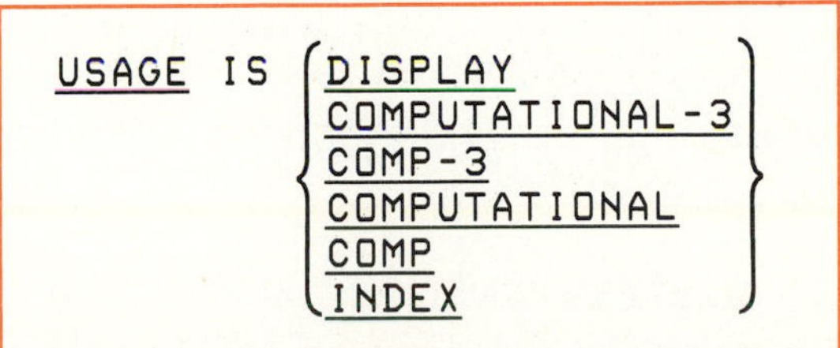
```
USAGE IS { DISPLAY
           COMPUTATIONAL-3
           COMP-3
           COMPUTATIONAL
           COMP
           INDEX }
```

This format indicates four types of USAGE. COMPUTATIONAL-3 and COMP-3 are two names for the same usage, as are COMPUTATIONAL and COMP. We shall cover USAGE IS DISPLAY in this chapter, and one of the other types of USAGE in each of the next three chapters.

DISPLAY stores data as one character per byte. If our choice of data format in storage is DISPLAY, we can achieve this in either of two ways. The first is to include a USAGE IS DISPLAY clause when we define each data item we want in that format.

```
05 FIELD-A        PIC 9(3)  VALUE ZEROS   USAGE IS DISPLAY.
```

The second and more common way is to leave the USAGE clause off. When there is no USAGE clause, DISPLAY is assumed. Thus, all of the storage in the programs of Chapters 2, 3, and 4 has been DISPLAY.

Let us look at what the storage contents are for a few data items. Study each item and relate it to the chart in Figure 4–42. Remember, what is shown is the hexadecimal representation of binary storage.

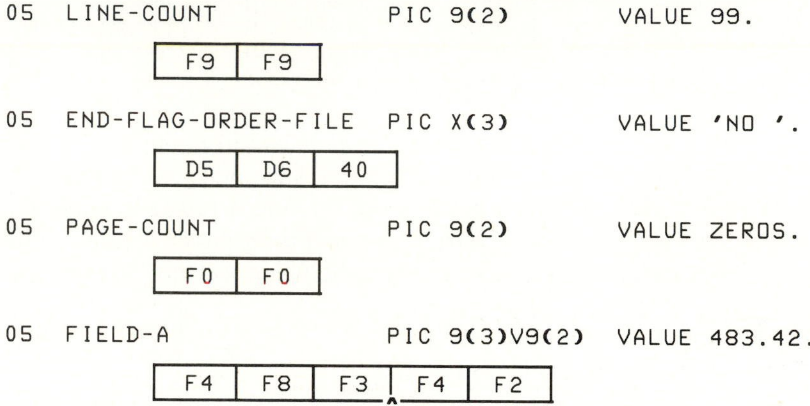

```
05  LINE-COUNT             PIC 9(2)        VALUE 99.
          | F9 | F9 |
05  END-FLAG-ORDER-FILE    PIC X(3)        VALUE 'NO '.
          | D5 | D6 | 40 |
05  PAGE-COUNT             PIC 9(2)        VALUE ZEROS.
          | F0 | F0 |
05  FIELD-A                PIC 9(3)V9(2)   VALUE 483.42.
          | F4 | F8 | F3 ^ F4 | F2 |
```

DISPLAY format is suitable for alphanumeric data and for some numeric data items. It is not, however, the most efficient format for data items to be used in calculations. In Chapter 5 we introduce the USAGE IS COMP-3 option of the USAGE clause and explain its advantage for data items use in calculations.

SUMMARY

The COBOL emphasis in this chapter has been on decision making and calculations. The following are formats for the COBOL verbs used.

The IF Statement

Format

```
IF {identifier-1       } IS [NOT] {GREATER THAN} {identifier-1       }
   {literal-1          }          {>           } {literal-1          }
   {arithmetic-exp-1   }          {LESS THAN   } {arithmetic-exp-1   }
                                  {<           }
                                  {EQUAL  TO   }
                                  {=           }
```

The COMPUTE Statement

Format

```
COMPUTE identifier-1 [ROUNDED] [identifier-2 [ROUNDED]] . . . =
{identifier-n         }
{literal-1            }
{arithmetic expression}
```

Arithmetic Operators

SYMBOL	MEANING
Binary Arithmetic Operators	
+	Addition
−	Subtraction
*	Multiplication
/	Division
**	Exponentiation
Unary Arithmetic Operators	
+	Multiplication by +1
−	Multiplication by −1

The ADD Statement

Format 1

```
     {identifier-1}  [identifier-2]
ADD  {literal-1   }  [literal-2   ]  . . .TO identifier-m

[ROUNDED] [identifier-n [ROUNDED]] . . .
```

Format 2

```
     {identifier-1} {identifier-2} [identifier-3]
ADD  {literal-1   } {literal-2   } [literal-3   ]  . . . GIVING

identifier-m [ROUNDED] [identifier-n [ROUNDED]] . . .
```

The SUBTRACT Statement

Format 1

```
          {identifier-1} [identifier-2]
SUBTRACT  {literal-1   } [literal-2   ]  . . . FROM identifier-m

[ROUNDED] [identifier-n [ROUNDED]] . . .
```

Format 2

```
         {identifier-1} [identifier-2]           {identifier-m}
SUBTRACT {literal-1   } [literal-2   ]  . . . FROM {literal-m   }

GIVING identifier-n [ROUNDED] [identifier-o [ROUNDED]] . . .
```

The MULTIPLY Statement

Format 1

```
         {identifier-1}
MULTIPLY {literal-1   }  BY identifier-2 [ROUNDED] [identifier-3

[ROUNDED]] . . .
```

Format 2

```
MULTIPLY {identifier-1} BY {identifier-2} GIVING identifier-3
         {literal-1   }    {literal-2   }
[ROUNDED] [identifier-4 [ROUNDED]] . . .
```

The DIVIDE Statement

Format 1

```
DIVIDE {identifier-1} INTO identifier-2 [ROUNDED] [identifier-3
       {literal-1   }
    [ROUNDED]] . . .
```

Format 2

```
DIVIDE {identifier-1} {INTO} {identifier-2} GIVING
       {literal-1   } {  BY} {literal-2   }
identifier-3 [ROUNDED] [identifier-4 [ROUNDED]] . . .
```

Format 3

```
DIVIDE {identifier-1} {INTO} {identifier-2} GIVING
       {literal-1   } {  BY} {literal-2   }
identifier-3 [ROUNDED] [REMAINDER identifier-4]
```

AND/OR

AND—Both conditions must be true for the compound condition to be true

OR—At least one of the conditions must be true for the compound condition to be true

Order of evaluation:

Parentheses
Arithmetic expressions
Relational operators
NOT
AND
OR

EXERCISES

I. For each COBOL statement listed, determine whether its syntax is valid or invalid.

______ **1.** ADD FIELD-A TO FIELD-B FIELD-C.
______ **2.** ADD FIELD-C TO 10.
______ **3.** SUBTRACT FIELD-A FIELD-B FROM FIELD-C ROUNDED.
______ **4.** SUBTRACT 1 FROM FIELD-B.
______ **5.** SUBTRACT FIELD-A FROM FIELD-B ROUNDED GIVING FIELD-C.
______ **6.** MULTIPLY 12 BY FIELD-B.
______ **7.** MULTIPLY 10 BY 16 GIVING 160.
______ **8.** MULTIPLY FIELD-A BY 10.
______ **9.** DIVIDE 10 INTO FIELD-A.
______ **10.** DIVIDE FIELD-A FIELD-B BY FIELD-C.

______ **11.** DIVIDE FIELD-A BY FIELD-B GIVING FIELD-C ROUNDED.
______ **12.** COMPUTE FIELD-A = (FIELD-B + 10) / FIELD-C).
______ **13.** COMPUTE FIELD-A ROUNDED = FIELD-B.
______ **14.** COMPUTE FIELD-A = 14.

II. For each of the following algebraic formulas, write a matching COBOL COMPUTE statement.
Example

X = A + B
COMPUTE X = A + B

1. $X = A + 1$
2. $X = AB$
3. $X = A^2$
4. $X = \frac{A + B}{C}$
5. $X = 3A - B$
6. $X = 6AB$
7. $X = A(C - 5)$
8. $X = A - 3 + AC$

III. For each of the following, write a COBOL ADD, SUBTRACT, MULTIPLY, or DIVIDE statement.
1. $X = A + B - C$
2. $X = A^2$
3. $X = A - B - C$
4. $X = \frac{A}{2}$
5. $X = \frac{A}{B}$
6. $X = 2A$

IV. Determine the value of FIELD-A after each of the following COMPUTE statements is executed.
1. COMPUTE FIELD-A = 10 * 5 + 2.
2. COMPUTE FIELD-A = 6 + 3 − 1 * 5.
3. COMPUTE FIELD-A = 12 + 20 / 5.
4. COMPUTE FIELD-A = 5 * 9 / 3.
5. COMPUTE FIELD-A = 10 + 2 * 6 + 1.
6. COMPUTE FIELD-A = 6 + 5 * 2 * 10.

V. From the following flowchart segments, code the matching COBOL IFs.

1.

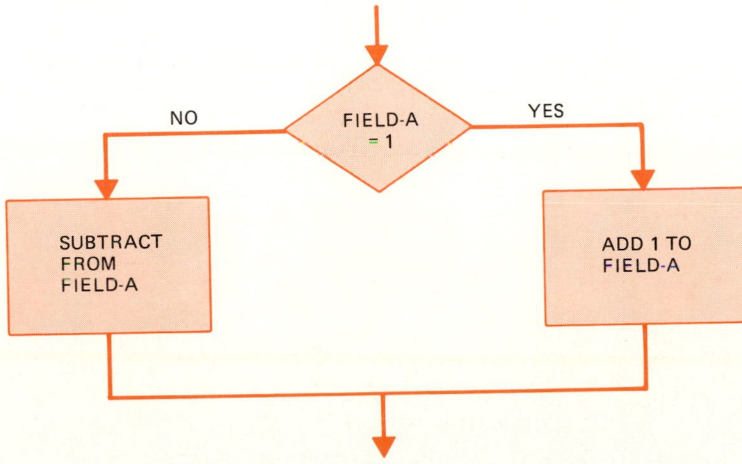

2.

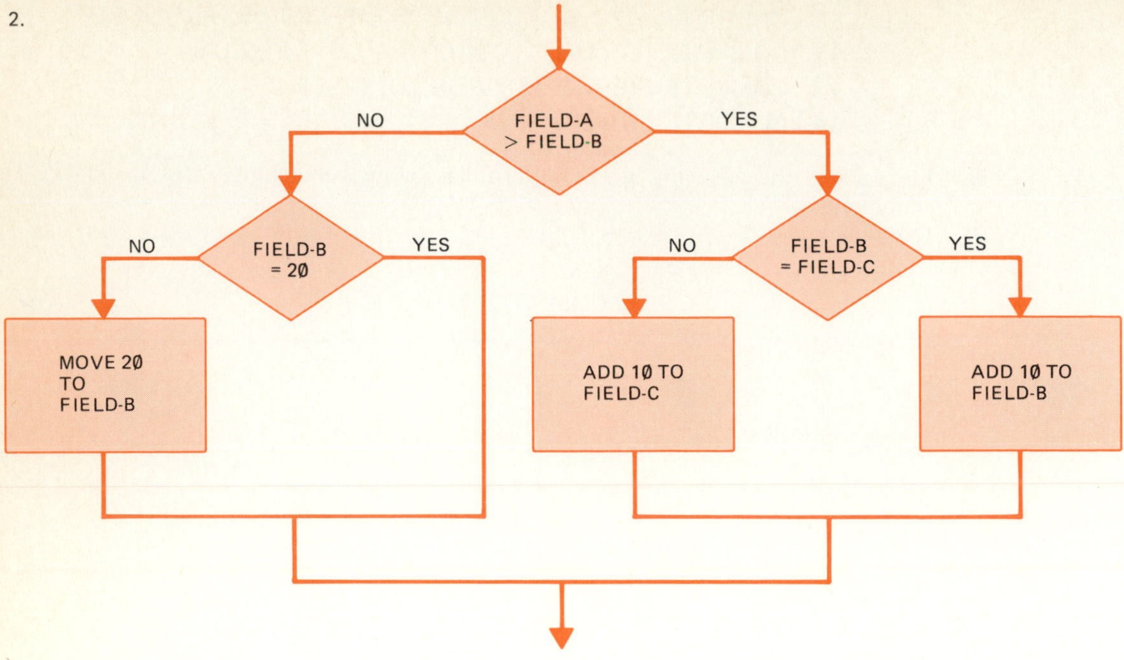

VI. For each of the following, write the COBOL PROCEDURE DIVISION code.

1. XYZ Corporation has decided that a freight charge should be calculated for each of their orders, based on the total price of the order. The freight charges to be assessed are as follows:

TOTAL PRICE	FREIGHT CHARGE
$0–$100.00	7% of the total price
$100.01–$500.00	5% of the total price
Over $500.00	No freight charge

Use the following data names:

TOTAL-PRICE
FREIGHT-CHARGE

2. XYZ Corporation has decided to give bonus checks to some of its employees. An employee will receive a bonus equal to 20 times his or her hourly pay rate if

(a) The employee is in Department Number 516 or 598, and
(b) The employee's hourly rate of pay is more than $6.00

Use the following data names:

HOURLY-PAY-RATE
TOTAL-BONUS
DEPARTMENT-NBR

PROJECTS

For each of the following specifications and input record layouts, design a print chart and code a COBOL program that satisfies the specification.

PROJECT 4–1 Payroll

PROGRAM SPECIFICATION

Program Name: PAY4

Program Function:

The program will produce a printed report of all employees in Division 1, and all employees in 4 whose gross pay per week is less than $750.00.

Input Files:

I. PAYROLL-FILE

INPUT DEVICE:	DISK
FILE ORGANIZATION:	SEQUENTIAL
RECORD LENGTH:	80 BYTES
FILE SEQUENCE:	ASCENDING ON DIVISION / DEPARTMENT

Output Files:

I. PRINT-FILE

OUTPUT DEVICE:	PRINTER
RECORD LENGTH:	133 BYTES

Processing Requirements:

For each record from the payroll file, calculate the gross pay (gross pay = pay rate × hours worked). The record should be included in the output report if it is from Division 1 or 4, and the gross pay is less than $750.00.

Totals for credit union deduction, medical insurance deduction, and gross pay should be accumulated and printed at the end of the report.

Output Requirements:

The following are formatting requirements for the report:

1. Each page of the report should contain:
   (a) a main heading which contains the company name, the report name, the current date, and a page number.
   (b) column headings which describe the items printed underneath them.
2. Detail lines should include all fields from the input and the gross pay.

3. Detail lines should be double spaced.
4. Total lines should be double spaced.

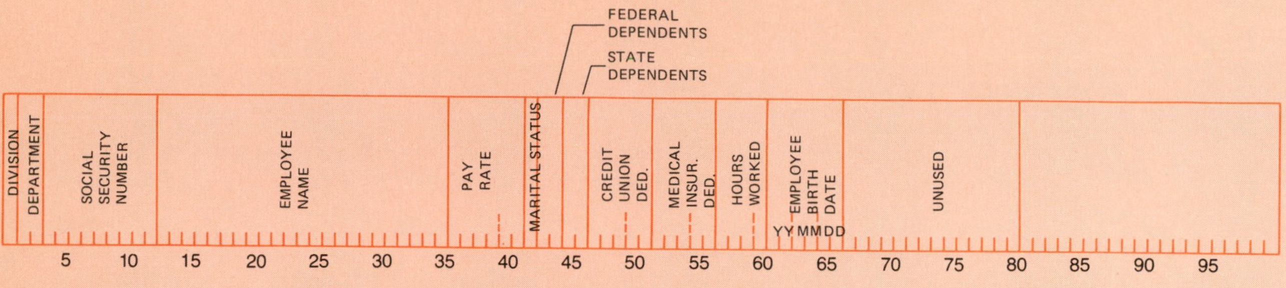

PROJECT 4–2 Inventory

PROGRAM SPECIFICATION

Program Name: INV4

Program Function:

The program will produce a printed report of all inventory items of types 1, 2, and 3 wherein the quantity on hand is less than the reorder level.

Input Files:

I. INVENTORY-FILE

INPUT DEVICE:	DISK
FILE ORGANIZATION:	SEQUENTIAL
RECORD LENGTH:	80 BYTES
FILE SEQUENCE:	ASCENDING ON INVENTORY STOCK NUMBER

Output Files:

I. PRINT-FILE

OUTPUT DEVICE:	PRINTER
RECORD LENGTH:	133 BYTES

Processing Requirements:

A record should be included in the output report if it is of either type 1, 2, or 3, and the quantity on hand is less than the reorder level.

Totals for the quantity on hand and the quantity on order should be accumulated and printed at the end of the report.

Output Requirements:

The following are formatting requirements for the report:

1. Each page of the report should contain:
   (a) a main heading which contains the company name, the report name, the current date, and a page number.
   (b) column headings which describe the items printed underneath them.
2. Detail lines should include all fields from the input.

3. Detail lines should be double spaced.
4. Total lines should be double spaced.

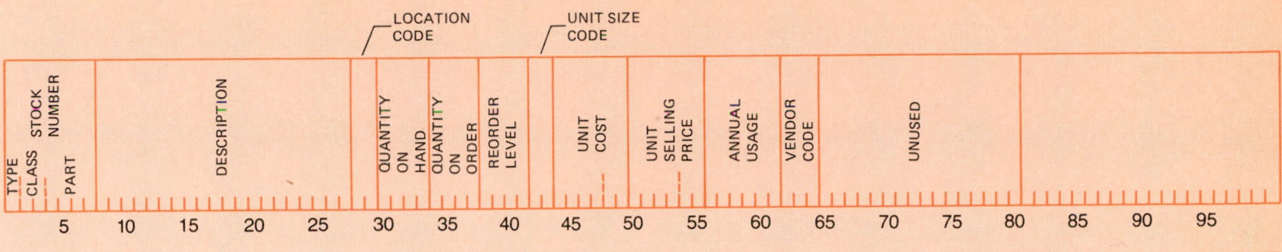

PROJECT 4–3 Accounts Payable

PROGRAM SPECIFICATION

Program Name: AP4

Program Function:

The program will produce a printed report of all invoices due within 10 days of 10–30–87. This date is used in place of the current date in order to produce consistent output whenever the program is executed.

Input Files:

I. ACCOUNTS-PAYABLE-FILE

INPUT DEVICE:	DISK
FILE ORGANIZATION:	SEQUENTIAL
RECORD LENGTH:	80 BYTES
FILE SEQUENCE:	ASCENDING ON DIVISION CONTROL-NBR

Output Files:

I. PRINT-FILE

OUTPUT DEVICE:	PRINTER
RECORD LENGTH:	133 BYTES

Processing Requirements:

For each record from the accounts payable file, calculate the difference between the due date and 10–30–87. The record should be included in the output report if the difference is 10 days or less.

Totals for invoice amount, invoice tax, invoice labor, invoice freight, and invoice hard goods should be accumulated and printed at the end of the report.

Output Requirements

The following are formatting requirements for the report:

1. Each page of the report should contain:
   (a) a main heading which contains the company name, the report name, the current date, and a page number.
   (b) column headings which describe the items printed underneath them.

2. Detail lines should include all fields from the input and the numerical difference between the two dates.
3. Detail lines should be double spaced.
4. Total lines should be double spaced.

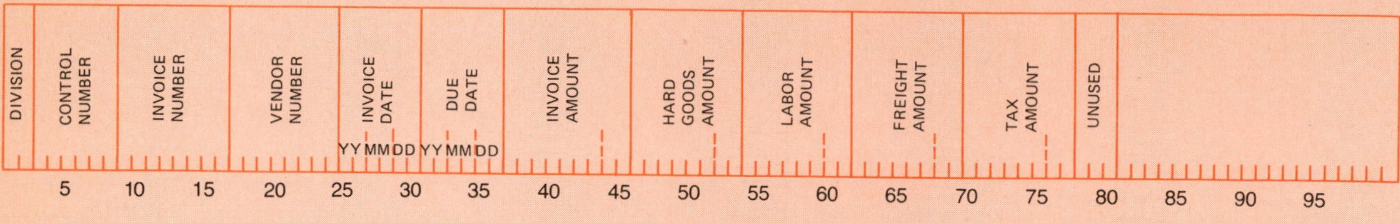

PROJECT 4–4 Pension

PROGRAM SPECIFICATION

Program Name: PEN4

Program Function:

The program will produce a printed report of all pension records wherein the employee is over 60 years of age with eight or more years of service to the company.

Input Files:

I. PENSION-FILE

INPUT DEVICE:	DISK
FILE ORGANIZATION:	SEQUENTIAL
RECORD LENGTH:	80 BYTES
FILE SEQUENCE:	ASCENDING ON SOCIAL SECURITY NUMBER

Output Files:

I. PRINT-FILE

OUTPUT DEVICE:	PRINTER
RECORD LENGTH:	133 BYTES

Processing Requirements:

For each record from the pension file, calculate the age and number of full years of service for each employee as of 10–30–87. This date is used in place of the current date to produce consistent output each time the program is executed. The record should be included in the output report if the age is 60 or greater and the number of years of service is 8 or greater.

Totals of gross salary, employee contribution, employer contribution, and balance forward should be accumulated and printed at the end of the report.

Output Requirements

The following are formatting requirements for the report:

1. Each page of the report should contain:
   (a) a main heading which contains the company name, the report name, the current date, and a page number.
   (b) column headings which describe the items printed underneath them.
2. Detail lines should include all fields from the input and the age and years of service.

3. Detail lines should be double spaced.
4. Total lines should be double spaced.

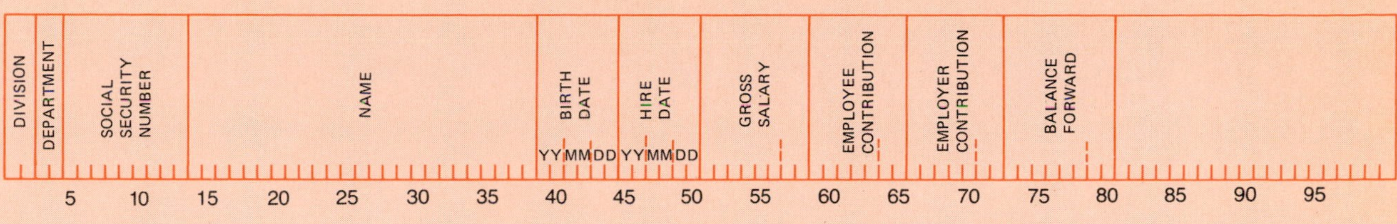

PROJECT 4–5 Bill of Materials

PROGRAM SPECIFICATION

Program Name: BOM4

Program Function:

This program will produce a printed report of all bill-of-materials records wherein the product line is less than 100 and the extended cost (quantity times cost) is greater than $5.00.

Input Files:

I. BILL-OF-MATERIALS-FILE

INPUT DEVICE:	DISK
FILE ORGANIZATION:	SEQUENTIAL
RECORD LENGTH:	55 BYTES
FILE SEQUENCE:	ASCENDING ON PRODUCT LINE PART NUMBER

Output Files:

I. PRINT-FILE

OUTPUT DEVICE:	PRINTER
RECORD LENGTH:	133 BYTES

Processing Requirements:

For each record from the bill-of-materials file, calculate the extended cost (quantity times cost). The record should be included in the output report if the product line is less than 100 and the extended cost is greater than $5.00.

The total of extended cost should be accumulated and printed at the end of the report.

Output Requirements

The following are formatting requirements for the report:

1. Each page of the report should contain:
   (a) a main heading which contains the company name, the report name, the current date, and a page number.
   (b) column headings which describe the items printed underneath them.
2. Detail lines should include all fields from the input and the extended cost.

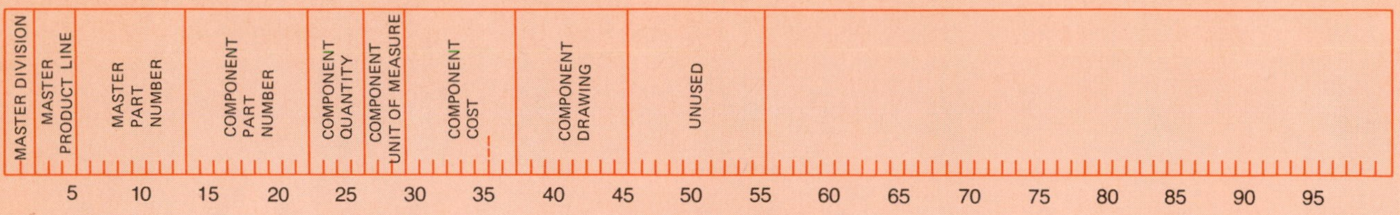

PROJECT 4–6 Manufacturing Cost

PROGRAM SPECIFICATION

Program Name: COST4

Program Function:

The program will produce a printed report of all cost records wherein the product line is greater than 100 and the total amount of all cost factors for a single part number is greater than $100.00.

Input Files:

I. COST-FILE

INPUT DEVICE:	DISK
FILE ORGANIZATION:	SEQUENTIAL
RECORD LENGTH:	75 BYTES
FILE SEQUENCE:	ASCENDING ON PRODUCT LINE PART NUMBER

Output Files:

I. PRINT-FILE

OUTPUT DEVICE:	PRINTER
RECORD LENGTH:	133 BYTES

Processing Requirements:

For each record from the cost file, calculate the total of the cost factors (steel, paint, hardware, packaging, and labor). The record should be included in the output report if the product line is greater than 100 and the total of the cost factors is greater than $100.00.

A count should be made of the records processed and should be printed at the end of the report.

Output Requirements

The following are formatting requirements for the report:

1. Each page of the report should contain:
   (a) a main heading which contains the company name, the report name, the current date, and a page number.
   (b) column headings which describe the items printed underneath them.
2. Detail lines should include all fields from the input and the total of all cost factors.

3. Detail lines should be double spaced.
4. The count of total records should be double spaced.

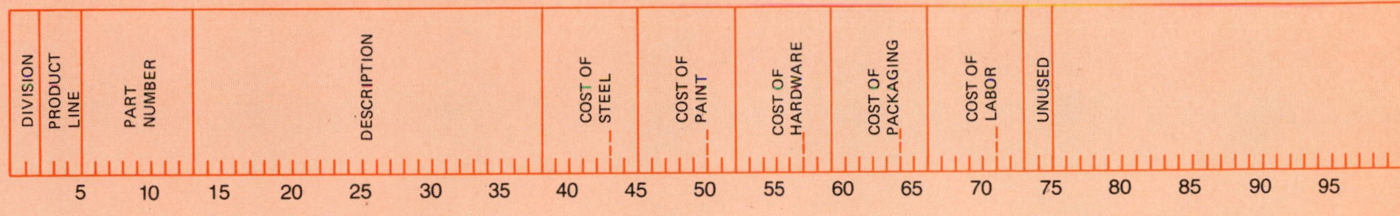

CHAPTER

5

Control Breaks, I

The programming logic concept presented in this chapter is the production of reports based on breaks (changes) in control fields. In the first program, a break in the control field (a branch of an organization) produces a page change so that each new branch starts on a new page. Final totals for quantity and extended price are also produced.

The second program produces a report with two levels of totals for quantity and extended price. The first level is by branch, the second by final totals. The technique for efficient accumulation of these two levels is called *rolling totals.*

The COBOL language emphasis is on output editing, which is the insertion of new characters and/or the replacement of existing characters in a data item. Some insertion characters are the dollar sign, decimal point, comma, plus sign, and minus sign. Some replacement characters are blanks and asterisks (for leading zeros). The use of condition-names (88 levels) and signed data is also included.

The debugging section presents diagnostics that might be generated by errors in the use of the output editing symbols or condition-names, a method of storing numeric data in a packed manner, and methods for tracing the execution steps of the program and displaying the values of data items.

PROGRAM SPECIFICATION: BREAK-1

The first programming project in this chapter is a listing of orders by branch. Each branch is to start on a new page. The report will include final totals of quantity and extended price. The program specification is shown in Figure 5–1.

Input Record Layout

The input record layout is shown in Figure 5–2. This is the same file used in previous projects, repeated here for convenience.

Print Chart

The print chart for the project is shown in Figure 5–3. It includes a final total line for quantity and extended price.

LOGIC FOR SINGLE-LEVEL BREAK AND FINAL TOTALS

The logic design for the BREAK-1 program is shown by means of a hierarchy chart in Figure 5–4, pseudocode in Figure 5–5, and a flowchart in Figure 5–6.

PROGRAM SPECIFICATION

Program Name: BREAK-1

Program Function:

The program will produce a printed report of an order file. The report will include final totals for quantity and extended price. Each branch will begin on a new page.

Input Files:

I. ORDER-FILE

INPUT DEVICE:	DISK
FILE ORGANIZATION:	SEQUENTIAL
RECORD LENGTH:	70 BYTES
FILE SEQUENCE:	ASCENDING ON BRANCH / SALES REP

Output Files:

I. PRINT-FILE

OUTPUT DEVICE:	PRINTER
RECORD LENGTH:	133 BYTES

Processing Requirements:

Each record read from the order file should be printed on one line of the output report. All input fields, except the customer purchase order number, are to be included on the output. The extended price is to be calculated for each order and printed on the output. (Extended price = quantity × unit price.)

Totals for quantity and extended price are to be accumulated and printed for the entire company.

Output Requirements:

The following are formatting requirements for the report:

1. Each page of the report should contain:
   (a) a main heading which includes the company name, the report name, the report date, and a page number.
   (b) column headings which describe the items printed underneath them.
2. Detail lines should include all fields from the input (except the customer purchase order number) and the extended price.
3. Detail lines should be double spaced.
4. Each new branch should begin on a new page.
5. The final total line should be double spaced.

FIGURE 5–1

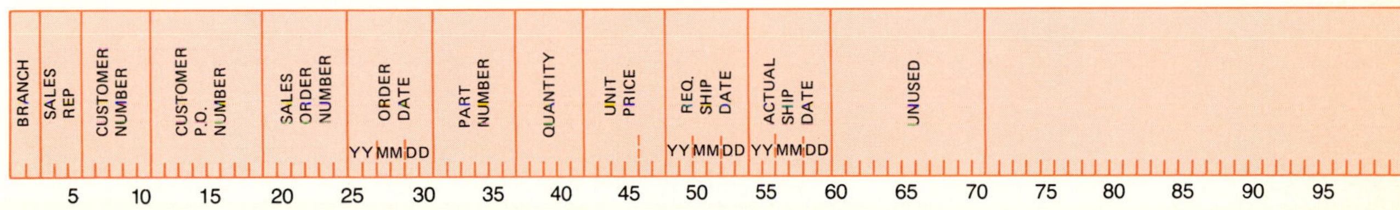

FIGURE 5–2

```
       DATE: XX/XX/XX                        PRODUCT DISTRIBUTION INC. - CURRENT ORDERS                           PAGE: ZZ9

              SALES CUSTOMER   SALES      ORDER      REQUESTED    ACTUAL      PART                  UNIT          EXTENDED
       BRANCH  REP   NUMBER   ORDER       DATE      SHIP DATE   SHIP DATE    NUMBER    QUANTITY     PRICE           PRICE

         99    999   99999    X XXXXX   99/99/99    99/99/99    99/99/99    XXXXXX      ZZ,ZZ9    $$,$$9.99    $$,$$$,$$9.99

         99    999   99999    X XXXXX   99/99/99    99/99/99    99/99/99    XXXXXX      ZZ,ZZ9    $$,$$9.99    $$,$$$,$$9.99


         FINAL TOTALS                                                                 ZZZ,ZZ9              $$$,$$$,$$9.99
```

FIGURE 5–3

Hierarchy Chart

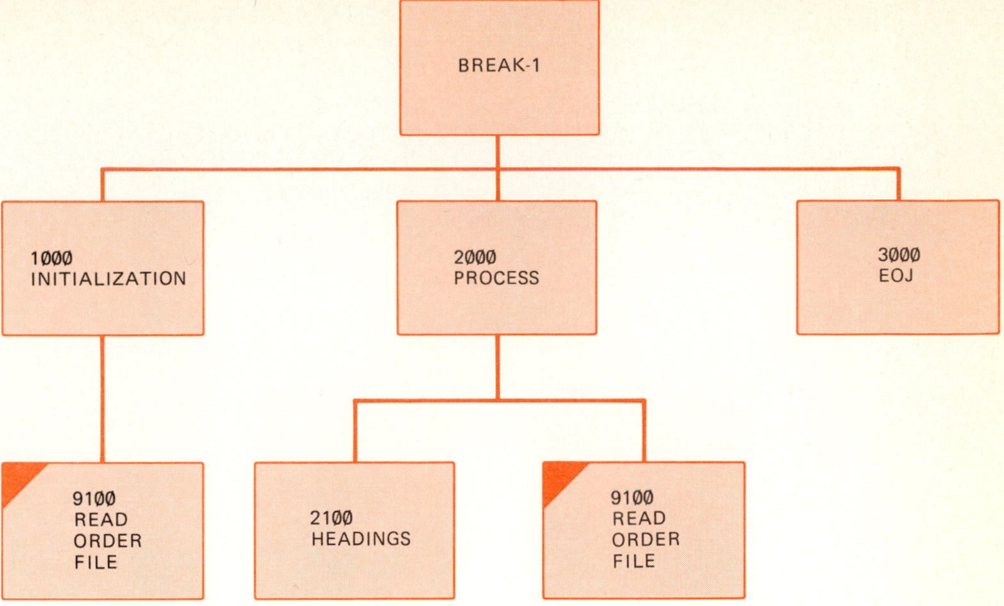

FIGURE 5–4

Pseudocode

```
MAIN LINE
      DO initialization
      DO WHILE more order records
            DO process
      ENDDO
      DO end of job
INITIALIZATION
      OPEN files
      MOVE date to heading
      DO read an order
      MOVE branch to branch hold
PROCESS
      IF branch = branch hold
           IF line count > 50
                DO headings
           ENDIF
      ELSE
            DO headings
            MOVE branch to branch hold
      ENDIF
      MOVE input to output
      CALCULATE extended price
      MOVE extended price to output
      ADD quantity to final quantity
      ADD extended price to final extended price
      WRITE detail line
      ADD 2 to line count
      DO read an order
HEADINGS
      ADD 1 to page count
      MOVE page count to output
      WRITE main heading line
```

FIGURE 5–5

cont. on next page

```
     WRITE column heading line one
     WRITE column heading line two
     MOVE 4 to line count
END OF JOB
     MOVE final quantity to output
     MOVE final extended price to output
     WRITE final total line
     CLOSE files
READ AN ORDER
     READ order file
```

FIGURE 5–5 cont.

Flowchart

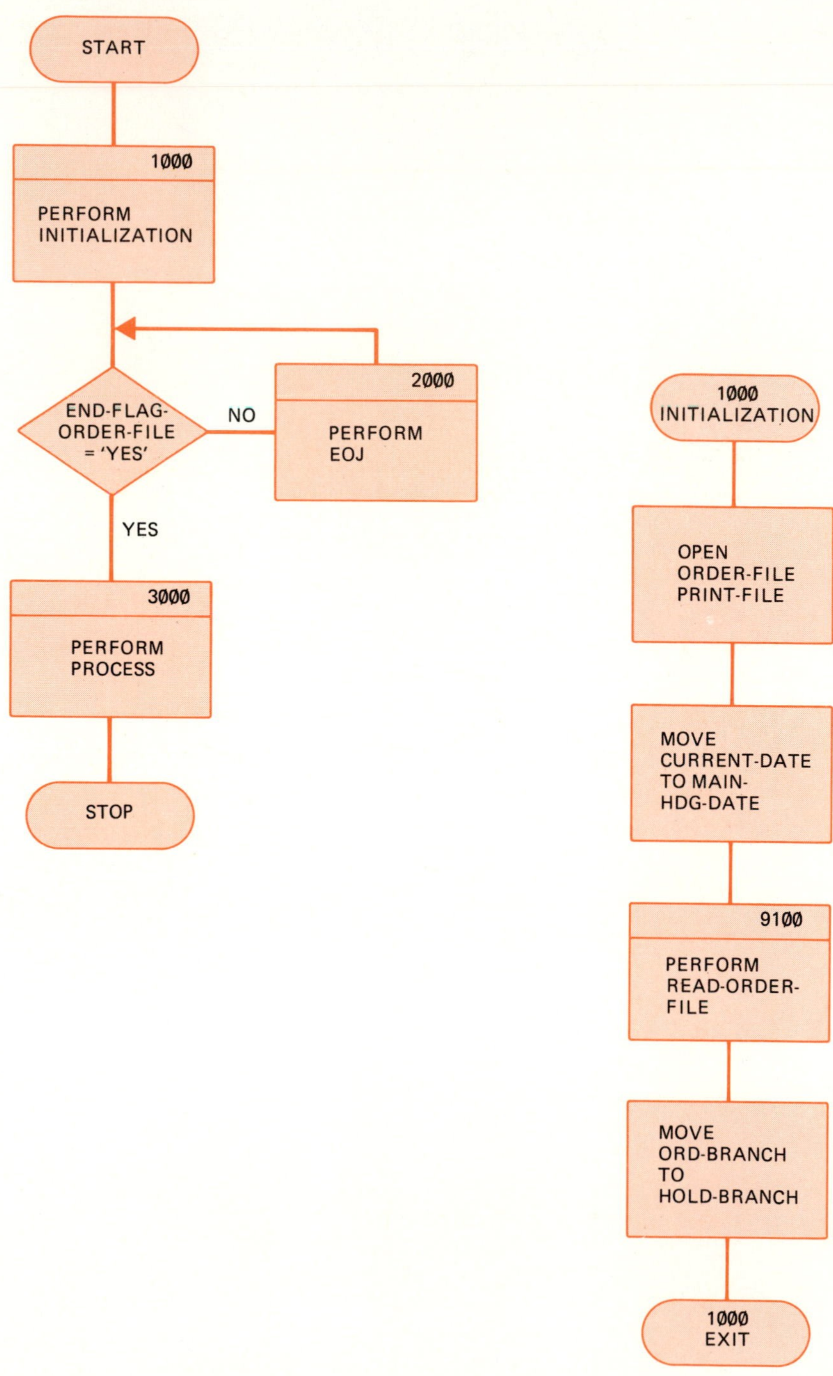

FIGURE 5–6

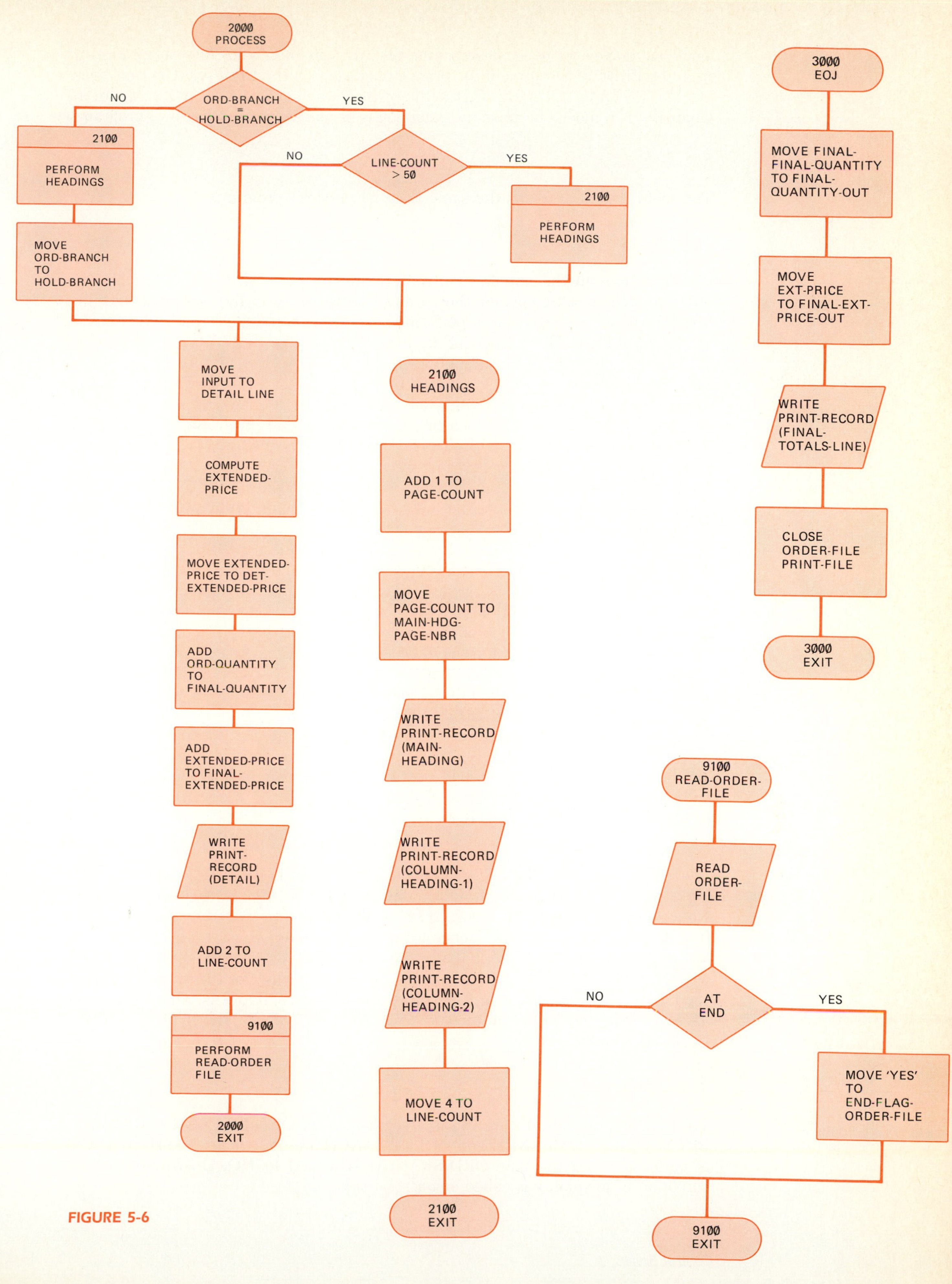
2000
PROCESS
ORD-BRANCH
=
HOLD-BRANCH
NO
YES
2100
PERFORM
HEADINGS
MOVE
ORD-BRANCH
TO
HOLD-BRANCH
LINE-COUNT
> 50
NO
YES
2100
PERFORM
HEADINGS
MOVE
INPUT TO
DETAIL LINE
COMPUTE
EXTENDED-
PRICE
MOVE EXTENDED-
PRICE TO DET-
EXTENDED-PRICE
ADD
ORD-QUANTITY
TO
FINAL-QUANTITY
ADD
EXTENDED-PRICE
TO FINAL-
EXTENDED-PRICE
WRITE
PRINT-
RECORD
(DETAIL)
ADD 2 TO
LINE-COUNT
9100
PERFORM
READ-ORDER
FILE
2000
EXIT
2100
HEADINGS
ADD 1 TO
PAGE-COUNT
MOVE
PAGE-COUNT TO
MAIN-HDG-
PAGE-NBR
WRITE
PRINT-RECORD
(MAIN-
HEADING)
WRITE
PRINT-RECORD
(COLUMN-
HEADING-1)
WRITE
PRINT-RECORD
(COLUMN-
HEADING-2)
MOVE 4 TO
LINE-COUNT
2100
EXIT
3000
EOJ
MOVE FINAL-
FINAL-QUANTITY
TO FINAL-
QUANTITY-OUT
MOVE
EXT-PRICE
TO FINAL-EXT-
PRICE-OUT
WRITE
PRINT-RECORD
(FINAL-
TOTALS-LINE)
CLOSE
ORDER-FILE
PRINT-FILE
3000
EXIT
9100
READ-ORDER-
FILE
READ
ORDER-
FILE
AT
END
NO
YES
MOVE 'YES'
TO
END-FLAG-
ORDER-FILE
9100
EXIT

FIGURE 5-6

Explanation of Logic

There are no new routines needed in the BREAK-1 program. Headings are performed from the PROCESS routine if the branch changes or if the LINE-COUNT exceeds 50. The EXTRACTED-RECORD routine which was in the EXTRACT program in Chapter 4 is removed because no extraction is necessary in the BREAK-1 program.

MAIN LINE

The main routine remains the same as in all previous programs.

1000-INITIALIZATION

The first steps in the initialization routine are the same as in the LEAD-TIME program. The files are opened, the current date is placed in the headings, and the first READ of the input file is performed. The last step (MOVE ORD-BRANCH TO HOLD-BRANCH) is a part of the logic necessary to cause a page change on the report each time the branch changes.

The data is in ascending order by branch. Therefore, records for one branch number are grouped together, and each time the branch changes the new branch will be a higher number. To determine when the value of a field has changed, the new value is compared with the previous value. Because each value for a data item is destroyed when the new one is read into the same area, a separate area is needed in which to save the old value. A field called HOLD-BRANCH has been created for this purpose. Note that only the field from the input which is needed for comparion is saved.

If the hold area is initialized to zero, the first value read for ORD-BRANCH is not likely to be equal to the value in the hold area. This difference (zero versus the value in the first record) indicates that it is time to change pages. Notice that there are now two things that can cause a page break: when the LINE-COUNT exceeds 50, and when the branch changes. Either of these things can produce the first set of headings. LINE-COUNT will produce the first set of headings if it is initialized to a value higher than 50. Also, the comparison of ORD-BRANCH and HOLD-BRANCH in 2000-PROCESS will cause the headings to print if HOLD-BRANCH is not equal to ORD-BRANCH.

Only one set of headings is needed at the beginning of the report. To avoid producing two sets of headings at that time, the hold area for the branch is updated after the first READ in 1000-INITIALIZATION. Updating of the hold area is done by placing the following code immediately after 9100-READ-ORDER-FILE is performed in 1000-INITIALIZATION:

```
MOVE ORD-BRANCH TO HOLD-BRANCH.
```

Now, in 2000-PROCESS, when the value of ORD-BRANCH from the first input record is compared against the value of HOLD-BRANCH, they will be equal. Notice that the first record was read *before* the value was moved to the hold area. It is not good programming practice to assume that one knows the first value that will be read and set the hold to that value in WORKING-STORAGE. The program would then be inflexible and would work only when the data for the branch selected came first. If the first branch is assumed to be 1, what happens when Branch 1 has no data due to a shutdown? (See Figure 5–7 for the logic of 1000-INITIALIZATION.)

2000-PROCESS

The first step in 2000-PROCESS is a comparison of ORD-BRANCH and HOLD-BRANCH. If ORD-BRANCH and HOLD-BRANCH are not equal, 2100-HEADINGS is performed and the new ORD-BRANCH is moved to HOLD-BRANCH. This condition of inequality is called a *control break*.

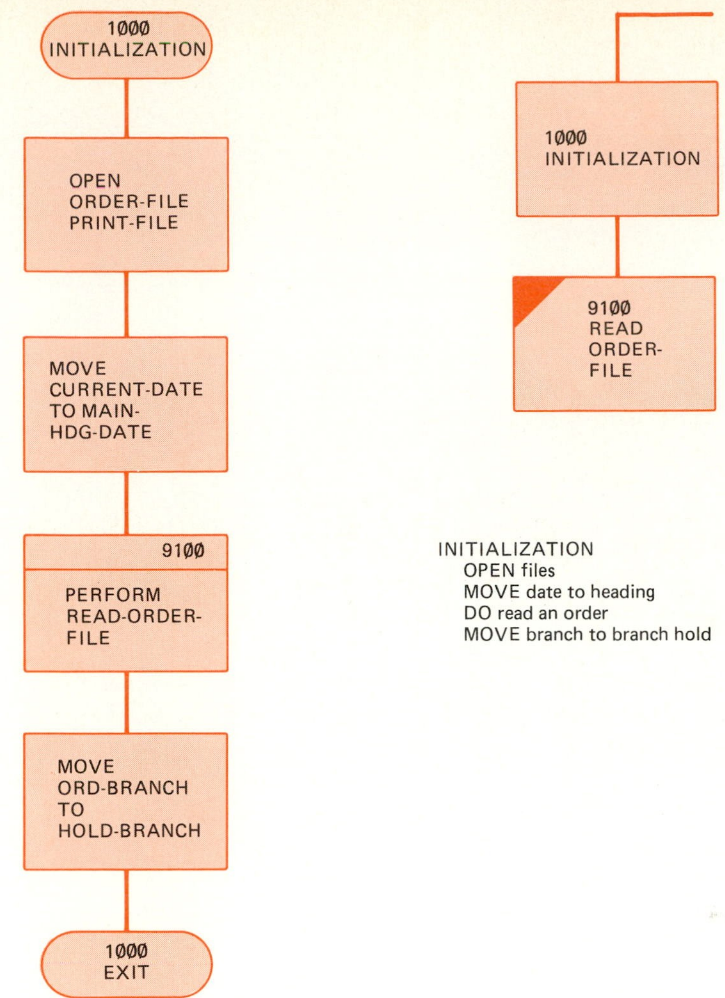

FIGURE 5–7

Because ORD-BRANCH was moved to HOLD-BRANCH after the READ in 1000-INITIALIZATION, the two will be equal during the processing of the first record, and for all remaining records of the same branch. Since ORD-BRANCH and HOLD-BRANCH are equal when the first record is processed, LINE-COUNT will be tested for a value greater than 50. LINE-COUNT is greater than 50 for the first record, so the first set of headings will be produced.

No matter which path is taken in the nested IF structure, control subsequently passes to MOVE INPUT TO OUTPUT. Each item from the input that is to be printed is moved individually to the detail line. Then, EXTENDED-PRICE is calculated and moved to an area on the detail line, and ORD-QUANTITY and EXTENDED-PRICE are added to the final totals.

Next, the detail line is written. The detail line that was just built is transferred to PRINT-RECORD and then to the printer. Then the routine that reads the next record is performed. After 2000-PROCESS is complete, control returns to the main routine to test END-FLAG-ORDER-FILE. If the READ was successful, END-FLAG-ORDER-FILE will still be NO and 2000-PROCESS will be executed again to process the record which was just read. (See Figure 5–8.)

At some point, ORD-BRANCH and HOLD-BRANCH will not be equal. This indicates the first record of a new branch. The inequality condition will cause a set of headings to be printed, so that the record with the new branch number will be printed on a new page. To ensure that each subsequent record for this new branch does not cause additional headings, the hold area is updated by moving

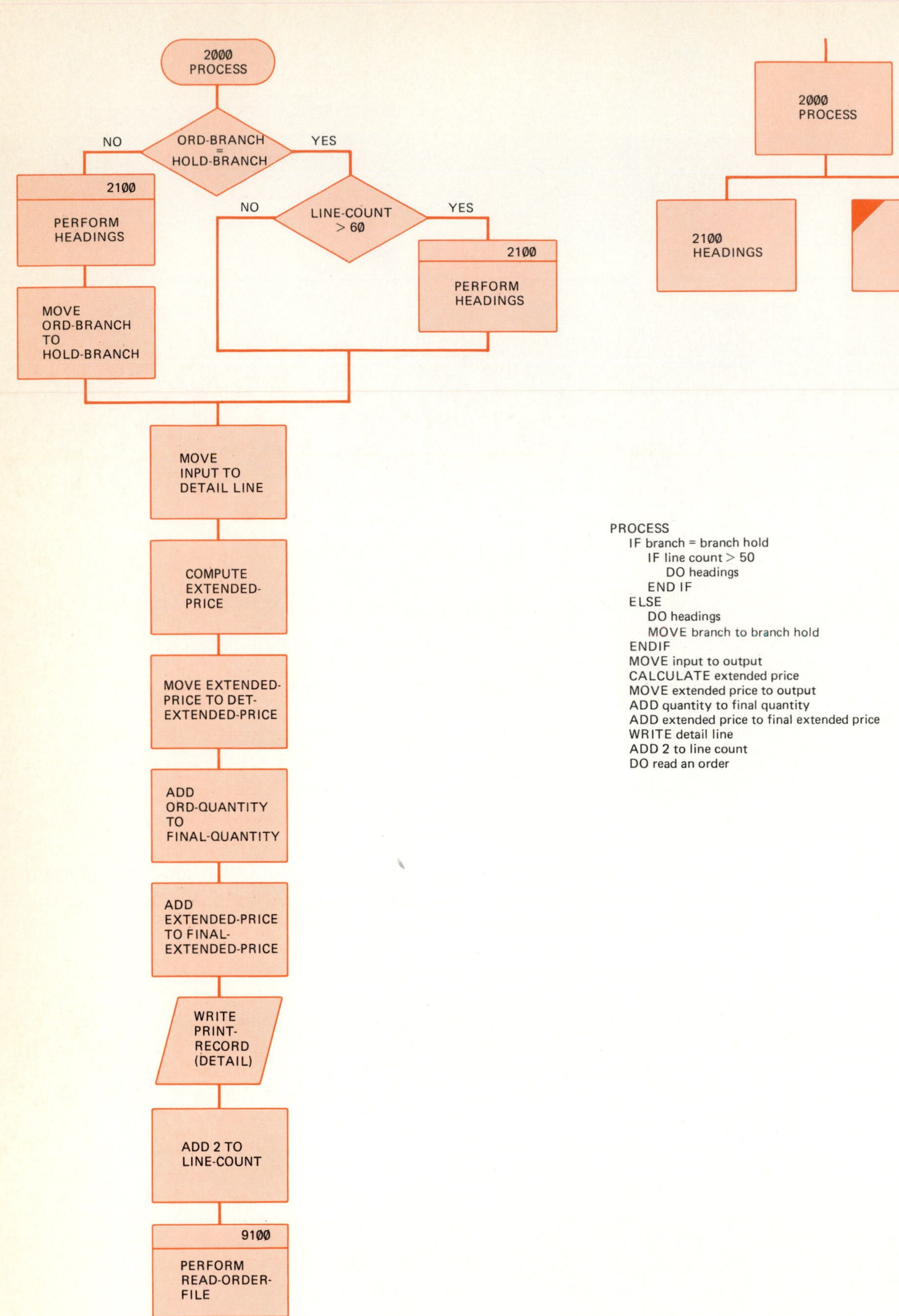


```
PROCESS
    IF branch = branch hold
        IF line count > 50
            DO headings
        END IF
    ELSE
        DO headings
        MOVE branch to branch hold
    ENDIF
    MOVE input to output
    CALCULATE extended price
    MOVE extended price to output
    ADD quantity to final quantity
    ADD extended price to final extended price
    WRITE detail line
    ADD 2 to line count
    DO read an order
```

FIGURE 5–8

ORD-BRANCH to HOLD-BRANCH. Figure 5–9 shows the contents of ORD-BRANCH and HOLD-BRANCH at various stages in the execution of the program.

FIGURE 5–9

ORD-BRANCH	HOLD-BRANCH	
?	0	At the beginning of execution
1	0	After the READ in 1000-INITIALIZATION
1	1	After MOVE ORD-BRANCH TO HOLD-BRANCH in 1000-INITIALIZATION
1	1	
1	1	As each record in Branch 1 is read
⋮	⋮	⋮
2	1	After the first record of Branch 2 is read
2	2	After headings are written and ORD-BRANCH is moved to HOLD-BRANCH

2100-HEADINGS

The routine 2100-HEADINGS will be performed from 2000-PROCESS under either of two conditions: (1) when LINE-COUNT is greater than 50, and (2) when there is a control break on ORD-BRANCH. Headings are written when LINE-COUNT exceeds 50 so that nothing is written over the perforations on the continuous-form paper. The COBOL instructions to write the headings will include a command to advance the paper to the top of a new page. Headings are also written when there is a change in ORD-BRANCH, since the specifications for the report ask that each branch begin on a new page.

After the headings are written, LINE-COUNT is set to 4. This has the effect of setting LINE-COUNT to zero and then adding 4 to it to account for the lines used by the headings. (See Figure 5–10 for the heading routine.)

3000-EOJ

Final totals which were accumulated as each record was processed are moved to output and written. The files are closed, and control returns to the main routine, where STOP RUN is encountered. (See Figure 5–11.)

9100-READ-ORDER-FILE

A record is read from the ORDER-FILE. If the READ is successful, the routine is complete. If the READ encounters the end-of-file indicator, 'YES' is moved to END-FLAG-ORDER-FILE. This routine is performed at the end of 2000-PROCESS just before returning to the main routine to test END-FLAG-ORDER-FILE. It is also performed once in 1000-INITIALIZATION. (See Figure 5–12.)

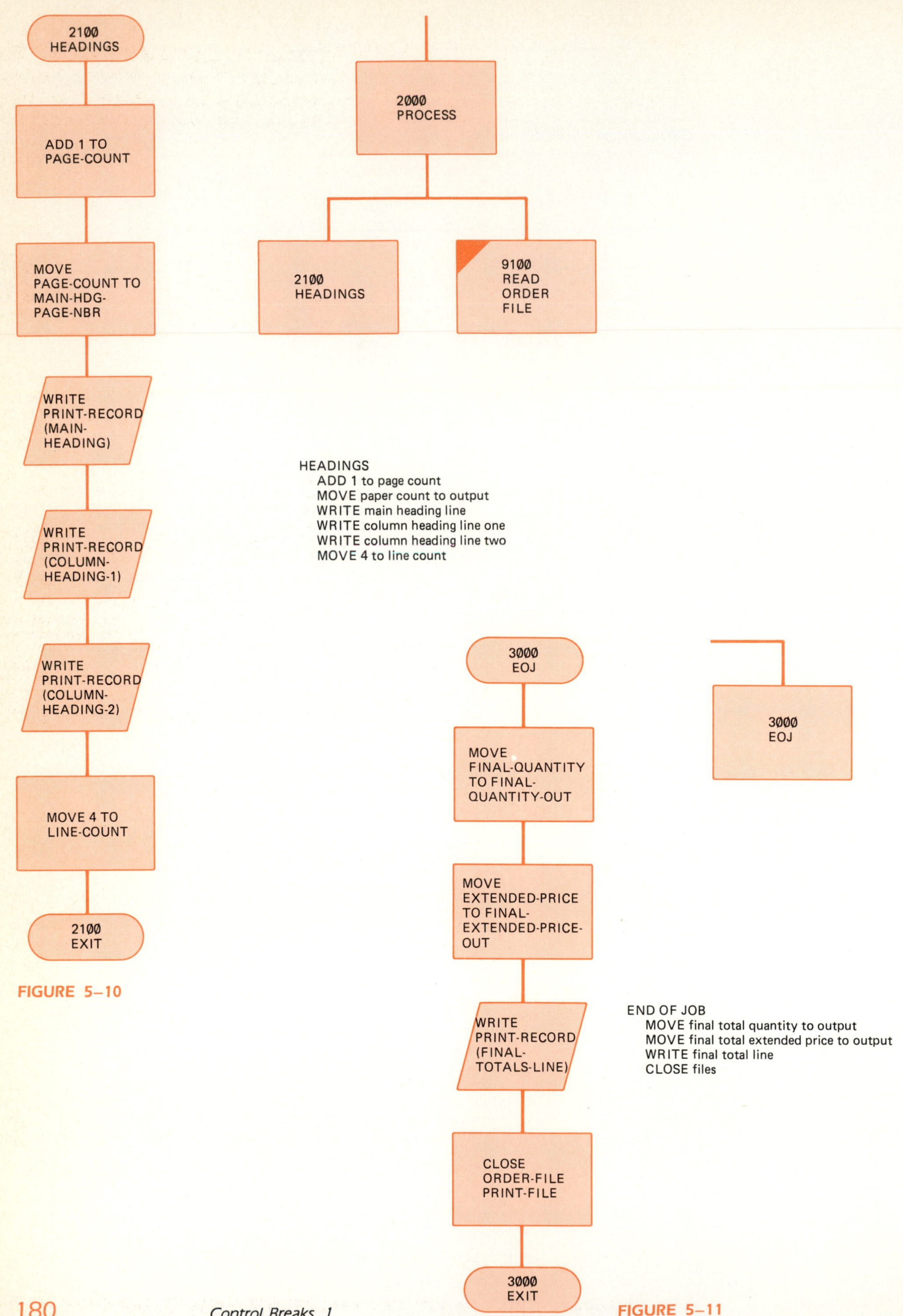

FIGURE 5–10

```
HEADINGS
    ADD 1 to page count
    MOVE paper count to output
    WRITE main heading line
    WRITE column heading line one
    WRITE column heading line two
    MOVE 4 to line count
```

```
END OF JOB
    MOVE final total quantity to output
    MOVE final total extended price to output
    WRITE final total line
    CLOSE files
```

FIGURE 5–11

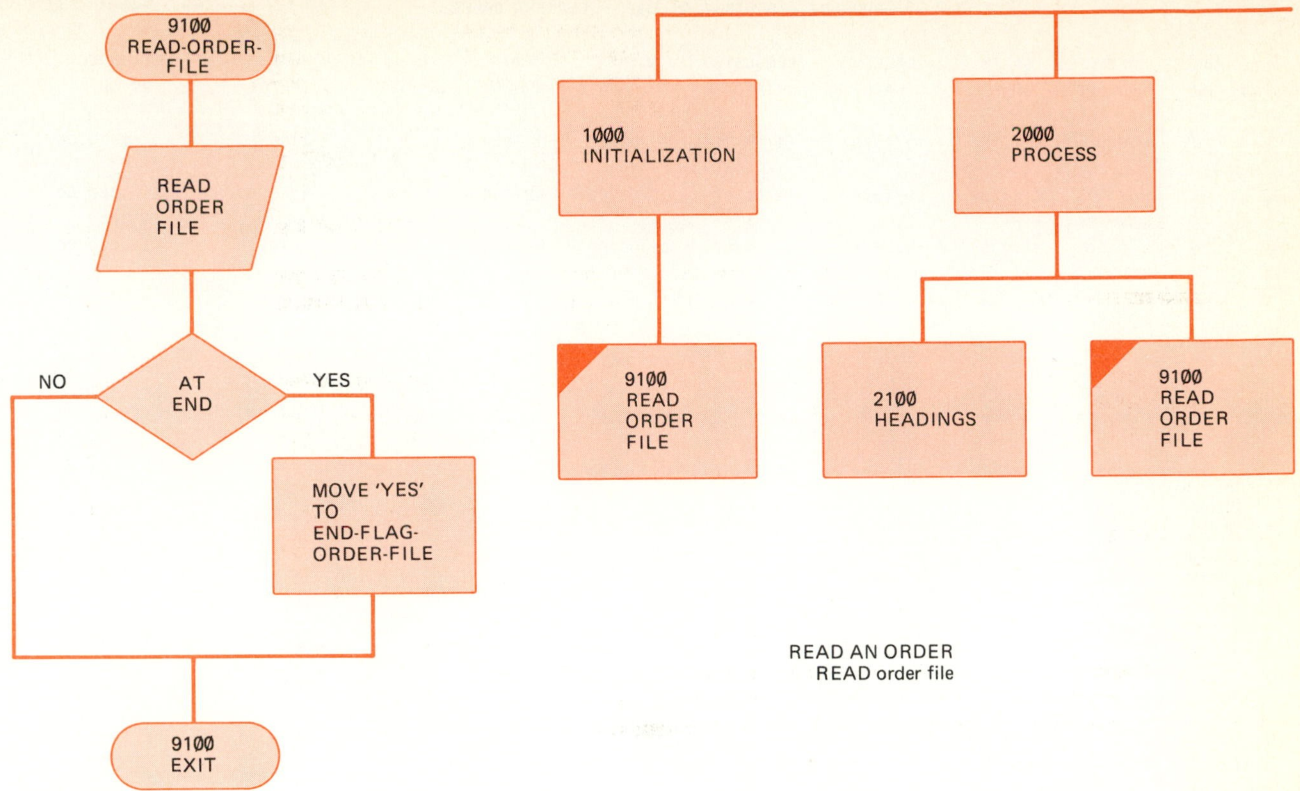

FIGURE 5–12

```
Ø12Ø1ØØ3ØØPO173   B123838710Ø25GN4Ø2AØØØØ1Ø45ØØØ871116ØØØØØØ
Ø12Ø1Ø47278372    G483888709 13WB7Ø2XØØØ9ØØ115ØØ8711Ø1ØØØØØØ
Ø12Ø1ØØ3ØØE1Ø12   B1233587110Ø5WB493EØØØØ2Ø54ØØØ871122ØØØØØØ
Ø3ØØ747300        H84777870223MF4Ø3TØØØØ5Ø4ØØØØ87Ø5Ø2ØØØØØØ
Ø3ØØ7ØØ378EBNER   H845798708 11VX922PØØ8ØØØØ1275891120ØØØØØØ
Ø3ØØ7739897747    B892888711Ø6MF848JØØØØ5Ø2145Ø88Ø13ØØØØØØØ
Ø3ØØ7ØØ28334567X  B342378710 3ØHL834EØØØ16Ø19ØØØ871121ØØØØØØ
Ø3ØØ747300        Y289Ø3870811VXØØ1LØØ2ØØØØ622Ø8712Ø3ØØØØØØ
Ø344Ø69481870341  GØ418Ø87Ø2Ø9JGØ4ØXØØØØ1Ø525ØØ88Ø619ØØØØØØ
Ø361182888P2783733B8433Ø871Ø25HL289BØØØ1ØØ234ØØ871113ØØØØØØ
Ø361128375T7838   T7829987Ø323JG563WØØØØ6Ø43ØØØ871Ø18ØØØØØØ
Ø36115Ø912        H6915Ø87Ø2Ø6MF848TØØØØ3Ø36ØØØ8712Ø1ØØØØØØ
Ø8174314Ø865      H4189187Ø412TK61ØLØØØ18ØØ78ØØ87Ø63ØØØØØØØ
Ø8174Ø18Ø5R7278   T2164287Ø81ØTK497XØØØ1ØØ118ØØ87113ØØØØØØØ
Ø8174Ø18Ø5R8322   Y211Ø587Ø6Ø1TN116TØØØØ1Ø3ØØØØ871221ØØØØØØ
Ø891562Ø54SCHUH   L5Ø681871108TK812EØØØØ6Ø573ØØ88Ø1Ø5ØØØØØØ
Ø891521Ø78        B71Ø45871ØØ1FV782TØØØØ3ØØ28ØØ871115ØØØØØØ
```

FIGURE 5–13

THE COBOL PROGRAM

Test Data

Test data for the BREAK-1 program is shown in Figure 5–13. It is the same data used in all the previous programs.

Sample Output

Sample output from the BREAK-1 program is shown in Figure 5–14. Three pages of output are produced, one for each branch which is included in the test data. Since this is test data, the pages are not as full as they would probably be if the report were run with actual data.

The Program

The complete COBOL BREAK-1 program is shown in Figure 5–15.

DATE: 11/09/87 PRODUCT DISTRIBUTION INC. - CURRENT ORDERS PAGE: 1

BRANCH	SALES REP	CUSTOMER NUMBER	SALES ORDER	ORDER DATE	REQUESTED SHIP DATE	ACTUAL SHIP DATE	PART NUMBER	QUANTITY	UNIT PRICE	EXTENDED PRICE
01	201	00300	B 12383	10/25/87	11/16/87	00/00/00	GN402A	1	$450.00	$450.00
01	201	04727	G 48388	09/13/87	11/01/87	00/00/00	WB702X	90	$115.00	$10,350.00
01	201	00300	B 12335	11/05/87	11/22/87	00/00/00	WB493E	2	$540.00	$1,080.00

DATE: 11/09/87 PRODUCT DISTRIBUTION INC. - CURRENT ORDERS PAGE: 2

BRANCH	SALES REP	CUSTOMER NUMBER	SALES ORDER	ORDER DATE	REQUESTED SHIP DATE	ACTUAL SHIP DATE	PART NUMBER	QUANTITY	UNIT PRICE	EXTENDED PRICE
03	007	47300	H 84777	02/23/87	05/02/87	00/00/00	MF403T	5	$400.00	$2,000.00
03	007	00378	H 84579	08/11/87	11/20/89	00/00/00	VX922P	800	$12.75	$10,200.00
03	007	73989	B 89288	11/06/87	01/30/88	00/00/00	MF848J	5	$214.50	$1,072.50
03	007	00283	B 34237	10/30/87	11/21/87	00/00/00	HL834E	16	$190.00	$3,040.00
03	007	47300	Y 28903	08/11/87	12/03/87	00/00/00	VX001L	200	$62.20	$12,440.00
03	440	69481	G 04180	02/09/87	06/19/88	00/00/00	JG040X	1	$525.00	$525.00
03	611	82888	B 84330	10/25/87	11/13/87	00/00/00	HL289B	10	$234.00	$2,340.00
03	611	28375	T 78299	03/23/87	10/18/87	00/00/00	JG563W	6	$430.00	$2,580.00
03	611	50912	H 69150	02/06/87	12/01/87	00/00/00	MF848T	3	$360.00	$1,080.00

DATE: 11/09/87 PRODUCT DISTRIBUTION INC. - CURRENT ORDERS PAGE: 3

BRANCH	SALES REP	CUSTOMER NUMBER	SALES ORDER	ORDER DATE	REQUESTED SHIP DATE	ACTUAL SHIP DATE	PART NUMBER	QUANTITY	UNIT PRICE	EXTENDED PRICE
08	174	31408	H 41891	04/12/87	06/30/87	00/00/00	TK610L	18	$78.00	$1,404.00
08	174	01805	T 21642	08/10/87	11/30/87	00/00/00	TK497X	10	$118.00	$1,180.00
08	174	01805	Y 21105	06/01/87	12/21/87	00/00/00	TN116T	1	$300.00	$300.00
08	915	62054	L 50681	11/08/87	01/05/88	00/00/00	TK812E	6	$573.00	$3,438.00
08	915	21078	B 71045	10/01/87	11/15/87	00/00/00	FV782T	3	$28.00	$84.00
FINAL TOTALS								1,177		$53,563.50

FIGURE 5–14

```
IDENTIFICATION DIVISION.

PROGRAM-ID.     BREAK-1.

AUTHOR.         HELEN HUMPHREYS.

INSTALLATION.   PRODUCT DISTRIBUTION INC.

DATE-WRITTEN.   Ø5/1Ø/87.

DATE-COMPILED.  Ø5/16/87.
```

FIGURE 5–15

FIGURE 5-15 cont.

```
*****************************************************************
*                                                               *
*    THIS PROGRAM WILL PRODUCE A PRINTED REPORT OF THE ORDER    *
*    FILE.  THE REPORT WILL INCLUDE FINAL TOTALS FOR QUANTITY   *
*    AND EXTENDED PRICE.  EACH BRANCH WILL BEGIN ON A NEW PAGE. *
*                                                               *
*****************************************************************

 ENVIRONMENT DIVISION.

 CONFIGURATION SECTION.

 SOURCE-COMPUTER.
        IBM-37Ø.
 OBJECT-COMPUTER.
        IBM-37Ø.

 INPUT-OUTPUT SECTION.
 FILE-CONTROL.
     SELECT ORDER-FILE ASSIGN TO DISK.
     SELECT PRINT-FILE ASSIGN TO PRINTER.

 DATA DIVISION.
 FILE SECTION.

 FD  ORDER-FILE
     LABEL RECORDS ARE STANDARD
     RECORD CONTAINS 7Ø CHARACTERS
     DATA RECORD IS ORDER-RECORD.

 Ø1  ORDER-RECORD.
     Ø5  ORD-BRANCH                PIC 9(2).
     Ø5  ORD-SALES-REP             PIC 9(3).
     Ø5  ORD-CUSTOMER-NBR          PIC 9(5).
     Ø5  ORD-CUST-PO-NBR           PIC X(8).
     Ø5  ORD-SALES-ORD-NBR         PIC X(6).
     Ø5  ORD-DATE.
         1Ø  ORD-YY                PIC 9(2).
         1Ø  ORD-MM                PIC 9(2).
         1Ø  ORD-DD                PIC 9(2).
     Ø5  ORD-PART-NBR              PIC X(6).
     Ø5  ORD-QUANTITY              PIC 9(5).
     Ø5  ORD-UNIT-PRICE            PIC 9(4)V9(2).
     Ø5  ORD-REQ-SHIP-DATE.
         1Ø  ORD-REQ-SHIP-YY       PIC 9(2).
         1Ø  ORD-REQ-SHIP-MM       PIC 9(2).
         1Ø  ORD-REQ-SHIP-DD       PIC 9(2).
     Ø5  ORD-ACT-SHIP-DATE.
         1Ø  ORD-ACT-SHIP-YY       PIC 9(2).
         1Ø  ORD-ACT-SHIP-MM       PIC 9(2).
         1Ø  ORD-ACT-SHIP-DD       PIC 9(2).
     Ø5  FILLER                    PIC X(11).

 FD  PRINT-FILE
     LABEL RECORDS ARE OMITTED
     RECORD CONTAINS 133 CHARACTERS
     DATA RECORD IS PRINT-RECORD.

 Ø1  PRINT-RECORD                  PIC X(133).

 WORKING-STORAGE SECTION.

 Ø1  HOLDS-COUNTERS-SWITCHES.
     Ø5  END-FLAG-ORDER-FILE       PIC X(3)        VALUE 'NO'.
     Ø5  LINE-COUNT                PIC 9(2)        VALUE 99.
     Ø5  PAGE-COUNT                PIC 9(3)        VALUE ZEROS.
     Ø5  HOLD-BRANCH               PIC 9(2)        VALUE ZEROS.

 Ø1  CALCULATED-FIELDS.
     Ø5  EXTENDED-PRICE            PIC 9(7)V9(2).

 Ø1  FINAL-TOTALS.
     Ø5  FINAL-QUANTITY            PIC 9(6)        VALUE ZEROS.
     Ø5  FINAL-EXT-PRICE           PIC 9(8)V9(2)   VALUE ZEROS.

 Ø1  MAIN-HEADING.
     Ø5  FILLER                    PIC X(7)        VALUE SPACES.
     Ø5  FILLER                    PIC X(6)        VALUE 'DATE:'.
     Ø5  MAIN-HDG-DATE             PIC X(8).
     Ø5  FILLER                    PIC X(25)       VALUE SPACES.
     Ø5  FILLER                    PIC X(42)
         VALUE 'PRODUCT DISTRIBUTION INC. - CURRENT ORDERS'.
     Ø5  FILLER                    PIC X(27)       VALUE SPACES.
     Ø5  FILLER                    PIC X(6)        VALUE 'PAGE:'.
```

FIGURE 5-15 cont.

```
           05  MAIN-HDG-PAGE-NBR         PIC ZZ9.
           05  FILLER                    PIC X(9)        VALUE SPACES.

       01  COLUMN-HEADING-1.
           05  FILLER                    PIC X(14)       VALUE SPACES.
           05  FILLER                    PIC X(5)        VALUE 'SALES'.
           05  FILLER                    PIC X(2)        VALUE SPACES.
           05  FILLER                    PIC X(8)        VALUE 'CUSTOMER'.
           05  FILLER                    PIC X(3)        VALUE SPACES.
           05  FILLER                    PIC X(5)        VALUE 'SALES'.
           05  FILLER                    PIC X(6)        VALUE SPACES.
           05  FILLER                    PIC X(5)        VALUE 'ORDER'.
           05  FILLER                    PIC X(6)        VALUE SPACES.
           05  FILLER                    PIC X(9)        VALUE
                                                         'REQUESTED'.
           05  FILLER                    PIC X(4)        VALUE SPACES.
           05  FILLER                    PIC X(6)        VALUE 'ACTUAL'.
           05  FILLER                    PIC X(6)        VALUE SPACES.
           05  FILLER                    PIC X(4)        VALUE 'PART'.
           05  FILLER                    PIC X(18)       VALUE SPACES.
           05  FILLER                    PIC X(4)        VALUE 'UNIT'.
           05  FILLER                    PIC X(9)        VALUE SPACES.
           05  FILLER                    PIC X(8)        VALUE 'EXTENDED'.
           05  FILLER                    PIC X(11)       VALUE SPACES.

       01  COLUMN-HEADING-2.
           05  FILLER                    PIC X(7)        VALUE SPACES.
           05  FILLER                    PIC X(6)        VALUE 'BRANCH'.
           05  FILLER                    PIC X(2)        VALUE SPACES.
           05  FILLER                    PIC X(3)        VALUE 'REP'.
           05  FILLER                    PIC X(4)        VALUE SPACES.
           05  FILLER                    PIC X(6)        VALUE 'NUMBER'.
           05  FILLER                    PIC X(4)        VALUE SPACES.
           05  FILLER                    PIC X(5)        VALUE 'ORDER'.
           05  FILLER                    PIC X(7)        VALUE SPACES.
           05  FILLER                    PIC X(4)        VALUE 'DATE'.
           05  FILLER                    PIC X(6)        VALUE SPACES.
           05  FILLER                    PIC X(9)        VALUE
                                                         'SHIP DATE'.
           05  FILLER                    PIC X(3)        VALUE SPACES.
           05  FILLER                    PIC X(9)        VALUE
                                                         'SHIP DATE'.
           05  FILLER                    PIC X(3)        VALUE SPACES.
           05  FILLER                    PIC X(6)        VALUE 'NUMBER'.
           05  FILLER                    PIC X(3)        VALUE SPACES.
           05  FILLER                    PIC X(8)        VALUE 'QUANTITY'.
           05  FILLER                    PIC X(6)        VALUE SPACES.
           05  FILLER                    PIC X(5)        VALUE 'PRICE'.
           05  FILLER                    PIC X(9)        VALUE SPACES.
           05  FILLER                    PIC X(5)        VALUE 'PRICE'.
           05  FILLER                    PIC X(9)        VALUE SPACES.

       01  DETAIL-LINE.
           05  FILLER                    PIC X(9)        VALUE SPACES.
           05  DET-BRANCH                PIC 9(2).
           05  FILLER                    PIC X(4)        VALUE SPACES.
           05  DET-SALES-REP             PIC 9(3).
           05  FILLER                    PIC X(4)        VALUE SPACES.
           05  DET-CUSTOMER-NBR          PIC 9(5).
           05  FILLER                    PIC X(4)        VALUE SPACES.
           05  DET-SALES-ORD-NBR         PIC XBXXXXX.
           05  FILLER                    PIC X(4)        VALUE SPACES.
           05  DET-ORDER-MM              PIC 9(2).
           05  FILLER                    PIC X(1)        VALUE '/'.
           05  DET-ORDER-DD              PIC 9(2).
           05  FILLER                    PIC X(1)        VALUE '/'.
           05  DET-ORDER-YY              PIC 9(2).
           05  FILLER                    PIC X(4)        VALUE SPACES.
           05  DET-REQ-SHIP-MM           PIC 9(2).
           05  FILLER                    PIC X(1)        VALUE '/'.
           05  DET-REQ-SHIP-DD           PIC 9(2).
           05  FILLER                    PIC X(1)        VALUE '/'.
           05  DET-REQ-SHIP-YY           PIC 9(2).
           05  FILLER                    PIC X(4)        VALUE SPACES.
           05  DET-ACT-SHIP-MM           PIC 9(2).
           05  FILLER                    PIC X(1)        VALUE '/'.
           05  DET-ACT-SHIP-DD           PIC 9(2).
           05  FILLER                    PIC X(1)        VALUE '/'.
           05  DET-ACT-SHIP-YY           PIC 9(2).
           05  FILLER                    PIC X(4)        VALUE SPACES.
           05  DET-PART-NBR              PIC X(6).
           05  FILLER                    PIC X(4)        VALUE SPACES.
           05  DET-QUANTITY              PIC ZZ,ZZ9.
           05  FILLER                    PIC X(4)        VALUE SPACES.
           05  DET-UNIT-PRICE            PIC $$,$$9.99.
```

FIGURE 5-15 cont.

```
           Ø5  FILLER                      PIC X(4)        VALUE SPACES.
           Ø5  DET-EXTENDED-PRICE          PIC $$,$$$,$$9.99.
           Ø5  FILLER                      PIC X(9)        VALUE SPACES.

       Ø1  FINAL-TOTALS-LINE.
           Ø5  FILLER                      PIC X(9)        VALUE SPACES.
           Ø5  FILLER                      PIC X(12)
                                           VALUE 'FINAL TOTALS'.
           Ø5  FILLER                      PIC X(66)       VALUE SPACES.
           Ø5  FINAL-QUANTITY-OUT          PIC ZZZ,ZZ9.
           Ø5  FILLER                      PIC X(16)       VALUE SPACES.
           Ø5  FINAL-EXT-PRICE-OUT         PIC $$$,$$$,$$9.99.
           Ø5  FILLER                      PIC X(9).

       PROCEDURE DIVISION.

           PERFORM 1ØØØ-INITIALIZATION.
           PERFORM 2ØØØ-PROCESS
               UNTIL END-FLAG-ORDER-FILE = 'YES'.
           PERFORM 3ØØØ-EOJ.
           STOP RUN.

       1ØØØ-INITIALIZATION.
           OPEN INPUT  ORDER-FILE
                OUTPUT PRINT-FILE.
           MOVE CURRENT-DATE TO MAIN-HDG-DATE.
           PERFORM 91ØØ-READ-ORDER-FILE.
           MOVE ORD-BRANCH TO HOLD-BRANCH.

       2ØØØ-PROCESS.
           IF ORD-BRANCH = HOLD-BRANCH
               IF LINE-COUNT > 5Ø
                   PERFORM 21ØØ-HEADINGS
               ELSE
                   NEXT SENTENCE
           ELSE
               PERFORM 21ØØ-HEADINGS
               MOVE ORD-BRANCH TO HOLD-BRANCH.
           MOVE ORD-BRANCH             TO DET-BRANCH.
           MOVE ORD-SALES-REP          TO DET-SALES-REP.
           MOVE ORD-CUSTOMER-NBR       TO DET-CUSTOMER-NBR.
           MOVE ORD-SALES-ORD-NBR      TO DET-SALES-ORD-NBR.
           MOVE ORD-YY                 TO DET-ORDER-YY.
           MOVE ORD-MM                 TO DET-ORDER-MM.
           MOVE ORD-DD                 TO DET-ORDER-DD.
           MOVE ORD-PART-NBR           TO DET-PART-NBR.
           MOVE ORD-QUANTITY           TO DET-QUANTITY.
           MOVE ORD-UNIT-PRICE         TO DET-UNIT-PRICE.
           MOVE ORD-REQ-SHIP-YY        TO DET-REQ-SHIP-YY.
           MOVE ORD-REQ-SHIP-MM        TO DET-REQ-SHIP-MM.
           MOVE ORD-REQ-SHIP-DD        TO DET-REQ-SHIP-DD.
           MOVE ORD-ACT-SHIP-YY        TO DET-ACT-SHIP-YY.
           MOVE ORD-ACT-SHIP-MM        TO DET-ACT-SHIP-MM.
           MOVE ORD-ACT-SHIP-DD        TO DET-ACT-SHIP-DD.
           COMPUTE EXTENDED-PRICE = ORD-UNIT-PRICE * ORD-QUANTITY.
           MOVE EXTENDED-PRICE         TO DET-EXTENDED-PRICE.
           ADD ORD-QUANTITY            TO FINAL-QUANTITY.
           ADD EXTENDED-PRICE          TO FINAL-EXT-PRICE.
           WRITE PRINT-RECORD FROM DETAIL-LINE
               AFTER ADVANCING 2 LINES.
           ADD 2 TO LINE-COUNT.
           PERFORM 91ØØ-READ-ORDER-FILE.

       21ØØ-HEADINGS.
           ADD 1 TO PAGE-COUNT.
           MOVE PAGE-COUNT TO MAIN-HDG-PAGE-NBR.
           WRITE PRINT-RECORD FROM MAIN-HEADING
               AFTER ADVANCING PAGE.
           WRITE PRINT-RECORD FROM COLUMN-HEADING-1
               AFTER ADVANCING 2 LINES.
           WRITE PRINT-RECORD FROM COLUMN-HEADING-2
               AFTER ADVANCING 1 LINE.
           MOVE 4 TO LINE-COUNT.

       3ØØØ-EOJ.
           MOVE FINAL-QUANTITY TO FINAL-QUANTITY-OUT.
           MOVE FINAL-EXT-PRICE TO FINAL-EXT-PRICE-OUT.
           WRITE PRINT-RECORD FROM FINAL-TOTALS-LINE
               AFTER ADVANCING 3 LINES.
           CLOSE ORDER-FILE
                 PRINT-FILE.

       91ØØ-READ-ORDER-FILE.
           READ ORDER-FILE
               AT END
                   MOVE 'YES' TO END-FLAG-ORDER-FILE.
```

NEW COBOL ELEMENTS

Signed Data

Although not used in the BREAK-1 program, signed numbers are introduced at this point for completion of coverage of output editing. (Signed numbers are used in the second programming project of the chapter.)

A numeric field may be signed or unsigned. For a signed field, an S is used as the first character in the PICTURE. The S does not add any bytes to the field size. For numeric fields where USAGE IS DISPLAY, the first half (zone half) of the rightmost byte is used to indicate whether a field is signed or unsigned and, if it is signed, whether it is positive or negative. Figure 5–16 shows how unsigned and signed numbers are represented in storage with the EBCDIC code when USAGE IS DISPLAY. In the zone half of the rightmost byte an F indicates an unsigned field, a C indicates a signed positive field, and a D indicates a signed negative field. Unsigned fields are assumed to be positive.

FIGURE 5–16

```
05  FIELD-A                        PIC 9(3)      VALUE 186.
05  FIELD-B                        PIC S9(3)     VALUE +186.
05  FIELD-C                        PIC S9(3)     VALUE -186.
```

FIELD-A	F	1	F	8	F	6	UNSIGNED
FIELD-B	F	1	F	8	C	6	POSITIVE
FIELD-C	F	1	F	8	D	6	NEGATIVE

If there is *any* possibility that a field may contain a negative number, it should be signed. The need to sign a field applies not only to the field itself, but also to any fields it is used with. The usefulness of signing an input field is lost if we multiply the signed field by a second field and place the result in an unsigned field. For assume that an input field is signed and contains negative data and that we multiply it by a field whose contents are positive. The result would be negative. However, if the result field is unsigned, the stored result will be considered positive.

When a signed field is printed, the PICTURE of the output field needs to carry evidence of the sign. There are a number of ways to do this, and we shall discuss them shortly.

SIGN Condition

Format

```
                        ⎧POSITIVE⎫
operand IS [NOT]        ⎨NEGATIVE⎬
                        ⎩ZERO    ⎭
```

The sign condition is tested in an IF statement. The test may be performed on a data-name which is numeric or on an arithmetic expression which contains at least one data-name. When made on a signed field, the test can produce any of the three results, POSITIVE, NEGATIVE, and ZERO. When performed on an unsigned field, the test will only produce a POSITIVE or ZERO result.

Division by zero is illegal in COBOL. The sign test may be used to avoid any such inadvertent division. It may also be used to avoid the use of negative numbers in a calculation where it is known that they would not produce a correct result.

Output Editing

Output editing is used to produce output that is easily readable. Input data and calculated data are often in a format that is not suitable for a printed report. For example, numeric fields contain leading zeros and do not include decimal points. Accordingly, output editing is used to format these data items for printing.

Output editing includes inserting new characters, suppressing existing characters, and/or replacing existing characters. Output editing is accomplished by a MOVE statement which moves an unedited data item to a data item with an edited picture.

The different types of output editing are (1) simple insertion, (2) special insertion, (3) fixed insertion, (4) floating insertion, (5) suppression of zeros, and (6) replacement with asterisks.

Simple Insertion

Simple insertion is suitable for alphabetic, alphanumeric, and numeric items. In simple insertion, the size of the edited field is increased by the number of insertion characters used. Figure 5–17 shows several examples of simple insertion. The symbols used to accomplish the task are as follows:

TYPE OF FIELD	SYMBOLS AVAILABLE
Alphabetic	B
Alphanumeric edited	B 0 /
Numeric edited	B 0 / ,

The editing character B will insert a space in the edited field. The remaining characters insert copies of themselves in the edited field (i.e., a slash will insert a slash, etc.)

FIGURE 5–17

ALPHABETIC (B)

Sending Field PICTURE	Value	Receiving Field PICTURE	Edited Value
A(8)	LEFTMOST	A(4)BA(4)	LEFT MOST
A(6)	INCOME	A(2)BA(4)	IN COME
A(4)	SIZE	B(3)A(4)	SIZE

ALPHANUMERIC EDITED (B 0 /)

Sending Field PICTURE	Value	Receiving Field PICTURE	Edited Value
X(7)	1234567	X(3)BX(4)	123 4567
X(6)	ABCDEF	0XX0XX0XX	0AB0CD0EF
X(6)	123456	XX/XX/XX	12/34/56

NUMERIC EDITED (B 0 / ,)

Sending Field PICTURE	Value	Receiving Field PICTURE	Edited Value
9(4)	1234	99,,99	12,,34
9(6)	123456	B999B999	123 456
9(6)	112233	99/99/99	11/22/33

Special Insertion

The period is the only special-insertion editing symbol. It is used to represent a decimal point in a numeric-edited picture. A V in a numeric picture will be aligned with the decimal point in the numeric-edited picture. COBOL can distinguish between the decimal point and the period which terminates a COBOL sentence because the period will always be followed by a space while the decimal point will not. The decimal point occupies a space on the print chart.

After alignment is made between the V and the decimal point, movement is from right to left on the integer portion, and from left to right on the decimal portion, of the number in the field. (See Figure 5–18.)

FIGURE 5–18

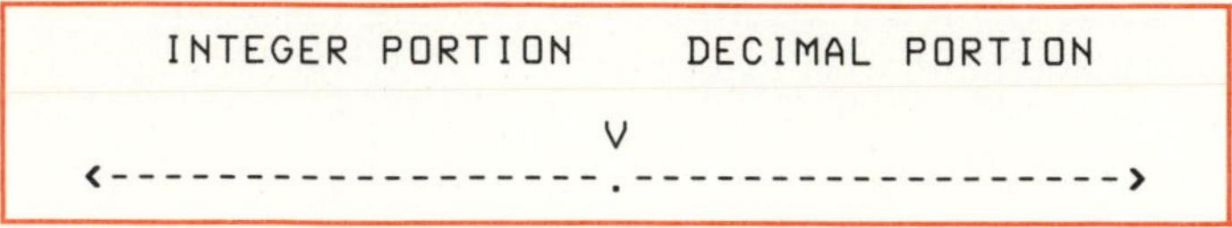

If the sending field is shorter than the receiving field on either side of the decimal, the receiving field is padded with zeros. If the sending field is longer than the receiving field on either side of the decimal, the extra digits in the sending field are truncated. (See Figure 5–19.)

FIGURE 5–19

Sending Field		Receiving Field	
PICTURE	Value	PICTURE	Value
9(4)V9(2)	1234‸56	9(4).9(2)	1234.56
9(5)V9(1)	12345‸6	9(4).9(2)	2345.60
9(3)V9(3)	123‸456	9(4).9(2)	0123.45

Fixed Insertion

The following are used as fixed-insertion symbols in numeric-edited items:

$	(currency symbol)
+ − CR DB	(sign-control symbol)

A numeric-edited picture can contain only one currency symbol and one sign-control symbol for fixed insertion. The + or − may be used on either the left or the right of a picture string. The CR or DB may only be used on the right of a picture string.

If only the $ is used, it must be the leftmost symbol in the picture. If both a + or − and a $ are used, then the + or − must be the leftmost symbol in the numeric-edited picture.

A + in an edited picture will produce a + on the output if the data in the sending field is positive or zero, and a − if the data in the sending field is negative. A −, CR, or DB will produce the same symbol on the output only if the sending field is negative. (See Figure 5–20.)

Floating Insertion

The following symbols are used as floating-insertion symbols in numeric-edited pictures:

$	(currency symbol)
+ −	(sign-control symbols)

A floating string consists of at least two of the same floating-insertion symbols. Although both a currency symbol and a sign-control symbol may be used as fixed

FIGURE 5–20

Sending Field		Receiving Field	
PICTURE	Value	PICTURE	Edited Value
S9(4)	+1234	9(4)+	1234+
S9(4)	+1234	9(4)-	1234
S9(4)	-1234	$9(4)+	$1234-
S9(4)	-0012	$9(4)-	$0012-
S9(4)	+1234	$9(4)CR	$1234
S9(4)	+1234	9(4)DB	1234
S9(4)	-1234	9(4)CR	1234CR
S9(4)	-1234	$9(4)DB	$1234DB
S9(4)	+0012	+$9(4)	+$0012
S9(4)	+1234	-9(4)	1234
S9(4)	-1234	+9(4)	-1234
S9(4)	-1234	-$9(4)	-$1234

symbols in the same picture string, only one or the other may be used as a floating string in a picture string. The leftmost character of the floating string represents an extra position for printing purposes. It should be used in addition to those positions which may be replaced by numeric data. (See Figures 5–21 and 5–22.)

FIGURE 5–21

```
|-->  The leftmost position at which the floating character
             can print.
|
||---->  The leftmost position where numeric data can print.
||
||     |->  The rightmost position at which the floating
||     |              character can print.
$$$$,$$9.99
```

FIGURE 5–22

Sending Field		Receiving Field	
PICTURE	Value	PICTURE	Edited Value
9(3)V9(2)	123‸45	$$$$.99	$123.45
S9(3)V9(2)	123‸45	++++.99	+123.45
9(5)V9(2)	00123‸45	$$$,$$$.99	$123.45
S9(5)V9(2)	00001‸23	+++,+++.99	+1.23
S9(2)V9(2)	-01‸23	$$$.99DB	$1.23DB
9(4)	0000	$$,$$$	
S9(4)	-0123	++,+++	-123

Suppression of Zeros and Replacement with Asterisks

Suppression of zeros and replacement of asterisks require that one or more of the characters Z and *, respectively, be present in the edit picture. Starting at the left, each leading zero is replaced by the appropriate replacement character until either (1) there are no more replacement characters in the edit string, or (2) the sending field contains nonzero data.

Commas embedded in the replacement characters in the edit string will be replaced with the replacement character. If Z's are used on both sides of a decimal point, the decimal point in the string will be replaced with a space when the value of the data is all zeros. If *'s are used on both sides of a decimal point, the decimal point will print when the value of the data is all zeros. Replacement of asterisks is often used when printing checks, so that the dollar amount on the check cannot easily be altered. (See Figure 5–23.)

Sending Field		Receiving Field	
PICTURE	Value	PICTURE	Edited Value
9(4)	0000	ZZZ9	0
9(4)	0012	***9	**12
S9(4)	-0012	ZZZZ+	12-
S9(4)	0000	ZZZZ-	
9(4)V99	0012^50	Z,ZZ9.99	12.50
9(4)V99	1234^50	*,**9.99	1,234.50
9(5)V99	12340^50	ZZ,ZZZ.ZZ	12,340.50
9(5)V99	00000^00	ZZ,ZZZ.ZZ	
9(5)V99	00000^00	**,***.**	******.**
S9(6)V99	+000000^50	$ZZZ,ZZ9.99CR	$ 0.50
S9(6)V99	-123400^50	$***,**9.99DB	$123,400.50DB

FIGURE 5–23

In the 1985 standard, a numeric-edited data item may be moved to a numeric or numeric-edited data item in order to remove editing characters from the sending field.

BLANK WHEN ZERO

Format

```
BLANK WHEN ZERO
```

The BLANK WHEN ZERO clause may be used with a numeric or numeric-edited data item in describing the item in the DATA DIVISION. It will cause the entire item to be filled with spaces if the contents of the field are zero. The clause is used primarily for printed output when blanks are preferred over having a zero field with edit characters such as a dollar sign or decimal point.

If BLANK WHEN ZERO is specified for a numeric item, that item is considered to be numeric edited and may not be used where a numeric field is required in a calculation or move. The BLANK WHEN ZERO clause may not be used when the asterisk (*) is the replacement item in an edit picture.

JUSTIFIED RIGHT

Format

```
{JUSTIFIED} RIGHT
{JUST     }
```

The JUSTIFIED RIGHT clause may be used with an elementary alphabetic or alphanumeric data item in describing it in the DATA DIVISION. It may not be specified for a numeric or numeric-edited data item.

When data is moved to a data item with the JUSTIFIED RIGHT clause, the data is aligned on the rightmost position and movement is from right to left. If the sending field is too long, its leftmost characters will be truncated. If the sending field is too short, the receiving field will be padded on the left with blanks. (See Figure 5–24.)

Notice the placement of the names in the output field; since the spaces following EBNER are a part of the sending field, they are included in the movement of data to the receiving field.

DESCRIPTION OF SENDING FIELD
```
     05  EMPLOYEE-NAME          PIC X(20).
```
ACTUAL DATA

```
GERALD J. MELLENTHIN
KELLY M. EBNER
```

DESCRIPTION OF RECEIVING FIELD
```
     05  EMPLOYEE-NAME-OUT      PIC X(30)   JUSTIFIED RIGHT.
```
PRINTED OUTPUT

```
          GERALD J. MELLENTHIN
                KELLY M. EBNER
```

FIGURE 5–24

PROGRAM SPECIFICATION: BREAK-2

The second programming project for this chapter includes subtotals of quantity and extended price for each branch, as well as final totals for the same fields. The program specifications are shown in Figure 5–25.

PROGRAM SPECIFICATION

Program Name: BREAK-2

Program Function:

The program will produce a printed listing of an order file. The report will include branch and final totals for quantity and extended price. Each branch will begin on a new page.

Input Files:

I. ORDER-FILE

INPUT DEVICE:	DISK
FILE ORGANIZATION:	SEQUENTIAL
RECORD LENGTH:	70 BYTES
FILE SEQUENCE:	ASCENDING ON BRANCH / SALES REP

Output Files:

I. PRINT-FILE

OUTPUT DEVICE:	PRINTER
RECORD LENGTH:	133 BYTES

Processing Requirements:

Each record read from the order file should be printed on one line of the output report. All input fields, except the customer purchase order number, are to be included on the output. The extended price is to be calculated for each order and printed on the output. (Extended price = quantity × unit price.)

Totals for quantity and extended price are to be accumulated and printed for each branch and for the entire company.

FIGURE 5–25

Output Requirements:

The following are formatting requirements for the report:

1. Each page of the report should contain:
   (a) a main heading which includes, the company name, the report name, the report date, and a page number.
   (b) column headings which describe the items printed underneath them.
2. Detail lines should include all fields from the input (except the customer purchase order number) and the extended price.
3. Detail lines should be double spaced.
4. Each new branch should begin on a new page.
5. Total lines should be double spaced.

FIGURE 5–25 cont.

Input Record Layout

The input record layout is shown in Figure 5–26. It is the same file used in previous projects, repeated here for convenience.

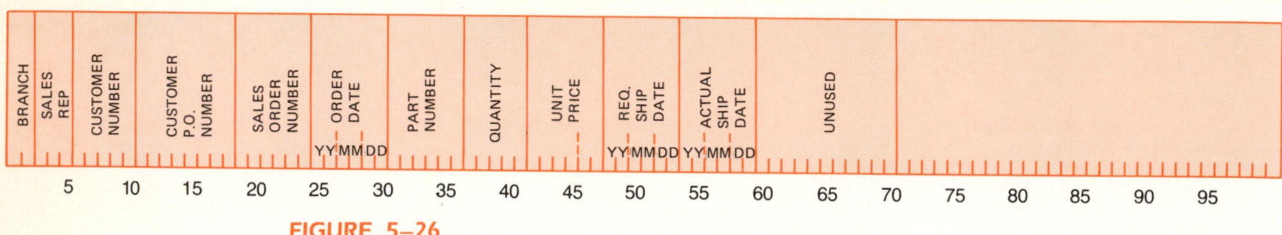

FIGURE 5–26

Print Chart

The print chart for the project is shown in Figure 5–27. It includes branch totals for quantity and extended price, neither of which was on the print chart of the previous, BREAK-1, project.

LOGIC FOR SINGLE-LEVEL BREAK WITH TOTALS

The logic design for the BREAK-2 program is shown by means of a hierarchy chart in Figure 5–28, pseudocode in Figure 5–29, and a flowchart in Figure 5–30.

Hierarchy Chart

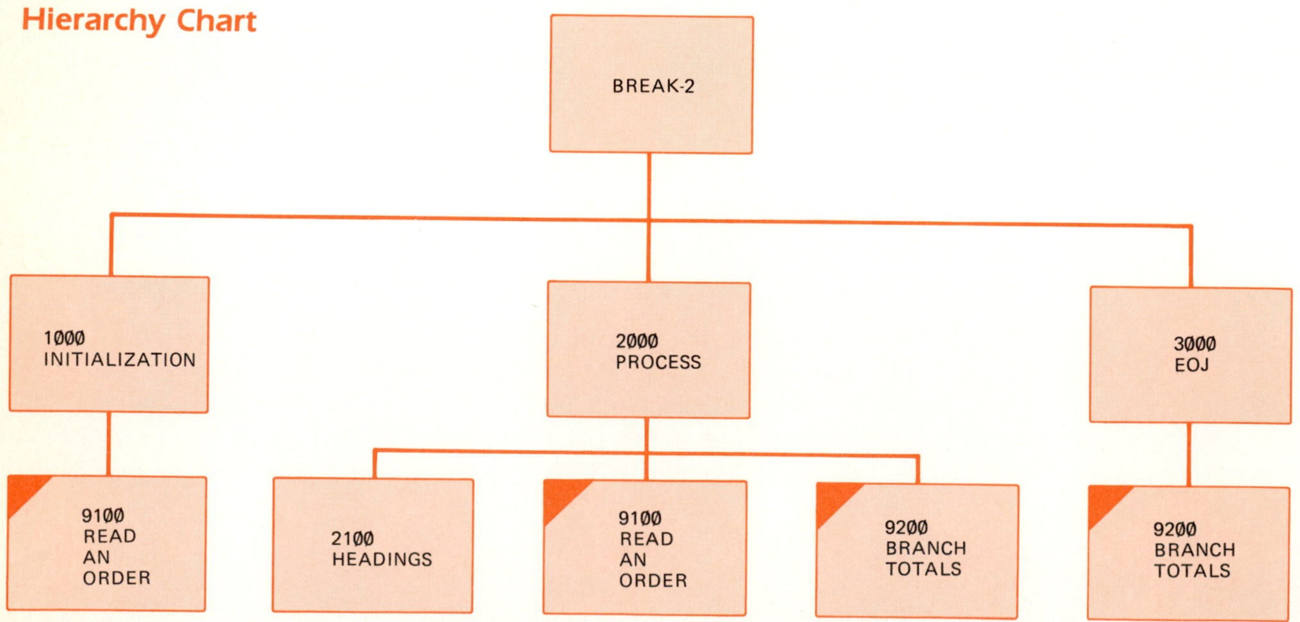

FIGURE 5–28

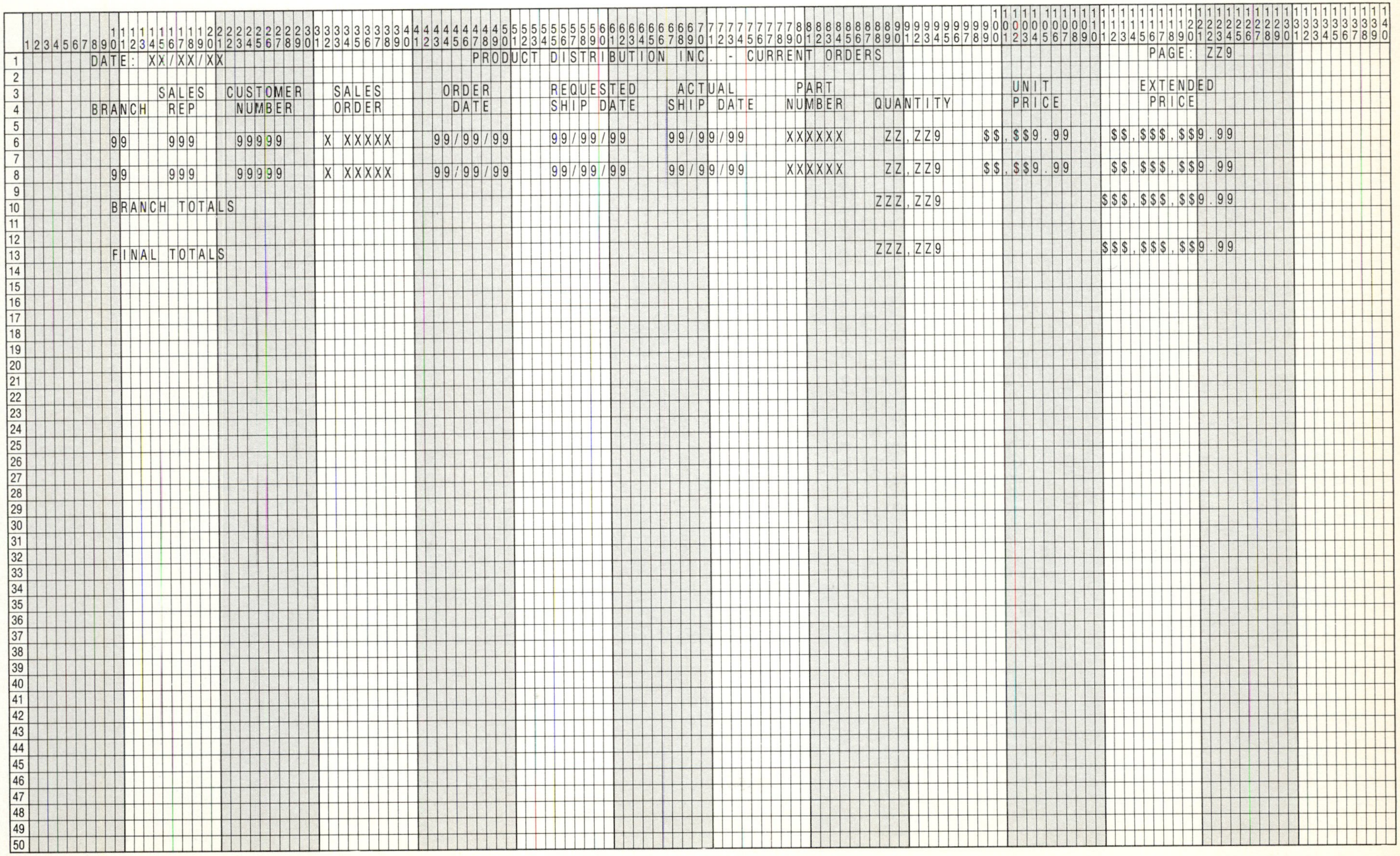

```
       DATE: XX/XX/XX                                         PRODUCT DISTRIBUTION INC. - CURRENT ORDERS                           PAGE: ZZ9

              SALES  CUSTOMER   SALES      ORDER      REQUESTED    ACTUAL      PART                  UNIT         EXTENDED
       BRANCH  REP    NUMBER    ORDER       DATE      SHIP DATE   SHIP DATE   NUMBER   QUANTITY      PRICE         PRICE

         99    999    99999    X XXXXX    99/99/99    99/99/99    99/99/99    XXXXXX    ZZ,ZZ9    $$,$$9.99    $$,$$$,$$9.99

         99    999    99999    X XXXXX    99/99/99    99/99/99    99/99/99    XXXXXX    ZZ,ZZ9    $$,$$9.99    $$,$$$,$$9.99

         BRANCH TOTALS                                                                 ZZZ,ZZ9                $$$,$$$,$$9.99


         FINAL TOTALS                                                                  ZZZ,ZZ9                $$$,$$$,$$9.99
```

FIGURE 5–27

Pseudocode

```
MAIN LINE
     DO initialization
     DO WHILE more order records
          DO process
     ENDDO
     DO end of job
INITIALIZATION
     OPEN files
     MOVE date to heading
     DO read an order
     MOVE branch to branch hold
PROCESS
     IF branch = branch hold
          IF line count > 50
               DO headings
          ENDIF
     ELSE
          DO branch totals
          DO headings
     ENDIF
     MOVE input to output
     CALCULATE extended price
     MOVE extended price to output
     ADD quantity to branch quantity
     ADD extended price to branch extended price
     WRITE detail line
     ADD 2 to line count
     DO read an order
HEADINGS
     ADD 1 to page count
     MOVE page count to output
     WRITE main heading line
     WRITE column heading line one
     WRITE column heading line two
     MOVE 4 to line count
END OF JOB
     DO branch totals
     MOVE final quantity to output
     MOVE final extended price to output
     WRITE final total line
     CLOSE files
READ AN ORDER
     READ order file
BRANCH TOTALS
     MOVE branch quantity to output
     MOVE branch extended price to output
     WRITE branch total line
     ADD branch quantity to final quantity
     ADD branch extended price to final extended
       price
     MOVE zeros to branch totals
     MOVE branch to branch hold
```

FIGURE 5–29

Flowchart

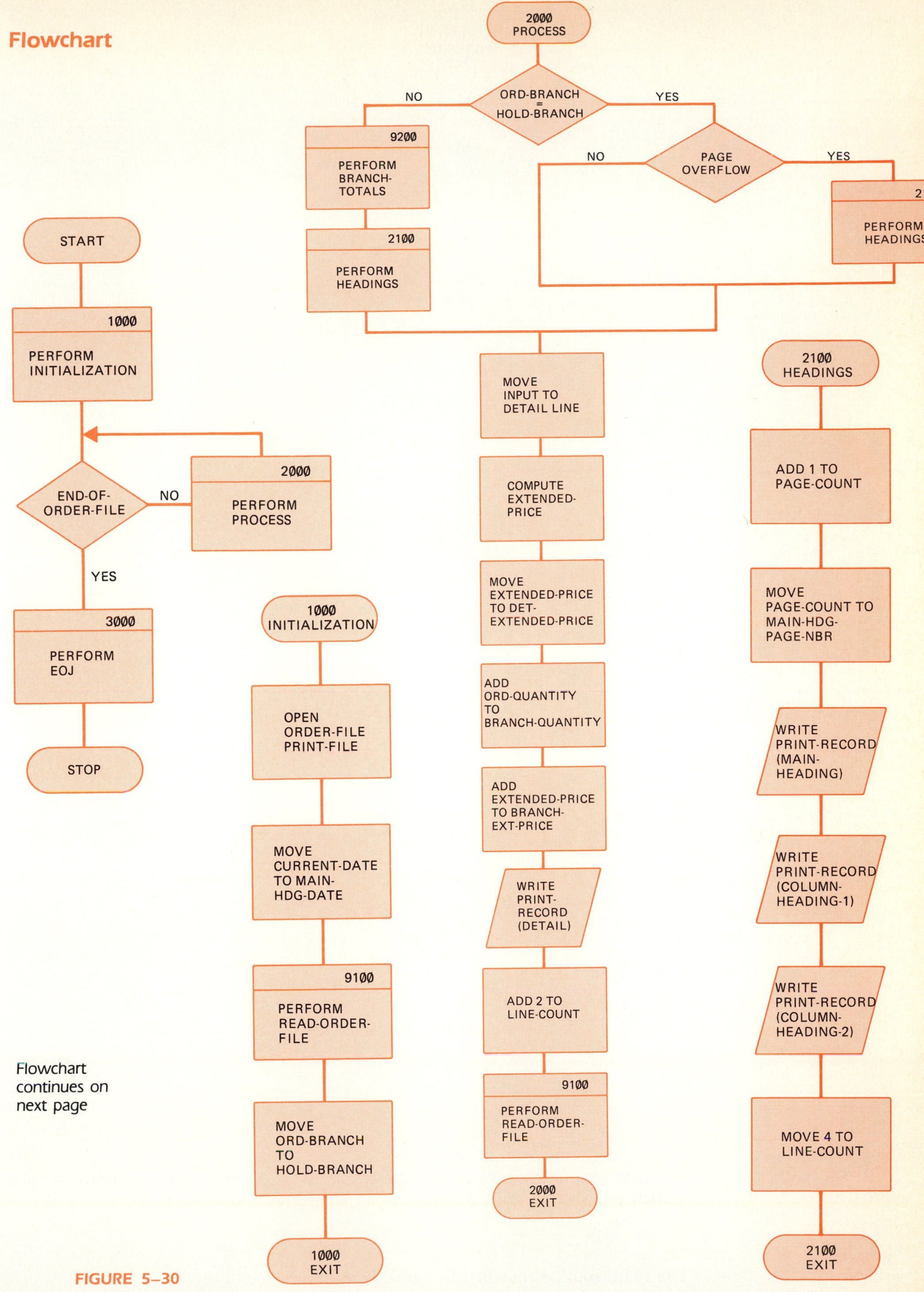

Flowchart continues on next page

FIGURE 5–30

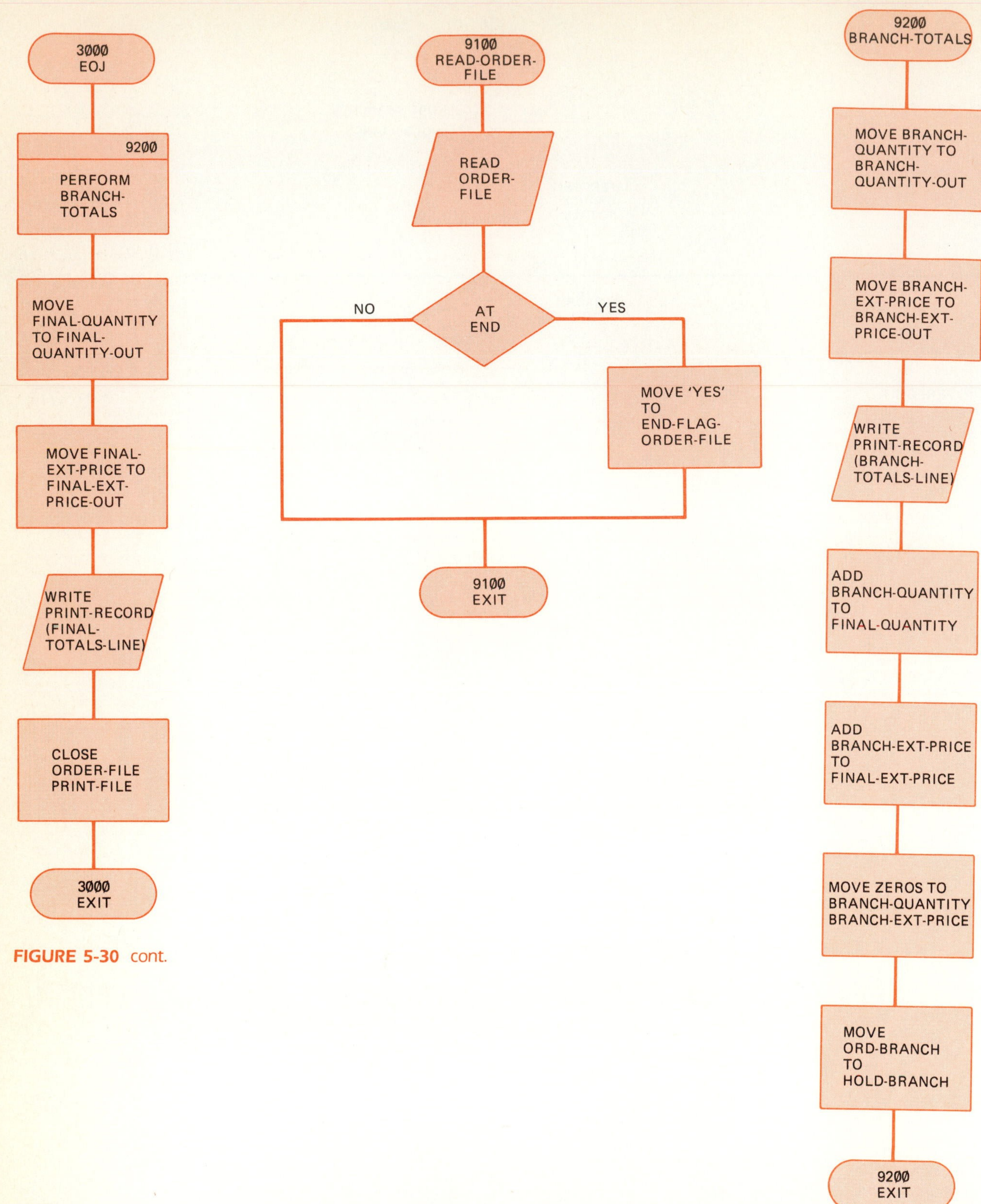

FIGURE 5-30 cont.

Explanation of Logic

One new routine is added to the logic of the BREAK-1 program in order to produce branch totals. This routine is performed when the branch changes.

MAIN LINE

The main routine remains the same as in all previous programs.

1000-INITIALIZATION

The steps in the initialization routine are the same as in the BREAK-1 program. The files are opened, the current date is placed in the headings, and the first READ of the input file is performed.

The last step moves ORD-BRANCH, from the first record, to HOLD-BRANCH. This is a part of the control-break logic which will let us know when there is a change in ORD-BRANCH. Recall that the specifications call for totals to be printed for each branch.

With the hold area initialized to zero, the first value read for ORD-BRANCH will probably not be equal to that of the hold area. This change (from zero to the value in the first record) indicates that it is time to print totals. However, since it is the first record that is being read, there are no totals ready to be printed. In order to circumvent this problem, the hold is updated after the first READ in 1000-INITIALIZATION. Then, in 2000-PROCESS, when the value from the first input record is compared against that of the hold area, the two will be equal and no totals will be printed.

Figure 5–31 shows the logic of the 1000-INITIALIZATION routine.

2000-PROCESS

In 2000-PROCESS, ORD-BRANCH is compared to HOLD-BRANCH. If ORD-BRANCH and HOLD-BRANCH are not equal, it is time for a control break which

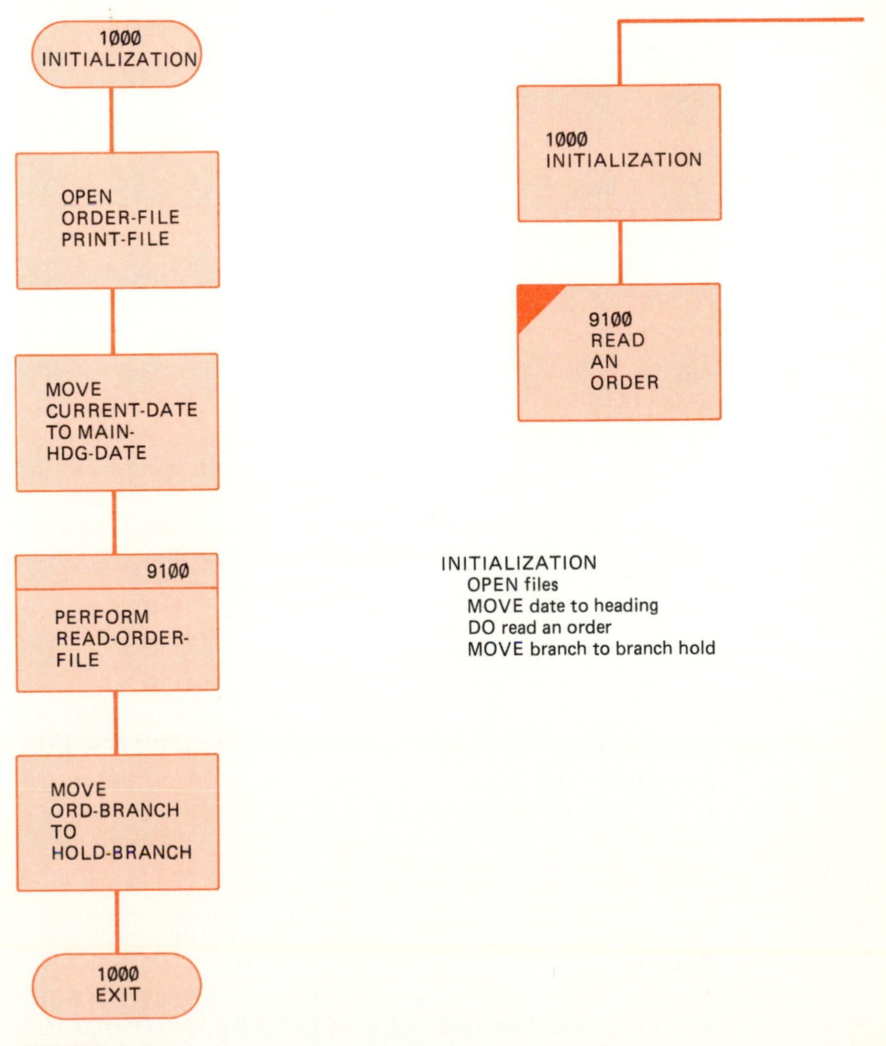

FIGURE 5–31

includes performing BRANCH-TOTALS and then HEADINGS. The BRANCH-TOTALS routine will print the branch totals, add them to the final totals, zero out branch totals, and move the new branch number to the hold area. In short, all actions that must be performed when the branch changes will be done.

If ORD-BRANCH and HOLD-BRANCH are equal, LINE-COUNT is tested. If LINE-COUNT is greater than 50, HEADINGS is performed before leaving the nested IF structure. In all cases the next step is to MOVE INPUT TO OUTPUT. Each item from the input that is to be printed is moved to the detail line. Also, EXTENDED-PRICE is calculated and moved to an area on the detail line.

EXTENDED-PRICE and ORD-QUANTITY are added to the totals of those amounts for the branch. These branch totals will later be added into final totals as the control break for ORD-BRANCH occurs. This is the rolling totals technique which consists of adding together the lower level totals to create the higher level totals.

Next, the detail line is written and the routine that reads the next record is performed. Then 2000-PROCESS is exited, and control returns to the main routine to test END-OF-ORDER-FILE. 2000-PROCESS will be repeated until the end of the file is encountered on the ORDER-FILE. In this program, a new technique is used to test END-FLAG-ORDER-FILE. This technique is explained under CONDITION-NAMES later in the chapter.

Figure 5–32 shows the logic of 2000-PROCESS.

2100-HEADINGS

Headings are produced when either LINE-COUNT exceeds 50 or there is a change of branch. The new branch begins on a new page. Since, at six lines per inch, there are 66 lines on an 11-inch page, limiting a page to 50 detail lines allow space for a top and bottom margin. MOVE 4 TO LINE-COUNT is used to reset LINE-COUNT. (See Figure 5–33.)

3000-EOJ

The first step in 3000-EOJ is to perform BRANCH-TOTALS. As long as there are records to read, totals are generated when there is a change in a control-break field (ORD-BRANCH). This change is tested for at the beginning of 2000-PROCESS, and totals routines are performed when appropriate. When the end-of-file indicator is encountered, 'YES' is moved to END-FLAG-ORDER-FILE. The test made in the main routine selects the YES path to perform 3000-EOJ. There is no opportunity to return to 2000-PROCESS and test for a change in the control fields. As a result, the last set of totals for each control-break field must be produced from 3000-EOJ.

After all lower level totals are printed, final totals are written. The files are then closed, and control returns to the main routine where STOP RUN is encountered.

Figure 5–34 shows the logic of 3000-EOJ.

9100-READ-ORDER-FILE

A record is read from the ORDER-FILE, and if the READ encounters the end-of-file indicator, 'YES' is moved to END-FLAG-ORDER-FILE. This routine is always performed just before returning to the main routine to test for END-OF-ORDER-FILE. (See Figure 5–35.)

9200-BRANCH-TOTALS

The routine 9200-BRANCH-TOTALS is performed when ORD-BRANCH changes. Branch totals are moved to output, printed, added to the final totals, then zeroed out so that the totals for the next branch may be accumulated using the same storage areas. The new value of ORD-BRANCH that caused the control break is then moved to the hold area. (See Figure 5–36.)

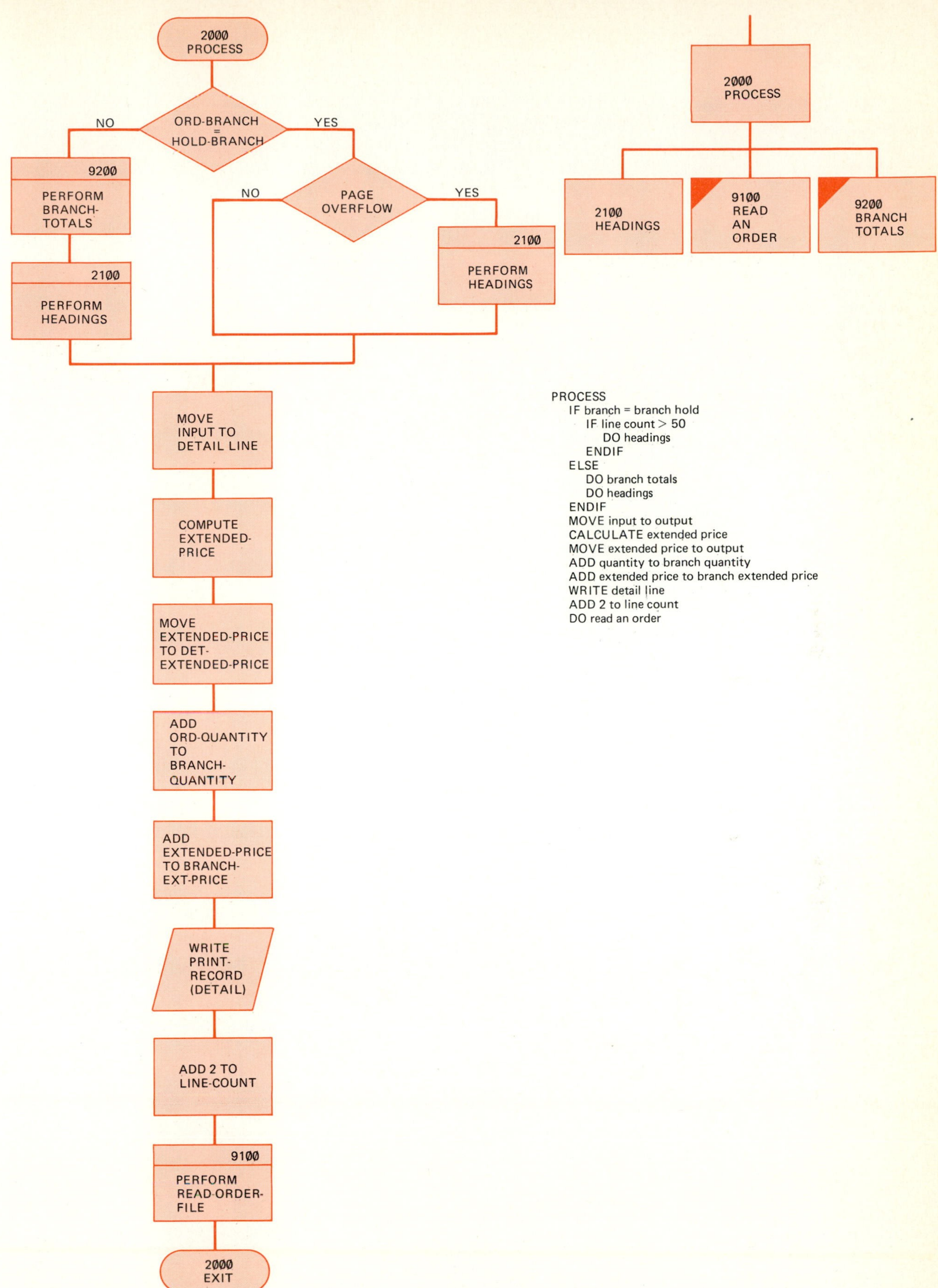
2000
PROCESS
ORD-BRANCH
=
HOLD-BRANCH
NO
YES
9200
PERFORM
BRANCH-
TOTALS
2100
PERFORM
HEADINGS
PAGE
OVERFLOW
NO
YES
2100
PERFORM
HEADINGS
MOVE
INPUT TO
DETAIL LINE
COMPUTE
EXTENDED-
PRICE
MOVE
EXTENDED-PRICE
TO DET-
EXTENDED-PRICE
ADD
ORD-QUANTITY
TO
BRANCH-
QUANTITY
ADD
EXTENDED-PRICE
TO BRANCH-
EXT-PRICE
WRITE
PRINT-
RECORD
(DETAIL)
ADD 2 TO
LINE-COUNT
9100
PERFORM
READ-ORDER-
FILE
2000
EXIT
2000
PROCESS
2100
HEADINGS
9100
READ
AN
ORDER
9200
BRANCH
TOTALS
PROCESS
IF branch = branch hold
IF line count > 50
DO headings
ENDIF
ELSE
DO branch totals
DO headings
ENDIF
MOVE input to output
CALCULATE extended price
MOVE extended price to output
ADD quantity to branch quantity
ADD extended price to branch extended price
WRITE detail line
ADD 2 to line count
DO read an order

FIGURE 5–32

Logic for Single-Level Break with Totals

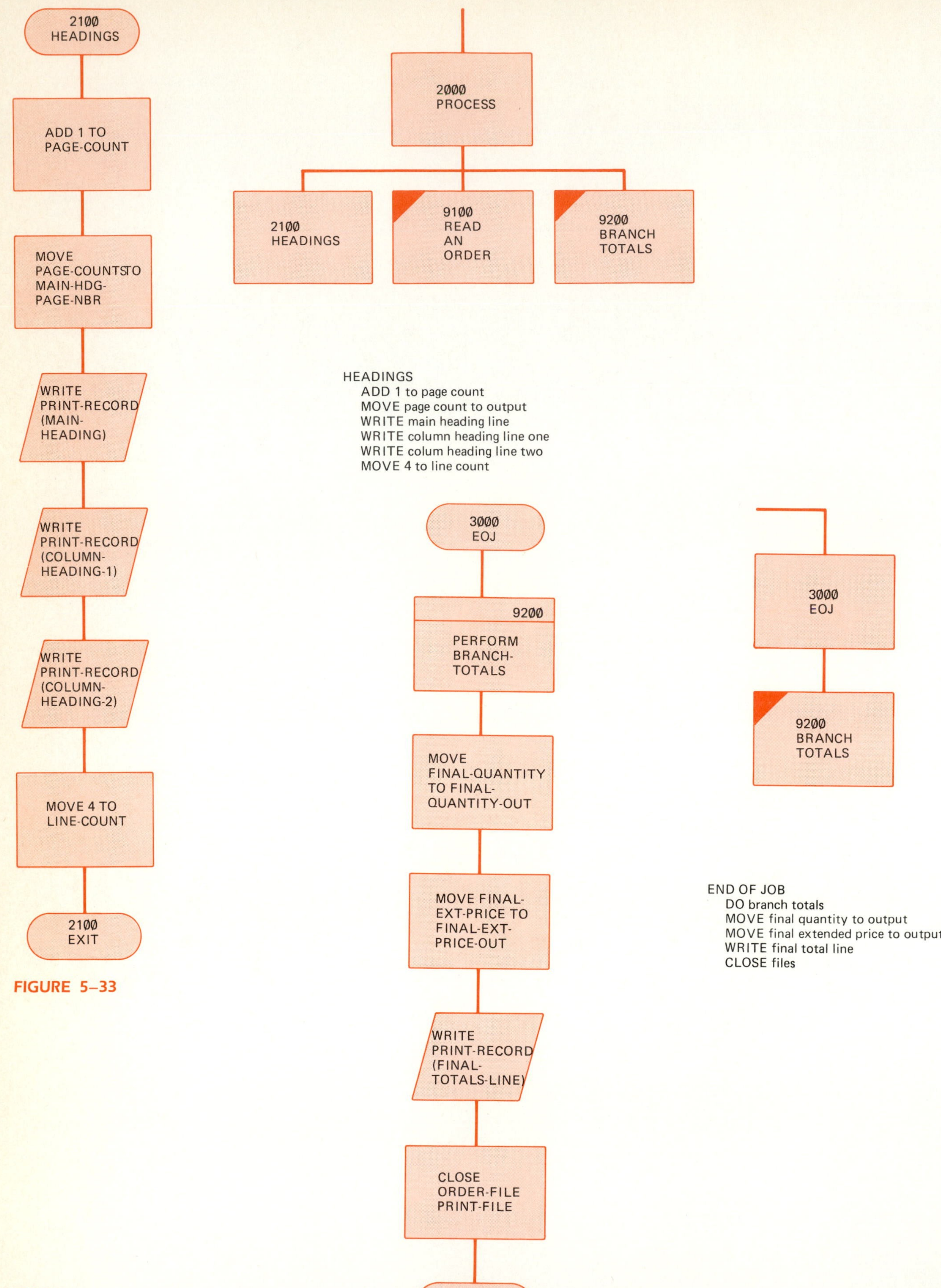

2100 HEADINGS
ADD 1 TO PAGE-COUNT
MOVE PAGE-COUNTSTO MAIN-HDG-PAGE-NBR
WRITE PRINT-RECORD (MAIN-HEADING)
WRITE PRINT-RECORD (COLUMN-HEADING-1)
WRITE PRINT-RECORD (COLUMN-HEADING-2)
MOVE 4 TO LINE-COUNT
2100 EXIT
2000 PROCESS
2100 HEADINGS
9100 READ AN ORDER
9200 BRANCH TOTALS
HEADINGS
ADD 1 to page count
MOVE page count to output
WRITE main heading line
WRITE column heading line one
WRITE colum heading line two
MOVE 4 to line count
3000 EOJ
9200
PERFORM BRANCH-TOTALS
MOVE FINAL-QUANTITY TO FINAL-QUANTITY-OUT
MOVE FINAL-EXT-PRICE TO FINAL-EXT-PRICE-OUT
WRITE PRINT-RECORD (FINAL-TOTALS-LINE)
CLOSE ORDER-FILE PRINT-FILE
3000 EXIT
3000 EOJ
9200 BRANCH TOTALS
END OF JOB
DO branch totals
MOVE final quantity to output
MOVE final extended price to output
WRITE final total line
CLOSE files

FIGURE 5–33

FIGURE 5–34

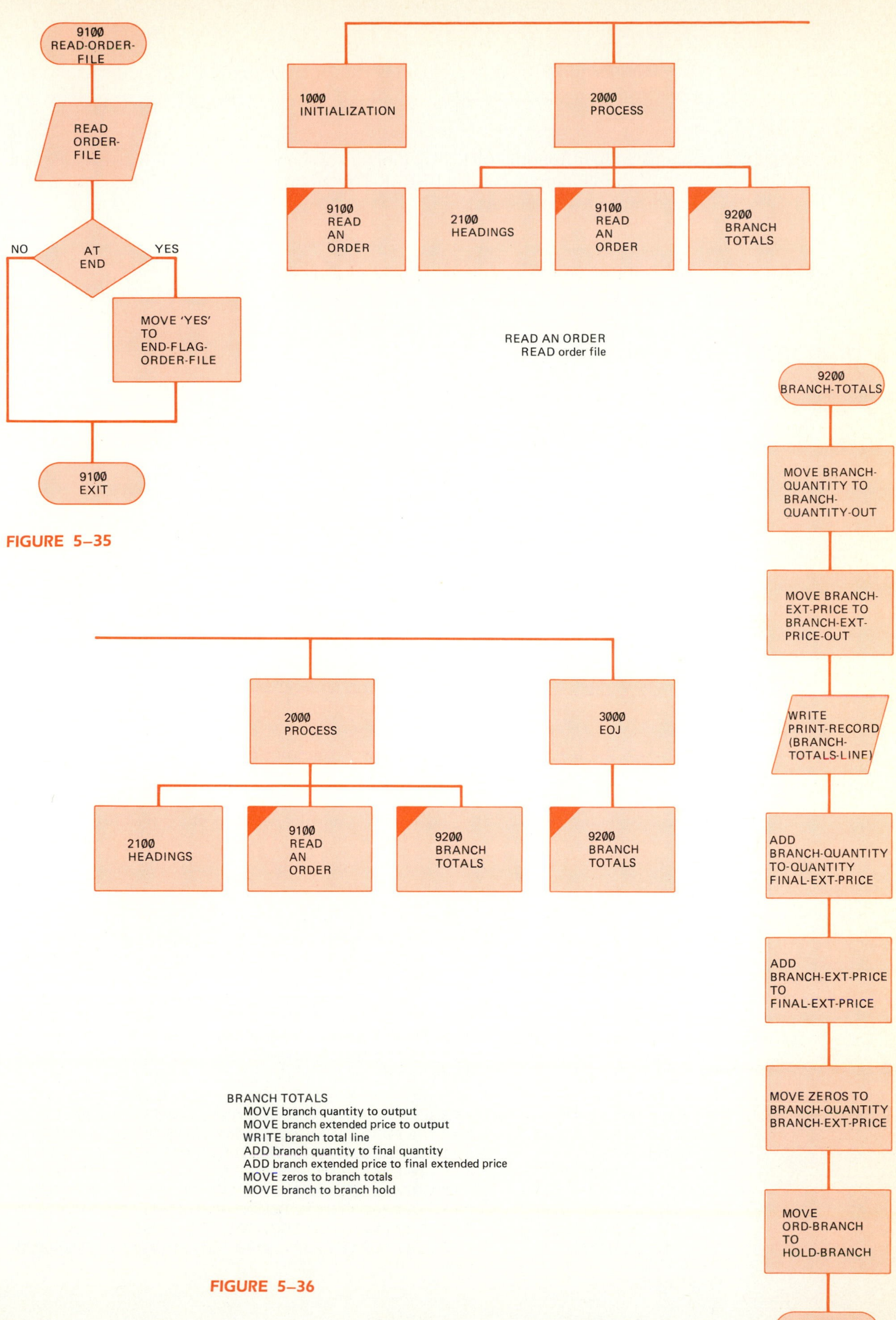
9100 READ-ORDER-FILE
READ ORDER-FILE
AT END
NO
YES
MOVE 'YES' TO END-FLAG-ORDER-FILE
9100 EXIT
1000 INITIALIZATION
2000 PROCESS
9100 READ AN ORDER
2100 HEADINGS
9100 READ AN ORDER
9200 BRANCH TOTALS
READ AN ORDER
READ order file
9200 BRANCH-TOTALS
MOVE BRANCH-QUANTITY TO BRANCH-QUANTITY-OUT
MOVE BRANCH-EXT-PRICE TO BRANCH-EXT-PRICE-OUT
WRITE PRINT-RECORD (BRANCH-TOTALS-LINE)
ADD BRANCH-QUANTITY TO-QUANTITY FINAL-EXT-PRICE
ADD BRANCH-EXT-PRICE TO FINAL-EXT-PRICE
MOVE ZEROS TO BRANCH-QUANTITY BRANCH-EXT-PRICE
MOVE ORD-BRANCH TO HOLD-BRANCH
9200 EXIT
2000 PROCESS
3000 EOJ
2100 HEADINGS
9100 READ AN ORDER
9200 BRANCH TOTALS
9200 BRANCH TOTALS
BRANCH TOTALS
MOVE branch quantity to output
MOVE branch extended price to output
WRITE branch total line
ADD branch quantity to final quantity
ADD branch extended price to final extended price
MOVE zeros to branch totals
MOVE branch to branch hold

FIGURE 5–35

FIGURE 5–36

THE COBOL PROGRAM

Test Data

Test data for the BREAK-2 program is shown in Figure 5–37. It is the same data used in the previous programs.

Sample Output

Sample output from the BREAK-2 program is shown in Figure 5–38. It is identical to the sample output for the BREAK-1 program shown in Figure 5–14, except that it includes branch totals.

The Program

The complete COBOL BREAK-2 program is shown in Figure 5–39.

NEW COBOL ELEMENTS

Condition-Names

Format

```
88 condition-name {VALUES ARE}
                  {VALUE  IS }

      literal-1 [ {THROUGH} literal-2]
                  {THRU   }

     [literal-3 [ {THROUGH} literal-4]...].
                  {THRU   }
```

A condition-name is a name associated with a value or series of values for a data item. It is used to make a comparison sound more English-like and to simplify the testing of a condition. A condition-name is preceded by the level number 88 and is placed immediately under the data item it applies to or under another 88-level entry for that same item. Thus, there may be multiple condition-names under one data item. Each 88-level entry has a condition-name and a VALUE clause. The VALUE clause indicates a value or series of values to be tested. VALUE clauses associated with 88 levels are allowed in the FILE SECTION and the WORKING-STORAGE SECTION, unlike VALUE clauses used to initialize fields, which are allowed only in the WORKING-STORAGE SECTION. (See Figure 5–40, page 207, for an example of 88-level entries.)

```
Ø1201ØØ3ØØPO173   B12383871Ø25GN4Ø2AØØØØ1Ø45ØØØ871116ØØØØØØØ
Ø1201Ø47278372    G48388870913WB7Ø2XØØØ9ØØ115ØØ871101ØØØØØØØ
Ø1201ØØ3ØØE1Ø12   B12335871105WB493EØØØØ2Ø54ØØØ871122ØØØØØØØ
Ø3ØØ747300        H84777870223MF4Ø3TØØØØ5Ø4ØØØØ87Ø5Ø2ØØØØØØØ
Ø3ØØ7ØØ378EBNER   H84579870811VX922PØØ8ØØØØ1275891120ØØØØØØØ
Ø3ØØ7739897747    B89288871106MF848JØØØØ5Ø2145Ø88Ø130ØØØØØØØ
Ø3ØØ7ØØ28334567X  B34237871Ø3ØHL834EØØØ16Ø19ØØØ871121ØØØØØØØ
Ø3ØØ747300        Y289Ø3870811VXØØ1LØØ2ØØØØ622Ø87120ØØØØØØØØ
Ø344Ø6948187Ø341  GØ418Ø87Ø2Ø9JGØ4ØXØØØØ1Ø525ØØ88Ø619ØØØØØØØ
Ø361182888P2783733B8433Ø871Ø25HL289BØØØ1ØØ234ØØ871113ØØØØØØØ
Ø361128375T7838   T7829987Ø323JG563WØØØØ6Ø43ØØØ871Ø18ØØØØØØØ
Ø36115Ø912        H6915Ø87Ø2Ø6MF848TØØØØ3Ø36ØØØ8712Ø1ØØØØØØØ
Ø817431408865     H4189187Ø412TK61ØLØØØ18ØØ78ØØ87Ø63ØØØØØØØØ
Ø8174Ø18Ø5R7278   T2164287Ø81ØTK497XØØØ1ØØ118ØØ87113ØØØØØØØØ
Ø8174Ø18Ø5R8322   Y211Ø587Ø6Ø1TN116TØØØØ1Ø3ØØØØ871221ØØØØØØØ
Ø891562Ø54SCHUH   L5Ø681871108TK812EØØØØ6Ø573ØØ88Ø1Ø5ØØØØØØØ
Ø891521Ø78        B71Ø45871ØØ1FV782TØØØØ3ØØ28ØØ871115ØØØØØØØ
```

FIGURE 5–37

DATE: 11/09/87 PRODUCT DISTRIBUTION INC. - CURRENT ORDERS PAGE: 1

BRANCH	SALES REP	CUSTOMER NUMBER	SALES ORDER	ORDER DATE	REQUESTED SHIP DATE	ACTUAL SHIP DATE	PART NUMBER	QUANTITY	UNIT PRICE	EXTENDED PRICE
01	201	00300	B 12383	10/25/87	11/16/87	00/00/00	GN402A	1	$450.00	$450.00
01	201	04727	G 48388	09/13/87	11/01/87	00/00/00	WB702X	90	$115.00	$10,350.00
01	201	00300	B 12335	11/05/87	11/22/87	00/00/00	WB493E	2	$540.00	$1,080.00
BRANCH TOTALS								93		$11,880.00

DATE: 11/09/87 PRODUCT DISTRIBUTION INC. - CURRENT ORDERS PAGE: 2

BRANCH	SALES REP	CUSTOMER NUMBER	SALES ORDER	ORDER DATE	REQUESTED SHIP DATE	ACTUAL SHIP DATE	PART NUMBER	QUANTITY	UNIT PRICE	EXTENDED PRICE
03	007	47300	H 84777	02/23/87	05/02/87	00/00/00	MF403T	5	$400.00	$2,000.00
03	007	00378	H 84579	08/11/87	11/20/89	00/00/00	VX922P	800	$12.75	$10,200.00
03	007	73989	B 89288	11/06/87	01/30/88	00/00/00	MF848J	5	$214.50	$1,072.50
03	007	00283	B 34237	10/30/87	11/21/87	00/00/00	HL834E	16	$190.00	$3,040.00
03	007	47300	Y 28903	08/11/87	12/03/87	00/00/00	VX001L	200	$62.20	$12,440.00
03	440	69481	G 04180	02/09/87	06/19/88	00/00/00	JG040X	1	$525.00	$525.00
03	611	82888	B 84330	10/25/87	11/13/87	00/00/00	HL289B	10	$234.00	$2,340.00
03	611	28375	T 78299	03/23/87	10/18/87	00/00/00	JG563W	6	$430.00	$2,580.00
03	611	50912	H 69150	02/06/87	12/01/87	00/00/00	MF848T	3	$360.00	$1,080.00
BRANCH TOTALS								1,046		$35,277.50

DATE: 11/09/87 PRODUCT DISTRIBUTION INC. - CURRENT ORDERS PAGE: 3

BRANCH	SALES REP	CUSTOMER NUMBER	SALES ORDER	ORDER DATE	REQUESTED SHIP DATE	ACTUAL SHIP DATE	PART NUMBER	QUANTITY	UNIT PRICE	EXTENDED PRICE
08	174	31408	H 41891	04/12/87	06/30/87	00/00/00	TK610L	18	$78.00	$1,404.00
08	174	01805	T 21642	08/10/87	11/30/87	00/00/00	TK497X	10	$118.00	$1,180.00
08	174	01805	Y 21105	06/01/87	12/21/87	00/00/00	TN116T	1	$300.00	$300.00
08	915	62054	L 50681	11/08/87	01/05/88	00/00/00	TK812E	6	$573.00	$3,438.00
08	915	21078	B 71045	10/01/87	11/15/87	00/00/00	FV782T	3	$28.00	$84.00
BRANCH TOTALS								38		$6,406.00
FINAL TOTALS								1,177		$53,563.50

FIGURE 5–38

```
IDENTIFICATION DIVISION.

PROGRAM-ID.    BREAK-2.

AUTHOR.        HELEN HUMPHREYS.

INSTALLATION.  PRODUCT DISTRIBUTION INC.

DATE-WRITTEN.  Ø5/23/87.

DATE-COMPILED. Ø5/31/87.

*****************************************************************
*                                                               *
*    THIS PROGRAM WILL PRODUCE A PRINTED LISTING OF THE ORDER   *
*    FILE.  THE REPORT WILL INCLUDE BRANCH AND FINAL TOTALS     *
*    FOR QUANTITY AND EXTENDED PRICE.  EACH BRANCH WILL BEGIN   *
*    ON A NEW PAGE.                                             *
*                                                               *
*****************************************************************

ENVIRONMENT DIVISION.

CONFIGURATION SECTION.

SOURCE-COMPUTER.
       IBM-37Ø.
OBJECT-COMPUTER.
       IBM-37Ø.

INPUT-OUTPUT SECTION.
FILE-CONTROL.
    SELECT ORDER-FILE ASSIGN TO DISK.
    SELECT PRINT-FILE ASSIGN TO PRINTER.

DATA DIVISION.
FILE SECTION.

FD  ORDER-FILE
    LABEL RECORDS ARE STANDARD
    RECORD CONTAINS 7Ø CHARACTERS
    DATA RECORD IS ORDER-RECORD.

Ø1  ORDER-RECORD.
    Ø5  ORD-BRANCH                  PIC 9(2).
    Ø5  ORD-SALES-REP               PIC 9(3).
    Ø5  ORD-CUSTOMER-NBR            PIC 9(5).
    Ø5  ORD-CUST-PO-NBR             PIC X(8).
    Ø5  ORD-SALES-ORD-NBR           PIC X(6).
    Ø5  ORD-DATE.
        1Ø  ORD-YY                  PIC 9(2).
        1Ø  ORD-MM                  PIC 9(2).
        1Ø  ORD-DD                  PIC 9(2).
    Ø5  ORD-PART-NBR                PIC X(6).
    Ø5  ORD-QUANTITY                PIC 9(5).
    Ø5  ORD-UNIT-PRICE              PIC 9(4)V9(2).
    Ø5  ORD-REQ-SHIP-DATE.
        1Ø  ORD-REQ-SHIP-YY         PIC 9(2).
        1Ø  ORD-REQ-SHIP-MM         PIC 9(2).
        1Ø  ORD-REQ-SHIP-DD         PIC 9(2).
    Ø5  ORD-ACT-SHIP-DATE.
        1Ø  ORD-ACT-SHIP-YY         PIC 9(2).
        1Ø  ORD-ACT-SHIP-MM         PIC 9(2).
        1Ø  ORD-ACT-SHIP-DD         PIC 9(2).
    Ø5  FILLER                      PIC X(11).

FD  PRINT-FILE
    LABEL RECORDS ARE OMITTED
    RECORD CONTAINS 133 CHARACTERS
    DATA RECORD IS PRINT-RECORD.

Ø1  PRINT-RECORD                    PIC X(133).

WORKING-STORAGE SECTION.

Ø1  HOLDS-COUNTERS-SWITCHES.
    Ø5  END-FLAG-ORDER-FILE         PIC X(3)        VALUE 'NO'.
        88  END-OF-ORDER-FILE                       VALUE 'YES'.
    Ø5  LINE-COUNT                  PIC 9(2)        VALUE 99.
        88  PAGE-OVERFLOW                           VALUE 51 THRU 99.
    Ø5  PAGE-COUNT                  PIC 9(3)        VALUE ZEROS.
```

FIGURE 5–39

FIGURE 5-39 cont.

```
           Ø5  HOLD-BRANCH              PIC 9(2)        VALUE ZEROS.

       Ø1  CALCULATED-FIELDS.
           Ø5  EXTENDED-PRICE           PIC 9(7)V9(2).

       Ø1  BRANCH-TOTALS.
           Ø5  BRANCH-QUANTITY          PIC 9(6)        VALUE ZEROS.
           Ø5  BRANCH-EXT-PRICE         PIC 9(8)V9(2)   VALUE ZEROS.

       Ø1  FINAL-TOTALS.
           Ø5  FINAL-QUANTITY           PIC 9(6)        VALUE ZEROS.
           Ø5  FINAL-EXT-PRICE          PIC 9(8)V9(2)   VALUE ZEROS.

       Ø1  MAIN-HEADING.
           Ø5  FILLER                   PIC X(7)        VALUE SPACES.
           Ø5  FILLER                   PIC X(6)        VALUE 'DATE:'.
           Ø5  MAIN-HDG-DATE            PIC X(8).
           Ø5  FILLER                   PIC X(25)       VALUE SPACES.
           Ø5  FILLER                   PIC X(42)
               VALUE 'PRODUCT DISTRIBUTION INC. - CURRENT ORDERS'.
           Ø5  FILLER                   PIC X(27)       VALUE SPACES.
           Ø5  FILLER                   PIC X(6)        VALUE 'PAGE:'.
           Ø5  MAIN-HDG-PAGE-NBR        PIC ZZ9.
           Ø5  FILLER                   PIC X(9)        VALUE SPACES.

       Ø1  COLUMN-HEADING-1.
           Ø5  FILLER                   PIC X(14)       VALUE SPACES.
           Ø5  FILLER                   PIC X(5)        VALUE 'SALES'.
           Ø5  FILLER                   PIC X(2)        VALUE SPACES.
           Ø5  FILLER                   PIC X(8)        VALUE 'CUSTOMER'.
           Ø5  FILLER                   PIC X(3)        VALUE SPACES.
           Ø5  FILLER                   PIC X(5)        VALUE 'SALES'.
           Ø5  FILLER                   PIC X(6)        VALUE SPACES.
           Ø5  FILLER                   PIC X(5)        VALUE 'ORDER'.
           Ø5  FILLER                   PIC X(6)        VALUE SPACES.
           Ø5  FILLER                   PIC X(9)        VALUE
                                                        'REQUESTED'.
           Ø5  FILLER                   PIC X(4)        VALUE SPACES.
           Ø5  FILLER                   PIC X(6)        VALUE 'ACTUAL'.
           Ø5  FILLER                   PIC X(6)        VALUE SPACES.
           Ø5  FILLER                   PIC X(4)        VALUE 'PART'.
           Ø5  FILLER                   PIC X(18)       VALUE SPACES.
           Ø5  FILLER                   PIC X(4)        VALUE 'UNIT'.
           Ø5  FILLER                   PIC X(9)        VALUE SPACES.
           Ø5  FILLER                   PIC X(8)        VALUE 'EXTENDED'.
           Ø5  FILLER                   PIC X(11)       VALUE SPACES.

       Ø1  COLUMN-HEADING-2.
           Ø5  FILLER                   PIC X(7)        VALUE SPACES.
           Ø5  FILLER                   PIC X(6)        VALUE 'BRANCH'.
           Ø5  FILLER                   PIC X(2)        VALUE SPACES.
           Ø5  FILLER                   PIC X(3)        VALUE 'REP'.
           Ø5  FILLER                   PIC X(4)        VALUE SPACES.
           Ø5  FILLER                   PIC X(6)        VALUE 'NUMBER'.
           Ø5  FILLER                   PIC X(4)        VALUE SPACES.
           Ø5  FILLER                   PIC X(5)        VALUE 'ORDER'.
           Ø5  FILLER                   PIC X(7)        VALUE SPACES.
           Ø5  FILLER                   PIC X(4)        VALUE 'DATE'.
           Ø5  FILLER                   PIC X(6)        VALUE SPACES.
           Ø5  FILLER                   PIC X(9)        VALUE
                                                        'SHIP DATE'.
           Ø5  FILLER                   PIC X(3)        VALUE SPACES.
           Ø5  FILLER                   PIC X(9)        VALUE
                                                        'SHIP DATE'.
           Ø5  FILLER                   PIC X(3)        VALUE SPACES.
           Ø5  FILLER                   PIC X(6)        VALUE 'NUMBER'.
           Ø5  FILLER                   PIC X(3)        VALUE SPACES.
           Ø5  FILLER                   PIC X(8)        VALUE 'QUANTITY'.
           Ø5  FILLER                   PIC X(6)        VALUE SPACES.
           Ø5  FILLER                   PIC X(5)        VALUE 'PRICE'.
           Ø5  FILLER                   PIC X(9)        VALUE SPACES.
           Ø5  FILLER                   PIC X(5)        VALUE 'PRICE'.
           Ø5  FILLER                   PIC X(9)        VALUE SPACES.

       Ø1  DETAIL-LINE.
           Ø5  FILLER                   PIC X(9)        VALUE SPACES.
           Ø5  DET-BRANCH               PIC 9(2).
           Ø5  FILLER                   PIC X(4)        VALUE SPACES.
           Ø5  DET-SALES-REP            PIC 9(3).
           Ø5  FILLER                   PIC X(4)        VALUE SPACES.
           Ø5  DET-CUSTOMER-NBR         PIC 9(5).
```

FIGURE 5-39 cont.

```
           Ø5  FILLER                     PIC X(4)        VALUE SPACES.
           Ø5  DET-SALES-ORD-NBR          PIC XBXXXXX.
           Ø5  FILLER                     PIC X(4)        VALUE SPACES.
           Ø5  DET-ORDER-MM               PIC 9(2).
           Ø5  FILLER                     PIC X(1)        VALUE '/'.
           Ø5  DET-ORDER-DD               PIC 9(2).
           Ø5  FILLER                     PIC X(1)        VALUE '/'.
           Ø5  DET-ORDER-YY               PIC 9(2).
           Ø5  FILLER                     PIC X(4)        VALUE SPACES.
           Ø5  DET-REQ-SHIP-MM            PIC 9(2).
           Ø5  FILLER                     PIC X(1)        VALUE '/'.
           Ø5  DET-REQ-SHIP-DD            PIC 9(2).
           Ø5  FILLER                     PIC X(1)        VALUE '/'.
           Ø5  DET-REQ-SHIP-YY            PIC 9(2).
           Ø5  FILLER                     PIC X(4)        VALUE SPACES.
           Ø5  DET-ACT-SHIP-MM            PIC 9(2).
           Ø5  FILLER                     PIC X(1)        VALUE '/'.
           Ø5  DET-ACT-SHIP-DD            PIC 9(2).
           Ø5  FILLER                     PIC X(1)        VALUE '/'.
           Ø5  DET-ACT-SHIP-YY            PIC 9(2).
           Ø5  FILLER                     PIC X(4)        VALUE SPACES.
           Ø5  DET-PART-NBR               PIC X(6).
           Ø5  FILLER                     PIC X(4)        VALUE SPACES.
           Ø5  DET-QUANTITY               PIC ZZ,ZZ9.
           Ø5  FILLER                     PIC X(4)        VALUE SPACES.
           Ø5  DET-UNIT-PRICE             PIC $$,$$9.99.
           Ø5  FILLER                     PIC X(4)        VALUE SPACES.
           Ø5  DET-EXTENDED-PRICE         PIC $$,$$$,$$9.99.
           Ø5  FILLER                     PIC X(9)        VALUE SPACES.

       Ø1  BRANCH-TOTALS-LINE.
           Ø5  FILLER                     PIC X(9)        VALUE SPACES.
           Ø5  FILLER                     PIC X(13)
                                          VALUE 'BRANCH TOTALS'.
           Ø5  FILLER                     PIC X(65)       VALUE SPACES.
           Ø5  BRANCH-QUANTITY-OUT        PIC ZZZ,ZZ9.
           Ø5  FILLER                     PIC X(16)       VALUE SPACES.
           Ø5  BRANCH-EXT-PRICE-OUT       PIC $$$,$$$,$$9.99.
           Ø5  FILLER                     PIC X(9).

       Ø1  FINAL-TOTALS-LINE.
           Ø5  FILLER                     PIC X(9)        VALUE SPACES.
           Ø5  FILLER                     PIC X(12)
                                          VALUE 'FINAL TOTALS'.
           Ø5  FILLER                     PIC X(66)       VALUE SPACES.
           Ø5  FINAL-QUANTITY-OUT         PIC ZZZ,ZZ9.
           Ø5  FILLER                     PIC X(16)       VALUE SPACES.
           Ø5  FINAL-EXT-PRICE-OUT        PIC $$$,$$$,$$9.99.
           Ø5  FILLER                     PIC X(9).

       PROCEDURE DIVISION.

           PERFORM 1ØØØ-INITIALIZATION.
           PERFORM 2ØØØ-PROCESS
               UNTIL END-OF-ORDER-FILE.
           PERFORM 3ØØØ-EOJ.
           STOP RUN.

       1ØØØ-INITIALIZATION.
           OPEN INPUT  ORDER-FILE
                OUTPUT PRINT-FILE.
           MOVE CURRENT-DATE TO MAIN-HDG-DATE.
           PERFORM 91ØØ-READ-ORDER-FILE.
           MOVE ORD-BRANCH TO HOLD-BRANCH.

       2ØØØ-PROCESS.
           IF ORD-BRANCH = HOLD-BRANCH
               IF PAGE-OVERFLOW
                   PERFORM 21ØØ-HEADINGS
               ELSE
                   NEXT SENTENCE
           ELSE
               PERFORM 92ØØ-BRANCH-TOTALS
               PERFORM 21ØØ-HEADINGS.
           MOVE ORD-BRANCH                TO DET-BRANCH.
           MOVE ORD-SALES-REP             TO DET-SALES-REP.
           MOVE ORD-CUSTOMER-NBR          TO DET-CUSTOMER-NBR.
           MOVE ORD-SALES-ORD-NBR         TO DET-SALES-ORD-NBR.
           MOVE ORD-YY                    TO DET-ORDER-YY.
           MOVE ORD-MM                    TO DET-ORDER-MM.
           MOVE ORD-DD                    TO DET-ORDER-DD.
```

FIGURE 5-39 cont.

```
           MOVE ORD-PART-NBR            TO DET-PART-NBR.
           MOVE ORD-QUANTITY            TO DET-QUANTITY.
           MOVE ORD-UNIT-PRICE          TO DET-UNIT-PRICE.
           MOVE ORD-REQ-SHIP-YY         TO DET-REQ-SHIP-YY.
           MOVE ORD-REQ-SHIP-MM         TO DET-REQ-SHIP-MM.
           MOVE ORD-REQ-SHIP-DD         TO DET-REQ-SHIP-DD.
           MOVE ORD-ACT-SHIP-YY         TO DET-ACT-SHIP-YY.
           MOVE ORD-ACT-SHIP-MM         TO DET-ACT-SHIP-MM.
           MOVE ORD-ACT-SHIP-DD         TO DET-ACT-SHIP-DD.
           COMPUTE EXTENDED-PRICE = ORD-UNIT-PRICE * ORD-QUANTITY.
           MOVE EXTENDED-PRICE          TO DET-EXTENDED-PRICE.
           ADD ORD-QUANTITY             TO BRANCH-QUANTITY.
           ADD EXTENDED-PRICE           TO BRANCH-EXT-PRICE.
           WRITE PRINT-RECORD FROM DETAIL-LINE
               AFTER ADVANCING 2 LINES.
           ADD 2 TO LINE-COUNT.
           PERFORM 9100-READ-ORDER-FILE.

       2100-HEADINGS.
           ADD 1 TO PAGE-COUNT.
           MOVE PAGE-COUNT TO MAIN-HDG-PAGE-NBR.
           WRITE PRINT-RECORD FROM MAIN-HEADING
               AFTER ADVANCING PAGE.
           WRITE PRINT-RECORD FROM COLUMN-HEADING-1
               AFTER ADVANCING 2 LINES.
           WRITE PRINT-RECORD FROM COLUMN-HEADING-2
               AFTER ADVANCING 1 LINE.
           MOVE 4 TO LINE-COUNT.

       3000-EOJ.
           PERFORM 9200-BRANCH-TOTALS.
           MOVE FINAL-QUANTITY TO FINAL-QUANTITY-OUT.
           MOVE FINAL-EXT-PRICE TO FINAL-EXT-PRICE-OUT.
           WRITE PRINT-RECORD FROM FINAL-TOTALS-LINE
               AFTER ADVANCING 3 LINES.
           CLOSE ORDER-FILE
                 PRINT-FILE.

       9100-READ-ORDER-FILE.
           READ ORDER-FILE
               AT END
                   MOVE 'YES' TO END-FLAG-ORDER-FILE.

       9200-BRANCH-TOTALS.
           MOVE BRANCH-QUANTITY         TO BRANCH-QUANTITY-OUT.
           MOVE BRANCH-EXT-PRICE        TO BRANCH-EXT-PRICE-OUT.
           WRITE PRINT-RECORD FROM BRANCH-TOTALS-LINE
               AFTER ADVANCING 2 LINES.
           ADD BRANCH-QUANTITY          TO FINAL-QUANTITY.
           ADD BRANCH-EXT-PRICE         TO FINAL-EXT-PRICE.
           MOVE ZEROS                   TO BRANCH-QUANTITY
                                           BRANCH-EXT-PRICE.
           MOVE ORD-BRANCH              TO HOLD-BRANCH.
```

```
05  ORD-BRANCH                      PIC 9(2).
    88  EASTERN-BRANCH                  VALUE 1.
    88  SOUTHERN-BRANCH                 VALUE 2.
    88  CENTRAL-BRANCH                  VALUE 3.
    88  ROCKY-MOUNTAIN-BRANCH           VALUE 4.
    88  WESTERN-BRANCH                  VALUE 5.
    88  VALID-BRANCH                    VALUE 1 THRU 5.
```

FIGURE 5–40

Testing Condition-names

Format

```
IF [NOT] condition-name . . .
```

When a condition-name is used in an IF statement, the computer generates a comparison of the current contents of the data item with the value(s) specified in the 88 level. Thus,

```
IF EASTERN-BRANCH . . .
```

will generate the comparison IF ORD-BRANCH = 1 . . . , and

```
IF VALID-BRANCH . . .
```

will generate the comparison IF ORD-BRANCH > 0 AND ORD-BRANCH < 6 . . . .

When a code is changed in the data, the change only needs to be made in one place—at the 88-level VALUE. Suppose that the code for the eastern branch was changed from 1 to 11 due to a reorganization of branches. We would then change the 88 level to

```
88 EASTERN-BRANCH                VALUE 11.
```

Any references to IF EASTERN-BRANCH in the program would then generate the appropriate comparison. If the alternative, IF ORD-BRANCH = 1, had been used, then each comparison would require changing to IF ORD-BRANCH = 11.

The VALUE clause in the 88 level must agree with the PICTURE clause if the condition-name is for an elementary item. If the condition-name is for a group item, the VALUE clause must be alphanumeric. (See Figure 5–41.)

FIGURE 5–41

```
05  ORIGIN-OF-SALE.
    88  INSIDE-SALE                        VALUE '00000' '00100'.
    88  OUTSIDE-SALE                       VALUE '01001' THRU
                                                 '05199'.
    10  ORD-BRANCH                   PIC   9(2).
        88  EASTERN-BRANCH                 VALUE 1.
        88  SOUTHERN-BRANCH                VALUE 2.
        88  CENTRAL-BRANCH                 VALUE 3.
        88  ROCKY-MOUNTAIN-BRANCH          VALUE 4.
        88  WESTERN-BRANCH                 VALUE 5.
        88  VALID-BRANCH                   VALUE 1 THRU 5.
    10  ORD-SALES-REP                PIC 9(3).
        88  SALES-REP                      VALUE 001 THRU 099.
        88  SALES-MANAGER                  VALUE 100 THRU 199.
```

For the data shown in the figure, the statement

```
IF INSIDE-SALE. . .
```

will generate the comparison

```
IF ORIGIN-OF-SALE = '00000' OR
   ORIGIN-OF-SALE = '00100'. . . .
```

In the BREAK-2 program a condition-name END-OF-ORDER-FILE is used with the data item END-FLAG-ORDER-FILE:

```
05  END-FLAG-ORDER-FILE        PIC X(3)   VALUE 'NO'.
    88  END-OF-ORDER-FILE                 VALUE 'YES'.
```

The 05-level entry is called a condition variable because of the 88-level entry under it. The condition variable (END-FLAG-ORDER-FILE) occupies three bytes of storage and is initialized with a value of 'NO'. This area of storage may be tested using the condition-name. Thus,

```
IF END-OF-ORDER-FILE . . .
```

will generate the comparison IF END-FLAG-ORDER-FILE = 'YES', which will be false until the file reaches an AT END condition and MOVE 'YES' TO END-FLAG-ORDER-FILE has been executed. Notice that (1) the 05 level reserves storage, whereas the 88 level does not, (2) EQUAL or = is not used with a condition-name, and (3) data is moved to the condition variable, not the condition-name.

DEBUGGING

Diagnostics

HIGH-ORDER TRUNCATION

This diagnostic generally points to a MOVE statement. It means that if the MOVE is made with the field sizes specified, digits may be lost on the left (high-order) side because the sending field is too large or the receiving field is too small. Remember that one *extra* $, +, or − must be coded along with those same symbols which will be replaced with digits.

To solve the problem, the programmer must

1. Determine the number of positions in the sending field.
2. Check to make sure that the sending field is the proper size. If it is from an input file, the programmer is not at liberty to change it.
3. Count the number of positions in the receiving field that may be replaced by digits. Is there the extra $, +, or − needed to print the symbol?
4. Consider the number of positions on both sides of the decimal position in both the sending and receiving fields.

CONDITION-NAME ILLEGAL AS USED

This diagnostic generally points to an IF statement in which the condition-name has been used with a relational operator.

To solve the problem, the programmer must

1. Determine the condition variable associated with the condition-name.
2. Check the erroneous statement to see whether the condition variable should have been used instead of the condition-name.
3. Rephrase the IF statement so that it does not contain relational operators if the intent was to use the condition-name.

__________ MAY NOT BE THE TARGET FIELD FOR __________ IN A MOVE STATEMENT

This diagnostic may occur when a field with editing characters is moved to a receiving field which also has editing characters.

To solve the problem, the programmer must

1. Check the sending field to see whether it is the correct one.
2. Remove all editing characters if the sending field is correct.

Packed Data

Format

```
USAGE IS COMPUTATIONAL-3
```

While USAGE IS DISPLAY is suitable for alphanumeric fields and some uses of numeric fields, there is a more machine-efficient choice for numeric fields which are used in calculations, edited for printed output, or used in numeric comparisons. In order to perform these operations, numeric data in display format is converted to a packed format before it is used.

There are two general ways for data to become packed. The first is for the programmer to describe the data as USAGE IS DISPLAY and let the computer pack the data when it needs to do so for use in certain instructions. The second is to include a USAGE IS COMP-3 or equivalent clause in the data description so that the data is stored in a packed format. USAGE IS COMP-3 is not part of ANSI

74 STANDARD COBOL; it is an extension to the language available on some compilers. The programmer should find out whether the facility exists in his or her installation.

Figure 5–42 shows the technique for converting display data to packed data. FIELD-A contains display data by default because no other USAGE is specified. FIELD-B is a packed field, since COMP-3 is specified. Thus, even though the PICTURE for FIELD-B specifies five numeric positions, only three bytes of storage are reserved for it. To accomplish the packing, the first and last halves of the rightmost byte are reversed and moved to the packed field, and then only the digit portion (the last half) of each remaining byte is moved.

FIGURE 5–42

```
IN THE DATA DIVISION
     05  FIELD-A              PIC 9(5)          VALUE 12345.
     05  FIELD-B              PIC 9(5)          COMP-3.
IN THE PROCEDURE DIVISION
     MOVE FIELD-A TO FIELD-B
```

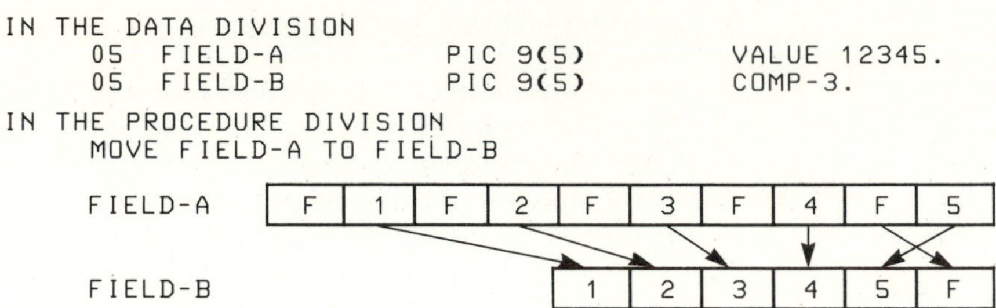

As is plain from the figure, data stored in a packed format generally uses less memory. To find the amount of memory required for packed data, one need merely perform one of the following calculations, depending on whether the PICTURE has an odd or even number of 9's, respectively:

(odd number of digits + 1) / 2
even number of digits / 2 + 1

If it is left to the computer to convert the data from DISPLAY to a COMPUTATIONAL-3 form, the number of steps required to execute this type of instruction has been increased. If data items are instead defined as COMP-3, then the computer does not have to generate the instruction steps necessary to pack the data.

If any COMP-3 fields are included in a record format, the data will take less space when stored on tape or disk. A description of an input record to be used in a program will specify any fields that are COMP-3. Note that the file already exists, and it either has fields that are stored in a packed format or it does not. Hence, a programmer working with an existing file may not arbitrarily decide to make a field in that file COMP-3.

The 1985 standard includes
USAGE IS PACKED-DECIMAL
The storage represents decimal values which use the minimum possible storage.

TRACE

Format

```
{READY}  TRACE
{RESET}
```

A COBOL student's early concerns are usually associated with diagnostics: one too many or one too few periods, one too many or one too few hyphens, a data-name that is not unique, or a data-name that is not defined. After a little programming experience the diagnostics are easier to understand, but a new set of problems arises as programs become more complex. The new problems might be things like

1. There is no output even though there are no diagnostics and the program attempted to execute, or
2. There is too much of something or not enough of something (like heading lines or total lines).

This is a short list, but it provides a place to start. In these cases you may be unsure of the logic path that was followed. Certainly, it is not what you hoped for. Unfortunately, it will turn out to be what you asked for. To solve the problem, you can trace the logic steps to find out whether (1) the wrong path is being taken, (2) steps have been omitted, or (3) extra steps have been included. You can do this by playing computer, i.e., following the PROCEDURE DIVISION instructions step by step, making notes and/or drawing diagrams as you go along.

Sometimes the logic problem becomes apparent after a few minutes. Sometimes it takes a few hours, and occasionally it takes a few days. After you have spent some time trying to trace the problem yourself without success, you can turn to a tool called TRACE that is available on most COBOL compilers.

READY TRACE turns a trace on, and RESET TRACE turns it off. If the command READY TRACE is coded in the PROCEDURE DIVISION, a trace of the logic flow of the program will begin when the instruction is encountered. Since student programs are normally small (hundreds of statements instead of thousands), READY TRACE is often placed immediately after the reserved words PROCEDURE DIVISION, and the entire PROCEDURE DIVISION is traced. The trace will end when the program ends. If you wish the trace to end sooner, you may insert the words RESET TRACE at the point in the logic where the trace is to stop. Terminate the statement with a period unless, of course, you are placing it inside an IF statement.

READY TRACE prints the paragraph-name of each paragraph the logic flow goes through. On some compilers an option allows the programmer to choose between the statement numbers of paragraph-names and the paragraph-names themselves. Presumably, the names will be self-explanatory and, therefore, much easier to follow than the numbers. The programmer should find out whether READY TRACE is available at his or her installation, what form it takes if it is, and what to use in its place if it is not.

Figure 5–43 shows the beginning of a READY TRACE on the BREAK-2 program. Only eight records are traced, three for the first branch and five for the second. Notice how the paragraph names are interspersed with the regular output produced by the program. Since COBOL does not count the lines used by READY TRACE, LINE-COUNT will appear not to be working. When READY TRACE is removed from the program, LINE-COUNT will work as it did before.

```
PROCEDURE DIVISION.
    READY TRACE.
    PERFORM 1000-INITIALIZATION.
      .
      .
      .
```

Since BREAK-2 is a working program, the steps shown by the trace are what we expect. But what if the program were not printing branch totals and, after looking at the logic, you cannot spot the problem. The comparison of ORD-BRANCH and HOLD-BRANCH *seems* correct, and the routine that writes the branch totals *seems* correct, but still you have no totals. If the problem is with the comparison, the trace will show that 9200-BRANCH-TOTALS is not being performed. If the trace shows that 9200-BRANCH-TOTALS is being performed, then the problem lies in the 9200-BRANCH-TOTALS routine. While READY TRACE will not solve the problem for you, it will help you isolate it.

```
1000-INITIALIZATION
9100-READ-ORDER-FILE
2000-PROCESS
2100-HEADINGS

-----------------------------------------------------------------------------------------------------------

      DATE: 11/09/87                         PRODUCT DISTRIBUTION INC. - CURRENT ORDERS                         PAGE:   1

              SALES  CUSTOMER   SALES     ORDER     REQUESTED    ACTUAL      PART                     UNIT        EXTENDED
      BRANCH  REP    NUMBER     ORDER     DATE      SHIP DATE    SHIP DATE   NUMBER   QUANTITY        PRICE       PRICE


        01    201    00300     B 12383   10/25/87   11/16/87     00/00/00    GN402A          1     $450.00          $450.00
9100-READ-ORDER-FILE
2000-PROCESS


        01    201    04727     G 48388   09/13/87   11/01/87     00/00/00    WB702X         90     $115.00       $10,350.00
9100-READ-ORDER-FILE
2000-PROCESS


        01    201    00300     B 12335   11/05/87   11/22/87     00/00/00    WB493E          2     $540.00        $1,080.00
9100-READ-ORDER-FILE
2000-PROCESS
9200-BRANCH-TOTALS


        BRANCH TOTALS                                                                   93                    $11,880.00
2100-HEADINGS

-----------------------------------------------------------------------------------------------------------

      DATE: 11/09/87                         PRODUCT DISTRIBUTION INC. - CURRENT ORDERS                         PAGE:   2

              SALES  CUSTOMER   SALES     ORDER     REQUESTED    ACTUAL      PART                     UNIT        EXTENDED
      BRANCH  REP    NUMBER     ORDER     DATE      SHIP DATE    SHIP DATE   NUMBER   QUANTITY        PRICE       PRICE


        03    007    47300     H 84777   02/23/87   05/02/87     00/00/00    MF403T          5     $400.00        $2,000.00
9100-READ-ORDER-FILE
2000-PROCESS


        03    007    00378     H 84579   08/11/87   11/20/89     00/00/00    VX922P        800      $12.75       $10,200.00
9100-READ-ORDER-FILE
2000-PROCESS


        03    007    73989     B 89288   11/06/87   01/30/88     00/00/00    MF848J          5     $214.50        $1,072.50
9100-READ-ORDER-FILE
2000-PROCESS


        03    007    00283     B 34237   10/30/87   11/21/87     00/00/00    HL834E         16     $190.00        $3,040.00
9100-READ-ORDER-FILE
2000-PROCESS


        03    007    47300     Y 28903   08/11/87   12/03/87     00/00/00    VX001L        200      $62.20       $12,440.00
9100-READ-ORDER-FILE
2000-PROCESS
```

FIGURE 5–43

Let us consider another situation where the program has begun to execute but is not producing any output. Without any output, it is difficult to guess which logic path is being taken or how far it got. READY TRACE will answer both of these questions for you.

Once you are confident you have found the problem, remove the READY TRACE command and run the program again. As is plain from Figure 5–43, the output will not be usable until the trace is removed.

DISPLAY

READY TRACE will tell you which paragraphs the program is passing through. Sometimes, however, this is not enough to pinpoint the problem. It may be that you know which instruction is causing the logic to take the wrong logic path, but you still cannot pinpoint why it is doing so. An example of this is a comparison with unexpected results. You may have used READY TRADE to pinpoint the statement causing the problem, but you still cannot understand what is going wrong. Suppose, for example, that the comparison between ORD-BRANCH and HOLD-BRANCH is such that the result is always equality, so that no branch totals are ever produced. Suppose further that this was discovered using a READY TRACE which found that 9200-BRANCH-TOTALS was never performed. Then DISPLAY statements can be added to the program to display the values of ORD-BRANCH and HOLD-BRANCH on the output listing. The programmer merely chooses the locations in the PROCEDURE DIVISION where it would be helpful to know the values. One spot would be just prior to the comparison. Then, every time the DISPLAY statement is executed, the values of the items specified will be displayed starting in the left margin. The output goes to the system output device unless you specify otherwise. For student programs, this is normally the printer. The DISPLAY statement has the following format:

Format

```
         ┌identifier-1┐   ┌identifier-2┐
DISPLAY  ┤            ├   │            │ . . .
         └literal-1   ┘   └literal-2   ┘
```

To display ORD-BRANCH and HOLD-BRANCH, any of the following could be used:

```
DISPLAY ORD-BRANCH HOLD-BRANCH
```

This statement will display the values of ORD-BRANCH and HOLD-BRANCH on the same line. This form is not recommended, since the values are not identified by name on the output and may be difficult to spot, especially if one or both of them are spaces.

```
DISPLAY 'ORD-BRANCH = ' ORD-BRANCH 'HOLD-BRANCH = '
  HOLD-BRANCH
```

This statement will display the literals ORD-BRANCH = and HOLD-BRANCH = followed by their values. Now we know where we expect the values to be, and it will be apparent if they are blank.

```
DISPLAY 'ORD-BRANCH = ' ORD-BRANCH
DISPLAY 'HOLD-BRANCH = ' HOLD-BRANCH
```

This coding is the clearest of the three to read. Each name and value has its own line; the printer advances a line automatically before printing the output for DISPLAY.

Notice that there are no periods after the DISPLAY statements. This is because DISPLAY statements are often inserted inside nested IFs. A period on such a display statement might cause diagnostics and would certainly change the logic of the IF statement. It is easier to form the habit of omitting periods on DISPLAY statements used for debugging purposes.

DISPLAY statements are often used as a debugging tool without the READY TRACE. Suppose a calculation of federal tax is producing incorrect results. Then if we display the fields involved in the calculation immediately before each step in it, we are likely to spot one or more fields whose value is not what was expected. Accordingly, to use the DISPLAY statement effectively, some thought must be given to which fields affect the calculation and at what point(s) in the execution it will be most beneficial to see the values.

Figure 5–44 gives an example of a DISPLAY statement used with a simplified tax calculation. It is assumed that the value of FEDERAL-TAX is already known. Because an incorrect value is being printed for FEDERAL-TAX, the DISPLAY statements shown were put in the program. The displayed data will alternate with the detail lines printed by the program because the DISPLAY statements will be executed once for every pass through PROCESS in the same way the WRITE for the detail line is.

An extra space is placed at the end of the literal so that the literal and the value will not run together when printed. Notice that the numbers are not edited; the values of the numeric fields used in the calculation are displayed. The programmer must pinpoint the position of the assumed decimal, since none is printed. Once the problem is solved, the DISPLAY statements are removed.

FIGURE 5–44

```
PROCEDURE DIVISION.
    DISPLAY 'NBR-DEP ' NBR OF DEPENDENTS
    DISPLAY 'FED-EXEMP ' FEDERAL EXEMPTION
    COMPUTE EXEMPTION-ALLOWED = NBR-OF-DEPENDENTS
      * FEDERAL-EXEMPTION / 24.
    DISPLAY 'EXEMP-ALLOWED ' EXEMPTION-ALLOWED
    DISPLAY 'GROSS-PAY ' GROSS-PAY
    DISPLAY 'TAX-RATE ' TAX-RATE
    COMPUTE FEDERAL-TAX = (GROSS-PAY - EXEMPTION-ALLOWED)
      * TAX-RATE.
```

OUTPUT

```
    NBR-DEP 03
    FED-EXEMP 100000
    EXEMP-ALLOWED 12500
    GROSS-PAY 86500
    TAX-RATE 250

518-64-4942   SARAH SAMUELSON   $865.00   $185.00   $680.00
```

SUMMARY

Signed Data

An S is used as the first character in the picture string for numeric data to indicate a signed data item. The contents of the data item may be tested using the following code:

Format

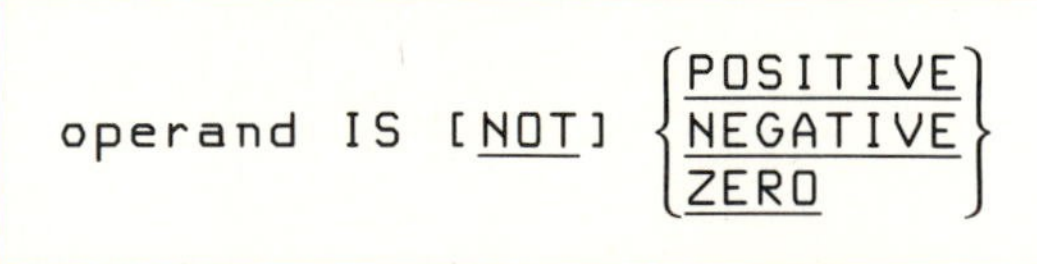

Output Editing

Simple Insertion

B 0 / ,

Special Insertion

. (period)

Fixed Insertion

$ + - CR DB

Floating Insertion

$ + -

Suppression of Zeros and Replacement of Asterisks

Z *

BLANK WHEN ZERO

Format

```
BLANK WHEN ZERO
```

JUSTIFIED RIGHT

Format

```
{JUSTIFIED} RIGHT
{JUST     }
```

Condition Names (88 Levels)

Format

```
                    {VALUES ARE}
88 condition-name   {VALUE  IS }

                 {THROUGH}
     literal-1 [ {THRU   }  literal-2]

                 {THROUGH}
    [literal-3 [ {THRU   }  literal-4]...].
```

Format

```
IF [NOT] condition-name . . .
```

Packed Data

Format

```
USAGE IS COMPUTATIONAL-3
```

TRACE

Format

```
{READY} TRACE
{RESET}
```

DISPLAY Format

```
             ┌identifier-1┐   ┌identifier-2┐
DISPLAY      └literal-1   ┘   └literal-2   ┘
```

EXERCISES

I. For each of the following, indicate what the resulting edited value would be after the contents of the sending field have been moved to the receiving field.

	SENDING FIELD		RECEIVING FIELD	
	Picture	Value	Picture	Edited Value
1.	X(5)	GREEN	X0XXXX	
2.	9(7)	461000	9,999,999	
3.	X(2)	AT	XBX	
4.	9(3)V9(2)	38100	9(2).9(1)	
5.	S9(3)	−142	−9(4)	
6.	S9(4)	+1000	9(4)DB	
7.	9(4)	6290	$9999	
8.	9(3)V9(2)	00025	$$$9.99	
9.	S9(3)	+185	999−	
10.	9(4)V9(1)	24000	Z,ZZZ.9	
11.	9(5)	00000	ZZZ99	
12.	9(3)V9(2)	00025	$$$$.99	
13.	S9(3)	+014	++++	
14.	9(4)V9(2)	001650	*,***.99	
15.	9(3)	000	$$$$	

II. Use the following condition entries, and assume that the current value of ORD-BRANCH is 03. Indicate which of the IF statements
(a) are valid in COBOL
(b) would test TRUE

```
05  ORD-BRANCH              PIC 9(2).
    88  EASTERN-BRANCH                    VALUE 1.
    88  SOUTHERN-BRANCH                   VALUE 2.
    88  CENTRAL-BRANCH                    VALUE 3.
    88  ROCKY-MOUNTAIN-BRANCH             VALUE 4.
    88  WESTERN-BRANCH                    VALUE 5.
    88  VALID-BRANCH                      VALUE 1 THRU 5.
```

1. IF ORD-BRANCH OR CENTRAL-BRANCH . . .
2. IF NOT SOUTHERN-BRANCH AND VALID-BRANCH. . .
3. IF EASTERN-BRANCH. . .
4. IF CENTRAL-BRANCH = 3. . .
5. IF EASTERN-BRANCH AND WESTERN-BRANCH. . .
6. IF NOT VALID-BRANCH. . .
7. IF CENTRAL-BRANCH OR WESTERN-BRANCH. . .
8. IF ORD-BRANCH = 3. . .

III. Use the following condition-name entries, and assume that the current value of ORD-MM is 02. Indicate which of the IF statements
(a) are valid in COBOL
(b) have a TRUE condition in them

```
05  ORD-MM                   PIC 99.
    88  VALID-MONTH                      VALUE 1 THRU 12.
    88  THIRTY-DAY-MONTH                 VALUE 4 6 9 11.
    88  THIRTY-ONE-DAY-MONTH             VALUE 1 3 5 7 8
                                           10 12.
```

```
88  JANUARY                  VALUE 1.
88  FEBRUARY                 VALUE 2.
88  MARCH                    VALUE 3.
88  APRIL                    VALUE 4.
88  MAY                      VALUE 5.
88  JUNE                     VALUE 6.
88  JULY                     VALUE 7.
88  AUGUST                   VALUE 8.
88  SEPTEMBER                VALUE 9.
88  OCTOBER                  VALUE 10.
88  NOVEMBER                 VALUE 11.
88  DECEMBER                 VALUE 12.
```

1. IF VALID-MONTH . . .
2. IF VALID-MONTH = 02 . . .
3. IF JANUARY . . .
4. IF ORD-MM = 02 . . .
5. IF THIRTY-DAY-MONTH . . .
6. IF NOT VALID-MONTH . . .
7. IF VALID-MONTH AND DECEMBER . . .
8. IF THIRTY-DAY-MONTH OR FEBRUARY . . .

PROJECTS

For each of the following specifications and input record layouts, design a print chart and code a COBOL program that satisfies the specification.

PROJECT 5–1 Payroll

PROGRAM SPECIFICATION

Program Name: PAY5

Program Function:

This program will produce a printed listing of a payroll file. The report will include totals by division and final totals for credit union deductions, medical insurance deductions, and gross pay.

Input Files:

I. PAYROLL-FILE

INPUT DEVICE:	DISK
FILE ORGANIZATION:	SEQUENTIAL
RECORD LENGTH:	80 BYTES
FILE SEQUENCE:	ASCENDING ON DIVISION/ DEPARTMENT

Output Files:

I. PRINT-FILE

OUTPUT DEVICE:	PRINTER
RECORD LENGTH:	133 BYTES

Processing Requirements:

Each record read from the input file should be printed on one line of the output report. Gross pay should be calculated for each record. (Gross pay = pay rate × hours worked.)

Totals of credit union deduction, medical insurance deduction, and gross pay are to be accumulated and printed for each division and for the entire company.

Output Requirements:

The following are formatting requirements for the report:

1. Each page of the report should contain:
   (a) a main heading which includes the company name, the report name, the report date, and a page number.
   (b) column headings which describe the items printed underneath them.
2. Detail lines should include all fields from the input and gross pay.
3. Detail lines should be double spaced.
4. Each new division should begin on a new page, with the page number reset (to 1).
5. Total lines should be double spaced.

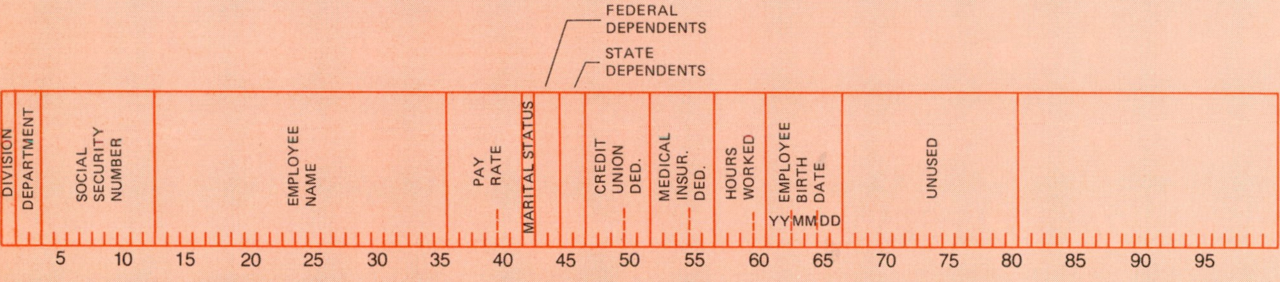

PROJECT 5–2 Inventory

PROGRAM SPECIFICATION

Program Name: INV5

Program Function:

The program will produce a printed listing of an inventory file. The report will include product totals and final totals for quantity on hand, quantity on order, and inventory cost.

Input Files:

I. INVENTORY-FILE

INPUT DEVICE:	DISK
FILE ORGANIZATION:	SEQUENTIAL
RECORD LENGTH:	80 BYTES
FILE SEQUENCE:	ASCENDING ON INVENTORY STOCK NUMBER

Output Files:

I. PRINT-FILE

OUTPUT DEVICE:	PRINTER
RECORD LENGTH:	133 BYTES

Processing Requirements:

Each record on the input file should be printed on the output report. Inventory cost should be calculated for each record. (Inventory cost = quantity on hand × inventory unit cost.)

Totals for quantity on hand, quantity on order, and inventory cost are to be accumulated and printed for each type of product and for the entire file.

Output Requirements:

The following are formatting requirements for the report:

1. Each page of the report should contain:
   (a) a main heading which includes the company name, the report name, the report date, and a page number.
   (b) column headings which describe the items printed underneath them.
2. Detail lines should include all fields from the input and the inventory cost.
3. Detail lines should be double spaced.
4. Each new type of product should begin on a new page.
5. Total lines should be double spaced.

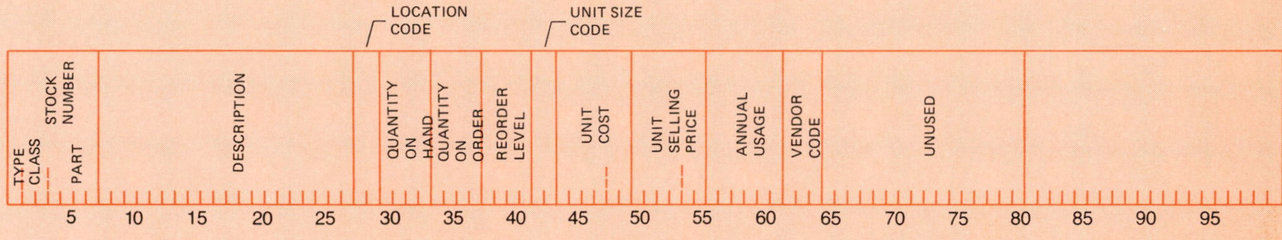

PROJECT 5–3 Accounts Payable

PROGRAM SPECIFICATION

Program Name: AP5

Program Function:

The program will produce a printed listing of an accounts payable file. The report will include division totals and final totals for amount, hard goods, labor, freight, and tax.

Input Files:

I. ACCOUNTS-PAYABLE-FILE

INPUT DEVICE:	DISK
FILE ORGANIZATION:	SEQUENTIAL
RECORD LENGTH:	80 BYTES
FILE SEQUENCE:	ASCENDING ON DIVISION / CONTROL NBR

Output Files:

I. PRINT-FILE

OUTPUT DEVICE:	PRINTER
RECORD LENGTH:	133 BYTES

Processing Requirements:

Each record on the input file should be printed on one line of the output report. Totals for amount, hard goods, labor, freight, and tax are to be accumulated and printed for each division and for the entire company.

Output Requirements:

The following are formatting requirements for the report:

1. Each page of the report should contain:
   (a) a main heading which includes the company name, the report name, the report date, and a page number.
   (b) column headings which describe the items printed underneath them.
2. Detail lines should include all fields from the input.
3. Detail lines should be double spaced.
4. Each new division should begin on a new page.
5. Total lines should be double spaced.

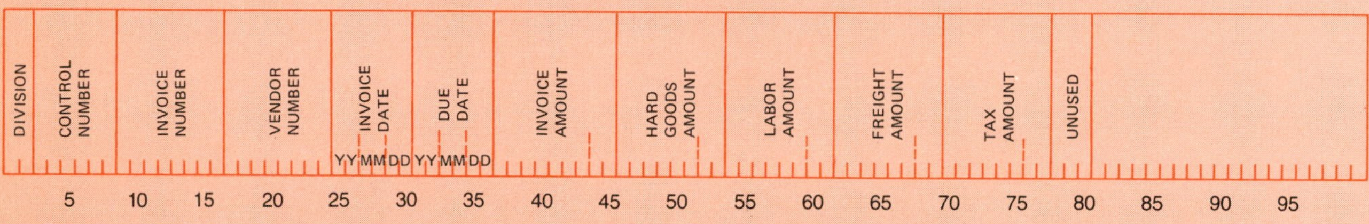

PROJECT 5–4 Pension

PROGRAM SPECIFICATION

Program Name: PEN5

Program Function:

The program will produce a printed report of a pension file. The report will include division totals and final totals for salary, employee contribution, employer contribution, and balance forward.

Input Files:

I. PENSION-FILE

INPUT DEVICE:	DISK
FILE ORGANIZATION:	SEQUENTIAL
RECORD LENGTH:	80 BYTES
FILE SEQUENCE:	ASCENDING ON DIVISION / DEPARTMENT

Output Files:

I. PRINT-FILE

OUTPUT DEVICE:	PRINTER
RECORD LENGTH:	133 BYTES

Processing Requirements:

Each record read from the pension file should be printed on one line of the output report. Totals for salary, employee contribution, employer contribution, and balance forward are to be accumulated and printed for each division and for the entire company.

Output Requirements:

The following are formatting requirements for the report:

1. Each page of the report should contain:
   (a) a main heading which includes the company name, the report name, the report date, and a page number.
   (b) column headings which describe the items printed underneath them.
2. Detail lines should include all fields from the input.
3. Detail lines should be double spaced.
4. Each new division should begin on a new page.
5. Total lines should be double spaced.

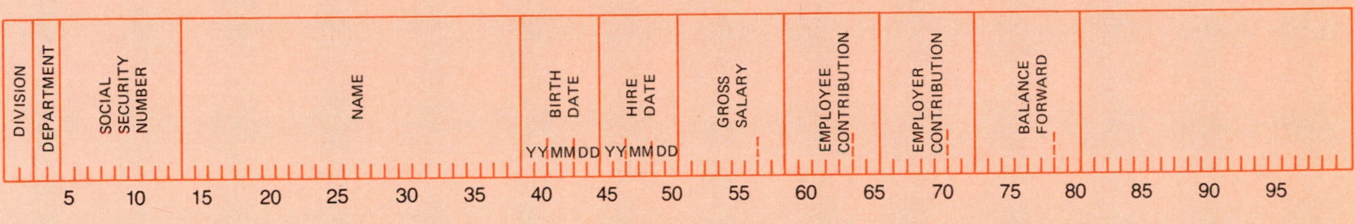

PROJECT 5–5 Bill of Materials

PROGRAM SPECIFICATION

Program Name: BOM5

Program Function:

The program will produce a printed report of a bill-of-materials file which will include the extended cost. The report will include division totals and final totals for extended cost.

Input Files:

I. BILL-OF-MATERIALS-FILE

INPUT DEVICE:	DISK
FILE ORGANIZATION:	SEQUENTIAL
RECORD LENGTH:	55 BYTES
FILE SEQUENCE:	ASCENDING ON DIVISION / PRODUCT LINE

Output Files:

I. PRINT-FILE

OUTPUT DEVICE:	PRINTER
RECORD LENGTH:	133 BYTES

Processing Requirements:

Each record from the bill-of-materials file should be printed on one line of the output report. Extended cost (quantity times cost) is to be calculated for each record. Totals for extended cost are to be accumulated and printed for each division and for the entire company.

Output Requirements:

The following are formatting requirements for the report:

1. Each page of the report should contain:

(a) a main heading which includes the company name, the report name, the report date, and a page number.
(b) column headings which describe the items printed underneath them.

2. Detail lines should include all fields from the input and the extended cost.
3. Detail lines should be double spaced.
4. Each new division should begin on a new page.
5. Total lines should be double spaced.

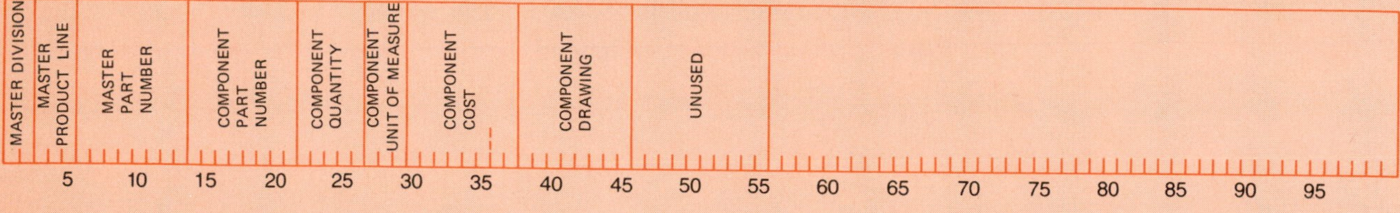

PROJECT 5–6 Cost

PROGRAM SPECIFICATION

Program Name: COST5

Program Function:

The program will produce a printed report of a cost file which will include the total for all cost factors. The report will separate the records by division and provide a count of records for each division.

Input Files:

I. COST-FILE

INPUT DEVICE:	DISK
FILE ORGANIZATION:	SEQUENTIAL
RECORD LENGTH:	75 BYTES
FILE SEQUENCE:	ASCENDING ON DIVISION / PRODUCT LINE

Output Files:

I. PRINT-FILE

OUTPUT DEVICE:	PRINTER
RECORD LENGTH:	133 BYTES

Processing Requirements:

Each record from the cost file should be printed on one line of the output report. The total for all cost factors should be calculated for each record. A count of the records for each division should be accumulated and printed after each division.

Output Requirements:

The following are formatting requirements for the report:

1. Each page of the report should contain:
   (a) a main heading which includes the company name, the report name, the report date, and a page number.
   (b) column headings which describe the items printed underneath them.
2. Detail lines should include all fields from the input and the total for the cost factors.

3. Detail lines should be double spaced.
4. Each new division should begin on a new page.
5. Total (count) lines should be double spaced.

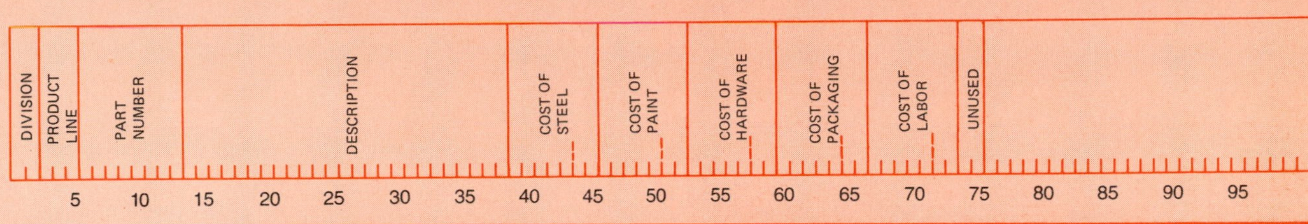

CHAPTER 6

Control Breaks, II

There are two control break programming projects in this chapter. The first program produces a report with multiple levels of totals (sales representative, branch, and final totals). The second program produces the same three levels of totals and also includes an extraction routine to select certain branches for inclusion on the report. It illustrates how to combine control breaks and extraction in a single program.

The new COBOL elements include the REDEFINES clause, the ACCEPT statement, the qualification of data-names, the CORRESPONDING option, the ON SIZE ERROR clause, the GO TO / DEPENDING ON statement, and the EVALUATE statement which is a part of the 1985 standard.

The debugging section provides an explanation of DATA EXCEPTIONS, a common cause of interruption while a program is executing. This section includes suggestions for finding the cause of a data exception.

PROGRAM SPECIFICATION: BREAK-3

The first programming project of this chapter produces a listing which includes subtotals of quantity and extended price for sales representatives and branches, as well as final totals. The program specification is shown in Figure 6–1.

Input Record Layout

The input record layout is shown in Figure 6–2. This is the same file used in previous projects, repeated here for convenience.

Print Chart

The print chart for the project is shown in Figure 6–3. It includes totals for quantity and extended price by sales representative and branch, and final totals for quantity and extended price.

LOGIC FOR BREAK-3 PROGRAM

The logic design for the BREAK-3 program is shown by means of a hierarchy chart in Figure 6–4, pseudocode in Figure 6–5, and a flowchart in Figure 6–6.

Flowchart

The complete flowchart is shown in Figure 6–6.

PROGRAM SPECIFICATION

Program Name: BREAK-3

Program Function:

The program will produce a printed listing of an order file. The report will include totals for quantity and extended price by sales representative and branch, and final totals for the same. Each branch will begin on a new page.

Input Files:

I. ORDER-FILE

INPUT DEVICE:	DISK
FILE ORGANIZATION:	SEQUENTIAL
RECORD LENGTH:	70 BYTES
FILE SEQUENCE:	ASCENDING ON BRANCH / SALES REP

Output Files:

I. PRINT-FILE

OUTPUT DEVICE:	PRINTER
RECORD LENGTH:	133 BYTES

Processing Requirements:

Each record read from the ORDER-FILE should be printed on one line of the output report. All fields except the customer purchase order number are to be included on the output. In addition, the extended price is to be calculated for each order and printed on the output. (Extended price = quantity × unit price.)

Totals for quantity and extended price are to be accumulated and printed for each sales representative, each branch, and the entire company.

Output Requirements:

The following are formatting requirements for the report:

1. Each page of the report should contain:
   (a) a main heading which includes the company name, the report name, the report date, and a page number.
   (b) column headings which describe the items printed underneath them.
2. Detail lines should include all fields from the input except the customer purchase order number. The extended price should also be included.
3. Detail lines should be double spaced.
4. Total lines for sales representative should be double spaced, with two additional blank lines after each total.
5. Each new branch should begin on a new page.
6. Final total lines should be triple spaced.

FIGURE 6–1

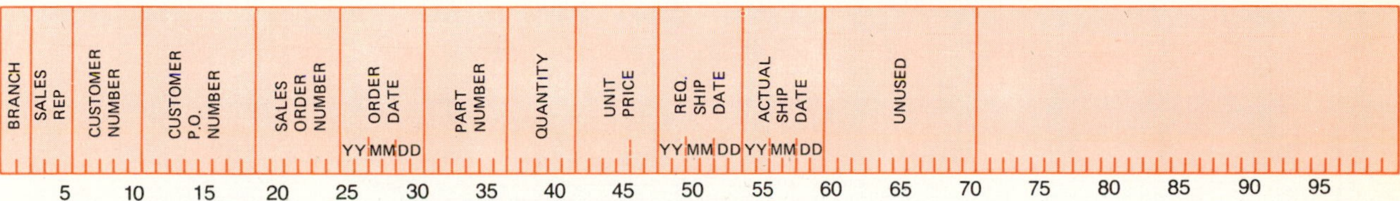

FIGURE 6–2

```
         DATE: XX/XX/XX                        PRODUCT DISTRIBUTION INC. - CURRENT ORDERS                           PAGE: ZZ9

                SALES   CUSTOMER    SALES      ORDER      REQUESTED     ACTUAL       PART                    UNIT          EXTENDED
         BRANCH  REP     NUMBER     ORDER       DATE      SHIP DATE    SHIP DATE    NUMBER   QUANTITY        PRICE           PRICE

           99    999     99999     XBXXXXX    99/99/99    99/99/99     99/99/99     XXXXXX    ZZ,ZZ9-    $$,$$9.99-   $$,$$$,$$9.99-

           99    999     99999     XBXXXXX    99/99/99    99/99/99     99/99/99     XXXXXX    ZZ,ZZ9-    $$,$$9.99-   $$,$$$,$$9.99-

           SALES REPRESENTATIVE TOTALS                                                       ZZZ,ZZ9-                 $$$,$$$,$$9.99-



           BRANCH TOTALS                                                                     ZZZ,ZZ9-                 $$$,$$$,$$9.99-


           FINAL TOTALS                                                                      ZZZ,ZZ9-                 $$$,$$$,$$9.99-
```

FIGURE 6–3

Hierarchy Chart

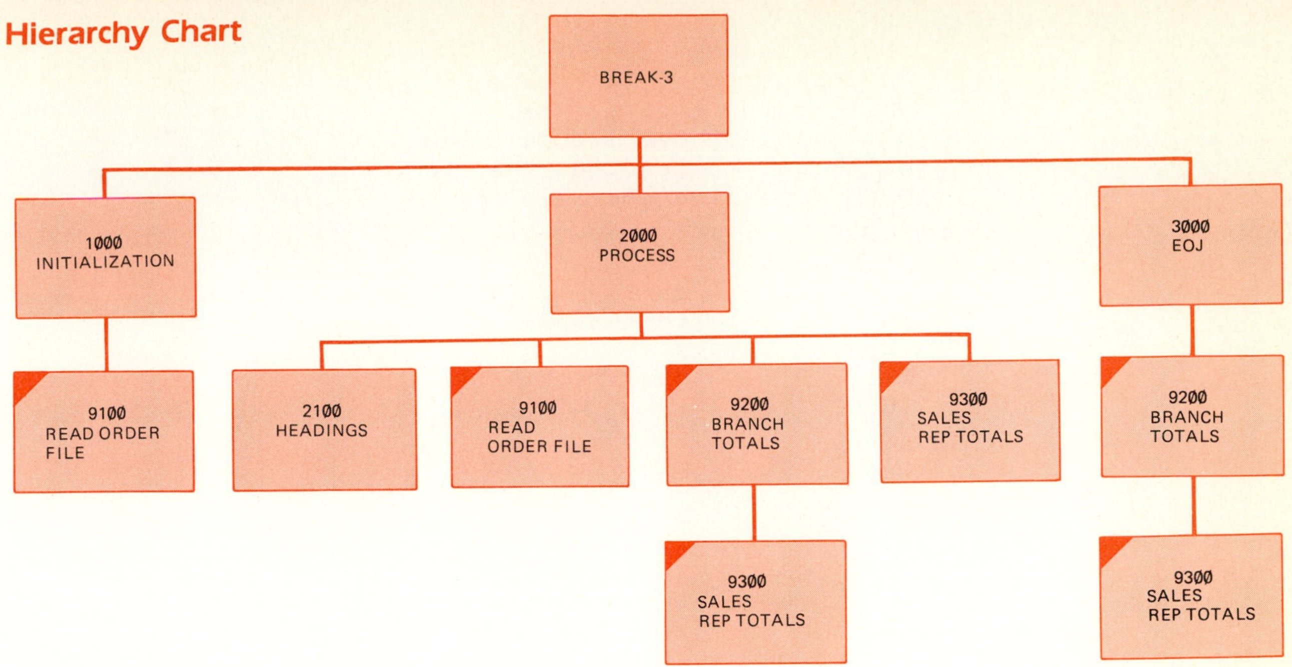

FIGURE 6–4

Pseudocode

```
MAIN LINE
     DO initialization
     DO WHILE more order records
          DO process
     ENDO
     DO end of job
INITIALIZATION
     OPEN files
     MOVE date to heading
     DO read an order
     MOVE branch to branch hold
     MOVE sales rep to sales rep hold
PROCESS
     IF branch = branch hold
          IF sales rep = sales rep hold
               IF page overflow
                    DO headings
               ENDIF
          ELSE
               DO sales rep totals
          ENDIF
     ELSE
          DO branch totals
          DO headings
     ENDIF
     MOVE input to output
     CALCULATE extended price
     MOVE extended price to output
     ADD quantity to sales rep quantity
     ADD extended price to sales rep extended price
     WRITE detail line
     ADD 2 to line count
     DO read an order
```

FIGURE 6–5

Logic for Break-3 Program

```
HEADINGS
     ADD 1 to page count
     MOVE page count to heading
     WRITE main heading line
     WRITE column heading line one
     WRITE column heading line two
     MOVE 4 to line count
END OF JOB
     DO branch totals
     MOVE final quantity to final quantity out
     MOVE final extended price to final extended
       price out
     WRITE final total line
     CLOSE files
READ AN ORDER
     READ order file
BRANCH TOTALS
     DO sales rep totals
     MOVE branch quantity to output
     MOVE branch extended price to output
     WRITE branch total line
     ADD branch quantity to final quantity
     ADD branch extended price to final extended
       price
     MOVE zeros to branch quantity, branch extended
       price
     MOVE branch to branch hold
SALES REP TOTALS
     MOVE sales rep quantity to output
     MOVE sales rep extended price to output
     WRITE sales rep total line
     WRITE blank line
     ADD 4 to line count
     ADD sales rep quantity to branch quantity
     ADD sales rep extended price to branch
       extended price
     MOVE zeros to sales rep quantity, sales rep
       extended price
     MOVE sales rep to sales rep hold
```

FIGURE 6–5 cont.

Explanation of Logic

MAIN LINE

The main routine remains the same as in all previous programs.

1000-INITIALIZATION

The first steps in the initialization routine are the same as in the BREAK-2 program. The files are opened, the current date is placed in the headings, and the first input record is read from the ORDER-FILE.

The last two steps are a part of the control-break logic. The program will accumulate totals for ORD-QUANTITY and EXTENDED-PRICE for each branch and for each sales representative within a branch. In order to do this, a test is made on each record read to determine when ORD-BRANCH and ORD-SALES-REP change.

To determine when the value of a field has changed, the new value is compared against the previous value. Since each value for a data item is destroyed when the new one is read into the same area, a separate area in storage is used to save the old value. Two fields, HOLD-BRANCH and HOLD-SALES-REP, will be used for this purpose. Note that only those fields from the input record which must be compared with fields from subsequent records are saved in the special storage area.

After the READ in the initialization routine, ORD-BRANCH and ORD-SALES-REP are moved to the hold areas:

```
MOVE ORD-BRANCH TO HOLD-BRANCH.
MOVE ORD-SALES-REP TO HOLD-SALES-REP.
```

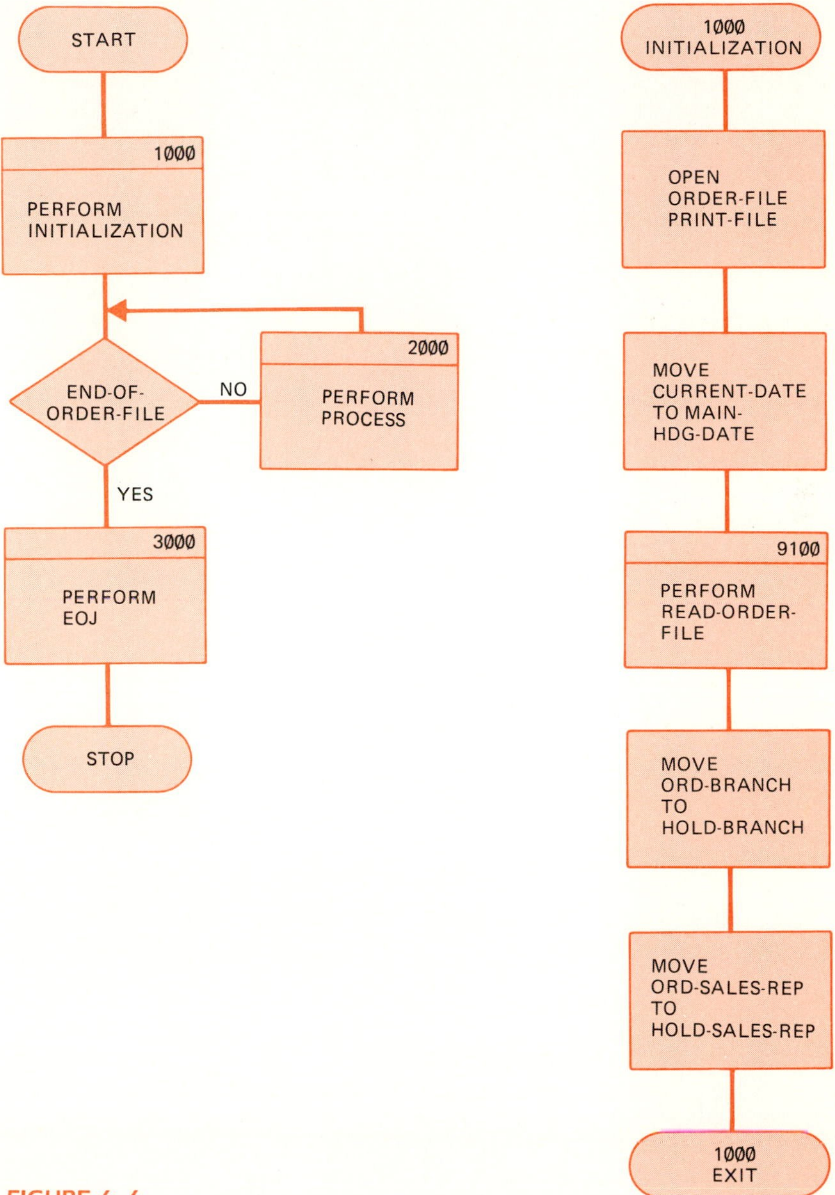

FIGURE 6–6

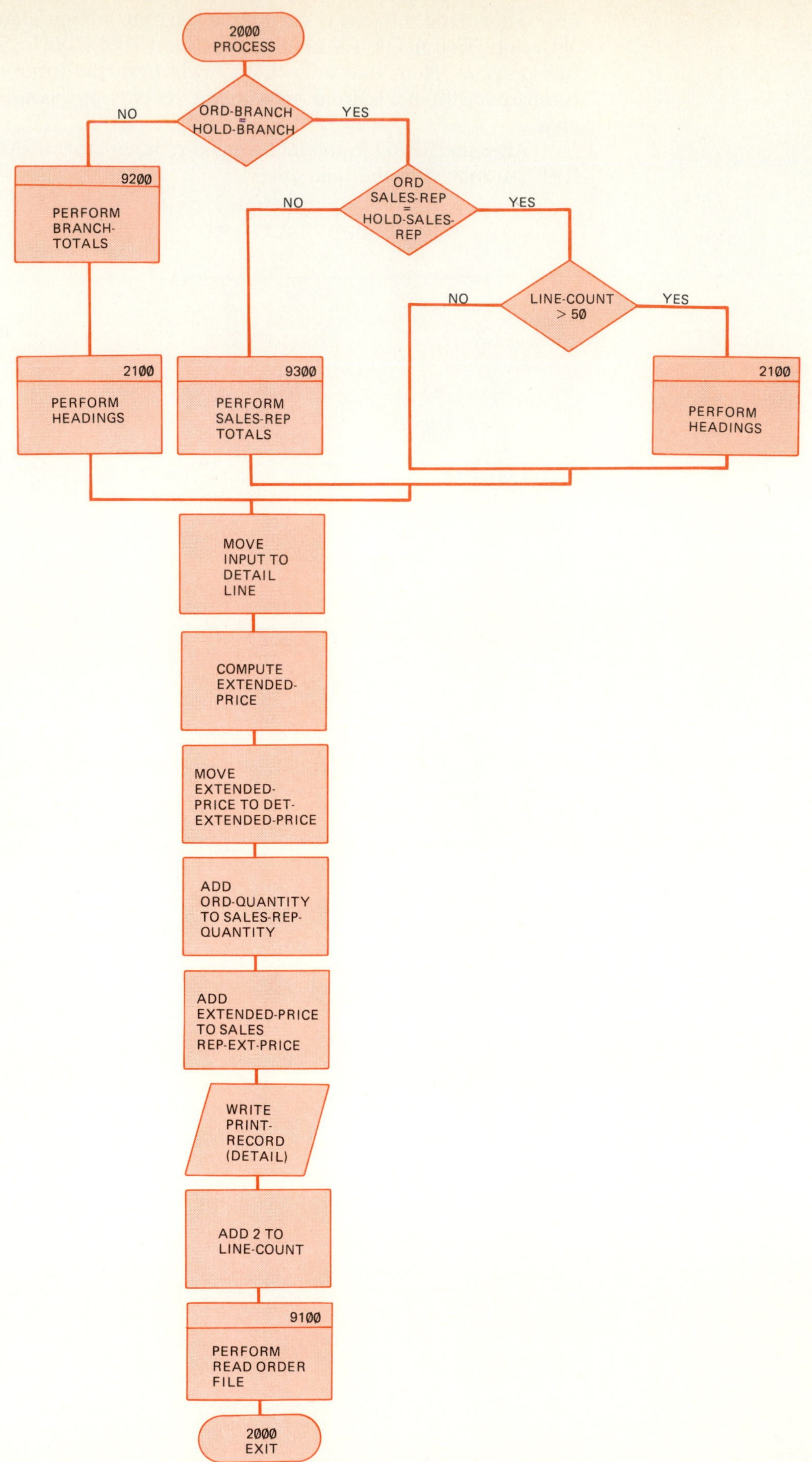

FIGURE 6–6 cont.

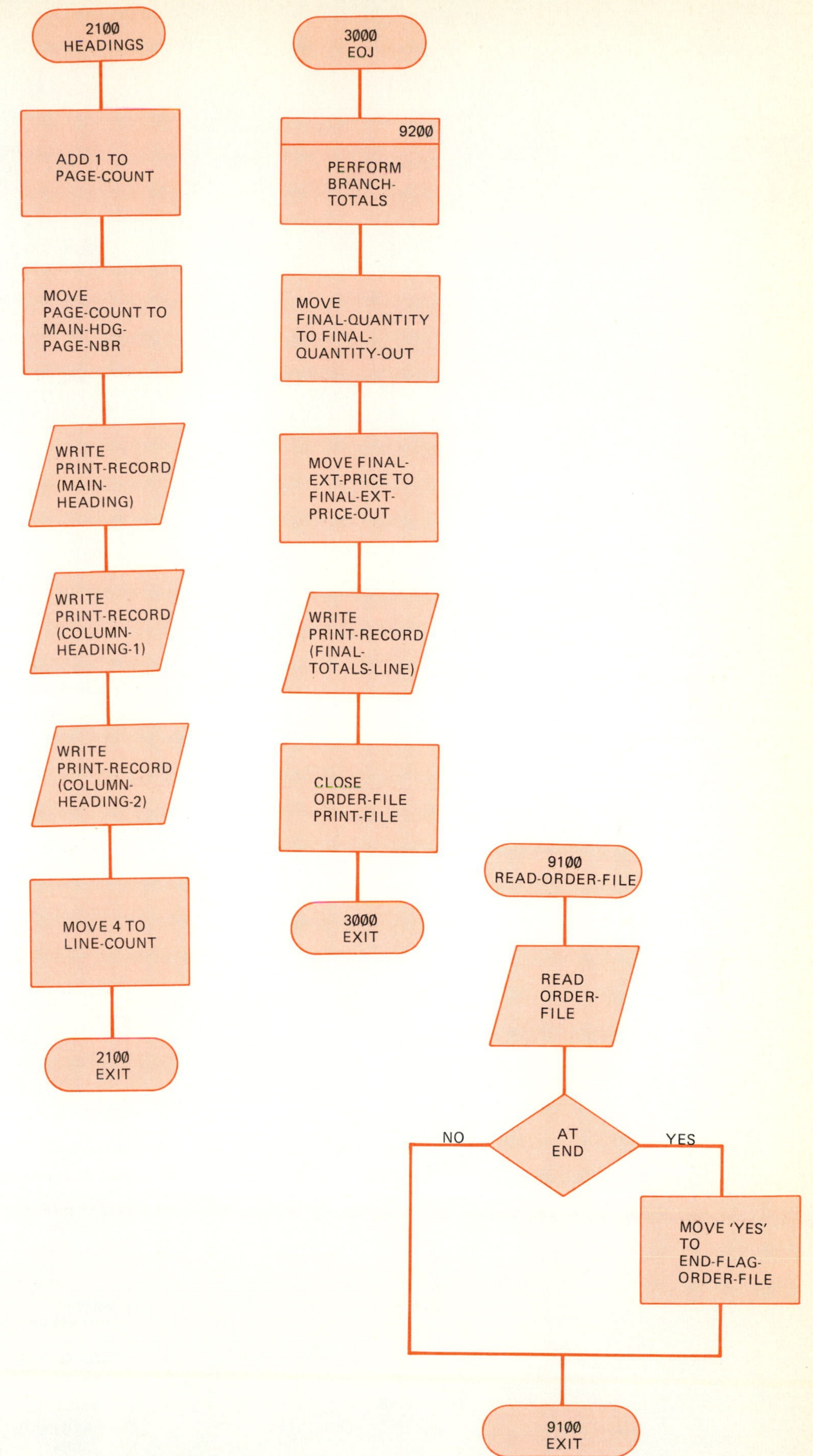

FIGURE 6–6 cont.

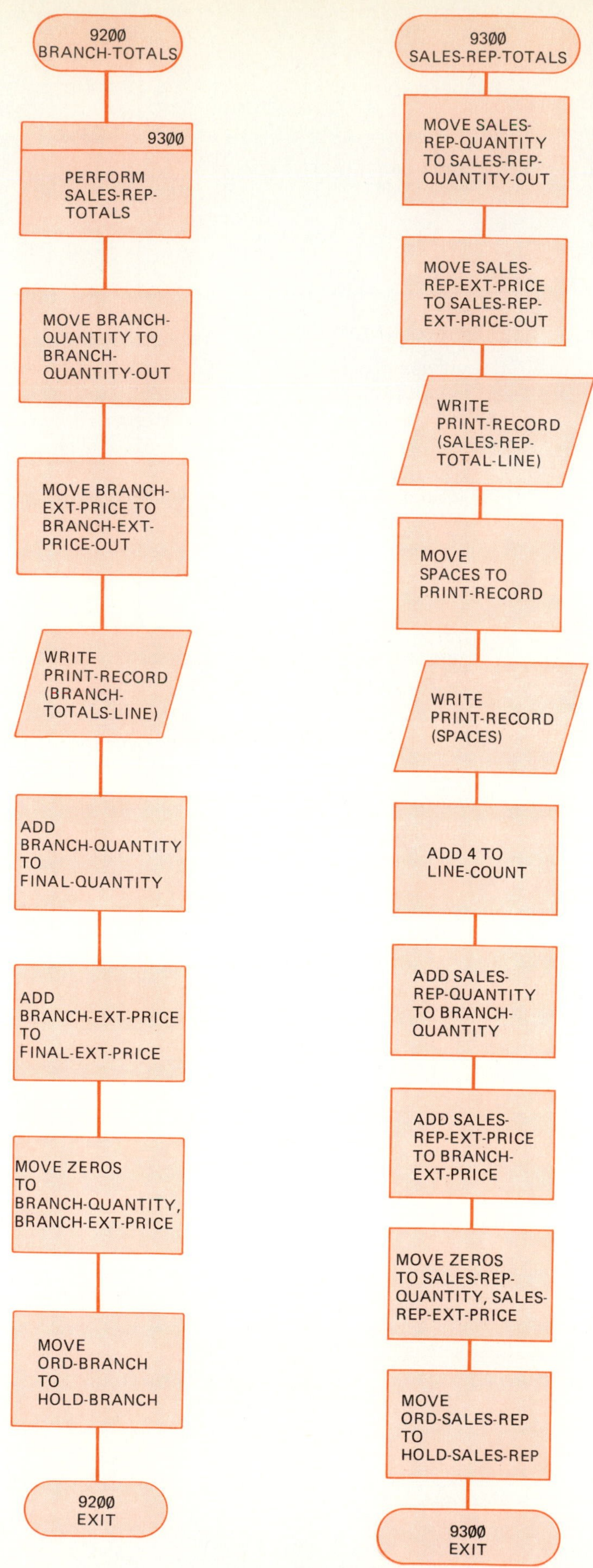

FIGURE 6–6 cont.

This prevents a control break from occurring the first time through 2000-PROCESS. Now, in 2000-PROCESS, when the values of ORD-BRANCH and ORD-SALES-REP from the first input record are compared against the values in the hold areas, they will be equal. Notice that the first record was read before the values were moved to the hold areas. (See Figure 6–7 for the COBOL code for 1000-INITIALIZATION.)

```
       1000-INITIALIZATION.
           OPEN INPUT  ORDER-FILE
                OUTPUT PRINT-FILE.
           MOVE CURRENT-DATE TO MAIN-HDG-DATE.
           PERFORM 9100-READ-ORDER-FILE.
           MOVE ORD-BRANCH TO HOLD-BRANCH.
           MOVE ORD-SALES-REP TO HOLD-SALES-REP.
```

FIGURE 6–7

2000-PROCESS

The first step in 2000-PROCESS is to determine whether a control break is necessary. The control fields ORD-BRANCH and ORD-SALES-REP are checked against the hold areas to determine whether they have changed. ORD-BRANCH is checked first because it is the higher level control field. If either field has changed, the appropriate break routine is performed. If there is no control break, LINE-COUNT is checked to determine whether a new page is needed.

Next, the input is moved to output (the detail line), and the extended price is calculated and moved to output. The extended price and quantity are then added to the sales representative totals, and the detail line is printed. The last thing in 2000-PROCESS is to read the ORDER-FILE. The routine will be repeated until there are no more records in the ORDER-FILE. (See Figure 6–8 for the COBOL code for 2000-PROCESS.)

```
       2000-PROCESS.
           IF ORD-BRANCH = HOLD-BRANCH
               IF ORD-SALES-REP = HOLD-SALES-REP
                   IF PAGE-OVERFLOW
                       PERFORM 2100-HEADINGS
                   ELSE
                       NEXT SENTENCE
               ELSE
                   PERFORM 9300-SALES-REP-TOTALS
           ELSE
               PERFORM 9200-BRANCH-TOTALS
               PERFORM 2100-HEADINGS.
           MOVE ORD-BRANCH              TO DET-BRANCH.
           MOVE ORD-SALES-REP           TO DET-SALES-REP.
           MOVE ORD-CUSTOMER-NBR        TO DET-CUSTOMER-NBR.
           MOVE ORD-SALES-ORD-NBR       TO DET-SALES-ORD-NBR.
           MOVE ORD-YY                  TO DET-ORDER-YY.
           MOVE ORD-MM                  TO DET-ORDER-MM.
           MOVE ORD-DD                  TO DET-ORDER-DD.
           MOVE ORD-PART-NBR            TO DET-PART-NBR.
           MOVE ORD-QUANTITY            TO DET-QUANTITY.
           MOVE ORD-UNIT-PRICE          TO DET-UNIT-PRICE.
           MOVE ORD-REQ-SHIP-YY         TO DET-REQ-SHIP-YY.
           MOVE ORD-REQ-SHIP-MM         TO DET-REQ-SHIP-MM.
           MOVE ORD-REQ-SHIP-DD         TO DET-REQ-SHIP-DD.
           MOVE ORD-ACT-SHIP-YY         TO DET-ACT-SHIP-YY.
           MOVE ORD-ACT-SHIP-MM         TO DET-ACT-SHIP-MM.
           MOVE ORD-ACT-SHIP-DD         TO DET-ACT-SHIP-DD.
           COMPUTE EXTENDED-PRICE = ORD-UNIT-PRICE * ORD-QUANTITY.
           MOVE EXTENDED-PRICE          TO DET-EXTENDED-PRICE.
           ADD ORD-QUANTITY             TO SALES-REP-QUANTITY.
           ADD EXTENDED-PRICE           TO SALES-REP-EXT-PRICE.
           WRITE PRINT-RECORD FROM DETAIL-LINE
               AFTER ADVANCING 2 LINES.
           ADD 2 TO LINE-COUNT.
           PERFORM 9100-READ-ORDER-FILE.
```

FIGURE 6–8

2100-HEADINGS

Routine 2100-HEADINGS is performed whenever LINE-COUNT exceeds 50 or there is a control break on ORD-BRANCH. The routine prints the headings and resets LINE-COUNT to 4. (See Figure 6–9.)

```
       21ØØ-HEADINGS.
           ADD 1 TO PAGE-COUNT.
           MOVE PAGE-COUNT TO MAIN-HDG-PAGE-NBR.
           WRITE PRINT-RECORD FROM MAIN-HEADING
               AFTER ADVANCING PAGE.
           WRITE PRINT-RECORD FROM COLUMN-HEADING-1
               AFTER ADVANCING 2 LINES.
           WRITE PRINT-RECORD FROM COLUMN-HEADING-2
               AFTER ADVANCING 1 LINE.
           MOVE 4 TO LINE-COUNT.
```

FIGURE 6–9

3000-EOJ

The end-of-job routine invokes 9200-BRANCH-TOTALS, which in turn invokes 9300-SALES-REP-TOTALS, together providing the last set of sales representative and branch totals. Then the final totals are moved to the output line and printed. Finally, the files are closed. (See Figure 6–10.)

```
       3ØØØ-EOJ.
           PERFORM 92ØØ-BRANCH-TOTALS.
           MOVE FINAL-QUANTITY TO FINAL-QUANTITY-OUT.
           MOVE FINAL-EXT-PRICE TO FINAL-EXT-PRICE-OUT.
           WRITE PRINT-RECORD FROM FINAL-TOTALS-LINE
               AFTER ADVANCING 3 LINES.
           CLOSE ORDER-FILE
                 PRINT-FILE.
```

FIGURE 6–10

9100-READ-ORDER-FILE

A record is read from the order file. If the read is successful, the routine is complete. If the read encounters the end-of-file indicator, 'YES' is moved to END-FLAG-ORDER-FILE. (See Figure 6–11.)

```
       91ØØ-READ-ORDER-FILE.
           READ ORDER-FILE
               AT END
                   MOVE 'YES' TO END-FLAG-ORDER-FILE.
```

FIGURE 6–11

9200-BRANCH-TOTALS

9200-BRANCH-TOTALS is performed when ORD-BRANCH changes. When ORD-BRANCH changes, ORD-SALES-REP also changes. 9200-BRANCH-TOTALS invokes 9300-SALES-REP-TOTALS, which prints out totals for the last sales representative in the previous branch, rolls the sales representative totals into the branch totals, zeroes out the sales representative totals, and moves the new ORD-SALES-REP to its hold area.

After control returns to 9200-BRANCH-TOTALS, the branch totals are moved to output, printed, added to the final totals, and then zeroed out so that they may be used to accumulate the totals for the next branch. The new ORD-BRANCH that caused the control break is then moved to its hold area. (See Figure 6–12.)

9300-SALES-REP-TOTALS

The 9300-SALES-REP-TOTALS routine is performed when ORD-SALES-REP changes. The sales representative totals for quantity and extended price are moved to output, printed, added into the next level of (branch) totals, and then zeroed

```
       9200-BRANCH-TOTALS.
           PERFORM 9300-SALES-REP-TOTALS.
           MOVE BRANCH-QUANTITY           TO BRANCH-QUANTITY-OUT.
           MOVE BRANCH-EXT-PRICE          TO BRANCH-EXT-PRICE-OUT.
           WRITE PRINT-RECORD FROM BRANCH-TOTALS-LINE
               AFTER ADVANCING 2 LINES.
           ADD BRANCH-QUANTITY            TO FINAL-QUANTITY.
           ADD BRANCH-EXT-PRICE           TO FINAL-EXT-PRICE.
           MOVE ZEROS                     TO BRANCH-QUANTITY
                                             BRANCH-EXT-PRICE.
           MOVE ORD-BRANCH                TO HOLD-BRANCH.
```

FIGURE 6–12

out. The new ORD-SALES-REP which caused the control break is moved to its hold area. (See Figure 6–13.)

```
       9300-SALES-REP-TOTALS.
           MOVE SALES-REP-QUANTITY        TO SALES-REP-QUANTITY-OUT.
           MOVE SALES-REP-EXT-PRICE       TO SALES-REP-EXT-PRICE-OUT.
           WRITE PRINT-RECORD FROM SALES-REP-TOTALS-LINE
               AFTER ADVANCING 2 LINES.
           MOVE SPACES TO PRINT-RECORD.
           WRITE PRINT-RECORD AFTER ADVANCING 2 LINES.
           ADD 4 TO LINE-COUNT.
           ADD SALES-REP-QUANTITY         TO BRANCH-QUANTITY.
           ADD SALES-REP-EXT-PRICE        TO BRANCH-EXT-PRICE.
           MOVE ZEROS                     TO SALES-REP-QUANTITY
                                             SALES-REP-EXT-PRICE.
           MOVE ORD-SALES-REP             TO HOLD-SALES-REP.
```

FIGURE 6–13

THE COBOL PROGRAM

Test Data

The test data for the BREAK-3 program is shown in Figure 6–14. It is the same data used in all the previous programs.

```
Ø1201ØØ3ØØPO173   B12383871Ø25GN4Ø2AØØØØ1Ø45ØØØ871116ØØØØØØ
Ø1201Ø47278372    G4838887Ø913WB7Ø2XØØØ9ØØ115ØØ8711Ø1ØØØØØØ
Ø1201ØØ3ØØE1Ø12   B123358711Ø5WB493EØØØØ2Ø54ØØØ871122ØØØØØØ
Ø3ØØ7473ØØ        H8477787Ø223MF4Ø3TØØØØ5Ø4ØØØØ87Ø5Ø2ØØØØØØ
Ø3ØØ7ØØ378EBNER   H8457987Ø811VX922PØØ8ØØØØ127589112ØØØØØØØ
Ø3ØØ7739897747    B892888711Ø6MF848JØØØØ5Ø2145Ø88Ø13ØØØØØØØ
Ø3ØØ7ØØ28334567X  B34237871Ø3ØHL834EØØØ16Ø19ØØØ871121ØØØØØØ
Ø3ØØ7473ØØ        Y289Ø387Ø811VXØØ1LØØ2ØØØØ622Ø8712Ø3ØØØØØØ
Ø344Ø6948187Ø341  GØ418Ø87Ø2Ø9JGØ4ØXØØØØ1Ø525ØØ88Ø619ØØØØØØ
Ø361182888P2783733B8433Ø871Ø25HL289BØØØ1ØØ234ØØ871113ØØØØØØ
Ø36112837 5T7838  T7829987Ø323JG563WØØØØ6Ø43ØØØ871Ø18ØØØØØØ
Ø36115Ø912        H6915Ø87Ø2Ø6MF848TØØØØ3Ø36ØØØ8712Ø1ØØØØØØ
Ø8174314Ø865      H4189187Ø412TK61ØLØØØ18ØØ78ØØ87Ø63ØØØØØØØ
Ø8174Ø18Ø5R7278   T2164287Ø81ØTK497XØØØ1ØØ118ØØ87113ØØØØØØØ
Ø8174Ø18Ø5R8322   Y211Ø587Ø6Ø1TN116TØØØØ1Ø3ØØØØ871221ØØØØØØ
Ø891562Ø54SCHUH   L5Ø6818711Ø8TK812EØØØØ6Ø573ØØ88Ø1Ø5ØØØØØØ
Ø891521Ø78        B71Ø45871ØØ1FV782TØØØØ3ØØ28ØØ871115ØØØØØØ
```

FIGURE 6–14

Sample Output

There are multiple pages of output because each branch begins on a new page. (See Figure 6–15.)

The Program

The COBOL code for the complete BREAK-3 program is shown in Figure 6–16.

DATE: 11/09/87 PRODUCT DISTRIBUTION INC. - CURRENT ORDERS PAGE: 1

BRANCH	SALES REP	CUSTOMER NUMBER	SALES ORDER	ORDER DATE	REQUESTED SHIP DATE	ACTUAL SHIP DATE	PART NUMBER	QUANTITY	UNIT PRICE	EXTENDED PRICE
01	201	00300	B 12383	10/25/87	11/16/87	00/00/00	GN402A	1	$450.00	$450.00
01	201	04727	G 48388	09/13/87	11/01/87	00/00/00	WB702X	90	$115.00	$10,350.00
01	201	00300	B 12335	11/05/87	11/22/87	00/00/00	WB493E	2	$540.00	$1,080.00
SALES REPRESENTATIVE TOTALS								93		$11,880.00
BRANCH TOTALS								93		$11,880.00

DATE: 11/09/87 PRODUCT DISTRIBUTION INC. - CURRENT ORDERS PAGE: 2

BRANCH	SALES REP	CUSTOMER NUMBER	SALES ORDER	ORDER DATE	REQUESTED SHIP DATE	ACTUAL SHIP DATE	PART NUMBER	QUANTITY	UNIT PRICE	EXTENDED PRICE
03	007	47300	H 84777	02/23/87	05/02/87	00/00/00	MF403T	5	$400.00	$2,000.00
03	007	00378	H 84579	08/11/87	11/20/89	00/00/00	VX922P	800	$12.75	$10,200.00
03	007	73989	B 89288	11/06/87	01/30/88	00/00/00	MF848J	5	$214.50	$1,072.50
03	007	00283	B 34237	10/30/87	11/21/87	00/00/00	HL834E	16	$190.00	$3,040.00
03	007	47300	Y 28903	08/11/87	12/03/87	00/00/00	VX001L	200	$62.20	$12,440.00
SALES REPRESENTATIVE TOTALS								1,026		$28,752.50
03	440	69481	G 04180	02/09/87	06/19/88	00/00/00	JG040X	1	$525.00	$525.00
SALES REPRESENTATIVE TOTALS								1		$525.00
03	611	82888	B 84330	10/25/87	11/13/87	00/00/00	HL289B	10	$234.00	$2,340.00
03	611	28375	T 78299	03/23/87	10/18/87	00/00/00	JG563W	6	$430.00	$2,580.00
03	611	50912	H 69150	02/06/87	12/01/87	00/00/00	MF848T	3	$360.00	$1,080.00
SALES REPRESENTATIVE TOTALS								19		$6,000.00
BRANCH TOTALS								1,046		$35,277.50

DATE: 11/09/87 PRODUCT DISTRIBUTION INC. - CURRENT ORDERS PAGE: 3

BRANCH	SALES REP	CUSTOMER NUMBER	SALES ORDER	ORDER DATE	REQUESTED SHIP DATE	ACTUAL SHIP DATE	PART NUMBER	QUANTITY	UNIT PRICE	EXTENDED PRICE
08	174	31408	H 41891	04/12/87	06/30/87	00/00/00	TK610L	18	$78.00	$1,404.00
08	174	01805	T 21642	08/10/87	11/30/87	00/00/00	TK497X	10	$118.00	$1,180.00
08	174	01805	Y 21105	06/01/87	12/21/87	00/00/00	TN116T	1	$300.00	$300.00
SALES REPRESENTATIVE TOTALS								29		$2,884.00
08	915	62054	L 50681	11/08/87	01/05/88	00/00/00	TK812E	6	$573.00	$3,438.00
08	915	21078	B 71045	10/01/87	11/15/87	00/00/00	FV782T	3	$28.00	$84.00
SALES REPRESENTATIVE TOTALS								9		$3,522.00
BRANCH TOTALS								38		$6,406.00
FINAL TOTALS								1,177		$53,563.50

FIGURE 6–15

```
       IDENTIFICATION DIVISION.

       PROGRAM-ID.    BREAK-3.

       AUTHOR.        HELEN HUMPHREYS.

       INSTALLATION.  PRODUCT DISTRIBUTION INC.

       DATE-WRITTEN.  Ø6/Ø1/87.

       DATE-COMPILED. Ø6/Ø8/87.

      ******************************************************************
      *                                                                *
      *    THIS PROGRAM WILL PRODUCE A PRINTED LISTING OF THE ORDER    *
      *    FILE.  THE REPORT WILL INCLUDE SALES REPRESENTATIVE,        *
      *    BRANCH, AND FINAL TOTALS FOR QUANTITY AND EXTENDED PRICE.   *
      *    EACH BRANCH WILL BEGIN ON A NEW PAGE.                       *
      *                                                                *
      ******************************************************************

       ENVIRONMENT DIVISION.

       CONFIGURATION SECTION.

       SOURCE-COMPUTER.
              IBM-37Ø.
       OBJECT-COMPUTER.
              IBM-37Ø.

       INPUT-OUTPUT SECTION.
       FILE-CONTROL.
           SELECT ORDER-FILE ASSIGN TO DISK.
           SELECT PRINT-FILE ASSIGN TO PRINTER.

       DATA DIVISION.
       FILE SECTION.

       FD  ORDER-FILE
           LABEL RECORDS ARE STANDARD
           RECORD CONTAINS 7Ø CHARACTERS
           DATA RECORD IS ORDER-RECORD.

       Ø1  ORDER-RECORD.
           Ø5  ORD-BRANCH               PIC 9(2).
           Ø5  ORD-SALES-REP            PIC 9(3).
           Ø5  ORD-CUSTOMER-NBR         PIC 9(5).
           Ø5  ORD-CUST-PO-NBR          PIC X(8).
           Ø5  ORD-SALES-ORD-NBR        PIC X(6).
           Ø5  ORD-DATE.
               1Ø  ORD-YY               PIC 9(2).
               1Ø  ORD-MM               PIC 9(2).
               1Ø  ORD-DD               PIC 9(2).
           Ø5  ORD-PART-NBR             PIC X(6).
           Ø5  ORD-QUANTITY             PIC S9(5).
           Ø5  ORD-UNIT-PRICE           PIC S9(4)V9(2).
           Ø5  ORD-REQ-SHIP-DATE.
               1Ø  ORD-REQ-SHIP-YY      PIC 9(2).
               1Ø  ORD-REQ-SHIP-MM      PIC 9(2).
               1Ø  ORD-REQ-SHIP-DD      PIC 9(2).
           Ø5  ORD-ACT-SHIP-DATE.
               1Ø  ORD-ACT-SHIP-YY      PIC 9(2).
               1Ø  ORD-ACT-SHIP-MM      PIC 9(2).
               1Ø  ORD-ACT-SHIP-DD      PIC 9(2).
           Ø5  FILLER                   PIC X(11).

       FD  PRINT-FILE
           LABEL RECORDS ARE OMITTED
           RECORD CONTAINS 133 CHARACTERS
           DATA RECORD IS PRINT-RECORD.

       Ø1  PRINT-RECORD                 PIC X(133).

       WORKING-STORAGE SECTION.

       Ø1  HOLDS-COUNTERS-SWITCHES.
           Ø5  END-FLAG-ORDER-FILE      PIC X(3)        VALUE 'NO'.
               88  END-OF-ORDER-FILE                    VALUE 'YES'.
           Ø5  LINE-COUNT               PIC 9(2)        VALUE 99.
               88  PAGE-OVERFLOW                        VALUE 51 THRU 99.
           Ø5  PAGE-COUNT               PIC 9(3)        VALUE ZEROS.
           Ø5  HOLD-BRANCH              PIC 9(2)        VALUE ZEROS.
```

FIGURE 6–16

```
           Ø5  HOLD-SALES-REP           PIC 9(3)        VALUE ZEROS.

       Ø1  CALCULATED-FIELDS.
           Ø5  EXTENDED-PRICE           PIC S9(7)V9(2).

       Ø1  SALES-REP-TOTALS.
           Ø5  SALES-REP-QUANTITY       PIC S9(6)       VALUE ZEROS.
           Ø5  SALES-REP-EXT-PRICE      PIC S9(8)V9(2)  VALUE ZEROS.

       Ø1  BRANCH-TOTALS.
           Ø5  BRANCH-QUANTITY          PIC S9(6)       VALUE ZEROS.
           Ø5  BRANCH-EXT-PRICE         PIC S9(8)V9(2)  VALUE ZEROS.

       Ø1  FINAL-TOTALS.
           Ø5  FINAL-QUANTITY           PIC S9(6)       VALUE ZEROS.
           Ø5  FINAL-EXT-PRICE          PIC S9(8)V9(2)  VALUE ZEROS.

       Ø1  MAIN-HEADING.
           Ø5  FILLER                   PIC X(7)        VALUE SPACES.
           Ø5  FILLER                   PIC X(6)        VALUE 'DATE:'.
           Ø5  MAIN-HDG-DATE            PIC X(8).
           Ø5  FILLER                   PIC X(25)       VALUE SPACES.
           Ø5  FILLER                   PIC X(42)
               VALUE 'PRODUCT DISTRIBUTION INC. - CURRENT ORDERS'.
           Ø5  FILLER                   PIC X(27)       VALUE SPACES.
           Ø5  FILLER                   PIC X(6)        VALUE 'PAGE:'.
           Ø5  MAIN-HDG-PAGE-NBR        PIC ZZ9.
           Ø5  FILLER                   PIC X(9)        VALUE SPACES.

       Ø1  COLUMN-HEADING-1.
           Ø5  FILLER                   PIC X(14)       VALUE SPACES.
           Ø5  FILLER                   PIC X(5)        VALUE 'SALES'.
           Ø5  FILLER                   PIC X(2)        VALUE SPACES.
           Ø5  FILLER                   PIC X(8)        VALUE 'CUSTOMER'.
           Ø5  FILLER                   PIC X(3)        VALUE SPACES.
           Ø5  FILLER                   PIC X(5)        VALUE 'SALES'.
           Ø5  FILLER                   PIC X(6)        VALUE SPACES.
           Ø5  FILLER                   PIC X(5)        VALUE 'ORDER'.
           Ø5  FILLER                   PIC X(6)        VALUE SPACES.
           Ø5  FILLER                   PIC X(9)        VALUE
                                                        'REQUESTED'.
           Ø5  FILLER                   PIC X(4)        VALUE SPACES.
           Ø5  FILLER                   PIC X(6)        VALUE 'ACTUAL'.
           Ø5  FILLER                   PIC X(6)        VALUE SPACES.
           Ø5  FILLER                   PIC X(4)        VALUE 'PART'.
           Ø5  FILLER                   PIC X(18)       VALUE SPACES.
           Ø5  FILLER                   PIC X(4)        VALUE 'UNIT'.
           Ø5  FILLER                   PIC X(9)        VALUE SPACES.
           Ø5  FILLER                   PIC X(8)        VALUE 'EXTENDED'.
           Ø5  FILLER                   PIC X(11)       VALUE SPACES.

       Ø1  COLUMN-HEADING-2.
           Ø5  FILLER                   PIC X(7)        VALUE SPACES.
           Ø5  FILLER                   PIC X(6)        VALUE 'BRANCH'.
           Ø5  FILLER                   PIC X(2)        VALUE SPACES.
           Ø5  FILLER                   PIC X(3)        VALUE 'REP'.
           Ø5  FILLER                   PIC X(4)        VALUE SPACES.
           Ø5  FILLER                   PIC X(6)        VALUE 'NUMBER'.
           Ø5  FILLER                   PIC X(4)        VALUE SPACES.
           Ø5  FILLER                   PIC X(5)        VALUE 'ORDER'.
           Ø5  FILLER                   PIC X(7)        VALUE SPACES.
           Ø5  FILLER                   PIC X(4)        VALUE 'DATE'.
           Ø5  FILLER                   PIC X(6)        VALUE SPACES.
           Ø5  FILLER                   PIC X(9)        VALUE
                                                        'SHIP DATE'.
           Ø5  FILLER                   PIC X(3)        VALUE SPACES.
           Ø5  FILLER                   PIC X(9)        VALUE
                                                        'SHIP DATE'.
           Ø5  FILLER                   PIC X(3)        VALUE SPACES.
           Ø5  FILLER                   PIC X(6)        VALUE 'NUMBER'.
           Ø5  FILLER                   PIC X(3)        VALUE SPACES.
           Ø5  FILLER                   PIC X(8)        VALUE 'QUANTITY'.
           Ø5  FILLER                   PIC X(6)        VALUE SPACES.
           Ø5  FILLER                   PIC X(5)        VALUE 'PRICE'.
           Ø5  FILLER                   PIC X(9)        VALUE SPACES.
           Ø5  FILLER                   PIC X(5)        VALUE 'PRICE'.
           Ø5  FILLER                   PIC X(9)        VALUE SPACES.

       Ø1  DETAIL-LINE.
           Ø5  FILLER                   PIC X(9)        VALUE SPACES.
           Ø5  DET-BRANCH               PIC 9(2).
           Ø5  FILLER                   PIC X(4)        VALUE SPACES.
```

FIGURE 6–16 cont.

```
           Ø5  DET-SALES-REP              PIC 9(3).
           Ø5  FILLER                     PIC X(4)        VALUE SPACES.
           Ø5  DET-CUSTOMER-NBR           PIC 9(5).
           Ø5  FILLER                     PIC X(4)        VALUE SPACES.
           Ø5  DET-SALES-ORD-NBR          PIC XBXXXXX.
           Ø5  FILLER                     PIC X(4)        VALUE SPACES.
           Ø5  DET-ORDER-MM               PIC 9(2).
           Ø5  FILLER                     PIC X(1)        VALUE '/'.
           Ø5  DET-ORDER-DD               PIC 9(2).
           Ø5  FILLER                     PIC X(1)        VALUE '/'.
           Ø5  DET-ORDER-YY               PIC 9(2).
           Ø5  FILLER                     PIC X(4)        VALUE SPACES.
           Ø5  DET-REQ-SHIP-MM            PIC 9(2).
           Ø5  FILLER                     PIC X(1)        VALUE '/'.
           Ø5  DET-REQ-SHIP-DD            PIC 9(2).
           Ø5  FILLER                     PIC X(1)        VALUE '/'.
           Ø5  DET-REQ-SHIP-YY            PIC 9(2).
           Ø5  FILLER                     PIC X(4)        VALUE SPACES.
           Ø5  DET-ACT-SHIP-MM            PIC 9(2).
           Ø5  FILLER                     PIC X(1)        VALUE '/'.
           Ø5  DET-ACT-SHIP-DD            PIC 9(2).
           Ø5  FILLER                     PIC X(1)        VALUE '/'.
           Ø5  DET-ACT-SHIP-YY            PIC 9(2).
           Ø5  FILLER                     PIC X(4)        VALUE SPACES.
           Ø5  DET-PART-NBR               PIC X(6).
           Ø5  FILLER                     PIC X(4)        VALUE SPACES.
           Ø5  DET-QUANTITY               PIC ZZ,ZZ9-.
           Ø5  FILLER                     PIC X(3)        VALUE SPACES.
           Ø5  DET-UNIT-PRICE             PIC $$,$$9.99-.
           Ø5  FILLER                     PIC X(3)        VALUE SPACES.
           Ø5  DET-EXTENDED-PRICE         PIC $$,$$$,$$9.99-.
           Ø5  FILLER                     PIC X(8)        VALUE SPACES.

       Ø1  SALES-REP-TOTALS-LINE.
           Ø5  FILLER                     PIC X(9)        VALUE SPACES.
           Ø5  FILLER                     PIC X(27)
               VALUE 'SALES REPRESENTATIVE TOTALS'.
           Ø5  FILLER                     PIC X(51)       VALUE SPACES.
           Ø5  SALES-REP-QUANTITY-OUT     PIC ZZZ,ZZ9-.
           Ø5  FILLER                     PIC X(15)       VALUE SPACES.
           Ø5  SALES-REP-EXT-PRICE-OUT    PIC $$$,$$$,$$9.99-.
           Ø5  FILLER                     PIC X(8).

       Ø1  BRANCH-TOTALS-LINE.
           Ø5  FILLER                     PIC X(9)        VALUE SPACES.
           Ø5  FILLER                     PIC X(13)
                                          VALUE 'BRANCH TOTALS'.
           Ø5  FILLER                     PIC X(65)       VALUE SPACES.
           Ø5  BRANCH-QUANTITY-OUT        PIC ZZZ,ZZ9-.
           Ø5  FILLER                     PIC X(15)       VALUE SPACES.
           Ø5  BRANCH-EXT-PRICE-OUT       PIC $$$,$$$,$$9.99-.
           Ø5  FILLER                     PIC X(8).

       Ø1  FINAL-TOTALS-LINE.
           Ø5  FILLER                     PIC X(9)        VALUE SPACES.
           Ø5  FILLER                     PIC X(12)
                                          VALUE 'FINAL TOTALS'.
           Ø5  FILLER                     PIC X(66)       VALUE SPACES.
           Ø5  FINAL-QUANTITY-OUT         PIC ZZZ,ZZ9-.
           Ø5  FILLER                     PIC X(15)       VALUE SPACES.
           Ø5  FINAL-EXT-PRICE-OUT        PIC $$$,$$$,$$9.99-.
           Ø5  FILLER                     PIC X(8).

       PROCEDURE DIVISION.

           PERFORM 1ØØØ-INITIALIZATION.
           PERFORM 2ØØØ-PROCESS
               UNTIL END-OF-ORDER-FILE.
           PERFORM 3ØØØ-EOJ.
           STOP RUN.

       1ØØØ-INITIALIZATION.
           OPEN INPUT  ORDER-FILE
                OUTPUT PRINT-FILE.
           MOVE CURRENT-DATE TO MAIN-HDG-DATE.
           PERFORM 91ØØ-READ-ORDER-FILE.
           MOVE ORD-BRANCH TO HOLD-BRANCH.
           MOVE ORD-SALES-REP TO HOLD-SALES-REP.

       2ØØØ-PROCESS.
           IF ORD-BRANCH = HOLD-BRANCH
               IF ORD-SALES-REP = HOLD-SALES-REP
```

FIGURE 6–16 cont.

```
                IF PAGE-OVERFLOW
                    PERFORM 21ØØ-HEADINGS
                ELSE
                    NEXT SENTENCE
            ELSE
                PERFORM 93ØØ-SALES-REP-TOTALS
        ELSE
            PERFORM 92ØØ-BRANCH-TOTALS
            PERFORM 21ØØ-HEADINGS.
        MOVE ORD-BRANCH             TO DET-BRANCH.
        MOVE ORD-SALES-REP          TO DET-SALES-REP.
        MOVE ORD-CUSTOMER-NBR       TO DET-CUSTOMER-NBR.
        MOVE ORD-SALES-ORD-NBR      TO DET-SALES-ORD-NBR.
        MOVE ORD-YY                 TO DET-ORDER-YY.
        MOVE ORD-MM                 TO DET-ORDER-MM.
        MOVE ORD-DD                 TO DET-ORDER-DD.
        MOVE ORD-PART-NBR           TO DET-PART-NBR.
        MOVE ORD-QUANTITY           TO DET-QUANTITY.
        MOVE ORD-UNIT-PRICE         TO DET-UNIT-PRICE.
        MOVE ORD-REQ-SHIP-YY        TO DET-REQ-SHIP-YY.
        MOVE ORD-REQ-SHIP-MM        TO DET-REQ-SHIP-MM.
        MOVE ORD-REQ-SHIP-DD        TO DET-REQ-SHIP-DD.
        MOVE ORD-ACT-SHIP-YY        TO DET-ACT-SHIP-YY.
        MOVE ORD-ACT-SHIP-MM        TO DET-ACT-SHIP-MM.
        MOVE ORD-ACT-SHIP-DD        TO DET-ACT-SHIP-DD.
        COMPUTE EXTENDED-PRICE = ORD-UNIT-PRICE * ORD-QUANTITY.
        MOVE EXTENDED-PRICE         TO DET-EXTENDED-PRICE.
        ADD ORD-QUANTITY            TO SALES-REP-QUANTITY.
        ADD EXTENDED-PRICE          TO SALES-REP-EXT-PRICE.
        WRITE PRINT-RECORD FROM DETAIL-LINE
            AFTER ADVANCING 2 LINES.
        ADD 2 TO LINE-COUNT.
        PERFORM 91ØØ-READ-ORDER-FILE.

    21ØØ-HEADINGS.
        ADD 1 TO PAGE-COUNT.
        MOVE PAGE-COUNT TO MAIN-HDG-PAGE-NBR.
        WRITE PRINT-RECORD FROM MAIN-HEADING
            AFTER ADVANCING PAGE.
        WRITE PRINT-RECORD FROM COLUMN-HEADING-1
            AFTER ADVANCING 2 LINES.
        WRITE PRINT-RECORD FROM COLUMN-HEADING-2
            AFTER ADVANCING 1 LINE.
        MOVE 4 TO LINE-COUNT.

    3ØØØ-EOJ.
        PERFORM 92ØØ-BRANCH-TOTALS.
        MOVE FINAL-QUANTITY TO FINAL-QUANTITY-OUT.
        MOVE FINAL-EXT-PRICE TO FINAL-EXT-PRICE-OUT.
        WRITE PRINT-RECORD FROM FINAL-TOTALS-LINE
            AFTER ADVANCING 3 LINES.
        CLOSE ORDER-FILE
              PRINT-FILE.

    91ØØ-READ-ORDER-FILE.
        READ ORDER-FILE
            AT END
                MOVE 'YES' TO END-FLAG-ORDER-FILE.

    92ØØ-BRANCH-TOTALS.
        PERFORM 93ØØ-SALES-REP-TOTALS.
        MOVE BRANCH-QUANTITY        TO BRANCH-QUANTITY-OUT.
        MOVE BRANCH-EXT-PRICE       TO BRANCH-EXT-PRICE-OUT.
        WRITE PRINT-RECORD FROM BRANCH-TOTALS-LINE
            AFTER ADVANCING 2 LINES.
        ADD BRANCH-QUANTITY         TO FINAL-QUANTITY.
        ADD BRANCH-EXT-PRICE        TO FINAL-EXT-PRICE.
        MOVE ZEROS                  TO BRANCH-QUANTITY
                                       BRANCH-EXT-PRICE.
        MOVE ORD-BRANCH             TO HOLD-BRANCH.

    93ØØ-SALES-REP-TOTALS.
        MOVE SALES-REP-QUANTITY     TO SALES-REP-QUANTITY-OUT.
        MOVE SALES-REP-EXT-PRICE    TO SALES-REP-EXT-PRICE-OUT.
        WRITE PRINT-RECORD FROM SALES-REP-TOTALS-LINE
            AFTER ADVANCING 2 LINES.
        MOVE SPACES TO PRINT-RECORD.
        WRITE PRINT-RECORD AFTER ADVANCING 2 LINES.
        ADD 4 TO LINE-COUNT.
        ADD SALES-REP-QUANTITY      TO BRANCH-QUANTITY.
        ADD SALES-REP-EXT-PRICE     TO BRANCH-EXT-PRICE.
        MOVE ZEROS                  TO SALES-REP-QUANTITY
                                       SALES-REP-EXT-PRICE.
        MOVE ORD-SALES-REP          TO HOLD-SALES-REP.
```

FIGURE 6–16 cont.

PROGRAM SPECIFICATION: BREAK-4

The second programming project of the chapter combines the previous control-break program with an extraction. Figure 6–17 gives the program specification.

PROGRAM SPECIFICATION

Program Name: BREAK-4

Program Function:

This program will produce a printed listing of an order file. This listing will include only branches 3 and 8. The report will include totals for quantity and extended price by sales representative and branch for Branches 3 and 8, and final totals for the same. Each branch will begin on a new page.

Input Files:

I. ORDER-FILE

INPUT DEVICE:	DISK
FILE ORGANIZATION:	SEQUENTIAL
RECORD LENGTH:	70 BYTES
FILE SEQUENCE:	ASCENDING ON BRANCH / SALES REP

Output Files:

I. PRINT-FILE

OUTPUT DEVICE:	PRINTER
RECORD LENGTH:	133 BYTES

Processing Requirements:

As the records are read from ORDER-FILE, only those records pertaining to Branches 3 and 8 are selected for the listing. All fields except customer purchase order number are to be included on the output. In addition, the extended price is to be calculated for each order and printed on the output. (Extended price = quantity × unit price.)

Totals for quantity and extended price are to be accumulated and printed for each sales representative, each branch, and the entire report.

Output Requirements:

The following are formatting requirements for the report:

1. Each page of the report should contain:
   (a) a main heading which includes the company name, the report name, the report date, and a page number.
   (b) column headings which describe the items printed underneath them.
2. Detail lines should include all fields from the input except the customer purchase order number. The extended price should also be included.
3. Detail lines should be double spaced.
4. Total lines for sales representative should be double spaced, with two additional blank lines after each total.
5. Each new branch should begin on a new page.
6. Final total lines should be triple spaced.

FIGURE 6–17

Input Record Layout

The input record layout is shown in Figure 6–18. This is the same file used in previous projects, repeated here for convenience.

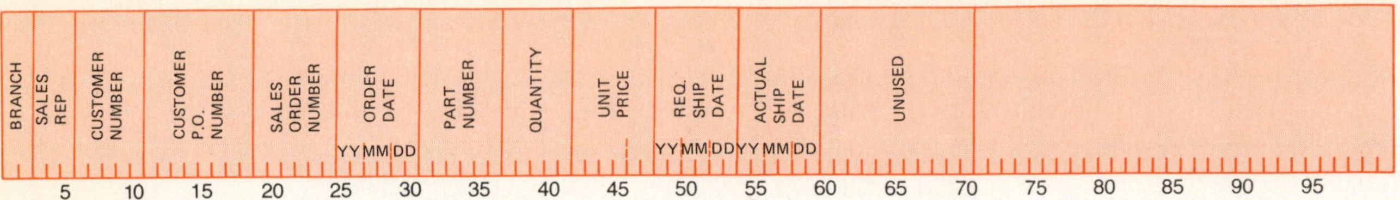

FIGURE 6–18

Print Chart

The print chart for the project is shown in Figure 6–19. It is identical to that used for the BREAK-3 program. The only significant difference between the two programs lies in which records are printed, not the format in which they are printed.

LOGIC FOR EXTRACT WITH MULTIPLE-LEVEL BREAKS AND TOTALS

The logic design for the BREAK-4 progam is shown by means of a hierarchy chart in Figure 6–20, pseudocode in Figure 6–21, and a flowchart in Figure 6–22.

Explanation of Logic

MAIN LINE

The main routine remains the same as in all previous programs. Indeed, changes to the BREAK-3 program were made in only three routines to produce the BREAK-4 program: 1000-INITIALIZATION, 2000-PROCESS, and 2100-EXTRACTED-RECORD. These changes were made in order to convert BREAK-3 into a program that extracts and prints records only for selected branches.

1000-INITIALIZATION

The initialization routine is the same as that for BREAK-3, except that the hold areas for branch and sales representative are not updated after performing 9100-READ-ORDER-FILE. This is because the fields and their hold areas are no longer compared in 2000-PROCESS, which is performed for every record. Rather, the comparison is made in 2100-EXTRACTED-RECORD, which is performed only for selected records. If the hold areas were updated in 1000-INITIALIZATION with the first record read, the extraction logic would work only if the first record was one of the extracted records. If the first record read were placed in the hold area, and if it were not for a selected branch, it would be of no value by the time a selected record was read.

To illustrate the point, suppose that there are nine branches numbered 1–9, but that the report is to be concerned only with Branches 3 and 8. If the branch number is saved for the first record read, the hold area will have a 1 in it. Consequently, this record will be rejected in 2000-PROCESS, and another record will be read. This reading and rejection will continue until a record from Branch 3 is read, at which point 2100-EXTRACTED-RECORD will be performed and the hold area will be compared with the current record read. Since the hold area will contain a 1 and the current branch is Branch 3, the inequality will result in a set of totals being printed for the first record. To avoid this premature set of totals, the hold area is left with a value of zero (established in WORKING-STORAGE) until the first record is selected. At *that* point, it is updated in 2100-EXTRACTED-RECORD. (See Figure 6–23.)

2000-PROCESS

The 2000-PROCESS routine is considerably smaller than it was in BREAK-3. Most of the statements there have been moved to 2100-EXTRACTED-RECORD. In 2000-PROCESS each record is tested to determine whether it refers to one of the selected branches. The IF statement uses a condition-name (EXTRACTED-BRANCH) for the test. If the record pertains to a selected branch, 2100-EXTRACTED-RECORD is performed. Regardless of the outcome of the test, 9100-READ-ORDER-FILE is performed to read the next record. (See Figure 6–24.)

```
          DATE: XX/XX/XX                      PRODUCT DISTRIBUTION INC. - CURRENT ORDERS                            PAGE: ZZ9

                 SALES  CUSTOMER   SALES     ORDER     REQUESTED    ACTUAL      PART                  UNIT          EXTENDED
         BRANCH   REP    NUMBER    ORDER      DATE     SHIP DATE   SHIP DATE  NUMBER   QUANTITY       PRICE           PRICE

           99    999     99999   XBXXXXX  99/99/99    99/99/99    99/99/99    XXXXXX    ZZ,ZZ9-   $$,$$9.99-  $$,$$$,$$9.99-

           99    999     99999   XBXXXXX  99/99/99    99/99/99    99/99/99    XXXXXX    ZZ,ZZ9-   $$,$$9.99-  $$,$$$,$$9.99-

           SALES REPRESENTATIVE TOTALS                                                 ZZZ,ZZ9-               $$$,$$$,$$9.99-



           BRANCH TOTALS                                                               ZZZ,ZZ9-               $$$,$$$,$$9.99-


           FINAL TOTALS                                                                ZZZ,ZZ9-               $$$,$$$,$$9.99-
```

FIGURE 6–19

Hierarchy Chart

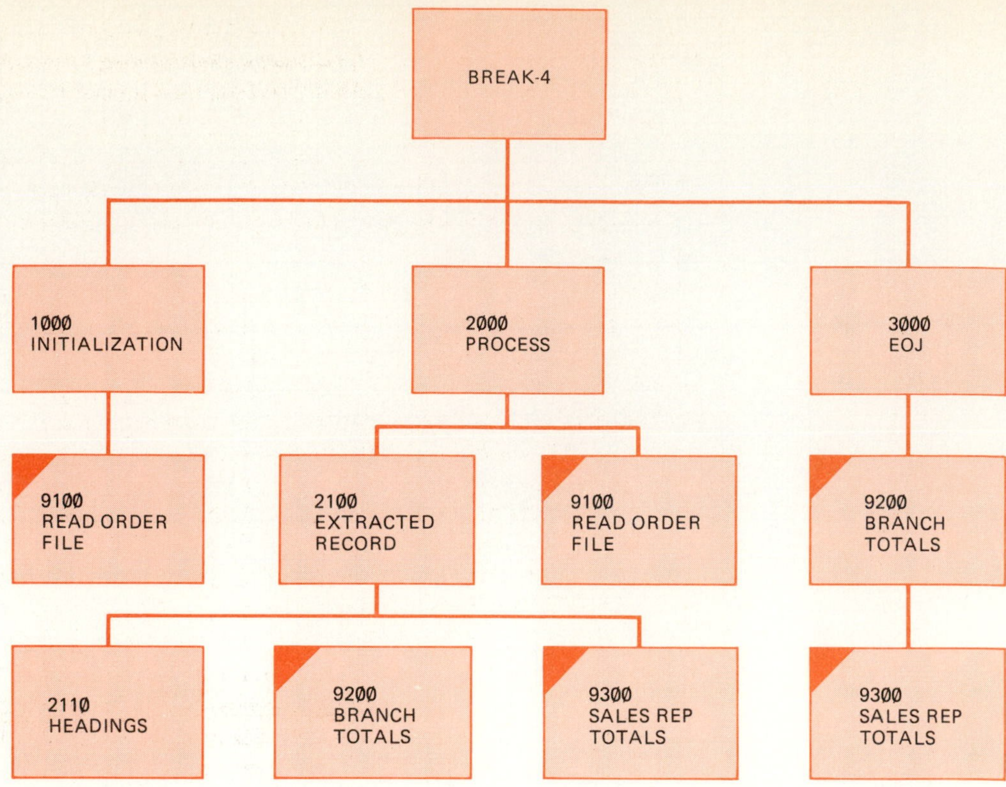

FIGURE 6–20

Pseudocode

```
MAIN LINE
     DO initialization
     DO WHILE more order records
          DO process
     ENDDO
     DO end of job
INITIALIZATION
     OPEN files
     MOVE date to heading
     DO read an order
PROCESS
     IF extracted branch
          DO extracted record
     ENDIF
     DO read an order
EXTRACTED RECORD
     IF branch hold = zero
          MOVE branch to branch hold
          MOVE sales rep to sales rep hold
     ENDIF
     IF branch = branch hold
          IF sales rep = sales rep hold
               IF page overflow
                    DO headings
               ENDIF
```

FIGURE 6–21

```
            ELSE
                 DO sales rep totals
            ENDIF
       ELSE
            DO branch totals
            DO headings
       ENDIF
       MOVE input to output
       CALCULATE extended price
       MOVE extended price to output
       ADD quantity to sales rep quantity
       ADD extended price to sales rep extended price
       WRITE detail line
       ADD 2 to line count
HEADINGS
       ADD 1 to page count
       MOVE page count to heading
       WRITE main heading line
       WRITE column heading line one
       WRITE column heading line two
       MOVE 4 to line count
END OF JOB
       DO branch totals
       MOVE final quantity to final quantity out
       MOVE final extended price to final extended
         price out
       WRITE final total line
       CLOSE files
READ AN ORDER
       READ order file
BRANCH TOTALS
       DO sales rep totals
       MOVE branch quantity to output
       MOVE branch extended price to output
       WRITE branch total line
       ADD branch quantity to final quantity
       ADD branch extended price to final extended
         price
       MOVE zeros to branch quantity, branch extended
         price
       MOVE branch to branch hold
SALES REP TOTALS
       MOVE sales rep quantity to output
       MOVE sales rep extended price to output
       WRITE sales rep total line
       WRITE blank line
       ADD 4 to line count
       ADD sales rep quantity to branch quantity
       ADD sales rep extended price to branch
         extended price
       MOVE zeros to sales rep quantity, sales rep
         extended price
       MOVE sales rep to sales rep hold
```

FIGURE 6–21 cont.

Flowchart

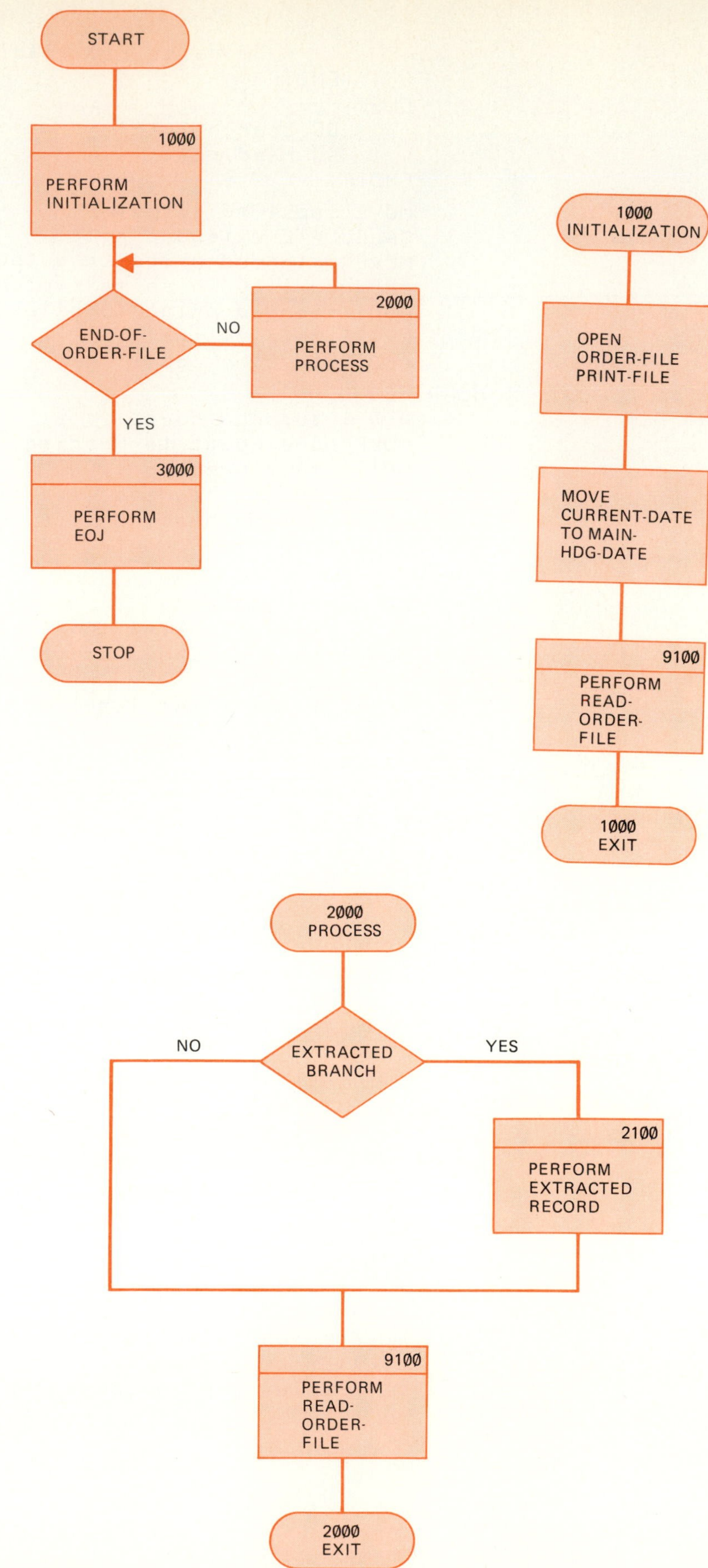

FIGURE 6–22

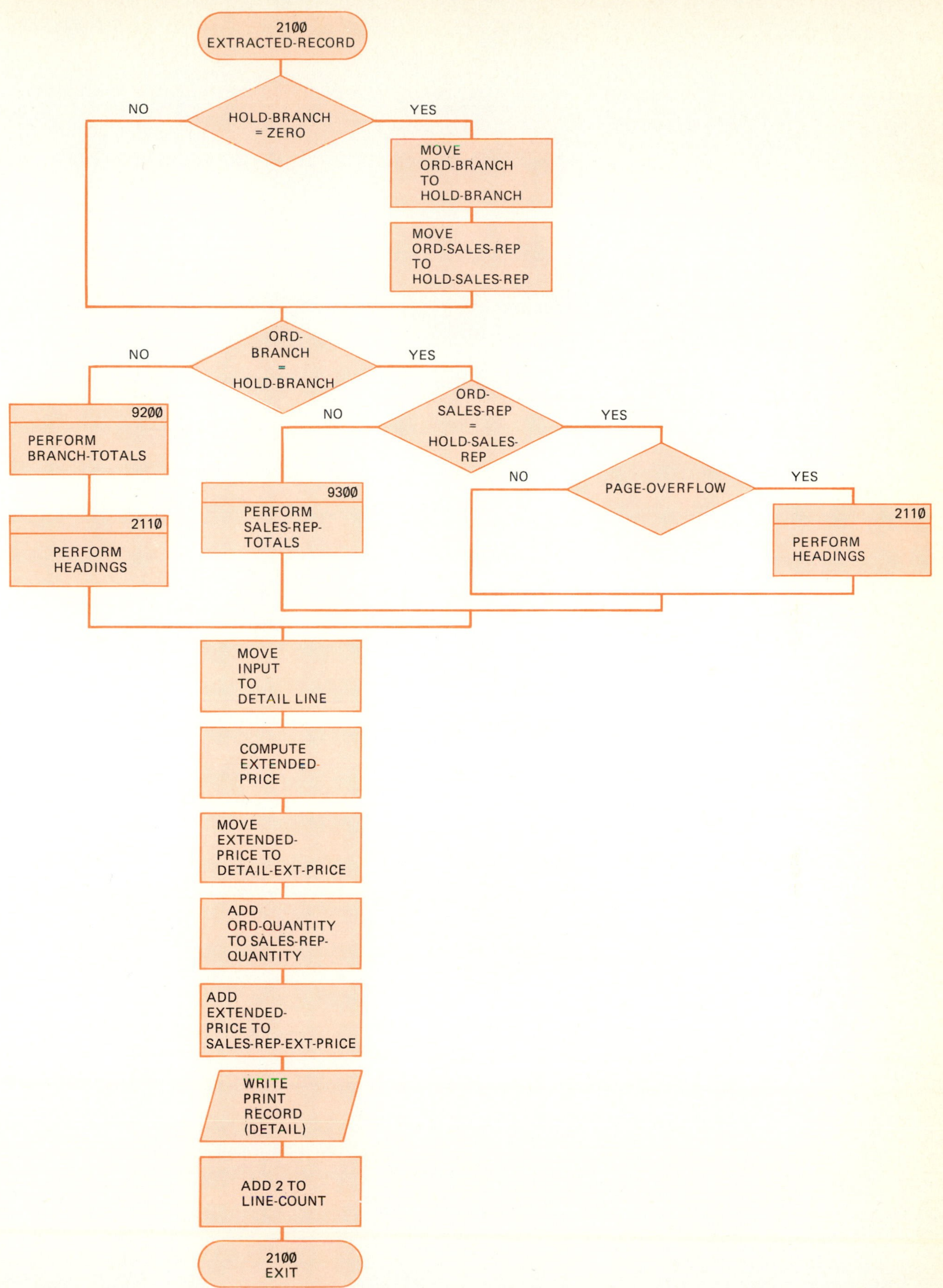

FIGURE 6–22 cont.

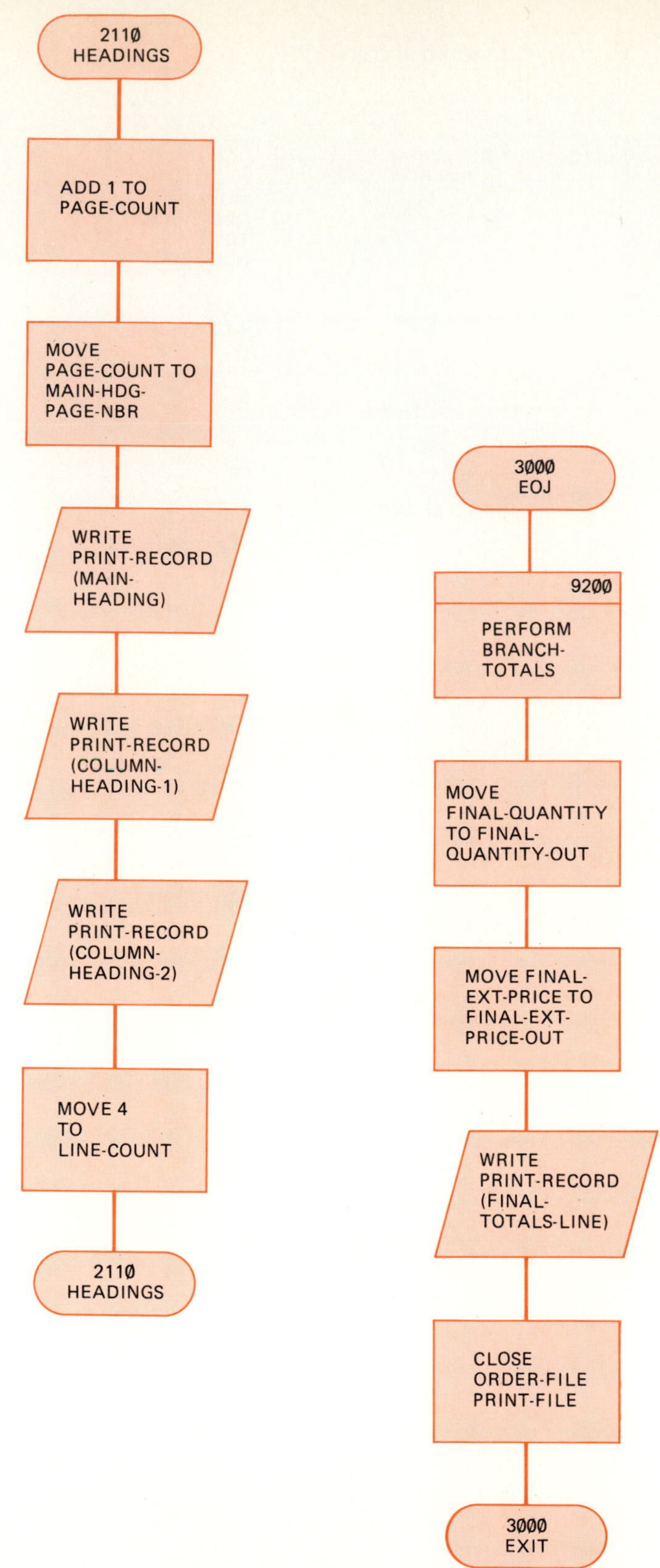

FIGURE 6–22 cont.

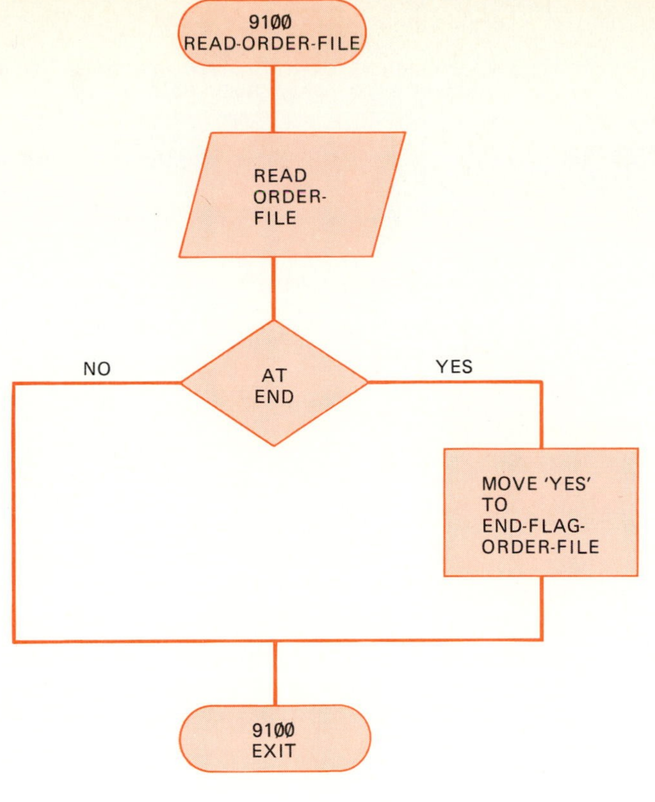

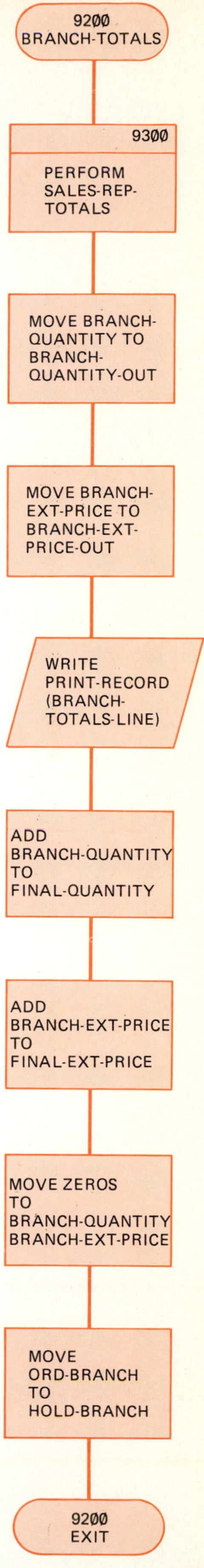

FIGURE 6–22 cont.

```
       1000-INITIALIZATION.
           OPEN INPUT  ORDER-FILE
                OUTPUT PRINT-FILE.
           MOVE CURRENT-DATE TO MAIN-HDG-DATE.
           PERFORM 9100-READ-ORDER-FILE.
```

FIGURE 6–23

```
       2000-PROCESS.
           IF EXTRACTED-BRANCH
               PERFORM 2100-EXTRACTED-RECORD.
           PERFORM 9100-READ-ORDER-FILE.
```

FIGURE 6–24

2100-EXTRACTED-RECORD

The first step in 2100-EXTRACTED-RECORD tests HOLD-BRANCH to determine whether it contains a value of ZERO. This will be true the first time the routine is performed, so that both the branch and sales representative hold areas will be updated. From this point on, the routine contains the same statements as 2000-PROCESS did in the BREAK-3 program, except that PERFORM 9100-READ-ORDER-FILE appears in 2000-PROCESS instead of here. The READ must be done in 2000-PROCESS so that it is performed every time an input record is processed. (See Figure 6–25.)

```
       2100-EXTRACTED-RECORD.
           IF HOLD-BRANCH = ZERO
               MOVE ORD-BRANCH TO HOLD-BRANCH
               MOVE ORD-SALES-REP TO HOLD-SALES-REP.
           IF ORD-BRANCH = HOLD-BRANCH
               IF ORD-SALES-REP = HOLD-SALES-REP
                   IF PAGE-OVERFLOW
                       PERFORM 2110-HEADINGS
                   ELSE
                       NEXT SENTENCE
               ELSE
                   PERFORM 9300-SALES-REP-TOTALS
           ELSE
               PERFORM 9200-BRANCH-TOTALS
               PERFORM 2110-HEADINGS.
           MOVE ORD-BRANCH            TO DET-BRANCH.
           MOVE ORD-SALES-REP         TO DET-SALES-REP.
           MOVE ORD-CUSTOMER-NBR      TO DET-CUSTOMER-NBR.
           MOVE ORD-SALES-ORD-NBR     TO DET-SALES-ORD-NBR.
           MOVE ORD-YY                TO DET-ORDER-YY.
           MOVE ORD-MM                TO DET-ORDER-MM.
           MOVE ORD-DD                TO DET-ORDER-DD.
           MOVE ORD-PART-NBR          TO DET-PART-NBR.
           MOVE ORD-QUANTITY          TO DET-QUANTITY.
           MOVE ORD-UNIT-PRICE        TO DET-UNIT-PRICE.
           MOVE ORD-REQ-SHIP-YY       TO DET-REQ-SHIP-YY.
           MOVE ORD-REQ-SHIP-MM       TO DET-REQ-SHIP-MM.
           MOVE ORD-REQ-SHIP-DD       TO DET-REQ-SHIP-DD.
           MOVE ORD-ACT-SHIP-YY       TO DET-ACT-SHIP-YY.
           MOVE ORD-ACT-SHIP-MM       TO DET-ACT-SHIP-MM.
           MOVE ORD-ACT-SHIP-DD       TO DET-ACT-SHIP-DD.
           COMPUTE EXTENDED-PRICE = ORD-UNIT-PRICE * ORD-QUANTITY.
           MOVE EXTENDED-PRICE        TO DET-EXTENDED-PRICE.
           ADD ORD-QUANTITY           TO SALES-REP-QUANTITY.
           ADD EXTENDED-PRICE         TO SALES-REP-EXT-PRICE.
           WRITE PRINT-RECORD FROM DETAIL-LINE
               AFTER ADVANCING 2 LINES.
           ADD 2 TO LINE-COUNT.
```

FIGURE 6–25

THE COBOL PROGRAM

Test Data

The test data for the BREAK-4 program appears in Figure 6–26.

```
Ø1201ØØ3ØØPO173   B1238387Ø25GN4Ø2AØØØØ1Ø45ØØØ871116ØØØØØØ
Ø1201Ø47278372    G4838887Ø913WB7Ø2XØØØ9ØØ115ØØ871101ØØØØØØ
Ø1201ØØ3ØØE1Ø12   B12335871105WB493EØØØØ2Ø54ØØØ871122ØØØØØØ
Ø3ØØ7473ØØ        H8477787Ø223MF4Ø3TØØØØ5Ø4ØØØØ87Ø5Ø2ØØØØØØ
Ø3ØØ7ØØ378EBNER   H8457987Ø811VX922PØØ8ØØØØ127589112ØØØØØØØ
Ø3ØØ7739897747    B89288871106MF848JØØØØ5Ø2145Ø88Ø13ØØØØØØØ
Ø3ØØ7ØØ28334567X  B3423787103ØHL834EØØØ16Ø19ØØØ871121ØØØØØØ
Ø3ØØ7473ØØ        Y289Ø387Ø811VXØØ1LØØ2ØØØØ622Ø8712Ø3ØØØØØØ
Ø344Ø6948187Ø341  GØ418Ø87Ø2Ø9JGØ4ØXØØØØ1Ø525ØØ88Ø619ØØØØØØ
Ø361182888P2783733B8433Ø871Ø25HL289BØØØ1ØØ234ØØ871113ØØØØØØ
Ø361128375T7838   T7829987Ø323JG563WØØØØ6Ø43ØØØ871Ø18ØØØØØØ
Ø36115Ø912        H6915Ø87Ø2Ø6MF848TØØØØ3Ø36ØØØ8712Ø1ØØØØØØ
Ø8174314Ø865      H4189187Ø412TK61ØLØØØ18ØØ78ØØ87Ø63ØØØØØØØ
Ø8174Ø18Ø5R7278   T2164287Ø81ØTK497XØØØ1ØØ118ØØ87113ØØØØØØØ
Ø8174Ø18Ø5R8322   Y211Ø587Ø6Ø1TN116TØØØØ1Ø3ØØØØ871221ØØØØØØ
Ø891562Ø54SCHUH   L5Ø681871108TK812EØØØØ6Ø573ØØ88Ø1Ø5ØØØØØØ
Ø891521Ø78        B71Ø45871ØØ1FV782TØØØØ3ØØ28ØØ871115ØØØØØØ
```

FIGURE 6–26

Sample Output

Sample output for BREAK-4 appears in Figure 6–27.

The Program

The complete COBOL BREAK-4 program appears in Figure 6–28.

DATE: 11/09/87 PRODUCT DISTRIBUTION INC. - CURRENT ORDERS PAGE: 1

BRANCH	SALES REP	CUSTOMER NUMBER	SALES ORDER	ORDER DATE	REQUESTED SHIP DATE	ACTUAL SHIP DATE	PART NUMBER	QUANTITY	UNIT PRICE	EXTENDED PRICE
03	007	47300	H 84777	02/23/87	05/02/87	00/00/00	MF403T	5	$400.00	$2,000.00
03	007	00378	H 84579	08/11/87	11/20/89	00/00/00	VX922P	800	$12.75	$10,200.00
03	007	73989	B 89288	11/06/87	01/30/88	00/00/00	MF848J	5	$214.50	$1,072.50
03	007	00283	B 34237	10/30/87	11/21/87	00/00/00	HL834E	16	$190.00	$3,040.00
03	007	47300	Y 28903	08/11/87	12/03/87	00/00/00	VX001L	200	$62.20	$12,440.00
SALES REPRESENTATIVE TOTALS								1,026		$28,752.50
03	440	69481	G 04180	02/09/87	06/19/88	00/00/00	JG040X	1	$525.00	$525.00
SALES REPRESENTATIVE TOTALS								1		$525.00
03	611	82888	B 84330	10/25/87	11/13/87	00/00/00	HL289B	10	$234.00	$2,340.00
03	611	28375	T 78299	03/23/87	10/18/87	00/00/00	JG563W	6	$430.00	$2,580.00
03	611	50912	H 69150	02/06/87	12/01/87	00/00/00	MF848T	3	$360.00	$1,080.00
SALES REPRESENTATIVE TOTALS								19		$6,000.00
BRANCH TOTALS								1,046		$35,277.50

FIGURE 6–27

DATE: 11/09/87 PRODUCT DISTRIBUTION INC. - CURRENT ORDERS PAGE: 2

BRANCH	SALES REP	CUSTOMER NUMBER	SALES ORDER	ORDER DATE	REQUESTED SHIP DATE	ACTUAL SHIP DATE	PART NUMBER	QUANTITY	UNIT PRICE	EXTENDED PRICE
08	174	31408	H 41891	04/12/87	06/30/87	00/00/00	TK610L	18	$78.00	$1,404.00
08	174	01805	T 21642	08/10/87	11/30/87	00/00/00	TK497X	10	$118.00	$1,180.00
08	174	01805	Y 21105	06/01/87	12/21/87	00/00/00	TN116T	1	$300.00	$300.00
SALES REPRESENTATIVE TOTALS								29		$2,884.00
08	915	62054	L 50681	11/08/87	01/05/88	00/00/00	TK812E	6	$573.00	$3,438.00
08	915	21078	B 71045	10/01/87	11/15/87	00/00/00	FV782T	3	$28.00	$84.00
SALES REPRESENTATIVE TOTALS								9		$3,522.00
BRANCH TOTALS								38		$6,406.00
FINAL TOTALS								1,084		$41,683.50

FIGURE 6–27 cont.

```
IDENTIFICATION DIVISION.

PROGRAM-ID.    BREAK-4.

AUTHOR.        HELEN HUMPHREYS.

INSTALLATION.  PRODUCT DISTRIBUTION INC.

DATE-WRITTEN.  Ø6/12/87.

DATE-COMPILED. Ø6/3Ø/87.

*****************************************************************
*                                                               *
*    THIS PROGRAM WILL PRODUCE A PRINTED LISTING OF THE ORDER   *
*    FILE.  THE REPORT WILL INCLUDE SALES REPRESENTATIVE,       *
*    BRANCH, AND FINAL TOTALS FOR QUANTITY AND EXTENDED PRICE.  *
*    EACH BRANCH WILL BEGIN ON A NEW PAGE.  ONLY BRANCHES 3     *
*    AND 8 WILL BE INCLUDED IN THE OUTPUT.                      *
*                                                               *
*****************************************************************

ENVIRONMENT DIVISION.

CONFIGURATION SECTION.

SOURCE-COMPUTER.
        IBM-37Ø.
OBJECT-COMPUTER.
        IBM-37Ø.

INPUT-OUTPUT SECTION.
FILE-CONTROL.
    SELECT ORDER-FILE ASSIGN TO DISK.
    SELECT PRINT-FILE ASSIGN TO PRINTER.

DATA DIVISION.
FILE SECTION.

FD  ORDER-FILE
    LABEL RECORDS ARE STANDARD
    RECORD CONTAINS 7Ø CHARACTERS
    DATA RECORD IS ORDER-RECORD.

Ø1  ORDER-RECORD.
    Ø5  ORD-BRANCH              PIC 9(2).
        88  EXTRACTED-BRANCH                    VALUES 3 8.
```

FIGURE 6–28

```
           Ø5  ORD-SALES-REP             PIC 9(3).
           Ø5  ORD-CUSTOMER-NBR          PIC 9(5).
           Ø5  ORD-CUST-PO-NBR           PIC X(8).
           Ø5  ORD-SALES-ORD-NBR         PIC X(6).
           Ø5  ORD-DATE.
               1Ø  ORD-YY                PIC 9(2).
               1Ø  ORD-MM                PIC 9(2).
               1Ø  ORD-DD                PIC 9(2).
           Ø5  ORD-PART-NBR              PIC X(6).
           Ø5  ORD-QUANTITY              PIC S9(5).
           Ø5  ORD-UNIT-PRICE            PIC S9(4)V9(2).
           Ø5  ORD-REQ-SHIP-DATE.
               1Ø  ORD-REQ-SHIP-YY       PIC 9(2).
               1Ø  ORD-REQ-SHIP-MM       PIC 9(2).
               1Ø  ORD-REQ-SHIP-DD       PIC 9(2).
           Ø5  ORD-ACT-SHIP-DATE.
               1Ø  ORD-ACT-SHIP-YY       PIC 9(2).
               1Ø  ORD-ACT-SHIP-MM       PIC 9(2).
               1Ø  ORD-ACT-SHIP-DD       PIC 9(2).
           Ø5  FILLER                    PIC X(11).

       FD  PRINT-FILE
           LABEL RECORDS ARE OMITTED
           RECORD CONTAINS 133 CHARACTERS
           DATA RECORD IS PRINT-RECORD.

       Ø1  PRINT-RECORD                  PIC X(133).

       WORKING-STORAGE SECTION.

       Ø1  HOLDS-COUNTERS-SWITCHES.
           Ø5  END-FLAG-ORDER-FILE       PIC X(3)        VALUE 'NO'.
               88  END-OF-ORDER-FILE                     VALUE 'YES'.
           Ø5  LINE-COUNT                PIC 9(2)        VALUE 99.
               88  PAGE-OVERFLOW                         VALUE 51 THRU 99.
           Ø5  PAGE-COUNT                PIC 9(3)        VALUE ZEROS.
           Ø5  HOLD-BRANCH               PIC 9(2)        VALUE ZEROS.
           Ø5  HOLD-SALES-REP            PIC 9(3)        VALUE ZEROS.

       Ø1  CALCULATED-FIELDS.
           Ø5  EXTENDED-PRICE            PIC S9(7)V9(2).

       Ø1  SALES-REP-TOTALS.
           Ø5  SALES-REP-QUANTITY        PIC S9(6)       VALUE ZEROS.
           Ø5  SALES-REP-EXT-PRICE       PIC S9(8)V9(2)  VALUE ZEROS.

       Ø1  BRANCH-TOTALS.
           Ø5  BRANCH-QUANTITY           PIC S9(6)       VALUE ZEROS.
           Ø5  BRANCH-EXT-PRICE          PIC S9(8)V9(2)  VALUE ZEROS.

       Ø1  FINAL-TOTALS.
           Ø5  FINAL-QUANTITY            PIC S9(6)       VALUE ZEROS.
           Ø5  FINAL-EXT-PRICE           PIC S9(8)V9(2)  VALUE ZEROS.

       Ø1  MAIN-HEADING.
           Ø5  FILLER                    PIC X(7)        VALUE SPACES.
           Ø5  FILLER                    PIC X(6)        VALUE 'DATE:'.
           Ø5  MAIN-HDG-DATE             PIC X(8).
           Ø5  FILLER                    PIC X(25)       VALUE SPACES.
           Ø5  FILLER                    PIC X(42)
               VALUE 'PRODUCT DISTRIBUTION INC. - CURRENT ORDERS'.
           Ø5  FILLER                    PIC X(27)       VALUE SPACES.
           Ø5  FILLER                    PIC X(6)        VALUE 'PAGE:'.
           Ø5  MAIN-HDG-PAGE-NBR         PIC ZZ9.
           Ø5  FILLER                    PIC X(9)        VALUE SPACES.

       Ø1  COLUMN-HEADING-1.
           Ø5  FILLER                    PIC X(14)       VALUE SPACES.
           Ø5  FILLER                    PIC X(5)        VALUE 'SALES'.
           Ø5  FILLER                    PIC X(2)        VALUE SPACES.
           Ø5  FILLER                    PIC X(8)        VALUE 'CUSTOMER'.
           Ø5  FILLER                    PIC X(3)        VALUE SPACES.
           Ø5  FILLER                    PIC X(5)        VALUE 'SALES'.
           Ø5  FILLER                    PIC X(6)        VALUE SPACES.
           Ø5  FILLER                    PIC X(5)        VALUE 'ORDER'.
           Ø5  FILLER                    PIC X(6)        VALUE SPACES.
           Ø5  FILLER                    PIC X(9)        VALUE
                                                         'REQUESTED'.
           Ø5  FILLER                    PIC X(4)        VALUE SPACES.
           Ø5  FILLER                    PIC X(6)        VALUE 'ACTUAL'.
           Ø5  FILLER                    PIC X(6)        VALUE SPACES.
           Ø5  FILLER                    PIC X(4)        VALUE 'PART'.
           Ø5  FILLER                    PIC X(18)       VALUE SPACES.
           Ø5  FILLER                    PIC X(4)        VALUE 'UNIT'.
```

FIGURE 6–28 cont.

```
           Ø5  FILLER                     PIC X(9)        VALUE SPACES.
           Ø5  FILLER                     PIC X(8)        VALUE 'EXTENDED'.
           Ø5  FILLER                     PIC X(11)       VALUE SPACES.

       Ø1  COLUMN-HEADING-2.
           Ø5  FILLER                     PIC X(7)        VALUE SPACES.
           Ø5  FILLER                     PIC X(6)        VALUE 'BRANCH'.
           Ø5  FILLER                     PIC X(2)        VALUE SPACES.
           Ø5  FILLER                     PIC X(3)        VALUE 'REP'.
           Ø5  FILLER                     PIC X(4)        VALUE SPACES.
           Ø5  FILLER                     PIC X(6)        VALUE 'NUMBER'.
           Ø5  FILLER                     PIC X(4)        VALUE SPACES.
           Ø5  FILLER                     PIC X(5)        VALUE 'ORDER'.
           Ø5  FILLER                     PIC X(7)        VALUE SPACES.
           Ø5  FILLER                     PIC X(4)        VALUE 'DATE'.
           Ø5  FILLER                     PIC X(6)        VALUE SPACES.
           Ø5  FILLER                     PIC X(9)        VALUE
                                                          'SHIP DATE'.
           Ø5  FILLER                     PIC X(3)        VALUE SPACES.
           Ø5  FILLER                     PIC X(9)        VALUE
                                                          'SHIP DATE'.
           Ø5  FILLER                     PIC X(3)        VALUE SPACES.
           Ø5  FILLER                     PIC X(6)        VALUE 'NUMBER'.
           Ø5  FILLER                     PIC X(3)        VALUE SPACES.
           Ø5  FILLER                     PIC X(8)        VALUE 'QUANTITY'.
           Ø5  FILLER                     PIC X(6)        VALUE SPACES.
           Ø5  FILLER                     PIC X(5)        VALUE 'PRICE'.
           Ø5  FILLER                     PIC X(9)        VALUE SPACES.
           Ø5  FILLER                     PIC X(5)        VALUE 'PRICE'.
           Ø5  FILLER                     PIC X(9)        VALUE SPACES.

       Ø1  DETAIL-LINE.
           Ø5  FILLER                     PIC X(9)        VALUE SPACES.
           Ø5  DET-BRANCH                 PIC 9(2).
           Ø5  FILLER                     PIC X(4)        VALUE SPACES.
           Ø5  DET-SALES-REP              PIC 9(3).
           Ø5  FILLER                     PIC X(4)        VALUE SPACES.
           Ø5  DET-CUSTOMER-NBR           PIC 9(5).
           Ø5  FILLER                     PIC X(4)        VALUE SPACES.
           Ø5  DET-SALES-ORD-NBR          PIC XBXXXXX.
           Ø5  FILLER                     PIC X(4)        VALUE SPACES.
           Ø5  DET-ORDER-MM               PIC 9(2).
           Ø5  FILLER                     PIC X(1)        VALUE '/'.
           Ø5  DET-ORDER-DD               PIC 9(2).
           Ø5  FILLER                     PIC X(1)        VALUE '/'.
           Ø5  DET-ORDER-YY               PIC 9(2).
           Ø5  FILLER                     PIC X(4)        VALUE SPACES.
           Ø5  DET-REQ-SHIP-MM            PIC 9(2).
           Ø5  FILLER                     PIC X(1)        VALUE '/'.
           Ø5  DET-REQ-SHIP-DD            PIC 9(2).
           Ø5  FILLER                     PIC X(1)        VALUE '/'.
           Ø5  DET-REQ-SHIP-YY            PIC 9(2).
           Ø5  FILLER                     PIC X(4)        VALUE SPACES.
           Ø5  DET-ACT-SHIP-MM            PIC 9(2).
           Ø5  FILLER                     PIC X(1)        VALUE '/'.
           Ø5  DET-ACT-SHIP-DD            PIC 9(2).
           Ø5  FILLER                     PIC X(1)        VALUE '/'.
           Ø5  DET-ACT-SHIP-YY            PIC 9(2).
           Ø5  FILLER                     PIC X(4)        VALUE SPACES.
           Ø5  DET-PART-NBR               PIC X(6).
           Ø5  FILLER                     PIC X(4)        VALUE SPACES.
           Ø5  DET-QUANTITY               PIC ZZ,ZZ9-.
           Ø5  FILLER                     PIC X(3)        VALUE SPACES.
           Ø5  DET-UNIT-PRICE             PIC $$,$$9.99-.
           Ø5  FILLER                     PIC X(3)        VALUE SPACES.
           Ø5  DET-EXTENDED-PRICE         PIC $$,$$$,$$9.99-.
           Ø5  FILLER                     PIC X(8)        VALUE SPACES.

       Ø1  SALES-REP-TOTALS-LINE.
           Ø5  FILLER                     PIC X(9)        VALUE SPACES.
           Ø5  FILLER                     PIC X(27)
               VALUE 'SALES REPRESENTATIVE TOTALS'.
           Ø5  FILLER                     PIC X(51)       VALUE SPACES.
           Ø5  SALES-REP-QUANTITY-OUT     PIC ZZZ,ZZ9-.
           Ø5  FILLER                     PIC X(15)       VALUE SPACES.
           Ø5  SALES-REP-EXT-PRICE-OUT PIC $$$,$$$,$$9.99-.
           Ø5  FILLER                     PIC X(8).

       Ø1  BRANCH-TOTALS-LINE.
           Ø5  FILLER                     PIC X(9)        VALUE SPACES.
           Ø5  FILLER                     PIC X(13)
                                          VALUE 'BRANCH TOTALS'.
           Ø5  FILLER                     PIC X(65)       VALUE SPACES.
           Ø5  BRANCH-QUANTITY-OUT        PIC ZZZ,ZZ9-.
           Ø5  FILLER                     PIC X(15)       VALUE SPACES.
```

FIGURE 6–28 cont.

```
    Ø5  BRANCH-EXT-PRICE-OUT    PIC $$$,$$$,$$9.99-.
    Ø5  FILLER                  PIC X(8).

Ø1  FINAL-TOTALS-LINE.
    Ø5  FILLER                  PIC X(9)        VALUE SPACES.
    Ø5  FILLER                  PIC X(12)
                                VALUE 'FINAL TOTALS'.
    Ø5  FILLER                  PIC X(66)       VALUE SPACES.
    Ø5  FINAL-QUANTITY-OUT      PIC ZZZ,ZZ9-.
    Ø5  FILLER                  PIC X(15)       VALUE SPACES.
    Ø5  FINAL-EXT-PRICE-OUT     PIC $$$,$$$,$$9.99-.
    Ø5  FILLER                  PIC X(8).

PROCEDURE DIVISION.

    PERFORM 1ØØØ-INITIALIZATION.
    PERFORM 2ØØØ-PROCESS
        UNTIL END-OF-ORDER-FILE.
    PERFORM 3ØØØ-EOJ.
    STOP RUN.

1ØØØ-INITIALIZATION.
    OPEN INPUT  ORDER-FILE
         OUTPUT PRINT-FILE.
    MOVE CURRENT-DATE TO MAIN-HDG-DATE.
    PERFORM 91ØØ-READ-ORDER-FILE.

2ØØØ-PROCESS.
     IF EXTRACTED-BRANCH
         PERFORM 21ØØ-EXTRACTED-RECORD.
     PERFORM 91ØØ-READ-ORDER-FILE.

21ØØ-EXTRACTED-RECORD.
    IF HOLD-BRANCH = ZERO
        MOVE ORD-BRANCH TO HOLD-BRANCH
        MOVE ORD-SALES-REP TO HOLD-SALES-REP.
    IF ORD-BRANCH = HOLD-BRANCH
        IF ORD-SALES-REP = HOLD-SALES-REP
            IF PAGE-OVERFLOW
                PERFORM 211Ø-HEADINGS
            ELSE
                NEXT SENTENCE
        ELSE
            PERFORM 93ØØ-SALES-REP-TOTALS
    ELSE
        PERFORM 92ØØ-BRANCH-TOTALS
        PERFORM 211Ø-HEADINGS.
    MOVE ORD-BRANCH             TO DET-BRANCH.
    MOVE ORD-SALES-REP          TO DET-SALES-REP.
    MOVE ORD-CUSTOMER-NBR       TO DET-CUSTOMER-NBR.
    MOVE ORD-SALES-ORD-NBR      TO DET-SALES-ORD-NBR.
    MOVE ORD-YY                 TO DET-ORDER-YY.
    MOVE ORD-MM                 TO DET-ORDER-MM.
    MOVE ORD-DD                 TO DET-ORDER-DD.
    MOVE ORD-PART-NBR           TO DET-PART-NBR.
    MOVE ORD-QUANTITY           TO DET-QUANTITY.
    MOVE ORD-UNIT-PRICE         TO DET-UNIT-PRICE.
    MOVE ORD-REQ-SHIP-YY        TO DET-REQ-SHIP-YY.
    MOVE ORD-REQ-SHIP-MM        TO DET-REQ-SHIP-MM.
    MOVE ORD-REQ-SHIP-DD        TO DET-REQ-SHIP-DD.
    MOVE ORD-ACT-SHIP-YY        TO DET-ACT-SHIP-YY.
    MOVE ORD-ACT-SHIP-MM        TO DET-ACT-SHIP-MM.
    MOVE ORD-ACT-SHIP-DD        TO DET-ACT-SHIP-DD.
    COMPUTE EXTENDED-PRICE = ORD-UNIT-PRICE * ORD-QUANTITY.
    MOVE EXTENDED-PRICE         TO DET-EXTENDED-PRICE.
    ADD ORD-QUANTITY            TO SALES-REP-QUANTITY.
    ADD EXTENDED-PRICE          TO SALES-REP-EXT-PRICE.
    WRITE PRINT-RECORD FROM DETAIL-LINE
        AFTER ADVANCING 2 LINES.
    ADD 2 TO LINE-COUNT.

211Ø-HEADINGS.
    ADD 1 TO PAGE-COUNT.
    MOVE PAGE-COUNT TO MAIN-HDG-PAGE-NBR.
    WRITE PRINT-RECORD FROM MAIN-HEADING
        AFTER ADVANCING PAGE.
    WRITE PRINT-RECORD FROM COLUMN-HEADING-1
        AFTER ADVANCING 2 LINES.
    WRITE PRINT-RECORD FROM COLUMN-HEADING-2
        AFTER ADVANCING 1 LINE.
    MOVE 4 TO LINE-COUNT.

3ØØØ-EOJ.
    PERFORM 92ØØ-BRANCH-TOTALS.
    MOVE FINAL-QUANTITY TO FINAL-QUANTITY-OUT.
```

FIGURE 6–28 cont.

```
           MOVE FINAL-EXT-PRICE TO FINAL-EXT-PRICE-OUT.
           WRITE PRINT-RECORD FROM FINAL-TOTALS-LINE
               AFTER ADVANCING 3 LINES.
           CLOSE ORDER-FILE
                 PRINT-FILE.

       9100-READ-ORDER-FILE.
           READ ORDER-FILE
               AT END
                   MOVE 'YES' TO END-FLAG-ORDER-FILE.

       9200-BRANCH-TOTALS.
           PERFORM 9300-SALES-REP-TOTALS.
           MOVE BRANCH-QUANTITY         TO BRANCH-QUANTITY-OUT.
           MOVE BRANCH-EXT-PRICE        TO BRANCH-EXT-PRICE-OUT.
           WRITE PRINT-RECORD FROM BRANCH-TOTALS-LINE
               AFTER ADVANCING 2 LINES.
           ADD BRANCH-QUANTITY          TO FINAL-QUANTITY.
           ADD BRANCH-EXT-PRICE         TO FINAL-EXT-PRICE.
           MOVE ZEROS                   TO BRANCH-QUANTITY
                                           BRANCH-EXT-PRICE.
           MOVE ORD-BRANCH              TO HOLD-BRANCH.

       9300-SALES-REP-TOTALS.
           MOVE SALES-REP-QUANTITY      TO SALES-REP-QUANTITY-OUT.
           MOVE SALES-REP-EXT-PRICE     TO SALES-REP-EXT-PRICE-OUT.
           WRITE PRINT-RECORD FROM SALES-REP-TOTALS-LINE
               AFTER ADVANCING 2 LINES.
           MOVE SPACES TO PRINT-RECORD.
           WRITE PRINT-RECORD AFTER ADVANCING 2 LINES.
           ADD 4 TO LINE-COUNT.
           ADD SALES-REP-QUANTITY       TO BRANCH-QUANTITY.
           ADD SALES-REP-EXT-PRICE      TO BRANCH-EXT-PRICE.
           MOVE ZEROS                   TO SALES-REP-QUANTITY
                                           SALES-REP-EXT-PRICE.
           MOVE ORD-SALES-REP           TO HOLD-SALES-REP.
```

FIGURE 6–28 cont.

NEW COBOL ELEMENTS

REDEFINES

Format

```
level-number data-name-1 REDEFINES data-name-2
```

COBOL allows an area of memory to have alternative data descriptions by using the REDEFINES clause. REDEFINES allows the *same* area of storage to be described in more than one way. Data-name-1 (the redefining area) and data-name-2 (the redefined area) must have the same level numbers and must be the same size. They may be either elementary or group items. In the following example, only five bytes of storage are used:

```
05 QUANTITY-OUT                          PIC ZZZZ9.
05 STOCK-ERROR REDEFINES QUANTITY-OUT    PIC X(5).
```

The first definition of the storage area specifies a numeric-edited data item. The second definition of the same area specifies an alphanumeric data item. If this pair of definitions were part of a print line, it would allow either a quantity or some alphanumeric characters to be printed in a single column of the print line. Remember, QUANTITY-OUT and STOCK-ERROR are two names for one area of storage.

Group items may also contain a REDEFINES clause. The redefinition ends when a level number less than or equal to the level number of the data-name which contains the REDEFINES clause is encountered. An area of storage may be redefined numerous times, but each redefinition must refer to the original entry. In Figure 6–29 the 30-byte storage area has three definitions, each of which subdivides the same 30 bytes in a different manner. Except for condition-names, no entries which give a new definition to the storage area may contain a VALUE clause.

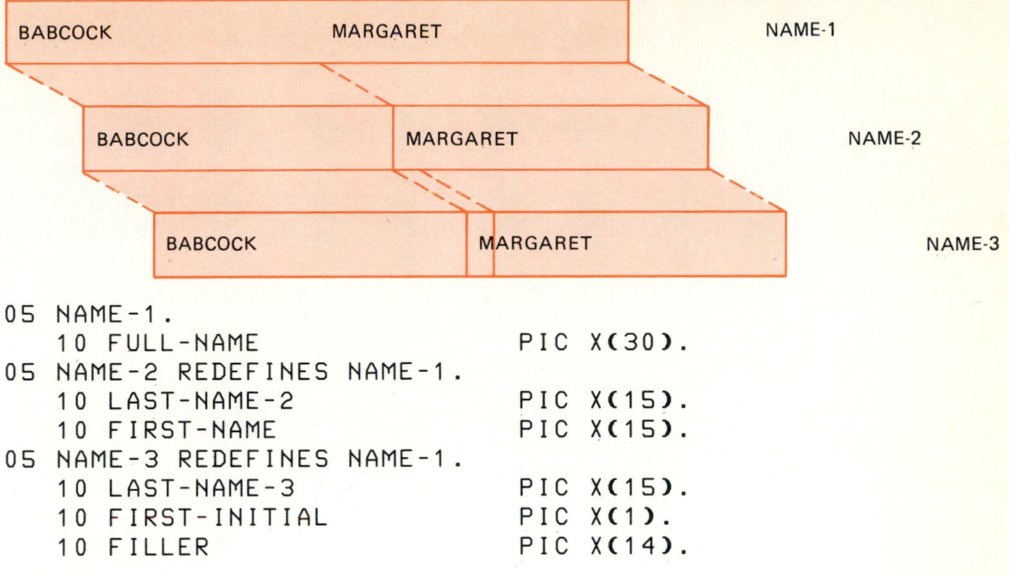


```
05 NAME-1.
   10 FULL-NAME                 PIC X(30).
05 NAME-2 REDEFINES NAME-1.
   10 LAST-NAME-2               PIC X(15).
   10 FIRST-NAME                PIC X(15).
05 NAME-3 REDEFINES NAME-1.
   10 LAST-NAME-3               PIC X(15).
   10 FIRST-INITIAL             PIC X(1).
   10 FILLER                    PIC X(14).
```

FIGURE 6–29

DATA RECORDS ARE

In the FILE SECTION a file may be described with multiple record formats. However, the REDEFINES clause is not used there with level-01 entries to indicate that they share the same area of storage. Rather, the DATA RECORDS ARE clause specifies that the record types occupy a common area in memory. The effect is the same as REDEFINES. (See Figure 6–30.)

```
FD   PARTS-FILE
     LABEL RECORDS ARE STANDARD
     DATA RECORDS ARE MASTER-PART-RECORD
                      TRANS-PART-RECORD.
     01 MASTER-PART-RECORD.
        05
        .
        .
        .
     01 TRANS-PART-RECORD.
        05
        .
        .
        .
```

FIGURE 6–30

The 1985 standard allows the item associated with the REDEFINES clause (the redefining area) to be *less than* or equal to the size of the redefined item.

DISPLAY

Format

```
DISPLAY {identifier-1} [identifier-2]
        {literal-1   } [literal-2   ] . . .[UPON mnemonic-name]
```

The DISPLAY statement transfers the contents of each identifier or the value of each literal to an output device. DISPLAY is useful in debugging a program, as it allows the current contents of an identifier to be printed as the program executes. The output from DISPLAY will be placed at the left margin of the paper and will usually be interspersed with output normally produced by the program's execution. It is recommended that a literal be used with each identifier to label the items printed. The DISPLAY statements used for debugging are removed from the program when debugging is complete. DISPLAY is also used to produce small amounts of normal output, such as the printing of an audit trail (counts of various actions taken, e.g., records read) at the end of a program. Literals that may be displayed include figurative constants (e.g., ZEROS, SPACES), except for ALL. Figure 6–31 has examples of DISPLAY statements and the output they produce. The COBOL code is indented to distinguish it from the DISPLAY output produced.

```
        DISPLAY 'NET PAY ' NET-PAY.
NET PAY 169860
```

```
        DISPLAY 'THE RECORD COUNT IS ' RECORD-COUNT.
THE RECORD COUNT IS 200
```

```
        DISPLAY 'YES PATH ON FIRST IF'
YES PATH ON FIRST IF
```

```
        DISPLAY 'PLEASE ENTER REPORT DATE' UPON
        CONSOLE.
    PLEASE ENTER REPORT DATE
        ACCEPT REPORT-DATE.
```

FIGURE 6–31

When UPON is specified, the programmer may specify the device that is to receive the output. A common use of UPON is to allow the programmer to send a message to the operator's console. If UPON is not specified, the system logical unit (normally a printer) is assumed.

The 1985 standard allows the use of the figurative constant ALL in a DISPLAY statement.

ACCEPT

Format

```
ACCEPT identifier [FROM mnemonic-name]
```

ACCEPT causes the transfer of data into an identifier (the storage area reserved by the program under that name) from a device. If the FROM option is specified, the device may be the system input device or the operator's console. If the FROM option is not specified, the system input device is assumed. The ACCEPT statement often follows a DISPLAY statement in a program. It allows the response of an operator to a question or command in the DISPLAY statement to become input to the program in which the ACCEPT statement occurs. An ACCEPT statement would follow the last DISPLAY statement in Figure 6–31, which requests a report date. The identifier following the word ACCEPT would be the storage area where the date entered by the operator would be stored.

Qualification

Format

```
{data-name-1   }  [ {OF} data-name-2] . . .
{condition-name}    {IN}
```

A data-name that is not unique can be made unique through the use of qualifiers. A qualifier is a group item which contains the data-name to be made unique. The two partial record descriptions shown in Figure 6–32 are from a single program. There are a number of identical data-names that appear in both records. If used in the PROCEDURE DIVISION without qualifiers, the data-names would generate the diagnostic DATA-NAME NOT UNIQUE. In order to avoid this error, one or more qualifiers are used.

```
01 CUSTOMER-RECORD
   05  NAME
   05  ADDRESS
       10 STREET
       10 CITY
       10 STATE
       10 ZIP
   05  SHIP-ADDRESS
       10 STREET
       10 CITY
       10 STATE
       10 ZIP
   05  TERMS
   05  CREDIT-LIMIT
```

```
01 CUSTOMER-LIST
   05  NAME
   05  ADDRESS
       10 STREET
       10 CITY
       10 STATE
       10 ZIP
   05  SHIP-ADDRESS
       10 STREET
       10 CITY
       10 STATE
       10 ZIP
   05  TERMS
   05  CREDIT-LIMIT
```

FIGURE 6–32

NAME appears in both record formats. In order to identify which NAME we are referring to, it may be qualified by

```
NAME OF CUSTOMER-RECORD
  or
NAME OF CUSTOMER-LIST
```

CITY appears twice in each record format. In order to identify which of the four occurrences is being referenced, it may be qualified by any of

```
CITY OF ADDRESS OF CUSTOMER-RECORD
CITY OF SHIP-ADDRESS OF CUSTOMER-RECORD
CITY OF ADDRESS OF CUSTOMER-LIST
CITY OF SHIP-ADDRESS OF CUSTOMER-LIST
```

The use of duplicate data-names and qualifiers creates more work than it saves in many instances. It is recommended that data-names be made unique through the use of prefixes in order to avoid the need for qualification.

The 1985 standard provides for 50 levels of qualification. The 1974 standard provided for only 5.

CORRESPONDING

The reserved word CORRESPONDING may be included in the formats for the MOVE, ADD, and SUBTRACT statements if the statements use group items as identifiers. The operation specified for the group items will be performed on any elementary items within the group which have the same name (and qualifiers). Figure 6–33 gives examples of the use of the CORRESPONDING option.

In order to use CORRESPONDING, a program must contain duplicate data-names. The advantages of using CORRESPONDING (potentially fewer MOVEs, ADDs, and SUBTRACTs when they can be done at the group level) must be weighed against the necessity of qualifying these data-names each time they are used in some other way in the program.

```
01 RECORD-1.
   05  QUANTITY.
       10 FIRST-QUARTER
       10 SECOND-QUARTER
       10 THIRD-QUARTER
       10 FOURTH-QUARTER
   05  RATE-1
   05  BALANCE
01 RECORD-2.
   05  QUANTITY.
       10 FIRST-QUARTER
       10 SECOND-QUARTER
       10 THIRD-QUARTER
       10 FOURTH-QUARTER
    05  RATE-2
    05  BALANCE
MOVE CORRESPONDING RECORD-1 TO RECORD-2.
ADD CORRESPONDING RECORD-1 TO RECORD-2.
SUBTRACT CORRESPONDING RECORD-1 FROM RECORD-2.
```

FIGURE 6–33

SIZE ERROR

Format

```
[ON SIZE ERROR imperative statement]
```

The result of a calculation may exceed the size of the result field that has been defined for it. COBOL provides a method to check for this condition. It is called SIZE ERROR, and it may be included in all arithmetic statements (i.e., ADD, SUBTRACT, MULTIPLY, DIVIDE, and COMPUTE statements). When included with an arithmetic statement, it is the last clause in the statement. Some examples are shown in Figure 6–34.

```
ADD FIELD-A TO FIELD-B
    ON SIZE ERROR
        DISPLAY 'SIZE ERROR IN ADD STATEMENT'
        DISPLAY 'FIELD-A ' FIELD-A
        DISPLAY 'FIELD-B ' FIELD-B.
MULTIPLY FIELD-A BY FIELD-B ROUNDED
    ON SIZE ERROR
        MOVE FIELD-A TO ERROR-FIELD-1
        MOVE FIELD-B TO ERROR-FIELD-2
        PERFORM SIZE-ERROR-RTN.
COMPUTE FIELD-X = FIELD-A / FIELD-B
    ON SIZE ERROR
        PERFORM SIZE-ERROR-RTN.
```

FIGURE 6–34

When SIZE ERROR is specified in an arithmetic statement, the following occur:

1. The calculation is performed in a work area. The result is decimal aligned and tested to determine whether it exceeds the largest value that may be stored in the result field.
2. If the answer is too large, it will not be placed in the result field and the statements following ON SIZE ERROR up to the period will be executed.
3. If the arithmetic statement has a ROUNDED clause, rounding takes place before the answer is checked for SIZE ERROR.

4. In ADD, SUBTRACT, and COMPUTE statements, only the final result is checked for SIZE ERROR. Intermediate as well as final results are checked in MULTIPLY and DIVIDE statements.
5. Division by zero causes a SIZE ERROR.

The 1985 standard allows both ON SIZE ERROR and NOT ON SIZE ERROR to be included in the formats for arithmetic statements.

GO TO/ DEPENDING ON

Format

```
GO TO procedure-name-1 [procedure-name-2] . . .
     DEPENDING ON identifier
```

GO TO/DEPENDING ON allows for the transfer of control to a procedure-name based on the value of an identifier. In this format, the procedure-names must be paragraph- or section-names in the PROCEDURE DIVISION and the identifier must represent an integer of four or less digits. COBOL will use the integer to determine which of the procedures to GO TO. If the integer has a value of 1, control is transferred to the first procedure-name in the list; if the integer has a value of 2, control is transferred to the second procedure-name in the list, and so on.

If the value of the identifier is less than or greater than the number of procedures in the list, no GO TO takes place and control drops to the next COBOL statement. Because GO TOs rather than PERFORMs are executed, there is no provision for return of control. Hence, care must be taken to assure that control is returned to the proper point in the logic. The example in Figure 6–35 demonstrates how control may be kept in a section to limit the disadvantages of using the GO TO statement. Notice that regardless of the path taken in the section, control ultimately passes to 1000-EXIT.

An EXIT statement is used in the figure to provide a common end point for the group of procedures. EXIT is a one-word statement. It must be the only statement in the paragraph. EXITs are used in COBOL to provide a destination for a GO TO statement. As a result, their use is limited in accordance with the restrictions placed on the use of GO TO within a facility. When EXITs are used, the PERFORM statement is changed to include the THRU option (e.g., PERFORM 1000-QUARTERLY-PROCESSING THRU 1000-EXIT).

```
    .
    PERFORM 1000-QUARTERLY-PROCESSING THRU 1000-EXIT.
    .
    .
    .
1000-QUARTERLY-PROCESSING SECTION.
    GO TO 1010-FIRST-QUARTER
          1020-SECOND-QUARTER
          1030-THIRD-QUARTER
          1040-FOURTH-QUARTER
          DEPENDING ON QUARTER.
    DISPLAY 'QUARTER NOT BETWEEN 1 AND 4' QUARTER.
    GO TO 1000-EXIT.
1010-FIRST-QUARTER.
    .
    .
    .
    GO TO 1000-EXIT.
```

FIGURE 6–35

```
1020-SECOND-QUARTER.
    .
    .
    .
    GO TO 1000-EXIT.
1030-THIRD-QUARTER.
    .
    .
    .
    GO TO 1000-EXIT.
1040-FOURTH-QUARTER.
    .
    .
    .
    GO TO 1000-EXIT.
1000-EXIT.
    EXIT.
```

FIGURE 6–35 cont.

EVALUATE

Format

```
EVALUATE {identifier-1}
         {expression-1}
  WHEN    condition-1   imperative-statement-1 . . .
  [WHEN OTHER imperative-statement-2]
END-EVALUATE
```

In the discussion of GO TO . . . DEPENDING ON it was necessary to use GO TOs to implement the case structure. The 1985 standard includes a new verb, EVALUATE, for implementing the case structure which does not require a GO TO. The example used for GO TO . . . DEPENDING ON is repeated using EVALUATE.

The routine will EVALUATE QUARTER and select a single routine listed between EVALUATE and END-EVALUATE depending on the value of QUARTER. The format above is only a partial format for EVALUATE. The full format is included in Appendix B.

```
EVALUATE QUARTER
    WHEN 1 PERFORM 1010-FIRST-QUARTER
    WHEN 2 PERFORM 1020-SECOND-QUARTER
    WHEN 3 PERFORM 1030-THIRD-QUARTER
    WHEN 4 PERFORM 1040-FOURTH-QUARTER
    WHEN OTHER DISPLAY 'QUARTER NOT BETWEEN 1 AND 4'
      QUARTER
END-EVALUATE.
```

DEBUGGING

Data Exceptions

A data exception is a common cause of program interruption. It occurs during the execution of a program. An attempt is made to utilize improper data in a calculation, numeric comparison, or output edit. The system tests data used for these purposes to ensure that it is numeric and that the value stored agrees with the USAGE given for the item in the DATA DIVISION. If the data fails the test, the program is interrupted and a data exception message is displayed.

Compilers and installations vary on the amount of information provided about a data exception. They also vary on the style in which the information is presented. The discussion that follows will be a general guide to why a data exception occurs and the steps necessary to correct it. The description given has an IBM orientation. The programmer should learn the specifics regarding data exception for his or her particular installation.

The following COBOL verbs are the ones most likely to produce a DATA EXCEPTION:

ADD
SUBTRACT
MULTIPLY
DIVIDE
COMPUTE
IF (numeric comparisons only)
MOVE (from a numeric to a numeric or numeric-edited field)

These instructions all require at least some of their operands to be numeric. In the following examples the data items that must be numeric are underlined.

```
COMPUTE X = A + B.
MOVE QUANTITY TO ZERO-SUPRESSED-QUANTITY.
IF NET-PAY < MINIMUM-PAY . . .
```

When used with an IBM mainframe, the numeric operands will likely have a USAGE of DISPLAY or of COMP-3 (packed). Remember, if no usage is given, the default is DISPLAY. For the instructions listed, the system requires that the data be in a packed format before the instruction is executed. If USAGE IS DISPLAY, the system will convert the data to a packed format. If USAGE IS COMP-3, the system assumes the data is already in a packed format. For packed numeric data to be valid, the right half of the rightmost byte must contain a valid sign (C, D, or F). All of the remaining half-bytes must be digits, 0 through 9. If the data item is not a valid packed numeric data item, the instruction will fail on a data exception.

How does inappropriate data end up in numeric fields? The answer constitutes a long list. Following are a few of the more common ways.

1. Data is read from a file that has not been through a thorough input edit where each field is checked for correctness. A READ is like a group move. The entire contents of the record are transferred as a single unit. No testing is done to ensure that the data matches the individual item descriptions in the record.
2. The programmer neglects to initialize a field that is supposed to contain a specific numeric value. For example, consider

   ```
   05 PAGE-COUNT     PIC 9(2).
   ```

   At some point in the program the logic will require that 1 be added to PAGE-COUNT. If PAGE-COUNT has not been initialized either by a VALUE clause in WORKING-STORAGE or a MOVE statement in the PROCEDURE DIVISION, its contents are unpredictable.
3. The record description written by the programmer contains an error and does not agree with the actual arrangement of data in the record.
4. The programmer moves the wrong thing to a field. An example would be moving SPACES when ZEROS were intended.
5. The programmer moves a group item when elementary items should have been moved. If an elementary numeric item is moved from a field whose USAGE IS DISPLAY to an elementary item whose USAGE IS COMP-3, the

data will be packed automatically. If the move is made with a group item, however, the field is considered alphanumeric even though it may consist of numeric elementary items. Since the move is alphanumeric, no packing takes place. The data description then says that the field contains packed data, but it does not; and when the field is to be used in a calculation, the system will not pack the data since the description indicates that it is already packed. As a result, when the data is checked, it will not contain the proper characters and a data exception will occur.

6. The programmer develops or uses an incorrect value for a subscript or index for a table (covered in Chapters 7 and 8). The value causes COBOL to calculate an incorrect location for the table element. As a result, an instruction the programmer intended to execute on the contents of a table element is attempted in an area of memory that may not contain numeric data.

When a data exception occurs, some or all of the following will be provided by the system:

1. The line number of the COBOL statement that was being executed when the DATA EXCEPTION occurred.
2. The assembler language instruction that was being executed. (Each COBOL statement generates multiple assembler language instructions.)
3. Either a display of the contents of the data items involved in the instruction, or information that will assist the programmer in locating the data items in a memory dump.
4. A memory dump.

The information provided allows the programmer to determine which fields from the instruction contain the improper data. The programmer must be able to inspect the field contents and determine whether they are numeric and properly packed. Determining which fields are at fault allows the programmer to narrow the search for the cause of the problem regarding those fields.

SUMMARY

REDEFINES

Format

```
level-number data-name-1 REDEFINES data-name-2
```

DISPLAY

Format

```
DISPLAY {identifier-1} [identifier-2]
        {literal-1   } [literal-2   ] . . .[UPON mnemonic-name]
```

ACCEPT

Format

```
ACCEPT identifier [FROM mnemonic-name]
```

Qualification

Format

```
{data-name-1    }  [ {OF} data-name-2] . . .
{condition-name }    {IN}
```

SIZE ERROR

Format

```
[ON SIZE ERROR imperative statement]
```

GO TO/ DEPENDING ON

Format

```
GO TO procedure-name-1 [procedure-name-2] . . .
    DEPENDING ON identifier
```

EVALUATE

Format

```
EVALUATE {identifier-1}
         {expression-1}
  WHEN    condition-1   imperative-statement-1 . . .
  [WHEN OTHER imperative-statement-2]
END-EVALUATE
```

EXERCISES

I. Indicate whether the following statements are true or false.

_____ **1.** A REDEFINES clause must immediately follow the data item which is being redefined.

_____ **2.** The ON SIZE ERROR clause may be used with a MOVE statement.

_____ **3.** When multiple control breaks occur in a program, they are performed in order from MAJOR BREAK to MINOR BREAK.

_____ **4.** Qualification may be used in order to reference a data-name which is not unique.

_____ **5.** Division by zero will cause a SIZE ERROR.

_____ **6.** In a control-break program, the data from each record is normally added to minor, intermediate, and final level totals in PROCESS.

_____ **7.** REDEFINES may be used on elementary items, but not on group items.

_____ **8.** Each DISPLAY statement may contain either an identifier or a literal, but not both.

_____ **9.** GO TO/DEPENDING ON allows control to drop to the next statement if the number of choices is less than the value of the identifier.

_____ **10.** Rounding, if specified, takes place after the value is checked for SIZE ERROR.

II. Determine whether each of the following data description entries is valid or invalid. Assume that the descriptions are in the WORKING-STORAGE SECTION.

1.
```
01  NAME.
    05  FIRST-NAME                  PIC X(10).
    05  MIDDLE-NAME                 PIC X(10).
    05  LAST-NAME                   PIC X(15).
01  INITIALS REDEFINES NAME.
    05  FIRST-INITIAL               PIC X(1).
    05  FILLER                      PIC X(9).
    05  MIDDLE-INITIAL              PIC X(1).
    05  FILLER                      PIC X(9).
    05  LAST-INITIAL                PIC X(1).
```

2.
```
01  PHONE-LIST-RECORD.
    05  NAME                        PIC X(25).
    05  PHONE-NUMBER                PIC 9(9).
        10  PHONE-NO REDEFINES PHONE-NUMBER.
            15  AREA-CODE           PIC 9(3).
            15  FILLER              PIC 9(6).
```

3.
```
01  STOCK-RECORD.
    05  STOCK-NUMBER                    PIC X(6).
    05  UNIT-PRICE                      PIC 9(5)V9(2).
    05  PRICE REDEFINES UNIT-PRICE.
        10  UNIT-PRICE-DOLLARS          PIC 9(5).
        10  UNIT-PRICE-CENTS            PIC 9(1).
```

4.
```
01  ORDER-HEADER.
    05  CUSTOMER-NAME                   PIC X(35).
    05  CUSTOMER-NUMBER                 PIC 9(5).
01  LINE-ITEM-RECORD REDEFINES ORDER-HEADER.
    05  STOCK-NUMBER                    PIC X(8).
    05  QUANTITY                        PIC 9(5).
    05  UNIT-PRICE                      PIC 9(5)V9(2).
    05  FILLER                          PIC X(20)
                                             VALUE SPACES.
```

5.
```
01  INVOICE-RECORD.
    05  INVOICE-NUMBER                  PIC 9(8).
    05  INVOICE-NO REDEFINES INVOICE-NUMBER
                                                 PIC X(8).
```

III. Using the following record descriptions and PROCEDURE DIVISION statements, determine the contents of the indicated data items.

```
01  INVOICE-HEADER.
    05  RECORD-TYPE                 PIC X(1).
    05  INVOICE-NUMBER              PIC 9(5).
    05  CUSTOMER-NAME               PIC X(10).
    05  INVOICE-DATE.
        10  INVOICE-YEAR            PIC 9(2).
        10  INVOICE-MONTH           PIC 9(2).
        10  INVOICE-DAY             PIC 9(2).
01  INVOICE-LINE-ITEM REDEFINES INVOICE-HEADER.
    05  RECORD-TYPE                 PIC X(1).
    05  STOCK-NUMBER                PIC X(8).
    05  QUANTITY                    PIC 9(5).
    05  UNIT-PRICE                  PIC 9(6)V9(2).

MOVE 'L' TO RECORD-TYPE OF INVOICE-HEADER.
MOVE 'SRWX454' TO STOCK-NUMBER.
MOVE 16 TO QUANTITY.
MOVE 1540.50 TO UNIT-PRICE.
```

_____ **1.** RECORD-TYPE OF INVOICE-LINE-ITEM
_____ **2.** INVOICE-YEAR
_____ **3.** INVOICE-MONTH
_____ **4.** INVOICE-DAY
_____ **5.** INVOICE-NUMBER
_____ **6.** QUANTITY
_____ **7.** CUSTOMER-NAME
_____ **8.** UNIT-PRICE
_____ **9.** STOCK-NUMBER

IV. Using the following record descriptions, determine whether the indicated references to data items will or will not be unique.

```
01 INVOICE-RECORD.
   05  STOCK-NUMBER              PIC X(8).
   05  QUANTITY                  PIC 9(5).
   05  UNIT-PRICE                PIC 9(6)V9(2).
01 INVENTORY-RECORD.
   05  STOCK-NUMBER              PIC X(8).
   05  UNIT-PRICE                PIC 9(6)V9(2).
   05  ON-HAND-AMOUNTS.
       10  QUANTITY              PIC 9(5).
       10  UNIT-COST             PIC 9(6)V9(2).
   05  ON-ORDER-AMOUNTS.
       10  QUANTITY              PIC 9(5).
       10  UNIT-COST             PIC 9(6)V9(2).
```

_____ **1.** QUANTITY OF INVOICE-RECORD.
_____ **2.** QUANTITY OF INVENTORY-RECORD.
_____ **3.** UNIT-COST OF ON-HAND-AMOUNTS.
_____ **4.** STOCK-NUMBER.
_____ **5.** UNIT-PRICE OF INVOICE-RECORD.
_____ **6.** ON-HAND-AMOUNTS.
_____ **7.** UNIT-COST OF INVENTORY-RECORD.
_____ **8.** QUANTITY OF ON-HAND-AMOUNTS.
_____ **9.** QUANTITY OF ON-HAND-AMOUNTS OF INVENTORY-RECORD.

V. Given the indicated values of TRANSACTION-TYPE, determine which procedure will be executed.

```
1000-PROCESS-TRANSACTION.
    GO TO 1020-WITHDRAWAL
          1040-DEPOSIT
          1050-TRANSFER
          1060-SERVICE-CHARGE
          DEPENDING ON TRANSACTION-TYPE.
    PERFORM 1090-TRANSACTION-TYPE-ERRORS.
    .
    .
    .
```

_____ **1.** TRANSACTION-TYPE = 2
_____ **2.** TRANSACTION-TYPE = 4
_____ **3.** TRANSACTION-TYPE = 0
_____ **4.** TRANSACTION-TYPE = 1
_____ **5.** TRANSACTION-TYPE = 5

PROJECTS

For each of the following specifications and input record layouts, design a print chart and code a COBOL program that satisfies the specification.

PROJECT 6–1 Payroll

PROGRAM SPECIFICATION

Program Name: PAY6

Program Function:

This program will produce a printed listing of a payroll file. The report will include department, division, and final totals for credit union deductions, medical insurance deductions, and gross pay.

Input Files:

I. PAYROLL-FILE

INPUT DEVICE:	DISK
FILE ORGANIZATION:	SEQUENTIAL
RECORD LENGTH:	80 BYTES
FILE SEQUENCE:	ASCENDING ON DIVISION / DEPARTMENT

Output Files:

I. PRINT-FILE

OUTPUT DEVICE:	PRINTER
RECORD LENGTH:	133 BYTES

Processing Requirements:

Each record read from the input file should be printed on one line of the output report. Gross pay should be calculated for each record. (Gross pay = pay rate × hours worked.)

Totals for credit union deduction, medical insurance deduction, and gross pay are to be accumulated and printed for each department, division, and the entire company.

Output Requirements:

The following are formatting requirements for the report:

1. Each page of the report should contain:
   (a) a main heading which includes the company name, the report name, the report date, and a page number.
   (b) column headings which describe the items printed underneath them.
2. Detail lines should include all fields from the input and gross pay.
3. Detail lines should be double spaced.
4. Department total lines should be double spaced, with two additional blank lines after each total.

5. Each new division should begin on a new page, with the page number reset to 1.
6. Final total lines should be triple spaced.

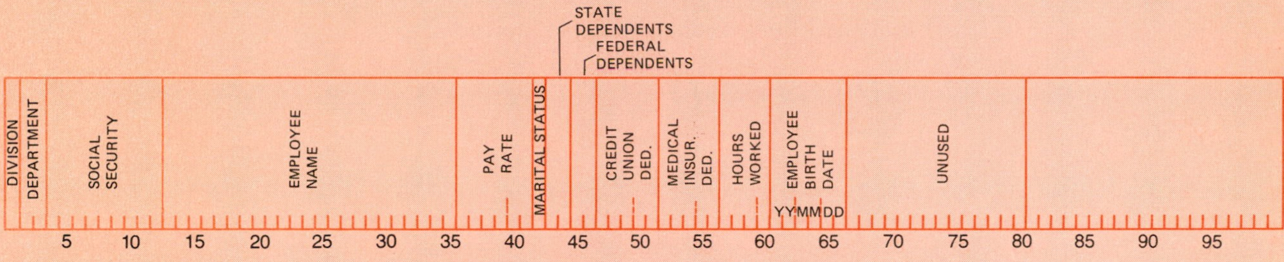

PROJECT 6–2 Inventory

PROGRAM SPECIFICATION

Program Name: INV6

Program Function:

The program will produce a printed listing of an inventory file. The report will include class, type, and final totals for quantity on hand, quantity on order, and inventory cost.

Input Files:

I. INVENTORY-FILE

INPUT DEVICE:	DISK
FILE ORGANIZATION:	SEQUENTIAL
RECORD LENGTH:	80 BYTES
FILE SEQUENCE:	ASCENDING ON INVENTORY STOCK NUMBER

Output Files:

I. PRINT-FILE

OUTPUT DEVICE:	PRINTER
RECORD LENGTH:	133 BYTES

Processing Requirements:

Each record on the input file should be printed on the output report. Inventory cost should be calculated for each record. (Inventory cost = quantity on hand × inventory unit cost.)

Totals for quantity on hand, quantity on order, and inventory cost are to be accumulated and printed for each product class and type, and for the entire file.

Output Requirements:

The following are formatting requirements for the report:

1. Each page of the report should contain:
   (a) a main heading which includes the company name, the report name, the report date, and a page number.
   (b) column headings which describe the items printed underneath them.
2. Detail lines should include all fields from the input and the inventory cost.

3. Detail lines should be double spaced.
4. Class total lines should be double spaced, with two additional blank lines after each total.
5. Each new product type should begin on a new page.
6. Final total lines should be triple spaced.

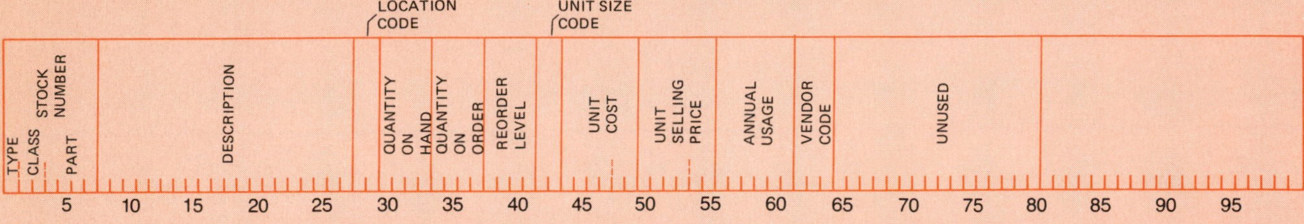

PROJECT 6–3 Accounts Payable

PROGRAM SPECIFICATION

Program Name: AP6

Program Function:

The program will produce a printed listing of an accounts payable file. The report will include control numbers, and division and final totals for amount, hard goods, labor, freight, and tax for Divisions 2 and 4 of the organization.

Input Files:

I. ACCOUNTS-PAYABLE-FILE

INPUT DEVICE:	DISK
FILE ORGANIZATION:	SEQUENTIAL
RECORD LENGTH:	80 BYTES
FILE SEQUENCE:	ASCENDING ON DIVISION / CONTROL NBR

Output Files:

I. PRINT-FILE

OUTPUT DEVICE:	PRINTER
RECORD LENGTH:	133 BYTES

Processing Requirements:

Each extracted record on the input file should be printed on one line of the output report. Totals for amount, hard goods, labor, freight, and tax are to be accumulated and printed for each control number within Divisions 2 and 4 for Divisions 2 and 4, as well as a final total including only Divisions 2 and 4.

Output Requirements:

The following are formatting requirements for the report:

1. Each page of the report should contain:
   (a) a main heading which includes the company name, the report name, the report date, and a page number.
   (b) column headings which describe the items printed underneath them.
2. Detail lines should include all fields from the input.

3. Detail lines should be double spaced.
4. Control number total lines should be double spaced, with two additional blank lines after each total.
5. Each new division should begin on a new page.
6. Final total lines should be triple spaced.

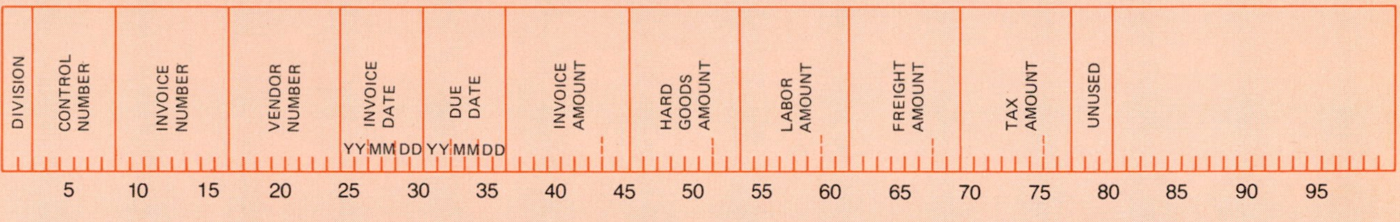

PROJECT 6–4 Pension

PROGRAM SPECIFICATION

Program Name: PEN6

Program Function:

The program will produce a printed report of a pension file. The report will include department, division, and final totals for salary, employee contribution, employer contribution, and balance forward for Divisions 1 and 3 of the organization.

Input Files:

I. PENSION-FILE

INPUT DEVICE:	DISK
FILE ORGANIZATION:	SEQUENTIAL
RECORD LENGTH:	80 BYTES
FILE SEQUENCE:	ASCENDING ON DIVISION / DEPARTMENT

Output Files:

I. PRINT-FILE

OUTPUT DEVICE:	PRINTER
RECORD LENGTH:	133 BYTES

Processing Requirements:

Each record read from the pension file should be printed on one line of the output report. Totals for salary, employee contribution, employer contribution, and balance forward are to be accumulated and printed for each department within Divisions 1 and 3, for Divisions 1 and 3, as well as final totals including Divisions 1 and 3.

Output Requirements:

The following are formatting requirements for the report:

1. Each page of the report should contain:
   (a) a main heading which includes the company name, the report name, the report date, and a page number.
   (b) column headings which describe the items printed underneath them.
2. Detail lines should include all fields from the input.

3. Detail lines should be double spaced.
4. Department total lines should be double spaced, with two additional blank lines after each total.
5. Each new division should begin on a new page.
6. Final total lines should be triple spaced.

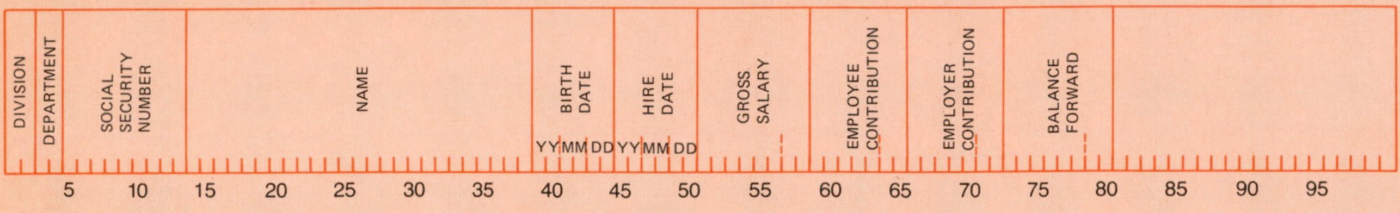

PROJECT 6–5 Bill of Materials

PROGRAM SPECIFICATION

Program Name: BOM6

Program Function:

The program will produce a printed report of a bill-of-materials file which will include the extended cost. The report will include product line, division, and final totals for extended cost.

Input Files:

I. BILL-OF-MATERIALS-FILE

INPUT DEVICE:	DISK
FILE ORGANIZATION:	SEQUENTIAL
RECORD LENGTH:	55 BYTES
FILE SEQUENCE:	ASCENDING ON DIVISION / PRODUCT LINE

Output Files:

I. PRINT-FILE

OUTPUT DEVICE:	PRINTER
RECORD LENGTH:	133 BYTES

Processing Requirements:

Each record from the bill-of-materials file should be printed on one line of the output report. Extended cost (quantity times cost) is to be calculated for each record. Totals of extended cost are to be accumulated and printed for each product line and division, and for the entire company.

Output Requirements:

The following are formatting requirements for the report:

1. Each page of the report should contain:
   (a) a main heading which includes the company name, the report name, the report date, and a page number.
   (b) column headings which describe the items printed underneath them.
2. Detail lines should include all fields from the input and the extended cost.
3. Detail lines should be double spaced.

4. Product line total lines should be double spaced, with two additional blank lines after each total.
5. Each new division should begin on a new page.
6. Final total lines should be triple spaced.

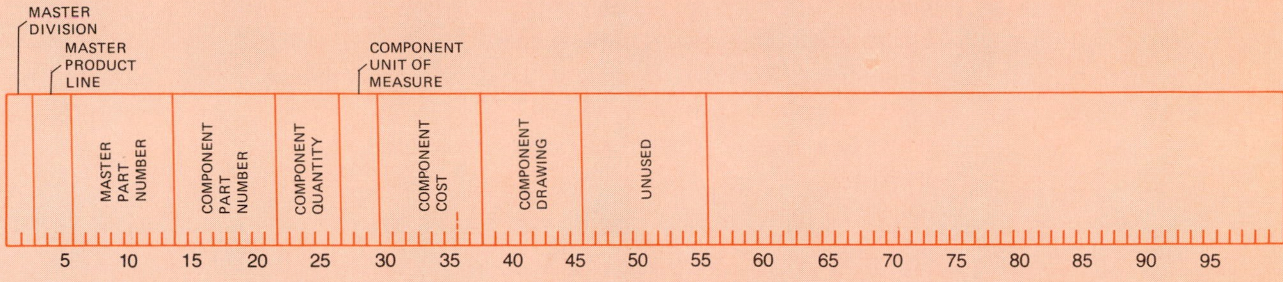

PROJECT 6–6 Cost

PROGRAM SPECIFICATION

Program Name: COST6

Program Function:

The program will produce a printed report of a cost file which will include the total for all cost factors. The report will separate the records by division and provide a count of records for each product line and division for those records from Divisions 1 and 5 whose product line is less than 100.

Input Files:

I. COST-FILE

INPUT DEVICE:	DISK
FILE ORGANIZATION:	SEQUENTIAL
RECORD LENGTH:	75 BYTES
FILE SEQUENCE:	ASCENDING ON DIVISION / PRODUCT LINE

Output Files:

I. PRINT-FILE

OUTPUT DEVICE:	PRINTER
RECORD LENGTH:	133 BYTES

Processing Requirements:

Each record from the cost file should be printed on one line of the output report. The total for all cost factors should be calculated for each record. A count of the records for each product line and division for those records of Divisions 1 and 5 whose product line is less than 100 should be accumulated and printed after the appropriate product line and division.

Output Requirements:

The following are formatting requirements for the report:

1. Each page of the report should contain:
   (a) a main heading which includes the company name, the report name, the report date, and a page number.
   (b) column headings which describe the items printed underneath them.
2. Detail lines should include all fields from the input and the total for the cost factors.
3. Detail lines should be double spaced.
4. Product total (count) lines should be double spaced, with two additional blank lines after each count.
5. Each new division should begin on a new page.
6. Final total (count) lines should be triple spaced.

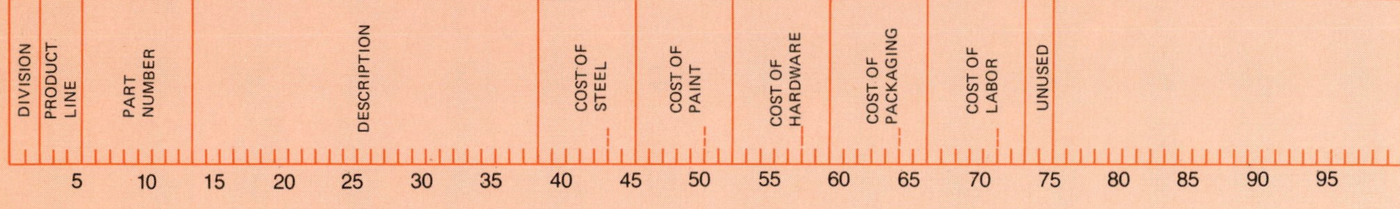

CHAPTER

7 Table Handling, I

The programming logic for this chapter is a continuation of the control break logic of Chapter 6. An additional set of branch totals is stored in a table so that the totals may be printed as a group at the end of the report.

An overview of when and how tables are loaded with data and the ways table data may be accessed is provided.

The COBOL language emphasis is on the structure of tables with one, two, and three dimensions. In the programming project, a one-dimensional table is loaded with branch totals. Printing techniques for one-, two-, and three-dimensional tables are demonstrated.

The debugging section includes diagnostics peculiar to programs containing tables. A third version of the USAGE clause, USAGE IS COMP, is explained.

PROGRAM SPECIFICATION: TABLE-1

A table for storing the branch totals of ORD-QUANTITY and EXTENDED-PRICE has been added to the BREAK-3 program presented in Chapter 6. Use of a table allows the printing of a summary of the branch totals at the end of the report in addition to the totals at the end of each branch. Figure 7–1 shows the program specification.

Input Record Layout

The input record layout is the same as that of all previous projects. It is repeated here for convenience. (See Figure 7–2).

Print Chart

There are two print charts for this project. The first is the listing of the ORDER-FILE with totals. It is similar to the print chart for the BREAK-4 program in Chapter 6. The second depicts the layout for the printing of the table of branch totals after all detail lines and other totals have been printed. (See Figure 7–3.)

PROGRAM SPECIFICATION

Program Name: TABLE-1

Program Function:

The program will produce a printed report in two parts:

1. The first part will be a listing of the order file. Totals for quantity and extended price will be printed for each sales representative, each branch, and the entire company.
2. The second part will be a summary of total quantity and total extended price by branch.

FIGURE 7–1

Input Files:

I. ORDER-FILE

INPUT DEVICE:	DISK
FILE ORGANIZATION:	SEQUENTIAL
RECORD LENGTH:	70 BYTES
FILE SEQUENCE:	ASCENDING ON BRANCH / SALES REP

Output Files:

I. PRINT-FILE

OUTPUT DEVICE:	PRINTER
RECORD LENGTH:	133 BYTES

Processing Requirements:

Each record read from the order file should be printed on one line of the output report. Extended price is to be calculated and printed on the output. (Extended price = quantity × unit price.)

Totals for quantity and extended price are to be accumulated and printed for each sales representative, each branch, and the entire company. Also, the branch totals are to be stored in a table and used to create the printed summary at the end of the job.

Output Requirements:

The following are formatting requirements for the report:

1. Each page of the report should contain:
   (a) a main heading which includes the company name, the report name, the report date, and a page number.
   (b) column headings which describe the items printed underneath them.
2. Detail lines should include all fields from the input except the customer purchase order number. The extended price should also be included.
3. Detail lines should be double spaced.
4. The sales representative and branch total lines should be double spaced. Two extra blank lines should be left after each sales representative total line. The final total line should be triple spaced.
5. Each new branch should begin on a new page.
6. The branch summary should begin on a new page.

FIGURE 7–1 cont.

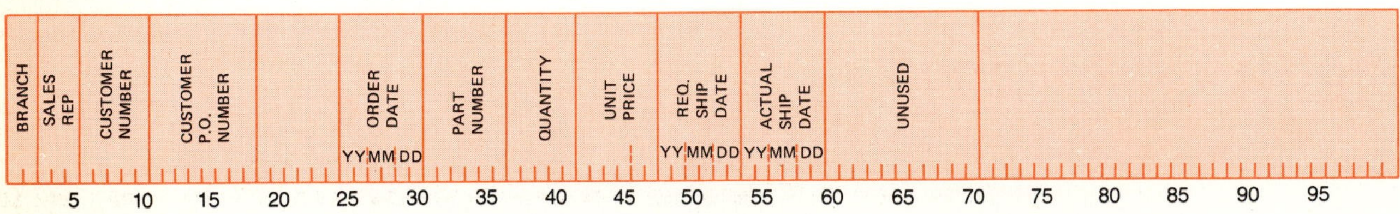

FIGURE 7–2

LOGIC FOR TABLE STORAGE OF TOTALS

A hierarchy chart for TABLES-1 is shown in Figure 7–4. Pseudocode and a flowchart are shown in Figures 7–5 and 7–6, respectively.

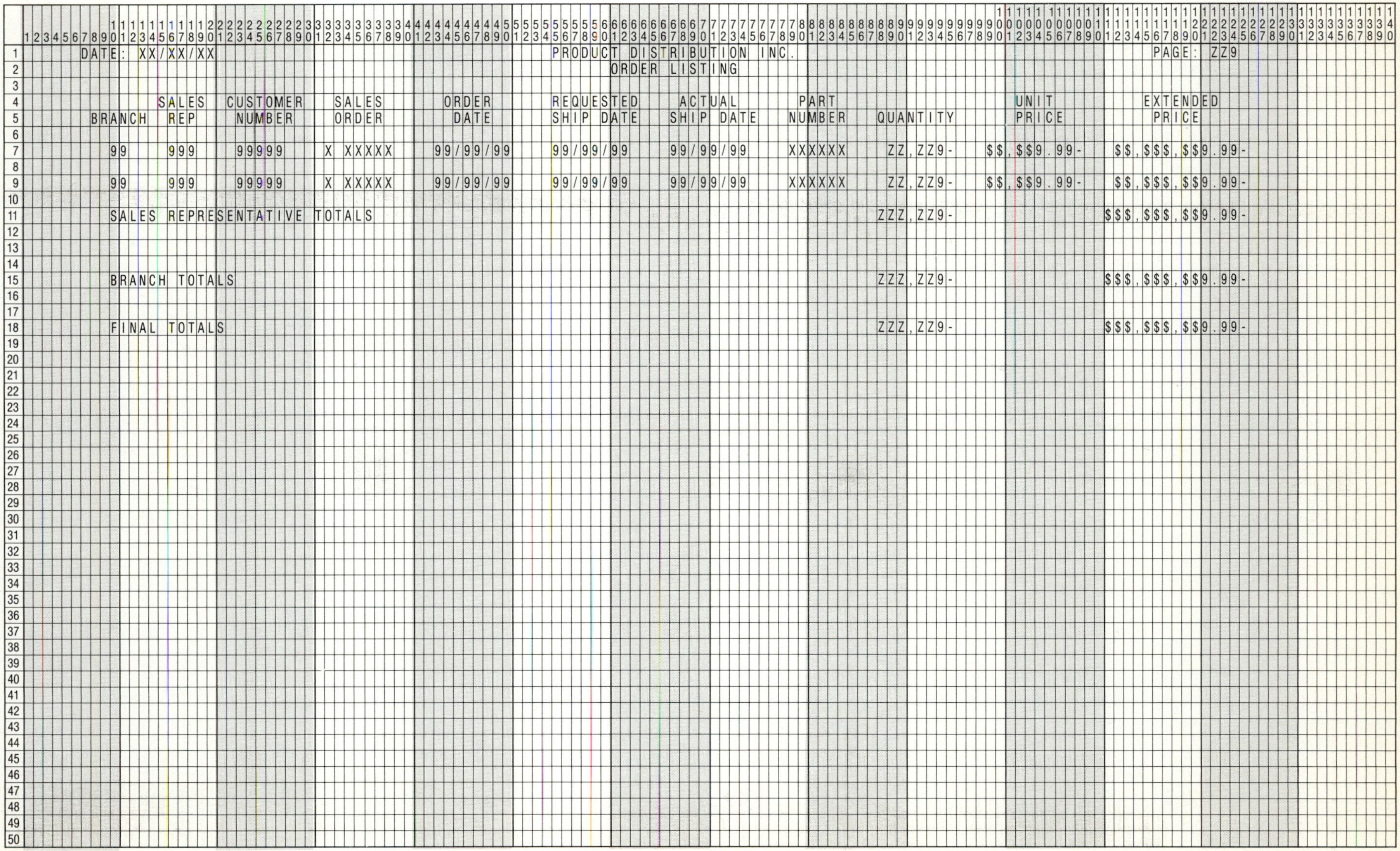

```
      DATE: XX/XX/XX                                  PRODUCT DISTRIBUTION INC.                                    PAGE: ZZ9
                                                            ORDER LISTING

              SALES  CUSTOMER   SALES      ORDER      REQUESTED    ACTUAL      PART                  UNIT         EXTENDED
       BRANCH  REP    NUMBER    ORDER       DATE      SHIP DATE   SHIP DATE   NUMBER   QUANTITY      PRICE          PRICE

         99    999    99999    X XXXXX    99/99/99    99/99/99    99/99/99    XXXXXX    ZZ,ZZ9-   $$,$$9.99-   $$,$$$,$$9.99-

         99    999    99999    X XXXXX    99/99/99    99/99/99    99/99/99    XXXXXX    ZZ,ZZ9-   $$,$$9.99-   $$,$$$,$$9.99-

         SALES REPRESENTATIVE TOTALS                                                   ZZZ,ZZ9-               $$$,$$$,$$9.99-



         BRANCH TOTALS                                                                 ZZZ,ZZ9-               $$$,$$$,$$9.99-


         FINAL TOTALS                                                                  ZZZ,ZZ9-               $$$,$$$,$$9.99-
```

FIGURE 7–3

```
       DATE: XX/XX/XX                                 PRODUCT DISTRIBUTION INC.                                     PAGE: ZZ9
                                                       ORDER SUMMARY BY BRANCH

                                                            QUANTITY         EXTENDED PRICE
                                                                             $$$,$$$,$$9.99-
                                        BRANCH Z9           ZZZ,ZZ9-
                                                                             $$$,$$$,$$9.99-
                                        BRANCH Z9           ZZZ,ZZ9-
```

FIGURE 7–3 cont.

Hierarchy Chart

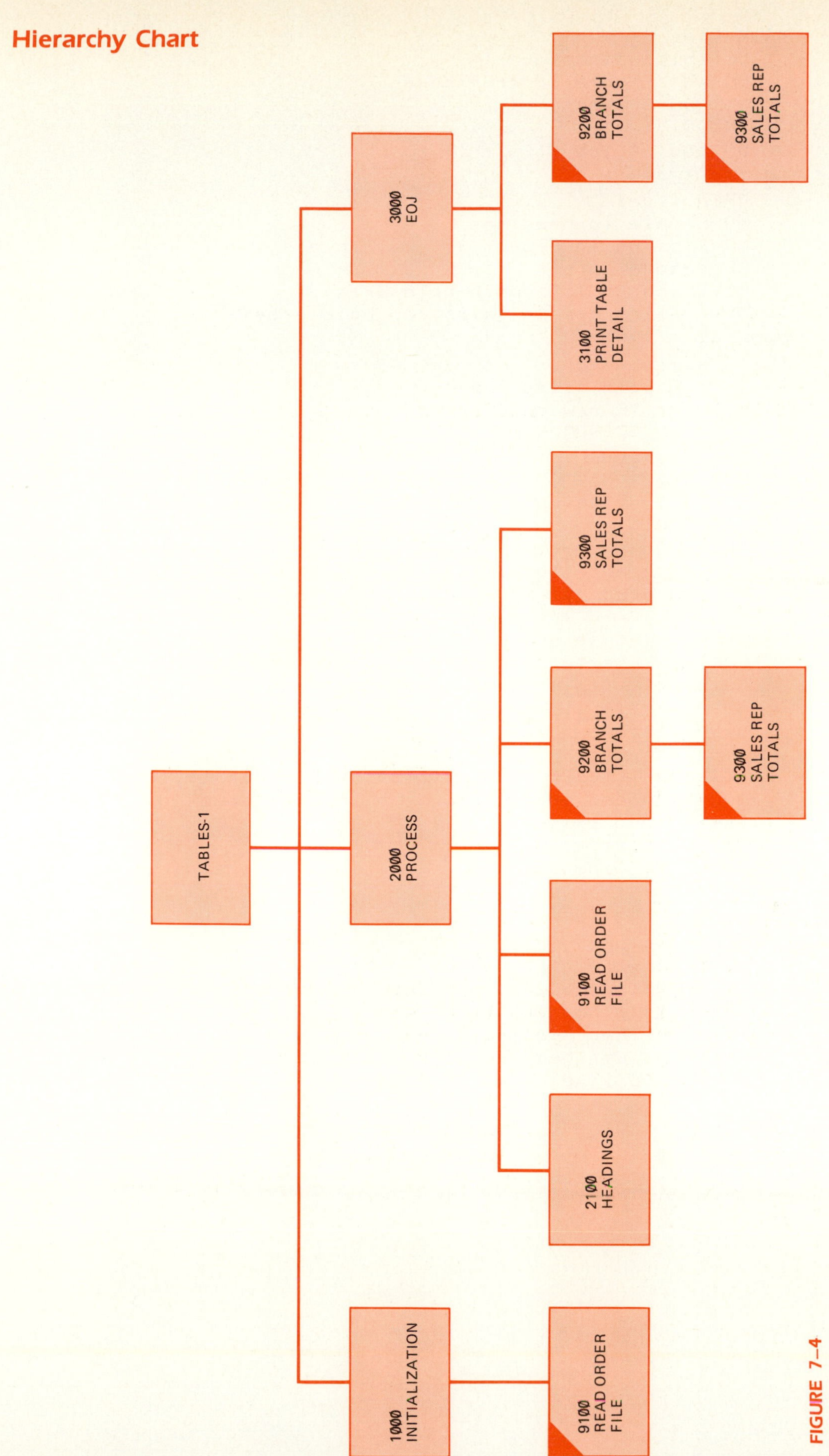

FIGURE 7–4

Pseudocode

```
MAIN LINE
   DO initialization
   DO WHILE more order records
       DO process
   ENDDO
   DO end of job
INITIALIZATION
   OPEN files
   MOVE date to headings
   MOVE zeros to branch totals table
   DO read an order
   MOVE branch to branch hold area
   MOVE sales rep to sales rep hold area
PROCESS
   IF same branch
       IF same sales rep
           IF new page needed
               DO headings
           ENDIF
       ELSE
           DO sales rep totals
       ENDIF
   ELSE
       DO branch totals
       DO headings
   ENDIF
   MOVE input to output
   CALCULATE extended price
   MOVE extended price to output
   ADD quantity to sales rep total quantity
   ADD extended price to sales rep total extended
     price
   ADD quantity to branch totals table quantity
   ADD extended price to branch totals table
     extended price
   WRITE detail line
   ADD 2 to line count
   DO read an order
HEADINGS
   ADD 1 to page count
   MOVE page count to output
   WRITE main heading line one
   WRITE main heading line two
   WRITE column heading line one
   WRITE column heading line two
   MOVE 4 to line count
```

FIGURE 7–5

```
END OF JOB
   DO branch totals
   MOVE final total quantity to output
   MOVE final total extended price to output
   WRITE final totals line
   ADD 1 to page count
   MOVE page count to output
   WRITE main heading line
   WRITE table heading line one
   WRITE table heading line two
   MOVE 1 to branch subscript
   DO WHILE branch subscript not > 10
       DO print table detail
       ADD 1 to branch subscript
   ENDDO
   CLOSE files
PRINT TABLE DETAIL
   MOVE branch subscript to output
   MOVE branch totals table quantity (branch
     subscript) to output
   MOVE branch totals table extended price (branch
     subscript) to output
   WRITE table detail line
READ AN ORDER
   READ order file
BRANCH TOTALS
   DO sales rep totals
   MOVE branch total quantity to output
   MOVE branch total extended price to output
   WRITE branch total line
   ADD branch total quantity to final total
     quantity
   ADD branch total extended price to final total
     extended price
   MOVE zeros to branch total quantity
   MOVE zeros to branch total extended price
   MOVE branch to branch hold area
SALES REP TOTALS
   MOVE sales rep total quantity to output
   MOVE sales rep total extended price to output
   WRITE sales rep total line
   WRITE blank line
   ADD 4 to line count
   ADD sales rep total quantity to branch total
     quantity
   ADD sales rep total extended price to branch
     total extended price
   MOVE zeros to sales rep total quantity
   MOVE zeros to sales rep total extended price
   MOVE sales rep to sales rep hold area
```

FIGURE 7–5 cont.

Flowchart

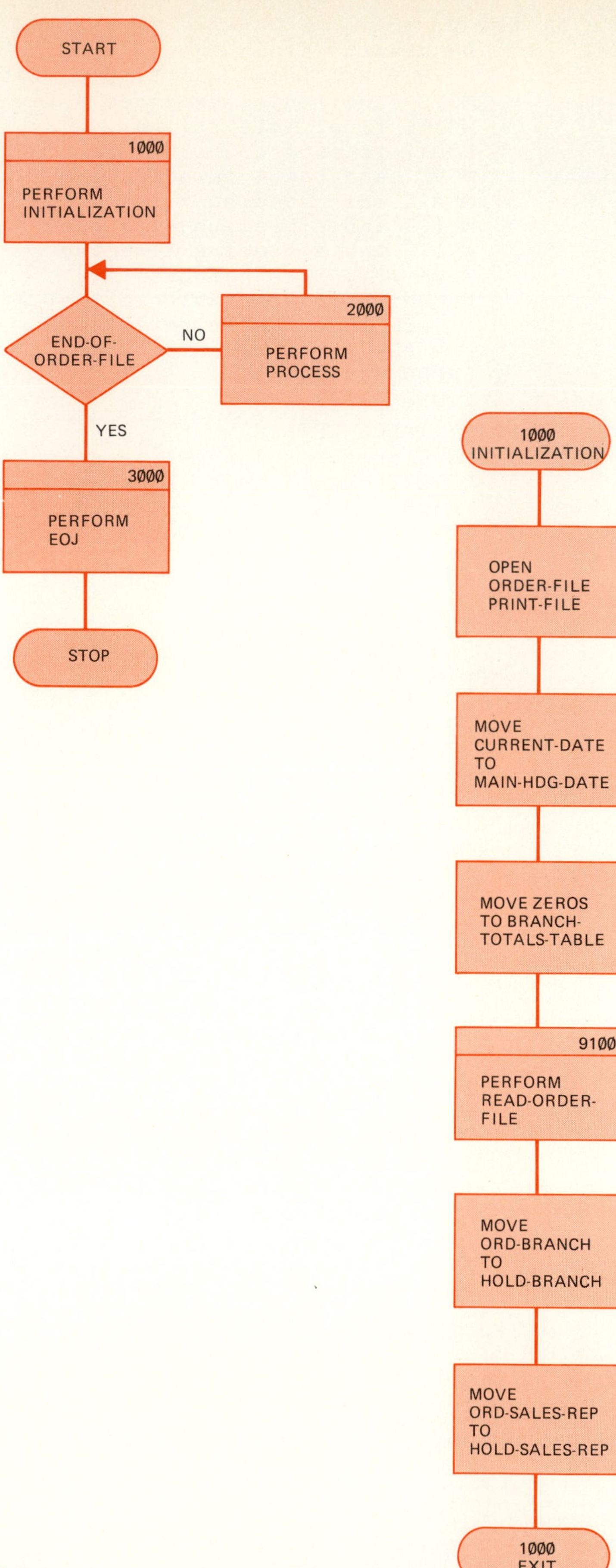

FIGURE 7–6

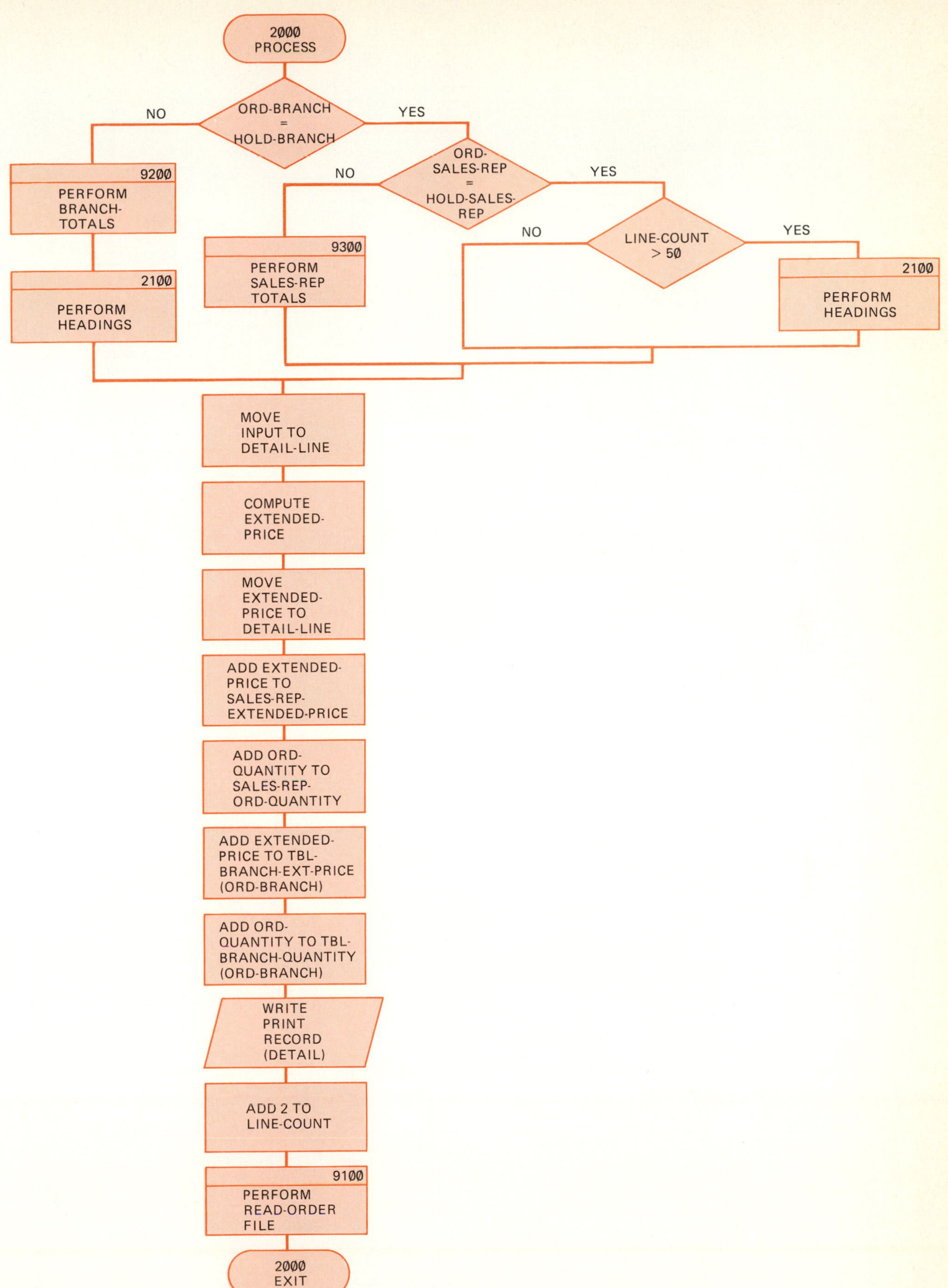

FIGURE 7–6 cont.

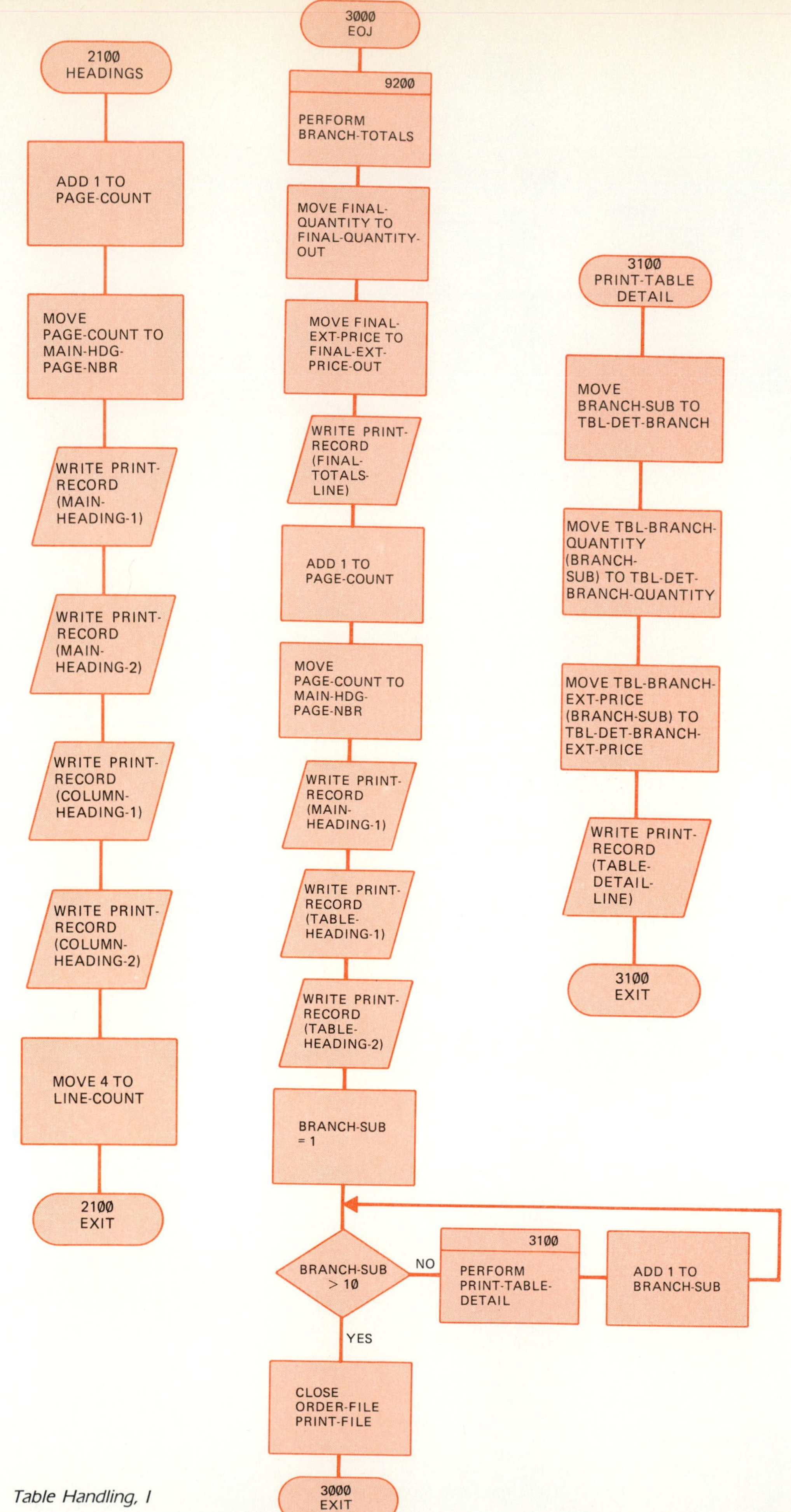

FIGURE 7–6 cont.

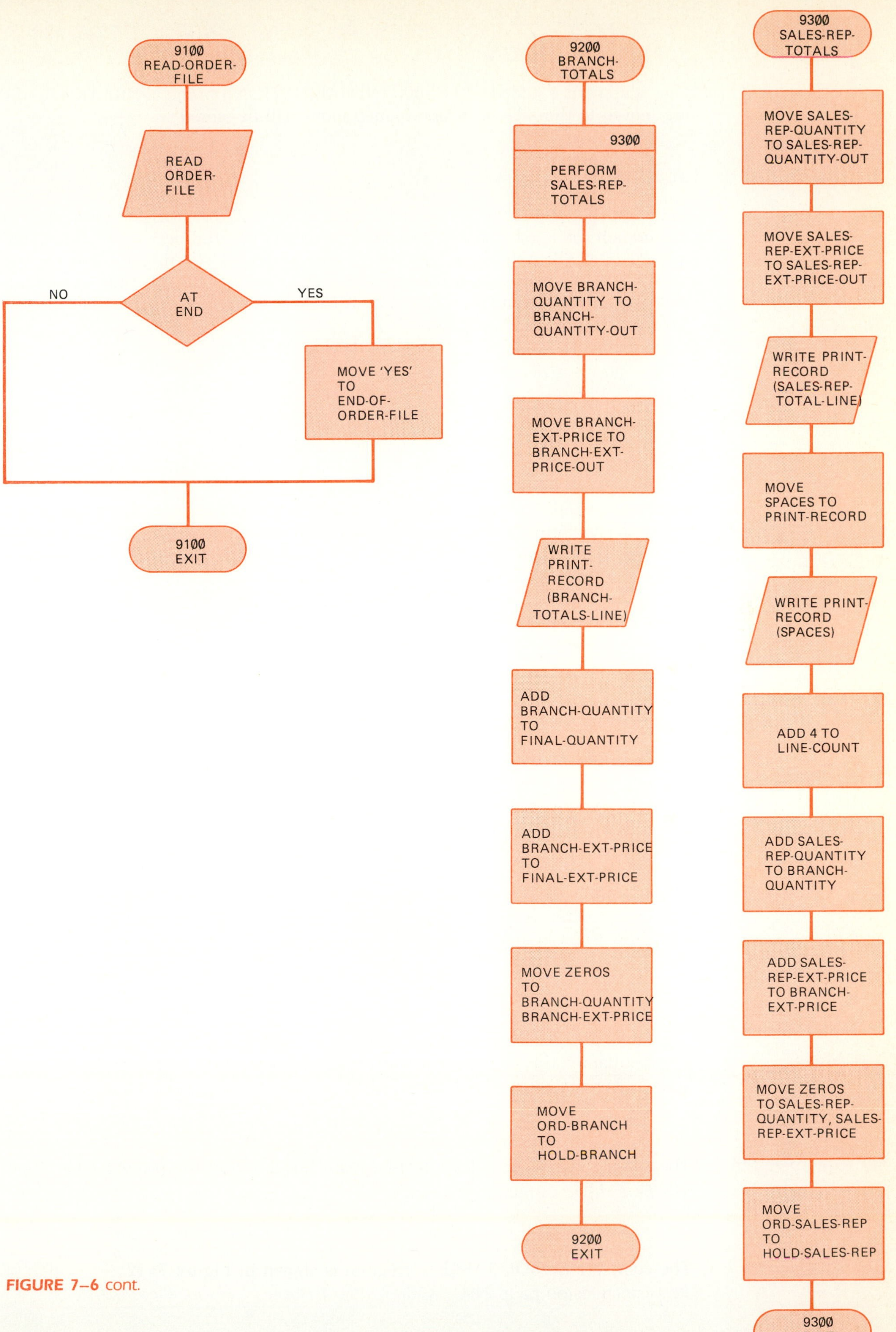

FIGURE 7–6 cont.

Explanation of Logic

1000-INITIALIZATION

One statement is added to the 1000-INITIALIZATION routine of BREAK-4: zeros are moved to the table in which branch totals will be stored.

2000-PROCESS

The only change to 2000-PROCESS from BREAK-4 is the provision for adding to the branch totals table as each record is processed. In the new ADD statements a word (ORD-BRANCH) is enclosed in parentheses. Used in this manner, the word is called a *subscript*. It identifies which part of the table the amount is being added to. An explanation of why ORD-BRANCH is used as a subscript is found later in the chapter. (See Figure 7–7.)

3000-EOJ

3000-EOJ varies from its counterpart in BREAK-3 in that 3100-PRINT-TABLE-DETAIL is performed toward the end of the routine. Headings for the table and 10 table detail lines are needed. COBOL uses PERFORM . . . VARYING to repeat a routine several times using a different value for a variable each time. (See Figure 7–8.) As shown in the program flowchart (Figure 7–6), in 3000-EOJ a counter is set to an initial value (BRANCH-SUB = 1) and then is tested to see whether it exceeds a limit (BRANCH-SUB > 10). If it does not, the routine is performed using the current value of BRANCH-SUB. After the routine is performed, the counter is incremented (ADD 1 to BRANCH-SUB) and the loop is repeated until the limit (BRANCH-SUB > 10) is exceeded.

3100-PRINT-TABLE-DETAIL

The routine 3100-PRINT-TABLE-DETAIL prepares and writes one print line using one row of data from the table. Each row in the table corresponds to one of the branches. Therefore, the counter BRANCH-SUB is used to keep track of the row being moved to the print line, and the value of BRANCH-SUB is printed to represent the branch. The quantity and extended price are moved from the table using the same counter to indicate which element (row) they should come from. Next, the line is written.

The routine is invoked by the EOJ routine. It will be performed 10 times, providing 10 table detail lines. (See Figure 7–9.)

THE COBOL PROGRAM

Test Data

The test data is the same as that used in all the previous programs. It is repeated here for convenience. (See Figure 7–10.)

Sample Output

The sample output includes a revised main heading and the printed table. (See Figure 7–11.)

The Program

The complete COBOL TABLE-1 program is shown in Figure 7–12.

(text continues on page 295)

```
2000-PROCESS.
    IF ORD-BRANCH = HOLD-BRANCH
        IF ORD-SALES-REP = HOLD-SALES-REP
            IF LINE-COUNT > 50
                PERFORM 2100-HEADINGS
            ELSE
                NEXT SENTENCE
        ELSE
            PERFORM 9300-SALES-REP-TOTALS
    ELSE
        PERFORM 9200-BRANCH-TOTALS
        PERFORM 2100-HEADINGS.
    MOVE ORD-BRANCH                 TO DET-BRANCH.
    MOVE ORD-SALES-REP              TO DET-SALES-REP.
    MOVE ORD-CUSTOMER-NBR           TO DET-CUSTOMER-NBR.
    MOVE ORD-SALES-ORD-NBR          TO DET-SALES-ORD-NBR.
    MOVE ORD-YY                     TO DET-ORDER-YY.
    MOVE ORD-MM                     TO DET-ORDER-MM.
    MOVE ORD-DD                     TO DET-ORDER-DD.
    MOVE ORD-PART-NBR               TO DET-PART-NBR.
    MOVE ORD-QUANTITY               TO DET-QUANTITY.
    MOVE ORD-UNIT-PRICE             TO DET-UNIT-PRICE.
    MOVE ORD-REQ-SHIP-YY            TO DET-REQ-SHIP-YY.
    MOVE ORD-REQ-SHIP-MM            TO DET-REQ-SHIP-MM.
    MOVE ORD-REQ-SHIP-DD            TO DET-REQ-SHIP-DD.
    MOVE ORD-ACT-SHIP-YY            TO DET-ACT-SHIP-YY.
    MOVE ORD-ACT-SHIP-MM            TO DET-ACT-SHIP-MM.
    MOVE ORD-ACT-SHIP-DD            TO DET-ACT-SHIP-DD.
    COMPUTE EXTENDED-PRICE = ORD-UNIT-PRICE * ORD-QUANTITY.
    MOVE EXTENDED-PRICE             TO DET-EXTENDED-PRICE.
    ADD ORD-QUANTITY                TO SALES-REP-QUANTITY.
    ADD EXTENDED-PRICE              TO SALES-REP-EXT-PRICE.
    ADD ORD-QUANTITY       TO TBL-BRANCH-QUANTITY (ORD-BRANCH).
    ADD EXTENDED-PRICE     TO TBL-BRANCH-EXT-PRICE (ORD-BRANCH).
    WRITE PRINT-RECORD FROM DETAIL-LINE
        AFTER ADVANCING 2 LINES.
    ADD 2 TO LINE-COUNT.
    PERFORM 9100-READ-ORDER-FILE.
```

FIGURE 7–7

```
3000-EOJ.
    PERFORM 9200-BRANCH-TOTALS.
    MOVE FINAL-QUANTITY TO FINAL-QUANTITY-OUT.
    MOVE FINAL-EXT-PRICE TO FINAL-EXT-PRICE-OUT.
    WRITE PRINT-RECORD FROM FINAL-TOTALS-LINE
        AFTER ADVANCING 3 LINES.
    ADD 1 TO PAGE-COUNT.
    MOVE PAGE-COUNT TO MAIN-HDG-PAGE-NBR.
    WRITE PRINT-RECORD FROM MAIN-HEADING-1
        AFTER ADVANCING PAGE.
    WRITE PRINT-RECORD FROM TABLE-HEADING-1
        AFTER ADVANCING 1 LINE.
    WRITE PRINT-RECORD FROM TABLE-HEADING-2
        AFTER ADVANCING 2 LINES.
    PERFORM 3100-PRINT-TABLE-DETAIL
        VARYING BRANCH-SUB FROM 1 BY 1
            UNTIL BRANCH-SUB > 10.
    CLOSE ORDER-FILE
          PRINT-FILE.
```

FIGURE 7–8

```
3100-PRINT-TABLE-DETAIL.
    MOVE BRANCH-SUB   TO TBL-DET-BRANCH.
    MOVE TBL-BRANCH-QUANTITY (BRANCH-SUB)
                      TO TBL-DET-BRANCH-QUANTITY.
    MOVE TBL-BRANCH-EXT-PRICE (BRANCH-SUB)
                      TO TBL-DET-BRANCH-EXT-PRICE.
    WRITE PRINT-RECORD FROM TABLE-DETAIL-LINE
        AFTER ADVANCING 2 LINES.
```

FIGURE 7–9

```
Ø1201ØØ3ØØPO173     B12383871Ø25GN4Ø2AØØØØ1Ø45ØØØ871116ØØØØØØ
Ø1201Ø47278372      G48388870913WB7Ø2XØØØ9ØØ115ØØ871101ØØØØØØ
Ø1201ØØ3ØØE1Ø12     B12335871105WB493EØØØØ2Ø54ØØØ871122ØØØØØØ
Ø3ØØ747300          H84777870223MF403TØØØØ5Ø4ØØØØ870502ØØØØØØ
Ø3ØØ7ØØ378EBNER     H84579870811VX922PØØ8ØØØØ127589112ØØØØØØØ
Ø3ØØ7739897747      B89288871106MF848JØØØØ5Ø2145Ø88013ØØØØØØØ
Ø3ØØ7ØØ28334567X    B34237871030HL834EØØØ16Ø19ØØØ871121ØØØØØØ
Ø3ØØ747300          Y28903870811VX001LØØ2ØØØØ622Ø871203ØØØØØØ
Ø344Ø69481870341    GØ418Ø87Ø2Ø9JGØ4ØXØØØØ1Ø525ØØ88Ø619ØØØØØØ
Ø361182888P2783733B84330871025HL289BØØØ1ØØ234ØØ871113ØØØØØØ
Ø361128375T7838     T78299870323JG563WØØØØ6Ø43ØØØ871018ØØØØØØ
Ø36115Ø912          H6915Ø87Ø2Ø6MF848TØØØØ3Ø36ØØØ871201ØØØØØØ
Ø817431408865       H41891870412TK61ØLØØØ18ØØ78ØØ87063ØØØØØØØ
Ø8174Ø18Ø5R7278     T2164287Ø81ØTK497XØØØ1ØØ118ØØ87113ØØØØØØØ
Ø8174Ø18Ø5R8322     Y211Ø587Ø6Ø1TN116TØØØØ1Ø3ØØØØ871221ØØØØØØ
Ø891562Ø54SCHUH     L5Ø681871108TK812EØØØØ6Ø573ØØ88Ø105ØØØØØØ
Ø891521Ø78          B71Ø4587100 1FV782TØØØØ3ØØ28ØØ871115ØØØØØØ
```

FIGURE 7–10

DATE: 11/09/87 PRODUCT DISTRIBUTION INC. PAGE: 1

ORDER LISTING

BRANCH	SALES REP	CUSTOMER NUMBER	SALES ORDER	ORDER DATE	REQUESTED SHIP DATE	ACTUAL SHIP DATE	PART NUMBER	QUANTITY	UNIT PRICE	EXTENDED PRICE
01	201	00300	B 12383	10/25/87	11/16/87	00/00/00	GN402A	1	$450.00	$450.00
01	201	04727	G 48388	09/13/87	11/01/87	00/00/00	WB702X	90	$115.00	$10,350.00
01	201	00300	B 12335	11/05/87	11/22/87	00/00/00	WB493E	2	$540.00	$1,080.00
SALES REPRESENTATIVE TOTALS								93		$11,880.00
BRANCH TOTALS								93		$11,880.00

DATE: 11/09/87 PRODUCT DISTRIBUTION INC. PAGE: 2

ORDER LISTING

BRANCH	SALES REP	CUSTOMER NUMBER	SALES ORDER	ORDER DATE	REQUESTED SHIP DATE	ACTUAL SHIP DATE	PART NUMBER	QUANTITY	UNIT PRICE	EXTENDED PRICE
03	007	47300	H 84777	02/23/87	05/02/87	00/00/00	MF403T	5	$400.00	$2,000.00
03	007	00378	H 84579	08/11/87	11/20/89	00/00/00	VX922P	800	$12.75	$10,200.00
03	007	73989	B 89288	11/06/87	01/30/88	00/00/00	MF848J	5	$214.50	$1,072.50
03	007	00283	B 34237	10/30/87	11/21/87	00/00/00	HL834E	16	$190.00	$3,040.00
03	007	47300	Y 28903	08/11/87	12/03/87	00/00/00	VX001L	200	$62.20	$12,440.00
SALES REPRESENTATIVE TOTALS								1,026		$28,752.50
03	440	69481	G 04180	02/09/87	06/19/88	00/00/00	JG040X	1	$525.00	$525.00
SALES REPRESENTATIVE TOTALS								1		$525.00

FIGURE 7–11

03	611	82888	B 84330	10/25/87	11/13/87	00/00/00	HL289B	10	$234.00	$2,340.00
03	611	28375	T 78299	03/23/87	10/18/87	00/00/00	JG563W	6	$430.00	$2,580.00
03	611	50912	H 69150	02/06/87	12/01/87	00/00/00	MF848T	3	$360.00	$1,080.00
SALES REPRESENTATIVE TOTALS								19		$6,000.00
BRANCH TOTALS								1,046		$35,277.50

DATE: 11/09/87 PRODUCT DISTRIBUTION INC. PAGE: 3

ORDER LISTING

BRANCH	SALES REP	CUSTOMER NUMBER	SALES ORDER	ORDER DATE	REQUESTED SHIP DATE	ACTUAL SHIP DATE	PART NUMBER	QUANTITY	UNIT PRICE	EXTENDED PRICE
08	174	31408	H 41891	04/12/87	06/30/87	00/00/00	TK610L	18	$78.00	$1,404.00
08	174	01805	T 21642	08/10/87	11/30/87	00/00/00	TK497X	10	$118.00	$1,180.00
08	174	01805	Y 21105	06/01/87	12/21/87	00/00/00	TN116T	1	$300.00	$300.00
SALES REPRESENTATIVE TOTALS								29		$2,884.00
08	915	62054	L 50681	11/08/87	01/05/88	00/00/00	TK812E	6	$573.00	$3,438.00
08	915	21078	B 71045	10/01/87	11/15/87	00/00/00	FV782T	3	$28.00	$84.00
SALES REPRESENTATIVE TOTALS								9		$3,522.00
BRANCH TOTALS								38		$6,406.00
FINAL TOTALS								1,177		$53,563.50

DATE: 11/09/87 PRODUCT DISTRIBUTION INC. PAGE: 4

ORDER SUMMARY BY BRANCH

	QUANTITY	EXTENDED PRICE
BRANCH 1	93	$11,880.00
BRANCH 2	0	$0.00
BRANCH 3	1,046	$35,277.50
BRANCH 4	0	$0.00
BRANCH 5	0	$0.00
BRANCH 6	0	$0.00
BRANCH 7	0	$0.00
BRANCH 8	38	$6,406.00
BRANCH 9	0	$0.00
BRANCH 10	0	$0.00

FIGURE 7–11 cont.

```
       IDENTIFICATION DIVISION.
       PROGRAM-ID.    TABLE-1.
       AUTHOR.        HELEN HUMPHREYS.
       INSTALLATION.  PRODUCT DISTRIBUTION INC.
       DATE-WRITTEN.  Ø7/12/87.
       DATE-COMPILED. Ø7/21/87.
      *****************************************************************
      *                                                               *
      *    THIS PROGRAM WILL PRODUCE A PRINTED REPORT IN TWO PARTS.   *
      *                                                               *
      *    -THE FIRST PART IS A LISTING OF THE ORDER FILE.  TOTALS    *
      *     FOR QUANTITY AND EXTENDED PRICE WILL BE PRINTED FOR       *
      *     EACH SALES REPRESENTATIVE, BRANCH, AND FOR THE ENTIRE     *
      *     COMPANY.                                                  *
      *                                                               *
      *    -THE SECOND PART IS A SUMMARY OF TOTAL QUANTITY AND TOTAL  *
      *     EXTENDED PRICE BY BRANCH.                                 *
      *                                                               *
      *****************************************************************
       ENVIRONMENT DIVISION.
       CONFIGURATION SECTION.
       SOURCE-COMPUTER.
              IBM-37Ø.
       OBJECT-COMPUTER.
              IBM-37Ø.
       INPUT-OUTPUT SECTION.
       FILE-CONTROL.
           SELECT ORDER-FILE ASSIGN TO DISK.
           SELECT PRINT-FILE ASSIGN TO PRINTER.
       DATA DIVISION.
       FILE SECTION.
       FD  ORDER-FILE
           LABEL RECORDS ARE STANDARD
           RECORD CONTAINS 7Ø CHARACTERS
           DATA RECORD IS ORDER-RECORD.
       Ø1  ORDER-RECORD.
           Ø5  ORD-BRANCH                PIC 9(2).
           Ø5  ORD-SALES-REP             PIC 9(3).
           Ø5  ORD-CUSTOMER-NBR          PIC 9(5).
           Ø5  ORD-CUST-PO-NBR           PIC X(8).
           Ø5  ORD-SALES-ORD-NBR         PIC X(6).
           Ø5  ORD-DATE.
               1Ø  ORD-YY                PIC 9(2).
               1Ø  ORD-MM                PIC 9(2).
               1Ø  ORD-DD                PIC 9(2).
           Ø5  ORD-PART-NBR              PIC X(6).
           Ø5  ORD-QUANTITY              PIC 9(5).
           Ø5  ORD-UNIT-PRICE            PIC 9(4)V9(2).
           Ø5  ORD-REQ-SHIP-DATE.
               1Ø  ORD-REQ-SHIP-YY       PIC 9(2).
               1Ø  ORD-REQ-SHIP-MM       PIC 9(2).
               1Ø  ORD-REQ-SHIP-DD       PIC 9(2).
           Ø5  ORD-ACT-SHIP-DATE.
               1Ø  ORD-ACT-SHIP-YY       PIC 9(2).
               1Ø  ORD-ACT-SHIP-MM       PIC 9(2).
               1Ø  ORD-ACT-SHIP-DD       PIC 9(2).
           Ø5  FILLER                    PIC X(11).
       FD  PRINT-FILE
           LABEL RECORDS ARE OMITTED
           RECORD CONTAINS 133 CHARACTERS
           DATA RECORD IS PRINT-RECORD.
       Ø1  PRINT-RECORD                  PIC X(133).
       WORKING-STORAGE SECTION.
       Ø1  HOLDS-COUNTERS-SWITCHES.
           Ø5  END-FLAG-ORDER-FILE       PIC X(3)        VALUE 'NO'.
```

FIGURE 7–12

```
           88  END-OF-ORDER-FILE                      VALUE 'YES'.
       Ø5  LINE-COUNT              PIC 9(2)           VALUE 99.
       Ø5  PAGE-COUNT              PIC 9(3)           VALUE ZEROS.
       Ø5  HOLD-BRANCH             PIC 9(2)           VALUE ZEROS.
       Ø5  HOLD-SALES-REP          PIC 9(3)           VALUE ZEROS.

   Ø1  CALCULATED-FIELDS.
       Ø5  EXTENDED-PRICE          PIC S9(7)V9(2).

   Ø1  SALES-REP-TOTALS.
       Ø5  SALES-REP-QUANTITY      PIC S9(6)          VALUE ZEROS.
       Ø5  SALES-REP-EXT-PRICE     PIC S9(8)V9(2)     VALUE ZEROS.

   Ø1  BRANCH-TOTALS.
       Ø5  BRANCH-QUANTITY         PIC S9(6)          VALUE ZEROS.
       Ø5  BRANCH-EXT-PRICE        PIC S9(8)V9(2)     VALUE ZEROS.

   Ø1  FINAL-TOTALS.
       Ø5  FINAL-QUANTITY          PIC S9(6)          VALUE ZEROS.
       Ø5  FINAL-EXT-PRICE         PIC S9(8)V9(2)     VALUE ZEROS.

   Ø1  BRANCH-TOTALS-TABLE.
       Ø5  TBL-BRANCH-ROW OCCURS 1Ø TIMES.
           1Ø  TBL-BRANCH-QUANTITY     PIC S9(6).
           1Ø  TBL-BRANCH-EXT-PRICE    PIC S9(7)V9(2).

   Ø1  BRANCH-SUB                  PIC S9(4)          COMP.


   Ø1  MAIN-HEADING-1.
       Ø5  FILLER                  PIC X(6)           VALUE SPACES.
       Ø5  FILLER                  PIC X(6)           VALUE 'DATE:'.
       Ø5  MAIN-HDG-DATE           PIC X(8).
       Ø5  FILLER                  PIC X(34)          VALUE SPACES.
       Ø5  FILLER                  PIC X(25)
           VALUE 'PRODUCT DISTRIBUTION INC.'.
       Ø5  FILLER                  PIC X(38)          VALUE SPACES.
       Ø5  FILLER                  PIC X(6)           VALUE 'PAGE:'.
       Ø5  MAIN-HDG-PAGE-NBR       PIC ZZ9.
       Ø5  FILLER                  PIC X(7)           VALUE SPACES.

   Ø1  MAIN-HEADING-2.
       Ø5  FILLER                  PIC X(6Ø)          VALUE SPACES.
       Ø5  FILLER                  PIC X(13)
                                   VALUE 'ORDER LISTING'.
       Ø5  FILLER                  PIC X(6Ø)          VALUE SPACES.

   Ø1  TABLE-HEADING-1.
       Ø5  FILLER                  PIC X(55)          VALUE SPACES.
       Ø5  FILLER                  PIC X(23)
                                   VALUE 'ORDER SUMMARY BY BRANCH'.
       Ø5  FILLER                  PIC X(55)          VALUE SPACES.

   Ø1  TABLE-HEADING-2.
       Ø5  FILLER                  PIC X(6Ø)          VALUE SPACES.
       Ø5  FILLER                  PIC X(8)           VALUE 'QUANTITY'.
       Ø5  FILER                   PIC X(1Ø)          VALUE SPACES.
       Ø5  FILLER                  PIC X(14)
                                   VALUE 'EXTENDED PRICE'.
       Ø5  FILLER                  PIC X(41)          VALUE SPACES.

   Ø1  COLUMN-HEADING-1.
       Ø5  FILLER                  PIC X(14)          VALUE SPACES.
       Ø5  FILLER                  PIC X(5)           VALUE 'SALES'.
       Ø5  FILLER                  PIC X(2)           VALUE SPACES.
       Ø5  FILLER                  PIC X(8)           VALUE 'CUSTOMER'.
       Ø5  FILLER                  PIC X(3)           VALUE SPACES.
       Ø5  FILLER                  PIC X(5)           VALUE 'SALES'.
       Ø5  FILLER                  PIC X(6)           VALUE SPACES.
       Ø5  FILLER                  PIC X(5)           VALUE 'ORDER'.
       Ø5  FILLER                  PIC X(6)           VALUE SPACES.
       Ø5  FILLER                  PIC X(9)           VALUE
                                                      'REQUESTED'.
       Ø5  FILLER                  PIC X(4)           VALUE SPACES.
       Ø5  FILLER                  PIC X(6)           VALUE 'ACTUAL'.
       Ø5  FILLER                  PIC X(6)           VALUE SPACES.
       Ø5  FILLER                  PIC X(4)           VALUE 'PART'.
       Ø5  FILLER                  PIC X(18)          VALUE SPACES.
       Ø5  FILLER                  PIC X(4)           VALUE 'UNIT'.
       Ø5  FILLER                  PIC X(9)           VALUE SPACES.
       Ø5  FILLER                  PIC X(8)           VALUE 'EXTENDED'.
       Ø5  FILLER                  PIC X(11)          VALUE SPACES.
```

FIGURE 7–12 cont.

```
       Ø1  COLUMN-HEADING-2.
           Ø5  FILLER                 PIC X(7)        VALUE SPACES.
           Ø5  FILLER                 PIC X(6)        VALUE 'BRANCH'.
           Ø5  FILLER                 PIC X(2)        VALUE SPACES.
           Ø5  FILLER                 PIC X(3)        VALUE 'REP'.
           Ø5  FILLER                 PIC X(4)        VALUE SPACES.
           Ø5  FILLER                 PIC X(6)        VALUE 'NUMBER'.
           Ø5  FILLER                 PIC X(4)        VALUE SPACES.
           Ø5  FILLER                 PIC X(5)        VALUE 'ORDER'.
           Ø5  FILLER                 PIC X(7)        VALUE SPACES.
           Ø5  FILLER                 PIC X(4)        VALUE 'DATE'.
           Ø5  FILLER                 PIC X(6)        VALUE SPACES.
           Ø5  FILLER                 PIC X(9)        VALUE
                                                      'SHIP DATE'.
           Ø5  FILLER                 PIC X(3)        VALUE SPACES.
           Ø5  FILLER                 PIC X(9)        VALUE
                                                      'SHIP DATE'.
           Ø5  FILLER                 PIC X(3)        VALUE SPACES.
           Ø5  FILLER                 PIC X(6)        VALUE 'NUMBER'.
           Ø5  FILLER                 PIC X(3)        VALUE SPACES.
           Ø5  FILLER                 PIC X(8)        VALUE 'QUANTITY'.
           Ø5  FILLER                 PIC X(6)        VALUE SPACES.
           Ø5  FILLER                 PIC X(5)        VALUE 'PRICE'.
           Ø5  FILLER                 PIC X(9)        VALUE SPACES.
           Ø5  FILLER                 PIC X(5)        VALUE 'PRICE'.
           Ø5  FILLER                 PIC X(9)        VALUE SPACES.

       Ø1  DETAIL-LINE.
           Ø5  FILLER                 PIC X(9)        VALUE SPACES.
           Ø5  DET-BRANCH             PIC 9(2).
           Ø5  FILLER                 PIC X(4)        VALUE SPACES.
           Ø5  DET-SALES-REP          PIC 9(3).
           Ø5  FILLER                 PIC X(4)        VALUE SPACES.
           Ø5  DET-CUSTOMER-NBR       PIC 9(5).
           Ø5  FILLER                 PIC X(4)        VALUE SPACES.
           Ø5  DET-SALES-ORD-NBR      PIC XBXXXXX.
           Ø5  FILLER                 PIC X(4)        VALUE SPACES.
           Ø5  DET-ORDER-MM           PIC 9(2).
           Ø5  FILLER                 PIC X(1)        VALUE '/'.
           Ø5  DET-ORDER-DD           PIC 9(2).
           Ø5  FILLER                 PIC X(1)        VALUE '/'.
           Ø5  DET-ORDER-YY           PIC 9(2).
           Ø5  FILLER                 PIC X(4)        VALUE SPACES.
           Ø5  DET-REQ-SHIP-MM        PIC 9(2).
           Ø5  FILLER                 PIC X(1)        VALUE '/'.
           Ø5  DET-REQ-SHIP-DD        PIC 9(2).
           Ø5  FILLER                 PIC X(1)        VALUE '/'.
           Ø5  DET-REQ-SHIP-YY        PIC 9(2).
           Ø5  FILLER                 PIC X(4)        VALUE SPACES.
           Ø5  DET-ACT-SHIP-MM        PIC 9(2).
           Ø5  FILLER                 PIC X(1)        VALUE '/'.
           Ø5  DET-ACT-SHIP-DD        PIC 9(2).
           Ø5  FILLER                 PIC X(1)        VALUE '/'.
           Ø5  DET-ACT-SHIP-YY        PIC 9(2).
           Ø5  FILLER                 PIC X(4)        VALUE SPACES.
           Ø5  DET-PART-NBR           PIC X(6).
           Ø5  FILLER                 PIC X(4)        VALUE SPACES.
           Ø5  DET-QUANTITY           PIC ZZ,ZZ9-.
           Ø5  FILLER                 PIC X(3)        VALUE SPACES.
           Ø5  DET-UNIT-PRICE         PIC $$,$$9.99-.
           Ø5  FILLER                 PIC X(3)        VALUE SPACES.
           Ø5  DET-EXTENDED-PRICE     PIC $$,$$$,$$9.99-.
           Ø5  FILLER                 PIC X(8)        VALUE SPACES.

       Ø1  SALES-REP-TOTALS-LINE.
           Ø5  FILLER                 PIC X(9)        VALUE SPACES.
           Ø5  FILLER                 PIC X(27)
               VALUE 'SALES REPRESENTATIVE TOTALS'.
           Ø5  FILLER                 PIC X(51)       VALUE SPACES.
           Ø5  SALES-REP-QUANTITY-OUT PIC ZZZ,ZZ9-.
           Ø5  FILLER                 PIC X(15)       VALUE SPACES.
           Ø5  SALES-REP-EXT-PRICE-OUT PIC $$$,$$$,$$9.99-.
           Ø5  FILLER                 PIC X(8).

       Ø1  BRANCH-TOTALS-LINE.
           Ø5  FILLER                 PIC X(9)        VALUE SPACES.
           Ø5  FILLER                 PIC X(13)
                                      VALUE 'BRANCH TOTALS'.
           Ø5  FILLER                 PIC X(65)       VALUE SPACES.
           Ø5  BRANCH-QUANTITY-OUT    PIC ZZZ,ZZ9-.
           Ø5  FILLER                 PIC X(15)       VALUE SPACES.
```

FIGURE 7–12 cont.

```
           Ø5  BRANCH-EXT-PRICE-OUT     PIC $$$,$$$,$$9.99-.
           Ø5  FILLER                   PIC X(8).

       Ø1  FINAL-TOTALS-LINE.
           Ø5  FILLER                   PIC X(9)        VALUE SPACES.
           Ø5  FILLER                   PIC X(12)
                                        VALUE 'FINAL TOTALS'.
           Ø5  FILLER                   PIC X(66)       VALUE SPACES.
           Ø5  FINAL-QUANTITY-OUT       PIC ZZZ,ZZ9-.
           Ø5  FILLER                   PIC X(15)       VALUE SPACES.
           Ø5  FINAL-EXT-PRICE-OUT      PIC $$$,$$$,$$9.99-.
           Ø5  FILLER                   PIC X(8).


       Ø1  TABLE-DETAIL-LINE.
           Ø5  FILLER                   PIC X(4Ø)       VALUE SPACES.
           Ø5  FILLER                   PIC X(7)        VALUE 'BRANCH'.
           Ø5  TBL-DET-BRANCH           PIC Z9.
           Ø5  FILLER                   PIC X(11)       VALUE SPACES.
           Ø5  TBL-DET-BRANCH-QUANTITY PIC ZZZ,ZZ9-.
           Ø5  FILLER                   PIC X(1Ø)       VALUE SPACES.
           Ø5  TBL-DET-BRANCH-EXT-PRICE    PIC $$$,$$$,$$9.99-.
           Ø5  FILLER                   PIC X(4Ø)       VALUE SPACES.

       PROCEDURE DIVISION.

           PERFORM 1ØØØ-INITIALIZATION.
           PERFORM 2ØØØ-PROCESS
               UNTIL END-OF-ORDER-FILE.
           PERFORM 3ØØØ-EOJ.
           STOP RUN.

       1ØØØ-INITIALIZATION.
           OPEN INPUT  ORDER-FILE
                OUTPUT PRINT-FILE.
           MOVE CURRENT-DATE TO MAIN-HDG-DATE.
           MOVE ZEROS TO BRANCH-TOTALS-TABLE.
           PERFORM 91ØØ-READ-ORDER-FILE.
           MOVE ORD-BRANCH TO HOLD-BRANCH.
           MOVE ORD-SALES-REP TO HOLD-SALES-REP.

       2ØØØ-PROCESS.
           IF ORD-BRANCH = HOLD-BRANCH
               IF ORD-SALES-REP = HOLD-SALES-REP
                   IF LINE-COUNT > 5Ø
                       PERFORM 21ØØ-HEADINGS
                   ELSE
                       NEXT SENTENCE
               ELSE
                   PERFORM 93ØØ-SALES-REP-TOTALS
           ELSE
               PERFORM 92ØØ-BRANCH-TOTALS
               PERFORM 21ØØ-HEADINGS.
           MOVE ORD-BRANCH               TO DET-BRANCH.
           MOVE ORD-SALES-REP            TO DET-SALES-REP.
           MOVE ORD-CUSTOMER-NBR         TO DET-CUSTOMER-NBR.
           MOVE ORD-SALES-ORD-NBR        TO DET-SALES-ORD-NBR.
           MOVE ORD-YY                   TO DET-ORDER-YY.
           MOVE ORD-MM                   TO DET-ORDER-MM.
           MOVE ORD-DD                   TO DET-ORDER-DD.
           MOVE ORD-PART-NBR             TO DET-PART-NBR.
           MOVE ORD-QUANTITY             TO DET-QUANTITY.
           MOVE ORD-UNIT-PRICE           TO DET-UNIT-PRICE.
           MOVE ORD-REQ-SHIP-YY          TO DET-REQ-SHIP-YY.
           MOVE ORD-REQ-SHIP-MM          TO DET-REQ-SHIP-MM.
           MOVE ORD-REQ-SHIP-DD          TO DET-REQ-SHIP-DD.
           MOVE ORD-ACT-SHIP-YY          TO DET-ACT-SHIP-YY.
           MOVE ORD-ACT-SHIP-MM          TO DET-ACT-SHIP-MM.
           MOVE ORD-ACT-SHIP-DD          TO DET-ACT-SHIP-DD.
           COMPUTE EXTENDED-PRICE = ORD-UNIT-PRICE * ORD-QUANTITY.
           MOVE EXTENDED-PRICE           TO DET-EXTENDED-PRICE.
           ADD ORD-QUANTITY              TO SALES-REP-QUANTITY.
           ADD EXTENDED-PRICE            TO SALES-REP-EXT-PRICE.
           ADD ORD-QUANTITY        TO TBL-BRANCH-QUANTITY (ORD-BRANCH).
           ADD EXTENDED-PRICE      TO TBL-BRANCH-EXT-PRICE (ORD-BRANCH).
           WRITE PRINT-RECORD FROM DETAIL-LINE
               AFTER ADVANCING 2 LINES.
           ADD 2 TO LINE-COUNT.
           PERFORM 91ØØ-READ-ORDER-FILE.

       21ØØ-HEADINGS.
           ADD 1 TO PAGE-COUNT.
```

FIGURE 7–12 cont.

```
    MOVE PAGE-COUNT TO MAIN-HDG-PAGE-NBR.
    WRITE PRINT-RECORD FROM MAIN-HEADING-1
        AFTER ADVANCING PAGE.
    WRITE PRINT-RECORD FROM MAIN-HEADING-2
        AFTER ADVANCING 1 LINE.
    WRITE PRINT-RECORD FROM COLUMN-HEADING-1
        AFTER ADVANCING 2 LINES.
    WRITE PRINT-RECORD FROM COLUMN-HEADING-2
        AFTER ADVANCING 1 LINE.
    MOVE 4 TO LINE-COUNT.

3000-EOJ.
    PERFORM 9200-BRANCH-TOTALS.
    MOVE FINAL-QUANTITY TO FINAL-QUANTITY-OUT.
    MOVE FINAL-EXT-PRICE TO FINAL-EXT-PRICE-OUT.
    WRITE PRINT-RECORD FROM FINAL-TOTALS-LINE
        AFTER ADVANCING 3 LINES.
    ADD 1 TO PAGE-COUNT.
    MOVE PAGE-COUNT TO MAIN-HDG-PAGE-NBR.
    WRITE PRINT-RECORD FROM MAIN-HEADING-1
        AFTER ADVANCING PAGE.
    WRITE PRINT-RECORD FROM TABLE-HEADING-1
        AFTER ADVANCING 1 LINE.
    WRITE PRINT-RECORD FROM TABLE-HEADING-2
        AFTER ADVANCING 2 LINES.
    PERFORM 3100-PRINT-TABLE-DETAIL
        VARYING BRANCH-SUB FROM 1 BY 1
            UNTIL BRANCH-SUB > 10.
    CLOSE ORDER-FILE
          PRINT-FILE.

3100-PRINT-TABLE-DETAIL.
    MOVE BRANCH-SUB   TO TBL-DET-BRANCH.
    MOVE TBL-BRANCH-QUANTITY (BRANCH-SUB)
                      TO TBL-DET-BRANCH-QUANTITY.
    MOVE TBL-BRANCH-EXT-PRICE (BRANCH-SUB)
                      TO TBL-DET-BRANCH-EXT-PRICE.
    WRITE PRINT-RECORD FROM TABLE-DETAIL-LINE
        AFTER ADVANCING 2 LINES.

9100-READ-ORDER-FILE.
    READ ORDER-FILE
        AT END
            MOVE 'YES' TO END-FLAG-ORDER-FILE.

9200-BRANCH-TOTALS.
    PERFORM 9300-SALES-REP-TOTALS.
    MOVE BRANCH-QUANTITY          TO BRANCH-QUANTITY-OUT.
    MOVE BRANCH-EXT-PRICE         TO BRANCH-EXT-PRICE-OUT.
    WRITE PRINT-RECORD FROM BRANCH-TOTALS-LINE
        AFTER ADVANCING 2 LINES.
    ADD BRANCH-QUANTITY           TO FINAL-QUANTITY.
    ADD BRANCH-EXT-PRICE          TO FINAL-EXT-PRICE.
    MOVE ZEROS                    TO BRANCH-QUANTITY
                                     BRANCH-EXT-PRICE.
    MOVE ORD-BRANCH               TO HOLD-BRANCH.

9300-SALES-REP-TOTALS.
    MOVE SALES-REP-QUANTITY       TO SALES-REP-QUANTITY-OUT.
    MOVE SALES-REP-EXT-PRICE      TO SALES-REP-EXT-PRICE-OUT.
    WRITE PRINT-RECORD FROM SALES-REP-TOTALS-LINE
        AFTER ADVANCING 2 LINES.
    MOVE SPACES TO PRINT-RECORD.
    WRITE PRINT-RECORD AFTER ADVANCING 2 LINES.
    ADD 4 TO LINE-COUNT.
    ADD SALES-REP-QUANTITY        TO BRANCH-QUANTITY.
    ADD SALES-REP-EXT-PRICE       TO BRANCH-EXT-PRICE.
    MOVE ZEROS                    TO SALES-REP-QUANTITY
                                     SALES-REP-EXT-PRICE.
    MOVE ORD-SALES-REP            TO HOLD-SALES-REP.
```

FIGURE 7–12 cont.

NEW COBOL ELEMENTS

Table Structure: OCCURS

Format

```
               {data-name}
level number   {FILLER   }  [OCCURS integer-2 TIMES] [PICture clause]
```

A table is a set of data items that share a common name and data description. Items are combined into a table because they are to be treated in a similar manner. An OCCURS clause is used to indicate how many items are in the set. The OCCURS clause is included in the data description entry in the DATA DIVISION and may be coded on any data description entry which has a level number 02 through 49. The OCCURS clause in effect defines the table.

One-Dimensional Tables

```
05  TABLE-B      OCCURS 5 TIMES    PIC 9(6).
```

Because TABLE-B contains only a single OCCURS clause it is a one-dimensional table. OCCURS 5 TIMES indicates that there are five elements in the table. TABLE-B reserves storage for five data items, each of which is a six-byte numeric data item. Thus, a total of 30 bytes of memory will be reserved for TABLE-B.

Since all five elements of TABLE-B share the same name, there needs to be a way to tell them apart. To identify a single table element, a subscript is used. A subscript is an integer denoting an element in the table—the first, second, third, and so on. A subscript may be a numeric literal or a data-name. It is enclosed in parentheses and placed after the table name to indicate which table element is being referenced. The following five table elements are identified by means of a numeric literal as the subscript:

```
TABLE-B (1)
TABLE-B (2)
TABLE-B (3)
TABLE-B (4)
TABLE-B (5)
```

The diagram of memory in Figure 7–13 shows how the 30 bytes reserved by the table would be divided up.

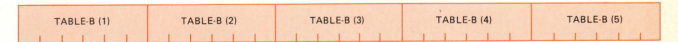

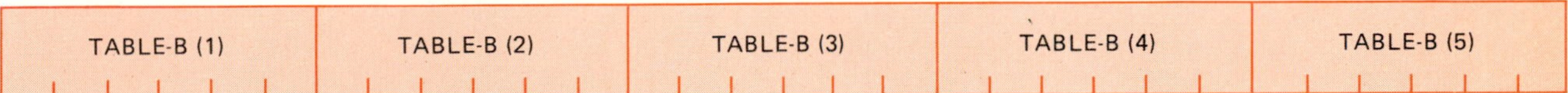

FIGURE 7–13

The 1985 standard allows a subscript to be a data-name followed by + or −, followed by an integer—for example,

```
MOVE ZERO TO TABLE-B (BRANCH + 1)
```

Notice that the value of the subscript in TABLE-B ranges from 1 to 5. The lowest possible value of a subscript in COBOL is +1; the highest should be equal to the number specified in the OCCURS clause for a given table.

A data item becomes a table when it has an OCCURS clause in its description. Any item described this way must have a subscript or an index when referenced in the PROCEDURE DIVISION in order to indicate which of the elements is being referenced. Indices are described in Chapter 8. If the subscript or index is left off, a diagnostic will be generated.

If a subscript is always a numeric literal, much of the advantage of grouping like data items together as a table is lost. As long as the first element of the table is coded as TABLE-B (1) and the second as TABLE-B (2), it will require as many lines of code to use the table elements as it would if they were not elements of a table and were simply five different data-names. Thus, to add to the table when literals are used as subscripts requires five ADD statements, and to move data into the table requires five MOVE statements.

Using a data-name as a subscript often allows the programmer to reduce the number of COBOL statements required to accomplish a task. Suppose that we wish to add QUANTITY from an input file to a table in such a way that the first element of the table (TABLE-B (1)) contains the total quantity for the first branch, the second table element (TABLE-B (2)) contains the total quantity for the second branch, and so on. Each input record contains a QUANTITY and a BRANCH. Each time a record is read, the following instruction may be executed:

```
ADD QUANTITY TO TABLE-B (BRANCH).
```

Since each input record contains a value for QUANTITY, it is available to be added to the table. The BRANCH from the input record will be used to determine which table element the quantity will be added to. Some sample input data is shown in figure 7–14. It is instructive to substitute the sample input values for the data-names in ADD QUANTITY TO TABLE-B (BRANCH) and see how the contents of the table change each time the ADD statement is executed. (A table of this type usually has all of its elements set to zero before a program is executed.)

INPUT DATA	
Quantity	Branch
40	1
80	1
300	1
60	2
10	3
500	3
50	4
40	4
90	4
75	5
50	5

ADD WITH VALUES SUBSTITUTED FOR THE DATA-NAMES QUANTITY AND BRANCH	TABLE				
ADD QUANTITY TO TABLE-B (BRANCH)					
THE TABLE BEFORE ANY ADDS	000000	000000	000000	000000	000000
ADD 40 TO TABLE-B (1).	000040	000000	000000	000000	000000
ADD 80 TO TABLE-B (1).	000120	000000	000000	000000	000000
ADD 300 TO TABLE-B (1).	000420	000000	000000	000000	000000
ADD 60 TO TABLE-B (2).	000420	000060	000000	000000	000000
ADD 10 TO TABLE-B (3).	000420	000060	000010	000000	000000
ADD 500 TO TABLE-B (3).	000420	000060	000510	000000	000000
ADD 50 TO TABLE-B (4).	000420	000060	000510	000050	000000
ADD 40 TO TABLE-B (4).	000420	000060	000510	000090	000000
ADD 90 TO TABLE-B (4).	000420	000060	000510	000180	000000
ADD 75 TO TABLE-B (5).	000420	000060	000510	000180	000075
ADD 50 TO TABLE-B (5).	000420	000060	000510	000180	000125

FIGURE 7–14

Rearranging the input data so that the records are not in sequence by BRANCH, and adding the input data into the table again makes it clear that using BRANCH as a subscript will fill the table properly whether the data is in sequence by branch or not. Each input record provides the data needed (BRANCH) to identify the proper table element. With one ADD statement any number of records in a file may be processed, and the number of elements in the table may be expanded, to accommodate any number of branches in an organization. Keep in mind, however, that if the records are rearranged so that they are not in sequence by BRANCH, the control-break portion of the program will not work properly.

It is possible to access the entire table at one time by adding a group item above the table. In Figure 7–15, TABLE-A is a group item, including all five TABLE-B elements in its definition. Thus, a reference to TABLE-A is a reference to 30 bytes of memory, and the table may be initialized by moving the figurative constant ZEROS to TABLE-A:

```
MOVE ZEROS TO TABLE-A.
01  TABLE-A.
    05  TABLE-B   OCCURS 5 TIMES   PIC 9(6).
```

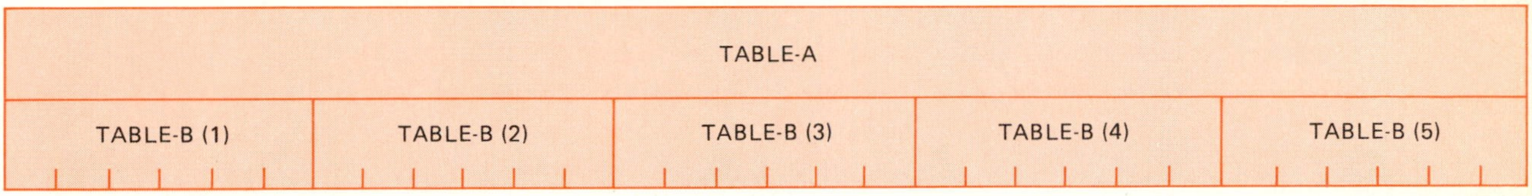

FIGURE 7–15

The table may also be initialized in WORKING-STORAGE by coding VALUE ZEROS on the group item, TABLE-A. COBOL does not allow a VALUE clause on the same line as an OCCURS clause, but a value clause may be placed on the group level, which does not have an OCCURS clause.

```
01  TABLE-A                  VALUE ZEROS.
    05  TABLE-B  OCCURS 5 TIMES PIC 9(6).
```

The preceding two methods of initializing a table will function correctly only when all numeric items in the table are USAGE IS DISPLAY.

A one-dimensional table may have more than one data-name associated with a single OCCURS clause. In the code in Figure 7–16, each of the five elements is divided into two pieces. TABLE-B is still a one-dimensional table with five elements, but now each element is a group item and has two subordinate data items.

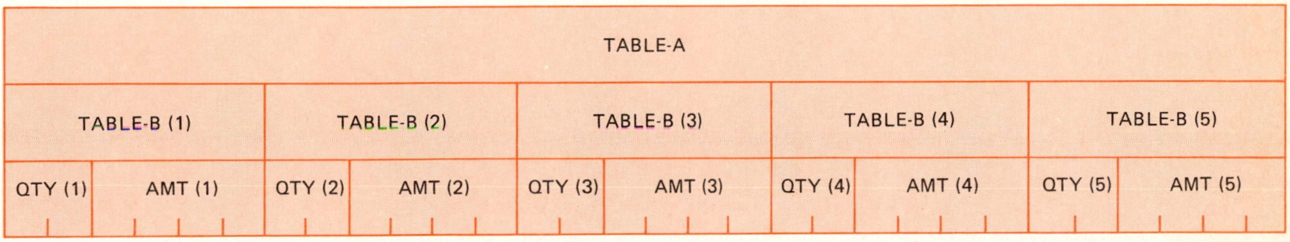

```
01  TABLE-A.
    05  TABLE-B OCCURS 5 TIMES
        10  QTY                  PIC 9(2).
        10  AMT                  PIC 9(4).
```

FIGURE 7–16

The table is still a 30-byte *one-dimensional* table. QTY and AMT are the two parts of each of the five table elements and hence require a subscript to identify which of these elements they are a part of. In order to add two values from an input record to QTY and AMT in TABLE-A, BRANCH is used as the subscript. The code would be as follows:

```
ADD QUANTITY TO QTY (BRANCH).
ADD AMOUNT TO AMT (BRANCH).
```

In the 1974 standard, VALUE clauses are not allowed on data items that are subordinate to a group item if the group item contains an OCCURS clause as, for example, do QTY and AMT.

The 1985 standard allows a VALUE clause on an entry that has an OCCURS clause or is subordinate to an entry that has an OCCURS clause.

Two-Dimensional Tables

In many instances, a one-dimensional table will not be adequate to store a particular set of data. Rather, the data may be easier to manipulate if it is stored in a two-dimensional table. Figure 7–17 gives an example of a two-dimensional table.

TABLE-A											
TABLE-B (1)			TABLE-B (2)			TABLE-B (3)			TABLE-B (4)		
TABLE-C (1, 1)	TABLE-C (1, 2)	TABLE-C (1, 3)	TABLE-C (2, 1)	TABLE-C (2, 2)	TABLE-C (2, 3)	TABLE-C (3, 1)	TABLE-C (3, 2)	TABLE-C (3, 3)	TABLE-C (4, 1)	TABLE-C (4, 2,)	TABLE-C (4, 3)

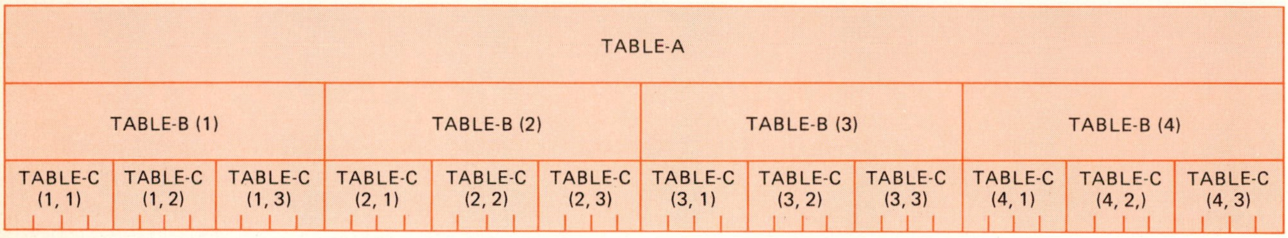

```
01  TABLE-A.
    05  TABLE-B    OCCURS 4 TIMES.
        10  TABLE-C     OCCURS 3 TIMES          PIC 9(4).
```

FIGURE 7–17

In the figure, TABLE-A is a group item, containing both TABLE-B and TABLE-C, and encompassing 48 bytes of storage. Since it is a group item, it is alphanumeric. Any reference to TABLE-A references all 48 bytes. No subscript is allowed in referring to TABLE-A in the PROCEDURE DIVISION. (See Figure 7–18.)

TABLE-A

FIGURE 7–18

TABLE-B, on the other hand, consists of four elements (OCCURS 4 TIMES), each of which is 12 bytes. Each element of TABLE-B is a group item, since each such element contains elements of TABLE-C. Thus, any reference to TABLE-B is a reference to 12 bytes of storage and requires one subscript. (See Figure 7–19.)

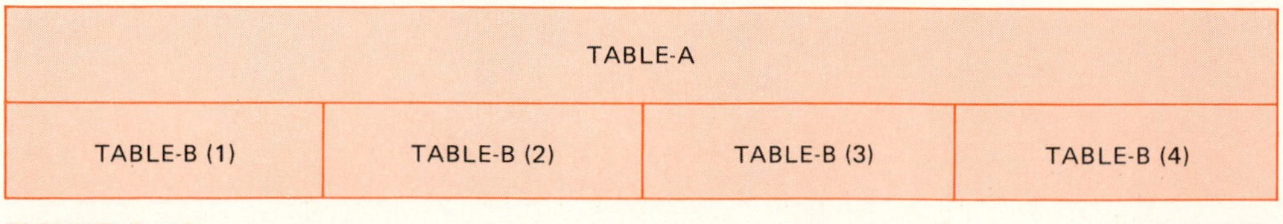

TABLE-A			
TABLE-B (1)	TABLE-B (2)	TABLE-B (3)	TABLE-B (4)

FIGURE 7–19

TABLE-A							
TABLE-B (1)				TABLE-B (2)			
TABLE-C (1, 1)	TABLE-C (1, 2)	TABLE-C (1, 3)	TABLE-C (1, 4)	TABLE-C (2, 1)	TABLE-C (2, 2)	TABLE-C (2, 3)	TABLE-C (2, 4)
(1, 1, 1) (1, 1, 2) (1, 1, 3)	(1, 2, 1) (1, 2, 2) (1, 2, 3)	(1, 3, 1) (1, 3, 2) (1, 3, 3)	(1, 4, 1) (1, 4, 2) (1, 4, 3)	(2, 1, 1) (2, 1, 2) (2, 1, 3)	(2, 2, 1) (2, 2, 2) (2, 2, 3)	(2, 3, 1) (2, 3, 2) (2, 3, 3)	(2, 4, 1) (2, 4, 2) (2, 4, 3)

← TABLE-D →

FIGURE 7–26

Accessing Table Data

Reference to a table element may occur in COBOL code in most places that a data item of the same type may occur. Some examples are shown in Figure 7–27. Although they employ numeric literals as subscripts, data-names are more likely to be used in an actual program. It is assumed that any statement which requires an elementary item is referencing the level of its table which has a PICTURE clause.

```
MOVE ZEROS TO TABLE-A.
COMPUTE TABLE-D (1, 3, 2) = QUANTITY * RATE.
MOVE QUANTITY TO TABLE-C (2, 1).
MOVE TABLE-C (2, 1) TO . . .
MULTIPLY PRICE BY TABLE-B (3).
IF TABLE-D (2, 2, 3) = ZERO . . .
```

FIGURE 7–27

To locate a table element in memory, the computer uses two pieces of data: (1) the memory location where the table begins, and (2) the distance into the table the particular element is located. The latter is referred to as *displacement* within the table and is calculated using subscripts. Displacement indicates how many bytes there are in front of a given element.

For example, suppose that TABLE-A begins at memory location 8,000 (base 10). Then TABLE-B (1) also begins at memory location 8,000, and both TABLE-A and TABLE-B (1) have a displacement of zero. TABLE-B (2) begins at memory location 8,006 and has a displacement of 6, meaning there are six bytes before it in the table. TABLE-B (3) begins at memory location 8,012 and has a displacement of 12, and so on. (See Figure 7–28.)

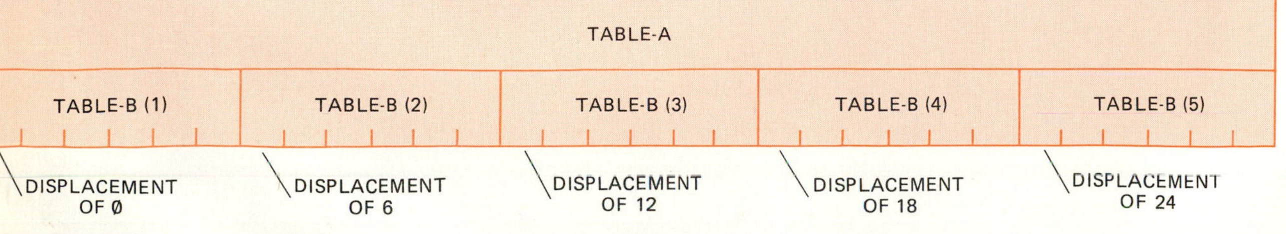

FIGURE 7–28

COBOL uses the information in the DATA DIVISION description of the table to calculate a displacement. It then adds the calculated displacement to the memory location of the beginning of the table. This gives the location of the table element. Let us use TABLE-B (4) as an example. The steps are:

Each element of TABLE-C is an elementary item with a PICTURE of 9(4). TABLE-C has three elements for each occurrence of TABLE-B, or a total of 12 elements, each of which is four bytes. Two subscripts are required to identify an element of TABLE-C. The first identifies an element of TABLE-B, the second the given element of TABLE-C. (See Figure 7–20.)

TABLE-A											
TABLE-B (1)			TABLE-B (2)			TABLE-B (3)			TABLE-B (4)		
TABLE-C (1, 1)	TABLE-C (1, 2)	TABLE-C (1, 3)	TABLE-C (2, 1)	TABLE-C (2, 2)	TABLE-C (2, 3)	TABLE-C (3, 1)	TABLE-C (3, 2)	TABLE-C (3, 3)	TABLE-C (4, 1)	TABLE-C (4, 2)	TABLE-C (4, 3)

FIGURE 7–20

Let us store a quantity in the two-dimensional TABLE-C. Data coming from an input record will contain both the amount to be added (QUANTITY) and the subscripts (REGION and BRANCH). In the following example, a comma followed by a space is used to separate the two subscripts. If desired, the comma may be omitted. The input data and ADD statements with the values substituted for the data-names are shown in Figure 7–21.

```
ADD QUANTITY TO TABLE-C (REGION, BRANCH).
```

INPUT DATA		
Quantity	Region	Branch
10	1	1
15	1	1
25	1	2
15	1	2
5	1	3
20	2	1
10	2	2
25	2	2
50	2	3
5	3	2
40	3	2
20	3	3
15	4	1
25	4	1
10	4	2
55	4	3
15	4	3

```
CONTENTS OF TABLE BEFORE ANY ADDS
```

0000	0000	0000	0000	0000	0000	0000	0000	0000	0000	0000	0000

```
ADD 10 TO TABLE-C (1, 1).
```

0010	0000	0000	0000	0000	0000	0000	0000	0000	0000	0000	0000

```
ADD 15 TO TABLE-C (1, 1).
```

0025	0000	0000	0000	0000	0000	0000	0000	0000	0000	0000	0000

```
ADD 25 TO TABLE-C (1, 2).
```

0025	0025	0000	0000	0000	0000	0000	0000	0000	0000	0000	0000

```
ADD 15 TO TABLE-C (1, 2).
```

0025	0040	0000	0000	0000	0000	0000	0000	0000	0000	0000	0000

```
ADD 5 TO TABLE-C (1, 3).
```

FIGURE 7–21

```
| 0025 | 0040 | 0005 | 0000 | 0000 | 0000 | 0000 | 0000 | 0000 | 0000 | 0000 | 0000 |
ADD 20 TO TABLE-C (2, 1).
| 0025 | 0040 | 0005 | 0020 | 0000 | 0000 | 0000 | 0000 | 0000 | 0000 | 0000 | 0000 |
ADD 10 TO TABLE-C (2, 2).
| 0025 | 0040 | 0005 | 0020 | 0010 | 0000 | 0000 | 0000 | 0000 | 0000 | 0000 | 0000 |
ADD 25 TO TABLE-C (2, 2).
| 0025 | 0040 | 0005 | 0020 | 0035 | 0000 | 0000 | 0000 | 0000 | 0000 | 0000 | 0000 |
ADD 50 TO TABLE-C (2, 3).
| 0025 | 0040 | 0005 | 0020 | 0035 | 0050 | 0000 | 0000 | 0000 | 0000 | 0000 | 0000 |
ADD 5 TO TABLE-C (3, 2).
| 0025 | 0040 | 0005 | 0020 | 0035 | 0050 | 0000 | 0005 | 0000 | 0000 | 0000 | 0000 |
ADD 40 TO TABLE-C (3, 2).
| 0025 | 0040 | 0005 | 0020 | 0035 | 0050 | 0000 | 0045 | 0000 | 0000 | 0000 | 0000 |
ADD 20 TO TABLE-C (3, 3).
| 0025 | 0040 | 0005 | 0020 | 0035 | 0050 | 0000 | 0045 | 0020 | 0000 | 0000 | 0000 |
ADD 15 TO TABLE-C (4, 1).
| 0025 | 0040 | 0005 | 0020 | 0035 | 0050 | 0000 | 0045 | 0020 | 0015 | 0000 | 0000 |
ADD 25 TO TABLE-C (4, 1).
| 0025 | 0040 | 0005 | 0020 | 0035 | 0050 | 0000 | 0045 | 0020 | 0040 | 0000 | 0000 |
ADD 10 TO TABLE-C (4, 2).
| 0025 | 0040 | 0005 | 0020 | 0035 | 0050 | 0000 | 0045 | 0020 | 0040 | 0010 | 0000 |
ADD 55 TO TABLE-C (4, 3).
| 0025 | 0040 | 0005 | 0020 | 0035 | 0050 | 0000 | 0045 | 0020 | 0040 | 0010 | 0055 |
ADD 15 TO TABLE-C (4, 3).
| 0025 | 0040 | 0005 | 0020 | 0035 | 0050 | 0000 | 0045 | 0020 | 0040 | 0010 | 0070 |
```

FIGURE 7–21 cont.

Three-Dimensional Tables

A two-dimensional table is essentially one table inside another. A three-dimensional table carries this concept one step further: it is a table inside a table which in turn is inside another table. (See Figure 7–22.)

```
01  TABLE-A.
    05  TABLE-B     OCCURS 2 TIMES.
        10  TABLE-C     OCCURS 4 TIMES.
            15  TABLE-D     OCCURS 3 TIMES      PIC 9(2).
```

In the figure, TABLE-A is a group item and includes 48 bytes of storage. It may not be subscripted when referred to in the PROCEDURE DIVISION. (See Figure 7–23.)

TABLE-B is also a group item. It consists of two elements, each of which represents 24 bytes of storage. References to TABLE-B must include one subscript in order to identify which of the two elements is being referred to. (See Figure 7–24.)

TABLE-C in turn is a group item which consists
element of TABLE-B. Since TABLE-B has two elemen
eight. References to TABLE-C require two subscripts, the
an element of TABLE-B and the second of which indicates
C within that element of TABLE-B. (See Figure 7–25.)

Finally, each element of TABLE-D is an elementary ite
9(2). TABLE-D has three elements for each element of TABLE
total of 24 elements. References to TABLE-D require three su
indicating an element of TABLE-B, the second an element of TA
third an element of TABLE-D. (See Figure 7–26.) A three-dimensio
be used to store data by branch, region, and salesperson.

> **Under the 1974 standard of COBOL, a maximum of three dimensions is for tables. The 1985 standard increases this to seven dimensions.**

TABLE-A							
TABLE-B (1)				TABLE-B (2)			
TABLE-C (1, 1)	TABLE-C (1, 2)	TABLE-C (1, 3)	TABLE-C (1, 4)	TABLE-C (2, 1)	TABLE-C (2, 2)	TABLE-C (2, 3)	TABE-C (2, 4)
(1, 1, 1) (1, 1, 2) (1, 1, 3)	(1, 2, 1) (1, 2, 2) (1, 2, 3)	(1, 3, 1) (1, 3, 2) (1, 3, 3)	(1, 4, 1) (1, 4, 2) (1, 4, 3)	(2, 1, 1) (2, 1, 2) (2, 1, 3)	(2, 2, 1) (2, 2, 2) (2, 2, 3)	(2, 3, 1) (2, 3, 2) (2, 3, 3)	(2, 4, 1) (2, 4, 2) (2, 4, 3)

TABLE-D

FIGURE 7–22

TABLE-A

FIGURE 7–23

TABLE-A	
TABLE-B (1)	TABLE-B (2)

FIGURE 7–24

TABLE-A							
TABLE-B (1)				TABLE-B (2)			
TABLE-C (1, 1)	TABLE-C (1, 2)	TABLE-C (1, 3)	TABLE-C (1, 4)	TABLE-C (2, 1)	TABLE-C (2, 2)	TABLE-C (2, 3)	TABI (2,

FIGURE 7–25

1. Subtract 1 from the subscript 4
− 1
3
2. Multiply by the size of an element * 6
18
3. Add the starting location of the table + 8,000
8,018

One is subtracted from the subscript so that the element to be located is not included in the calculation: the number of bytes located *ahead of* the element is the result desired.

Subscript Range

COBOL will not issue a diagnostic message if the subscript is too small or too large for the number of elements in the table. It proceeds instead with the calculation of the displacement and points to an area of memory outside the table. Using the table in Figure 7–28, let us execute the following instruction when BRANCH has a value of 8.

```
ADD QUANTITY TO TABLE-B (BRANCH).
```

8	(subscript)
− 1	
7	
* 6	(size of one element)
42	
+ 8,000	(beginning of TABLE-B)
8,042	

Since the last byte in the table is at location 8,029, COBOL will try to add QUANTITY to an area outside the table. Some possible results are as follows:

1. The area will be alphanumeric or have a different usage of numeric data than does TABLE-B, and the program will fail in trying to use the data. (See the discussion of data exceptions in Chapter 6.)
2. The area will contain numeric data of the same usage as TABLE-B, but the program will then produce the wrong answer in the wrong place. The value of the data item at location 8,042 will have been destroyed.

The moral of this example is that the programmer cannot depend on COBOL to use only subscripts that are in the proper range for the table. Instead, the value should be checked to see whether it lies within the range of the number of table elements before using it as a subscript.

Let us repeat the process of locating a data element in a table with a two-dimensional table. Figure 7–29 shows the calculations involved.

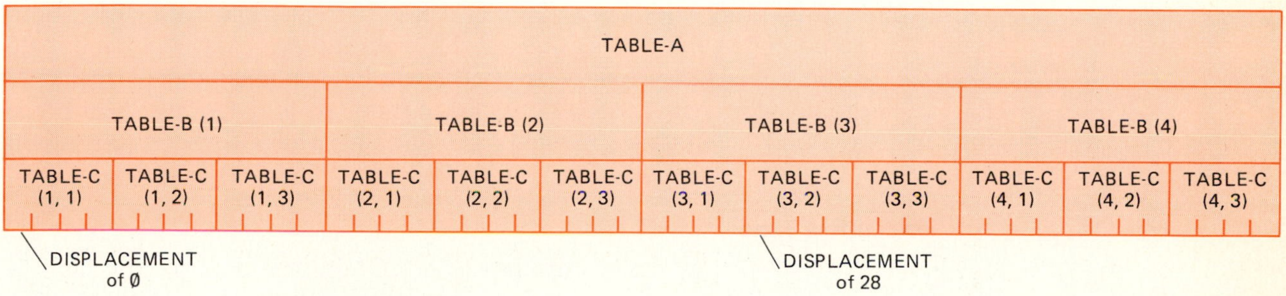

TABLE-A											
TABLE-B (1)			TABLE-B (2)			TABLE-B (3)			TABLE-B (4)		
TABLE-C (1, 1)	TABLE-C (1, 2)	TABLE-C (1, 3)	TABLE-C (2, 1)	TABLE-C (2, 2)	TABLE-C (2, 3)	TABLE-C (3, 1)	TABLE-C (3, 2)	TABLE-C (3, 3)	TABLE-C (4, 1)	TABLE-C (4, 2)	TABLE-C (4, 3)

DISPLACEMENT of Ø

DISPLACEMENT of 28

FIGURE 7–29

```
01  TABLE-A.
    05  TABLE-B     OCCURS 4 TIMES.
        10  TABLE-C     OCCURS 3 TIMES      PIC 9(4).

    ADD QUANTITY TO TABLE-C (REGION, BRANCH).
        REGION = 3
        BRANCH = 2
```

1. Subtract 1 from first subscript	3
	− 1
	2
2. Multiply by the size of an element (for TABLE-B)	* 12
	24
3. Subtract 1 from second subscript	2
	− 1
	1
4. Multiply by the size of an element (for TABLE-C)	* 4
	4
5. Add both answers to the origin of the table	8,000
	+ 24
	+ 4
	8,028

The technique is the same for a three-dimensional table, except that there is one more subscript from which to subtract 1. The result is then multiplied by the size of an element for the table the subscript represents, and the resulting product is added to the beginning location of the table along with the other two results. The reader should try a few combinations of subscripts to satisfy him- or herself that the technique works.

Overview of Table Handling

Loading Tables

In general, there are three times when program logic requires a table to be loaded (filled) with data.

Compile Time

The table data is coded in the DATA DIVISION using VALUE clauses, is compiled along with the rest of the program, and becomes a part of the object code. Data used in this manner should be of a permanent nature so that the program does not have to be recompiled to change it. An example of such data is the names of the months. Compile-time loading is discussed in Chapter 8.

Preprocess Time

Data is input from a keyboard or file, usually in the initialization routine. This technique is used when the data is of a less permanent nature; it provides the option of changing the data each time the program executes. The table data is loaded in the initialization routine so that it will be available as each record of the regular input files is processed. Examples of this type of data are freight rates, interest rates, and commission rates. This technique will also be discussed in Chapter 8.

Execution Time

Data is developed as records are processed. Often, the data for the table is the result of calculations made in processing input records. The result is then stored in the appropriate element of the table. This technique is used in the TABLE-1 program of this chapter for storing the totals by BRANCH of ORD-QUANTITY and EXTENDED-PRICE.

Accessing Tables

Three methods are in common use to access data in a table. The first is dependent on the location and the other two on the contents of an element.

Direct Access

Subscripts (or indices) are used to pinpoint the element required. Their value identifies the element by location regardless of its value. This technique was used in the TABLE-1 by means of the following statements:

```
ADD ORD-QUANTITY TO TBL-BRANCH-QUANTITY (ORD-BRANCH).
MOVE TBL-BRANCH-QUANTITY (BRANCH-SUB) TO
  TBL-DET-BRANCH-EXT-PRICE.
```

In the ADD statement, the subscript ORD-BRANCH is used to select the element to which ORD-QUANTITY will be added. The amount is added *directly* to the proper element without considering any others. When it is time to print the table, BRANCH-SUB is used as a counter and varied from 1 to 10 in order to directly access rows 1 through 10 and MOVE them from the table.

Linear or Serial Search

In order to search for an element in the table, a search argument (the value sought) is required. A linear search is started at some point in the table, and the search argument is compared against each element of the table until a match is found. The matching element in the table is called the *search function*. There are two methods of searching which may be used in a COBOL program. The first requires more effort from the programmer. A subscript is initialized with a value corresponding to the point in the table where the search should start. The programmer then compares the search argument with that table element. If they are equal, the search is over; if not, 1 is added to the subscript and the comparison is made again. This continues until a match is found for the search argument or the end of the table is reached. The second way uses the same principle, but employs the COBOL verb SEARCH which automatically incorporates some of the other steps. Both linear search techniques are discussed in Chapter 8.

Binary Search

A binary search can be performed only on a table that is in ascending or descending order on the search function. Binary searching is a very efficient method when used with large tables. The fact that the table is in order by search function allows the elimination of one-half of the table from the search after each attempt to match a search argument and a search function. To see how this works, suppose the table is in ascending order. Then the search is started at a table entry in the middle of the table. There are three possible results based on the comparison:

1. The table entries above the comparison are eliminated because their search functions are too low.
2. The table entries below the comparison are eliminated because their search functions are too high.
3. The search function of the compared entry matches the search argument. Then the compared entry is the entry we are looking for.

If a match is not found, the process is repeated by going to the middle of the remaining entries until either a match is found or there are no more entries to try. The binary search is discussed in Chapter 8.

Loading an Execution-Time Table

Sample Program

In the TABLE-1 program, ORD-QUANTITY and EXTENDED-PRICE are added to the table at execution time in 2000-PROCESS. ORD-BRANCH is used as the subscript. Each input record carries the data (directly or by calculation) to be added to the table and also the ORD-BRANCH subscript used to locate the table elements to which the data should be added. (See Figure 7–30).

An Alternative Approach

Adding to the table each time an input record is processed is not the most efficient approach. Rather, after the totals for an entire branch have been accumulated, they should be MOVEd or ADDed as a unit to the table. Using this approach requires that only one MOVE or ADD be executed for each field per branch, instead of one ADD per field per record. Indeed, it is because the transfer is done only once per field per branch into a unique table element that a MOVE can be used as well as an ADD. If it happened more than once per branch, only an ADD could be used, since any additional MOVEs to a single table element would overlay the first one.

To alter the TABLE-1 program in accordance with this approach, the statements used to add quantity and extended price to the table would be removed from 2000-PROCESS, and the following two statements would be added to 9200-BRANCH-TOTALS between the points where 9300-SALES-REP-TOTALS are performed and the branch totals are zeroed out:

```
ADD BRANCH-QUANTITY TO TBL-BRANCH-QUANTITY
  (HOLD-BRANCH).
ADD BRANCH-EXT-PRICE TO TBL-BRANCH-EXT-PRICE
  (HOLD-BRANCH).
```

Notice that it is the accumulated BRANCH- amounts rather than the input ORD- amounts that are being added to the table. This is done in 9200-BRANCH-TOTALS, where the records for a branch have just been processed and the branch totals are being printing and rolled into the final totals. This makes it possible to put the totals in the table with the execution of just one ADD per field per branch.

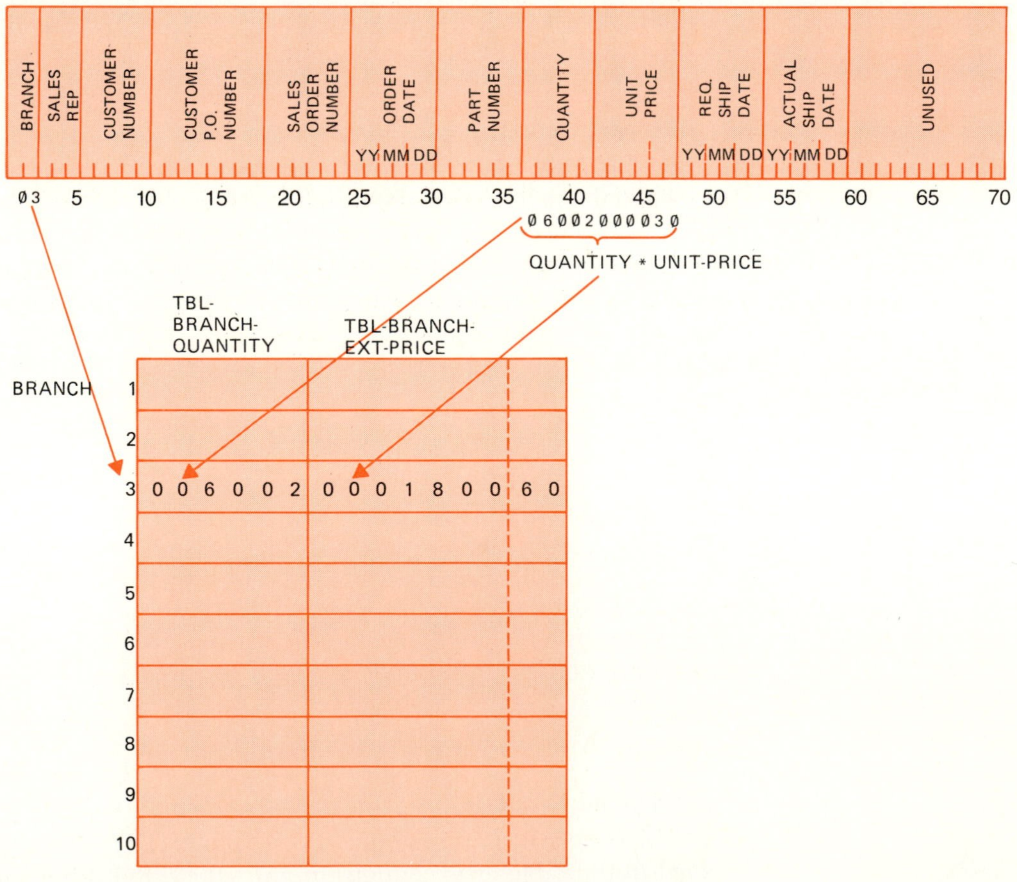

FIGURE 7–30

Notice also that the subscript has changed. In the original program it was ORD-BRANCH, so that each record provided the subscript. Now the totals are being added in the branch totals routine, which is performed because of a change in ORD-BRANCH. Assume the change was from an ORD-BRANCH of 1 to an ORD-BRANCH of 2. Then HOLD-BRANCH contains a 1 and ORD-BRANCH contains a 2. Now, the totals are for Branch 1. But then, if ORD-BRANCH were used as the subscript, the totals for Branch 1 would be put in the second element of TBL-BRANCH-ROW. To avoid this, the HOLD- is used as the subscript. It is used *before* it is updated by moving ORD-BRANCH to HOLD-BRANCH.

Writing Out a Table

In writing out a table, the major things to take into consideration are (1) the number of dimensions the table has, and (2) the form the output is to take. In what follows, we shall consider some of the possible combinations, starting with one-dimensional tables and working up to three-dimensional tables. The COBOL statement used most often for this purpose is PERFORM . . . VARYING.

PERFORM . . . VARYING

Format

```
                                  {THROUGH}
PERFORM procedure-name-1 [       {THRU   }  procedure-name-2]
                                       {literal-2   }
    VARYING identifier-1   FROM {identifier-2}
       {literal-3   }
    BY {identifier-3}   UNTIL condition-1

                                      {literal-5   }
    [AFTER identifier-4   FROM {identifier-5}
       {literal-6   }
    BY {identifier-6}   UNTIL condition-2

                                      {literal-8   }
    [AFTER identifier-7   FROM {identifier-8}
       {literal-9   }
    BY {identifier-9}  UNTIL condition-3]   ]
```

PERFORM . . . VARYING is used to perform a routine multiple times. It can increment or decrement one or more variables each time the routine is performed. This is particularly useful when a routine must be done more than once, with different values each time. (See Figure 7–31.) The general steps are as follows:

1. Initialize a variable.
2. Test for some condition.
3. If the condition is false, perform the routine, increment or decrement the variable, and return to step 2.
4. If the condition is true, pass to the statement following the PERFORM statement.

Up to three data items can be varied using PERFORM . . . VARYING. When several data items are varied, the one mentioned first is varied least often and the one mentioned last is varied most often.

In the 1985 standard, PERFORM . . . VARYING must allow at least six AFTER clauses. This allows seven subscripts to be varied and matches the maximum number of dimensions a table may have under the new standard.

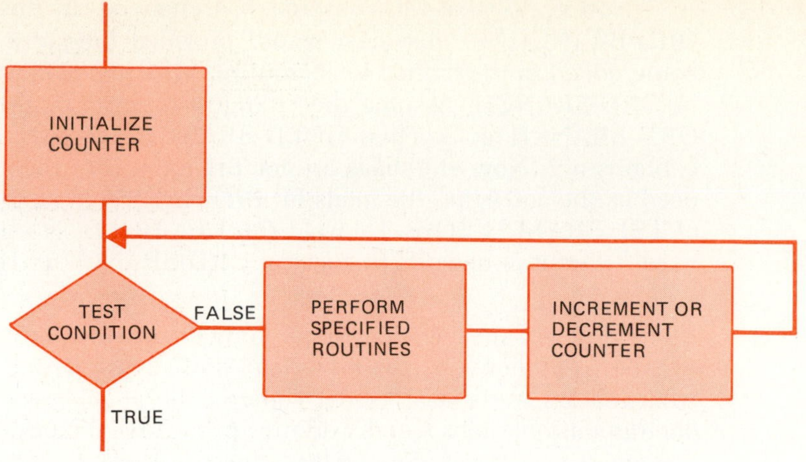

FIGURE 7–31

Writing a One-Dimensional Table

Consider a one-dimensional table containing quarterly sales, each quarter's sales to be printed on a separate line. Figure 7–32 shows the print chart. The storage definitions for the table and print line, and the PROCEDURE DIVISION code necessary to create the output follow.

The Table Definition

```
01  QUARTERLY-SALE-TABLE.
    05  QUARTERLY-SALES  OCCURS 4 TIMES
          PIC 9(6)V9(2).
```

The Print Line

```
01  TABLE-PRINT-LINE.
    05  FILLER          PIC X(20)     VALUE SPACES.
    05  FILLER          PIC X(8)      VALUE 'QUARTER '.
    05  QUARTER-OUT     PIC 9(1).
    05  FILLER          PIC X(20)     VALUE SPACES.
    05  QUARTERLY-SALES-OUT  PIC ZZZZ9.99.
    05  FILLER          PIC X(21)     VALUE SPACES.
```

The Procedure Division

```
3400-WRITE-Q-SALES-TABLE.
    WRITE PRINT-RECORD FROM TABLE-HEADING-LINE
        AFTER ADVANCING PAGE.
    PERFORM 3410-WRITE-Q-SALES-LINE
        VARYING QUARTER FROM 1 BY 1
            UNTIL QUARTER > 4.

3410-WRITE-Q-SALES-LINE.
    MOVE QUARTER TO QUARTER-OUT.
    MOVE QUARTERLY-SALES (QUARTER) TO
      QUARTERLY-SALES-OUT.
    WRITE PRINT-RECORD FROM TABLE-PRINT-LINE
      AFTER ADVANCING 2 LINES.
```

Paragraph 3400-WRITE-Q-SALES-TABLE prints the heading line for the table. The PERFORM . . . VARYING in it causes 3410-WRITE-Q-SALES-LINE to be performed four times. The value of QUARTER is initialized to 1 (FROM 1),

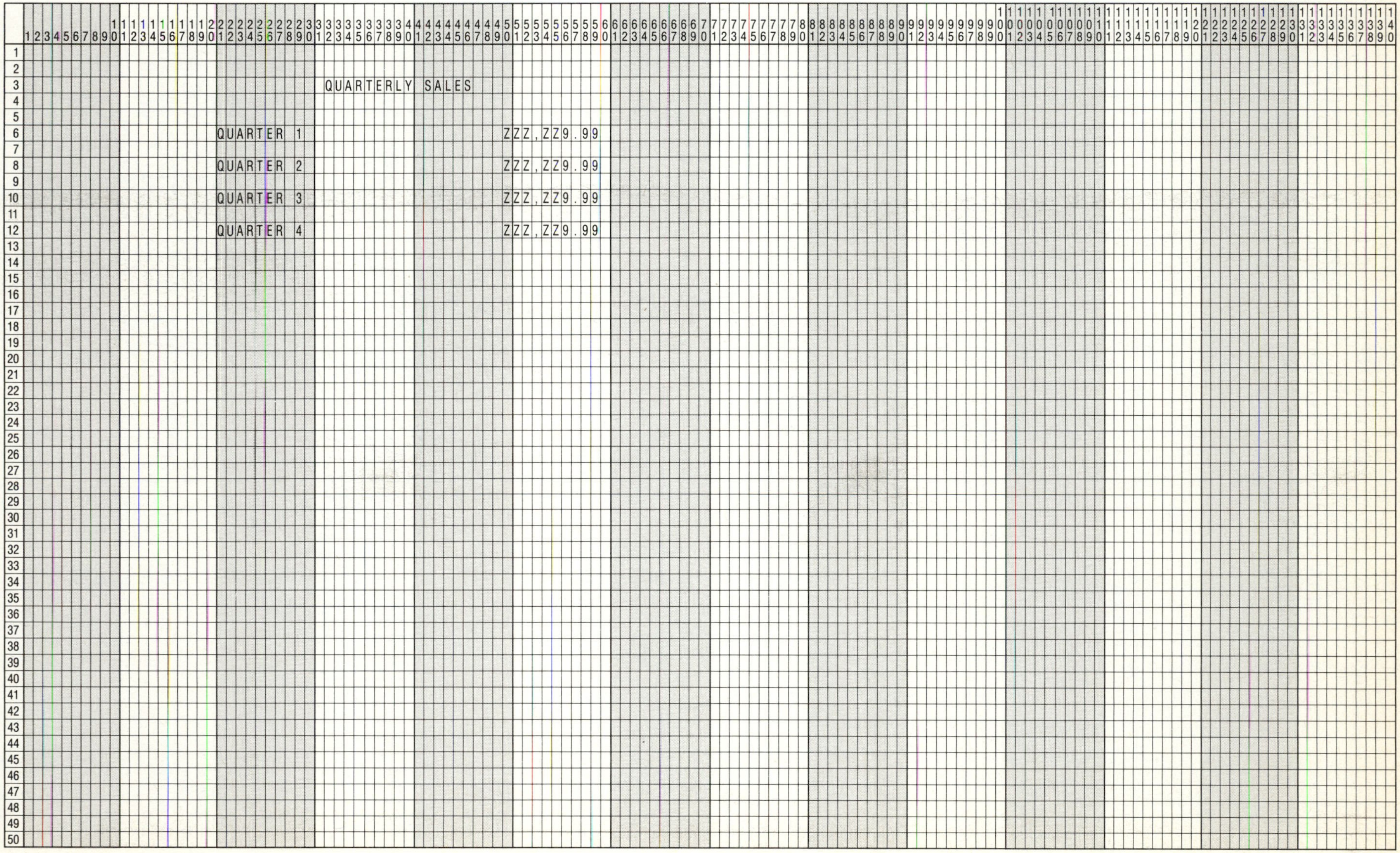

```
                               QUARTERLY SALES


                    QUARTER 1                     ZZZ,ZZ9.99

                    QUARTER 2                     ZZZ,ZZ9.99

                    QUARTER 3                     ZZZ,ZZ9.99

                    QUARTER 4                     ZZZ,ZZ9.99
```

FIGURE 7–32

and QUARTER is incremented by 1 (BY 1) each time the paragraph is performed. The paragraph is performed until QUARTER exceeds the limit (UNTIL QUARTER > 4). With PERFORM . . . VARYING, the increment or decrement is done after execution of the procedure. Thus, after performing the paragraph for the fourth time, QUARTER is incremented to five. This makes the test condition true and the PERFORM . . . VARYING complete. (See Figure 7–33.)

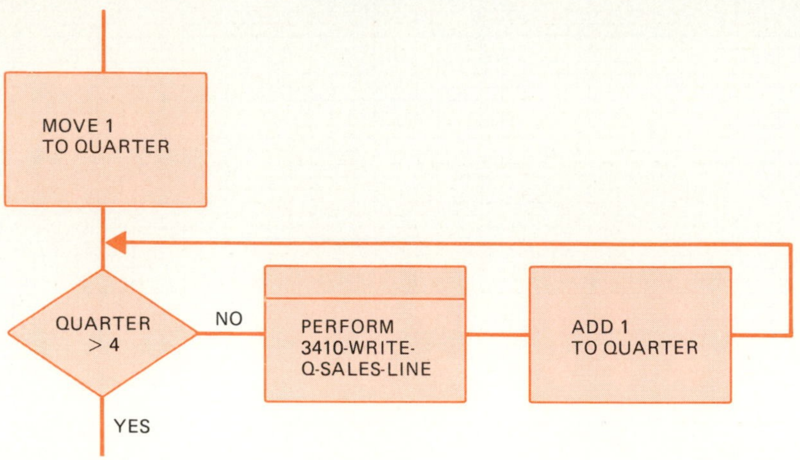

FIGURE 7–33

Let us look at how the ability to vary QUARTER assists in the printing of the table. The data-name QUARTER was chosen as a reminder that each line represents a quarter. QUARTER is used as a counter twice in 3410-WRITE-Q-SALES-LINE, first to MOVE the number of the quarter to an area in the print line, and second as a subscript to control which element of QUARTERLY-SALES is moved to an area in the print line.

Often, one-dimensional tables have multiple subordinate data elements for each occurrence of a table element. Such a table and the code necessary to write it on paper follow. The print chart is shown in Figure 7–34.

The Table Definition

```
01  QUARTERLY-TAX-WITHHOLDING.
    05  QUARTERLY-TAXES OCCURS 4 TIMES.
        10  FICA-EMPLOYER    PIC 9(6)V9(2).
        10  FICA-EMPLOYEE    PIC 9(6)V9(2).
        10  FUTA             PIC 9(4)V9(2).
        10  FED-INCOME-TAX   PIC 9(8)V9(2).
```

The Print Line

```
01  TAX-TABLE-PRINT-LINE.
    05  FILLER               PIC X(8)     VALUE SPACES.
    05  QUARTER              PIC 9(1).
    05  FILLER               PIC X(6)     VALUE SPACES.
    05  FICA-EMPLOYER-OUT    PIC ZZZ,ZZ9.99.
    05  FILLER               PIC X(6)     VALUE SPACES.
    05  FICA-EMPLOYEE-OUT    PIC ZZZ,ZZ9.99.
    05  FILLER               PIC X(6)     VALUE SPACES.
    05  FUTA-OUT             PIC Z,ZZ9.99.
    05  FILLER               PIC X(6)     VALUE SPACES.
    05  FED-INCOME-TAX-OUT   PIC ZZ,ZZZ,ZZ9.99.
    05  FILLER               PIC X(6)     VALUE SPACES.
```

```
                         QUARTERLY TAXES

                  FICA             FICA                        FEDERAL
    QUARTER     EMPLOYER         EMPLOYEE          FUTA       INCOME TAX

          9    ZZZ,ZZ9.99       ZZZ,ZZ9.99      Z,ZZ9.99    ZZ,ZZZ,ZZ9.99

          9    ZZZ,ZZ9.99       ZZZ,ZZ9.99      Z,ZZ9.99    ZZ,ZZZ,ZZ9.99
```

FIGURE 7–34

The Procedure Division

```
3500-WRITE-Q-TAX-TABLE.
    WRITE PRINT-RECORD FROM MAIN-HEADING
        AFTER ADVANCING PAGE.
    WRITE PRINT-RECORD FROM COL-HEADING-1
        AFTER ADVANCING 3 LINES.
    WRITE PRINT-RECORD FROM COL-HEADING-2
        AFTER ADVANCING 1 LINE.
    PERFORM 3510-WRITE-Q-TAX-LINE
        VARYING QUARTER FROM 1 BY 1
            UNTIL QUARTER IS > 4.

3510-WRITE-Q-TAX-LINE.
    MOVE QUARTER TO QUARTER-OUT.
    MOVE FICA-EMPLOYER (QUARTER)  TO FICA-EMPLOYER-OUT.
    MOVE FICA-EMPLOYEE (QUARTER)  TO FICA-EMPLOYEE-OUT.
    MOVE FUTA (QUARTER)           TO FUTA-OUT.
    MOVE-FED-INCOME-TAX (QUARTER) TO FED-INCOME-TAX-OUT.
    WRITE PRINT-RECORD FROM TAX-TABLE-PRINT-LINE
        AFTER ADVANCING 2 LINES.
```

Since each element of QUARTERLY-TAXES has four subordinate fields, four MOVEs are needed to transfer each element of the table to a print line. Each data-name used from the table is subscripted by QUARTER to indicate which element the data-name is part of. The first time 3510-WRITE-Q-TAX-LINE is performed, QUARTER will have the value 1. Each of the four data items subordinate to the first element of QUARTERLY-TAXES, as well as the digit 1, which QUARTER represents on this pass, will be moved to the print line.

Notice that the major difference between this and the previous example is the increased number of MOVE statements because of the four data items subordinate to QUARTERLY-TAXES. In both cases, however, references to table elements use a single subscript since the table is one-dimensional.

Writing a Two-Dimensional Table

Suppose that an organization's net pay is stored in a two-dimensional table by division and department. Suppose further that the table is to be printed in the EOJ routine. The print chart is shown in Figure 7–35. The storage definition of the table and print line, and the PROCEDURE DIVISION code follow.

The Print Chart

The Table Definition

```
01  NET-PAY-TABLE.
    05  DIVISION-ELEMENT        OCCURS 10 TIMES.
        10  DEPARTMENT-ELEMENT OCCURS 5 TIMES
                PIC 9(8)V9(2).
```

The Print Line

```
01  NET-PAY-TABLE-LINE.
    05  FILLER          PIC X(10)     VALUE SPACES.
    05  FILLER          PIC X(9)      VALUE
                                        'DIVISION '.
    05  DIVISION-OUT    PIC 9(1).
    05  FILLER          PIC X(8)      VALUE SPACES.
    05  DEPT-1-OUT      PIC ZZ,ZZZ,ZZ9.99.
    05  FILLER          PIC X(8)      VALUE SPACES.
    05  DEPT-2-OUT      PIC ZZ,ZZZ,ZZ9.99.
```

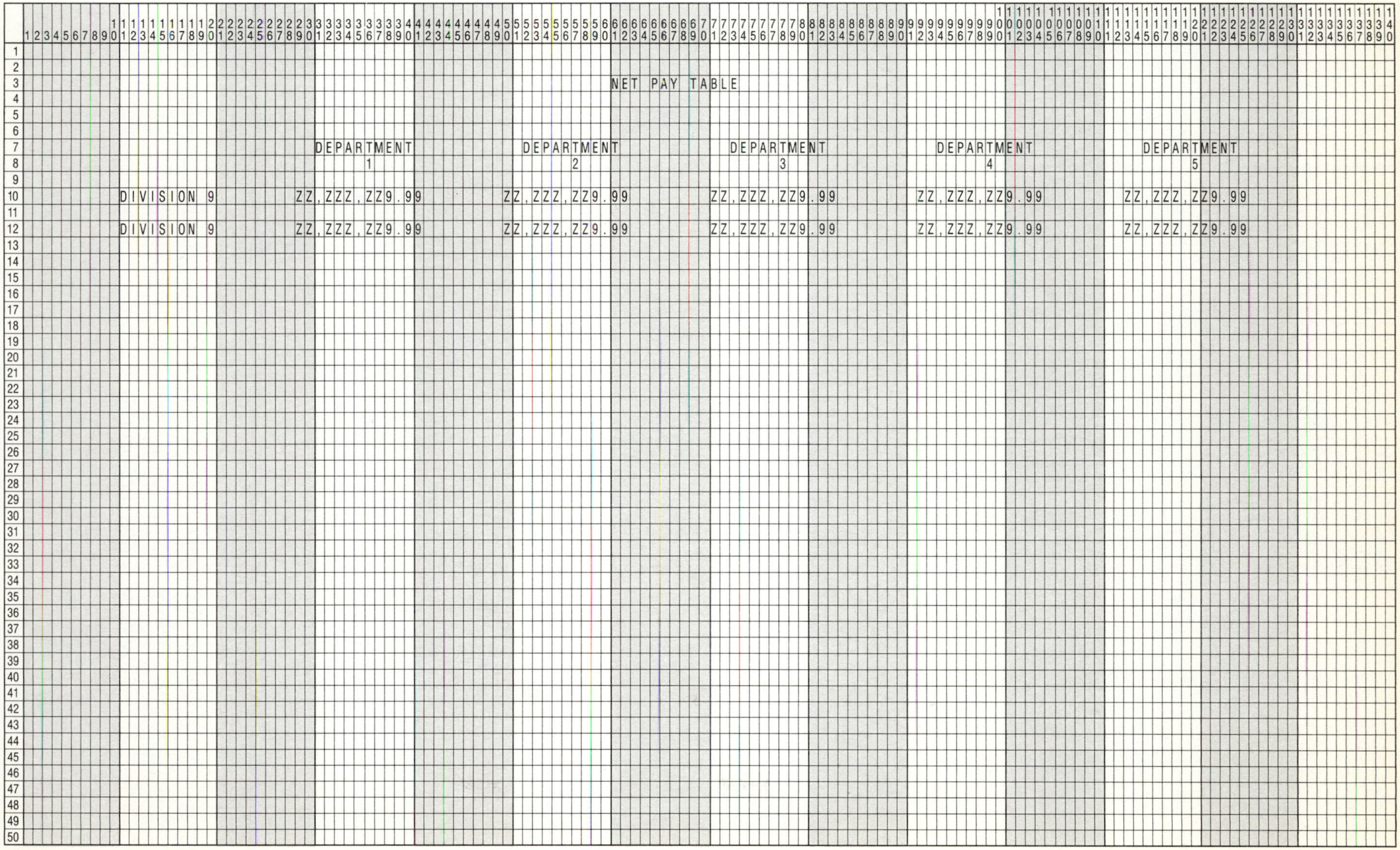

```
                                                                NET PAY TABLE

                                   DEPARTMENT                DEPARTMENT                DEPARTMENT                DEPARTMENT                DEPARTMENT
                                       1                         2                         3                         4                         5

              DIVISION 9         ZZ,ZZZ,ZZ9.99             ZZ,ZZZ,ZZ9.99             ZZ,ZZZ,ZZ9.99             ZZ,ZZZ,ZZ9.99             ZZ,ZZZ,ZZ9.99

              DIVISION 9         ZZ,ZZZ,ZZ9.99             ZZ,ZZZ,ZZ9.99             ZZ,ZZZ,ZZ9.99             ZZ,ZZZ,ZZ9.99             ZZ,ZZZ,ZZ9.99
```

FIGURE 7–35

```
    05  FILLER           PIC X(8)      VALUE SPACES.
    05  DEPT-3-OUT       PIC ZZ,ZZZ,ZZ9.99.
    05  FILLER           PIC X(8)      VALUE SPACES.
    05  DEPT-4-OUT       PIC ZZ,ZZZ,ZZ9.99.
    05  FILLER           PIC X(8)      VALUE SPACES.
    05  DEPT-5-OUT       PIC ZZ,ZZZ,ZZ9.99.
    05  FILLER           PIC X(8).
```

The Procedure Division

```
3000-EOJ.
    .
    .
    .
    WRITE PRINT-RECORD FROM TABLE-HEADING
        AFTER ADVANCING PAGE.
    WRITE PRINT-RECORD FROM COL-HEADING-1
        AFTER ADVANCING 3 LINES.
    WRITE PRINT-RECORD FROM COL-HEADING-2
        AFTER ADVANCING 1 LINE.
    PERFORM 3200-WRITE-NET-PAY-LINE
        VARYING DIV-SUB FROM 1 BY 1
            UNTIL DIV-SUB > 10.
    .
    .
    .
3200-WRITE-NET-PAY-LINE.
    MOVE DIV-SUB TO DIVISION-OUT.
    MOVE DEPARTMENT-ELEMENT (DIV-SUB, 1) TO
      DEPT-1-OUT.
    MOVE DEPARTMENT-ELEMENT (DIV-SUB, 2) TO
      DEPT-2-OUT.
    MOVE DEPARTMENT-ELEMENT (DIV-SUB, 3) TO
      DEPT-3-OUT.
    MOVE DEPARTMENT-ELEMENT (DIV-SUB, 4) TO
      DEPT-4-OUT.
    MOVE DEPARTMENT-ELEMENT (DIV-SUB, 5) TO
      DEPT-5-OUT.
    WRITE PRINT-RECORD FROM NET-PAY-TABLE-LINE
        AFTER ADVANCING 2 LINES.
```

The word DEPARTMENT and the department numbers are provided in the column headings. The word DIVISION is a literal in the table detail line. The division number is provided by the subscript being varied (DIV-SUB). When the first line is prepared and printed in 3200-WRITE-NET-PAY-LINE, DIV-SUB will have a value of 1. This value is moved to DIVISION-OUT and represents the division number of the printed output. The second time 3200-WRITE-NET-PAY-LINE is performed, DIV-SUB will have a value of 2, then 3, and so on.

DIV-SUB is also used as the first of two subscripts to move data from the table. The first subscript represents the division, the second the department. DIV-SUB has a new value each time 3200-WRITE-NET-PAY-LINE is performed. This means that the data for a new division is transferred each time the routine is performed. The elements for each department within a division are identified by the second subscript, which is given as a literal (1 through 5). There are five different data-names for table elements on the print line; therefore, five MOVEs are required.

A Table within a Detail Line

The next example uses the same table definition and print chart as in Figure 7–35, but the detail line is described differently in WORKING-STORAGE. On the print chart, the FILLER of X(8) and the PICTURE of ZZ,ZZZ,ZZ9.99 are repeated five times. This portion of the print line has been turned into a table which has five elements. Figure 7–36 shows the new version of the print line and the PROCEDURE DIVISION code that moves the two-dimensional table to the one-dimensional table on the print line.

The Print Line

```
01  NET-PAY-TABLE-LINE2.
    05  FILLER             PIC X(10)   VALUE SPACES.
    05  FILLER             PIC X(9)    VALUE
                                         'DIVISION '.
    05  DIVISION-OUT       PIC 9(1).
    05  DEPT-TABLE-OUT                 VALUE SPACES.
        10  DEPT-ELEMENT-OUT           OCCURS 5 TIMES.
            15  FILLER   PIC X(8).
            15  TABLE-NET-PAY-OUT     PIC ZZ,ZZZ,ZZ9.99.
    05  FILLER             PIC X(8)    VALUE SPACES.
```

The Procedure Division

```
3000-EOJ.
    .
    .
    .
    WRITE PRINT-RECORD FROM TABLE-HEADING
        AFTER ADVANCING PAGE.
    WRITE PRINT-RECORD FROM COL-HEADING-1
        AFTER ADVANCING 3 LINES.
    WRITE PRINT-RECORD FROM COL-HEADING-2
        AFTER ADVANCING 1 LINE.
    PERFORM 3200-WRITE-NET-PAY-LINE
        VARYING DIV-SUB FROM 1 BY 1
            UNTIL DIV-SUB > 10.
3200-WRITE-NET-PAY-LINE.
    MOVE DIV-SUB TO DIVISION-OUT.
    PERFORM 3210-FILL-LINE
        VARYING DEPT-SUB FROM 1 BY 1
            UNTIL DEPT-SUB > 5.
    WRITE PRINT-RECORD FROM NET-PAY-TABLE-LINE2
        AFTER ADVANCING 2 LINES.

3210-FILL-LINE.
    MOVE DEPT-ELEMENT (DIV-SUB, DEPT-SUB) TO
        TABLE-NET-PAY-OUT (DEPT-SUB).
```

FIGURE 7–36

Only the portion of the detail line that is repetitive was turned into a table. A group name, DEPT-TABLE-OUT, was given to this portion. This allows the use of VALUE SPACES at the group level or MOVE SPACES to the group level as a part of the initialization. The 01 level could not be used for the initialization because the word DIVISION would be destroyed if MOVE SPACES TO NET-PAY-TABLE-LINE2 were used. The 10 level was necessary to establish an OCCURS clause. The two 15 levels represent the repeating pattern.

Rather than five MOVE statements with a literal as the second subscript, now there is one MOVE which is performed five times using a variable as the second subscript. 3000-EOJ performs 3200-WRITE-NET-PAY-LINE 10 times (once for each division). 3200-WRITE-NET-PAY-LINE in turn performs 3210-FILL-LINE five times (once for each department), DEPT-SUB assuming the values 1 through 5 in turn with each performance. This is the equivalent of the five MOVE statements in the previous example.

```
                                        SALES TABLE FOR REGION 9



                                    SALESPERSON                     SALESPERSON                     SALESPERSON                     SALESPERSON
                                         1                               2                               3                               4

               BRANCH 9           ZZ,ZZZ,ZZ9.99                   ZZ,ZZZ,ZZ9.99                   ZZ,ZZZ,ZZ9.99                   ZZ,ZZZ,ZZ9.99

               BRANCH 9           ZZ,ZZZ,ZZ9.99                   ZZ,ZZZ,ZZ9.99                   ZZ,ZZZ,ZZ9.99                   ZZ,ZZZ,ZZ9.99
```

FIGURE 7–37

Writing a Three-Dimensional Table

In writing a three-dimensional table, one dimension is usually transferred to the headings. Thus, given a three-dimensional table with information on states, counties, and cities, the name or number of the state would be incorporated in the heading. The counties and cities would then form the rows and columns. This would result in the printing of multiple two-dimensional tables, one for each state. Each table would then occupy all or part of a page.

Following are two examples of printing three-dimensional tables. Both use the same table definition, which includes sales data for regions, branches, and salespersons. In both examples, the word REGION is transferred to the headings. In the first example, each row of the output represents a branch and each column a salesperson. In the second example, each row represents a salesperson and each column a branch. Figure 7–37 shows the print chart and Figure 7–38 gives the COBOL code to write the first table.

The preceding routines print six two-dimensional tables, one for each occurrence of REGION-ELEMENT. This is controlled by the PERFORM . . . VARYING statement in 3000-EOJ: 3200-WRITE-REGION-TABLE is performed varying the first (REGION-SUB) of three subscripts.

In 3200-WRITE-REGION-TABLE, REGION-SUB is moved to an area in the main heading. This heading and the two column headings are then written. Note that the column headings include the salesperson numbers. Next, the 3210-WRITE-BRANCH-LINE routine is performed varying the second subscript (BRANCH-SUB).

In 3210-WRITE-BRANCH-LINE, BRANCH-SUB is moved to BRANCH-OUT to represent the branch number. Then four MOVE statements are used to transfer each of the salesperson elements for that branch. A literal is used as the subscript representing the salesperson. The line representing the salespersons for one branch of one region is then written.

The table subscripts for Region 1 are shown in Figure 7–39. When the last subscript is varied the most rapidly, as in the COBOL code in Figure 7–38, the table elements are moved out in the order shown in Figure 7–39.

The Print Chart

The Table Definition

```
01  SALES-TABLE.
    05  REGION-ELEMENT     OCCURS 6 TIMES.
        10  BRANCH-ELEMENT     OCCURS 7 TIMES.
            15  SALESPERSON-ELEMENT   OCCURS 4 TIMES
                    PIC 9(8)V9(2).
```

The Print Line

```
01  BRANCH-TABLE-LINE.
    05  FILLER               PIC X(12)   VALUE SPACES.
    05  FILLER               PIC X(7)    VALUE
                                            'BRANCH '.
    05  BRANCH-OUT           PIC 9(1).
    05  FILLER               PIC X(12)   VALUE SPACES.
    05  SALESPERSON-1-OUT    PIC ZZ,ZZZ,ZZ9.99.
    05  FILLER               PIC X(12)   VALUE SPACES.
    05  SALESPERSON-2-OUT    PIC ZZ,ZZZ,ZZ9.99.
    05  FILLER               PIC X(12)   VALUE SPACES.
    05  SALESPERSON-3-OUT    PIC ZZ,ZZZ,ZZ9.99.
    05  FILLER               PIC X(12)   VALUE SPACES.
    05  SALESPERSON-4-OUT    PIC ZZ,ZZZ,Z99.99.
    05  FILLER               PIC X(13)   VALUE SPACES.
```

FIGURE 7–38

The Procedure Division

```
3000-EOJ.
    .
    .
    .
    PERFORM 3200-WRITE-REGION-TABLE
        VARYING REGION-SUB FROM 1 BY 1
            UNTIL REGION-SUB > 6.

3200-WRITE-REGION-TABLE.
    MOVE REGION-SUB TO REGION-OUT.
    WRITE PRINT-RECORD FROM MAIN-HEADING
        AFTER ADVANCING PAGE.
    WRITE PRINT-RECORD FROM COL-HEADING-1
        AFTER ADVANCING 3 LINES.
    WRITE PRINT-RECORD FROM COL-HEADING-2
        AFTER ADVANCING 1 LINE.
    PERFORM 3210-WRITE-BRANCH-LINE
        VARYING BRANCH-SUB FROM 1 BY 1
            UNTIL BRANCH-SUB > 7.

3210-WRITE-BRANCH-LINE.
    MOVE BRANCH-SUB TO BRANCH-OUT.
    MOVE SALESPERSON-ELEMENT (REGION-SUB,
      BRANCH-SUB, 1) TO SALESPERSON-1-OUT.
    MOVE SALESPERSON-ELEMENT (REGION-SUB,
      BRANCH-SUB, 2) TO SALESPERSON-2-OUT.
    MOVE SALESPERSON-ELEMENT (REGION-SUB,
      BRANCH-SUB, 3) TO SALESPERSON-3-OUT.
    MOVE SALESPERSON-ELEMENT (REGION-SUB,
      BRANCH-SUB, 4) TO SALESPERSON-4-OUT.
    WRITE PRINT-RECORD FROM BRANCH-TABLE-LINE
        AFTER ADVANCING 2 LINES.
```

FIGURE 7–38 cont.

1 ←	1, 1, 1	1, 1, 2	1, 1, 3	1, 1, 4
2 ←	1, 2, 1	1, 2, 2	1, 2, 3	1, 2, 4
3 ←	1, 3, 1	1, 3, 2	1, 3, 3	1, 3, 4
4 ←	1, 4, 1	1, 4, 2	1, 4, 3	1, 4, 4
5 ←	1, 5, 1	1, 5, 2	1, 5, 3	1, 5, 4
6 ←	1, 6, 1	1, 6, 2	1, 6, 3	1, 6, 4
7 ←	1, 7, 1	1, 7, 2	1, 7, 3	1, 7, 4

FIGURE 7–39

The report can also be printed with sales representatives as the rows and branches as the columns. (See Figure 7–40.) To use the same table definition and produce this output, the table elements must be transferred in a different order. Since only Region 1 is used in both examples, it remains constant. In the previous example, the third subscript was varied first. Here, the second subscript is varied first. Figure 7–41 shows the COBOL code; the order in which the elements are moved is shown in Figure 7–42.

```
                                                   SALES TABLE FOR REGION 9



                        BRANCH           BRANCH          BRANCH          BRANCH          BRANCH          BRANCH          BRANCH
                           1                2               3               4               5               6               7

     SALESPERSON 9  ZZ,ZZZ,ZZ9.99   ZZ,ZZZ,ZZ9.99   ZZ,ZZZ,ZZ9.99   ZZ,ZZZ,ZZ9.99   ZZ,ZZZ,ZZ9.99   ZZ,ZZZ,ZZ9.99   ZZ,ZZZ,ZZ9.99

     SALESPERSON 9  ZZ,ZZZ,ZZ9.99   ZZ,ZZZ,ZZ9.99   ZZ,ZZZ,ZZ9.99   ZZ,ZZZ,ZZ9.99   ZZ,ZZZ,ZZ9.99   ZZ,ZZZ,ZZ9.99   ZZ,ZZZ,ZZ9.99
```

FIGURE 7–40

The Print Chart

The Table Definition

```
01  SALES-TABLE.
    05  REGION-ELEMENT                  OCCURS 6 TIMES.
        10  BRANCH-ELEMENT              OCCURS 7 TIMES.
            15  SALESPERSON-ELEMENT     OCCURS 4 TIMES
                    PIC 9(8)V9(2).
```

The Print Line

```
01  SALESPERSON-TABLE-LINE.
    05  FILLER              PIC X(4)    VALUE SPACES.
    05  FILLER              PIC X(12)   VALUE
                                          'SALESPERSON '.
    05  SALESPERSON-OUT     PIC 9(1).
    05  FILLER              PIC X(3)    VALUE SPACES.
    05  BRANCH-1-OUT        ZZ,ZZZ,ZZ9.99.
    05  FILLER              PIC X(3)    VALUE SPACES.
    05  BRANCH-2-OUT        ZZ,ZZZ,ZZ9.99.
    05  FILLER              PIC X(3)    VALUE SPACES.
    05  BRANCH-3-OUT        ZZ,ZZZ,ZZ9.99.
    05  FILLER              PIC X(3)    VALUE SPACES.
    05  BRANCH-4-OUT        ZZ,ZZZ,ZZ9.99.
    05  FILLER              PIC X(3)    VALUE SPACES.
    05  BRANCH-5-OUT        ZZ,ZZZ,ZZ9.99.
    05  FILLER              PIC X(3)    VALUE SPACES.
    05  BRANCH-6-OUT        ZZ,ZZZ,ZZ9.99.
    05  FILLER              PIC X(3)    VALUE SPACES.
    05  BRANCH-7-OUT        ZZ,ZZZ,ZZ9.99.
    05  FILLER              PIC X(4)    VALUE SPACES.
```

The Procedure Division

```
3000-EOJ.
    .
    .
    .
    PERFORM 3200-WRITE-REGION-TABLE
        VARYING REGION-SUB FROM 1 BY 1
            UNTIL REGION-SUB > 6.
    .
    .
    .
3200-WRITE-REGION-TABLE.
    MOVE REGION-SUB TO REGION-OUT.
    WRITE PRINT-RECORD FROM MAIN-HEADING
        AFTER ADVANCING PAGE.
    WRITE PRINT-RECORD FROM COL-HEADING-1
        AFTER ADVANCING 3 LINES.
    WRITE PRINT-RECORD FROM COL-HEADING-2
        AFTER ADVANCING 1 LINE.
    PERFORM 3210-WRITE-SALESPERSON-LINE
        VARYING SALESPERSON-SUB FROM 1 BY 1
            UNTIL SALESPERSON-SUB > 4.
3210-WRITE-SALESPERSON-LINE.
    MOVE SALESPERSON-SUB TO SALESPERSON-OUT.
    MOVE SALESPERSON-ELEMENT (REGION-SUB, 1,
      SALESPERSON-SUB)
        TO BRANCH-1-OUT.
    MOVE SALESPERSON-ELEMENT (REGION-SUB, 2,
      SALESPERSON-SUB)
        TO BRANCH-2-OUT.
```

FIGURE 7–41

```
MOVE SALESPERSON-ELEMENT (REGION-SUB, 3,
  SALESPERSON-SUB)
    TO BRANCH-3-OUT.
MOVE SALESPERSON-ELEMENT (REGION-SUB, 4,
  SALESPERSON-SUB)
    TO BRANCH-4-OUT.
MOVE SALESPERSON-ELEMENT (REGION-SUB, 5,
  SALESPERSON-SUB)
    TO BRANCH-5-OUT.
MOVE SALESPERSON-ELEMENT (REGION-SUB, 6,
  SALESPERSON-SUB)
    TO BRANCH-6-OUT.
MOVE SALESPERSON-ELEMENT (REGION-SUB, 7,
  SALESPERSON-SUB)
    TO BRANCH-7-OUT.
WRITE PRINT-RECORD FROM SALESPERSON-TABLE-LINE
    AFTER ADVANCING 2 LINES.
```

FIGURE 7–41 cont.

```
   1            2            3            4
   ↑            ↑            ↑            ↑
   |            |            |            |
1, 1, 1      1, 1, 2      1, 1, 3      1, 1, 4
1, 2, 1      1, 2, 2      1, 2, 3      1, 2, 4
1, 3, 1      1, 3, 2      1, 3, 3      1, 3, 4
1, 4, 1      1, 4, 2      1, 4, 3      1, 4, 4
1, 5, 1      1, 5, 2      1, 5, 3      1, 5, 4
1, 6, 1      1, 6, 2      1, 6, 3      1, 6, 4
1, 7, 1      1, 7, 2      1, 7, 3      1, 7, 4
```

FIGURE 7–42

DEBUGGING

Diagnostics

The following diagnostics are common in working with tables:

```
SUBSCRIPT MUST BE INTEGRAL DATA-NAME OR LITERAL
```

COBOL requires that a subscript be both numeric and an integer. To correct the problem, the programmer should

1. Find the data item denoting the subscript in the DATA DIVISION and check whether it is numeric.
2. Change the data item to numeric if it is not. If for any reason the data item *must* also be alphanumeric, use a REDEFINES clause.
3. Change the data item to an integer (no implied decimal point) if it is already numeric.

```
DATA-NAME IS NOT DEFINED AS SUBSCRIPTED OR INDEXED
```

A subscript has been placed on a data-name that is not a table element. To correct the problem, the programmer should

1. Find the data-name mentioned in the diagnostic in the DATA DIVISION. No OCCURS clause will be associated with the name.
2. Either take the subscript off, if the data-name is correct, or change the data-name to the one that requires a subscript.

```
REQUIRES 1 LEVEL OF SUBSCRIPTING
```

A reference has been made to a data item representing a table element, and it has either no subscript or too many subscripts.

To correct the problem, the programmer should

1. Check whether the data-name is the one intended.
2. Find the table in the DATA DIVISION if the data-name is the one intended. The data-name either has an OCCURS clause or is subordinate to a data-name that does. The OCCURS clause tells how many elements there are with the name. The programmer must indicate *which one* is desired by using a subscript.
3. Eliminate any extra subscripts. The diagnostic is saying that, for the data name chosen, there must be one and only one subscript. Has the correct data-name in fact been chosen?

```
REQUIRES 2 LEVELS OF SUBSCRIPTING
```

The data-name in the diagnostic either has too few or too many subscripts. To correct the problem, the programmer should

1. Find the data-name in the DATA DIVISION.
2. Check whether the data-name is the one intended.
3. Provide a subscript for each OCCURS clause that the data-name has or is subordinate to.

USAGE IS COMPUTATIONAL

Format

```
[USAGE IS] COMPUTATIONAL
```

The computational option is used to indicate that storage is for binary data items. The USAGE IS COMP clause reserves two, four, or eight bytes of storage. The amount of storage depends upon the number of positions indicated in the PICTURE clause in accordance with the following:

PICTURE Clause	Storage Reserved
9(1) through 9(4)	2 bytes
9(5) through 9(9)	4 bytes
9(10) through 9(18)	8 bytes

Positive Numbers

For data items whose USAGE IS COMP, the decimal digits are converted directly to their binary equivalents using powers of 2 for place values. If the hexadecimal equivalent of the binary is provided (as in a memory dump), the conversion is made using powers of 16. The binary and hexadecimal equivalents of the decimal number 36 are shown in the following diagram:

DECIMAL 36 REPRESENTED AS A BINARY NUMBER

32,768	16,384	8,192	4,096	2,048	1,024	512	256	128	64	32	16	8	4	2	1
0	0	0	0	0	0	0	0	0	0	1	0	0	1	0	0

DECIMAL 36 REPRESENTED AS A HEXADECIMAL NUMBER

4,096	256	16	1
0	0	2	4

Negative Numbers

The sign for a computational item is stored in the leftmost bit, with 0 denoting a positive value and 1 a negative value. Negative numbers are stored in two's complement form. Thus, in order to store, say, the decimal number negative 36, first the 36 is converted to binary or hexadecimal. The equivalent in binary of a positive decimal 36 is 0000 0000 0010 0100. The equivalent in hexadecimal is 24. To convert a number to the two's complement form, (1) subtract the number from the highest number in the number base, and (2) add 1 to the result. For decimal 36, the operation is as follows:

BINARY	HEXADECIMAL
1111 1111 1111 1111	FFFF
0000 0000 0010 0100	0024
1111 1111 1101 1011	FFDB
+1	+1
1111 1111 1101 1100	FFDC

The preceding results indicate, respectively, the binary value in memory and the hexadecimal representation of the binary value of the decimal number 36. The 1 in the leftmost bit of the binary form indicates that the number is negative and, therefore, in two's complement form. To convert the negative number found in storage back to the original value, (1) subtract it from the highest number in the number base, (2) add 1 to the result, and (3) affix a minus sign thereto. The procedure is as follows:

BINARY		HEXADECIMAL
1111 1111 1111 1111		FFFF
− 1111 1111 1101 1100	or	− FFDC
0000 0000 0010 0011		0023
+1		+1
− 0000 0000 0010 0100		− 0024

The results are both equal to the decimal number 36.

Subscripts should be defined using USAGE IS COMPUTATIONAL. COBOL always converts a subscript to binary before it is used. Defining the subscript as COMP keeps the program from having to perform the conversion during execution.

SUMMARY

Table Structure: OCCURS

Format

```
               {data-name}
level number   {FILLER   }   [OCCURS integer-2 TIMES] [PICTURE clause]
```

Perform . . . Varying

Format

```
                               {THROUGH}
PERFORM procedure-name-1  [    {THRU   }  procedure-name-2]
                                          {literal-2   }
        VARYING identifier-1    FROM      {identifier-2}
           {literal-3   }
        BY {identifier-3}    UNTIL condition-1
                                          {literal-5   }
        [AFTER identifier-4   FROM        {identifier-5}
           {literal-6   }
        BY {identifier-6}    UNTIL condition-2
                                          {literal-8   }
        [AFTER identifier-7   FROM        {identifier-8}
           {literal-9   }
        BY {identifier-9}  UNTIL condition-3]   ]
```

USAGE IS COMPUTATIONAL

Format

```
[USAGE IS] COMPUTATIONAL
```

EXERCISES

I. Given the following table described for storage, perform the calculations. Place each answer in the proper table element. The results should be cumulative.

```
01  AMOUNT-TABLE          VALUE ZEROS.
    05  ROW-ELEMENT       OCCURS 4 TIMES.
        10  COL-ELEMENT   OCCURS 3 TIMES     PIC 9(5).
```

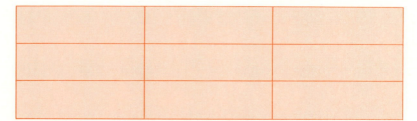

```
ADD 15 TO COL-ELEMENT (2, 1).
ADD 40 TO COL-ELEMENT (4, 2).
ADD 10 TO COL-ELELENT (1, 3).
ADD 25 TO COL-ELEMENT (3, 2).
ADD COL-ELEMENT (3, 2) TO COL-ELEMENT (4, 2).
ADD COL-ELEMENT (4, 2) TO COL-ELEMENT (1, 3).
SUBTRACT COL-ELEMENT (3, 2) FROM COL-ELEMENT (1, 3).
```

II. Using the storage description of the following table, fill in the names (with subscripts) and displacement for each element in the table diagram.

```
01  RATE-TABLE.
    05  COUNTY-ELEMENT                OCCURS 3 TIMES.
        10  CITY-ELEMENT              OCCURS 2 TIMES.
            15  CATEGORY-ELEMENT      OCCURS 3 TIMES
                    PIC V999.
```

III. Answer the true/false questions that follow each table.

```
01   TABLE-A.
     05   TABLE-B OCCURS 4 TIMES     PIC 9(3).
```

_____ **1.** TABLE-A is a numeric data item.
_____ **2.** TABLE-B (3) has a displacement of 8.
_____ **3.** TABLE-A can have only 1 subscript.
_____ **4.** TABLE-A has 4 elements.
_____ **5.** TABLE-A includes 12 bytes.

```
01   QUANTITY-TABLE.
     05   ROW-ELEMENT           OCCURS 5 TIMES.
          10   COL-ELEMENT      OCCURS 8 TIMES     PIC 9(6).
```

_____ **6.** ROW-ELEMENT requires 2 subscripts when referenced.
_____ **7.** ROW-ELEMENT is an element of a one-dimensional table.
_____ **8.** COL-ELEMENT (8, 5) is valid.
_____ **9.** COL-ELEMENT (3, 3) has a displacement of 102.
_____ **10.** ROW-ELEMENT is alphanumeric.

```
01   NET-PAY-TABLE.
     05   DIV-ELEMENT                     OCCURS 10 TIMES.
          10   DEPT-ELEMENT               OCCURS 5 TIMES.
               15   EXEMPTION-ELEMENT     OCCURS 2 TIMES
                        PIC 9(5)V9(2).
```

_____ **11.** The displacement of DEPT-ELEMENT (8, 4) is 532.
_____ **12.** There are 100 occurrences of EXEMPTION-ELEMENT.
_____ **13.** Each DIV-ELEMENT is 50 bytes.
_____ **14.** DEPT-ELEMENT is alphanumeric.
_____ **15.** The displacement of DIV-ELEMENT (4) is 150.

IV. Indicate whether each of the following tables is most likely to be loaded at
(a) compile time
(b) preprocess time
(c) execution time

_____ **1.** The names of the months.
_____ **2.** NET-PAY per pay period.
_____ **3.** The names of the days of the week.
_____ **4.** Current interest rates on Treasury bills.
_____ **5.** The names of states.
_____ **6.** Freight rates.
_____ **7.** Sales tax by month.
_____ **8.** The prime interest rate.
_____ **9.** Commissions earned by salespersons.
_____ **10.** Miles between locations.

V. Given the storage description of the following table and the general form of its output design, write the code necessary to print the table. Define a print line to move table items to. Given the table names and the names you created for the print line, write the PROCEDURE DIVISION code.

```
01   PRICE-TABLE.
     05   BRANCH ROW          OCCURS 5 TIMES.
          10   SALES-REP-COL  OCCURS 4 TIMES
                    PIC 99V99.
```

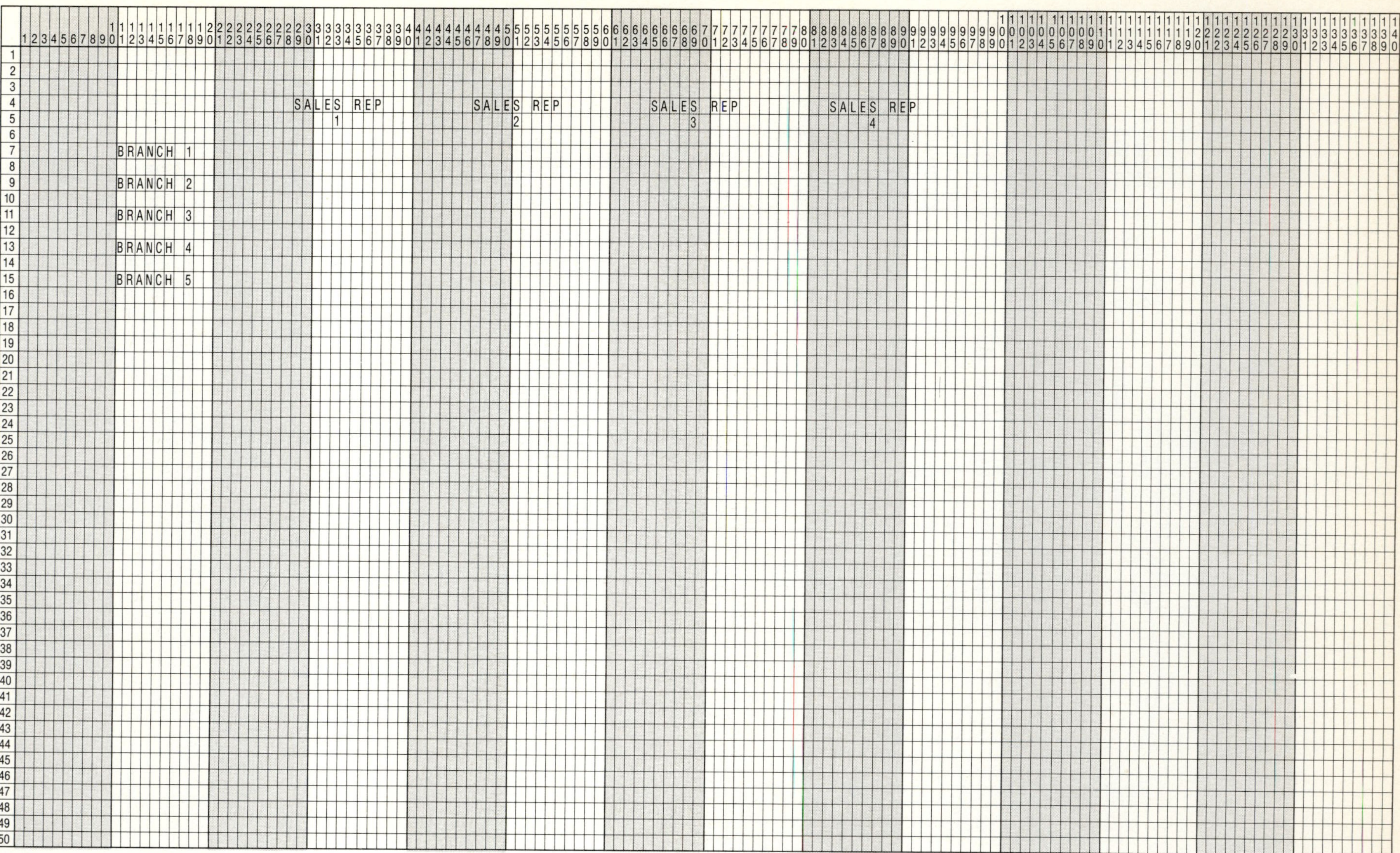
SALES REP
1
SALES REP
2
SALES REP
3
SALES REP
4
BRANCH 1
BRANCH 2
BRANCH 3
BRANCH 4
BRANCH 5

	SALES REP 1	SALES REP 2	SALES REP 3	SALES REP 4
Branch 1 Branch 2 Branch 3 Branch 4 Branch 5				

PROJECTS

For each of the following specifications and input record layouts, design a print chart and code a COBOL program that satisfies the specification.

PROJECT 7–1 Payroll

PROGRAM SPECIFICATION

Program Name: PAY7

Program Function:

This program will produce a printed report in two parts. The first part will be a listing of each payroll record, including totals for credit union deductions, medical insurance deductions, and gross pay for each department and division, and for the entire report. The second part of the report will be a summary of gross pay by division.

Input Files:

I. PAYROLL-FILE

INPUT DEVICE:	DISK
FILE ORGANIZATION:	SEQUENTIAL
RECORD LENGTH:	80 BYTES
FILE SEQUENCE:	ASCENDING ON DIVISION/ DEPARTMENT

Output Files:

I. PRINT-FILE

OUTPUT DEVICE:	PRINTER
RECORD LENGTH:	133 BYTES

Processing Requirements:

Each record read from the payroll file should be printed on one line of the output report. Gross pay is to be calculated and included on the output. (Gross pay = pay rate × hours worked.)

Totals for credit union deductions, medical insurance deductions, and gross pay are to be accumulated and printed for each department, each division, and the entire report. Also, the division gross pay totals are to be stored in a table and used to create the printed summary at the end of the job.

Output Requirements:

The following are formatting requirements for the report:

1. Each page of the report should contain:
   (a) a main heading which includes the company name, the report name, the report date, and a page number.
   (b) column headings which describe the items printed underneath them.
2. Detail lines should include all fields from the input and gross pay.
3. Detail lines should be double spaced.
4. Total lines should be double spaced.
5. Each new division should begin on a new page.
6. The division summary should begin on a new page.

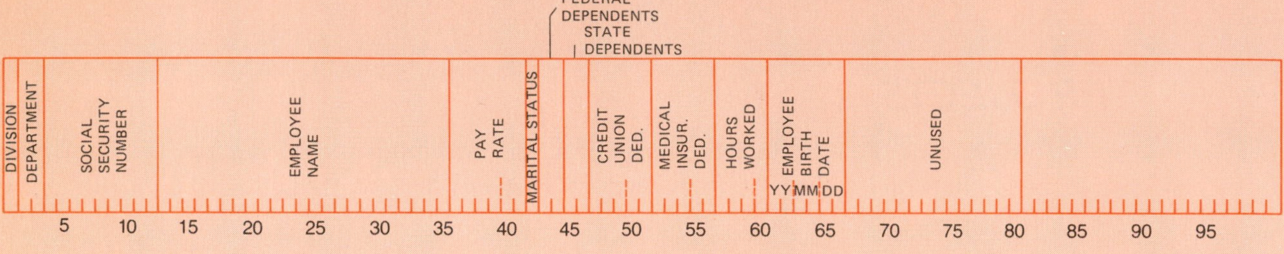

PROJECT 7–2 Inventory

PROGRAM SPECIFICATION

Program Name: INV7

Program Function:

This program will produce a printed report that is a summary by inventory type of quantity on hand, quantity on order, and inventory cost.

Input Files:

I. INVENTORY-FILE

INPUT DEVICE:	DISK
FILE ORGANIZATION:	SEQUENTIAL
RECORD LENGTH:	80 BYTES
FILE SEQUENCE:	ASCENDING ON INVENTORY STOCK NUMBER

Output Files:

I. PRINT-FILE

OUTPUT DEVICE:	PRINTER
RECORD LENGTH:	133 BYTES

Processing Requirements:

For each record read from the inventory file, quantity on hand, quantity on order, and inventory cost are added to a table by inventory type. (Inventory cost = quantity on hand × inventory unit cost.) After all records have been processed, the report is printed.

Output Requirements:

The following are formatting requirements for the report:

1. The report should have:
   (a) a main heading which includes the company name, the report name, and the report date.
   (b) column headings which describe the items printed underneath them.
2. Summary lines should be double spaced.

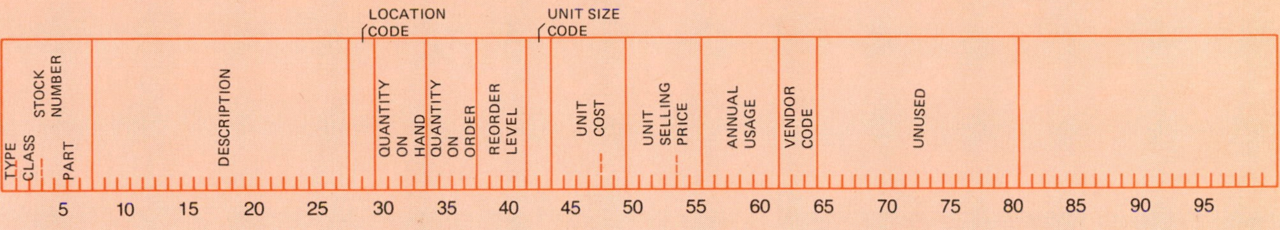

PROJECT 7–3 Accounts Payable

PROGRAM SPECIFICATION

Program Name: AP7

Program Function:

The program will produce a summary report of an accounts payable file. The report will include division totals for amount, hard goods, labor, freight, and tax.

Input Files:

I. ACCOUNTS-PAYABLE-FILE

INPUT DEVICE:	DISK
FILE ORGANIZATION:	SEQUENTIAL
RECORD LENGTH:	80 BYTES
FILE SEQUENCE:	ASCENDING ON DIVISION / CONTROL NBR

Output Files:

I. PRINT-FILE

OUTPUT DEVICE:	PRINTER
RECORD LENGTH:	133 BYTES

Processing Requirements:

Each record on the input file should be printed on one line of the output report. Division totals of amount, hard goods, labor, freight, and tax are to be accumulated in a table and printed as a summary.

Output Requirements:

The following are formatting requirements for the report:

1. Each page of the report should contain:
   (a) a main heading which includes the company name, the report name, the report date, and a page number.

(b) column headings which describe the items printed underneath them.

2. Summary lines should be double spaced.

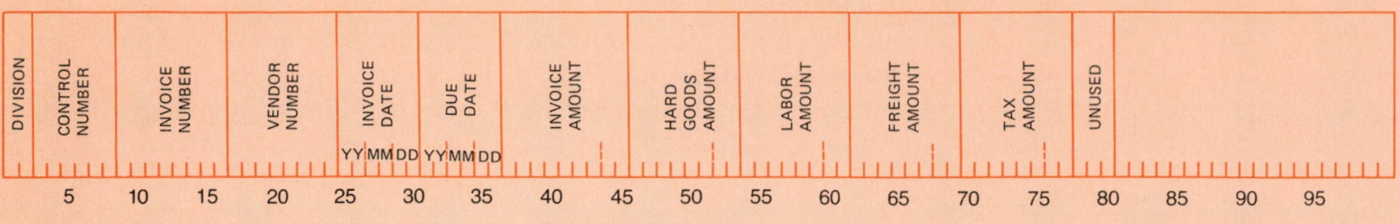

PROJECT 7–4 Pension

PROGRAM SPECIFICATION

Program Name: PEN7

Program Function:

This program will produce a printed report in two parts. The first part will be a listing of each pension record, including division and final totals for salary, employee contribution, employer contribution, and balance forward. The second part will be a summary of the balance forward by division.

Input Files:

I. PENSION-FILE

INPUT DEVICE:	DISK
FILE ORGANIZATION:	SEQUENTIAL
RECORD LENGTH:	80 BYTES
FILE SEQUENCE:	ASCENDING ON DIVISION / DEPARTMENT

Output Files:

I. PRINT-FILE

OUTPUT DEVICE:	PRINTER
RECORD LENGTH:	133 BYTES

Processing Requirements:

Each record read from the pension file should be printed on one line of the output report. Totals for salary, employee contribution, employer contribution, and balance forward are to be accumulated and printed for each division and for the entire company. Balance forward totals by division are to be stored in a table and used to create a printed summary of the balance forward at the end of the job.

Output Requirements:

The following are formatting requirements for the report:

1. Each page of the report should contain:
   (a) a main heading which includes the company name, the report name, the report date, and a page number.
   (b) column headings which describe the items printed underneath them.
2. Detail lines should include all fields from the input.
3. Detail lines should be double spaced.
4. Each new division should begin on a new page.

5. Total lines should be double spaced.
6. The division summary should begin on a new page.

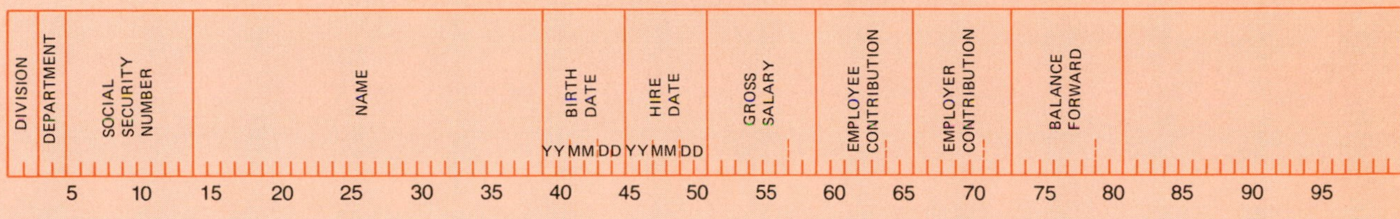

PROJECT 7–5 Bill of Materials

PROGRAM SPECIFICATION

Program Name: BOM7

Program Function:

The program will produce a printed report of a bill-of-materials file which will include the extended cost. The report will include division, product line, and final totals for extended cost. A summary will be printed of the extended cost by division and product line.

Input Files:

I. BILL-OF-MATERIALS-FILE

INPUT DEVICE:	DISK
FILE ORGANIZATION:	SEQUENTIAL
RECORD LENGTH:	55 BYTES
FILE SEQUENCE:	ASCENDING ON DIVISION / PRODUCT LINE

Output Files:

I. PRINT-FILE

OUTPUT DEVICE:	PRINTER
RECORD LENGTH:	133 BYTES

Processing Requirements:

Each record from the bill-of-materials file should be printed on one line of the output report. Extended cost (quantity times cost) is to be calculated for each record. Totals for extended cost are to be accumulated and printed for each division and product line, and for the entire company. Totals for extended cost are to be stored in a table by division and product line. The table should be used to create a summary at the end of the job.

Output Requirements:

The following are formatting requirements for the report:

1. Each page of the report should contain:
   (a) a main heading which includes the company name, the report name, the report date, and a page number.
   (b) column headings which describe the items printed underneath them.
2. Detail lines should include all fields from the input and extended cost.
3. Detail lines should be double spaced.

4. Each new division should begin on a new page.
5. Total lines should be double spaced.
6. The summary should begin on a new page.

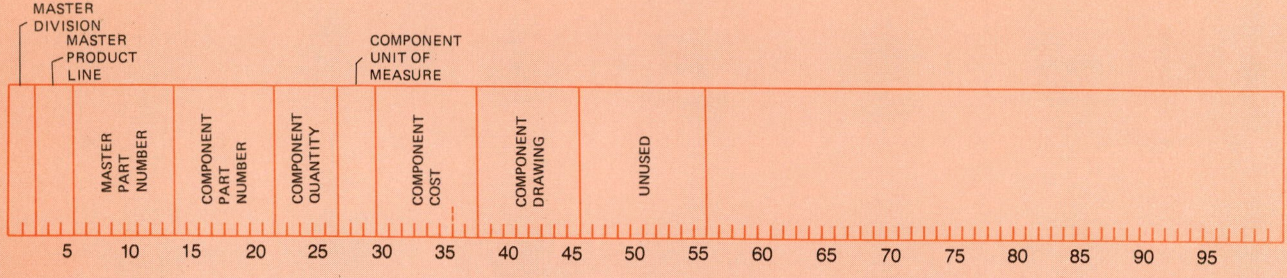

PROJECT 7–6 Cost

PROGRAM SPECIFICATION

Program Name: COST7

Program Function:

The program will produce a printed report of a cost file which will include the total for all cost factors. The report will separate the records by division and provide a count of records for each division. The count will be printed at the end of the report.

Input Files:

I. COST-FILE

INPUT DEVICE:	DISK
FILE ORGANIZATION:	SEQUENTIAL
RECORD LENGTH:	75 BYTES
FILE SEQUENCE:	ASCENDING ON DIVISION / PRODUCT LINE

Output Files:

I. PRINT-FILE

OUTPUT DEVICE:	PRINTER
RECORD LENGTH:	133 BYTES

Processing Requirements:

Each record from the cost file should be printed on one line of the output report. The total for all cost factors should be calculated for each record. A count of the records for each division should be accumulated in a table and printed at the end of the job.

Output Requirements:

The following are formatting requirements for the report:

1. Each page of the report should contain:
   (a) a main heading which includes the company name, the report name, the report date, and a page number.
   (b) column headings which describe the items printed underneath them.
2. Detail lines should include all fields from the input and the total for all cost factors.

3. Detail lines should be double spaced.
4. Each new division should begin on a new page.
5. The count of records by division should begin on a new page.
6. Total (count) lines should be double spaced.

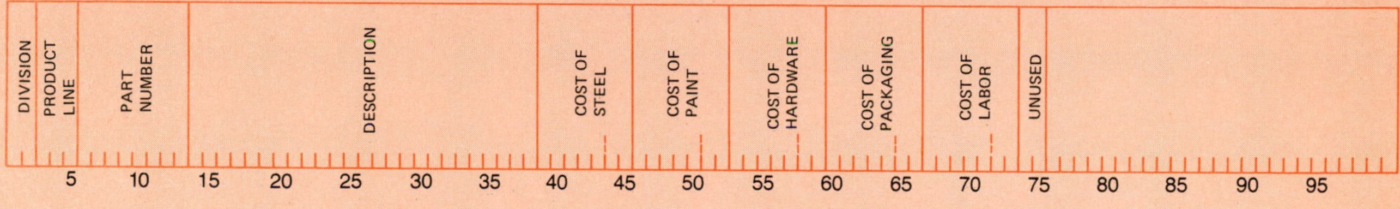

CHAPTER

8 Table Handling, II

The programming logic of this chapter deals with input editing. Input editing includes testing the contents of each field in a record to ensure that the data in the record is valid. The IF statement is reviewed, with emphasis on its use in editing. The programming project of the chapter deals with input editing performed on the ORDER-FILE used in the previous chapters. Programming logic for loading and searching tables is also included in the project.

The new COBOL language elements focus on table handling. They include loading compile- and preprocess-time tables and searching tables using serial and binary searches. Additional uses of the IF statement are presented for use in input editing.

The debugging section includes diagnostics associated with searching tables. The creation of test data is also discussed.

PROGRAM SPECIFICATION: EDIT

The programming project for this chapter is to perform input editing on a file. A listing of the errors found by means of editing is created so that these errors may be corrected. The program specification is shown in Figure 8–1.

PROGRAM SPECIFICATION

Program Name: EDIT

Program Function:

The program will edit input records from an order file. Each field in the order record will be tested for validity. Items that are not valid will be identified on a printed report.

Input Files:

I. ORDER-FILE

INPUT DEVICE:	DISK
FILE ORGANIZATION:	SEQUENTIAL
RECORD LENGTH:	70 BYTES
FILE SEQUENCE:	ASCENDING ON BRANCH / SALES REP

II. PARTS-FILE

INPUT DEVICE:	DISK
FILE ORGANIZATION:	SEQUENTIAL
RECORD LENGTH:	45 BYTES
FILE SEQUENCE:	ASCENDING ON PART NBR

FIGURE 8–1

Output Files:

I. PRINT-FILE

OUTPUT DEVICE: PRINTER
RECORD LENGTH: 133 BYTES

Processing Requirements:

The fields in ORDER-RECORD are to be tested and should meet the criteria listed after each field name. Tables containing all of the valid values are to be used to edit ORD-SALES-REP and ORD-PART-NBR.

ORD-BRANCH
- Numeric
- Range of 1 to 10

ORD-SALES-REP
- Numeric
- Exists in the sales representative table

ORD-CUSTOMER-NBR
- Numeric

ORD-CUST-PO-NBR
- No test necessary, no data need be present

ORD-SALES-ORD-NBR
- Must be present (not equal to spaces)

ORD-DATE
- Valid date

ORD-PART-NBR
- Exists in the parts file
- Must be an active part number

ORD-QUANTITY
- Numeric

ORD-UNIT-PRICE
- Numeric

ORD-REQ-SHIP-DATE
- Valid date

ORD-ACT-SHIP-DATE
- Zeros

The entire record is to be printed when the first erroneous field is encountered. For any additional erroneous fields in the same record, only the error message is to be printed.

Output Requirements:

The following are formatting requirements for the report:

1. Each page of the report should contain:
   (a) a main heading which includes the company name, the report name, the report date, and a page number.
   (b) column headings which describe the items printed underneath them.
2. All fields plus an error message are to be printed for the first error found in each record. These lines should be double spaced.
3. Only an error message is to be printed for each additional error in the same record. These lines should be single spaced.

FIGURE 8–1 cont.

Input Record Layouts

The input record layouts are shown in Figure 8–2. The first layout is for ORDER-RECORD, which is the same file as used in previous projects and is repeated here for convenience. The second layout is for PARTS-RECORD which depicts records from the PARTS-FILE which will be read in the initialization routine and loaded into a table. The table with the part numbers will be used to edit ORD-PART-NBR to assure that each part is an existing, active part.

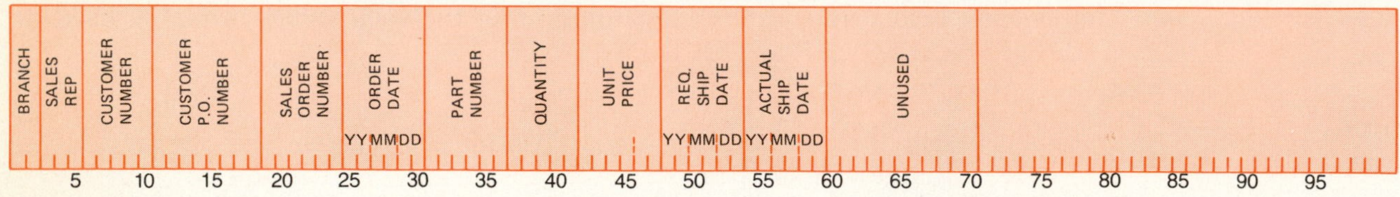

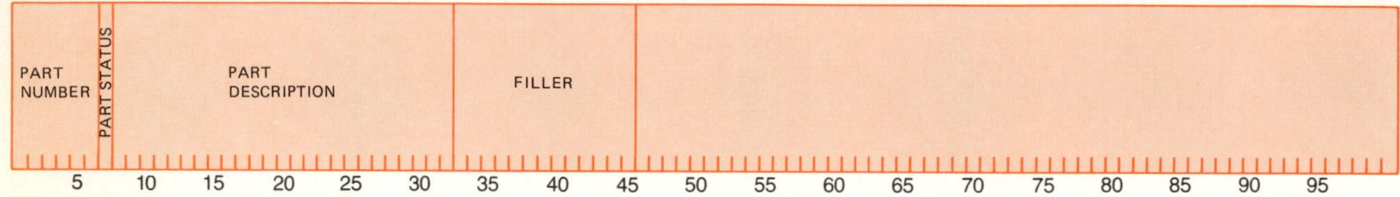

FIGURE 8–2

Print Chart

The print chart for the project is shown in Figure 8–3. Note that two types of detail lines are produced: (1) information about a record plus an error message, and (2) an error message only.

LOGIC FOR INPUT-EDIT USING TABLE

A hierarchy chart for the program is shown in Figure 8–4. Pseudocode and a flowchart are shown in Figures 8–5 and 8–6, respectively.

Explanation of Logic

1000-INITIALIZATION

In this initialization routine, a new approach is taken to placing the current date in the heading. Rather than the number of the month, the name of the month will be used. The names of the months have been placed in a table (coded as literals in a VALUE clause), and the number of the month (from CURRENT-DATE) will be used to access the correct element of the table. The element of the table containing the month name is then moved to the main heading.

1000-INITIALIZATION is also used to load table data into memory from an input file. The first step in this loading process is an initial read of PARTS-FILE. Following this read is a loop where the data read is moved to the appropriate element of the table in memory, and then a new data record is read. The loop continues until the end of PARTS-FILE is reached. A PERFORM . . . VARYING statement is used to control the loop. The table data will be used to edit part numbers from ORDER-FILE.

The last step in 1000-INITIALIZATION is to perform the initial read of ORDER-FILE. This record will be edited in the 2000-EDIT routine. The COBOL code for this routine is shown in Figure 8–7.

(text continued on page 347)

```
XXXXXXXXX 99, 9999                                        COMPANY NAME                                                  PAGE: ZZ9
                                                     ORDER FILE ERROR REPORT

         SALES          CUSTOMER   SALES      ORDER                      UNIT    REQUESTED   ACTUAL
 BRANCH   REP   CUST#     PO#      ORDER#     DATE     PART#     QTY     PRICE   SHIP DATE  SHIP DATE     ERROR MESSAGE

   XX     XXX   XXXXXX  XXXXXXXXX  XXXXXX   XX XX XX   XXXXXX   XXXXX   XXXXXX   XX XX XX   XX XX XX  X----------------------------X

   XX     XXX   XXXXXX  XXXXXXXXX  XXXXXX   XX XX XX   XXXXXX   XXXXX   XXXXXX   XX XX XX   XX XX XX  X----------------------------X
                                                                                                      X----------------------------X
                                                                                                      X----------------------------X
                                                                                                      X----------------------------X
```

FIGURE 8–3

Hierarchy Chart

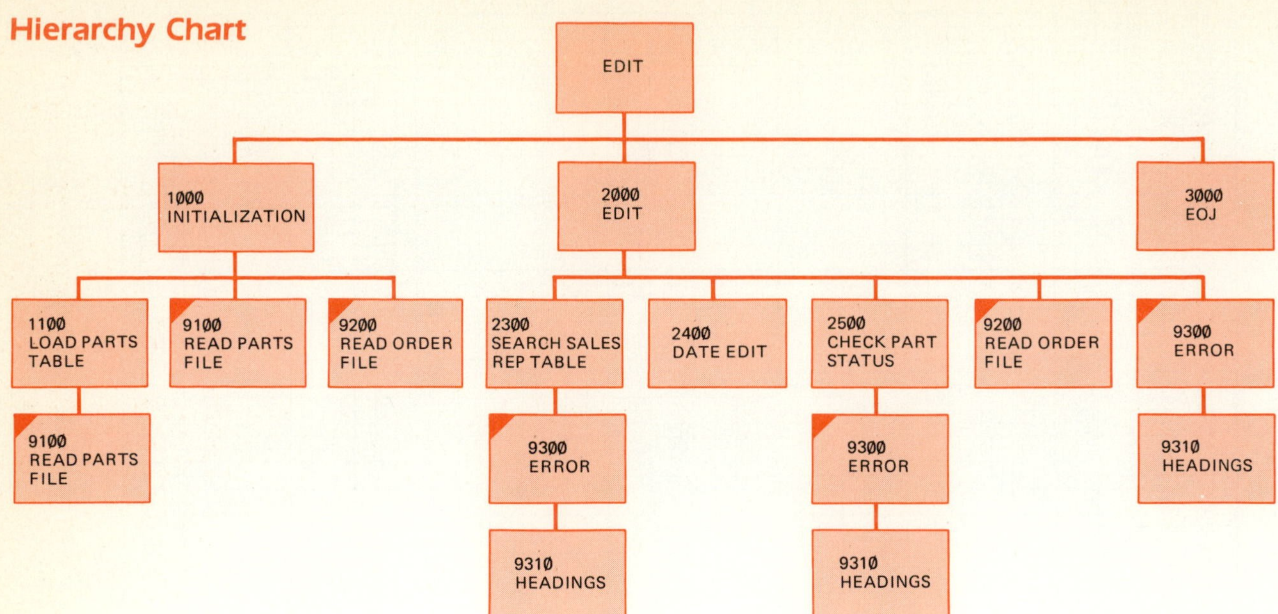

FIGURE 8–4

Pseudocode

```
MAIN LINE
     DO initialization
     DO WHILE more order records
          DO edit
     ENDDO
     DO eoj
     END
INITIALIZATION
     OPEN files
     MOVE date to heading
     DO read parts file
     MOVE 1 to part subscript
     DO WHILE more parts records
          DO load parts table
          ADD 1 to part subscript
     ENDDO
     DO read order file
LOAD PARTS TABLE
     MOVE part number to table
     MOVE part status to table
     DO read parts file
EDIT
     MOVE 'no' to error switch
     IF order branch is numeric
          IF valid branch
          ELSE
               MOVE 'branch out of range' to error
                 message
               DO error
          ENDIF
```

FIGURE 8–5

```
ELSE
     MOVE 'branch is not numeric' to error
       message
     DO error
ENDIF
IF order sales rep is numeric
     DO search sales rep table
ELSE
     MOVE 'sales rep nbr is not numeric' to
       error message
     DO error
ENDIF
IF order customer number is numeric
ELSE
     MOVE 'customer number is not numeric' to
       error message
     DO error
ENDIF
IF order sales order number = spaces
     MOVE 'sales order number is missing' to
       error message
     DO error
ENDIF
MOVE order date to date edit area
DO date edit
IF date error
     MOVE 'order date is invalid' to error
       message
     DO error
ENDIF
SEARCH part number table for order part number
IF found
     DO check part status
ELSE
     MOVE 'invalid part number--not in file'
       to error message
     DO error
ENDIF
IF order quantity is numeric
ELSE
     MOVE 'quantity is not numeric' to error
       message
     DO error
ENDIF
IF order unit price is numeric
ELSE
     MOVE 'unit price is not numeric' to error
       message
     DO error
ENDIF
MOVE order requested ship date to date edit
  area
DO date edit
```

FIGURE 8–5 cont.

```
        IF date error
             MOVE 'requested ship date is invalid' to
               error message
             DO error
        ENDIF
        IF order actual ship date = zeros
        ELSE
             MOVE 'actual ship date must be zero' to
               error message
             DO error
        ENDIF
        DO read order file
   SEARCH SALES REP TABLE
        SEARCH sales rep table for sales rep nbr
        IF found
        ELSE
             MOVE 'sales rep nbr not in table' to
               error message
             DO error
        ENDIF
   DATE EDIT
        MOVE 'no' to date error switch
        IF valid date
        ELSE
             MOVE 'yes' to date error switch
        ENDIF
   CHECK PART STATUS
        IF part discontinued
             MOVE 'part is discontinued' to error
               message
             DO error
        ENDIF
   EOJ
        CLOSE files
   READ PARTS FILE
        READ parts file
   READ ORDER FILE
        READ order file
   ERROR
        IF line count > 50
             DO headings
        ENDIF
        IF error switch = 'no'
             MOVE input to detail line
             MOVE error message to detail line 1
             WRITE detail line 1
             ADD 2 to line count
             MOVE 'yes' to error switch
        ELSE
             MOVE error message to detail line 2
             WRITE detail line 2
             ADD 1 to line count
```

FIGURE 8–5 cont.

```
        ENDIF

    HEADINGS
        ADD 1 to page count
        MOVE page count to main heading
        WRITE main heading line 1
        WRITE main heading line 2
        WRITE column heading line 1
        WRITE column heading line 2
        MOVE 5 to line count
```

FIGURE 8–5 cont.

Flowchart

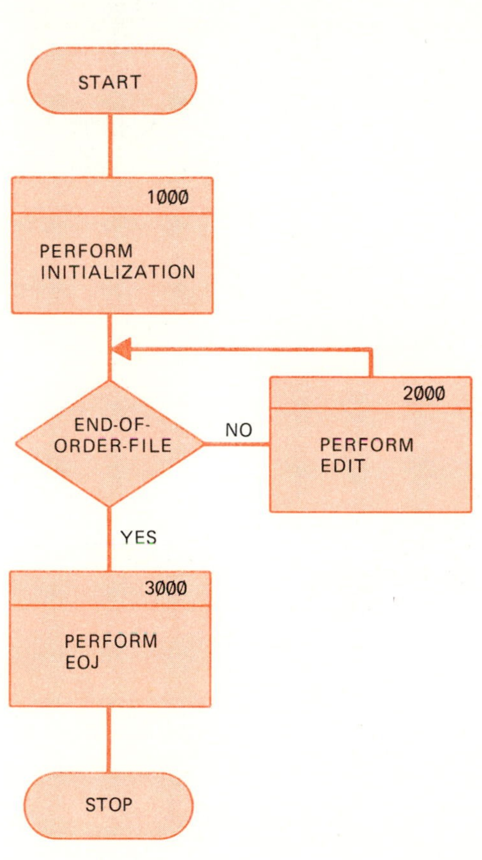

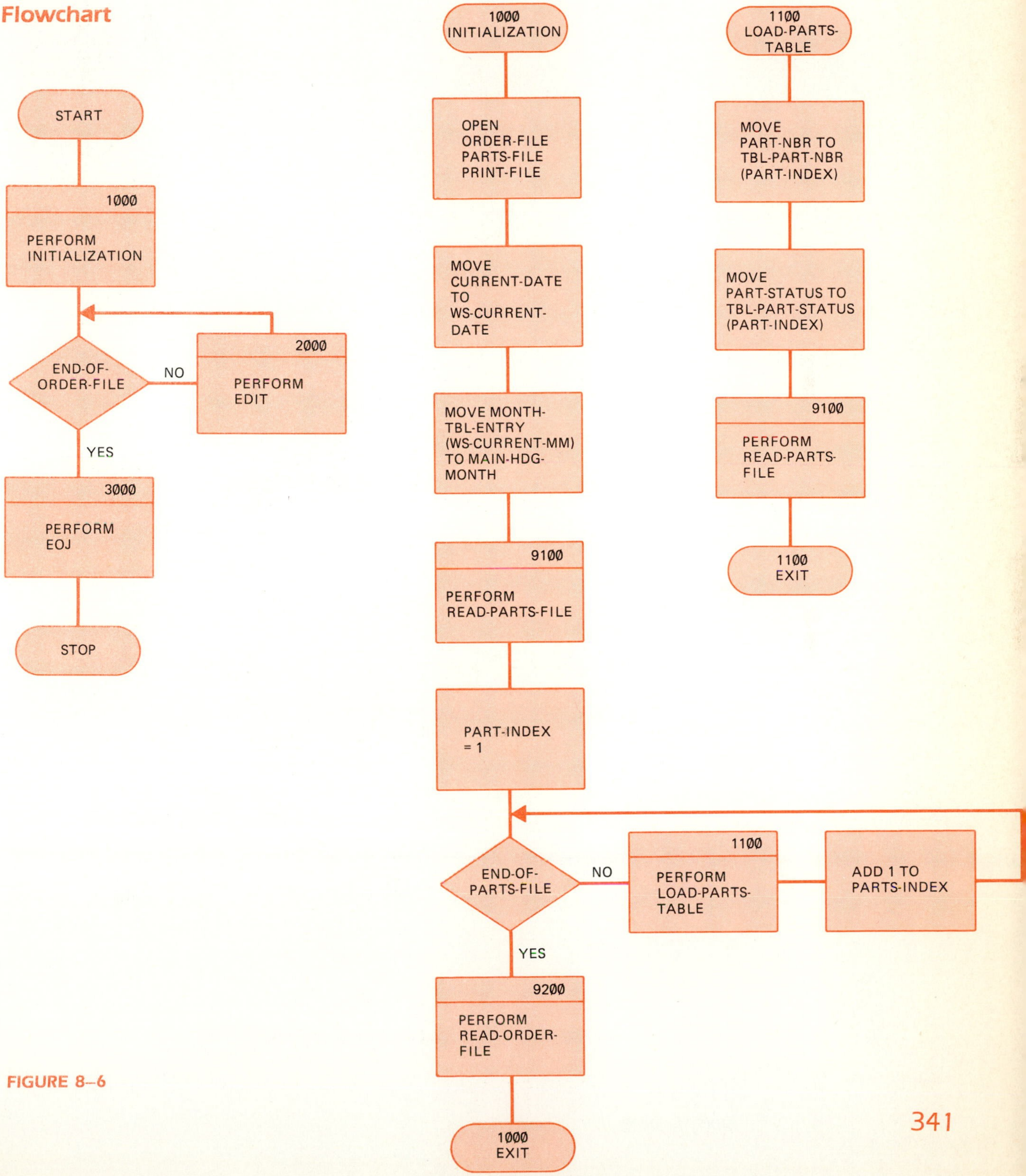

START
1000
PERFORM INITIALIZATION
END-OF-ORDER-FILE
NO
2000
PERFORM EDIT
YES
3000
PERFORM EOJ
STOP
1000 INITIALIZATION
OPEN ORDER-FILE PARTS-FILE PRINT-FILE
MOVE CURRENT-DATE TO WS-CURRENT-DATE
MOVE MONTH-TBL-ENTRY (WS-CURRENT-MM) TO MAIN-HDG-MONTH
9100
PERFORM READ-PARTS-FILE
PART-INDEX = 1
END-OF-PARTS-FILE
NO
1100
PERFORM LOAD-PARTS-TABLE
ADD 1 TO PARTS-INDEX
YES
9200
PERFORM READ-ORDER-FILE
1000 EXIT
1100 LOAD-PARTS-TABLE
MOVE PART-NBR TO TBL-PART-NBR (PART-INDEX)
MOVE PART-STATUS TO TBL-PART-STATUS (PART-INDEX)
9100
PERFORM READ-PARTS-FILE
1100 EXIT

FIGURE 8–6

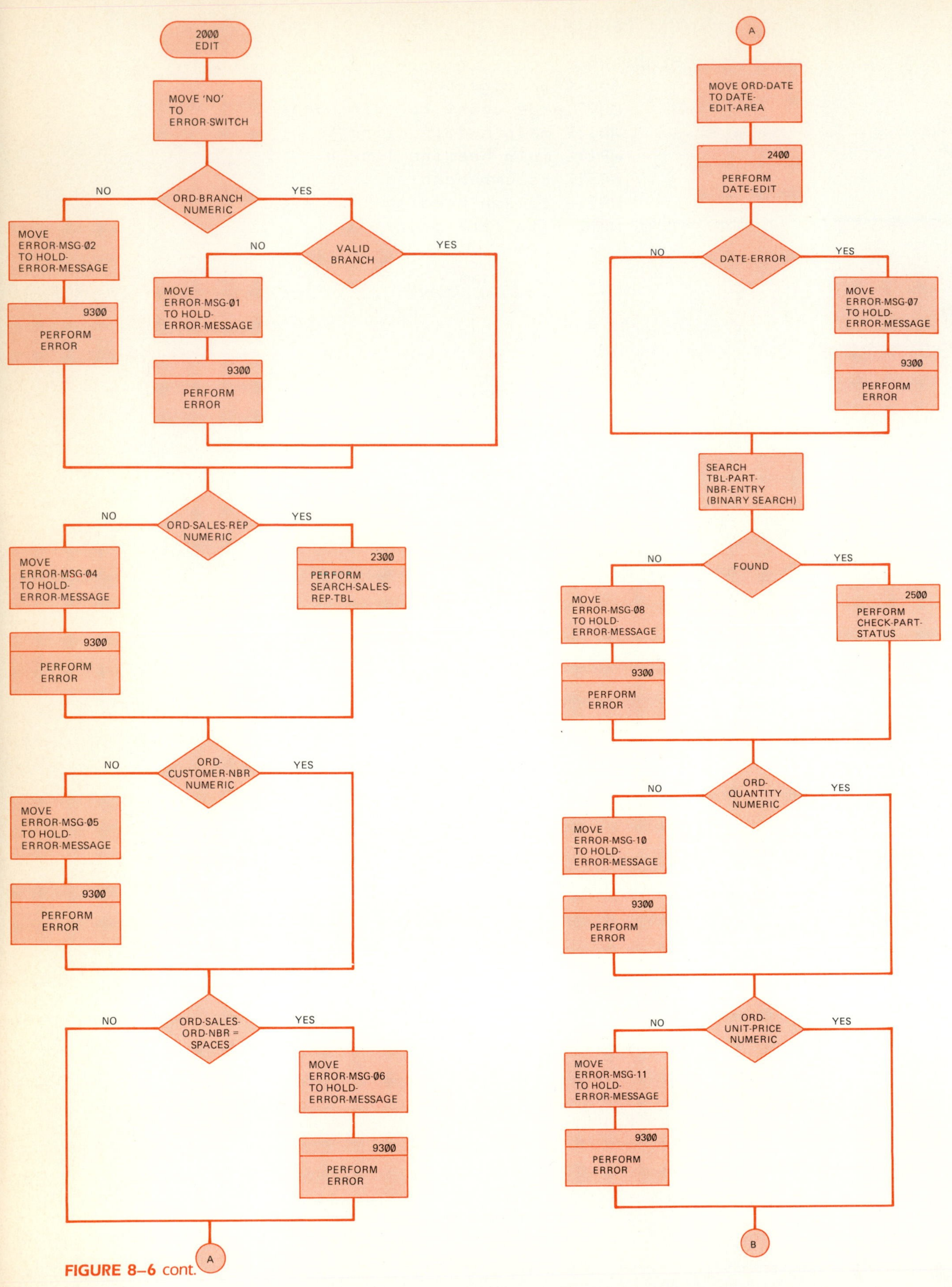

FIGURE 8–6 cont.

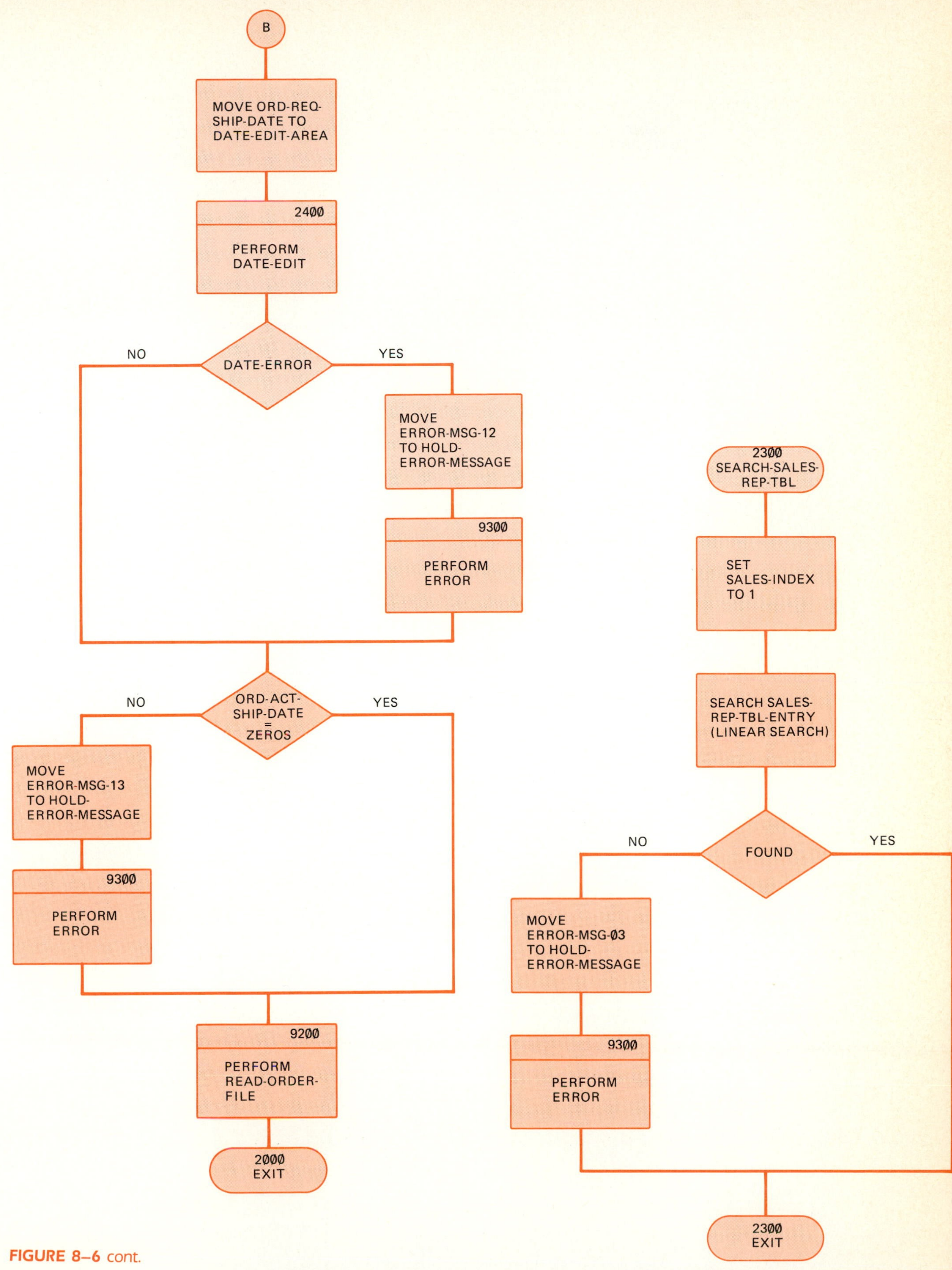

FIGURE 8–6 cont.

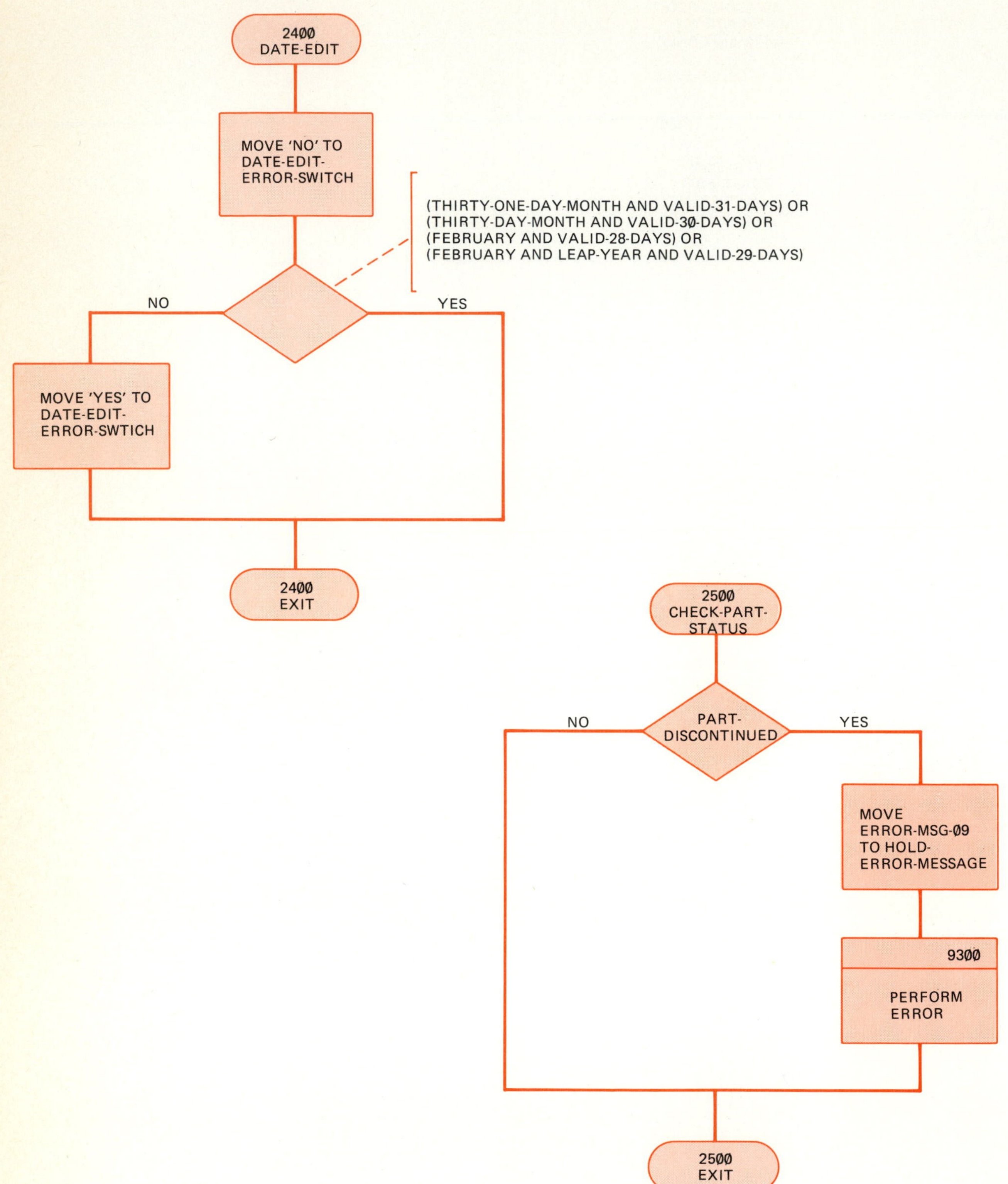

FIGURE 8–6 cont.

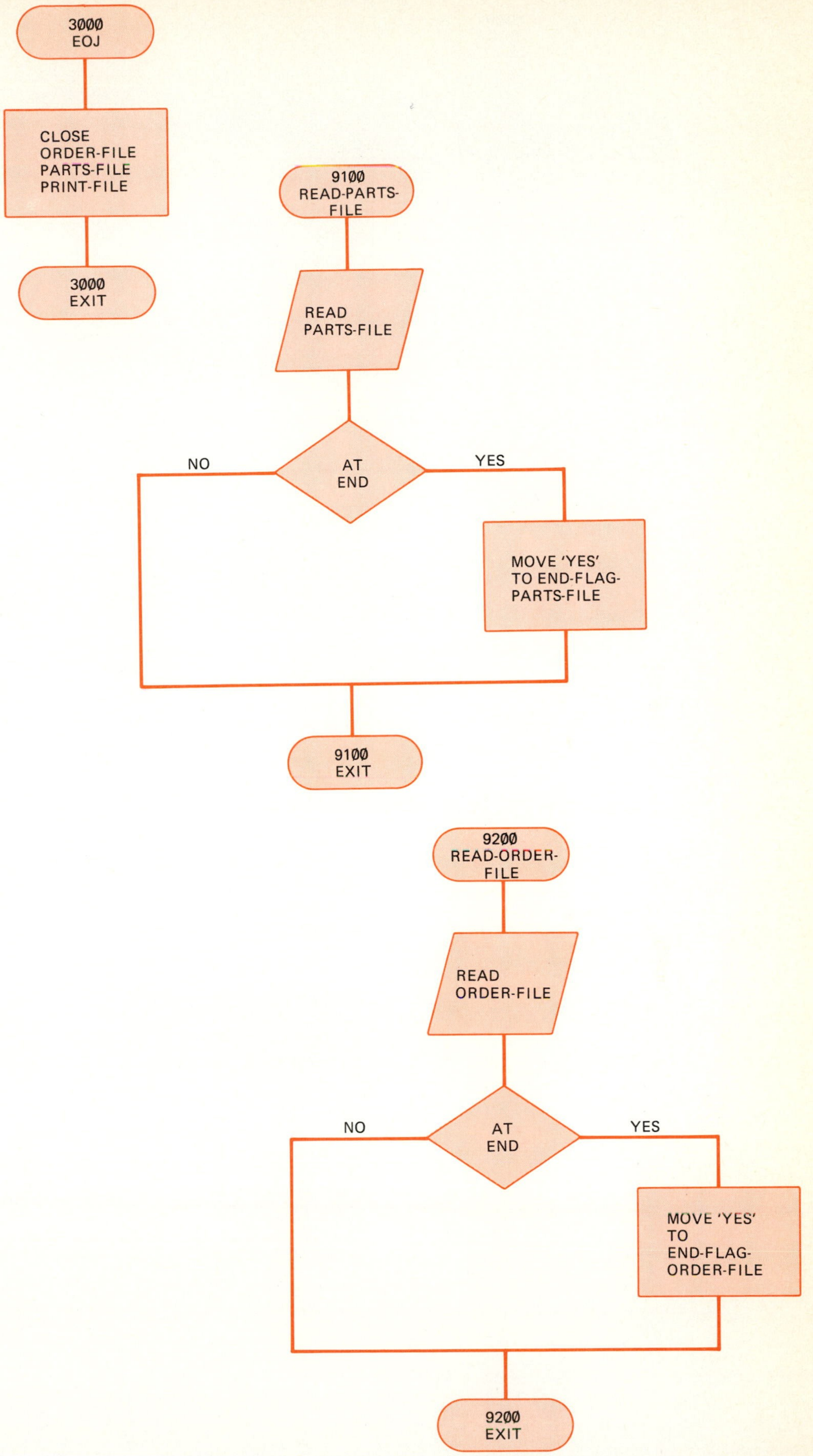

FIGURE 8–6 cont.

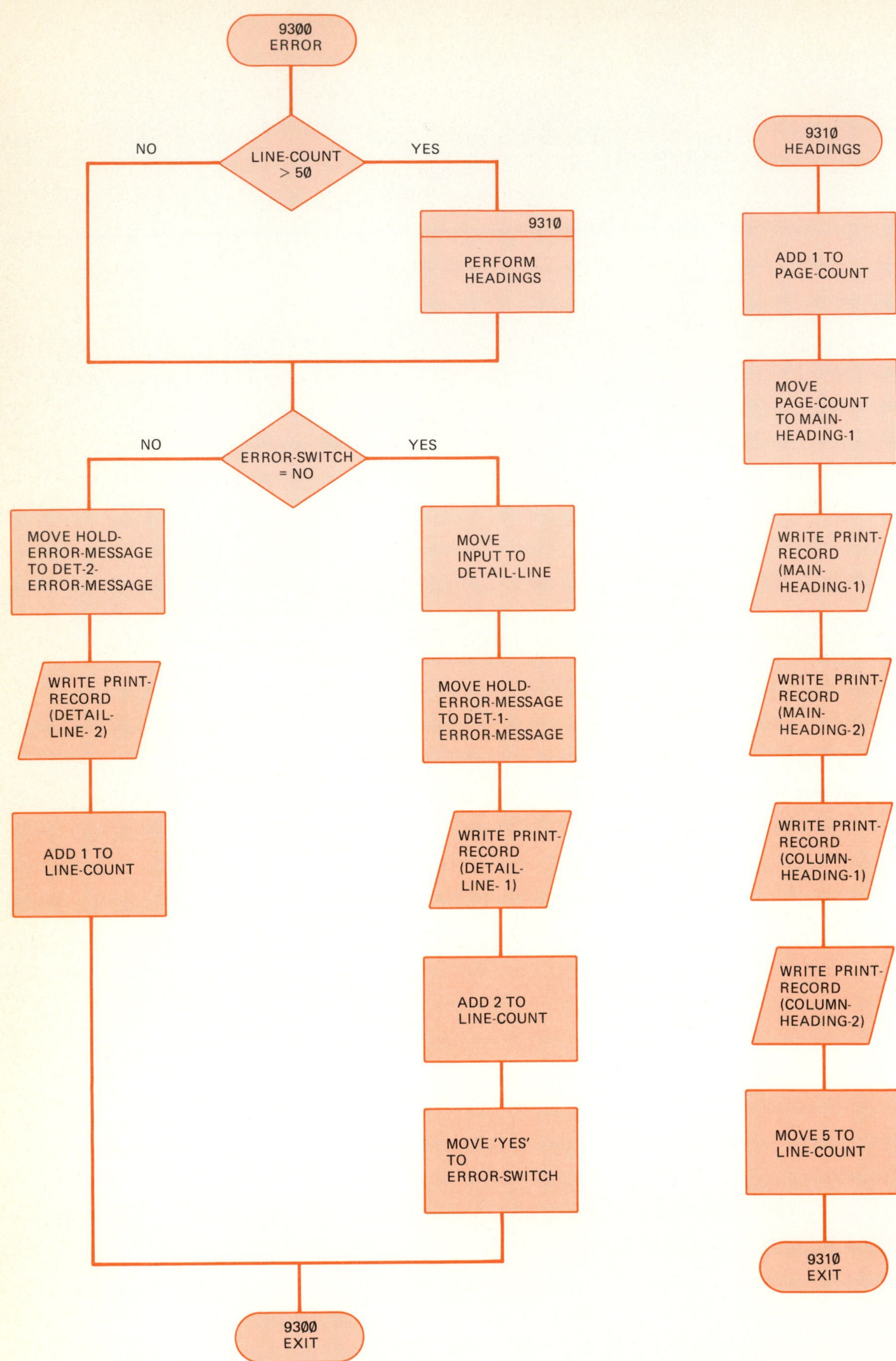

FIGURE 8–6 cont.

```
       1000-INITIALIZATION.
           OPEN INPUT  ORDER-FILE
                       PARTS-FILE
                OUTPUT PRINT-FILE.
           MOVE CURRENT-DATE                     TO WS-CURRENT-DATE.
           MOVE MONTH-TBL-ENTRY (WS-CURRENT-MM)  TO MAIN-HDG-MONTH.
           MOVE WS-CURRENT-DD                    TO MAIN-HDG-DAY.
           MOVE WS-CURRENT-YY                    TO MAIN-HDG-YEAR.
           PERFORM 9100-READ-PARTS-FILE.
           IF NOT END-OF-PARTS-FILE
               PERFORM 1100-LOAD-PARTS-TABLE
                   VARYING PART-INDEX FROM 1 BY 1
                       UNTIL END-OF-PARTS-FILE.
           PERFORM 9200-READ-ORDER-FILE.
```

FIGURE 8–7

1100-LOAD-PARTS-TABLE

The routine 1100-LOAD-PARTS-TABLE uses a record from PARTS-FILE and moves both the part number and part status of the item in question to a table in memory. The routine is invoked by 1000-INITIALIZATION, where it is controlled by a PERFORM . . . VARYING statement which increments the value of PART-INDEX each time the routine is performed. PART-INDEX then points to a new table element where the data should be placed each time the MOVEs in the routine are made. (See Figure 8–8.)

```
       1100-LOAD-PARTS-TABLE.
           MOVE PART-NBR      TO TBL-PART-NBR (PART-INDEX).
           MOVE PART-STATUS   TO TBL-PART-STATUS (PART-INDEX).
           PERFORM 9100-READ-PARTS-FILE.
```

FIGURE 8–8

2000-EDIT

A series of tests is performed on each record to ensure that each field in the record contains valid data. The program specification lists the criteria for each field. If a field passes the tests for valid data, tests are performed on the next field until all fields in the record have been tested.

If a field does not pass the test, an error message is moved to a hold area and an error routine is performed. The error routine prints data from the record and a message identifying the error.

Some of the fields are tested only to ensure that they contain numeric data. In these fields, any numeric value is considered valid. Other fields are tested for specific numeric values or ranges of values. The branch number and the shipping date are examples of the latter type of field. The sales order number is checked only for spaces. It is a field that normally contains alphanumeric data, so a test for whether it is numeric is not appropriate.

Two fields, ORD-SALES-REP and ORD-PART-NBR, are validated using table data. ORD-SALES-REP uses a compile-time table which contains the numbers of all current sales representatives. A routine, 2300-SEARCH-SALES-REP-TBL, is performed for each record. This routine goes through the sales representative table looking to match ORD-SALES-REP from the current record with an entry in the table. If a match is found, ORD-SALES-REP is considered valid. If no match is found, an error routine is performed.

The second field, ORD-PART-NBR, uses a table which was loaded from 1000-INITIALIZATION to ensure that the part number from each record is both valid and active. The table contains all part numbers and their status. The table is searched for a match with the part number from each record. If the part number is located in the table, the part number is valid. A second test is then performed to check whether the part is active. All discontinued parts have a 'D' in this field. If the part cannot be located in the table, or if it can be located but has a 'D' status, an error message is generated.

ORD-ACT-SHIP-DATE is tested for zeros, the presence of which means that the order has not been shipped yet. A new order which is to be added to the ORDER-FILE must not have been shipped. Anything else in this field at this point is considered invalid. (See Figure 8–9.)

```
       2000-EDIT.
           MOVE 'NO' TO ERROR-SWITCH.

           IF ORD-BRANCH IS NUMERIC
               IF VALID-BRANCH
                   NEXT SENTENCE
               ELSE
                   MOVE ERROR-MSG-01 TO HOLD-ERROR-MESSAGE
                   PERFORM 9300-ERROR
           ELSE
               MOVE ERROR-MSG-02 TO HOLD-ERROR-MESSAGE
               PERFORM 9300-ERROR.

           IF ORD-SALES-REP IS NUMERIC
               PERFORM 2300-SEARCH-SALES-REP-TBL
           ELSE
               MOVE ERROR-MSG-04 TO HOLD-ERROR-MESSAGE
               PERFORM 9300-ERROR.

           IF ORD-CUSTOMER-NBR IS NUMERIC
               NEXT SENTENCE
           ELSE
               MOVE ERROR-MSG-05 TO HOLD-ERROR-MESSAGE
               PERFORM 9300-ERROR.

           IF ORD-SALES-ORD-NBR = SPACES
               MOVE ERROR-MSG-06 TO HOLD-ERROR-MESSAGE
               PERFORM 9300-ERROR.

           MOVE ORD-DATE TO DATE-EDIT-AREA.
           PERFORM 2400-DATE-EDIT.
           IF DATE-ERROR
               MOVE ERROR-MSG-07 TO HOLD-ERROR-MESSAGE
               PERFORM 9300-ERROR.

           SEARCH ALL TBL-PART-NBR-ENTRY
               AT END
                   MOVE ERROR-MSG-08 TO HOLD-ERROR-MESSAGE
                   PERFORM 9300-ERROR
               WHEN TBL-PART-NBR (PART-INDEX) = ORD-PART-NBR
                   PERFORM 2500-CHECK-PART-STATUS.

           IF ORD-QUANTITY IS NUMERIC
               NEXT SENTENCE
           ELSE
               MOVE ERROR-MSG-10 TO HOLD-ERROR-MESSAGE
               PERFORM 9300-ERROR.

           IF ORD-UNIT-PRICE IS NUMERIC
               NEXT SENTENCE
           ELSE
               MOVE ERROR-MSG-11 TO HOLD-ERROR-MESSAGE
               PERFORM 9300-ERROR.

           MOVE ORD-REQ-SHIP-DATE TO DATE-EDIT-AREA.
           PERFORM 2400-DATE-EDIT.
           IF DATE-ERROR
               MOVE ERROR-MSG-12 TO HOLD-ERROR-MESSAGE
               PERFORM 9300-ERROR.

           IF ORD-ACT-SHIP-DATE = ZEROS
               NEXT SENTENCE
           ELSE
               MOVE ERROR-MSG-13 TO HOLD-ERROR-MESSAGE
               PERFORM 9300-ERROR.

           PERFORM 9200-READ-ORDER-FILE.
```

FIGURE 8–9

2300-SEARCH-SALES-REP-TBL

2300-SEARCH-SALES-REP-TBL searches the sales representative table looking to match ORD-SALES-REP from the current record with an entry in the table. If a match is found, ORD-SALES-REP is considered valid. The search is a serial search in which ORD-SALES-REP is compared with each table element, starting with the first and proceeding in a sequential manner until a match is found or the end of the table is reached. (See Figure 8–10.)

```
        2300-SEARCH-SALES-REP-TBL.
            SET SALES-INDEX TO 1.
            SEARCH SALES-REP-TBL-ENTRY
                AT END
                    MOVE ERROR-MSG-03 TO HOLD-ERROR-MESSAGE
                    PERFORM 9300-ERROR
                WHEN SALES-REP-TBL-ENTRY (SALES-INDEX) = ORD-SALES-REP
                    NEXT SENTENCE.
```

FIGURE 8–10

2400-DATE-EDIT

Condition names (88 levels) are used to assist in editing dates. The date is moved to a date editing area in the 2000-EDIT routine, and then 2400-DATE-EDIT is performed. Each portion of the data description (the year, month, and day) has been provided with condition names whose values lie within the ranges of those elements. This allows a less complicated and more English-like test for the various ranges. (See Figure 8–11.)

```
        2400-DATE-EDIT.
            MOVE 'NO' TO DATE-EDIT-ERROR-SWITCH.
            IF (THIRTY-ONE-DAY-MONTH AND VALID-31-DAYS)  OR
               (THIRTY-DAY-MONTH AND VALID-30-DAYS)      OR
               (FEBRUARY AND VALID-28-DAYS)              OR
               (FEBRUARY AND LEAP-YEAR AND VALID-29-DAYS)
                NEXT SENTENCE
            ELSE
                MOVE 'YES' TO DATE-EDIT-ERROR-SWITCH.
```

FIGURE 8–11

2500-CHECK-PART-STATUS

Once a part number from the input record has been located in the table, a test is performed to ensure that it is an active part number. (See Figure 8–12.)

```
        2500-CHECK-PART-STATUS.
            IF PART-DISCONTINUED (PART-INDEX)
                MOVE ERROR-MSG-09 TO HOLD-ERROR-MESSAGE
                PERFORM 9300-ERROR.
```

FIGURE 8–12

3000-EOJ

The only action necessary in 3000-EOJ is to close the files. (See Figure 8–13.)

```
        3000-EOJ.
            CLOSE ORDER-FILE
                  PARTS-FILE
                  PRINT-FILE.
```

FIGURE 8–13

9100-READ-PARTS-FILE

The routine 9100-READ-PARTS-FILE is performed initially from 1000-INITIALIZATION and repeatedly from 1100-LOAD-PARTS-TABLE until the end of the file is reached. The data read is loaded into a table in WORKING-STORAGE for use in subsequent editing. (See Figure 8–14.)

```
9100-READ-PARTS-FILE.
    READ PARTS-FILE
        AT END
            MOVE 'YES' TO END-FLAG-PARTS-FILE.
```

FIGURE 8–14

9200-READ-ORDER-FILE

9200-READ-ORDER-FILE is performed initially from 1000-INITIALIZATION and repeatedly from 2000-EDIT until the end of file is reached. (See Figure 8–15.)

```
9200-READ-ORDER-FILE.
    READ ORDER-FILE
        AT END
            MOVE 'YES' TO END-FLAG-ORDER-FILE.
```

FIGURE 8–15

9300-ERROR

The error routine handles the printing of error messages. Two types of detail lines are produced. If the error is the first for a record, a full detail line which includes the input data and an error message is printed. For any subsequent errors for the same record, a second detail line is used which prints only the error message. A switch (ERROR-SWITCH) is used to determine whether an error is the first for a record. The switch is set to 'NO' at the beginning of 2000-EDIT and is changed to 'YES' the first time the error routine is performed for any given record. (See Figure 8–16.)

```
9300-ERROR.

    IF LINE-COUNT > 50
        PERFORM 9310-HEADINGS.

    IF ERROR-SWITCH = 'NO'
        MOVE ORD-BRANCH          TO DET-BRANCH
        MOVE ORD-SALES-REP       TO DET-SALES-REP
        MOVE ORD-CUSTOMER-NBR    TO DET-CUSTOMER-NBR
        MOVE ORD-CUST-PO-NBR     TO DET-CUST-PO-NBR
        MOVE ORD-SALES-ORD-NBR   TO DET-SALES-ORD-NBR
        MOVE ORD-YY              TO DET-ORDER-YY
        MOVE ORD-MM              TO DET-ORDER-MM
        MOVE ORD-DD              TO DET-ORDER-DD
        MOVE ORD-PART-NBR        TO DET-PART-NBR
        MOVE ORD-QUANTITY        TO DET-QUANTITY
        MOVE ORD-UNIT-PRICE      TO DET-UNIT-PRICE
        MOVE ORD-REQ-SHIP-YY     TO DET-REQ-SHIP-YY
        MOVE ORD-REQ-SHIP-MM     TO DET-REQ-SHIP-MM
        MOVE ORD-REQ-SHIP-DD     TO DET-REQ-SHIP-DD
        MOVE ORD-ACT-SHIP-YY     TO DET-ACT-SHIP-YY
        MOVE ORD-ACT-SHIP-MM     TO DET-ACT-SHIP-MM
        MOVE ORD-ACT-SHIP-DD     TO DET-ACT-SHIP-DD
        MOVE HOLD-ERROR-MESSAGE TO DET-1-ERROR-MESSAGE
        WRITE PRINT-RECORD FROM DETAIL-LINE-1
            AFTER ADVANCING 2 LINES
        ADD 2 TO LINE-COUNT
        MOVE 'YES' TO ERROR-SWITCH
    ELSE
        MOVE HOLD-ERROR-MESSAGE TO DET-2-ERROR-MESSAGE
        WRITE PRINT-RECORD FROM DETAIL-LINE-2
            AFTER ADVANCING 1 LINE
        ADD 1 TO LINE-COUNT.
```

FIGURE 8–16

9310-HEADINGS

The routine 9310-HEADINGS is an ordinary heading routine. It does, however, print the month name rather than the month number. The name is placed in the heading line in 1000-INITIALIZATION. (See Figure 8–17.)

```
       9310-HEADINGS.
           ADD 1 TO PAGE-COUNT.
           MOVE PAGE-COUNT TO MAIN-HDG-PAGE-NBR.
           WRITE PRINT-RECORD FROM MAIN-HEADING-1
               AFTER ADVANCING PAGE.
           WRITE PRINT-RECORD FROM MAIN-HEADING-2
               AFTER ADVANCING 1 LINE.
           WRITE PRINT-RECORD FROM COLUMN-HEADING-1
               AFTER ADVANCING 2 LINES.
           WRITE PRINT-RECORD FROM COLUMN-HEADING-2
               AFTER ADVANCING 1 LINE.
           MOVE 5 TO LINE-COUNT.
```

FIGURE 8–17

THE COBOL PROGRAM

Test Data

The two sets of test data for the EDIT program are shown in Figure 8–18. The ORDER-FILE data is similar to the data in all the previous chapters, except that a number of errors have been incorporated into it. The second data set is the PARTS-FILE. It is used to load a table which is in turn used to validate part numbers.

ORDER-FILE

```
Ø12Ø1ØØ3ØØPO173         87Ø229GL4Ø2AØØØØ!Ø45ØØØ871116ØØØØØØ
Ø1354Ø47278372    G4838887Ø913WB7Ø2XØØØ9ØØ115ØØ871101ØØØØØØ
Ø12Ø1ØØ3ØØE1Ø12   B12335871105WB493EØØØØ2Ø54ØØØ871122ØØØØØØ
Ø3ØØ747300        H8477787Ø223MF4Ø3TØØØØ5Ø4ØØØØ87Ø5Ø2ØØØØØØ
 3ØØ7ØØ378EBNER   H84579      VX922PØØ8ØØØØ12758U112ØØØØØØØ
Ø3ØØ7739897747    B89288871106MF848JØØØØ5Ø2145Ø88Ø13ØØØØØØØ
Ø3ØØ7ØØ28334567X  B34237871Ø3ØHL834EØØØ16Ø19ØØØ871121ØØØØØØ
Ø3   473ØØ        Y289Ø387Ø811VXØØ1LØØ2ØØØØ622Ø8712Ø38711Ø8
Ø344Ø6948187Ø341  GØ418Ø87Ø2Ø9JGØ4ØXØØØØ1Ø%@%))88Ø619ØØØØØØ
Ø361182888P2783733B8433Ø871Ø25HL289BØØØ1ØØ234ØØ871113ØØØØØØ
Ø361128375T7838   T7829987Ø323JG563WØØØØ6Ø43ØØØ871Ø18ØØØØØØ
Ø36115Ø912        H6915Ø87Ø2Ø6MF848TØØØØ3Ø36ØØØ8712Ø1ØØØØØØ
Ø8174314Ø865      H4189187Ø412GN448TØØØ18ØØ78ØØ87Ø63ØØØØØØØ
Ø8174Ø18Ø5R7278   T2164287Ø81ØTK497XØØØ1ØØ118ØØ87113ØØØØØØØ
Ø8174E18Ø5R8322   Y211Ø58716Ø1TN116TØØØØ1Ø3ØØØØ871221ØØØØØØ
Ø891562Ø54SCHUH   L5Ø6818711Ø8TK812EØØØØ6Ø573ØØ88Ø1Ø5ØØØØØØ
1891521Ø78        B71Ø458719Ø1FV782TØØØØ3ØØ28ØØ871115ØØØØØØ
```

PARTS-FILE

```
FVØ4ØX DROP HANDLEBARS
FV563W HANDLEBAR TAPE - BLACK
FV782T TOURING PEDALS
FV848J RACING PEDALS
GN1Ø9T FRONT DERAILLEUR
GN116T REAR DERAILLEUR
GN4Ø2A JAPANESE COMPONENT GROUP
GN4Ø3T CANVAS TOURING SHOES
GN448TDLEATHER RACING SHOES
HL289B WIND RESISTANCE TRAINER
HL834E BICYCLE REPAIR STAND
HL911PDLEATHER RACING HELMET
JGØ4ØX TOURING FRAMESET - 25 IN.
JG563W TOURING FRAMESET - 19 IN.
MF4Ø3T RACING FRAMESET - 23 IN.
MF848J CAR TOP BICYCLE CARRIER
MF848T BIKE MECHANICS TOOL KIT
TK497X 7ØØ X 25C WHEELS (2)
TK61ØL 68  X 42T CRANKSET
TK812E TOURING BICYCLE - 23 IN.
TN116T WHEEL TRUING STAND
VXØØ1L SIDEPULL BRAKES
VX533T 27 X 1 IN. TUBE
VX922P 27 X 1 IN. TIRE
VX926P 27 X 1 1/4 IN. TIRE
VX932P 7ØØ X 25C TIRE
WB493E ITALIAN COMPONENT GROUP
WB7Ø2X 7ØØ X 25 C WHEELS (2)
```

FIGURE 8–18

Sample Output

Sample output is shown in Figure 8–19.

NOVEMBER 09, 1987 PRODUCT DISTRIBUTION INC. PAGE: 1

ORDER FILE ERROR REPORT

BRANCH	SALES REP	CUST#	CUSTOMER PO#	SALES ORDER#	ORDER DATE	PART#	QTY	UNIT PRICE	REQUESTED SHIP DATE	ACTUAL SHIP DATE	ERROR MESSAGE
01	201	00300	P0173		02 29 87	GL402A	0000!	045000	11 16 87	00 00 00	SALES ORDER# IS MISSING ORDER DATE IS INVALID INVALID PART#, NOT IN FILE QUANTITY IS NOT NUMERIC
01	354	04727	8372	G48388	09 13 87	WB702X	00090	011500	11 01 87	00 00 00	SALES REP# NOT ON TABLE
3	007	00378	EBNER	H84579		VX922P	00800	001275	11 20 8U	00 00 00	BRANCH IS NOT NUMERIC ORDER DATE IS INVALID
03		47300		Y28903	08 11 87	VX001L	00200	006220	12 03 87	11 08 87	SALES REP# IS NOT NUMERIC ACTUAL SHIP DATE MUST BE ZERO
03	440	69481	870341	G04180	02 09 87	JG040X	00001	0%@%))	06 19 88	00 00 00	UNIT PRICE IS NOT NUMERIC
08	174	31408	65	H41891	04 12 87	GN448T	00018	007800	06 30 87	00 00 00	PART IS DISCONTINUED
08	174	E1805	R8322	Y21105	16 01 87	TN116T	00001	030000	12 21 87	00 00 00	CUSTOMER# IS NOT NUMERIC ORDER DATE IS INVALID
18	915	21078		B71045	19 01 87	FV782T	00003	002800	11 15 87	00 00 00	BRANCH OUT OF RANGE ORDER DATE IS INVALID

FIGURE 8–19

The Program

The complete COBOL EDIT program is shown in Figure 8–20.

```
 IDENTIFICATION DIVISION.

 PROGRAM-ID.    EDIT.

 AUTHOR.        HELEN HUMPHREYS.

 INSTALLATION.  PRODUCT DISTRIBUTION INC.

 DATE-WRITTEN.  Ø8/Ø6/87.

 DATE-COMPILED. Ø8/18/87.

 INSTALLATION.  PRODUCT DISTRIBUTION INC.

*****************************************************************
*                                                               *
*    THIS PROGRAM EDITS INPUT FOR THE ORDER-FILE.  EACH FIELD   *
*    IN THE ORDER-RECORD IS TESTED FOR VALIDITY.  ITEMS THAT    *
*    ARE NOT VALID WILL BE IDENTIFIED ON A PRINTED REPORT.      *
*                                                               *
*****************************************************************

 ENVIRONMENT DIVISION.

 CONFIGURATION SECTION.

 SOURCE-COMPUTER.
     IBM-37Ø.
 OBJECT-COMPUTER.
     IBM-37Ø.

 INPUT-OUTPUT SECTION.
 FILE-CONTROL.
     SELECT ORDER-FILE ASSIGN TO DISK.
     SELECT PARTS-FILE ASSIGN TO DISK.
     SELECT PRINT-FILE ASSIGN TO PRINTER.

 DATA DIVISION.
```

FIGURE 8–20

```
       FILE SECTION.

       FD  ORDER-FILE
           LABEL RECORDS ARE STANDARD
           RECORD CONTAINS 7Ø CHARACTERS
           DATA RECORD IS ORDER-RECORD.

       Ø1  ORDER-RECORD.
           Ø5  ORD-BRANCH                PIC X(2).
               88  VALID-BRANCH              VALUES 'Ø1' THRU '1Ø'.
           Ø5  ORD-SALES-REP             PIC X(3).
           Ø5  ORD-CUSTOMER-NBR          PIC X(5).
           Ø5  ORD-CUST-PO-NBR           PIC X(8).
           Ø5  ORD-SALES-ORD-NBR         PIC X(6).
           Ø5  ORD-DATE.
               1Ø  ORD-YY                PIC X(2).
               1Ø  ORD-MM                PIC X(2).
               1Ø  ORD-DD                PIC X(2).
           Ø5  ORD-PART-NBR              PIC X(6).
           Ø5  ORD-QUANTITY              PIC X(5).
           Ø5  ORD-UNIT-PRICE            PIC X(6).
           Ø5  ORD-REQ-SHIP-DATE.
               1Ø  ORD-REQ-SHIP-YY       PIC X(2).
               1Ø  ORD-REQ-SHIP-MM       PIC X(2).
               1Ø  ORD-REQ-SHIP-DD       PIC X(2).
           Ø5  ORD-ACT-SHIP-DATE.
               1Ø  ORD-ACT-SHIP-YY       PIC X(2).
               1Ø  ORD-ACT-SHIP-MM       PIC X(2).
               1Ø  ORD-ACT-SHIP-DD       PIC X(2).
           Ø5  FILLER                    PIC X(11).

       FD  PARTS-FILE
           LABEL RECORDS ARE STANDARD
           RECORD CONTAINS 45 CHARACTERS
           DATA RECORD IS PARTS-RECORD.

       Ø1  PARTS-RECORD.
           Ø5  PART-NBR                  PIC X(6).
           Ø5  PART-STATUS               PIC X(1).
           Ø5  PART-DESCRIPTION          PIC X(25).
           Ø5  FILLER                    PIC X(13).

       FD  PRINT-FILE
           LABEL RECORDS ARE OMITTED
           RECORD CONTAINS 133 CHARACTERS
           DATA RECORD IS PRINT-RECORD.

       Ø1  PRINT-RECORD                  PIC X(133).

       WORKING-STORAGE SECTION.

       Ø1  HOLDS-COUNTERS-SWITCHES.
           Ø5  END-FLAG-ORDER-FILE       PIC X(3)        VALUE 'NO'.
               88  END-OF-ORDER-FILE                     VALUE 'YES'.
           Ø5  END-FLAG-PARTS-FILE       PIC X(3)        VALUE 'NO'.
               88  END-OF-PARTS-FILE                     VALUE 'YES'.
           Ø5  DATE-EDIT-ERROR-SWITCH    PIC X(3).
               88  DATE-ERROR                            VALUE 'YES'.
           Ø5  ERROR-SWITCH              PIC X(3).
           Ø5  LINE-COUNT                PIC 9(2)        VALUE 99.
           Ø5  PAGE-COUNT                PIC 9(3)        VALUE ZEROS.
           Ø5  HOLD-ERROR-MESSAGE        PIC X(3Ø).

       Ø1  WS-CURRENT-DATE.
           Ø5  WS-CURRENT-MM             PIC 9(2).
           Ø5  FILLER                    PIC X(1).
           Ø5  WS-CURRENT-DD             PIC 9(2).
           Ø5  FILLER                    PIC X(1).
           Ø5  WS-CURRENT-YY             PIC 9(2).

       Ø1  DATE-EDIT-AREA.
           Ø5  DATE-EDIT-YY              PIC X(2).
               88  LEAP-YEAR                 VALUES 'ØØ' 'Ø4' 'Ø8' '12'
                                                    '16' '2Ø' '24' '28'
                                                    '32' '36' '4Ø' '44'
                                                    '48' '52' '56' '6Ø'
                                                    '64' '68' '72' '76'
                                                    '8Ø' '84' '88' '92'
                                                    '96'.
           Ø5  DATE-EDIT-MM              PIC X(2).
               88  FEBRUARY                  VALUE 'Ø2'.
               88  THIRTY-DAY-MONTH          VALUE 'Ø4' 'Ø6' 'Ø9' '11'.
```

FIGURE 8–20 cont.

```
            88  THIRTY-ONE-DAY-MONTH     VALUE 'Ø1' 'Ø3' 'Ø5' 'Ø7'
                                               'Ø8' '1Ø' '12'.
        Ø5  DATE-EDIT-DD               PIC X(2).
            88  VALID-28-DAYS              VALUES 'Ø1' THRU '28'.
            88  VALID-29-DAYS              VALUES 'Ø1' THRU '29'.
            88  VALID-3Ø-DAYS              VALUES 'Ø1' THRU '3Ø'.
            88  VALID-31-DAYS              VALUES 'Ø1' THRU '31'.

    Ø1  MONTH-DATA.
        Ø5  FILLER                     PIC X(9)    VALUE 'JANUARY'.
        Ø5  FILLER                     PIC X(9)    VALUE 'FEBRUARY'.
        Ø5  FILLER                     PIC X(9)    VALUE 'MARCH'.
        Ø5  FILLER                     PIC X(9)    VALUE 'APRIL'.
        Ø5  FILLER                     PIC X(9)    VALUE 'MAY'.
        Ø5  FILLER                     PIC X(9)    VALUE 'JUNE'.
        Ø5  FILLER                     PIC X(9)    VALUE 'JULY'.
        Ø5  FILLER                     PIC X(9)    VALUE 'AUGUST'.
        Ø5  FILLER                     PIC X(9)    VALUE 'SEPTEMBER'.
        Ø5  FILLER                     PIC X(9)    VALUE 'OCTOBER'.
        Ø5  FILLER                     PIC X(9)    VALUE 'NOVEMBER'.
        Ø5  FILLER                     PIC X(9)    VALUE 'DECEMBER'.

    Ø1  MONTH-TABLE REDEFINES MONTH-DATA.
        Ø5  MONTH-TBL-ENTRY  OCCURS 12 TIMES  PIC X(Ø9).

    Ø1  SALES-REP-DATA.
        Ø5  FILLER                     PIC 9(3)    VALUE ØØ7.
        Ø5  FILLER                     PIC 9(3)    VALUE 816.
        Ø5  FILLER                     PIC 9(3)    VALUE 2Ø1.
        Ø5  FILLER                     PIC 9(3)    VALUE 611.
        Ø5  FILLER                     PIC 9(3)    VALUE 353.
        Ø5  FILLER                     PIC 9(3)    VALUE 44Ø.
        Ø5  FILLER                     PIC 9(3)    VALUE 174.
        Ø5  FILLER                     PIC 9(3)    VALUE 915.

    Ø1  SALES-REP-TABLE REDEFINES SALES-REP-DATA.
        Ø5  SALES-REP-TBL-ENTRY OCCURS 8 TIMES
                                INDEXED BY SALES-INDEX
                                PIC 9(3).

    Ø1  PART-NBR-TABLE.
        Ø5  TBL-PART-NBR-ENTRY   OCCURS 2ØØ TIMES
                                 INDEXED BY PART-INDEX
                                 ASCENDING KEY IS TBL-PART-NBR.
            1Ø  TBL-PART-NBR     PIC X(6).
            1Ø  TBL-PART-STATUS  PIC X(1).
                88  PART-DISCONTINUED              VALUE 'D'.

    Ø1  EDIT-ERROR-MESSAGES.
        Ø5  ERROR-MSG-Ø1               PIC X(3Ø)       VALUE
                                       'BRANCH OUT OF RANGE'.
        Ø5  ERROR-MSG-Ø2               PIC X(3Ø)       VALUE
                                       'BRANCH IS NOT NUMERIC'.
        Ø5  ERROR-MSG-Ø3               PIC X(3Ø)       VALUE
                                       'SALES REP# NOT ON TABLE'.
        Ø5  ERROR-MSG-Ø4               PIC X(3Ø)       VALUE
                                       'SALES REP# IS NOT NUMERIC'.
        Ø5  ERROR-MSG-Ø5               PIC X(3Ø)       VALUE
                                       'CUSTOMER# IS NOT NUMERIC'.
        Ø5  ERROR-MSG-Ø6               PIC X(3Ø)       VALUE
                                       'SALES ORDER# IS MISSING'.
        Ø5  ERROR-MSG-Ø7               PIC X(3Ø)       VALUE
                                       'ORDER DATE IS INVALID'.
        Ø5  ERROR-MSG-Ø8               PIC X(3Ø)       VALUE
                                       'INVALID PART#, NOT IN FILE'.
        Ø5  ERROR-MSG-Ø9               PIC X(3Ø)       VALUE
                                       'PART IS DISCONTINUED'.
        Ø5  ERROR-MSG-1Ø               PIC X(3Ø)       VALUE
                                       'QUANTITY IS NOT NUMERIC'.
        Ø5  ERROR-MSG-11               PIC X(3Ø)       VALUE
                                       'UNIT PRICE IS NOT NUMERIC'.
        Ø5  ERROR-MSG-12               PIC X(3Ø)       VALUE
                                       'REQUESTED SHIP DATE IS INVALID'.
        Ø5  ERROR-MSG-13               PIC X(3Ø)       VALUE
                                       'ACTUAL SHIP DATE MUST BE ZERO'.

    Ø1  MAIN-HEADING-1.
        Ø5  FILLER                     PIC X(1)        VALUE SPACES.
        Ø5  MAIN-HDG-MONTH             PIC X(9).
        Ø5  FILLER                     PIC X(1)        VALUE SPACES.
        Ø5  MAIN-HDG-DAY               PIC 9(2).
        Ø5  FILLER                     PIC X(4)        VALUE ', 19'.
```

FIGURE 8–20 cont.

```
           Ø5  MAIN-HDG-YEAR           PIC 9(2).
           Ø5  FILLER                  PIC X(35)       VALUE SPACES.
           Ø5  FILLER                  PIC X(25)       VALUE
                                       'PRODUCT DISTRIBUTION INC.'.
           Ø5  FILLER                  PIC X(44)       VALUE SPACES.
           Ø5  FILLER                  PIC X(6)        VALUE 'PAGE:'.
           Ø5  MAIN-HDG-PAGE-NBR       PIC ZZ9.
           Ø5  FILLER                  PIC X(1)        VALUE SPACES.

       Ø1  MAIN-HEADING-2.
           Ø5  FILLER                  PIC X(55)       VALUE SPACES.
           Ø5  FILLER                  PIC X(23)       VALUE
                                       'ORDER FILE ERROR REPORT'.
           Ø5  FILLER                  PIC X(55)       VALUE SPACES.

       Ø1  COLUMN-HEADING-1.
           Ø5  FILLER                  PIC X(9)        VALUE SPACES.
           Ø5  FILLER                  PIC X(5)        VALUE 'SALES'.
           Ø5  FILLER                  PIC X(1Ø)       VALUE SPACES.
           Ø5  FILLER                  PIC X(8)        VALUE 'CUSTOMER'.
           Ø5  FILLER                  PIC X(3)        VALUE SPACES.
           Ø5  FILLER                  PIC X(5)        VALUE 'SALES'.
           Ø5  FILLER                  PIC X(6)        VALUE SPACES.
           Ø5  FILLER                  PIC X(5)        VALUE 'ORDER'.
           Ø5  FILLER                  PIC X(22)       VALUE SPACES.
           Ø5  FILLER                  PIC X(4)        VALUE 'UNIT'.
           Ø5  FILLER                  PIC X(4)        VALUE SPACES.
           Ø5  FILLER                  PIC X(9)        VALUE
                                                       'REQUESTED'.
           Ø5  FILLER                  PIC X(3)        VALUE SPACES.
           Ø5  FILLER                  PIC X(6)        VALUE 'ACTUAL'.
           Ø5  FILLER                  PIC X(34)       VALUE SPACES.

       Ø1  COLUMN-HEADING-2.
           Ø5  FILLER                  PIC X(1)        VALUE SPACES.
           Ø5  FILLER                  PIC X(6)        VALUE 'BRANCH'.
           Ø5  FILLER                  PIC X(3)        VALUE SPACES.
           Ø5  FILLER                  PIC X(3)        VALUE 'REP'.
           Ø5  FILLER                  PIC X(3)        VALUE SPACES.
           Ø5  FILLER                  PIC X(5)        VALUE 'CUST#'.
           Ø5  FILLER                  PIC X(5)        VALUE SPACES.
           Ø5  FILLER                  PIC X(3)        VALUE 'PO#'.
           Ø5  FILLER                  PIC X(6)        VALUE SPACES.
           Ø5  FILLER                  PIC X(6)        VALUE 'ORDER#'.
           Ø5  FILLER                  PIC X(5)        VALUE SPACES.
           Ø5  FILLER                  PIC X(4)        VALUE 'DATE'.
           Ø5  FILLER                  PIC X(5)        VALUE SPACES.
           Ø5  FILLER                  PIC X(5)        VALUE 'PART#'.
           Ø5  FILLER                  PIC X(5)        VALUE SPACES.
           Ø5  FILLER                  PIC X(3)        VALUE 'QTY'.
           Ø5  FILLER                  PIC X(5)        VALUE SPACES.
           Ø5  FILLER                  PIC X(5)        VALUE 'PRICE'.
           Ø5  FILLER                  PIC X(3)        VALUE SPACES.
           Ø5  FILLER                  PIC X(9)        VALUE
                                                       'SHIP DATE'.
           Ø5  FILLER                  PIC X(2)        VALUE SPACES.
           Ø5  FILLER                  PIC X(9)        VALUE
                                                       'SHIP DATE'.
           Ø5  FILLER                  PIC X(5)        VALUE SPACES.
           Ø5  FILLER                  PIC X(13)       VALUE
                                                       'ERROR MESSAGE'.
           Ø5  FILLER                  PIC X(14)       VALUE SPACES.

       Ø1  DETAIL-LINE-1.
           Ø5  FILLER                  PIC X(3)        VALUE SPACES.
           Ø5  DET-BRANCH              PIC X(2).
           Ø5  FILLER                  PIC X(5)        VALUE SPACES.
           Ø5  DET-SALES-REP           PIC X(3).
           Ø5  FILLER                  PIC X(3)        VALUE SPACES.
           Ø5  DET-CUSTOMER-NBR        PIC X(5).
           Ø5  FILLER                  PIC X(3)        VALUE SPACES.
           Ø5  DET-CUST-PO-NBR         PIC X(8).
           Ø5  FILLER                  PIC X(3)        VALUE SPACES.
           Ø5  DET-SALES-ORD-NBR       PIC X(6).
           Ø5  FILLER                  PIC X(3)        VALUE SPACES.
           Ø5  DET-ORDER-MM            PIC X(2).
           Ø5  FILLER                  PIC X(1)        VALUE SPACES.
           Ø5  DET-ORDER-DD            PIC X(2).
           Ø5  FILLER                  PIC X(1)        VALUE SPACES.
           Ø5  DET-ORDER-YY            PIC X(2).
           Ø5  FILLER                  PIC X(3)        VALUE SPACES.
           Ø5  DET-PART-NBR            PIC X(6).
```

FIGURE 8–20 cont.

```
           Ø5  FILLER                  PIC X(3)        VALUE SPACES.
           Ø5  DET-QUANTITY            PIC X(5).
           Ø5  FILLER                  PIC X(3)        VALUE SPACES.
           Ø5  DET-UNIT-PRICE          PIC X(6).
           Ø5  FILLER                  PIC X(3)        VALUE SPACES.
           Ø5  DET-REQ-SHIP-MM         PIC X(2).
           Ø5  FILLER                  PIC X(1)        VALUE SPACES.
           Ø5  DET-REQ-SHIP-DD         PIC X(2).
           Ø5  FILLER                  PIC X(1)        VALUE SPACES.
           Ø5  DET-REQ-SHIP-YY         PIC X(2).
           Ø5  FILLER                  PIC X(3)        VALUE SPACES.
           Ø5  DET-ACT-SHIP-MM         PIC X(2).
           Ø5  FILLER                  PIC X(1)        VALUE SPACES.
           Ø5  DET-ACT-SHIP-DD         PIC X(2).
           Ø5  FILLER                  PIC X(1)        VALUE SPACES.
           Ø5  DET-ACT-SHIP-YY         PIC X(2).
           Ø5  FILLER                  PIC X(2)        VALUE SPACES.
           Ø5  DET-1-ERROR-MESSAGE     PIC X(3Ø).
           Ø5  FILLER                  PIC X(1)        VALUE SPACES.

       Ø1  DETAIL-LINE-2.
           Ø5  FILLER                  PIC X(1Ø2)      VALUE SPACES.
           Ø5  DET-2-ERROR-MESSAGE     PIC X(3Ø).
           Ø5  FILLER                  PIC X(1)        VALUE SPACES.

       PROCEDURE DIVISION.

           PERFORM 1ØØØ-INITIALIZATION.
           PERFORM 2ØØØ-EDIT
               UNTIL END-OF-ORDER-FILE.
           PERFORM 3ØØØ-EOJ.
           STOP RUN.

       1ØØØ-INITIALIZATION.
           OPEN INPUT  ORDER-FILE
                       PARTS-FILE
                OUTPUT PRINT-FILE.
           MOVE CURRENT-DATE                      TO WS-CURRENT-DATE.
           MOVE MONTH-TBL-ENTRY (WS-CURRENT-MM)   TO MAIN-HDG-MONTH.
           MOVE WS-CURRENT-DD                     TO MAIN-HDG-DAY.
           MOVE WS-CURRENT-YY                     TO MAIN-HDG-YEAR.
           PERFORM 91ØØ-READ-PARTS-FILE.
           IF NOT END-OF-PARTS-FILE
               PERFORM 11ØØ-LOAD-PARTS-TABLE
                   VARYING PART-INDEX FROM 1 BY 1
                       UNTIL END-OF-PARTS-FILE.
           PERFORM 92ØØ-READ-ORDER-FILE.

       11ØØ-LOAD-PARTS-TABLE.
           MOVE PART-NBR      TO TBL-PART-NBR (PART-INDEX).
           MOVE PART-STATUS   TO TBL-PART-STATUS (PART-INDEX).
           PERFORM 91ØØ-READ-PARTS-FILE.

       2ØØØ-EDIT.
           MOVE 'NO' TO ERROR-SWITCH.

           IF ORD-BRANCH IS NUMERIC
               IF VALID-BRANCH
                   NEXT SENTENCE
               ELSE
                   MOVE ERROR-MSG-Ø1 TO HOLD-ERROR-MESSAGE
                   PERFORM 93ØØ-ERROR
           ELSE
               MOVE ERROR-MSG-Ø2 TO HOLD-ERROR-MESSAGE
               PERFORM 93ØØ-ERROR.

           IF ORD-SALES-REP IS NUMERIC
               PERFORM 23ØØ-SEARCH-SALES-REP-TBL
           ELSE
               MOVE ERROR-MSG-Ø4 TO HOLD-ERROR-MESSAGE
               PERFORM 93ØØ-ERROR.

           IF ORD-CUSTOMER-NBR IS NUMERIC
               NEXT SENTENCE
           ELSE
               MOVE ERROR-MSG-Ø5 TO HOLD-ERROR-MESSAGE
               PERFORM 93ØØ-ERROR.

           IF ORD-SALES-ORD-NBR = SPACES
               MOVE ERROR-MSG-Ø6 TO HOLD-ERROR-MESSAGE
               PERFORM 93ØØ-ERROR.
```

FIGURE 8–20 cont.

```
    MOVE ORD-DATE TO DATE-EDIT-AREA.
    PERFORM 24ØØ-DATE-EDIT.
    IF DATE-ERROR
        MOVE ERROR-MSG-Ø7 TO HOLD-ERROR-MESSAGE
        PERFORM 93ØØ-ERROR.

    SEARCH ALL TBL-PART-NBR-ENTRY
        AT END
            MOVE ERROR-MSG-Ø8 TO HOLD-ERROR-MESSAGE
            PERFORM 93ØØ-ERROR
        WHEN TBL-PART-NBR (PART-INDEX) = ORD-PART-NBR
            PERFORM 25ØØ-CHECK-PART-STATUS.

    IF ORD-QUANTITY IS NUMERIC
        NEXT SENTENCE
    ELSE
        MOVE ERROR-MSG-1Ø TO HOLD-ERROR-MESSAGE
        PERFORM 93ØØ-ERROR.

    IF ORD-UNIT-PRICE IS NUMERIC
        NEXT SENTENCE
    ELSE
        MOVE ERROR-MSG-11 TO HOLD-ERROR-MESSAGE
        PERFORM 93ØØ-ERROR.

    MOVE ORD-REQ-SHIP-DATE TO DATE-EDIT-AREA.
    PERFORM 24ØØ-DATE-EDIT.
    IF DATE-ERROR
        MOVE ERROR-MSG-12 TO HOLD-ERROR-MESSAGE
        PERFORM 93ØØ-ERROR.

    IF ORD-ACT-SHIP-DATE = ZEROS
        NEXT SENTENCE
    ELSE
        MOVE ERROR-MSG-13 TO HOLD-ERROR-MESSAGE
        PERFORM 93ØØ-ERROR.

    PERFORM 92ØØ-READ-ORDER-FILE.


23ØØ-SEARCH-SALES-REP-TBL.
    SET SALES-INDEX TO 1.
    SEARCH SALES-REP-TBL-ENTRY
        AT END
            MOVE ERROR-MSG-Ø3 TO HOLD-ERROR-MESSAGE
            PERFORM 93ØØ-ERROR
        WHEN SALES-REP-TBL-ENTRY (SALES-INDEX) = ORD-SALES-REP
            NEXT SENTENCE.

24ØØ-DATE-EDIT.
    MOVE 'NO' TO DATE-EDIT-ERROR-SWITCH.
    IF (THIRTY-ONE-DAY-MONTH AND VALID-31-DAYS)  OR
       (THIRTY-DAY-MONTH AND VALID-3Ø-DAYS)      OR
       (FEBRUARY AND VALID-28-DAYS)              OR
       (FEBRUARY AND LEAP-YEAR AND VALID-29-DAYS)
        NEXT SENTENCE
    ELSE
        MOVE 'YES' TO DATE-EDIT-ERROR-SWITCH.

25ØØ-CHECK-PART-STATUS.
    IF PART-DISCONTINUED (PART-INDEX)
        MOVE ERROR-MSG-Ø9 TO HOLD-ERROR-MESSAGE
        PERFORM 93ØØ-ERROR.

3ØØØ-EOJ.
    CLOSE ORDER-FILE
          PARTS-FILE
          PRINT-FILE.

91ØØ-READ-PARTS-FILE.
    READ PARTS-FILE
        AT END
            MOVE 'YES' TO END-FLAG-PARTS-FILE.

92ØØ-READ-ORDER-FILE.
    READ ORDER-FILE
        AT END
            MOVE 'YES' TO END-FLAG-ORDER-FILE.
```

FIGURE 8–20 cont.

```
       9300-ERROR.

           IF LINE-COUNT > 50
               PERFORM 9310-HEADINGS.

           IF ERROR-SWITCH = 'NO'
               MOVE ORD-BRANCH          TO DET-BRANCH
               MOVE ORD-SALES-REP       TO DET-SALES-REP
               MOVE ORD-CUSTOMER-NBR    TO DET-CUSTOMER-NBR
               MOVE ORD-CUST-PO-NBR     TO DET-CUST-PO-NBR
               MOVE ORD-SALES-ORD-NBR   TO DET-SALES-ORD-NBR
               MOVE ORD-YY              TO DET-ORDER-YY
               MOVE ORD-MM              TO DET-ORDER-MM
               MOVE ORD-DD              TO DET-ORDER-DD
               MOVE ORD-PART-NBR        TO DET-PART-NBR
               MOVE ORD-QUANTITY        TO DET-QUANTITY
               MOVE ORD-UNIT-PRICE      TO DET-UNIT-PRICE
               MOVE ORD-REQ-SHIP-YY     TO DET-REQ-SHIP-YY
               MOVE ORD-REQ-SHIP-MM     TO DET-REQ-SHIP-MM
               MOVE ORD-REQ-SHIP-DD     TO DET-REQ-SHIP-DD
               MOVE ORD-ACT-SHIP-YY     TO DET-ACT-SHIP-YY
               MOVE ORD-ACT-SHIP-MM     TO DET-ACT-SHIP-MM
               MOVE ORD-ACT-SHIP-DD     TO DET-ACT-SHIP-DD
               MOVE HOLD-ERROR-MESSAGE TO DET-1-ERROR-MESSAGE
               WRITE PRINT-RECORD FROM DETAIL-LINE-1
                   AFTER ADVANCING 2 LINES
               ADD 2 TO LINE-COUNT
               MOVE 'YES' TO ERROR-SWITCH
           ELSE
               MOVE HOLD-ERROR-MESSAGE TO DET-2-ERROR-MESSAGE
               WRITE PRINT-RECORD FROM DETAIL-LINE-2
                   AFTER ADVANCING 1 LINE
               ADD 1 TO LINE-COUNT.


       9310-HEADINGS.
           ADD 1 TO PAGE-COUNT.
           MOVE PAGE-COUNT TO MAIN-HDG-PAGE-NBR.
           WRITE PRINT-RECORD FROM MAIN-HEADING-1
               AFTER ADVANCING PAGE.
           WRITE PRINT-RECORD FROM MAIN-HEADING-2
               AFTER ADVANCING 1 LINE.
           WRITE PRINT-RECORD FROM COLUMN-HEADING-1
               AFTER ADVANCING 2 LINES.
           WRITE PRINT-RECORD FROM COLUMN-HEADING-2
               AFTER ADVANCING 1 LINE.
           MOVE 5 TO LINE-COUNT.
```

FIGURE 8–20 cont.

NEW COBOL ELEMENTS

Editing

Programming would be simpler if we could depend on all data to be valid. Because of errors and misunderstandings, however, data is often less than perfect. Input editing involves the testing of data to ensure that the data is valid.

In an on-line system, testing may be done at the point of entry of the data, allowing for rejection of invalid data and requesting reentry of the data. In a batch system, editing may take place after a file is created but before the file is used in normal production. A special type of program whose only purpose is to edit the file may be executed first. This program will identify errors so that they may be corrected. In an edit program, tests are made on each data item based on the criteria set for that data item. Input edits should be as thorough as possible in order to limit the amount of incorrect data entering the system. Editing may include tests for the following:

1. Class (numeric or alphabetic)
2. Range
3. Reasonableness
4. Presence
5. Existence
6. Consistency

Class

Format

```
IF identifier is [NOT] { ALPHABETIC }
                       { NUMERIC    }
```

The class test allows us to find out whether the *contents* of a data item are of the type we desire them to be. For example, the programmer may have specified that a field is numeric by using a PICTURE of 9(3). However, this definition in no way guarantees that the data contained in that field will actually be numeric. This is because, in executing a READ statement or a group MOVE, COBOL does not check the data being placed into the elementary items to see whether the actual data type matches the data type of the PICTURE clause. Accordingly, it is possible to have nonnumeric data in fields which are described as numeric. It is important, then, to distinguish between the description of the data (what type of data the field should contain) and the actual data (what type of data the field in fact contains). In order to make sure that the actual data agrees with the description of the data item, we use the class test.

The word ALPHABETIC in a class test tests for the presence of the letters A–Z and the space. If any other character is found in the field, the field will fail an alphabetic class test. This test may be made on an alphabetic (A) or alphanumeric (X) field.

Tests for NUMERIC may be made on data items which have been defined as either numeric (9) or alphanumeric (X). The NUMERIC class test tests for the presence of the digits 0–9. If the PICTURE clause contains a sign, any valid sign is allowed in the data. If the PICTURE clause does not contain a sign, then none is allowed in the data.

Data items intended to be used in a calculation, for numeric output editing, or as a subscript must be numeric. A class test for NUMERIC will result in a true or false condition and cannot cause a data exception.

In the 1985 standard, the ALPHABETIC test is true for a data item that contains uppercase letters, lowercase letters, and/or the space character. Two new tests are the ALPHABETIC-UPPER tests, which requires the data to be uppercase and/or a space, and the ALPHABETIC-LOWER test, which requires the data to be lowercase and/or a space. The 1974 standard allowed only uppercase data, and/or the space in the ALPHABETIC test.

Range

Often, it is not enough to assure that data is numeric or alphanumeric. Many times, a data item cannot be considered valid unless it falls within a range of values. Some examples are dates, rates, and fields to be used as subscripts. When a field is used as a subscript, it may not be zero nor may it be greater than the number of elements in the table as specified in the OCCURS clause.

There are two general approaches to testing whether data falls within a certain range, one for fields defined as alphanumeric and one for fields defined as numeric. Since the former is the simpler of the two, fields in an editing program are often arbitrarily declared alphanumeric even though it is intended that they contain numeric data. Figure 8–21 shows two ways of testing an alphanumeric field for a range of values. The first uses relational tests, the second a condition-name.

```
05  BRANCH-SUB               PIC X(3).
IF BRANCH-SUB > '099' AND BRANCH-SUB NOT > '800'...
```

or

```
05  BRANCH-SUB               PIC X(3).
    88  VALID-SUB            VALUES ARE '100' THRU '800'.
IF VALID-SUB...
```

FIGURE 8–21

Recall that we are using these fields only for editing purposes in the EDIT program. So an alphanumeric description of the field will do, even though the name implies that the field will be used as a subscript. The description of the same data in a program where the data item is used for purposes other than editing may describe the data item as numeric.

Testing data described as numeric in an editing program involves comparing numeric fields. Should such a comparison be made when the actual data is not numeric, a data exception will occur. To avoid the data exception, numeric data items are tested first with a NUMERIC class test and then for the range using a nested IF. In this way, the range test will not be made unless the data proves to be numeric. (See Figure 8–22.)

```
05  ORD-SUB                  PIC 9(3).
IF ORD-SUB IS NUMERIC
    IF ORD-SUB > 99 AND ORD-SUB NOT > 800
        . . .
    ELSE
        . . .
ELSE
    . . .
```

or

```
05  ORD-SUB                  PIC 9(3).
    88 VALID-SUB             VALUES 100 THRU 800.
IF ORD-SUB IS NUMERIC
    IF VALID-SUB
        . . .
    ELSE
        . . .
ELSE
    . . .
```

FIGURE 8–22

In Figure 8–22, the field is tested first with a NUMERIC class test and then for the range. The range test is made only if the data in the field is numeric. Using a condition-name in the second method does not eliminate the need to nest the IFs, since the condition-name will generate the same numeric comparison the data-names would undergo.

The two approaches may be combined by defining the data item as alphanumeric and still retaining the NUMERIC class test. The edit would then continue to work properly even if the definition of the data item were later changed to numeric in a revision of the program.

Reasonableness

Sometimes only specific values are reasonable in a field. The idea is similar to that of a range, where one or more values might be acceptable while others are not. Thus, zero is not an acceptable value for a field that will be used as a subscript or a divisor.

The test for ORD-ACT-SHIP-DATE = ZEROS is an example from the EDIT program of a situation where zeros are reasonable. The zeros in the data item indicate that no actual shipping date has been provided; therefore, this record belongs in ORDER-FILE.

Presence

Fields whose data should be alphanumeric are often difficult to prove very much about. These fields may have a specific range or set of values to test for, or we may simply want to assure ourselves that there is something other than spaces in the field. A common test is the one made in EDIT:

```
IF ORD-SALES-ORD-NBR = SPACES
```

If the results of this test indicate that the field contains only spaces, the field is in error. If *any* other characters are present, the condition will test out false.

Existence

Some data items have such a large number of possible values that a table or an additional file containing those values is the most practical way to store the values used for comparison.

The EDIT program makes use of two tables to validate fields from ORDER-FILE: a compile-time table containing all valid sales representative numbers, and a preprocess-time table that will be loaded from a file containing all valid part numbers. Each time an ORDER-RECORD is read, these tables are searched for a match with ORD-SALES-REP and ORD-PART-NBR, respectively. If a match is found, the data is considered to be valid. When a part number is located in the table, an additional test is made using the table data to determine whether the part is active or discontinued.

Consistency

Sometimes comparisons are made between more than one field in a single record, a field in a record and a table element, or fields from two different files in order to determine whether the data is consistent. For example, a code indicating a salaried employee would not be consistent with an overtime amount in a single payroll record.

Indexing

In Chapter 7, tables were loaded and then accessed for printing using subscripts to identify each element as it was used. Another technique for identifying individual elements in a table is called *indexing*. In this chapter we shall use both subscripting and indexing.

Format

```
data-name-1 OCCURS integer-2 TIMES

[ { ASCENDING  } KEY IS data-name-2 [data-name-3]. . .]. . .
  { DESCENDING }

[INDEXED BY index-name-1 [index-name-2]. . .]
```

In order to use an index, the name of the index is normally established as a part of the table definition in the DATA DIVISION, whereupon COBOL reserves storage space for the index. Contrast this with a subscript, where no mention of the subscript is included in the table definition and storage for the subscript is reserved elsewhere in WORKING-STORAGE. In Figure 8–23, QTY-SUB defines four bytes of storage whose name implies that it will be used as a subscript with QUANTITY-TABLE. The connection between QTY-SUB and QUANTITY-TABLE exists only in the mind of the programmer; COBOL does not make the connection. STOCK-INDEX, on the other hand, is associated by COBOL with STOCK-NUMBER-TABLE.

TABLE WITH INDEX DEFINED

```
    01   STOCK-NUMBER-TABLE.
         05   STOCK-ELEMENT OCCURS 5 TIMES
                            INDEXED BY STOCK-INDEX  PIC 9(8).
```

TABLE WITH SUBSCRIPT DEFINED

```
    01   SUBSCRIPTS.
         05   QTY-SUB        PIC 9(4).
              .
              .
              .
    01   QUANTITY-TABLE.
         05 QUANTITY-ELEMENT  OCCURS 5 TIMES  PIC 9(8).
```

FIGURE 8–23

One difference between a subscript and an index is the form in which they are stored. A subscript is stored as an integer representing an ordinal occurrence of a table element—the first second, third, and so on. In order to locate the element in memory, the subscript(s) and element size(s) are used in a series of calculations which compute displacement. An index, however, is always stored in displacement form. In the table of Figure 8–24, note the difference between the contents of a subscript and an index in pointing to each element. Although the table is described as having an index, this does not prohibit the use of a subscript with the table instead.

```
01   STOCK-NUMBER-TABLE.
     05   STOCK-ELEMENT OCCURS 5 TIMES
                        INDEXED BY STOCK-INDEX  PIC 9(8).
01   SUBSCRIPTS.
     05   STOCK-SUB    PIC 9(4).
```

FIRST OCCURENCE OF STOCK-ELEMENT

```
STOCK-ELEMENT (STOCK-SUB)      STOCK-SUB = 1
STOCK-ELEMENT (STOCK-INDEX)    STOCK-INDEX = 0
```

SECOND OCCURENCE OF STOCK-ELEMENT

```
STOCK-ELEMENT (STOCK-SUB)      STOCK-SUB = 2
STOCK-ELEMENT (STOCK-INDEX)    STOCK-INDEX = 8
```

THIRD OCCURENCE OF STOCK-ELEMENT

```
STOCK-ELEMENT (STOCK-SUB)      STOCK-SUB = 3
STOCK-ELEMENT (STOCK-INDEX)    STOCK-INDEX = 16
```

FOURTH OCCURENCE OF STOCK-ELEMENT

```
STOCK-ELEMENT (STOCK-SUB)       STOCK-SUB = 4
STOCK-ELEMENT (STOCK-INDEX)    STOCK-INDEX = 24
```

FIFTH OCCURENCE OF STOCK-ELEMENT

```
STOCK-ELEMENT (STOCK-SUB)      STOCK-SUB = 5
STOCK-ELEMENT (STOCK-INDEX)    STOCK-INDEX = 32
```

FIGURE 8–24

The difference in storage techniques is invisible to the person writing a COBOL program. A programmer wanting to start at the beginning of a table would set the index to 1, just as a subscript would be initialized to 1. COBOL assigns a value of zero to an index when the index is set to 1; it assigns a 1 to a subscript started at 1.

In searching a table in a sequential manner, a subscript requires that COBOL perform the full calculation for displacement each time an element is to be located. An index, on the other hand, requires only that the size of an element be added to the current displacement. Because of this, indexing is more efficient than subscripting.

A subscript may be initialized or changed using a MOVE, READ, ACCEPT, COMPUTE, ADD, SUBTRACT, MULTIPLY, DIVIDE, or PERFORM . . . VARYING. An index may be initialized or changed using a SET, SEARCH, or PERFORM . . . VARYING.

The 1985 standard allows both an index and a subscript to be used in a single set of subscripts to reference an occurrence of a multidimensional table.

The SET Statement

Format 1

```
SET  { index-name-1  [ index-name-2 ] . . . }  TO { index-name-3 }
     { identifier-1  [ identifier-2 ] . . . }     { identifier-3 }
                                                  { literal-1    }
```

Format 1 of the SET statement is used primarily to initialize an index. In this format, the sending field follows the word TO and may be an index-name, an identifier, or a numeric literal. Whichever one is used must represent an integer.

The identifier referred to in the SET format may be described in the DATA DIVISION as having USAGE IS INDEX. This type of USAGE reserves storage in the same form as the INDEXED BY clause. The storage is not, however, automatically associated with a table, as it is with INDEXED BY. The usage clause may be written at either the group or the elementary level. However, it is always the elementary items that are considered index data items. An index data item may be used only in a SEARCH, SET, or relational IF statement.

Figure 8–25 shows the valid combinations for Format 1 of the SET statement. An explanation of each follows:

SENDING FIELD	RECEIVING FIELD		
	Index-Name	Index Data Item	Integer Data Item
index-name (INDEXED BY)	V	V	V
index data item (USAGE IS INDEX)	V	V	
integer data item	V		
integer literal	V		

FIGURE 8–25

```
SET index-name-1 TO index-name-3
```

This SET causes COBOL to calculate an occurrence based on the displacement in index-name-3 and use that occurrence to calculate a displacement for the same occurrence in the table indexed by index-name-1. This displacement is then placed in index-name-1.

```
SET index-name-1 TO identifier-3
```

When USAGE IS INDEX for identifier-3, the displacement in identifier-3 is placed unchanged in index-name-1. No conversion takes place.

```
SET index-name-1 TO identifier-3
```

When USAGE IS DISPLAY or USAGE IS COMP-3 for identifier-3, the integer value of identifier-3 is considered an occurrence and a displacement is calculated for the table indexed by index-name-1. This displacement is placed in index-name-1.

```
SET index-name-1 TO literal-1
```

The literal is considered an occurrence, and a displacement is calculated for the table indexed by index-name-1. This displacement is placed in index-name-1.

```
SET identifier-1 TO index-name-3
```

When USAGE IS INDEX for identifier-1, the displacement in index-name-3 is placed unchanged in identifier-1.

```
SET identifier-1 TO index-name-3
```

When USAGE IS DISPLAY or USAGE IS COMP-3 for identifier-1, the displacement in index-name-1 is used to calculate an occurrence, which is then placed in identifier-1.

```
SET identifier-1 TO identifier-3
```

In this format, the usage of both identifiers must be INDEX. Identifier-3 is placed in identifier-1, and no conversion takes place.

Format 2

```
SET index-name-4 [index-name-5] . . .}  {UP BY  }  {identifier-4}
                                        {DOWN BY}  {literal-2   }
```

Format 2 is used to increment or decrement index-names by the amount specified in the identifier or literal. Any identifier used must be an elementary item containing integer data. Any literal used must be an integer.

Loading Tables

Compile-Time Tables

Sometimes the data to be stored in a table is of a permanent nature, changing so seldom that the table data can be made a part of the program itself rather than being accessed from some other source each time the program is executed. When table data is included as a part of the program code, it is often called a *compile-time* table. Some characteristics of a compile-time table are as follows:

1. The data is of a permanent nature.
2. VALUE clauses are used to store the table data.
3. A REDEFINES clause is used with OCCURS clauses to redescribe the same area of storage.

COBOL does not allow a VALUE clause to coexist with an OCCURS clause in the same data item description. To avoid using both in one statement, the usual technique is to redefine the area, putting the VALUE clauses in the first definition and the OCCURS clause(s) in the second.

A compile-time table may use either a subscript or an index to identify the individual elements of the table. There are two compile-time tables in the EDIT program of this chapter. The first is a table containing the names of the months, wherein a subscript is used to provide direct access to the appropriate row in the table. The month portion of CURRENT-DATE is used as the subscript. (See Figure 8–26.)

```
01  MONTH-DATA.
    05  FILLER      PIC X(9)  VALUE 'JANUARY  '.
    05  FILLER      PIC X(9)  VALUE 'FEBRUARY '.
    05  FILLER      PIC X(9)  VALUE 'MARCH    '.
    05  FILLER      PIC X(9)  VALUE 'APRIL    '.
    05  FILLER      PIC X(9)  VALUE 'MAY      '.
    05  FILLER      PIC X(9)  VALUE 'JUNE     '.
    05  FILLER      PIC X(9)  VALUE 'JULY     '.
    05  FILLER      PIC X(9)  VALUE 'AUGUST   '.
    05  FILLER      PIC X(9)  VALUE 'SEPTEMBER'.
    05  FILLER      PIC X(9)  VALUE 'OCTOBER  '.
    05  FILLER      PIC X(9)  VALUE 'NOVEMBER '.
    05  FILLER      PIC X(9)  VALUE 'DECEMBER '.

01  MONTH-TABLE REDEFINES MONTH-DATA.
    05  MONTH-TBL-ENTRY  OCCURS 12 TIMES      PIC X(9).
```

FIGURE 8–26

In the table, MONTH-DATA is a group item which includes 108 bytes of storage. Each of the 12 month names uses nine bytes of that storage. (See Figure 8–27.)

```
01  MONTH-DATA.

    05  FILLER  PIC X(9)  VALUE 'JANUARY  '.     | JANUARY   |
    05  FILLER  PIC X(9)  VALUE 'FEBRUARY '.     | FEBRUARY  |
    05  FILLER  PIC X(9)  VALUE 'MARCH    '.     | MARCH     |
    05  FILLER  PIC X(9)  VALUE 'APRIL    '.     | APRIL     |
    05  FILLER  PIC X(9)  VALUE 'MAY      '.     | MAY       |
    05  FILLER  PIC X(9)  VALUE 'JUNE     '.     | JUNE      |
    05  FILLER  PIC X(9)  VALUE 'JULY     '.     | JULY      |
    05  FILLER  PIC X(9)  VALUE 'AUGUST   '.     | AUGUST    |
    05  FILLER  PIC X(9)  VALUE 'SEPTEMBER'.     | SEPTEMBER |
    05  FILLER  PIC X(9)  VALUE 'OCTOBER  '.     | OCTOBER   |
    05  FILLER  PIC X(9)  VALUE 'NOVEMBER '.     | NOVEMBER  |
    05  FILLER  PIC X(9)  VALUE 'DECEMBER '.     | DECEMBER  |
```

FIGURE 8–27

MONTH-TABLE is a group item which describes the *same* 108 bytes of storage that MONTH-DATA does. MONTH-TABLE contains a table with 12 elements (MONTH-TBL-ENTRY), each of which is nine bytes in length. The size of each element coincides with the space occupied by the name of each month. (See Figure 8–28.)

The month portion of CURRENT-DATE is used as the subscript to identify the table element containing the matching month name. To isolate the month from CURRENT-DATE, CURRENT-DATE is moved to WS-CURRENT-DATE, providing a value for WS-CURRENT-MM which ranges from 01 to 12. When used as a subscript, WS-CURRENT-MM will identify the appropriate table element. (See Figure 8–29.)

Subscripts are often provided by data that serves another purpose in the program. Here, CURRENT-DATE is so used. In Chapter 7, ORD-BRANCH, part of the input record, was used as a subscript.

The second compile-time table in program EDIT is composed of sales representative numbers. This table is used in the editing of ORDER-FILE to validate the sales representative number. The data in this table is of a less permanent

```
MONTH-TABLE.
     MONTH-TBL-ENTRY (1)      JANUARY
     MONTH-TBL-ENTRY (2)      FEBRUARY
     MONTH-TBL-ENTRY (3)      MARCH
     MONTH-TBL-ENTRY (4)      APRIL
     MONTH-TBL-ENTRY (5)      MAY
     MONTH-TBL-ENTRY (6)      JUNE
     MONTH-TBL-ENTRY (7)      JULY
     MONTH-TBL-ENTRY (8)      AUGUST
     MONTH-TBL-ENTRY (9)      SEPTEMBER
     MONTH-TBL-ENTRY (10)     OCTOBER
     MONTH-TBL-ENTRY (11)     NOVEMBER
     MONTH-TBL-ENTRY (12)     DECEMBER
```

FIGURE 8–28

```
01  WS-CURRENT-DATE.
    05  WS-CURRENT-MM          PIC 9(2).
    05  FILLER                 PIC X(1).
    05  WS-CURRENT-DD          PIC 9(2).
    05  FILLER                 PIC X(1).
    05  WS-CURRENT-YY          PIC 9(2).

MOVE CURRENT-DATE TO WS-CURRENT-DATE.
MOVE MONTH-TBL-ENTRY (WS-CURRENT-MM) TO MAIN-HDG-MONTH.
```

FIGURE 8–29

nature. Each time the company gains or loses a sales representative, the program must be recompiled to keep the table current. The decision to make the sales representative table a compile-time table would be based on a very stable work force.

The sales representative table uses VALUE clauses to store the sales representative numbers. The storage area is then redefined so that an OCCURS clause may be used. (See Figure 8–30.)

```
01  SALES-REP-DATA.
    05  FILLER        PIC 9(3)        VALUE 007.
    05  FILLER        PIC 9(3)        VALUE 816.
    05  FILLER        PIC 9(3)        VALUE 201.
    05  FILLER        PIC 9(3)        VALUE 611.
    05  FILLER        PIC 9(3)        VALUE 353.
    05  FILLER        PIC 9(3)        VALUE 440.
    05  FILLER        PIC 9(3)        VALUE 174.
    05  FILLER        PIC 9(3)        VALUE 915.

01  SALES-REP-TABLE REDEFINES SALES-REP-DATA.
    05  SALES-REP-TBL-ENTRY    OCCURS 8 TIMES
                               INDEXED BY SALES-INDEX
                               PIC 9(3).
```

FIGURE 8–30

The table specifies an index, SALES-INDEX, that may be used with it. Specifying an index as a part of the table description causes storage to be reserved for the index by the system. The programmer must not then reserve storage for this index.

A serial search will be used to locate the sales representative number. Recall that this type of search uses a search argument, the value sought, and compares that argument against each table element one after another until a match is found. In the EDIT program the search argument is a sales representative number (ORD-SALES-REP). ORD-SALES-REP will be compared with each element in the table until a match is found. If no match is found, an error message requested by the programmer will be printed. The COBOL code to accomplish this search will be covered shortly in the section on searching tables.

We see, then, that one of the compile-time tables in the EDIT program is accessed using a subscript for direct addressing, the other using an index and a serial search. The fact that a table was stored at compile time does not restrict how it may be accessed. Indeed, any access method may be applied to a compile-time table.

Preprocess-Time Tables

A preprocess-time table is a table whose values are loaded in the initialization routine of a program. The table data may be read from a file or entered through a keyboard. The data is then moved to the area of memory reserved for the table. A program loop is created, often using PERFORM . . . VARYING, so that each record of the table data can be read and placed in the table in memory. A decision is made to choose this method of loading a table when the table data is available before the program is executed but changes too often to be suitable for a compile-time table.

The method of loading a preprocess-time table is shown by the following code in the EDIT program:

```
01  PART-NBR-TABLE.
    05  TBL-PART-NBR-ENTRY     OCCURS 200 TIMES
                              INDEXED BY PART-INDEX
                              ASCENDING KEY IS TBL-PART-NBR.
    10  TBL-PART-NBR          PIC X(6).
    10  TBL-PART-STATUS       PIC X(1).
        88  PART-DISCONTINUED          VALUE 'D'.
```

Notice that there are no VALUE clauses used to initialize this table. The only VALUE clause is associated with a condition-name. Storage for 200 elements is established, each element having two data items. TBL-PART-NBR and TBL-PART-STATUS.

The data for this table is contained in PARTS-FILE. Transfer of the data from the file to the area of memory reserved for the table is done in 1000-INITIALIZATION. PARTS-FILE is opened as INPUT, and the first record is read from that file. Each record contains three data items: PART-NBR, PART-STATUS, and PART-DESCRIPTION. Only two of these items, PART-NBR and PART-STATUS, will be moved to the table. The routine 1100-LOAD-PARTS-TABLE moves the two items and invokes the routine to read the next parts record (9100-READ-PARTS-FILE). 1100-LOAD-PARTS-TABLE is controlled by a PERFORM . . . VARYING in 1000-INITIALIZATION and will be repeated until the end of PARTS-FILE is reached:

```
1000-INITIALIZATION.
         .
         .
         .
     PERFORM 9100-READ-PARTS-FILE.
     IF NOT END-OF-PARTS-FILE
         PERFORM 1100-LOAD-PARTS-FILE
             VARYING PART-INDEX FROM 1 BY 1
                 UNTIL END-OF-PARTS-FILE.
```

9100-READ-PARTS-FILE reads a record from PARTS-FILE. When the end-of-file indicator is encountered, 'YES' is moved to END-FLAG-PARTS-FILE. END-OF-PARTS-FILE, tested in the preceding PERFORM . . . VARYING, is a condition-name associated with END-FLAG-PARTS-FILE:

```
05  END-FLAG-PARTS-FILE       PIC X(3)         VALUE 'NO'.
    88  END-OF-PARTS-FILE     VALUE 'YES'.
```

Notice that PART-INDEX is used in the MOVE statement to determine which elements of the table the contents of PART-NBR and PART-STATUS should be placed in. In this example, either a subscript defined separately in WORKING-STORAGE by the programmer or PART-INDEX could have been used in the MOVE statement. Use of either subscripts or indices could be controlled with a PERFORM . . . VARYING and would point to the correct table element. While either could have been used for loading the table, an index is necessary in the table definition because of the way in which the table is accessed later in the program:

```
01  PART-NBR-TABLE.
    05  TBL-PART-NBR-ENTRY OCCURS 200 TIMES
                           INDEXED BY PART-INDEX
                           ASCENDING KEY IS TBL-PART-NBR.
        10  TBL-PART-NBR  PIC X(6).
        10  TBL-PART-STATUS  PIC X(1).
            88  PART-DISCONTINUED       VALUE 'D'.
```

In addition to the INDEXED BY clause, PART-NBR-TABLE has an ASCENDING KEY clause. This clause specifies that the table will be in ascending order by TBL-PART-NBR. This will allow the use of a binary search to access elements of the table. This search technique will be covered in the next section. Note that if the table is to be in ascending order by TBL-PART-NBR, the file from which it is loaded should also be in ascending order by TBL-PART-NBR.

Searching Tables

Serial Search

Format

```
                                  {identifier-2}
SEARCH identifier-1 [VARYING      {index-name-1}]

    [AT END imperative-statement-1]

    WHEN condition-1 {imperative-statement-2}
                     {NEXT SENTENCE         }

    [WHEN condition-2 {imperative-statement-3}
                      {NEXT SENTENCE         }  ] . . .
```

A serial search compares a search argument (what is sought) against each element of a table in a sequential manner until a match is found or the end of the table is reached. The search may begin at any point in the table. The word SET or a PERFORM . . . VARYING may be used to establish the starting point for the search. Figure 8–31 contains the DATA DIVISION definition of the sales representative table of the EDIT program and the PROCEDURE DIVISION routine used to search the table.

In the EDIT program, SET SALES-INDEX TO 1 starts the displacement with a value of zero. The index then points to the first element of the table with which the index is associated.

SEARCH specifies the table whose elements we wish to search. With the index set for the beginning of the table, each element of the table will be tested using the condition specified in the WHEN clause. When this condition is true, the search stops and any statements after the WHEN up until the period are

```
01  SALES-REP-DATA.
    05  FILLER         PIC 9(3)         VALUE 007.
    05  FILLER         PIC 9(3)         VALUE 816.
    05  FILLER         PIC 9(3)         VALUE 201.
    05  FILLER         PIC 9(3)         VALUE 611.
    05  FILLER         PIC 9(3)         VALUE 353.
    05  FILLER         PIC 9(3)         VALUE 440.
    05  FILLER         PIC 9(3)         VALUE 174.
    05  FILLER         PIC 9(3)         VALUE 915.

01  SALES-REP-TABLE REDEFINES SALES-REP-DATA.
    05  SALES-REP-TBL-ENTRY   OCCURS 8 TIMES
                              INDEXED BY SALES-INDEX
                              PIC 9(3).

2300-SEARCH-SALES-REP-TBL.
    SET SALES-INDEX TO 1.
    SEARCH SALES-REP-TBL-ENTRY
        AT END
            MOVE ERROR-MSG-03 TO HOLD-ERROR-MESSAGE
            PERFORM 2200-ERROR
        WHEN SALES-REP-TBL-ENTRY (SALES-INDEX) =
                                            ORD-SALES-REP
            NEXT SENTENCE.
```

FIGURE 8–31

executed. If the search reaches the end of the table without finding a true condition, the statements which are after the AT END but before the WHEN are executed.

In some circumstances, finding a true condition for the WHEN statement is considered complete success, and arriving at the AT END situation is considered failure. This is especially the case when we need to find only one item that meets the criteria in the table. However, consider a situation where there may be multiple items in the table that meet the criteria. In this case success comes only after all of the items have been located. Since the search stops when one item is located, we need a method of beginning the search again on the next element and continuing this procedure until AT END is reached. In this case AT END is our objective, and a true WHEN condition means only that one matching entry was found. The code for such a search is shown in Figure 8–32. Notice that the index is SET UP BY 1 before the search is continued. Otherwise the search would keep finding the first matching entry over and over again.

```
TABLE-RTN.
    .
    .
    .
    MOVE 'OFF' TO TABLE-FLAG.
    SET COURSE-INDEX TO 1.
    PERFORM TABLE-SEARCH
        UNTIL TABLE-FLAG = 'ON'.
    .
    .
    .
TABLE-SEARCH.
    SEARCH COURSE-TABLE
        AT END
            MOVE 'ON' TO TABLE-FLAG
        WHEN INPUT-COURSE = COURSE-NBR (COURSE-INDEX)
            MOVE COURSE-NAME (COURSE-INDEX) TO
              COURSE-OUT
            WRITE PRINT-RECORD FROM DETAIL-LINE
                AFTER ADVANCING 2 LINES.
    SET COURSE-INDEX UP BY 1.
```

FIGURE 8–32

For a serial search, the table data does not have to be in any particular order. On average, a serial search must test one-half of the items in a table before a true condition is found. If it is known that some of the items in the table will be accessed more often than others, they should be placed near the beginning of the table to speed up processing.

Each WHEN clause used with a serial search may contain any condition or combination of conditions allowed by COBOL. A serial search allows multiple WHEN clauses. If a WHEN is satisfied, the remaining WHEN's will not be tested.

Binary Search

Format

```
SEARCH ALL identifier-1
   [AT END imperative-statement-1]
          {relation-condition-1}
   WHEN   {condition-name-1    }

           {relation-condition-2
    [AND   {condition-name-2          ] . . .

   [imperative-statement-2]
   [NEXT SENTENCE         ]
```

The binary search is suitable for large ordered tables, in which it significantly reduces the number of comparisons necessary to locate an item. Figure 8–33 shows the maximum number of comparisons necessary to locate an item with a binary search as a function of the number of elements in the table.

TABLE ELEMENTS	COMPARISONS
1	1
3	2
7	3
15	4
31	5
63	6
127	7
255	8
511	9
1,023	10
2,047	11
4,095	12
8,191	13
16,383	14
32,767	15

FIGURE 8–33

To see how a binary search works, suppose we have a table in ascending order. The first step is to divide the table in half and compare the search argument against an element from the middle of the table. This element will likely be greater or less than the item we are looking for. If it is equal to the item, then the search is over on the first try. If the element is greater than the search argument, then every element following it will also be greater and, therefore, will not be what we are looking for. But then we can ignore the last half of the table and concentrate on the first half. A second attempt to find a match is then made by splitting the first half of the table in half and comparing against the middle item. If the table element is greater than the search argument, the matching item must be in the first one-fourth of the table. If the table element equals the search argument, the search is complete. If the table element is less than the search argument, the matching item must be in the second one-fourth of the table. The process continues until the item is found or determined to be missing.

To illustrate, suppose that we are looking for a value of 134 (the search argument) in a table arranged in ascending order, as shown in Figure 8–34. The middle element (144) is compared against the search argument first and is found to be larger than it. Next, the middle element for the first half of the table (131) is tested and found to be too small. So the remaining segment is split, and 138 is located. The value of this element is too large, so the table is split again and 134 is located.

```
123
125
126
128
129
131  ←—2nd comparison
134  ←—4th comparison
136
138  ←—3rd comparison
139
142
144  ←—1st comparison
147
149
151
153
156
158
160
163
165
168
170
```

FIGURE 8–34

Although the programmer may code each step of the binary search, COBOL itself provides a binary search with the use of the words SEARCH ALL. In order to use a binary search on a table, the table needs to be in either ascending or descending order and the definition of the table must include a KEY clause which specifies the order. (See Figure 8–35.) If a SEARCH ALL is done on a table which is not in order, the results of the search will not be correct because the search may not be able to find a table element which is actually in the table.

```
 01   PART-NBR-TABLE.
      05   TBL-PART-NBR-ENTRY        OCCURS 200 TIMES
                                     INDEXED BY PART-INDEX
                               ASCENDING KEY IS TBL-PART-NBR.
           10   TBL-PART-NBR         PIC X(6).
           10   TBL-PART-STATUS      PIC X(1).
                88   PART DISCONTINUED          VALUE 'D'.
 2000-EDIT.
       SEARCH ALL TBL-PART-NBR-ENTRY
            AT END
                 MOVE ERROR-MSG-08 TO HOLD-ERROR-MESSAGE
                 PERFORM 2200-ERROR
            WHEN TBL-PART-NBR (PART-INDEX) = ORD-PART-NBR
                 PERFORM 2500-CHECK-PART-STATUS.
```

FIGURE 8–35

Notice that no SET statement precedes the SEARCH ALL statement in the figure. This is because COBOL determines the appropriate setting for the index before beginning the search. The word ALL following the word SEARCH is a signal to COBOL that a binary search is requested.

Only one WHEN may be used with a binary search, and the relation specified therein is limited to equality. If a condition-name is used, the condition-name must be associated with a single value. Compound conditions may then be formed using AND.

Figure 8–36 compares the features of COBOL serial and binary searches.

COMPARISON OF SERIAL AND BINARY SEARCHES	
Serial	Binary
No KEY clause required in table definition	KEY clause required in table definition
SET used to prepare index before search begins	No SET needed; COBOL will prepare index before search begins
Search may begin anywhere in table	Search encompasses entire table
SEARCH	SEARCH ALL
Multiple WHENs allowed	Only one WHEN allowed
Any valid condition may be used	Only equality (=) or a condition-name with a single value associated with it may be used

FIGURE 8–36

Programmer-Written Searches

Both the serial and the binary search may be written in COBOL without using the reserved words SEARCH or SEARCH ALL. Figure 8–37 shows the COBOL code for a serial search. Prior to the routines shown, a record containing an ACCOUNT-NUMBER was read in an initialization routine, and the value 100 was moved to NBR-OF-TABLE-ELEMENTS in the same routine.

```
SEARCH-ROUTINE.
     MOVE 1 TO SEARCH-SUBSCRIPT.
     MOVE 'OFF' TO STOP-SWITCH.
     PERFORM SEARCH-LOOP
          UNTIL STOP-SWITCH = 'ON'.
SEARCH-LOOP-ROUTINE.
     IF SEARCH-SUBSCRIPT > NBR-OF-TABLE-ELEMENTS
          MOVE 'ON' TO STOP-SWITCH
          MOVE 'NO RECORD FOUND' TO ERROR-MESSAGE-OUT
          WRITE PRINT-RECORD FROM ERROR-LINE
               AFTER ADVANCING 2 LINES
     ELSE
          IF ACCOUNT-ELEMENT (SEARCH-SUBSCRIPT) =
               ACCOUNT-NUMBER
               MOVE 'ON' TO STOP-SWITCH
          ELSE
               ADD TO SEARCH-SUBSCRIPT.
```

FIGURE 8–37

The code for a programmer-designed binary search is shown in Figure 8–38. Prior to this search, PART-NUMBER was read in the program's initialization routine and an initial value was provided for NBR-OF-ELEMENTS.

```
BINARY-SEARCH-ROUTINE.
     MOVE 1 TO FIRST-ELEMENT.
     MOVE NBR-OF-ELEMENTS TO LAST-ELEMENT.
     MOVE 'OFF' TO END-OF-SEARCH.
     PERFORM SEARCH-LOOP-ROUTINE
          UNTIL END-OF-SEARCH = 'ON'.

SEARCH-LOOP-ROUTINE.
     IF FIRST-ELEMENT > LAST-ELEMENT
          MOVE 'RECORD NOT FOUND' TO MESSAGE-OUT
          WRITE PRINT-RECORD FROM MESSAGE-LINE
               AFTER ADVANCING 2 LINES
          MOVE 'ON' TO END-OF-SEARCH
     ELSE
          COMPUTE SUBSCRIPT = FIRST-ELEMENT + LAST-ELEMENT / 2
          IF PART-TABLE (SUBSCRIPT) = PART-NUMBER
               MOVE 'RECORD FOUND' TO MESSAGE-OUT
               WRITE PRINT-RECORD FROM MESSAGE-LINE
                    AFTER ADVANCING 2 LINES
               MOVE 'ON' TO END-OF-SEARCH
          ELSE
               IF PART-TABLE (SUBSCRIPT) < PART-NUMBER
                    COMPUTE FIRST-ELEMENT = SUBSCRIPT + 1
               ELSE
                    COMPUTE LAST-ELEMENT = SUBSCRIPT - 1.
```

FIGURE 8–38

DEBUGGING

Diagnostics

Following are some diagnostics that may appear in working with the new COBOL elements in this chapter.

```
SET STATEMENT REQUIRES OPERAND AFTER TO, TO BE AN
INDEX-NAME, INDEX DATA-NAME, NUMERIC INTEGRAL DATA-NAME
OR POSITIVE INTEGRAL NUMERIC LITERAL.
```

In the process of setting an index to some value, the programmer has used a data-item with an inappropriate description. The format for the SET statement allows:

1. *an index-name.* An index-name is a name defined using the INDEXED BY clause in the definition of a table.
2. *an identifier.* The identifier may be an index data-name or a numeric integral data-name. An index data-name is a data-item whose description includes a USAGE IS INDEX clause. A numeric integral data-name is a data-name whose PICTURE indicates that the field will contain an integer value. (No decimal positions are allowed.)
3. *a literal.* The literal must be both positive and an integer.

```
SET STATEMENT REQUIRES OPERAND AFTER UP BY OR DOWN BY TO BE
NUMERIC INTEGRAL DATA-NAME OR POSITIVE INTEGRAL NUMERIC
LITERAL.
```

The operand following BY represents the amount by which the index-name will be incremented or decremented. Whether a data-name or a literal is used, it must represent an integer.

```
SEARCH HAS EITHER SUBSCRIPTED OR INDEXED IDENTIFIER-1 OR AN
ILLEGAL OPERAND.
```

The operand following the word SEARCH must be a table name (a data-name that has been defined with an OCCURS clause). The table name should be used only as identifier-1. It should not be subscripted or indexed when used after the word SEARCH.

```
INVALID CONDITION OR FORMULA IN SEARCH ALL
```

SEARCH ALL has limits on the conditions that may be tested in the WHEN clause. If a relation is tested, it must be the equality (=) relation. If a condition-name is used, the 88 level name must have only a single value associated with it, and not a range or group of values.

Testing Considerations

A correct program is one which creates the correct output in all situations. It is a program which functions correctly for all combinations of input. Because of the size and complexity of computer programs, it is unrealistic to assume that a program will be created without any errors.

The goal of the programmer is to produce a program which is as free of error as possible. Programs are tested in order to find the errors that exist in them. If good test data is used and the test results are thoroughly checked, most of the errors in a program should be caught.

Test Data

In creating test data, we need to create data which will test the boundary conditions on the data. Boundary conditions are those conditions which are on the border between acceptable and unacceptable data. For example, in the EDIT program, ORD-BRANCH may be between '01' and '10'. Thus, boundary conditions for ORD-BRANCH are '00', '01', '10', and '11'. It is important to test each of these because errors are more likely to occur around the boundaries of the data than elsewhere. In the EDIT program, we must assure that the program recognizes '01' and '10' as valid branches and that it recognizes '00' and '11' as invalid branches.

Also, in creating test data, it is important to be sure that all of the paths which are possible through each of the decision structures in the program will be executed. For example, when ORD-BRANCH is checked for validity, there are three possible paths through the nested IF statement. (See Figure 8–39.) In order to execute all three paths, the test data must include (1) a nonnumeric branch, (2) a numeric but invalid branch, and (3) a numeric and valid branch.

SUMMARY

In this chapter, input editing has been used to illustrate table handling. Table loading at compile time and at preprocess time has been discussed, as has accessing of table elements using serial and binary searches.

Input editing may include tests for (1) class, (2) range, (3) reasonableness, (4) presence, (5) existence, and (6) consistency.

Class Test

Format

```
IF identifier IS [NOT] { ALPHABETIC }
                       { NUMERIC    }
```

INDEX and KEY Clauses

In order to use the SEARCH verb, an index is required. The following format shows how an index may be defined as part of a table definition. SEARCH ALL requires that the table to be searched be in either ascending or descending order and have a KEY clause. This is also shown in the format.

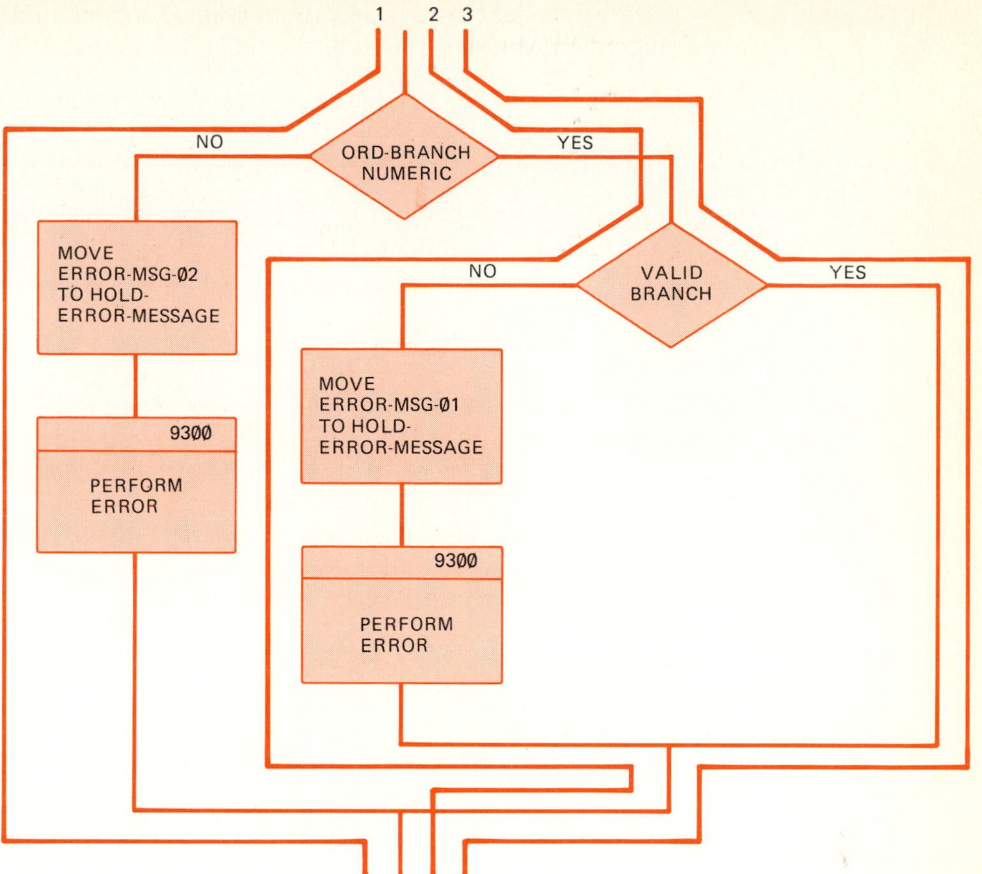

FIGURE 8–39

Format

```
data-name-1 OCCURS integer-2 TIMES
[ {ASCENDING } KEY IS data-name-2 [data-name-3]. . .]. . .
  {DESCENDING}
[INDEXED BY index-name-1 [index-name-2]. . .]
```

SET

Two formats of the SET statement are used to initialize and increment or decrement indices.

Format 1

```
SET {index-name-1 [index-name-2] . . .} TO {index-name-3}
    {identifier-1 [identifier-2] . . .}    {identifier-3}
                                           {literal-1   }
```

Format 2

```
SET index-name-4 [index-name-5] . . .} {UP BY  } {identifier-4}
                                       {DOWN BY} {literal-2   }
```

Serial Search

A serial search starts at a given point in a table and tests each element until a match is found or the end of the table is reached.

Format

```
                                      {identifier-2  }
SEARCH identifier-1 [VARYING {index-name-1 }]
    [AT END imperative-statement-1]
    WHEN condition-1 {imperative-statement-2}
                     {NEXT SENTENCE         }
    [WHEN condition-2 {imperative-statement-3}
                      {NEXT SENTENCE         }
                                                  ] . . .
```

Binary Search

A binary search is used only on ordered tables. It divides the table repeatedly, eliminating one-half of the table after each comparison. In tables with more than a few elements, the technique uses fewer comparisons to fine the correct element.

Format

```
SEARCH ALL identifier-1
    [AT END imperative-statement-1]
          {relation-condition-1}
    WHEN  {condition-name-1    }
          {relation-condition-2}
    [AND  {condition-name-2    }    ] . . .
    [imperative-statement-2]
    [NEXT SENTENCE         ]
```

EXERCISES

I. Given the following table, provide the displacement calculated as the result of each SET statement. Each question should use the answer of the previous question as the starting value if one is necessary.

```
01  SALES-TABLE.
    05  SALES-AMOUNTS    OCCURS 12 TIMES
                         INDEXED BY SALES-INDEX
                         PIC 9(6)V9(2).
```

_____ **1.** SET SALES-INDEX TO 1.

_____ **2.** SET SALES-INDEX UP BY 1.

_____ **3.** SET SALES-INDEX TO 4.

_____ **4.** SET SALES-INDEX DOWN BY 2.

_____ **5.** SET SALES-INDEX TO 10.

II. Given the following items in a DATA DIVISION, indicate whether the receiving item in each SET statement will be an exact copy of the sending item.

```
01  SALES-TABLE.
    05  SALES-AMOUNTS    OCCURS 12 TIMES
                         INDEXED BY SALES-INDEX
                         PIC 9(6)V9(2).
```

```
01  MONTH-TABLE.
    05  MONTH-NAME       OCCURS 12 TIMES
                         INDEXED BY MONTH-INDEX
                         PIC X(9).
01  HOLD-AREAS.
    05  HOLD-INDEX       PIC 9(4)  USAGE IS INDEX.
    05  HOLD-AREA        PIC 9(4).
```

_____ 1. SET SALES-INDEX TO HOLD-INDEX.

_____ 2. SET SALES-INDEX TO HOLD-AREA.

_____ 3. SET SALES-INDEX TO MONTH-INDEX.

_____ 4. SET HOLD-INDEX TO SALES-INDEX.

_____ 5. SET MONTH-INDEX TO SALES-INDEX.

III. Following is part of the definition of a compile-time table containing a month number and a sales amount with two decimal positions. Complete the part of the definition that contains the OCCURS clause.

```
01  MONTH-SALES-TABLE.
    05  FILLER          PIC X(10)   VALUE '0100482316'.
    05  FILLER          PIC X(10)   VALUE '0200516880'.
    05  FILLER          PIC X(10)   VALUE '0300524195'.
    05  FILLER          PIC X(10)   VALUE '0400498634'.
    05  FILLER          PIC X(10)   VALUE '0500561972'.
    05  FILLER          PIC X(10)   VALUE '0600584635'.
    05  FILLER          PIC X(10)   VALUE '0700516824'.
    05  FILLER          PIC X(10)   VALUE '0800529263'.
    05  FILLER          PIC X(10)   VALUE '0900485691'.
    05  FILLER          PIC X(10)   VALUE '1000476180'.
    05  FILLER          PIC X(10)   VALUE '1100528676'.
    05  FILLER          PIC X(10)   VALUE '1200501892'.
```

IV. Using the table completed in question 3 and the CURRENT-DATE, write the PROCEDURE DIVISION code to access the hypothetical firm's sales amount for June using three techniques: direct access, a linear search, and a binary search.

PROJECTS

For each of the following specifications and input record layouts, design a print chart and code a COBOL program that satisfies the specification.

PROJECT 8–1 Payroll

PROGRAM SPECIFICATION

Program Name: PAY8

Program Function:

The program will edit input records from a PAYROLL-FILE. Each field of the records in the PAYROLL-FILE will be tested for validity. Items that are not valid will be identified on a printed report.

Input Files:

I. PAYROLL-FILE

INPUT DEVICE:	DISK
FILE ORGANIZATION:	SEQUENTIAL
RECORD LENGTH:	80 BYTES
FILE SEQUENCE:	ASCENDING ON DIVISION/ DEPARTMENT

Output Files:

I. PRINT-FILE

OUTPUT DEVICE:	PRINTER
RECORD LENGTH:	133 BYTES

Processing Requirements:

Each field of the PAYROLL-RECORD is to be tested and should meet the criteria listed after it.

DIVISION
- Numeric
- Range 1–5

DEPARTMENT
- Numeric
- Range 1–10

SOCIAL-SECURITY-NUMBER
- Numeric

PAY-RATE
- Numeric

MARITAL-STATUS
- M or S

FEDERAL-DEPENDENTS
- Numeric

STATE-DEPENDENTS
- Numeric

CREDIT-UNION-DEDUCTION
- Numeric

MEDICAL-INSURANCE-DEDUCTION
- Numeric

HOURS-WORKED
- Numeric
- Less than 80

EMPLOYEE-BIRTH-DATE
- Valid date

Output Requirements:

The following are formatting requirements for the report:

1. Each page of the report should contain:
   (a) a main heading which includes the company name, the report name, the report date, and a page number.
   (b) column headings which describe the items printed underneath them.
2. All fields, plus an error message, are to be printed for the first error found in each record. These lines should be double spaced.

3. Only an error message is to be printed for each additional error for the same record. These lines should be single spaced.

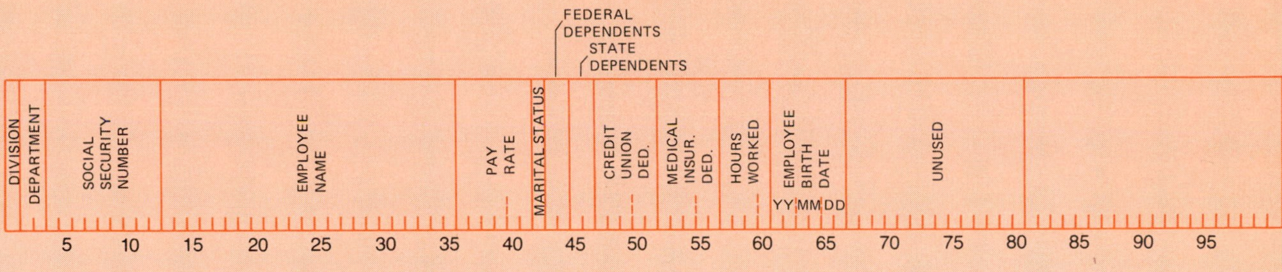

PROJECT 8–2 Inventory

PROGRAM SPECIFICATION

Program Name: INV8

Program Function:

The program will edit input records from an INVENTORY-FILE. Each field of the records in the INVENTORY-FILE will be tested for validity. Items that are not valid will be identified on a printed report.

Input Files:

I. INVENTORY-FILE

INPUT DEVICE:	DISK
FILE ORGANIZATION:	SEQUENTIAL
RECORD LENGTH:	80 BYTES
FILE SEQUENCE:	ASCENDING ON INVENTORY STOCK NUMBER

II. VENDOR-FILE

INPUT DEVICE:	DISK
FILE ORGANIZATION:	SEQUENTIAL
RECORD LENGTH:	80 BYTES
FILE SEQUENCE:	ASCENDING ON VENDOR CODE

Output Files:

I. PRINT-FILE

OUTPUT DEVICE:	PRINTER
RECORD LENGTH:	133 BYTES

Processing Requirements:

Each field of the INVENTORY-RECORD is to be tested and should meet the criteria listed after it. Tables containing all valid values are to be used to edit LOCATION-CODE, UNIT-SIZE-CODE, and VENDOR-CODE.

STOCK-NUMBER
    Numeric
DESCRIPTION
    Not equal to spaces

LOCATION-CODE
    Exists in the location code table
QUANTITY-ON-HAND
    Numeric
QUANTITY-ON-ORDER
    Numeric
REORDER-LEVEL
    Numeric
    Not greater than 1000
UNIT-SIZE-CODE
    Exists in size code table
UNIT-COST
    Numeric
UNIT-SELLING-PRICE
    Numeric
ANNUAL-USAGE
    Numeric
VENDOR-CODE
    Exists in the vendor file

Output Requirements:

The following are formatting requirements for the report:

1. Each page of the report should contain:
   (a) a main heading which includes the company name, the report name, the report date, and a page number.
   (b) column headings which describe the items printed underneath them.
2. All fields, plus an error message, are to be printed for the first error found in each record. These lines should be double spaced.
3. Only an error message is to be printed for each additional error for the same record. These lines should be single spaced.

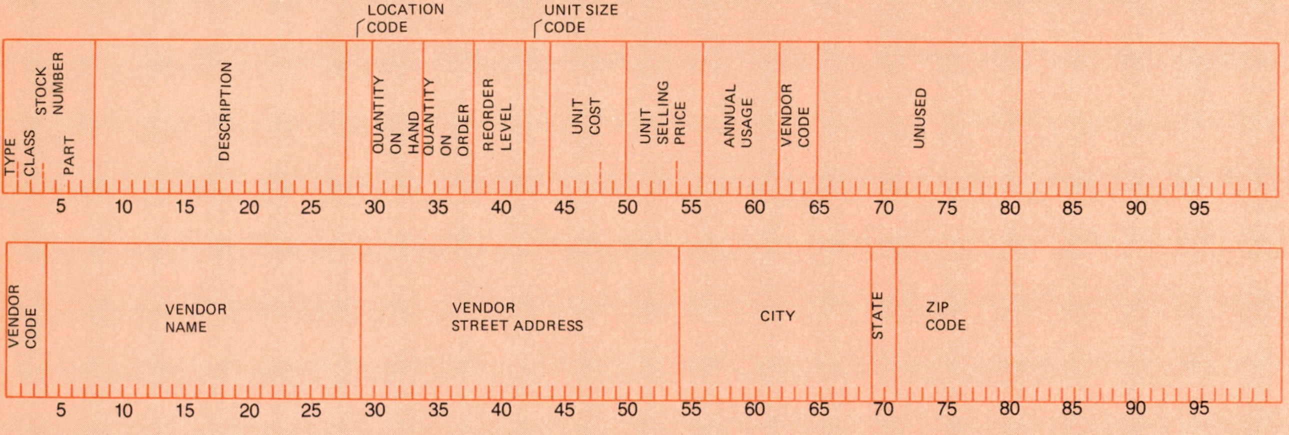

PROJECT 8–3 Accounts Payable

PROGRAM SPECIFICATION

Program Name: AP8

Program Function:

The program will edit input records from an ACCOUNTS-PAYABLE-FILE. Each field of the records in the ACCOUNTS-PAYABLE-FILE will be tested for validity. Items that are not valid will be identified on a printed report.

Input Files:

I. ACCOUNTS-PAYABLE-FILE

INPUT DEVICE:	DISK
FILE ORGANIZATION:	SEQUENTIAL
RECORD LENGTH:	80 BYTES
FILE SEQUENCE:	ASCENDING ON DIVISION / CONTROL NBR

II. VENDOR-FILE

INPUT DEVICE:	DISK
FILE ORGANIZATION:	SEQUENTIAL
RECORD LENGTH:	90 BYTES
FILE SEQUENCE:	ASCENDING ON VENDOR NUMBER

Output Files:

I. PRINT-FILE

OUTPUT DEVICE:	PRINTER
RECORD LENGTH:	133 BYTES

Processing Requirements:

Each field of the ACCOUNTS-PAYABLE-RECORD is to be tested and should meet the criteria listed after it. Tables containing all valid values are to be used to edit VENDOR-NUMBER. HARD-GOODS-AMOUNT, LABOR-AMOUNT, FREIGHT-AMOUNT, and TAX-AMOUNT are to be totaled and should equal INVOICE-AMOUNT.

- DIVISION
  - Numeric
  - Range 1–10
- CONTROL-NUMBER
  - Numeric
- INVOICE-NUMBER
  - Numeric
- VENDOR-NUMBER
  - Exists in vendor file
- INVOICE-DATE
  - Valid date
- DUE-DATE
  - Valid date
- INVOICE-AMOUNT
  - Numeric
- HARD-GOODS-AMOUNT
  - Numeric
- LABOR-AMOUNT
  - Numeric
- FREIGHT-AMOUNT
  - Numeric
- TAX-AMOUNT
  - Numeric

Output Requirements:

The following are formatting requirements for the report:

1. Each page of the report should contain:
   (a) a main heading which includes the company name, the report name, the report date, and a page number.

(b) column headings which describe the items printed underneath them.

2. All fields, plus an error message, are to be printed for the first error found in each record. These lines should be double spaced.
3. Only an error message is to be printed for each additional error for the same record. These lines should be single spaced.

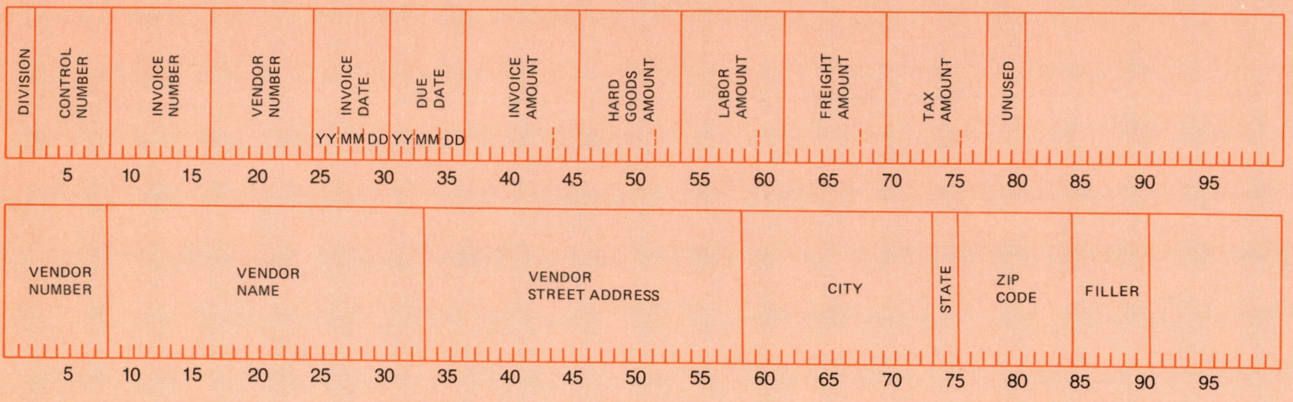

PROJECT 8–4 Pension

PROGRAM SPECIFICATION

Program Name: PEN8

Program Function:

The program will edit input records from a PENSION-FILE. Each field of the records in the PENSION-FILE will be tested for validity. Items that are not valid will be identified on a printed report.

Input Files:

I. PENSION-FILE

INPUT DEVICE:	DISK
FILE ORGANIZATION:	SEQUENTIAL
RECORD LENGTH:	80 BYTES
FILE SEQUENCE:	ASCENDING ON DIVISION / DEPARTMENT

II. PAYROLL FILE

INPUT DEVICE:	DISK
FILE ORGANIZATION:	SEQUENTIAL
RECORD LENGTH:	80
FILE SEQUENCE:	ASCENDING ON DIVISION / DEPARTMENT

Output Files:

I. PRINT-FILE

OUTPUT DEVICE:	PRINTER
RECORD LENGTH:	133 BYTES

Processing Requirements:

Each field of the PENSION-RECORD is to be tested and should meet the criteria listed after it. Tables containing all valid values are to be used to edit SOCIAL-SECURITY-NUMBER.

- DIVISION
  - Numeric
  - Range 1–10
- DEPARTMENT
  - Numeric
  - Range 1–10
- SOCIAL-SECURITY-NUMBER
  - Numeric
  - Exists on payroll file
- NAME
  - Not equal to spaces
- BIRTH-DATE
  - Valid date
- HIRE-DATE
  - Valid date
- GROSS-SALARY
  - Numeric
  - Not greater than 200,000
- EMPLOYEE-CONTRIBUTION
  - Numeric
- EMPLOYER-CONTRIBUTION
  - Numeric
- BALANCE-FORWARD
  - Numeric
  - Positive

Output Requirements:

The following are formatting requirements for the report:

1. Each page of the report should contain:
   (a) a main heading which includes the company name, the report name, the report date, and a page number.
   (b) column headings which describe the items printed underneath them.
2. All fields, plus an error message, are to be printed for the first error found in each record. These lines should be double spaced.
3. Only an error message is to be printed for each additional error for the same record. These lines should be single spaced.

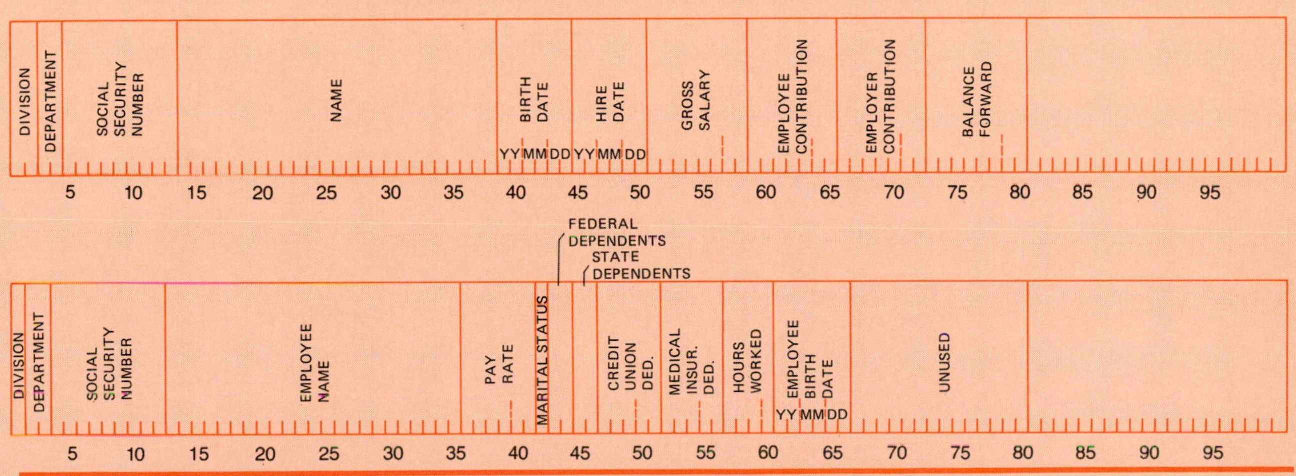

PROGRAM SPECIFICATION

Program Name: BOM8

Program Function:

The program will edit input records from a BILL-OF-MATERIALS-FILE. Each field of the records in the BILL-OF-MATERIALS-FILE will be tested for validity. Items that are not valid will be identified on a printed report.

Input Files:

I. BILL-OF-MATERIALS-FILE

INPUT DEVICE:	DISK
FILE ORGANIZATION:	SEQUENTIAL
RECORD LENGTH:	55 BYTES
FILE SEQUENCE:	ASCENDING ON INVENTORY STOCK NUMBER

II. PART NUMBER-FILE

INPUT DEVICE:	DISK
FILE ORGANIZATION:	SEQUENTIAL
RECORD LENGTH:	45 BYTES
FILE SEQUENCE:	ASCENDING ON PART-NUMBER

Output Files:

I. PRINT-FILE

OUTPUT DEVICE:	PRINTER
RECORD LENGTH:	133 BYTES

Processing Requirements:

Each field of the BILL-OF-MATERIALS-FILE is to be tested and should meet the criteria listed after it. Tables containing all valid values are to be used to edit MASTER-PRODUCT-LINE, MASTER-PART-NUMBER, COMPONENT-PART-NUMBER, and COMPONENT-UNIT-OF-MEASURE.

MASTER-DIVISION
- Numeric
- Range 1–10

MASTER-PRODUCT-LINE
- Numeric
- Exists in product line table

MASTER-PART-NUMBER
- Numeric
- Exists in master part number file

COMPONENT-PART-NUMBER
- Numeric
- Exists in part number file

COMPONENT-QUANTITY
- Numeric

COMPONENT-UNIT-OF-MEASURE
- Exists in unit of measure table

COMPONENT-COST
- Numeric

COMPONENT-DRAWING
Not equal to spaces

Output Requirements:

The following are formatting requirements for the report:

1. Each page of the report should contain:
   (a) a main heading which includes the company name, the report name, the report date, and a page number.
   (b) column headings which describe the items printed underneath them.
2. All fields, plus an error message, are to be printed for the first error found in each record. These lines should be double spaced.
3. Only an error message is to be printed for each additional error for the same record. These lines should be single spaced.

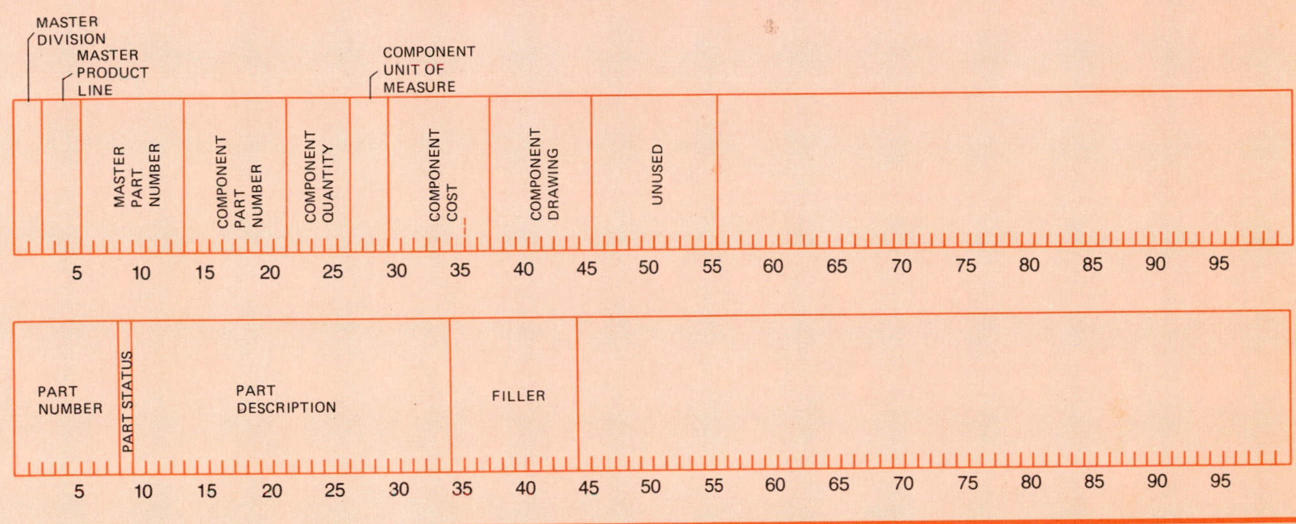

PROJECT 8–6 Cost

PROGRAM SPECIFICATION

Program Name: COST8

Program Function:

The program will edit input records from a COST-FILE. Each field of the records in the COST-FILE will be tested for validity. Items that are not valid will be identified on a printed report.

Input Files:

I. COST-FILE

INPUT DEVICE:	DISK
FILE ORGANIZATION:	SEQUENTIAL
RECORD LENGTH:	75 BYTES
FILE SEQUENCE:	ASCENDING ON DIVISION / PRODUCT LINE

II. PART-NUMBER-FILE

INPUT DEVICE:	DISK
FILE ORGANIZATION:	SEQUENTIAL
RECORD LENGTH:	45 BYTES
FILE SEQUENCE:	ASCENDING ON PART-NUMBER

Output Files:

I. PRINT-FILE

OUTPUT DEVICE:	PRINTER
RECORD LENGTH:	133 BYTES

Processing Requirements:

Each field of the COST-RECORD is to be tested and should meet the criteria listed after it. Tables consisting of all valid values are to be used to edit PRODUCT-LINE and PART-NUMBER.

- DIVISION
  - Numeric
  - Range 1–10
- PRODUCT-LINE
  - Numeric
  - Exists in product line table
- PART-NUMBER
  - Numeric
  - Exists in part number file
- DESCRIPTION
  - Not equal to spaces
- COST-OF-STEEL
  - Numeric
- COST-OF-PAINT
  - Numeric
- COST-OF-HARDWARE
  - Numeric
- COST-OF-PACKAGING
  - Numeric
- COST-OF-LABOR
  - Numeric

Output Requirements:

The following are formatting requirements for the report:

1. Each page of the report should contain:
   (a) a main heading which includes the company name, the report name, the report date, and a page number.
   (b) column headings which describe the items printed underneath them.
2. All fields, plus an error message, are to be printed for the first error found in each record. These lines should be double spaced.
3. Only an error message is to be printed for each additional error for the same record. These lines should be single spaced.

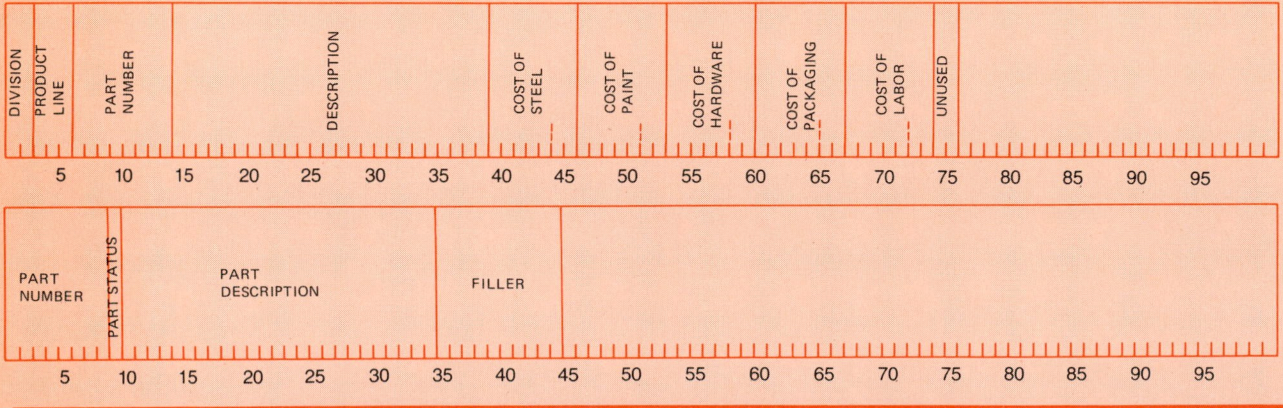

CHAPTER 9

Maintenance of Sequential Files

This chapter presents the logic for updating sequential files. The first program updates an order file by placing a shipping date in the field for the actual shipping date. A date file and a shipping file are used to determine the date of shipment and which orders have been shipped.

The second program is designed to maintain the above-mentioned order file. Maintenance is performed using a transaction file which contains data for ADDS, CHANGES, and DELETES to the order file.

There are no new COBOL elements in this chapter.

INTRODUCTION

Master files whose organization is sequential require periodic maintenance to keep them current. The transactions which reflect the changes to be made to the master file are accumulated in a transaction file, and then, using file-matching techniques, the master and transaction files are processed in order to produce a new version of the master file. These file-matching techniques require that each file have at least one field in common (called a key field). Furthermore, the files must be in sequence on those fields. Comparisons of the contents of the key fields are made using a record from each file, and the relationship between the fields, as well as the type of transaction, determines the action to be taken.

A new, updated sequential file must be created. Files whose organization is sequential cannot accommodate the insertion of new records, deletion of unneeded records, or rewriting of changed records on the original file.

There are two programming projects in this chapter. The first updates the actual shipping date in an order file for orders shipped on a particular day and produces a report of the orders shipped for that day. This program is designed to accommodate only one transaction for each record on the master file. The second program is a sequential-file maintenance program which adds new orders, deletes cancelled orders, and changes selected fields in unshipped orders. This program uses a technique which allows multiple transactions for each record on the master file.

PROGRAM SPECIFICATION: SHIPMENT

The first programming project updates the ORD-ACT-SHIP-DATE field of the ORDER-FILE of the previous chapter by placing a shipping date in the field to replace the zeros that indicate an unshipped order. The program specification is shown in Figure 9–1.

PROGRAM SPECIFICATION

Program Name: SHIPMENT

Program Function:

This program updates the ORDER-FILE using ORD-ACT-SHIP-DATE to indicate that orders have been shipped. The program will calculate an extended price and list all orders shipped. A final total for the extended price will be produced.

Input Files:

I. ORDER-FILE

INPUT DEVICE:	DISK
FILE ORGANIZATION:	SEQUENTIAL
RECORD LENGTH:	70 BYTES
FILE SEQUENCE:	ASCENDING ON SALES ORDER NUMBER

II. SHIP-FILE

INPUT DEVICE:	DISK
FILE ORGANIZATION:	SEQUENTIAL
RECORD LENGTH:	20 BYTES
FILE SEQUENCE:	ASCENDING ON SALES ORDER NUMBER

III. DATE-FILE

INPUT DEVICE:	DISK
FILE ORGANIZATION:	SEQUENTIAL
RECORD LENGTH:	10 BYTES
FILE SEQUENCE:	NONE (SINGLE RECORD FILE)

Output Files:

I. NEW-ORDER-FILE

OUTPUT DEVICE:	DISK
FILE ORGANIZATION:	SEQUENTIAL
RECORD LENGTH:	70 BYTES
FILE SEQUENCE:	ASCENDING ON SALES ORDER NUMBER

II. PRINT-FILE

OUTPUT DEVICE:	PRINTER
RECORD LENGTH:	133 BYTES

Processing Requirements:

DATE-FILE will contain a single record which contains a shipping date. SHIP-FILE contains order numbers for orders shipped on that date. The program will read the ORDER-FILE and create a new version of it (NEW-ORDER-FILE). For orders that are in SHIP-FILE, the matching record from ORDER-FILE is to be updated with the shipping date. That is, the shipping date from DATE-FILE is to be placed in the actual shipping date field in the order record. A detail line should be printed on the shipment report for each order which is updated. The extended price must be calculated for each line, printed, and totaled for the entire report. If an order number exists in SHIP-FILE but there is no matching order number in ORDER-FILE, this is an error and should be noted on the shipment error report.

FIGURE 9-1

Output Requirements:

Each order shipped should appear on the shipment report, and each record from the ORDER-FILE should appear on the NEW-ORDER-FILE.

The following are formatting requirements for the report:

1. Each page of the report should contain:
   (a) a main heading which includes the company name, the report name, the report date, and a page number.
   (b) column headings which describe the items printed underneath them.
2. Detail lines should include the sales order number, part number, quantity, and extended price.
3. Detail lines should be double spaced.
4. Final totals should be triple spaced.

The shipment error report should be on a separate page at the end of the shipment report. The error report will list all order numbers which were in SHIP-FILE but were not in ORDER-FILE.

FIGURE 9-1 cont.

Input Record Layout

The input record layouts for ORDER-FILE, SHIP-FILE, and DATE-FILE are shown in Figure 9–2. The record layout for NEW-ORDER-FILE is identical to that for ORDER-FILE.

ORDER-FILE:

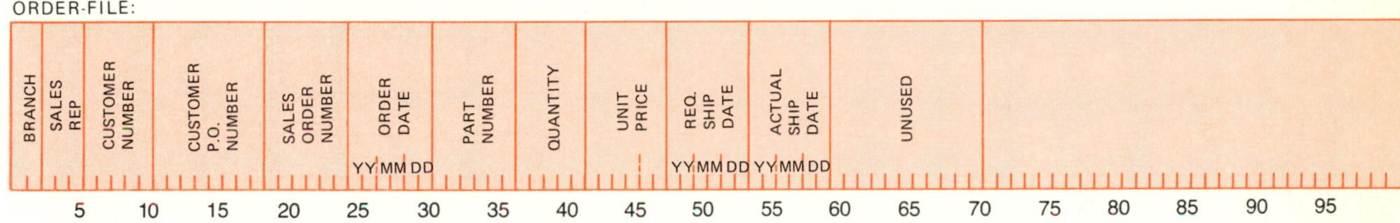

SHIP-FILE:

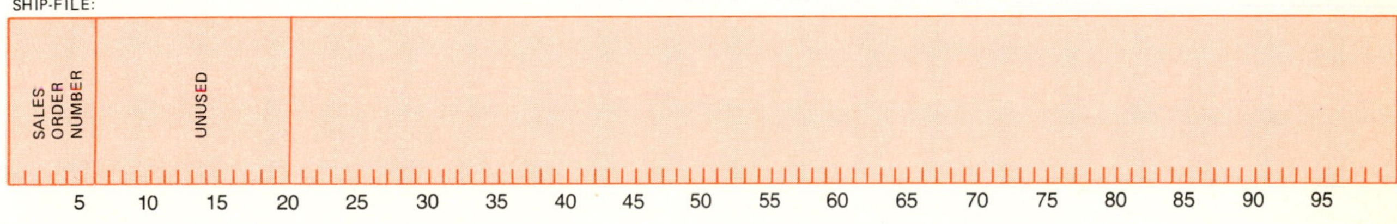

DATE-FILE:

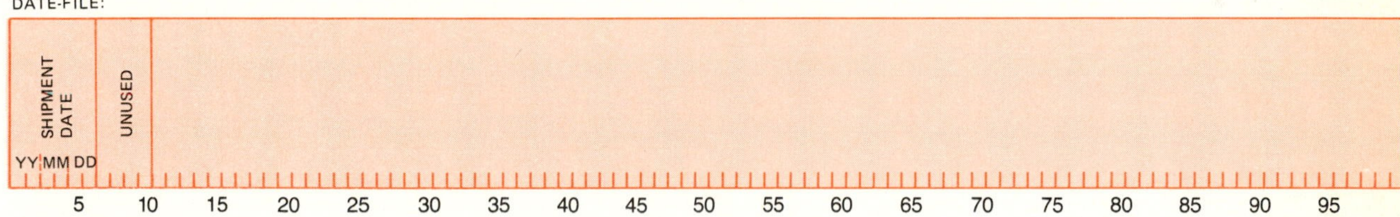

FIGURE 9–2

Print Chart

The print charts for the shipment report and the error report are shown in Figure 9–3.

LOGIC FOR SEQUENTIAL-FILE MAINTENANCE WITH CHANGES ONLY

A hierarchy chart for SHIPMENT is shown in Figure 9–4, and pseudocode and a flowchart for the same are shown in Figures 9–5 and 9–6, respectively.

(*text continued on page 401*)

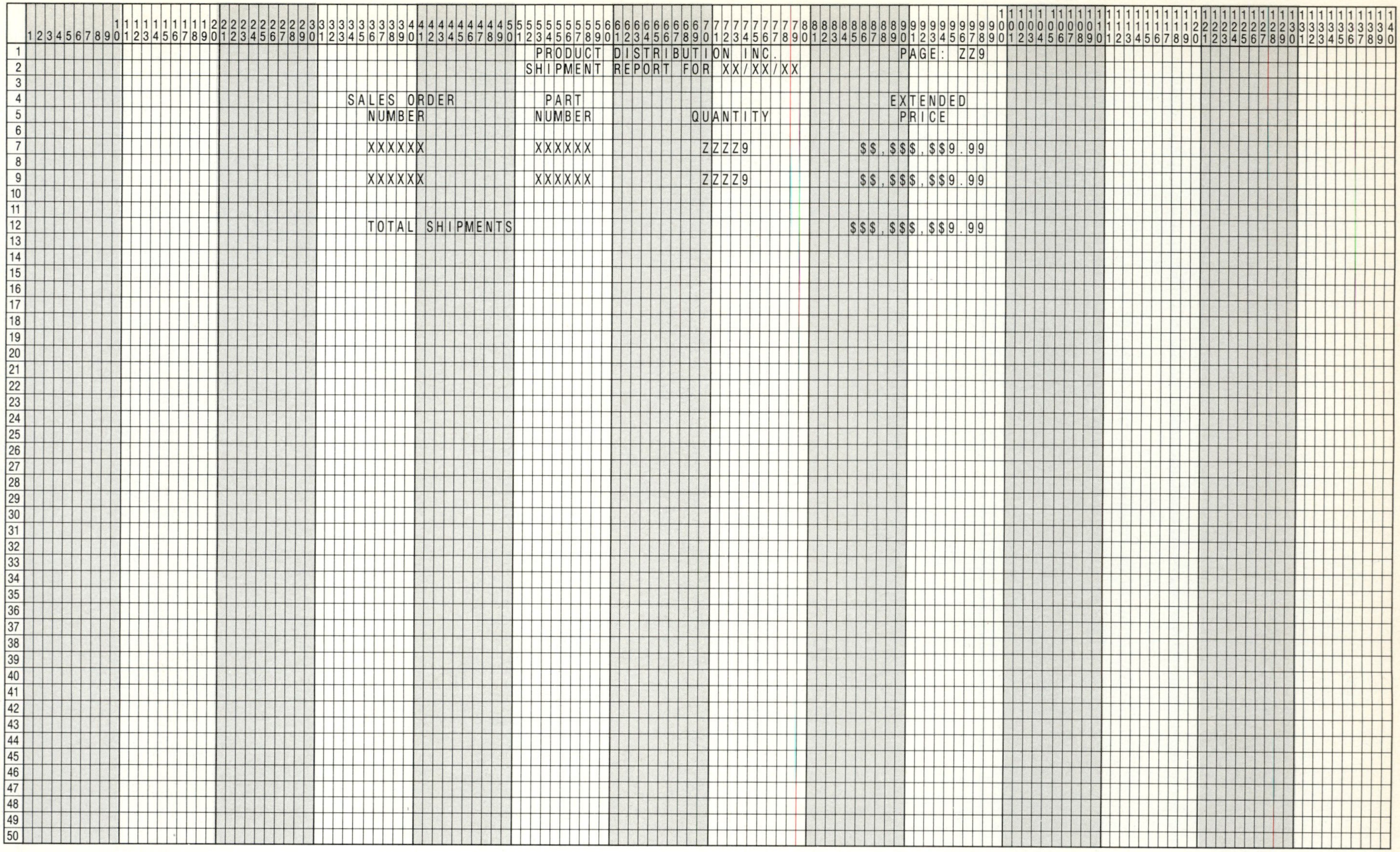

```
                                                    PRODUCT DISTRIBUTION INC.              PAGE: ZZ9
                                                   SHIPMENT REPORT FOR XX/XX/XX

                                SALES ORDER           PART                                 EXTENDED
                                  NUMBER             NUMBER           QUANTITY              PRICE

                                  XXXXXX             XXXXXX             ZZZZ9        $$,$$$,$$9.99

                                  XXXXXX             XXXXXX             ZZZZ9        $$,$$$,$$9.99


                                  TOTAL SHIPMENTS                                   $$$,$$$,$$9.99
```

FIGURE 9–3

```
                                                                          PRODUCT DISTRIBUTION INC.                    PAGE: ZZ9
                                                                           SHIPMENT ERROR REPORT

                                          THE FOLLOWING SALES ORDER NUMBERS DO NOT EXIST IN THE ORDER FILE:

                                                                                XXXXXX

                                                                                XXXXXX
```

FIGURE 9-3 cont.

Hierarchy Chart

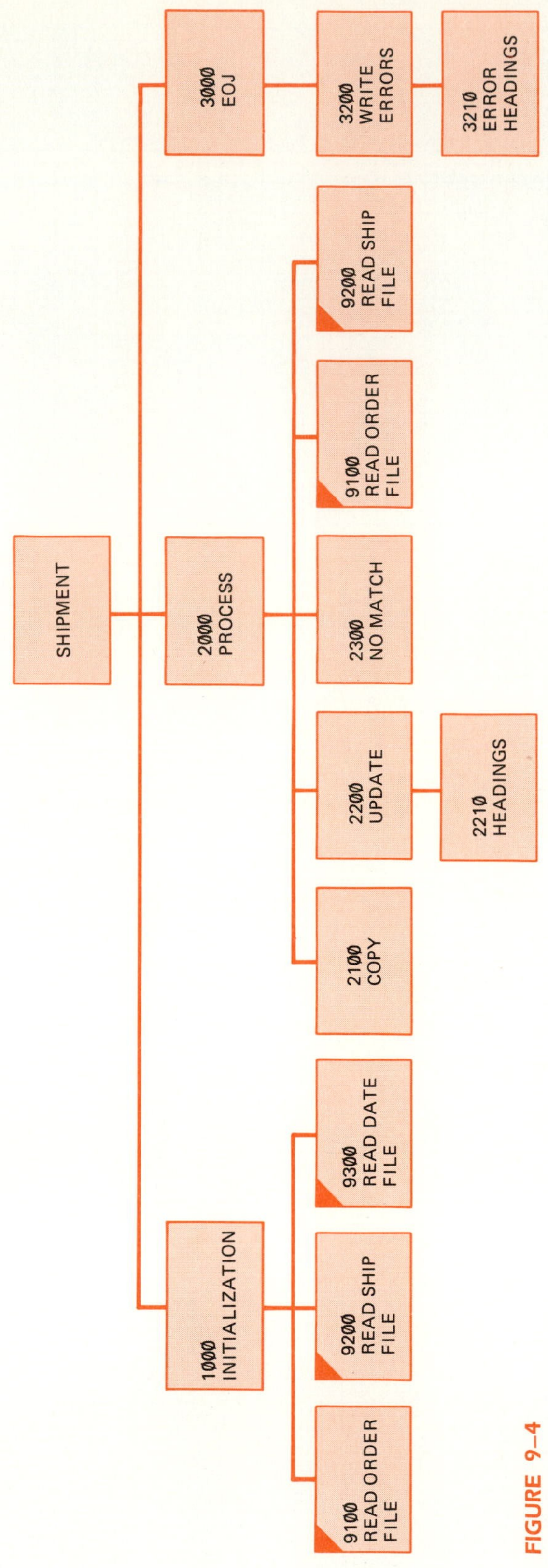

FIGURE 9–4

Pseudocode

```
MAIN LINE
     DO initialization
     DO while more order records or more ship
       records
          DO process
     ENDDO
     DO end of job

INITIALIZATION
     OPEN files
     DO read order file
     DO read ship file
     DO read date file
     MOVE date to heading

PROCESS
     IF sales order number < ship order number
          DO copy
          DO read order file
     ELSE
          IF sales order number = ship order number
               DO update
               DO read order file
               DO read ship file
          ELSE
               DO no match
               DO read ship file
          ENDIF
     ENDIF

COPY
     WRITE new order record

UPDATE
     MOVE input to output
     CALCULATE extended price
     MOVE extended price to output
     ADD extended price to final extended price
     IF page overflow
          DO headings
     ENDIF
     WRITE detail line
     ADD 2 to line count
     MOVE ship date to order actual ship date
     WRITE new order record

HEADINGS
     ADD 1 to page count
     MOVE page count to heading
     WRITE main heading line 1
     WRITE main heading line 2
     WRITE column heading line 1
     WRITE column heading line 2
     MOVE 5 to line count

NO MATCH
     ADD 1 to error subscript
     ADD 1 to number of errors
     MOVE sales order number to error table
       (error subscript)
```

FIGURE 9–5

```
END OF JOB
     MOVE final extended price to output
     WRITE final total line
     MOVE 99 to line count
     IF number of errors > zero
          DO WHILE error subscript > number of
            errors
               DO write errors
          ENDDO
     ELSE
          MOVE 'none' to output
          WRITE error detail line
     ENDIF
     CLOSE files

WRITE ERRORS
     IF page overflow
          DO error headings
     ENDIF
     MOVE error table (error subscript) to output
     WRITE error detail line
     ADD 2 to line count

ERROR HEADINGS
     ADD 1 to page count
     MOVE page count to heading
     WRITE main heading 1
     WRITE error heading 2
     WRITE error heading 3
     MOVE 4 to line count

READ ORDER FILE
     IF end of order file
     ELSE
          READ order file
          IF end of order file
               MOVE 'yes' to end flag order file
               MOVE a high value to sales order
               number
          ENDIF
     ENDIF

READ SHIP FILE
     IF end of ship file
     ELSE
          READ ship file
          IF end of ship file
               MOVE 'yes' to end flag ship file
               MOVE a high value to ship sales or-
               der number
          ENDIF
     ENDIF

READ DATE FILE
     READ date file
     IF end of file
          MOVE 'yes' to end flag date file
     ENDIF
```

FIGURE 9-5 cont.

Flowchart

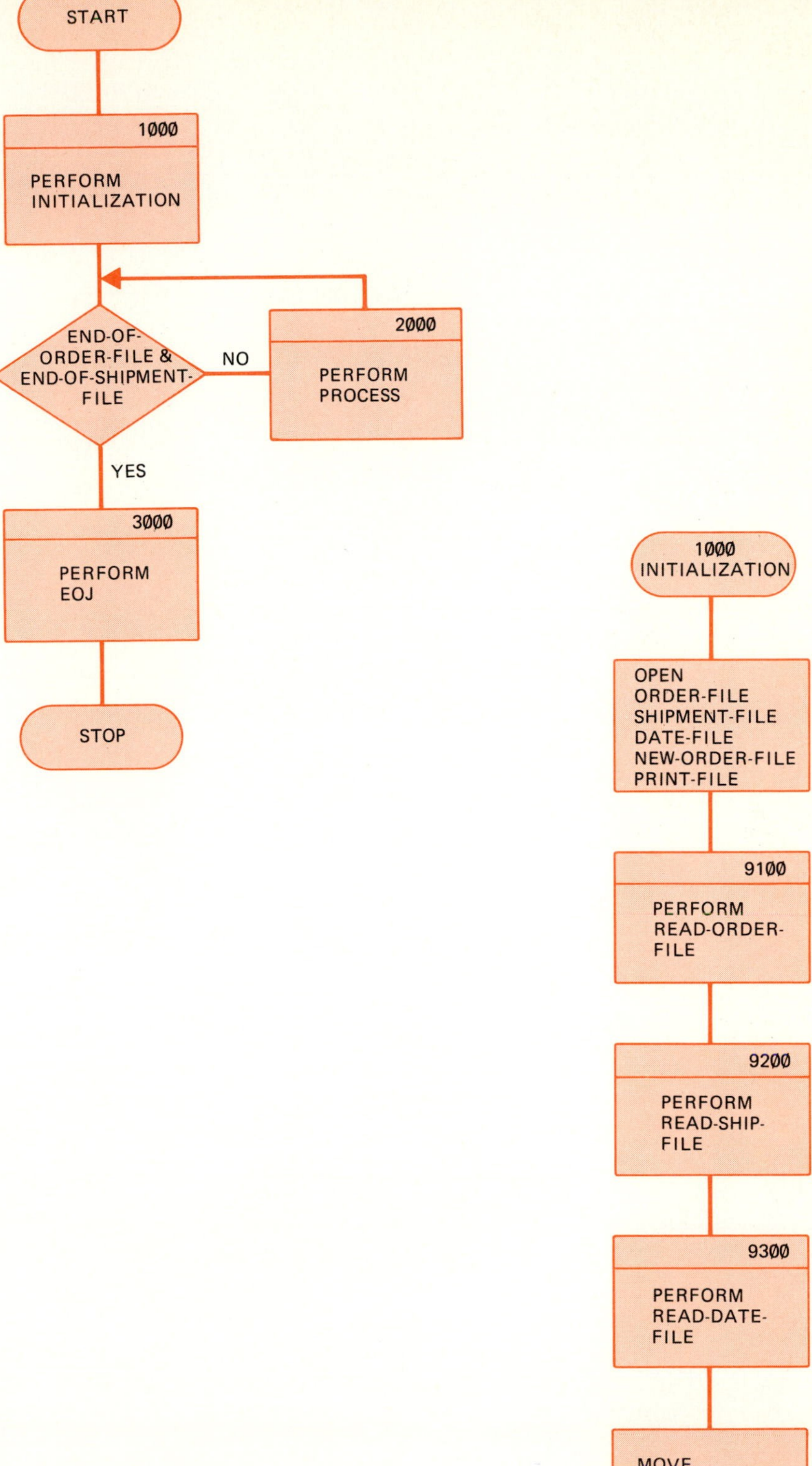

FIGURE 9–6

Logic for Sequential-File Maintenance with Changes Only

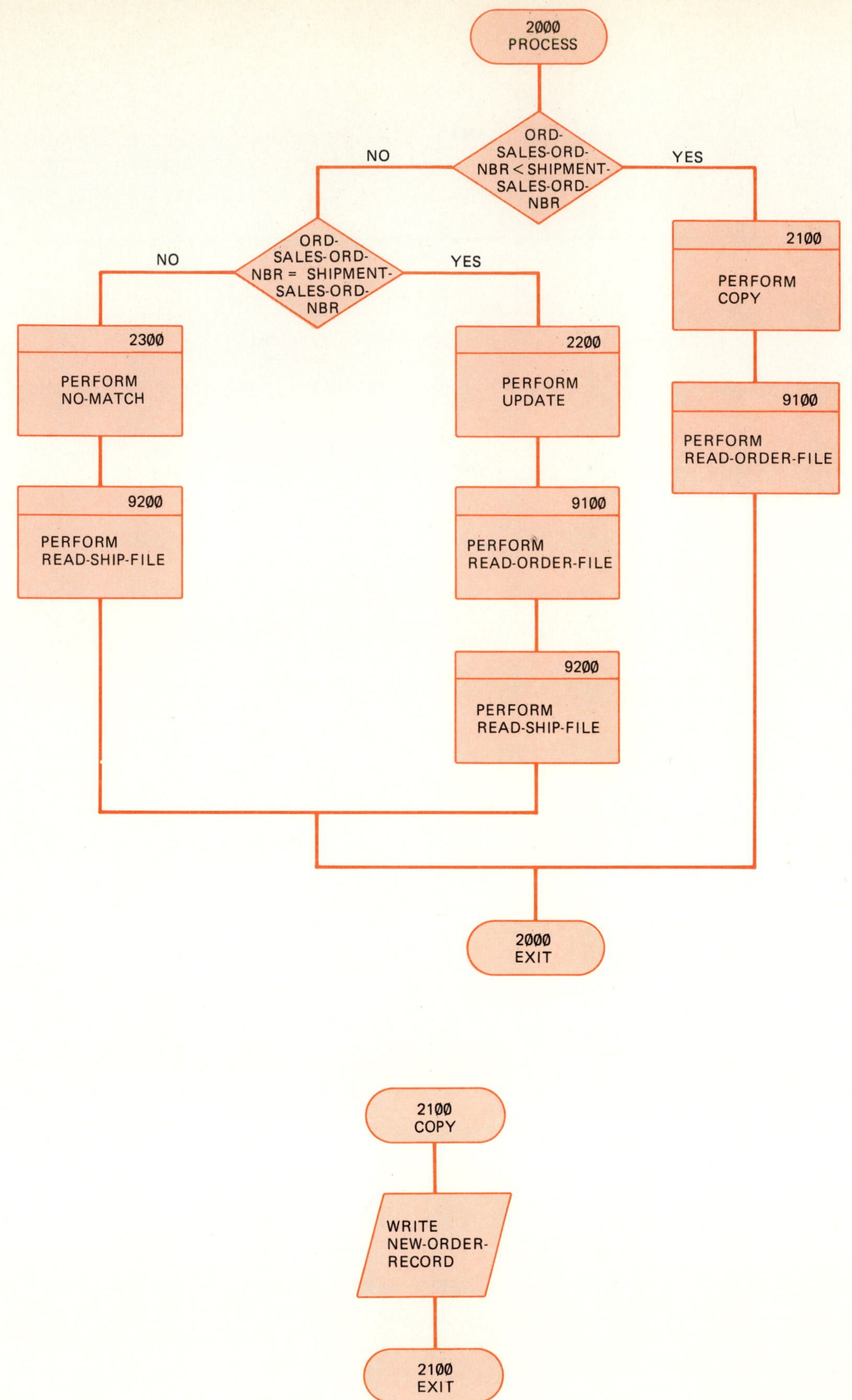

FIGURE 9-6 cont.

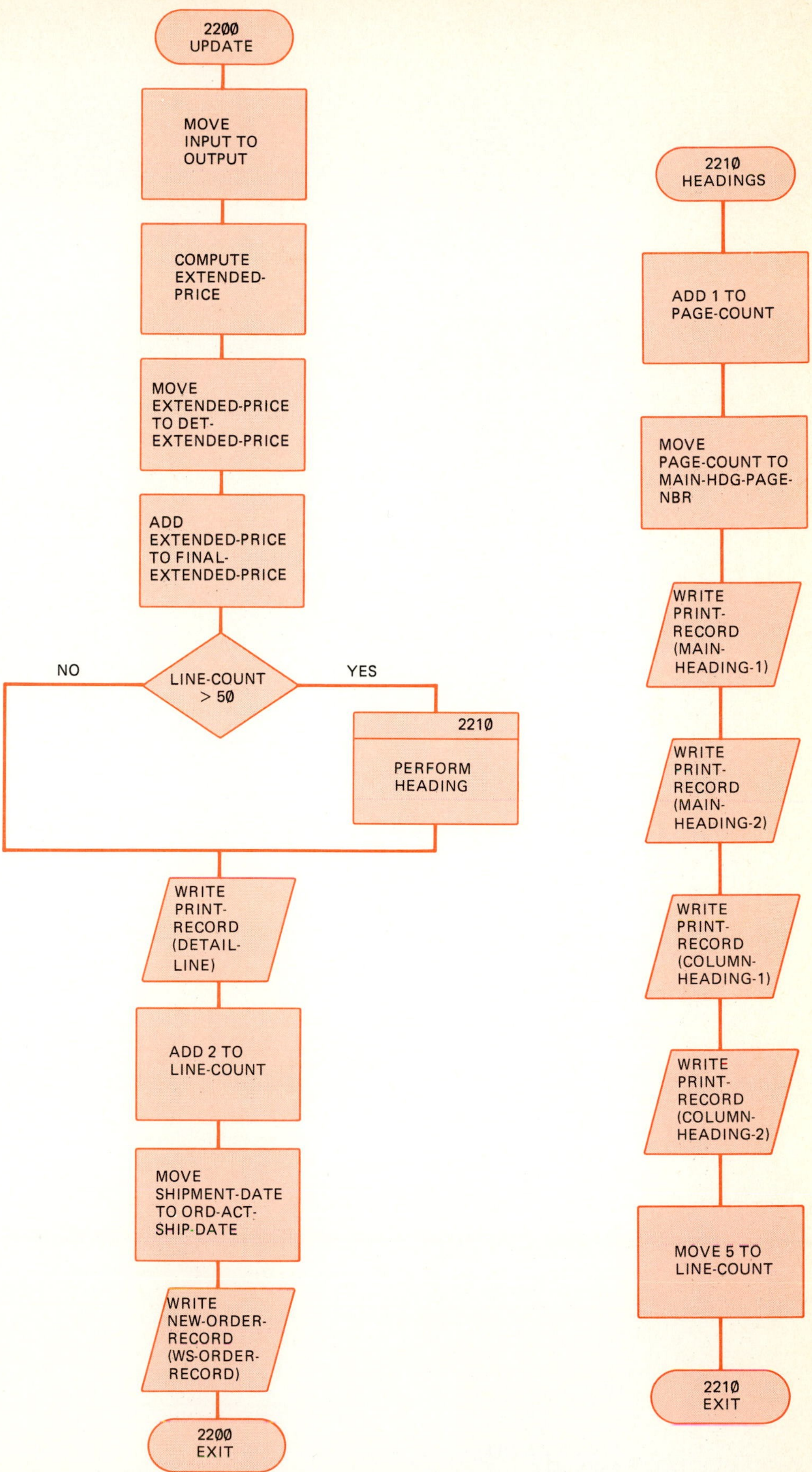

FIGURE 9-6 cont.

Logic for Sequential-File Maintenance with Changes Only

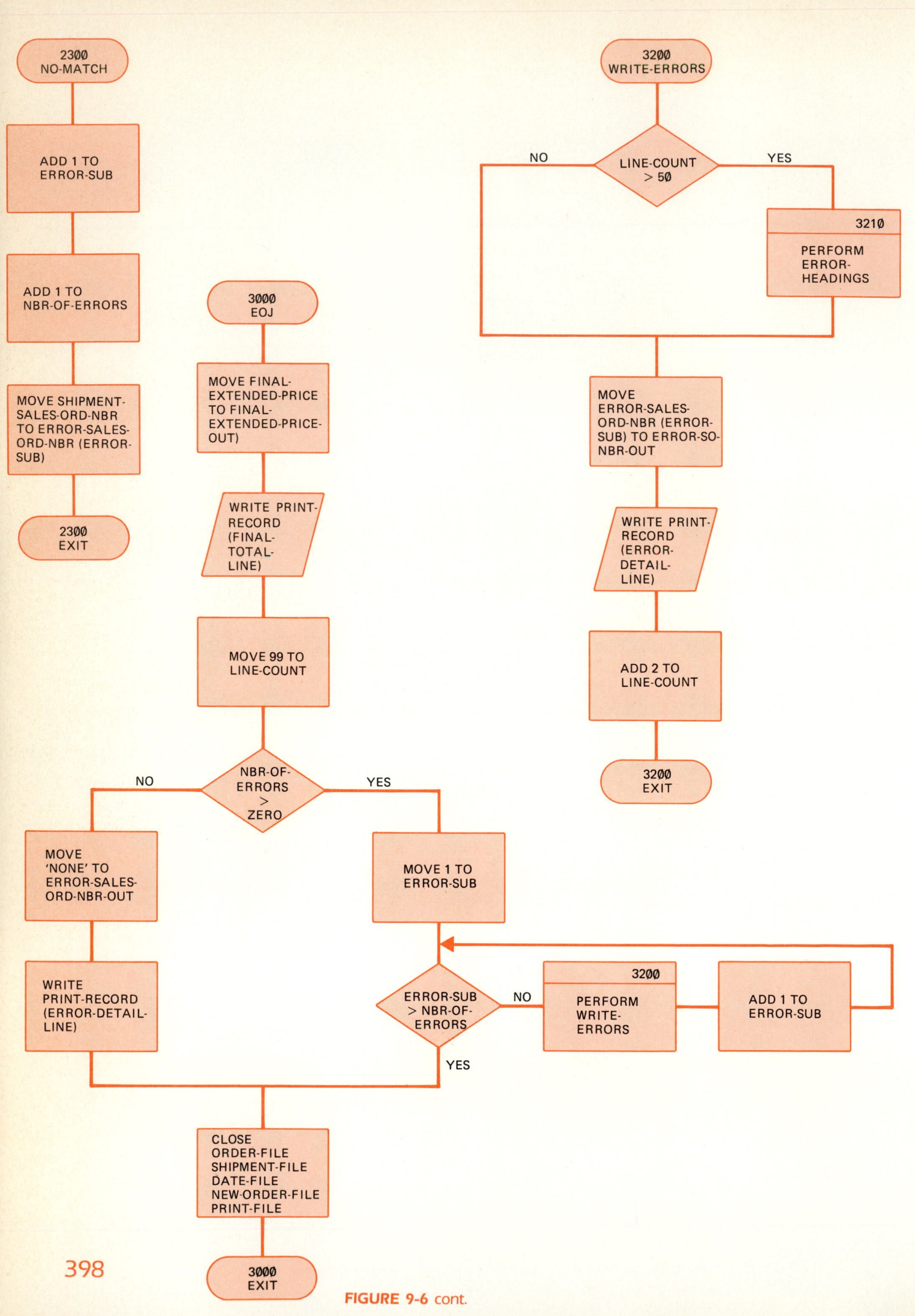

FIGURE 9-6 cont.

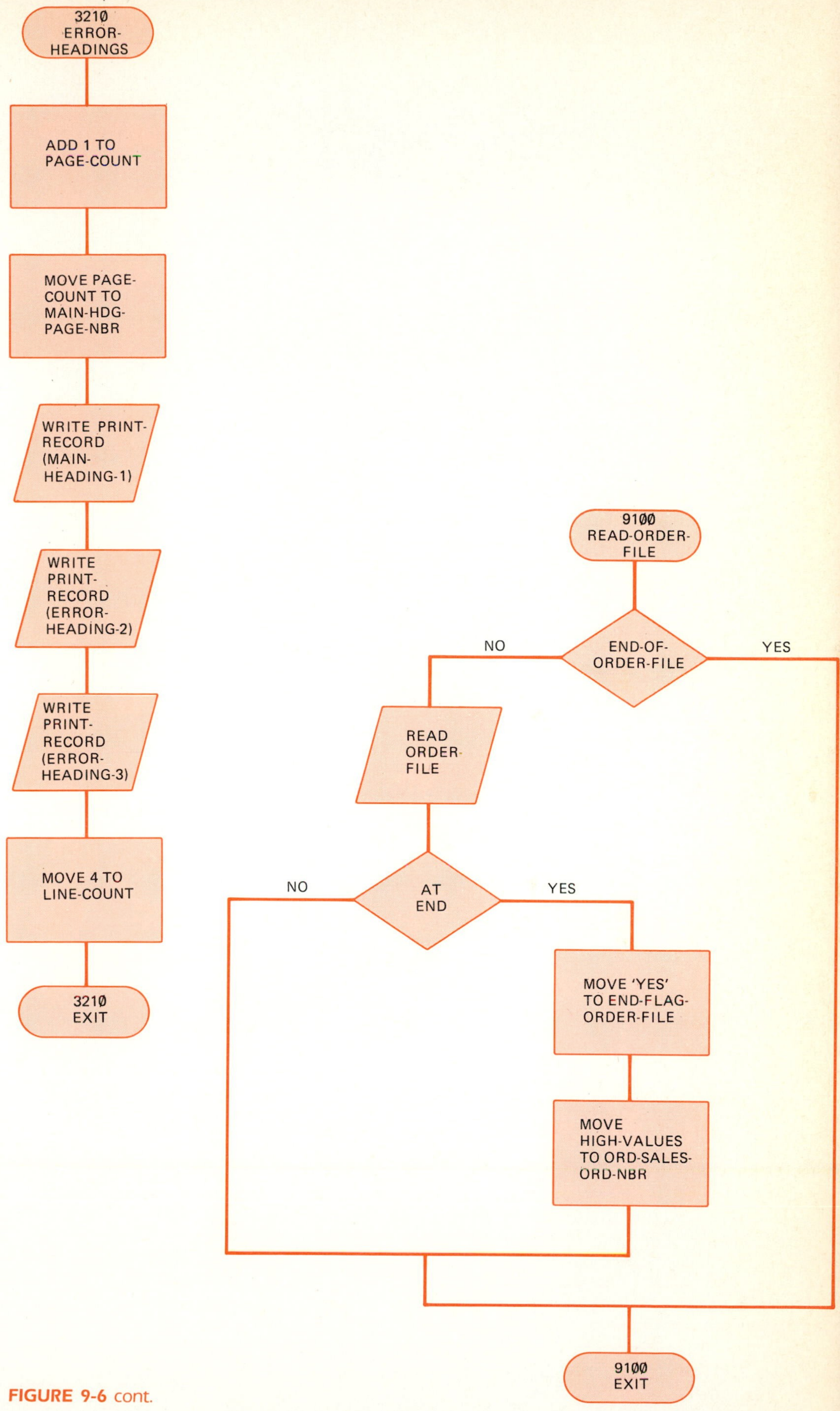

FIGURE 9-6 cont.

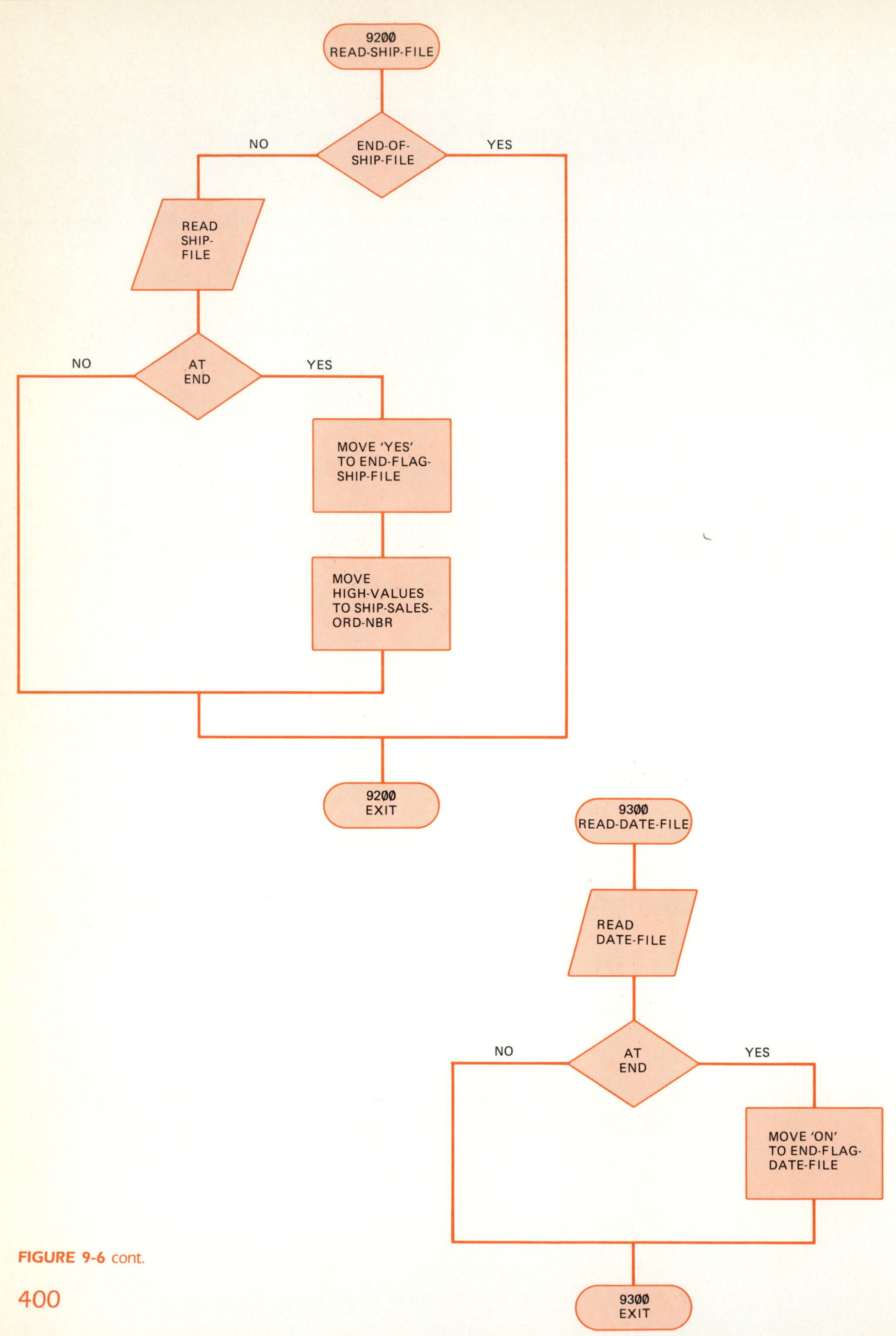

FIGURE 9-6 cont.

Explanation of Logic

Sequential Update

A sequential update requires at least two files: a master file and one or more transaction files. Each of the files must be in sequence on a key field. In the master file, each key field must be unique; however, transaction files may have multiple records where the key fields have the same value. If there are to be multiple transactions with the same value in the key field, logic for this situation must be included in the program design.

In a simple sequential update with a master file and one transaction file containing only changes for the master file, a record is read from each file and the key values are compared. Consider the following numbers by way of explanation.

MASTER	TRANSACTION
500	510
510	520
530	/*
/*	

If the master file key field (500) is less than the transaction file key field (510), there is no transaction for the master, as long as the files are in the same ascending or descending sequence. The master record in question may accordingly be written to the new master file without change, and a new master record is read.

MASTER	TRANSACTION
500	510
510	520
530	/*
/*	

Comparison of the two key fields now indicates a condition of equality. Hence, any changes present on the transaction record are transferred to the master record, and the master record is written to the new master file. Since the comparison results in the processing of both a master record and a transaction record, a new record is read from each file.

MASTER	TRANSACTION
500	510
510	520
530	/*
/*	

Comparison of the two fields now indicates a master (530) greater than a transaction (520). This means that there is a transaction with no master record corresponding to it. In a transaction file that contains only changes for the master file, this is an error. So an error message is printed, and a new transaction is read. The attempt to read the transaction file results in an end-of-file condition, and HIGH-VALUES is moved to the transaction key field, whereupon a flag is set to indicate that the transaction file has been processed.

MASTER	TRANSACTION
500	510
510	520
530	/* ←— Hexadecimal FFFFFF (HIGH-VALUES)

Comparison of the two fields now indicates that the master key field (530) is less than the transaction key field (Hex FFFFFF). This means that no transaction record exists for the master record. So the master record is written to the new master file, and a new master record is read. The attempt to read the master file results in an end-of-file condition, and HIGH-VALUES is moved to the master key field, whereupon a flag is set to indicate that the master file has been processed. At this point the flags for both files are set, and processing will be completed in the end-of-job routine.

In the SHIPMENT program, the ORDER-FILE (master) is updated using a SHIP-FILE (transaction) and a DATE-FILE. The date record contains the shipping date for the group of orders in the SHIP-FILE. Transactions from the SHIP-FILE that have a matching sales order number in the ORDER-FILE indicate an order that has been shipped.

MAIN LINE

The main routine has been changed from that of previous programs to accommodate the two input files used in the matching process. Both of the files must reach their end in order for processing to be complete. Accordingly, each file has its own end flag and 2000-PROCESS is performed until the end flags are set for both of the files. (See Figure 9–7.)

```
           PERFORM 1000-INITIALIZATION.
           PERFORM 2000-PROCESS
               UNTIL END-OF-ORDER-FILE AND END-OF-SHIP-FILE.
           PERFORM 3000-EOJ.
           STOP RUN.
```

FIGURE 9–7

1000-INITIALIZATION

The initialization routine uses three input files: the ORDER-FILE, SHIP-FILE, and DATE-FILE. Each record in the SHIP-FILE represents an order that has been shipped. The single record in the DATE-FILE represents the date of shipment for the group of orders under consideration. 2000-PROCESS will compare records from the SHIP-FILE with records from the ORDER-FILE, and if there is a match, the date from the DATE-FILE will be inserted in ORD-ACT-SHIP-DATE.

All of the files are opened, and a record is read from each of them. Since there is only one record in the DATE-FILE, no additional record will be read from this file, and the date will be available in the input area throughout the program. The first records from the ORDER-FILE and SHIP-FILE will be compared in 2000-PROCESS. (See Figure 9–8.)

```
       1000-INITIALIZATION.
           OPEN INPUT  ORDER-FILE
                       SHIP-FILE
                       DATE-FILE
                OUTPUT NEW-ORDER-FILE
                       PRINT-FILE.
           PERFORM 9100-READ-ORDER-FILE.
           PERFORM 9200-READ-SHIP-FILE.
           PERFORM 9300-READ-DATE-FILE.
           MOVE SHIPMENT-YY  TO MAIN-HDG-SHIP-YY.
           MOVE SHIPMENT-MM  TO MAIN-HDG-SHIP-MM.
           MOVE SHIPMENT-DD  TO MAIN-HDG-SHIP-DD.
```

FIGURE 9–8

2000-PROCESS

In 2000-PROCESS, the sales order numbers from the ORDER-FILE and the SHIP-FILE are compared. The objective is to locate and update any records in the ORDER-FILE which have a matching record in the SHIP-FILE. All records read from the ORDER-FILE are to be written to NEW-ORDER-FILE whether they are updated or not.

There are three possible outcomes for the comparison. If the sales order number in the ORDER-FILE is less than the sales order number in the SHIP-FILE, there is no matching record in the SHIP-FILE for the current ORDER-RECORD. Since both files are in ascending order, if the current SHIP-FILE record is greater than the ORDER-FILE record, all remaining records in the SHIP-FILE will also be greater. The record from the ORDER-FILE will then be written to the NEW-ORDER-FILE without any changes because the order has not been shipped. This is done in the 2100-COPY routine. At this point, the record from the ORDER-FILE has been processed and the record from the SHIP-FILE has not. In order to have a record from each file available for comparison when 2000-PROCESS is next entered, a new record is read from the ORDER-FILE. This is done in 9100-READ-ORDER-FILE.

A second outcome of the comparison is that the sales order number of the ORDER-FILE will be equal to the sales order number of the SHIP-FILE. If this is so, the ORDER-RECORD will be updated with the shipping date to indicate that the order in question has been shipped, a detail line will be printed on the shipment report, and the updated record will be written to the NEW-ORDER-FILE. This is all done in 2200-UPDATE. At this point both an ORDER-RECORD and a SHIP-RECORD have been processed, so a new record is read from both files by performing 9100-READ-ORDER-FILE and 9200-READ-SHIP-FILE.

The third possible outcome of the comparison is that the sales order number from the ORDER-FILE will be greater than the sales order number from the SHIP-FILE. This would indicate that there is no record on the ORDER-FILE to match the record from the SHIP-FILE, an error condition. For how can an order that doesn't exist be shipped? In this case the SHIP-SALES-ORD-NBR is saved in a table of errors in 2300-NO-MATCH which will be printed after the input files have been processed, and since a record from the SHIP-FILE has been processed (as an error), a new record is read from the SHIP-FILE in 9200-READ-SHIP-FILE.

At the completion of 2000-PROCESS, a record from each file is again available for comparison when the routine is reentered. If the end of either file is reached in an attempt to read the file, HIGH-VALUES is placed in the sales order number field for the file in question and is used in the next comparison. (See Figure 9–9 for the COBOL code for 2000-PROCESS.)

```
2000-PROCESS.
    IF ORD-SALES-ORD-NBR < SHIP-SALES-ORD-NBR
        PERFORM 2100-COPY
        PERFORM 9100-READ-ORDER-FILE
    ELSE
        IF ORD-SALES-ORD-NBR  = SHIP-SALES-ORD-NBR
            PERFORM 2200-UPDATE
            PERFORM 9100-READ-ORDER-FILE
            PERFORM 9200-READ-SHIP-FILE
        ELSE
            PERFORM 2300-NO-MATCH
            PERFORM 9200-READ-SHIP-FILE.
```

FIGURE 9–9

2100-COPY

When the key field in the master file is less than the key field in the transaction file, there is no transaction for the master in question. This means that the record from the ORDER-FILE does not require any updating and is written without changes to the NEW-ORDER-FILE. (See Figure 9–10.)

```
2100-COPY.
    WRITE NEW-ORDER-RECORD FROM WS-ORDER-RECORD.
```

FIGURE 9–10

2200-UPDATE

The routine 2200-UPDATE is executed when the sales order number from the ORDER-FILE matches the sales order number from the SHIP-FILE. This means that an order has been shipped. Accordingly, a detail line is prepared for the shipment report, the shipment date is moved to ORD-ACT-SHIP-DATE, and the record with its new date is written to the NEW-ORDER-FILE. (See Figure 9–11.)

```
       2200-UPDATE.
           MOVE ORD-SALES-ORD-NBR         TO DET-SALES-ORD-NBR.
           MOVE ORD-PART-NBR              TO DET-PART-NBR.
           MOVE ORD-QUANTITY              TO DET-QUANTITY.
           COMPUTE EXTENDED-PRICE = ORD-QUANTITY * ORD-UNIT-PRICE.
           MOVE EXTENDED-PRICE            TO DET-EXTENDED-PRICE.
           ADD EXTENDED-PRICE             TO FINAL-EXTENDED-PRICE.
           IF LINE-COUNT > 50
               PERFORM 2210-HEADINGS.
           WRITE PRINT-RECORD FROM DETAIL-LINE
               AFTER ADVANCING 2 LINES.
           ADD 2 TO LINE-COUNT.
           MOVE SHIPMENT-DATE TO ORD-ACT-SHIP-DATE.
           WRITE NEW-ORDER-RECORD FROM WS-ORDER-RECORD.
```

FIGURE 9–11

2210-HEADINGS

2210-HEADINGS is one of two heading routines. It is performed when headings are required on the shipment report. The other heading routine provides headings for the error report. (See Figure 9–12.)

```
       2210-HEADINGS.
           ADD 1 TO PAGE-COUNT.
           MOVE PAGE-COUNT TO MAIN-HDG-PAGE-NBR.
           WRITE PRINT-RECORD FROM MAIN-HEADING-1
               AFTER ADVANCING PAGE.
           WRITE PRINT-RECORD FROM MAIN-HEADING-2
               AFTER ADVANCING 1 LINE.
           WRITE PRINT-RECORD FROM COLUMN-HEADING-1
               AFTER ADVANCING 2 LINES.
           WRITE PRINT-RECORD FROM COLUMN-HEADING-2
               AFTER ADVANCING 1 LINE.
           MOVE 5 TO LINE-COUNT.
```

FIGURE 9–12

2300-NO-MATCH

The routine 2300-NO-MATCH is performed when a record from the SHIP-FILE has no match in the ORDER-FILE. A table is used to store the SHIP-SALES-ORD-NBR, and a count is kept of the number of errors. The error table will be printed out after the input files have been processed. (See Figure 9–13.)

```
       2300-NO-MATCH.
           ADD 1 TO ERROR-SUB.
           ADD 1 TO NBR-OF-ERRORS.
           MOVE SHIP-SALES-ORD-NBR TO
                ERROR-SALES-ORD-NBR (ERROR-SUB).
```

FIGURE 9–13

3000-EOJ

The final totals for the shipment report are printed, and the line count is reset to a high number. A test is made to see whether there are errors to be printed. If there are, 3200-WRITE-ERRORS is performed until all errors have been printed. If there are no errors, a message is printed to indicate this. In either case, the files are closed and control returns to the main routine. (See Figure 9–14.)

```
       3000-EOJ.
           MOVE FINAL-EXTENDED-PRICE  TO FINAL-EXTENDED-PRICE-OUT.
           WRITE PRINT-RECORD FROM FINAL-TOTAL-LINE
               AFTER ADVANCING 3 LINES.
           MOVE 99 TO LINE-COUNT.
           IF NBR-OF-ERRORS > ZERO
               PERFORM 3200-WRITE-ERRORS
                   VARYING ERROR-SUB FROM 1 BY 1
                       UNTIL ERROR-SUB > NBR-OF-ERRORS
           ELSE
               MOVE 'NONE' TO ERROR-SO-NBR-OUT
               WRITE PRINT-RECORD FROM ERROR-DETAIL-LINE
                   AFTER ADVANCING 2 LINES.
           CLOSE ORDER-FILE
                 SHIP-FILE
                 DATE-FILE
                 NEW-ORDER-FILE
                 PRINT-FILE.
```

FIGURE 9–14

3200-WRITE-ERRORS

3200-WRITE-ERRORS prepares and prints an error detail line. (See Figure 9–15.)

```
       3200-WRITE-ERRORS.
           IF LINE-COUNT > 50
               PERFORM 3210-ERROR-HEADINGS.
           MOVE ERROR-SALES-ORD-NBR (ERROR-SUB) TO ERROR-SO-NBR-OUT.
           WRITE PRINT-RECORD FROM ERROR-DETAIL-LINE
               AFTER ADVANCING 2 LINES.
           ADD 2 TO LINE-COUNT.
```

FIGURE 9–15

3210-ERROR-HEADINGS

3210-ERROR-HEADING is the second of the two heading routines. It is used for the error report. (See Figure 9–16.)

```
       3210-ERROR-HEADINGS.
           ADD 1 TO PAGE-COUNT.
           MOVE PAGE-COUNT TO MAIN-HDG-PAGE-NBR.
           WRITE PRINT-RECORD FROM MAIN-HEADING-1
               AFTER ADVANCING PAGE.
           WRITE PRINT-RECORD FROM ERROR-HEADING-2
               AFTER ADVANCING 1 LINE.
           WRITE PRINT-RECORD FROM ERROR-HEADING-3
               AFTER ADVANCING 2 LINES.
           MOVE 4 TO LINE-COUNT.
```

FIGURE 9–16

9100-READ-ORDER-FILE

The routine 9100-READ-ORDER-FILE reads a record from the ORDER-FILE. Since a read may be requested from a file after there are no more records to be read in the file, a test is made prior to the read to determine whether the end of the file has already been reached. If it has, the routine is complete; if it has not, a read is executed. If this read then encounters an end-of-file condition, 'YES' is moved to END-FLAG-ORDER-FILE and HIGH-VALUES is moved to the key field of the record. If the ORDER-FILE ends before the SHIP-FILE, then all remaining records on the SHIP-FILE are in error since there cannot be a match for them in the ORDER-FILE. This situation will be handled in 2000-PROCESS, since ORDER-FILE will then have HIGH-VALUES in its key field and every subsequent comparison with a record from the SHIP-FILE will result in the sales order number of ORDER-FILE being greater than the sales order number of SHIP-FILE. (See Figure 9–17.)

```
       9100-READ-ORDER-FILE.
           IF END-OF-ORDER-FILE
               NEXT SENTENCE
           ELSE
               READ ORDER-FILE INTO WS-ORDER-RECORD
                   AT END
                       MOVE 'YES'        TO END-FLAG-ORDER-FILE
                       MOVE HIGH-VALUES TO ORD-SALES-ORD-NBR.
```

FIGURE 9–17

9200-READ-SHIP-FILE

9200-READ-SHIP-FILE reads a record from the SHIP-FILE. If the end of the file has already been reached, the routine is complete. If it has not, a record is read from the SHIP-FILE. If the end of the file is encountered on this attempt, 'YES' is moved to END-FLAG-SHIP-FILE and HIGH-VALUES is moved to SHIP-SALES-ORD-NBR. In case the SHIP-FILE ends before the ORDER-FILE, all remaining records on the ORDER-FILE represent orders that have not been shipped. Since SHIP-SALES-ORD-NBR has HIGH-VALUES, all comparisons in 2000-PROCESS will then result in ORD-SALES-ORD-NBR being less than SHIP-SALES-ORD-NBR, and 2100-COPY will be performed for all the remaining records in the ORDER-FILE. (See Figure 9–18.)

```
       9200-READ-SHIP-FILE.
           IF END-OF-SHIP-FILE
               NEXT SENTENCE
           ELSE
               READ SHIP-FILE INTO WS-SHIP-RECORD
                   AT END
                       MOVE 'YES'        TO END-FLAG-SHIP-FILE
                       MOVE HIGH-VALUES TO SHIP-SALES-ORD-NBR.
```

FIGURE 9–18

9300-READ-DATE-FILE

The routine 9300-READ-DATE-FILE is performed only once, from 1000-INITIALIZATION. The date is moved to a heading for the shipment report and is also available in the input area throughout the program for use in updating ORD-ACT-SHIP-DATE. (See Figure 9–19.)

```
       9300-READ-DATE-FILE.
           READ DATE-FILE INTO WS-DATE-RECORD
               AT END
                   MOVE 'YES' TO END-FLAG-DATE-FILE.
```

FIGURE 9–19

THE COBOL PROGRAM

Test Data Test data for the ORDER-FILE, SHIP-FILE, and DATE-FILE are shown in Figure 9–20.

Sample Output Sample output for the shipment and error reports and a listing of the data from the NEW-ORDER-FILE are shown in Figure 9–21.

The Program The complete COBOL SHIPMENT program is shown in Figure 9–22.

ORDER-FILE

```
Ø12Ø1ØØ3ØØE1Ø12   B123358711Ø5WB493EØØØØ2Ø54ØØØ871122ØØØØØØ
Ø12Ø1ØØ3ØØPO173   B12383871Ø25GN4Ø2AØØØØ1Ø45ØØØ871116ØØØØØØ
Ø3ØØ7ØØ2834567X   B34237871Ø3ØHL834EØØØ16Ø19ØØØ871121ØØØØØØ
Ø891521Ø78        B71Ø45871ØØ1FV782TØØØØ3ØØ28ØØ871115ØØØØØØ
Ø361182888P2783733B8433Ø871Ø25HL289BØØØ1ØØ234ØØ871113ØØØØØØ
Ø3ØØ7739897747    B892888711Ø6MF848JØØØØ5Ø2145Ø88Ø13ØØØØØØØ
Ø344Ø6948187Ø341  GØ418Ø87Ø2Ø9JGØ4ØXØØØØ1Ø525ØØ88Ø619ØØØØØØ
Ø12Ø1Ø47278372    G4838887Ø913WB7Ø2XØØØ9ØØ115ØØ8711Ø1ØØØØØØ
Ø8174314Ø865      H4189187Ø412TK61ØLØØØ18ØØ78ØØ87Ø63ØØØØØØØ
Ø36115Ø912        H6915Ø87Ø2Ø6MF848TØØØØ3Ø36ØØØ8712Ø1ØØØØØØ
Ø3ØØ7ØØ378EBNER   H8457987Ø811VX922PØØ8ØØØØ127589112ØØØØØØØ
Ø3ØØ7473ØØ        H8477787Ø223MF4Ø3TØØØØ5Ø4ØØØØ87Ø5Ø2ØØØØØØ
Ø891562Ø54SCHUH   L5Ø6818711Ø8TK812EØØØØ6Ø573ØØ88Ø1Ø5ØØØØØØ
Ø8174Ø18Ø5R7278   T2164287Ø81ØTK497XØØØ1ØØ118ØØ87113ØØØØØØØ
Ø361128375T7838   T7829987Ø323JG563WØØØØ6Ø43ØØØ871Ø18ØØØØØØ
Ø8174Ø18Ø5R8322   Y211Ø587Ø6Ø1TN116TØØØØ1Ø3ØØØØ871221ØØØØØØ
Ø3ØØ7473ØØ        Y289Ø387Ø811VXØØ1LØØ2ØØØØ622Ø8712Ø3ØØØØØØ
```

SHIP-FILE

```
B71Ø45
B8433Ø
GØ4189
G48388
H41891
T21642
```

DATE-FILE

```
8711Ø9
```

FIGURE 9–20

```
                    PRODUCT DISTRIBUTION INC.            PAGE:   1
                   SHIPMENT REPORT FOR 11/09/87

SALES ORDER          PART                                EXTENDED
  NUMBER            NUMBER           QUANTITY              PRICE

  B71045            FV782T               3                   $84.00

  B84330            HL289B              10                $2,340.00

  G48388            WB702X              90               $10,350.00

  H41891            TK610L              18                $1,404.00

  T21642            TK497X              10                $1,180.00


  TOTAL SHIPMENTS                                        $15,358.00
---------------------------------------------------------------------------

                    PRODUCT DISTRIBUTION INC.            PAGE:   2
                      SHIPMENT ERROR REPORT

THE FOLLOWING SALES ORDER NUMBERS DO NOT EXIST ON THE ORDER FILE:

                             G04189
```

FIGURE 9–21

NEW-ORDER-FILE

```
Ø12Ø1ØØ3ØØE1Ø12   B123358711Ø5WB493EØØØØ2Ø54ØØØ871122ØØØØØØ
Ø12Ø1ØØ3ØØPO173   B12383871Ø25GN4Ø2AØØØØ1Ø45ØØØ871116ØØØØØØ
Ø3ØØ7ØØ28334567X  B34237871Ø3ØHL834EØØØ16Ø19ØØØ871121ØØØØØØ
Ø891521Ø78        B71Ø45871ØØ1FV782TØØØØ3ØØ28ØØ8711158711Ø9
Ø3611828888P2783733B8433Ø871Ø25HL289BØØØ1ØØ234ØØ8711138711Ø9
Ø3ØØ7739897747    B892888711Ø6MF848JØØØØ5Ø2145Ø88Ø13ØØØØØØØ
Ø344Ø69481870341  GØ418Ø87Ø2Ø9JGØ4ØXØØØØ1Ø525ØØ88Ø619ØØØØØØ
Ø12Ø1Ø47278372    G4838887Ø913WB7Ø2XØØØ9ØØ115ØØ8711Ø18711Ø9
Ø81743140865      H4189187Ø412TK61ØLØØØ18ØØ78ØØ87Ø63Ø8711Ø9
Ø36115Ø912        H6915Ø87Ø2Ø6MF848TØØØØ3Ø36ØØØ8712Ø1ØØØØØØ
Ø3ØØ7ØØ378EBNER   H8457987Ø811VX922PØØ8ØØØØ1275891120ØØØØØØ
Ø3ØØ747300        H8477787Ø223MF4Ø3TØØØØ5Ø4ØØØØ87Ø5Ø2ØØØØØØ
Ø891562Ø54SCHUH   L5Ø681871108TK812EØØØØ6Ø573ØØ88Ø1Ø5ØØØØØØ
Ø8174Ø18Ø5R7278   T2164287Ø81ØTK497XØØØ1ØØ118ØØ87113Ø871109
Ø361128375T7838   T7829987Ø323JG563WØØØØ6Ø43ØØØ871Ø18ØØØØØØ
Ø8174Ø18Ø5R8322   Y211Ø587Ø6Ø1TN116TØØØØ1Ø3ØØØØ871221ØØØØØØ
Ø3ØØ747300        Y289Ø387Ø811VXØØ1LØØ2ØØØØ622Ø8712Ø3ØØØØØØ
```

FIGURE 9-21 cont.

```
       IDENTIFICATION DIVISION.

       PROGRAM-ID.    SHIPMENT.

       AUTHOR.        HELEN HUMPHREYS.

       INSTALLATION.  PRODUCT DISTRIBUTION INC.

       DATE-WRITTEN.  Ø9/Ø3/87.

       DATE-COMPILED. Ø9/1Ø/87.

      *****************************************************************
      *                                                               *
      *   THE PROGRAM UPDATES THE ORDER-FILE TO INDICATE THAT ORDERS  *
      *   HAVE BEEN SHIPPED.  THIS PROGRAM WILL PRODUCE A PRINTED     *
      *   REPORT LISTING THE ORDERS SHIPPED.                          *
      *                                                               *
      *****************************************************************

       ENVIRONMENT DIVISION.

       CONFIGURATION SECTION.

       SOURCE-COMPUTER.
           IBM-37Ø.
       OBJECT-COMPUTER.
           IBM-37Ø.

       INPUT-OUTPUT SECTION.
       FILE-CONTROL.
           SELECT ORDER-FILE     ASSIGN TO DISK.
           SELECT SHIP-FILE      ASSIGN TO DISK.
           SELECT DATE-FILE      ASSIGN TO DISK.
           SELECT NEW-ORDER-FILE ASSIGN TO DISK.
           SELECT PRINT-FILE     ASSIGN TO PRINTER.

       DATA DIVISION.
       FILE SECTION.

       FD  ORDER-FILE
           LABEL RECORDS ARE STANDARD
           RECORD CONTAINS 7Ø CHARACTERS
           DATA RECORD IS ORDER-RECORD.

```

FIGURE 9–22

```
       Ø1  ORDER-RECORD                  PIC X(7Ø).

       FD  SHIP-FILE
           LABEL RECORDS ARE STANDARD
           RECORD CONTAINS 2Ø CHARACTERS
           DATA RECORD IS SHIP-RECORD.

       Ø1  SHIP-RECORD                   PIC X(2Ø).

       FD  DATE-FILE
           LABEL RECORDS ARE STANDARD
           RECORD CONTAINS 1Ø CHARACTERS
           DATA RECORD IS DATE-RECORD.

       Ø1  DATE-RECORD                   PIC X(1Ø).

       FD  NEW-ORDER-FILE
           LABEL RECORDS ARE STANDARD
           RECORD CONTAINS 7Ø CHARACTERS
           DATA RECORD IS NEW-ORDER-RECORD.

       Ø1  NEW-ORDER-RECORD              PIC X(7Ø).

       FD  PRINT-FILE
           LABEL RECORDS ARE OMITTED
           RECORD CONTAINS 133 CHARACTERS
           DATA RECORD IS PRINT-RECORD.

       Ø1  PRINT-RECORD                  PIC X(133).

       WORKING-STORAGE SECTION.

       Ø1  WS-ORDER-RECORD.
           Ø5  ORD-BRANCH                PIC 9(2).
           Ø5  ORD-SALES-REP             PIC 9(3).
           Ø5  ORD-CUSTOMER-NBR          PIC 9(5).
           Ø5  ORD-CUST-PO-NBR           PIC X(8).
           Ø5  ORD-SALES-ORD-NBR         PIC X(6).
           Ø5  ORD-DATE.
               1Ø  ORD-YY                PIC X(2).
               1Ø  ORD-MM                PIC X(2).
               1Ø  ORD-DD                PIC X(2).
           Ø5  ORD-PART-NBR              PIC X(6).
           Ø5  ORD-QUANTITY              PIC 9(5).
           Ø5  ORD-UNIT-PRICE            PIC 9(4)V9(2).
           Ø5  ORD-REQ-SHIP-DATE.
               1Ø  ORD-REQ-SHIP-YY       PIC X(2).
               1Ø  ORD-REQ-SHIP-MM       PIC X(2).
               1Ø  ORD-REQ-SHIP-DD       PIC X(2).
           Ø5  ORD-ACT-SHIP-DATE.
               1Ø  ORD-ACT-SHIP-YY       PIC X(2).
               1Ø  ORD-ACT-SHIP-MM       PIC X(2).
               1Ø  ORD-ACT-SHIP-DD       PIC X(2).
           Ø5  FILLER                    PIC X(11).

       Ø1  WS-SHIP-RECORD.
           Ø5  SHIP-SALES-ORD-NBR        PIC X(6).
           Ø5  FILLER                    PIC X(14).

       Ø1  WS-DATE-RECORD.
           Ø5  SHIPMENT-DATE.
               1Ø  SHIPMENT-YY           PIC X(2).
               1Ø  SHIPMENT-MM           PIC X(2).
               1Ø  SHIPMENT-DD           PIC X(2).
           Ø5  FILLER                    PIC X(4).

       Ø1  WS-SWITCHES.
           Ø5  END-FLAG-ORDER-FILE       PIC X(3)        VALUE 'NO'.
               88  END-OF-ORDER-FILE                     VALUE 'YES'.
           Ø5  END-FLAG-SHIP-FILE        PIC X(3)        VALUE 'NO'.
               88  END-OF-SHIP-FILE                      VALUE 'YES'.
           Ø5  END-FLAG-DATE-FILE        PIC X(3)        VALUE 'NO'.
               88  END-OF-DATE-FILE                      VALUE 'YES'.

       Ø1  WS-COUNTERS.
           Ø5  LINE-COUNT                PIC 9(2)        VALUE 99.
           Ø5  PAGE-COUNT                PIC 9(3)        VALUE ZEROS.
           Ø5  NBR-OF-ERRORS             PIC 9(3)        VALUE ZEROS.
```

FIGURE 9–22 cont.

```
       Ø1  WS-SUBSCRIPTS.
           Ø5  ERROR-SUB               PIC 9(4)       COMP SYNC
                                                      VALUE ZERO.

       Ø1  CALCULATED-FIELDS.
           Ø5  EXTENDED-PRICE          PIC 9(7)V9(2).

       Ø1  TOTAL-FIELDS.
           Ø5  FINAL-EXTENDED-PRICE    PIC 9(8)V9(2)  VALUE ZEROS.

       Ø1  ERROR-TABLE.
           Ø5  ERROR-SALES-ORD-NBR     PIC X(6)      OCCURS 2ØØ TIMES.

       Ø1  MAIN-HEADING-1.
           Ø5  FILLER                  PIC X(52)      VALUE SPACES.
           Ø5  FILLER                  PIC X(25)      VALUE
                                       'PRODUCT DISTRIBUTION INC.'.
           Ø5  FILLER                  PIC X(12)      VALUE SPACES.
           Ø5  FILLER                  PIC X(6)       VALUE 'PAGE:'.
           Ø5  MAIN-HDG-PAGE-NBR       PIC ZZ9.
           Ø5  FILLER                  PIC X(35)      VALUE SPACES.

       Ø1  MAIN-HEADING-2.
           Ø5  FILLER                  PIC X(51)      VALUE SPACES.
           Ø5  FILLER                  PIC X(2Ø)      VALUE
                                       'SHIPMENT REPORT FOR '.
           Ø5  MAIN-HDG-SHIP-MM        PIC X(2).
           Ø5  FILLER                  PIC X(1)       VALUE '/'.
           Ø5  MAIN-HDG-SHIP-DD        PIC X(2).
           Ø5  FILLER                  PIC X(1)       VALUE '/'.
           Ø5  MAIN-HDG-SHIP-YY        PIC X(2).
           Ø5  FILLER                  PIC X(55)      VALUE SPACES.

       Ø1  COLUMN-HEADING-1.
           Ø5  FILLER                  PIC X(33)      VALUE SPACES.
           Ø5  FILLER                  PIC X(11)      VALUE
                                                      'SALES ORDER'.
           Ø5  FILLER                  PIC X(9)       VALUE SPACES.
           Ø5  FILLER                  PIC X(4)       VALUE 'PART'.
           Ø5  FILLER                  PIC X(31)      VALUE SPACES.
           Ø5  FILLER                  PIC X(8)       VALUE 'EXTENDED'.
           Ø5  FILLER                  PIC X(37)      VALUE SPACES.

       Ø1  COLUMN-HEADING-2.
           Ø5  FILLER                  PIC X(35)      VALUE SPACES.
           Ø5  FILLER                  PIC X(6)       VALUE 'NUMBER'.
           Ø5  FILLER                  PIC X(11)      VALUE SPACES.
           Ø5  FILLER                  PIC X(6)       VALUE 'NUMBER'.
           Ø5  FILLER                  PIC X(1Ø)      VALUE SPACES.
           Ø5  FILLER                  PIC X(8)       VALUE 'QUANTITY'.
           Ø5  FILLER                  PIC X(13)      VALUE SPACES.
           Ø5  FILLER                  PIC X(5)       VALUE 'PRICE'.
           Ø5  FILLER                  PIC X(39)      VALUE SPACES.

       Ø1  DETAIL-LINE.
           Ø5  FILLER                  PIC X(35)      VALUE SPACES.
           Ø5  DET-SALES-ORD-NBR       PIC X(6).
           Ø5  FILLER                  PIC X(11)      VALUE SPACES.
           Ø5  DET-PART-NBR            PIC X(6).
           Ø5  FILLER                  PIC X(11)      VALUE SPACES.
           Ø5  DET-QUANTITY            PIC ZZZZ9.
           Ø5  FILLER                  PIC X(11)      VALUE SPACES.
           Ø5  DET-EXTENDED-PRICE      PIC $$,$$$,$$9.99.
           Ø5  FILLER                  PIC X(35)      VALUE SPACES.

       Ø1  FINAL-TOTAL-LINE.
           Ø5  FILLER                  PIC X(35)      VALUE SPACES.
           Ø5  FILLER                  PIC X(15)      VALUE
                                       'TOTAL SHIPMENTS'.
           Ø5  FILLER                  PIC X(34)      VALUE SPACES.
           Ø5  FINAL-EXTENDED-PRICE-OUT    PIC $$$,$$$,$$9.99.
           Ø5  FILLER                  PIC X(35)      VALUE SPACES.

       Ø1  ERROR-HEADING-2.
           Ø5  FILLER                  PIC X(53)      VALUE SPACES.
           Ø5  FILLER                  PIC X(21)      VALUE
               'SHIPMENT ERROR REPORT'.
           Ø5  FILLER                  PIC X(53)      VALUE SPACES.

       Ø1  ERROR-HEADING-3.
           Ø5  FILLER                  PIC X(34)      VALUE SPACES.
           Ø5  FILLER                  PIC X(65)      VALUE
               'THE FOLLOWING SALES ORDER NUMBERS DO NOT EXIST ON THE OR
```

FIGURE 9-22 cont.

```
      -         'DER FILE:'.
            Ø5  FILLER                    PIC X(34)       VALUE SPACES.

        Ø1  ERROR-DETAIL-LINE.
            Ø5  FILLER                    PIC X(63)       VALUE SPACES.
            Ø5  ERROR-SO-NBR-OUT          PIC X(6).
            Ø5  FILLER                    PIC X(64)       VALUE SPACES.


        PROCEDURE DIVISION.

            PERFORM 1ØØØ-INITIALIZATION.
            PERFORM 2ØØØ-PROCESS
                UNTIL END-OF-ORDER-FILE AND END-OF-SHIP-FILE.
            PERFORM 3ØØØ-EOJ.
            STOP RUN.

        1ØØØ-INITIALIZATION.
            OPEN INPUT  ORDER-FILE
                        SHIP-FILE
                        DATE-FILE
                 OUTPUT NEW-ORDER-FILE
                        PRINT-FILE.
            PERFORM 91ØØ-READ-ORDER-FILE.
            PERFORM 92ØØ-READ-SHIP-FILE.
            PERFORM 93ØØ-READ-DATE-FILE.
            MOVE SHIPMENT-YY  TO MAIN-HDG-SHIP-YY.
            MOVE SHIPMENT-MM  TO MAIN-HDG-SHIP-MM.
            MOVE SHIPMENT-DD  TO MAIN-HDG-SHIP-DD.

        2ØØØ-PROCESS.
            IF ORD-SALES-ORD-NBR < SHIP-SALES-ORD-NBR
                PERFORM 21ØØ-COPY
                PERFORM 91ØØ-READ-ORDER-FILE
            ELSE
                IF ORD-SALES-ORD-NBR  = SHIP-SALES-ORD-NBR
                    PERFORM 22ØØ-UPDATE
                    PERFORM 91ØØ-READ-ORDER-FILE
                    PERFORM 92ØØ-READ-SHIP-FILE
                ELSE
                    PERFORM 23ØØ-NO-MATCH
                    PERFORM 92ØØ-READ-SHIP-FILE.

        21ØØ-COPY.
            WRITE NEW-ORDER-RECORD FROM WS-ORDER-RECORD.

        22ØØ-UPDATE.
            MOVE ORD-SALES-ORD-NBR        TO DET-SALES-ORD-NBR.
            MOVE ORD-PART-NBR             TO DET-PART-NBR.
            MOVE ORD-QUANTITY             TO DET-QUANTITY.
            COMPUTE EXTENDED-PRICE = ORD-QUANTITY * ORD-UNIT-PRICE.
            MOVE EXTENDED-PRICE           TO DET-EXTENDED-PRICE.
            ADD EXTENDED-PRICE            TO FINAL-EXTENDED-PRICE.
            IF LINE-COUNT > 5Ø
                PERFORM 221Ø-HEADINGS.
            WRITE PRINT-RECORD FROM DETAIL-LINE
                AFTER ADVANCING 2 LINES.
            ADD 2 TO LINE-COUNT.
            MOVE SHIPMENT-DATE TO ORD-ACT-SHIP-DATE.
            WRITE NEW-ORDER-RECORD FROM WS-ORDER-RECORD.

        221Ø-HEADINGS.
            ADD 1 TO PAGE-COUNT.
            MOVE PAGE-COUNT TO MAIN-HDG-PAGE-NBR.
            WRITE PRINT-RECORD FROM MAIN-HEADING-1
                AFTER ADVANCING PAGE.
            WRITE PRINT-RECORD FROM MAIN-HEADING-2
                AFTER ADVANCING 1 LINE.
            WRITE PRINT-RECORD FROM COLUMN-HEADING-1
                AFTER ADVANCING 2 LINES.
            WRITE PRINT-RECORD FROM COLUMN-HEADING-2
                AFTER ADVANCING 1 LINE.
            MOVE 5 TO LINE-COUNT.

        23ØØ-NO-MATCH.
            ADD 1 TO ERROR-SUB.
            ADD 1 TO NBR-OF-ERRORS.
            MOVE SHIP-SALES-ORD-NBR TO
                 ERROR-SALES-ORD-NBR (ERROR-SUB).

        3ØØØ-EOJ.
            MOVE FINAL-EXTENDED-PRICE  TO FINAL-EXTENDED-PRICE-OUT.
            WRITE PRINT-RECORD FROM FINAL-TOTAL-LINE
                AFTER ADVANCING 3 LINES.
```

FIGURE 9-22 cont.

```
           MOVE 99 TO LINE-COUNT.
           IF NBR-OF-ERRORS > ZERO
               PERFORM 3200-WRITE-ERRORS
                   VARYING ERROR-SUB FROM 1 BY 1
                       UNTIL ERROR-SUB > NBR-OF-ERRORS
           ELSE
               MOVE 'NONE' TO ERROR-SO-NBR-OUT
               WRITE PRINT-RECORD FROM ERROR-DETAIL-LINE
                   AFTER ADVANCING 2 LINES.
           CLOSE ORDER-FILE
                 SHIP-FILE
                 DATE-FILE
                 NEW-ORDER-FILE
                 PRINT-FILE.

       3200-WRITE-ERRORS.
           IF LINE-COUNT > 50
               PERFORM 3210-ERROR-HEADINGS.
           MOVE ERROR-SALES-ORD-NBR (ERROR-SUB) TO ERROR-SO-NBR-OUT.
           WRITE PRINT-RECORD FROM ERROR-DETAIL-LINE
               AFTER ADVANCING 2 LINES.
           ADD 2 TO LINE-COUNT.

       3210-ERROR-HEADINGS.
           ADD 1 TO PAGE-COUNT.
           MOVE PAGE-COUNT TO MAIN-HDG-PAGE-NBR.
           WRITE PRINT-RECORD FROM MAIN-HEADING-1
               AFTER ADVANCING PAGE.
           WRITE PRINT-RECORD FROM ERROR-HEADING-2
               AFTER ADVANCING 1 LINE.
           WRITE PRINT-RECORD FROM ERROR-HEADING-3
               AFTER ADVANCING 2 LINES.
           MOVE 4 TO LINE-COUNT.

       9100-READ-ORDER-FILE.
           IF END-OF-ORDER-FILE
               NEXT SENTENCE
           ELSE
               READ ORDER-FILE INTO WS-ORDER-RECORD
                   AT END
                       MOVE 'YES'       TO END-FLAG-ORDER-FILE
                       MOVE HIGH-VALUES TO ORD-SALES-ORD-NBR.

       9200-READ-SHIP-FILE.
           IF END-OF-SHIP-FILE
               NEXT SENTENCE
           ELSE
               READ SHIP-FILE INTO WS-SHIP-RECORD
                   AT END
                       MOVE 'YES'       TO END-FLAG-SHIP-FILE
                       MOVE HIGH-VALUES TO SHIP-SALES-ORD-NBR.

       9300-READ-DATE-FILE.
           READ DATE-FILE INTO WS-DATE-RECORD
               AT END
                   MOVE 'YES' TO END-FLAG-DATE-FILE.
```

FIGURE 9-22 cont.

PROGRAM SPECIFICATION: ORDER-MAINT

The program specification for the second programming project of this chapter is given in Figure 9–23.

PROGRAM SPECIFICATION

Program Name: ORDER-MAINT

Program Function:

This program updates ORDER-FILE of the previous program. It will add records to the file, delete records from the file, and change the data in existing records. The program will also produce a printed report which lists the updates to the file.

Input Files:

I. ORDER-FILE

INPUT DEVICE:	DISK
FILE ORGANIZATION:	SEQUENTIAL
RECORD LENGTH:	70 BYTES
FILE SEQUENCE:	ASCENDING ON SALES ORDER NUMBER

II. TRANSACTION-FILE

INPUT DEVICE:	DISK
FILE ORGANIZATION:	SEQUENTIAL
RECORD LENGTH:	71 BYTES
FILE SEQUENCE:	ASCENDING ON SALES ORDER NUMBER

Output Files:

I. NEW-ORDER-FILE

OUTPUT DEVICE:	DISK
FILE ORGANIZATION:	SEQUENTIAL
RECORD LENGTH:	70 BYTES
FILE SEQUENCE:	ASCENDING ON SALES ORDER NUMBER

II. PRINT-FILE

OUTPUT DEVICE:	PRINTER
RECORD LENGTH:	133 BYTES

Processing Requirements:

The ORDER-FILE is to be updated by adding, changing, and deleting the appropriate order records based on the transaction records found in the TRANSACTION-FILE. No changes are allowed to orders that already have a date in ORD-ACT-SHIP-DATE. The updated version of the ORDER-FILE should be written to NEW-ORDER-FILE. A printed report should be made listing added records, changed records (before and after the change), deleted records, and all records found to be in error. An appropriate message should be printed for each line.

Output Requirements:

The NEW-ORDER-FILE should reflect any changes which occur as a result of applying the TRANSACTION-FILE to the ORDER-FILE.

The output report should include a detail line for each addition, change, deletion, and error transacted. Changed records should be printed before and after the changes are made. Changed fields should be highlighted using an underline of asterisks.

The following are formatting requirements for the report:

1. Each page of the report should contain:
   (a) a main heading which includes the company name, the report name, the report date, and a page number.
   (b) column headings which describe the items printed underneath them.
2. Detail lines should include all fields from the appropriate input record as well as a message indicating the type of transaction or error condition.
3. Detail lines should be double spaced.
4. Each "after change" line should have the changes highlighted with an underline of asterisks.

FIGURE 9-23

Input Record Layout

The input record layouts for the ORDER-FILE and the TRANSACTION-FILE are shown in Figure 9–24. The record layout for NEW-ORDER-FILE is identical to the layout for ORDER-FILE.

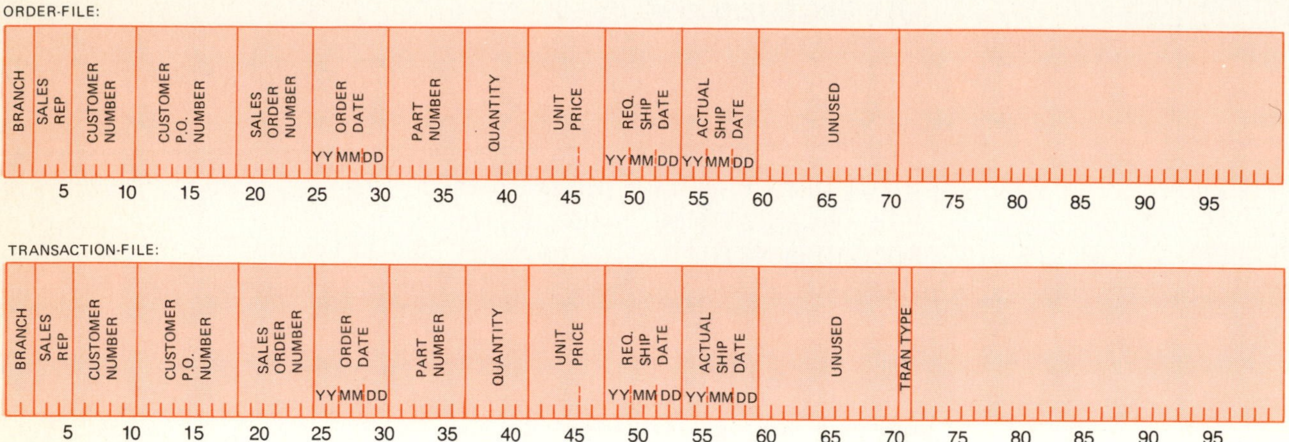

Print Chart

The print chart for the ORDER-MAINT program is shown in Figure 9–25.

LOGIC FOR SEQUENTIAL-FILE MAINTENANCE WITH ADDS, CHANGES, AND DELETES

A hierarchy chart for ORDER-MAINT is shown in Figure 9–26. Pseudocode and a flowchart for the same are shown in Figures 9–27 and 9–28, respectively.

Explanation of Logic

Sequential-File Maintenance

The objective of sequential-file maintenance is to bring a master file up to current status. This is done through the use of one or more transaction files which contain addition, change, and deletion records. An example of a master file is a personnel file meant to contain records of active employees only. The transaction file in that case would contain addition records representing newly hired employees; change records representing changes in name, address, telephone number, and so on; and deletion records representing employees who have been terminated.

A master file intended for sequential-file maintenance must be in sequence on a key field that is unique in each record. Any transaction files to be applied against the master must be in the same sequence on the given key field. However, there may be multiple transactions with the same key field.

If a master file is a sequential file, a new output file must be created to contain the updated version of the file. This is because sequential-file processing on tape or disk does not allow for additions, changes, or deletions to an existing master file.

In updating a master file by means of a transaction file, a record is made available from each file and the key fields are compared. In general terms, the results of the comparison and the appropriate actions are as follows:

MASTER KEY FIELD < TRANSACTION KEY FIELD

There is no transaction for the master. The master is copied to the new master file and another master record is read.

MASTER KEY FIELD = TRANSACTION KEY FIELD

(text continued on page 430)

```
  DATE: XX/XX/XX                                      PRODUCT DISTRIBUTION INC.                                           PAGE: ZZ9
                                                          MAINTENANCE REPORT

   SALES         SLS           CUSTOMER   ORDER     PART             UNIT      REQ     ACTUAL
   ORDER  BRANCH REP   CUST#     PO#       DATE    NUMBER    QTY     PRICE     SHIP     SHIP         MESSAGE

  X XXXXX   XX   XXX   XXXXX   XXXXXXXX   XXXXXX   XXXXXX    XXXXX   XXXXXX    XXXXXX  XXXXXX   XXXXXXXXXXXXXXXXXXXXXXXXXXXXXXXXXXXX

  X XXXXX   XX   XXX   XXXXX   XXXXXXXX   XXXXXX   XXXXXX    XXXXX   XXXXXX    XXXXXX  XXXXXX   XXXXXXXXXXXXXXXXXXXXXXXXXXXXXXXXXXXX
            **   ***   *****   ********   ******   ******    *****   ******    ******  ******
```

FIGURE 9–25

Hierarchy Chart

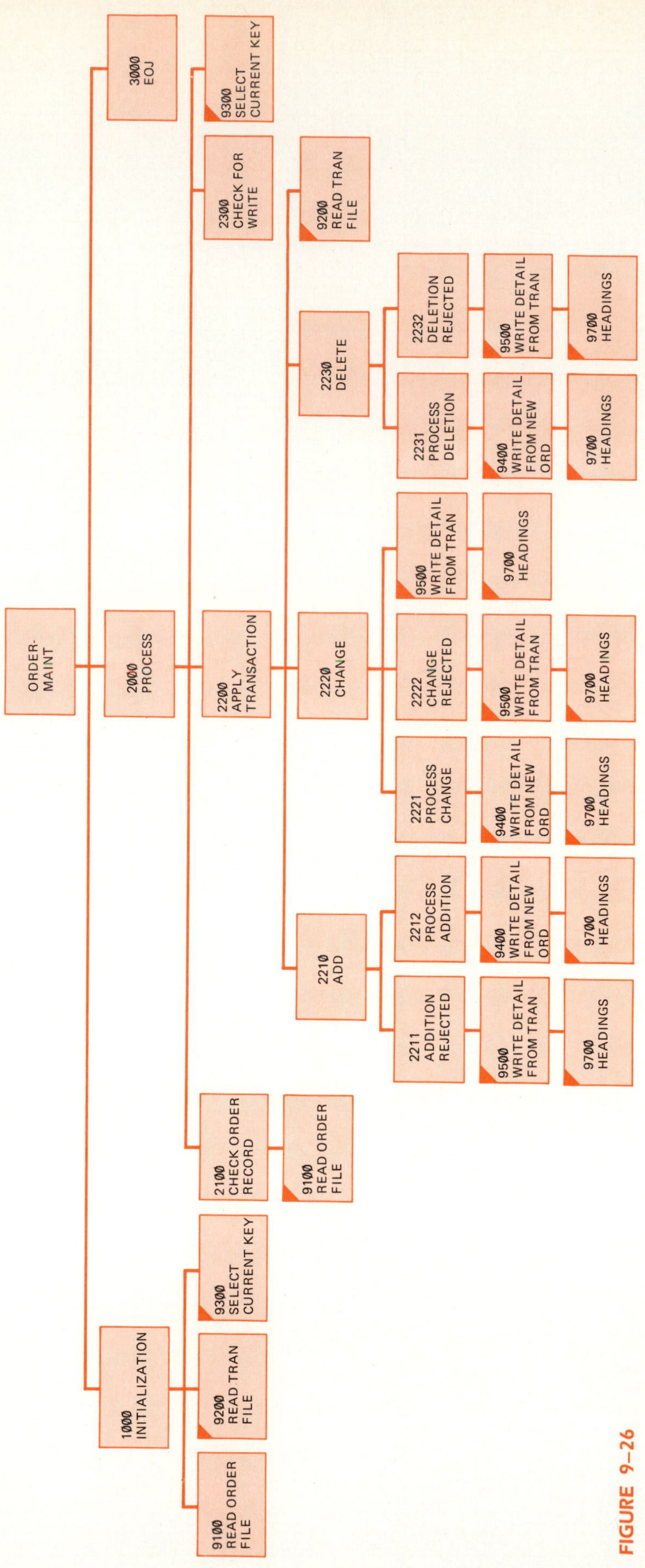

FIGURE 9–26

Pseudocode

```
MAIN LINE
     DO initialization
     DO WHILE more order records or more
       transaction records
          DO process
     ENDDO
     DO end of job

INITIALIZATION
     OPEN files
     MOVE date to heading
     DO read order file
     DO read transaction file
     DO select current key

PROCESS
     DO check order record
     DO WHILE transaction sales order number =
       current processing key
          DO apply transaction
     ENDDO
     DO check for write
     DO select current key

CHECK ORDER RECORD
     IF order sales order number = current
       processing key
          MOVE order record to new order record
          MOVE 'yes' to new order exists flag
          DO read order file
     ELSE
          MOVE 'no' to new order exists flag
     ENDIF

APPLY TRANSACTION
     IF addition
          DO add
     ELSE
          IF change
               DO change
          ELSE
               IF deletion
                    DO delete
               ENDIF
          ENDIF
     ENDIF
     DO read transaction file

ADD
     IF new order exists
          DO add rejected
     ELSE
          DO process add
     ENDIF

ADD REJECTED
     ADD 1 to number of errors
     MOVE 'add error' to detail message
     DO write detail from transaction record
```

FIGURE 9–27

```
PROCESS ADD
     MOVE tran record to new order record
     MOVE 'yes' to new order exists flag
     MOVE 'added' to detail message
     DO write detail from new order record
     ADD 1 to number of adds

CHANGE
     IF new order exists
          IF new order ship date = zero
               DO process changes
          ELSE
               ADD 1 to number of change errors
               MOVE 'change error' to detail message
               DO write detail from transaction record
          ENDIF
     ELSE
          DO change rejected
     ENDIF

PROCESS CHANGES
     ADD 1 to number of changes
     MOVE 'before changes' to detail message
     DO write detail from new order
     IF tran branch not equal to spaces
          MOVE tran branch to new order branch
          MOVE asterisks to asterisk branch
     ENDIF
     IF tran sales rep not equal to spaces
          MOVE tran sales rep to new order sales rep
          MOVE asterisks to asterisk sales rep
     ENDIF
     IF tran customer number not equal to spaces
          MOVE tran customer number to new order customer
            number
          MOVE asterisks to asterisk customer number
     ENDIF
     IF tran customer PO number not equal to spaces
          MOVE tran customer PO number to new order
            customer PO number
          MOVE asterisks to asterisk customer PO number
     ENDIF
     IF tran order date not equal to spaces
          MOVE tran order date to new order date
          MOVE asterisks to asterisk order date
     ENDIF
     IF tran part number not equal to spaces
          MOVE tran part number to new order part number
          MOVE asterisks to asterisk part number
     ENDIF
     IF quantity not equal to spaces
          MOVE tran quantity to new order quantity
          MOVE asterisks to asterisk quantity
     ENDIF
     IF tran unit price not equal to spaces
          MOVE tran unit price to new order unit price
          MOVE asterisks to asterisk unit price
     ENDIF
```

FIGURE 9-27 cont.

```
     IF tran req ship date not equal to spaces
          MOVE tran req ship date to new order req ship
            date
          MOVE asterisks to asterisk req ship date
     ENDIF
     IF tran actual ship date not equal to spaces
          MOVE tran actual ship date to new order actual
            ship date
          MOVE asterisks to asterisk actual ship date
     ENDIF
     MOVE 'after changes' to detail message
     DO write detail from new order record
     WRITE asterisk line
     ADD 1 to line count
     MOVE spaces to asterisk line

CHANGE REJECTED
     ADD 1 to number of change errors
     MOVE 'change error' to detail message
     DO write detail from transaction record

DELETE
     IF new order exists
          DO process delete
     ELSE
          DO delete rejected
     ENDIF

PROCESS DELETE
     MOVE 'no' to new order exists flag
     ADD 1 to number of deletes
     MOVE 'delete' to detail message
     DO write detail from new order record

DELETE REJECTED
     ADD 1 to number of delete errors
     MOVE 'delete error' to detail message
     DO write detail from transaction record

CHECK FOR WRITE
     IF new order exists
          WRITE new order record
          ADD 1 to number of orders written
     ENDIF

END OF JOB
     WRITE asterisk line
     DISPLAY counters
     CLOSE files

READ ORDER FILE
     IF end of order file
     ELSE
          READ order file
          IF end of file
               MOVE 'yes' to end flag order file
```

FIGURE 9-27 cont.

```
                    MOVE a high value to order sales
                      order number
               ENDIF
          ENDIF
          IF not end of order file
               ADD 1 to number of orders read
          ENDIF

     READ TRANSACTION FILE
          IF end of tran file
          ELSE
               READ tran file
               IF end of tran file
                    MOVE 'yes' to end flag tran file
                    MOVE a high value to tran sales
                      order number
               ENDIF
          ENDIF
          IF not end of tran file
               ADD 1 to number of tran read
          ENDIF

     SELECT CURRENT KEY
          IF order sales order number < tran sales
            order number
               MOVE order sales order number to current
                 processing key
          ELSE
               MOVE tran sales order number to current
                 processing key
          ENDIF

     WRITE DETAIL FROM NEW ORD
          MOVE new order to detail line
          IF line count > 50
               DO headings
          ENDIF
          WRITE detail line
          ADD 2 to line count

     WRITE DETAIL FROM TRAN
          MOVE tran to detail line
          IF line count > 50
               DO headings
          ENDIF
          WRITE detail line
          ADD 2 to line count

     HEADINGS
          ADD 1 to page count
          MOVE page count to heading
          WRITE main heading 1
          WRITE main heading 2
          WRITE column heading 1
          WRITE column heading 2
          MOVE 5 to line count
```

FIGURE 9-27 cont.

Flowchart

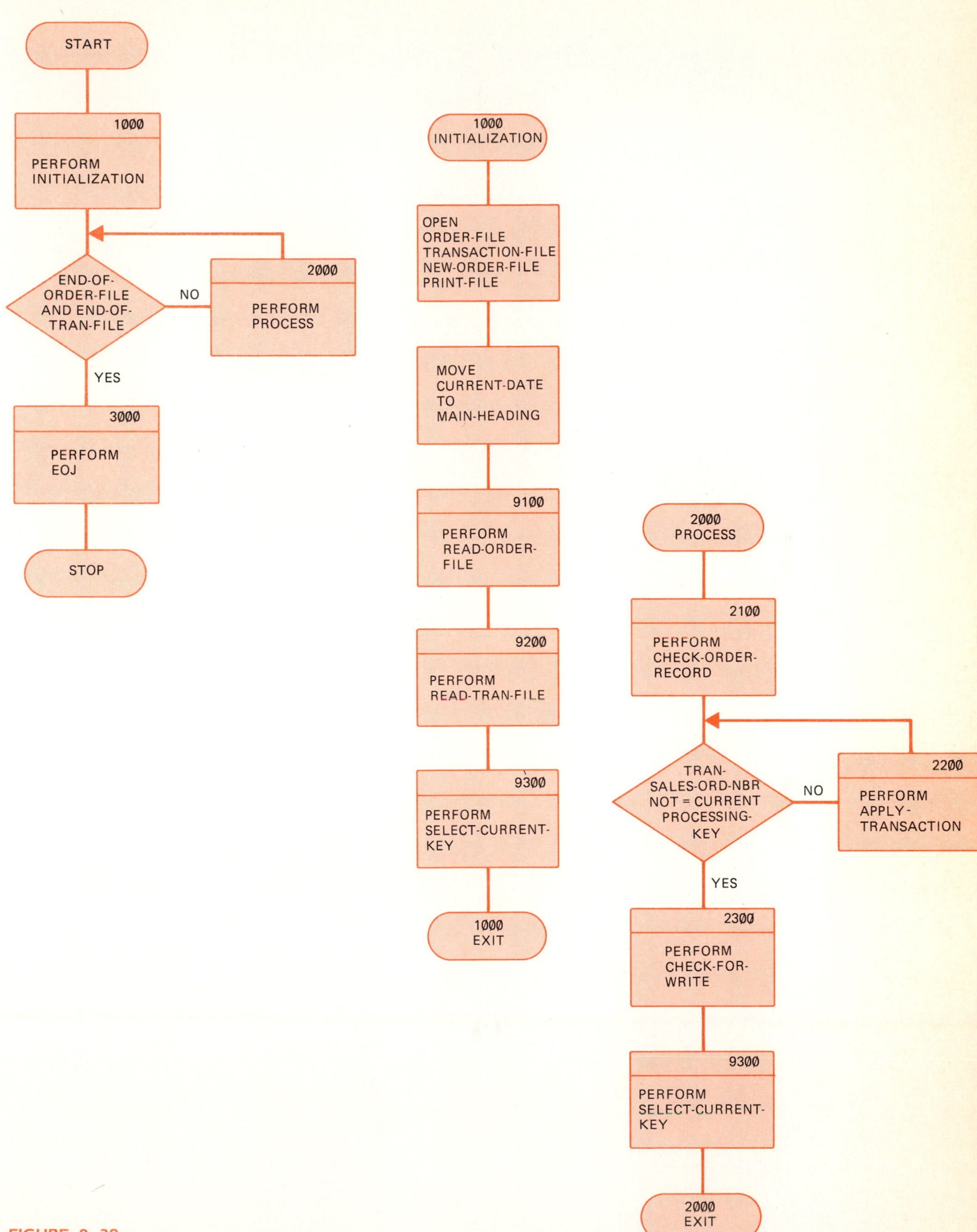

FIGURE 9–28

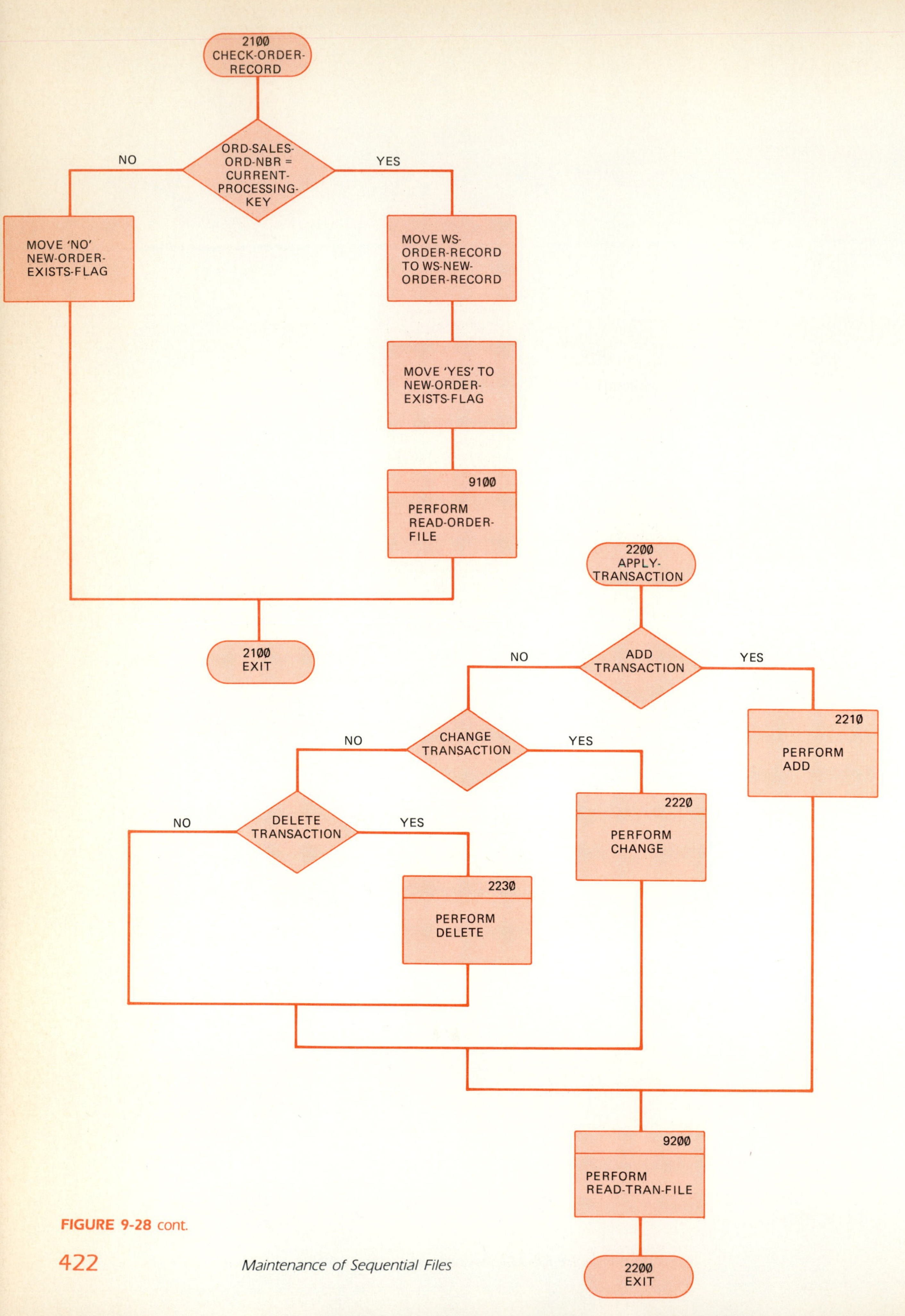

FIGURE 9-28 cont.

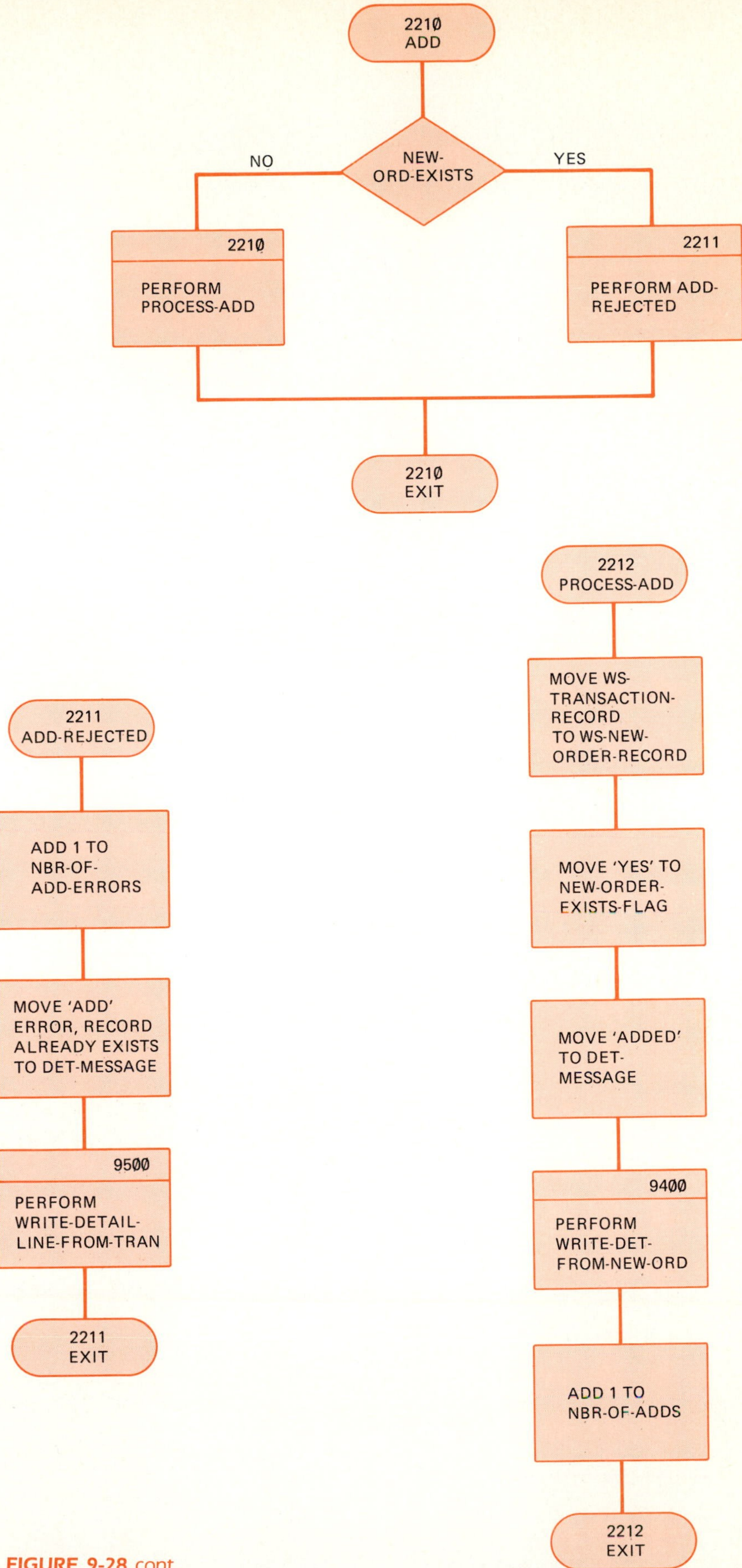

FIGURE 9-28 cont.

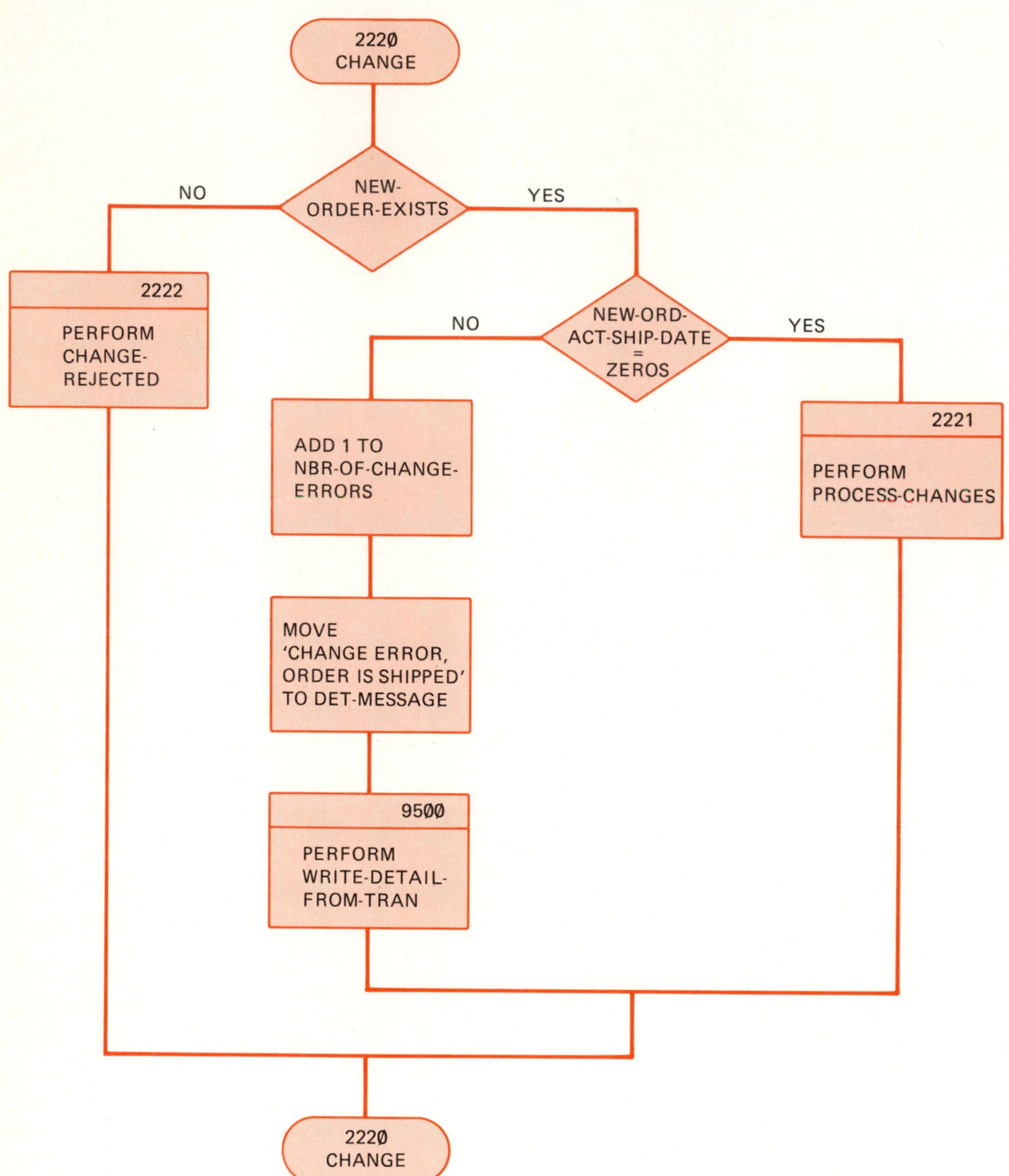

FIGURE 9-28 cont.

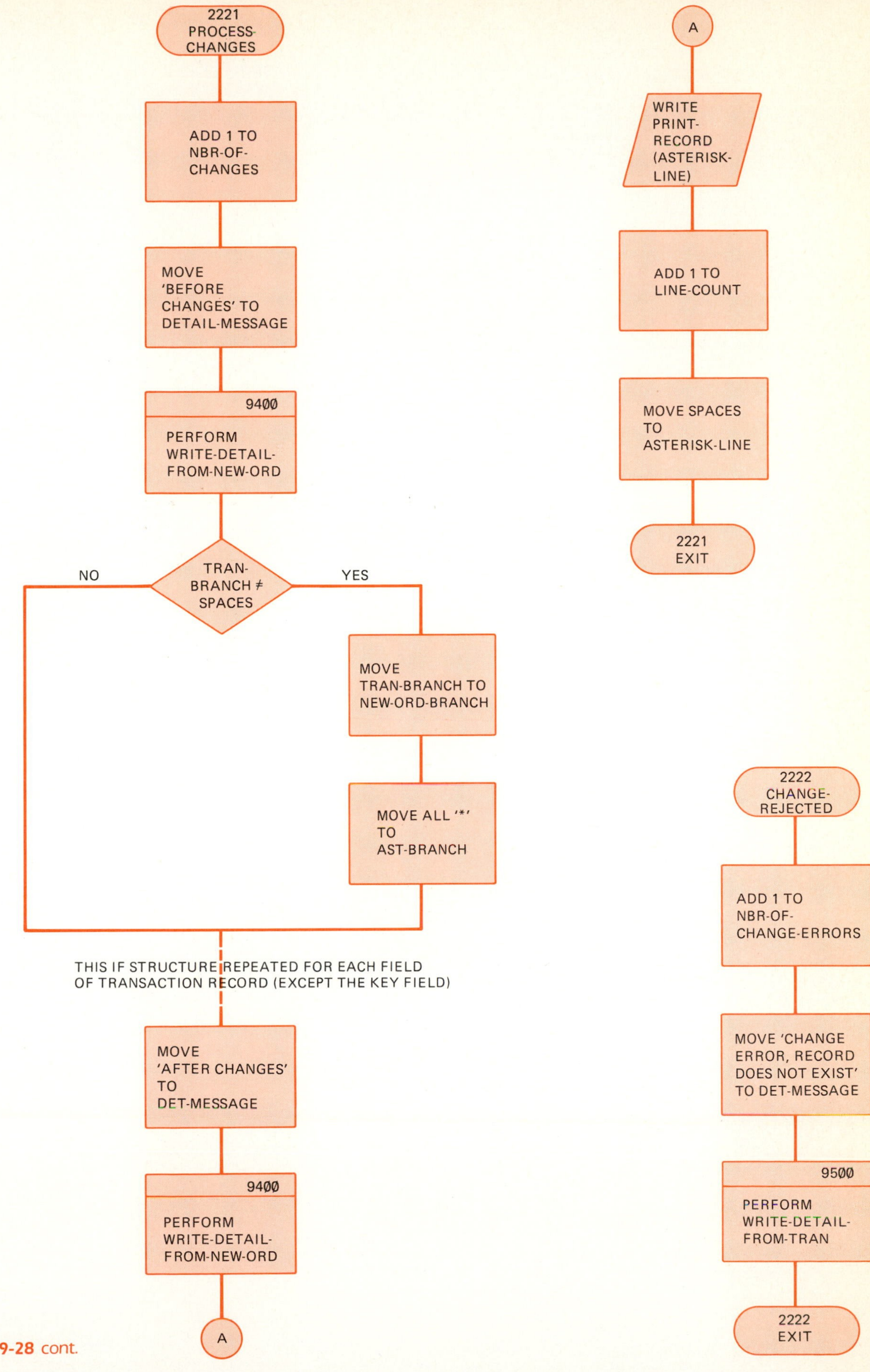

FIGURE 9-28 cont.

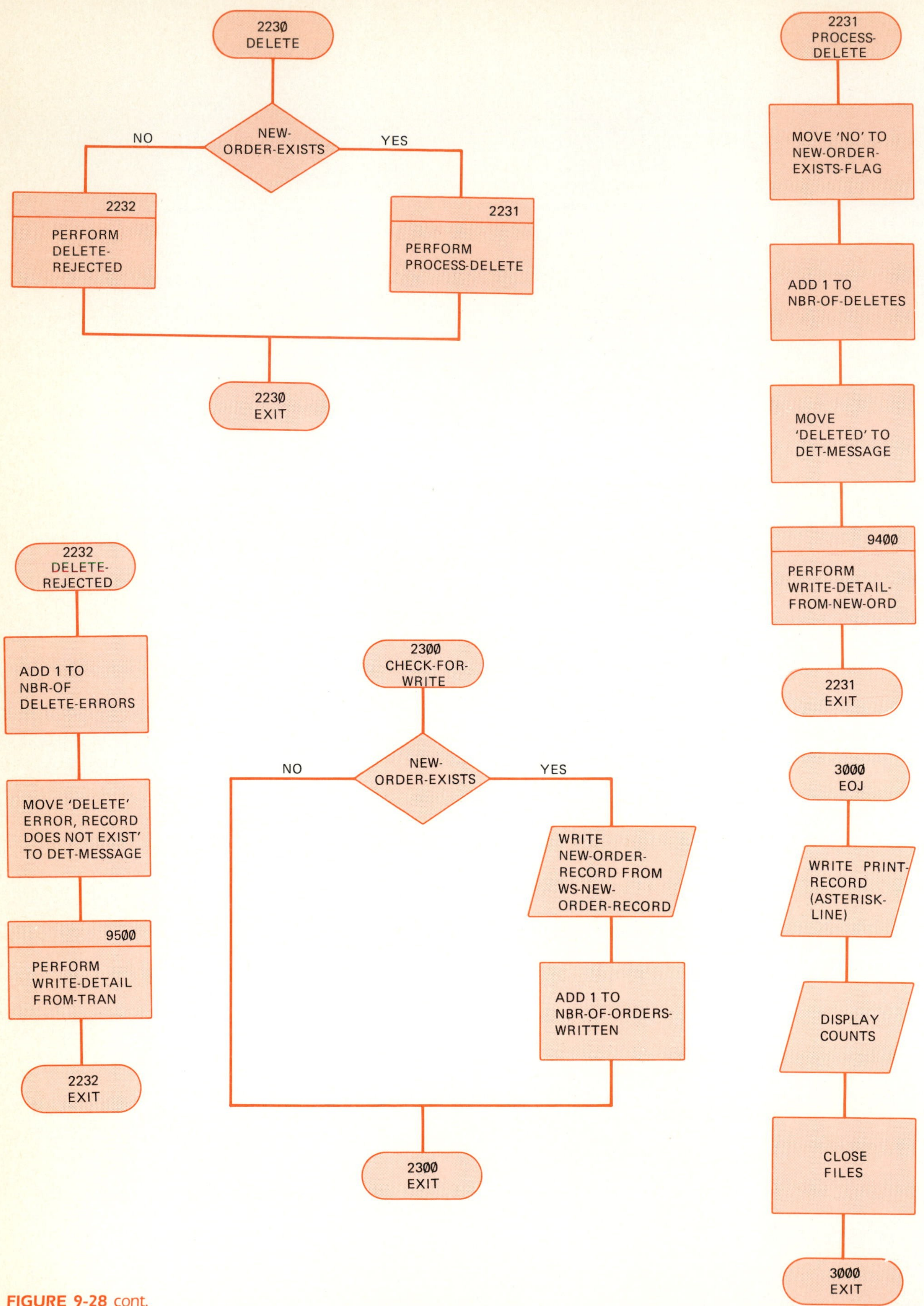

FIGURE 9-28 cont.

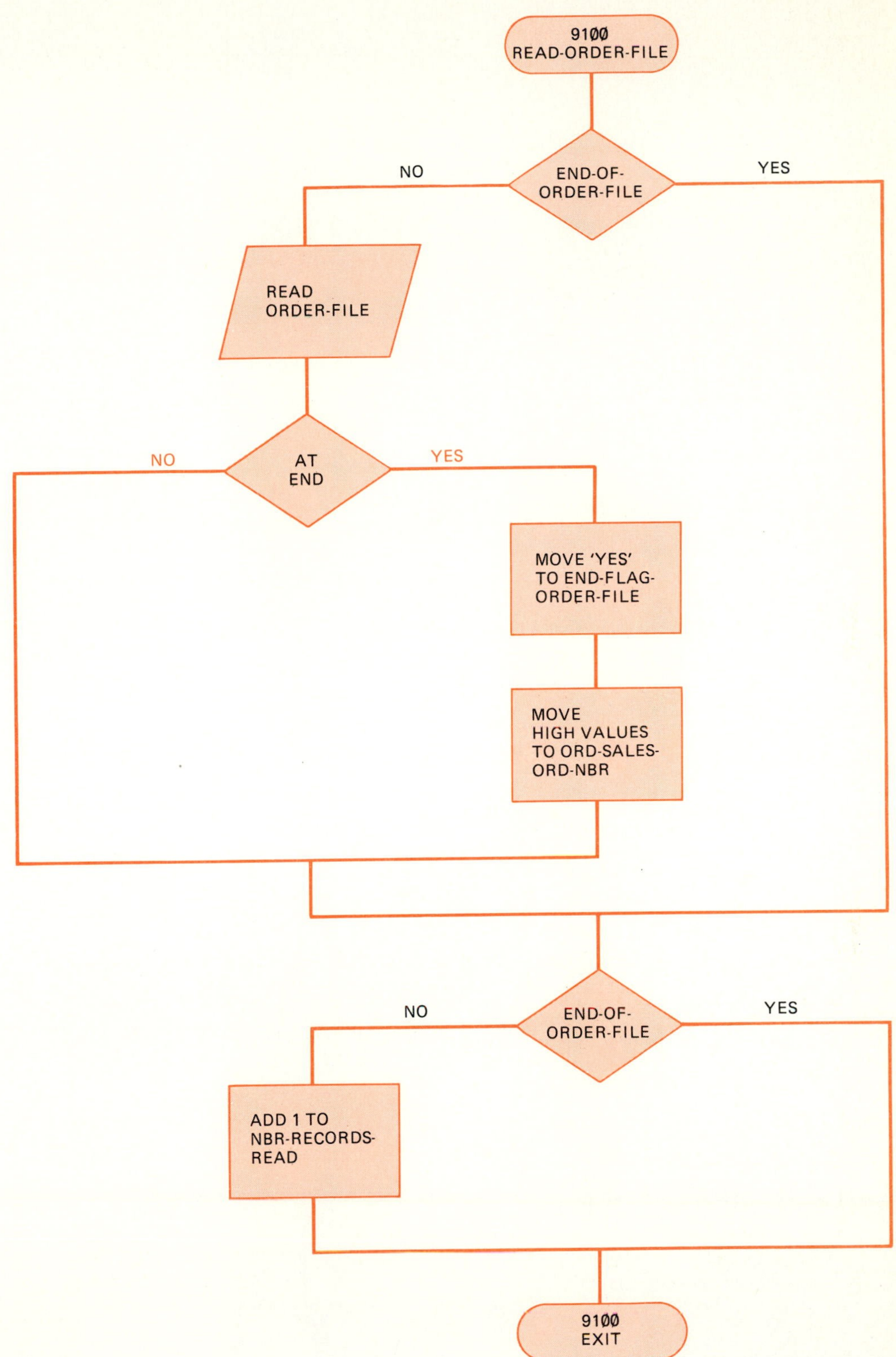

FIGURE 9-28 cont.

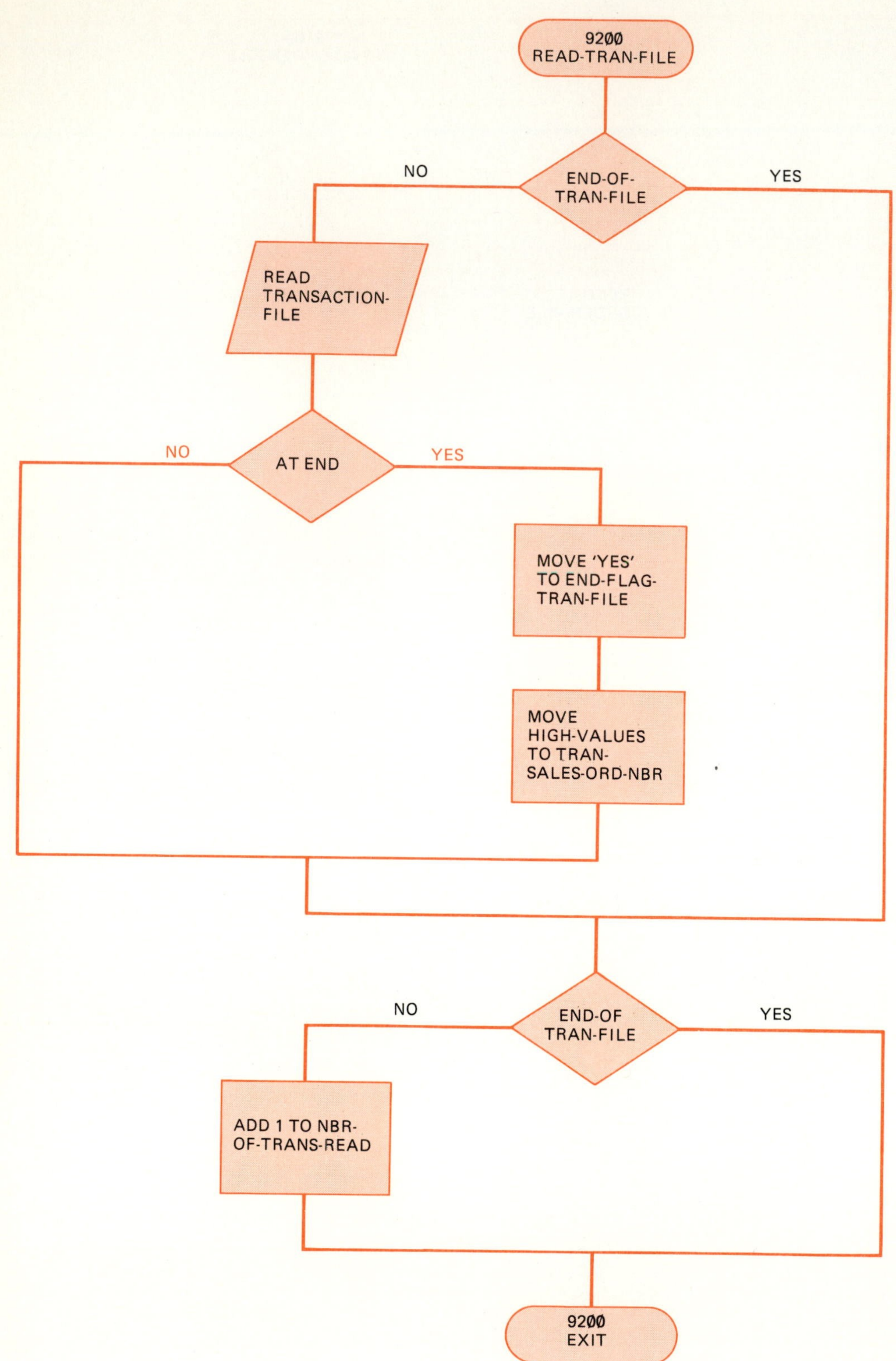

FIGURE 9-28 cont.

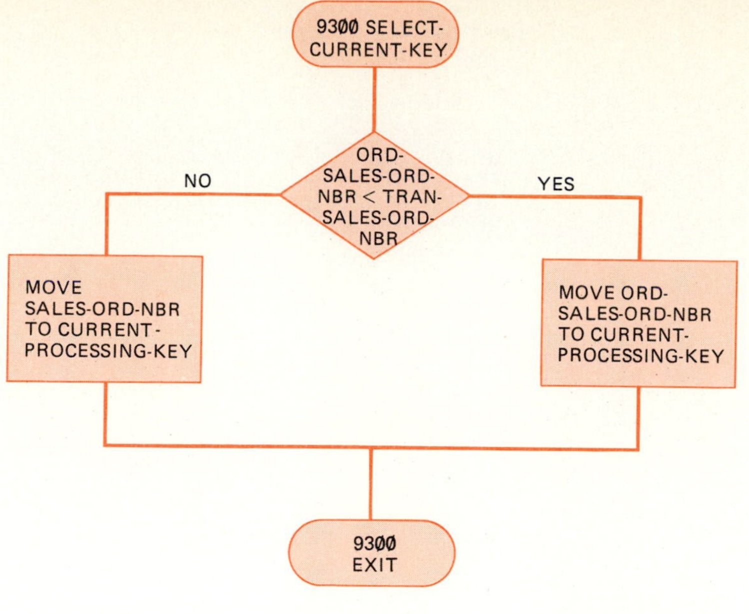

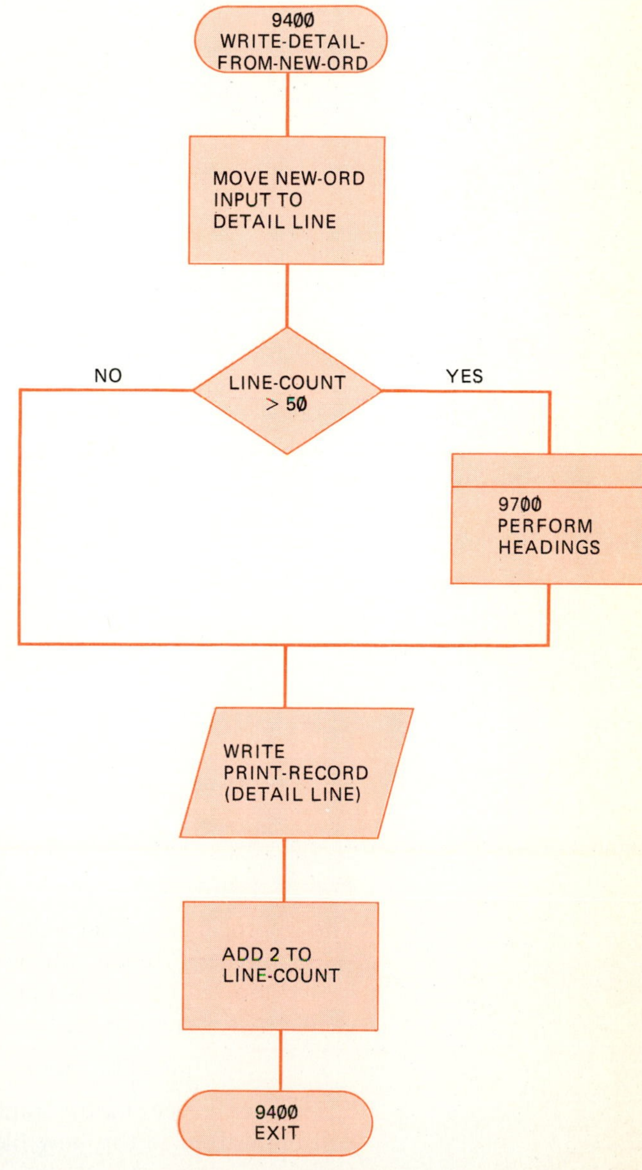

FIGURE 9-28 cont.

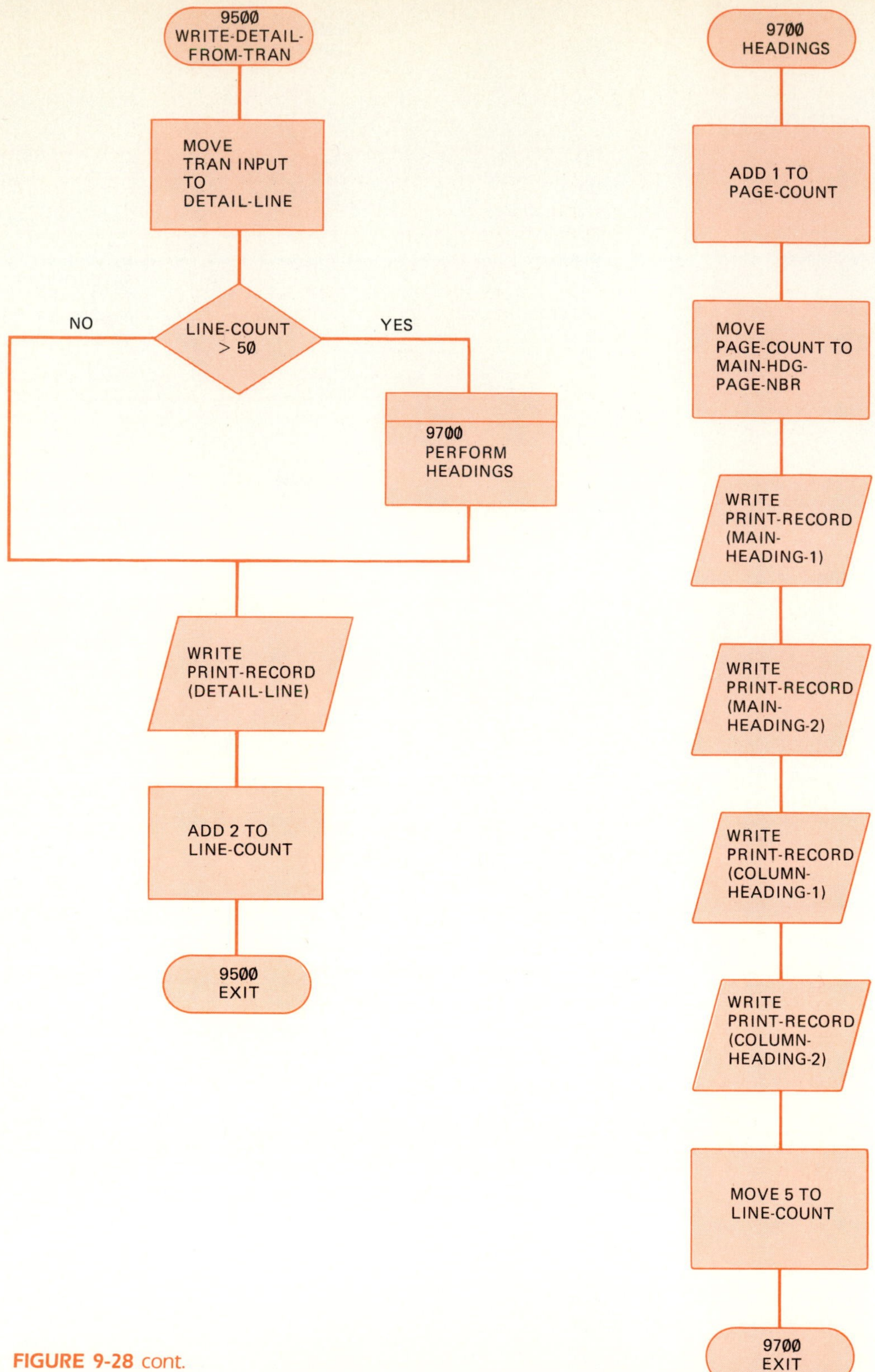

FIGURE 9-28 cont.

The appropriate action will depend on the type of transaction. If it is a change, the appropriate fields will be updated and the updated version of the record will be written onto the new master file. If it is a deletion, no write will take place. In either case, a new record will be read from the two input files.

MASTER KEY FIELD > TRANSACTION KEY FIELD

There is no master for the transaction. If the transaction is an addition, the transaction will be written to the new file and a new transaction record will be read.

Sequential-file maintenance must be able to handle error conditions as well as additions, changes, and deletions. Master files are usually created using a transaction file that has been edited, and in any given instance the current transaction file will also have been through an input edit. As might be expected, certain errors can be discovered only when the two files are used together. For example, a record from the transaction file may be an addition, yet a record with the same value in the key field may already be in the master file. Or a record from the transaction file may be a change or deletion, yet there may be no record with a matching key field in the master file. Such errors are normally listed on a report so that a correction may be made before the next run of the file maintenance program.

The ORDER-MAINT program is a file maintenance program for the ORDER-FILE. New orders are added, changes are made to existing orders, and cancelled orders are deleted.

MAIN LINE

The main routine is written to accommodate two input files that are to be matched against each other. Both of the files must reach their end in order for processing to be complete. Accordingly, each file has its own end flag, and 2000-PROCESS is performed until the end flags for both files have been set. (See Figure 9–29.)

```
           PERFORM 1000-INITIALIZATION.
           PERFORM 2000-PROCESS
               UNTIL END-OF-ORDER-FILE AND END-OF-TRAN-FILE.
           PERFORM 3000-EOJ.
           STOP RUN.
```

FIGURE 9–29

1000-INITIALIZATION

The two input files of the program are the master file (ORDER-FILE) and transaction file (TRANSACTION-FILE). The transaction file contains records used to maintain the ORDER-FILE. These records contain additions, changes, and deletions to the ORDER-FILE. The program also has two output files. NEW-ORDER-FILE is a disk file which will reflect the changes to ORDER-FILE after the additions, changes, and deletions from the transaction file are processed. PRINT-FILE will be used to provide a listing of these changes, as well as of any errors.

Since the two files are to be matched against each other, a record is read from each file in 1000-INITIALIZATION. The key fields for the two files (sales order number) are then compared in 9300-SELECT-KEY, and the lower one becomes the current processing key. If the key fields are equal, either one may be used. In this case, the code in 9300-SELECT-KEY uses the key field from the transaction file. (See Figure 9–30.)

```
       1000-INITIALIZATION.
           OPEN INPUT  ORDER-FILE
                       TRANSACTION-FILE
                OUTPUT NEW-ORDER-FILE
                       PRINT-FILE.
           MOVE CURRENT-DATE TO MAIN-HDG-DATE.
           PERFORM 9100-READ-ORDER-FILE.
           PERFORM 9200-READ-TRAN-FILE.
           PERFORM 9300-SELECT-CURRENT-KEY.
```

FIGURE 9–30

2000-PROCESS

When 2000-PROCESS is entered, a current processing key has already been selected. This key is the key value (order number) which the current execution of the 2000-PROCESS routine will process. When 2000-PROCESS is complete, the master record with this key (if it exists) and all transaction records with this key (if they exist) will have been processed.

The first step in 2000-PROCESS is to compare the master file key (ORD-SALES-ORD-NBR) against the current processing key to determine whether a master record exists with the current processing key. This is done in 2100-CHECK-ORDER-RECORD. If a master record (an order) exists with this key, then the ORDER-RECORD is moved to NEW-ORDER-RECORD, a flag (NEW-ORDER-EXISTS-FLAG) is set to 'YES', and the next record is read from the ORDER-FILE. If a master record with this key does not exist, then NEW-ORDER-EXISTS-FLAG is set to 'NO'.

The second step in 2000-PROCESS is to apply records from the transaction file until the transaction record key field is not equal to the current processing key. If the transaction key is not equal to the current processing key, there are no transaction records for this master record, and this step is bypassed. If the transaction key is equal to the current processing key, then there are transactions to be processed. If the NEW-ORDER-EXISTS-FLAG is set to 'YES', then there is a master record in NEW-ORDER-RECORD to process these transactions against. If the NEW-ORDER-EXISTS-FLAG is set to 'NO', the transactions to be processed have no matching master record. In this case, unless there is an error, the first transaction must be an addition.

After the transactions (if any) are applied, 2300-CHECK-FOR-WRITE tests NEW-ORDER-EXISTS-FLAG. If it is 'YES', the NEW-ORDER-RECORD is written and a new current processing key is selected. Remember, if the first master was placed in NEW-ORDER-RECORD, then a new master was read; if a transaction was applied or found to be in error, then a new transaction was read. (See Figure 9–31.)

```
       2000-PROCESS.
           PERFORM 2100-CHECK-ORDER-RECORD.
           PERFORM 2200-APPLY-TRANSACTION
               UNTIL TRAN-SALES-ORD-NBR NOT = CURRENT-PROCESSING-KEY
           PERFORM 2300-CHECK-FOR-WRITE.
           PERFORM 9300-SELECT-CURRENT-KEY.
```

FIGURE 9–31

2100-CHECK-ORDER-RECORD

The routine 2100-CHECK-ORDER-RECORD is performed every time 2000-PROCESS is performed. A new current processing key is selected at the end of 1000-INITIALIZATION and 2000-PROCESS and is available each time 2000-PROCESS is entered. 2100-CHECK-ORDER-RECORD checks the sales order number from the master file to see whether it is equal to the current processing key. If it is, then the master key field is either lower than or equal to the transaction key field. If the master key field is equal to the current processing key, the master record is moved to NEW-ORDER-RECORD and 'YES' is moved to NEW-ORDER-EXISTS-FLAG. The record may then be written to the NEW-ORDER-FILE without change if there are no matching transactions, or some transactions may be applied to it causing it to be changed or deleted. In either case, the next ORDER-RECORD is read.

If the master key field is not equal to the current processing key, 'NO' is moved to NEW-ORDER-EXISTS-FLAG. This means that the transaction record is less then the master record and the transaction sales order number was selected as the current processing key. When 2100-CHECK-ORDER is complete and control returns to 2000-PROCESS, an attempt will be made to apply this transaction. Since NEW-ORDER-EXISTS-FLAG indicates that no order exists to apply the transaction against, there will be an error if the transaction is a change or a deletion. On the other hand, if the transaction is an addition, it is proper that no order should already exist on the ORDER-FILE. (See Figure 9–32.)

```
        2100-CHECK-ORDER-RECORD.
             IF ORD-SALES-ORD-NBR = CURRENT-PROCESSING-KEY
                 MOVE WS-ORDER-RECORD TO WS-NEW-ORDER-RECORD
                 MOVE 'YES' TO NEW-ORDER-EXISTS-FLAG
                 PERFORM 9100-READ-ORDER-FILE
             ELSE
                 MOVE 'NO' TO NEW-ORDER-EXISTS-FLAG.
```

FIGURE 9–32

2200-APPLY-TRANSACTION

Routine 2200-APPLY-TRANSACTION is performed from 2000-PROCESS if the transaction sales order number is equal to the current processing key. This condition of equality occurs either because there are transactions to match with the master record or because there is a transaction without a master record. In either case, the transaction is tested to determine whether it is an addition, change, or deletion, since a separate routine is performed for each of these. After the appropriate routine is selected and performed, the next transaction record is read.

Each of the three routines 2210-ADD, 2220-CHANGE, and 2230-DELETE will determine whether a transaction of that type should be applied to the master or whether it is in error. (See Figure 9–33.)

```
        2200-APPLY-TRANSACTION.
            IF ADD-TRANSACTION
                PERFORM 2210-ADD
            ELSE
                IF CHANGE-TRANSACTION
                    PERFORM 2220-CHANGE
                ELSE
                    IF DELETE-TRANSACTION
                        PERFORM 2230-DELETE.
            PERFORM 9200-READ-TRAN-FILE.
```

FIGURE 9–33

2210-ADD

If NEW-ORDER-EXISTS-FLAG contains a 'YES', the current transaction should not be applied because an order already exists with this key. In this case, 2211-ADD-REJECTED will be performed. If NEW-ORDER-EXISTS-FLAG contains a 'NO', an addition is appropriate and 2212-PROCESS-ADD will be performed. (See Figure 9–34.)

```
        2210-ADD.
            IF NEW-ORDER-EXISTS
                PERFORM 2211-ADD-REJECTED
            ELSE
                PERFORM 2212-PROCESS-ADD.
```

FIGURE 9–34

2211-ADD-REJECTED

The routine 2211-ADD-REJECTED is performed when a transaction is an addition, but an order with the same sales order number already exists in the ORDER-FILE. An appropriate message is placed in the detail line, and the detail line is printed using the data from the transaction record. (See Figure 9–35.)

```
        2211-ADD-REJECTED.
            ADD 1 TO NBR-OF-ADD-ERRORS.
            MOVE 'ADD ERROR - RECORD ALREADY EXISTS' TO DET-MESSAGE.
            PERFORM 9500-WRITE-DETAIL-FROM-TRAN.
```

FIGURE 9–35

2212-PROCESS-ADD

2212-PROCESS-ADD is performed when a transaction is an addition and a record with the current key does not already exist. The data from the transaction record is moved to the NEW-ORDER-RECORD, and the NEW-ORDER-EXISTS-FLAG is set to 'YES'. A detail line is then printed showing the record added. (See Figure 9–36.)

```
2212-PROCESS-ADD.
    MOVE WS-TRANSACTION-RECORD TO WS-NEW-ORDER-RECORD.
    MOVE 'YES' TO NEW-ORDER-EXISTS-FLAG.
    MOVE 'ADDED' TO DET-MESSAGE.
    PERFORM 9400-WRITE-DETAIL-FROM-NEW-ORD.
    ADD 1 TO NBR-OF-ADDS.
```

FIGURE 9–36

2220-CHANGE

The 2220-CHANGE routine is performed from APPLY-TRANSACTION. If NEW-ORDER-EXISTS-FLAG is equal to 'YES' and the record in NEW-ORDER-RECORD has a shipping date of zeros, the change will be processed in 2221-PROCESS-CHANGES. If the order is available but has already been shipped, a detail line using data from the transaction record is written indicating that the transaction is in error. This is because no changes are allowed to an order that has already been shipped. If NEW-ORDER-EXISTS-FLAG is equal to 'NO', there is no record to be changed and 2222-CHANGE-REJECTED is performed. (See Figure 9–37.)

```
2220-CHANGE.
    IF NEW-ORDER-EXISTS
        IF NEW-ORD-ACT-SHIP-DATE = ZEROS
            PERFORM 2221-PROCESS-CHANGES
        ELSE
            ADD 1 TO NBR-OF-CHANGE-ERRORS
            MOVE 'CHANGE ERROR - ORDER IS SHIPPED' TO DET-MESSAGE
            PERFORM 9500-WRITE-DETAIL-FROM-TRAN
    ELSE
        PERFORM 2222-CHANGE-REJECTED.
```

FIGURE 9–37

2221-PROCESS-CHANGES

The routine 2221-PROCESS-CHANGES is performed when the transaction to be applied is a change, a NEW-ORDER-RECORD exists to apply it against, and the NEW-ORDER-RECORD has zeros for the actual shipping date. The record waiting to be changed in NEW-ORDER-RECORD is printed with a message indicating that it is "before changes." Then each field in the transaction record (except the key field) is checked for spaces. For any field that is not equal to spaces, the data from that field is moved to the corresponding field in NEW-ORDER-RECORD, overlaying (changing) the original data for ORDER-RECORD. Asterisks are then moved to an asterisk line which is used to highlight the changed field on the listing.

The data from NEW-ORDER-RECORD is then printed again, this time with an "after changes" message, and the asterisk line is printed to highlight the changes. Finally, spaces are moved to the asterisk line to clear it for use with the next record to be changed. (See Figure 9–38.)

2222-CHANGE-REJECTED

2222-CHANGE-REJECTED is performed when the transaction key field is equal to the current processing key, but there is no record in the NEW-ORDER-RECORD available for processing. A detail line is written indicating the error. (See Figure 9–39.)

```
2221-PROCESS-CHANGES.

    ADD 1 TO NBR-OF-CHANGES.
    MOVE 'BEFORE CHANGES' TO DET-MESSAGE.
    PERFORM 9400-WRITE-DETAIL-FROM-NEW-ORD.

    IF TRAN-BRANCH NOT = SPACES
        MOVE TRAN-BRANCH TO NEW-ORD-BRANCH
        MOVE ALL '*' TO AST-BRANCH.

    IF TRAN-SALES-REP NOT = SPACES
        MOVE TRAN-SALES-REP TO NEW-ORD-SALES-REP
        MOVE ALL '*' TO AST-SALES-REP.

    IF TRAN-CUSTOMER-NBR NOT = SPACES
        MOVE TRAN-CUSTOMER-NBR TO NEW-ORD-CUSTOMER-NBR
        MOVE ALL '*' TO AST-CUSTOMER-NBR.

    IF TRAN-CUST-PO-NBR NOT = SPACES
        MOVE TRAN-CUST-PO-NBR TO NEW-ORD-CUST-PO-NBR
        MOVE ALL '*' TO AST-CUST-PO-NBR.

    IF TRAN-ORD-DATE NOT = SPACES
        MOVE TRAN-ORD-DATE TO NEW-ORD-DATE
        MOVE ALL '*' TO AST-ORD-DATE.

    IF TRAN-PART-NBR NOT = SPACES
        MOVE TRAN-PART-NBR TO NEW-ORD-PART-NBR
        MOVE ALL '*' TO AST-PART-NBR.

    IF TRAN-QUANTITY NOT = SPACES
        MOVE TRAN-QUANTITY TO NEW-ORD-QUANTITY
        MOVE ALL '*' TO AST-QUANTITY.

    IF TRAN-UNIT-PRICE NOT = SPACES
        MOVE TRAN-UNIT-PRICE TO NEW-ORD-UNIT-PRICE
        MOVE ALL '*' TO AST-UNIT-PRICE.

    IF TRAN-REQ-SHIP-DATE NOT = SPACES
        MOVE TRAN-REQ-SHIP-DATE TO NEW-ORD-REQ-SHIP-DATE
        MOVE ALL '*' TO AST-REQ-SHIP-DATE.

    IF TRAN-ACT-SHIP-DATE NOT = SPACES
        MOVE TRAN-ACT-SHIP-DATE TO NEW-ORD-ACT-SHIP-DATE
        MOVE ALL '*' TO AST-ACT-SHIP-DATE.

    MOVE 'AFTER CHANGES' TO DET-MESSAGE.
    PERFORM 9400-WRITE-DETAIL-FROM-NEW-ORD.
    WRITE PRINT-RECORD FROM ASTERISK-LINE
        AFTER ADVANCING 1 LINE.
    ADD 1 TO LINE-COUNT.
    MOVE SPACES TO ASTERISK-LINE.
```

FIGURE 9–38

```
2222-CHANGE-REJECTED.
    ADD 1 TO NBR-OF-CHANGE-ERRORS.
    MOVE 'CHANGE ERROR - RECORD DOES NOT EXIST' TO DET-MESSAGE.
    PERFORM 9500-WRITE-DETAIL-FROM-TRAN.
```

FIGURE 9–39

2230-DELETE

The 2230-DELETE routine is performed from APPLY-TRANSACTIONS if the transaction type is 'D'. If a matching ORDER-RECORD has been placed in NEW-ORDER-RECORD awaiting possible transactions, 2231-PROCESS-DELETE will be performed. If there is no ORDER-RECORD waiting to be processed, 2232-DELETE-REJECTED will be performed. (See Figure 9–40.)

```
2230-DELETE.
    IF NEW-ORDER-EXISTS
        PERFORM 2231-PROCESS-DELETE
    ELSE
        PERFORM 2232-DELETE-REJECTED.
```

FIGURE 9–40

2231-PROCESS-DELETE

2231-PROCESS-DELETE changes the status of the record in NEW-ORDER-RECORD by moving 'NO' to NEW-ORDER-EXISTS-FLAG. This ensures that the record will not be written to the new file when 2300-CHECK-FOR-WRITE is performed. A detail line is printed indicating a deleted record. (See Figure 9–41.)

```
       2231-PROCESS-DELETE.
           MOVE 'NO' TO NEW-ORDER-EXISTS-FLAG.
           ADD 1 TO NBR-OF-DELETES.
           MOVE 'DELETED' TO DET-MESSAGE.
           PERFORM 9400-WRITE-DETAIL-FROM-NEW-ORD.
```

FIGURE 9–41

2232-DELETE-REJECTED

When the transaction to be applied is a deletion and NEW-ORDER-EXISTS-FLAG indicates that no order is available, 2232-DELETE-REJECTED is executed. A detail line indicating the error is written using data from the transaction record. (See Figure 9–42.)

```
       2232-DELETE-REJECTED.
           ADD 1 TO NBR-OF-DELETE-ERRORS.
           MOVE 'DELETE ERROR - RECORD DOES NOT EXIST' TO DET-MESSAGE.
           PERFORM 9500-WRITE-DETAIL-FROM-TRAN.
```

FIGURE 9–42

2300-CHECK-FOR-WRITE

2300-CHECK-FOR-WRITE is performed from 2000-PROCESS. It is performed after all transactions for the current processing key have been processed. This routine uses a switch to determine whether or not a record exists in NEW-ORDER-RECORD which should be written to NEW-ORDER-FILE. If it exists it will be written to the NEW-ORDER-FILE.

Some of the circumstances in which the record would be written to NEW-ORDER-FILE are (1) the master was less than the transaction, (2) the master was equal to the transaction and a transaction was a change, or (3) the master was greater than the transaction and a transaction is an addition. If the master was equal to the transaction and the transaction type was a deletion, 'NO' will have been moved to NEW-ORDER-EXISTS-FLAG and therefore no order record will be written. (See Figure 9–43.)

```
       2300-CHECK-FOR-WRITE.
           IF NEW-ORDER-EXISTS
               WRITE NEW-ORDER-RECORD FROM WS-NEW-ORDER-RECORD
               ADD 1 TO NBR-OF-ORDERS-WRITTEN.
```

FIGURE 9–43

3000-EOJ

3000-EOJ uses DISPLAY to list the counts kept for each possible outcome of the file processing. After the counts are displayed, the files are closed. (See Figure 9–44.)

9100-READ-ORDER-FILE

Since the end of one file may be reached while there is still processing to do on the other file, routine 9100-READ-ORDER-FILE may be performed after the end of the ORDER-FILE has been reached. A test is made first to see whether the

```
3000-EOJ.
    WRITE PRINT-RECORD FROM ASTERISK-LINE AFTER ADVANCING PAGE.
    DISPLAY 'NBR-OF-ADDS              ' NBR-OF-ADDS.
    DISPLAY 'NBR-OF-ADD-ERRORS        ' NBR-OF-ADD-ERRORS.
    DISPLAY 'NBR-OF-CHANGES           ' NBR-OF-CHANGES.
    DISPLAY 'NBR-OF-CHANGE-ERRORS     ' NBR-OF-CHANGE-ERRORS.
    DISPLAY 'NBR-OF-DELETES           ' NBR-OF-DELETES.
    DISPLAY 'NBR-OF-DELETE-ERRORS     ' NBR-OF-DELETE-ERRORS.
    DISPLAY 'NBR-OF-ORDERS-READ       ' NBR-OF-ORDERS-READ.
    DISPLAY 'NBR-OF-TRANS-READ        ' NBR-OF-TRANS-READ.
    DISPLAY 'NBR-OF-ORDERS-WRITTEN    ' NBR-OF-ORDERS-WRITTEN.
    CLOSE ORDER-FILE
          TRANSACTION-FILE
          NEW-ORDER-FILE
          PRINT-FILE.
```

FIGURE 9–44

end of the file has already been reached. If it has, the routine is complete; otherwise a READ is executed. If the READ encounters the end-of-file indicator, 'YES' is moved to END-FLAG-ORDER-FILE and HIGH-VALUES is placed in the master file key field (ORD-SALES-ORD-NBR). This will make the ORDER-FILE key field greater than the transaction file key field in future selections of the current processing key. If the read is successful, the number of records read is incremented by 1. (See Figure 9–45.)

```
9100-READ-ORDER-FILE.

    IF END-OF-ORDER-FILE
        NEXT SENTENCE
    ELSE
        READ ORDER-FILE INTO WS-ORDER-RECORD
            AT END
                MOVE 'YES'       TO END-FLAG-ORDER-FILE
                MOVE HIGH-VALUES TO ORD-SALES-ORD-NBR.

    IF NOT END-OF-ORDER-FILE
        ADD 1 TO NBR-OF-ORDERS-READ.
```

FIGURE 9–45

9200-READ-TRAN-FILE

The end of the transaction file may be reached while there are still records to be processed in the ORDER-FILE. As a result, 9200-READ-TRAN-FILE may be performed after the end of the transaction file has already been reached. Accordingly, a test is performed to determine whether the end of the file has been reached. If it has, the routine is complete; if it has not, the transaction file will be read. If the READ encounters an end-of-file indicator, 'YES' is moved to END-FLAG-TRAN-FILE and HIGH-VALUES is moved to the transaction file key field (TRAN-SALES-ORD-NBR). This will make the transaction file key field greater than the master file key field in future selections of the current processing key. (See Figure 9–46.)

```
9200-READ-TRAN-FILE.

    IF END-OF-TRAN-FILE
        NEXT SENTENCE
    ELSE
        READ TRANSACTION-FILE INTO WS-TRANSACTION-RECORD
            AT END
                MOVE 'YES'       TO END-FLAG-TRAN-FILE
                MOVE HIGH-VALUES TO TRAN-SALES-ORD-NBR.

    IF NOT END-OF-TRAN-FILE
        ADD 1 TO NBR-OF-TRANS-READ.
```

FIGURE 9–46

9300-SELECT-CURRENT-KEY

Routine 9300-SELECT-CURRENT-KEY is performed at the end of 1000-INITIALIZATION and 2000-PROCESS. It determines which of the available sales order numbers from the master and transaction files is lower. The lower one then becomes the current processing key. If the two numbers are equal, the transaction field is used. (See Figure 9–47.)

```
       9300-SELECT-CURRENT-KEY.
           IF ORD-SALES-ORD-NBR < TRAN-SALES-ORD-NBR
               MOVE ORD-SALES-ORD-NBR TO CURRENT-PROCESSING-KEY
           ELSE
               MOVE TRAN-SALES-ORD-NBR TO CURRENT-PROCESSING-KEY.
```

FIGURE 9–47

9400-WRITE-DETAIL-FROM-NEW-ORD

9400-WRITE-DETAIL-FROM-NEW-ORD is used to print detail lines for additions, changes, and deletions. (See Figure 9–48.)

```
       9400-WRITE-DETAIL-FROM-NEW-ORD.
           MOVE NEW-ORD-SALES-ORD-NBR    TO DET-SALES-ORD-NBR.
           MOVE NEW-ORD-BRANCH           TO DET-BRANCH.
           MOVE NEW-ORD-SALES-REP        TO DET-SALES-REP.
           MOVE NEW-ORD-CUSTOMER-NBR     TO DET-CUSTOMER-NBR.
           MOVE NEW-ORD-CUST-PO-NBR      TO DET-CUST-PO-NBR.
           MOVE NEW-ORD-DATE             TO DET-ORD-DATE.
           MOVE NEW-ORD-PART-NBR         TO DET-PART-NBR.
           MOVE NEW-ORD-QUANTITY         TO DET-QUANTITY.
           MOVE NEW-ORD-UNIT-PRICE       TO DET-UNIT-PRICE.
           MOVE NEW-ORD-REQ-SHIP-DATE    TO DET-REQ-SHIP-DATE.
           MOVE NEW-ORD-ACT-SHIP-DATE    TO DET-ACT-SHIP-DATE.
           IF LINE-COUNT > 50
               PERFORM 9700-HEADINGS.
           WRITE PRINT-RECORD FROM DETAIL-LINE
               AFTER ADVANCING 2 LINES.
           ADD 2 TO LINE-COUNT.
```

FIGURE 9–48

9500-WRITE-DETAIL-FROM-TRAN

9500-WRITE-DETAIL-FROM-TRAN will print a detail line for all rejected additions, changes, and deletions. (See Figure 9–49.)

```
       9500-WRITE-DETAIL-FROM-TRAN.
           MOVE TRAN-SALES-ORD-NBR       TO DET-SALES-ORD-NBR.
           MOVE TRAN-BRANCH              TO DET-BRANCH.
           MOVE TRAN-SALES-REP           TO DET-SALES-REP.
           MOVE TRAN-CUSTOMER-NBR        TO DET-CUSTOMER-NBR.
           MOVE TRAN-CUST-PO-NBR         TO DET-CUST-PO-NBR.
           MOVE TRAN-ORD-DATE            TO DET-ORD-DATE.
           MOVE TRAN-PART-NBR            TO DET-PART-NBR.
           MOVE TRAN-QUANTITY            TO DET-QUANTITY.
           MOVE TRAN-UNIT-PRICE          TO DET-UNIT-PRICE.
           MOVE TRAN-REQ-SHIP-DATE       TO DET-REQ-SHIP-DATE.
           MOVE TRAN-ACT-SHIP-DATE       TO DET-ACT-SHIP-DATE.
           IF LINE-COUNT > 50
               PERFORM 9700-HEADINGS.
           WRITE PRINT-RECORD FROM DETAIL-LINE
               AFTER ADVANCING 2 LINES.
           ADD 2 TO LINE-COUNT.
```

FIGURE 9–49

9700-HEADINGS

The 9700-HEADINGS routine is performed as needed from both 9400-WRITE-DETAIL-FROM-NEW-ORD and 9500-WRITE-DETAIL-FROM-TRAN. (See Figure 9–50.)

```
           9700-HEADINGS.
               ADD 1 TO PAGE-COUNT.
               MOVE PAGE-COUNT TO MAIN-HDG-PAGE-NBR.
               WRITE PRINT-RECORD FROM MAIN-HEADING-1
                   AFTER ADVANCING PAGE.
               WRITE PRINT-RECORD FROM MAIN-HEADING-2
                   AFTER ADVANCING 1 LINE.
               WRITE PRINT-RECORD FROM COLUMN-HEADING-1
                   AFTER ADVANCING 2 LINES.
               WRITE PRINT-RECORD FROM COLUMN-HEADING-2
                   AFTER ADVANCING 1 LINE.
               MOVE 5 TO LINE-COUNT.
```

FIGURE 9–50

THE COBOL PROGRAM

Test Data

Test data for the ORDER-FILE and the TRANSACTION-FILE are shown in Figure 9–51.

ORDER-FILE

```
Ø1201ØØ3ØØE1Ø12      B123358711Ø5WB493EØØØØ2Ø54ØØØ871122ØØØØØØ
Ø1201ØØ3ØØPO173      B12383871Ø25GN4Ø2AØØØØ1Ø45ØØØ871116ØØØØØØ
Ø3ØØ7ØØ28334567X     B34237871Ø3ØHL834EØØØ16Ø19ØØØ871121ØØØØØØ
Ø891521Ø78           B71Ø45871ØØ1FV782TØØØØ3ØØ28ØØ8711158711Ø9
Ø361182888P2783733B8433Ø871Ø25HL289BØØØ1ØØ234ØØ8711138711Ø9
Ø3ØØ7739897747       B892888711Ø6MF848JØØØØ5Ø2145Ø88Ø13ØØØØØØØ
Ø344Ø69481870341     GØ418Ø87Ø2Ø9JGØ4ØXØØØØ1Ø525ØØ88Ø619ØØØØØØ
Ø1201Ø47278372       G4838887Ø913WB7Ø2XØØØ9ØØ115ØØ8711Ø1871109
Ø817431408ØØ65       H4189187Ø412TK61ØLØØØ18ØØ78ØØ87Ø63Ø871109
Ø36115Ø912           H6915Ø87Ø2Ø6MF848TØØØØ3Ø36ØØØ8712Ø1ØØØØØØ
Ø3ØØ7ØØ378EBNER      H8457987Ø811VX922PØØ8ØØØØ127589112ØØØØØØØ
Ø3ØØ747300           H8477787Ø223MF4Ø3TØØØØ5Ø4ØØØØ87Ø5Ø2ØØØØØØ
Ø891562Ø54SCHUH      L5Ø6818711Ø8TK812EØØØØ6Ø573ØØ88Ø1Ø5ØØØØØØ
Ø8174Ø18Ø5R7278      T2164287Ø81ØTK497XØØØ1ØØ118ØØ87113Ø871109
Ø361128375T7838      T7829987Ø323JG563WØØØØ6Ø43ØØØ871Ø18ØØØØØØ
Ø8174Ø18Ø5R8322      Y211Ø587Ø6Ø1TN116TØØØØ1Ø3ØØØØ871221ØØØØØØ
Ø3ØØ7473ØØ           Y289Ø387Ø811VXØØ1LØØ2ØØØØ622Ø8712Ø3ØØØØØØ
```

TRANSACTION-FILE

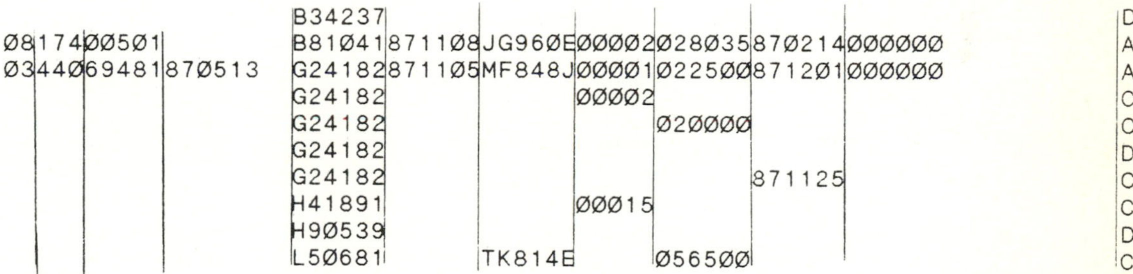

```
                              B34237                                              D
Ø8174ØØ5Ø1                    B81Ø41871108JG96ØEØØØØ2Ø28Ø3587Ø214ØØØØØØ           A
Ø344Ø69481870513              G241828711Ø5MF848JØØØØ1Ø225ØØ8712Ø1ØØØØØØ           A
                              G24182            ØØØØ2                             C
                              G24182                 Ø2ØØØØ                       C
                              G24182                                              D
                              G24182                       871125                 C
                              H41891            ØØØ15                             C
                              H9Ø539                                              D
                              L5Ø681      TK814E     Ø565ØØ                       C
```

FIGURE 9–51

Sample Output

Sample output for the listing and the NEW-ORDER-FILE are shown in Figure 9–52.

```
DATE: 11/09/87                                 PRODUCT DISTRIBUTION INC.                                  PAGE:   1
                                                   MAINTENANCE REPORT

 SALES          SLS          CUSTOMER    ORDER    PART               UNIT     REQ     ACTUAL
 ORDER  BRANCH REP   CUST#     PO#       DATE    NUMBER   QTY        PRICE    SHIP    SHIP         MESSAGE

B 34237   03   007   00283   34567X     871030   HL834E   00016     019000   871121   000000   DELETED

B 81041   08   174   00501              871108   JG960E   00002     028035   870214   000000   ADDED

G 24182   03   440   69481   870513     871105   MF848J   00001     022500   871201   000000   ADDED

G 24182   03   440   69481   870513     871105   MF848J   00001     022500   871201   000000   BEFORE CHANGES

G 24182   03   440   69481   870513     871105   MF848J   00002     022500   871201   000000   AFTER CHANGES
                                                          *****

G 24182   03   440   69481   870513     871105   MF848J   00002     022500   871201   000000   BEFORE CHANGES

G 24182   03   440   69481   870513     871105   MF848J   00002     020000   871201   000000   AFTER CHANGES
                                                                   *******

G 24182   03   440   69481   870513     871105   MF848J   00002     020000   871201   000000   DELETED

G 24182                                                                      871125            CHANGE ERROR - RECORD DOES NOT EXIST

H 41891                                                   00015                                CHANGE ERROR - ORDER IS SHIPPED

H 90539                                                                                        DELETE ERROR - RECORD DOES NOT EXIST

L 50681   08   915   62054   SCHUH      871108   TK812E   00006     057300   880105   000000   BEFORE CHANGES

L 50681   08   915   62054   SCHUH      871108   TK814E   00006     056500   880105   00000  AFTER CHANGES
                                                 ******            *******
-------------------------------------------------------------------------------------------------------------------------
NBR-OF-ADDS              00002
NBR-OF-ADD-ERRORS        00000
NBR-OF-CHANGES           00003
NBR-OF-CHANGE-ERRORS     00002
NBR-OF-DELETES           00002
NBR-OF-DELETE-ERRORS     00001
NBR-OF-ORDERS-READ       00017
NBR-OF-TRANS-READ        00010
NBR-OF-ORDERS-WRITTEN    00017
```

FIGURE 9–52

NEW-ORDER FILE

```
Ø1201ØØ3ØØE1Ø12      B12335871105WB493EØØØØ2Ø54ØØØ871122ØØØØØØ
Ø1201ØØ3ØØPO173      B12383871Ø25GN4Ø2AØØØØ1Ø45ØØØ871116ØØØØØØ
Ø891521Ø78           B71Ø45871ØØ1FV782TØØØØ3ØØ28ØØ871115871109
Ø8174ØØ5Ø1           B81Ø41871108JG96ØEØØØØ2Ø28Ø3587Ø214ØØØØØØ
Ø361182888P2783733B8433Ø871Ø25HL289BØØØ1ØØ234ØØ871113871109
Ø3ØØ7739897747       B89288871106MF848JØØØØ5Ø2145Ø88Ø13ØØØØØØØ
Ø344Ø6948187Ø341     GØ418Ø87Ø2Ø9JGØ4ØXØØØØ1Ø525ØØ88Ø619ØØØØØØ
Ø12Ø1Ø47278372       G4838887Ø913WB7Ø2XØØØ9ØØ115ØØ8711Ø1871109
Ø81743140865         H4189187Ø412TK61ØLØØØ18ØØ78ØØ87Ø63Ø871109
Ø36115Ø912           H6915Ø87Ø2Ø6MF848TØØØØ3Ø36ØØØ8712Ø1ØØØØØØ
Ø3ØØ7ØØ378EBNER      H8457987Ø811VX922PØØ8ØØØØ127589112ØØØØØØØ
Ø3ØØ747300           H8477787Ø223MF4Ø3TØØØØ5Ø4ØØØØ87Ø5Ø2ØØØØØØ
Ø891562Ø54SCHUH      L5Ø681871108TK814EØØØØ6Ø565ØØ88Ø1Ø5ØØØØØØ
Ø8174Ø18Ø5R7278      T2164287Ø81ØTK497XØØØ1ØØ118ØØ87113Ø871109
Ø361128375T7838      T7829987Ø323JG563WØØØØ6Ø43ØØØ871Ø18ØØØØØØ
Ø8174Ø18Ø5R8322      Y211Ø587Ø6Ø1TN116TØØØØ1Ø3ØØØØ871221ØØØØØØ
Ø3ØØ747300           Y289Ø387Ø811VXØØ1LØØ2ØØØØ622Ø8712Ø3ØØØØØØ
```

FIGURE 9–52 cont.

The Program

The complete COBOL ORDER-MAINT program is shown in Figure 9–53.

```
       IDENTIFICATION DIVISION.

       PROGRAM-ID.    ORDER-MAINT.

       AUTHOR.        HELEN HUMPHREYS.

       INSTALLATION.  PRODUCT DISTRIBUTION INC.

       DATE-WRITTEN.  Ø9/12/87.

       DATE-COMPILED. Ø9/25/87.

      *****************************************************************
      *                                                               *
      *    THIS PROGRAM UPDATES THE ORDER-FILE.  THIS PROGRAM WILL    *
      *    ADD RECORDS TO THE FILE, DELETE RECORDS FROM THE FILE,     *
      *    AND CHANGE THE DATA IN EXISTING RECORDS.  THIS PROGRAM     *
      *    WILL ALSO PRODUCE A PRINTED REPORT WHICH LISTS THE UPDATES *
      *    TO THE FILE.                                               *
      *                                                               *
      *****************************************************************

       ENVIRONMENT DIVISION.

       CONFIGURATION SECTION.

       SOURCE-COMPUTER.
           IBM-37Ø.
       OBJECT-COMPUTER.
```

FIGURE 9–53

```
               IBM-37Ø.

           INPUT-OUTPUT SECTION.
           FILE-CONTROL.
               SELECT ORDER-FILE          ASSIGN TO DISK.
               SELECT TRANSACTION-FILE    ASSIGN TO DISK.
               SELECT NEW-ORDER-FILE      ASSIGN TO DISK.
               SELECT PRINT-FILE          ASSIGN TO PRINTER.

           DATA DIVISION.
           FILE SECTION.

           FD  ORDER-FILE
               LABEL RECORDS ARE STANDARD
               RECORD CONTAINS 7Ø CHARACTERS
               DATA RECORD IS ORDER-RECORD.

           Ø1  ORDER-RECORD                     PIC X(7Ø).

           FD  TRANSACTION-FILE
               LABEL RECORDS ARE STANDARD
               RECORD CONTAINS 71 CHARACTERS
               DATA RECORD IS TRANSACTION-RECORD.

           Ø1  TRANSACTION-RECORD               PIC X(71).

           FD  NEW-ORDER-FILE
               LABEL RECORDS ARE STANDARD
               RECORD CONTAINS 7Ø CHARACTERS
               DATA RECORD IS NEW-ORDER-RECORD.

           Ø1  NEW-ORDER-RECORD                 PIC X(7Ø).

           FD  PRINT-FILE
               LABEL RECORDS ARE OMITTED
               RECORD CONTAINS 133 CHARACTERS
               DATA RECORD IS PRINT-RECORD.

           Ø1  PRINT-RECORD                     PIC X(133).

           WORKING-STORAGE SECTION.

           Ø1  WS-ORDER-RECORD.
               Ø5  ORD-BRANCH                   PIC 9(2).
               Ø5  ORD-SALES-REP                PIC 9(3).
               Ø5  ORD-CUSTOMER-NBR             PIC 9(5).
               Ø5  ORD-CUST-PO-NBR              PIC X(8).
               Ø5  ORD-SALES-ORD-NBR            PIC X(6).
               Ø5  ORD-DATE.
                   1Ø  ORD-YY                   PIC X(2).
                   1Ø  ORD-MM                   PIC X(2).
                   1Ø  ORD-DD                   PIC X(2).
               Ø5  ORD-PART-NBR                 PIC X(6).
               Ø5  ORD-QUANTITY                 PIC 9(5).
               Ø5  ORD-UNIT-PRICE               PIC 9(4)V9(2).
               Ø5  ORD-REQ-SHIP-DATE.
                   1Ø  ORD-REQ-SHIP-YY          PIC X(2).
                   1Ø  ORD-REQ-SHIP-MM          PIC X(2).
                   1Ø  ORD-REQ-SHIP-DD          PIC X(2).
               Ø5  ORD-ACT-SHIP-DATE.
                   1Ø  ORD-ACT-SHIP-YY          PIC X(2).
                   1Ø  ORD-ACT-SHIP-MM          PIC X(2).
                   1Ø  ORD-ACT-SHIP-DD          PIC X(2).
               Ø5  FILLER                       PIC X(11).

           Ø1  WS-TRANSACTION-RECORD.
               Ø5  TRAN-BRANCH                  PIC X(2).
               Ø5  TRAN-SALES-REP               PIC X(3).
               Ø5  TRAN-CUSTOMER-NBR            PIC X(5).
               Ø5  TRAN-CUST-PO-NBR             PIC X(8).
               Ø5  TRAN-SALES-ORD-NBR           PIC X(6).
               Ø5  TRAN-ORD-DATE.
                   1Ø  TRAN-ORD-YY              PIC X(2).
                   1Ø  TRAN-ORD-MM              PIC X(2).
                   1Ø  TRAN-ORD-DD              PIC X(2).
               Ø5  TRAN-PART-NBR                PIC X(6).
               Ø5  TRAN-QUANTITY                PIC X(5).
               Ø5  TRAN-UNIT-PRICE              PIC X(6).
               Ø5  TRAN-REQ-SHIP-DATE.
                   1Ø  TRAN-REQ-SHIP-YY         PIC X(2).
                   1Ø  TRAN-REQ-SHIP-MM         PIC X(2).
                   1Ø  TRAN-REQ-SHIP-DD         PIC X(2).
```

FIGURE 9-53 cont.

```
           Ø5  TRAN-ACT-SHIP-DATE.
               1Ø  TRAN-ACT-SHIP-YY      PIC X(2).
               1Ø  TRAN-ACT-SHIP-MM      PIC X(2).
               1Ø  TRAN-ACT-SHIP-DD      PIC X(2).
           Ø5  FILLER                    PIC X(11).
           Ø5  TRAN-TYPE                 PIC X(1).
               88  ADD-TRANSACTION                  VALUE 'A'.
               88  CHANGE-TRANSACTION               VALUE 'C'.
               88  DELETE-TRANSACTION               VALUE 'D'.

       Ø1  WS-NEW-ORDER-RECORD.
           Ø5  NEW-ORD-BRANCH                PIC X(2).
           Ø5  NEW-ORD-SALES-REP             PIC X(3).
           Ø5  NEW-ORD-CUSTOMER-NBR          PIC X(5).
           Ø5  NEW-ORD-CUST-PO-NBR           PIC X(8).
           Ø5  NEW-ORD-SALES-ORD-NBR         PIC X(6).
           Ø5  NEW-ORD-DATE.
               1Ø  NEW-ORD-YY                PIC X(2).
               1Ø  NEW-ORD-MM                PIC X(2).
               1Ø  NEW-ORD-DD                PIC X(2).
           Ø5  NEW-ORD-PART-NBR              PIC X(6).
           Ø5  NEW-ORD-QUANTITY              PIC X(5).
           Ø5  NEW-ORD-UNIT-PRICE            PIC X(6).
           Ø5  NEW-ORD-REQ-SHIP-DATE.
               1Ø  NEW-ORD-REQ-SHIP-YY       PIC X(2).
               1Ø  NEW-ORD-REQ-SHIP-MM       PIC X(2).
               1Ø  NEW-ORD-REQ-SHIP-DD       PIC X(2).
           Ø5  NEW-ORD-ACT-SHIP-DATE.
               1Ø  NEW-ORD-ACT-SHIP-YY       PIC X(2).
               1Ø  NEW-ORD-ACT-SHIP-MM       PIC X(2).
               1Ø  NEW-ORD-ACT-SHIP-DD       PIC X(2).
           Ø5  FILLER                        PIC X(11).

       Ø1  WS-SWITCHES.
           Ø5  END-FLAG-ORDER-FILE       PIC X(3)        VALUE 'NO'.
               88  END-OF-ORDER-FILE                     VALUE 'YES'.
           Ø5  END-FLAG-TRAN-FILE        PIC X(3)        VALUE 'NO'.
               88  END-OF-TRAN-FILE                      VALUE 'YES'.
           Ø5  NEW-ORDER-EXISTS-FLAG     PIC X(3).
               88  NEW-ORDER-EXISTS                      VALUE 'YES'.

       Ø1  WS-COUNTERS.
           Ø5  LINE-COUNT                PIC 9(2)        VALUE 99.
           Ø5  PAGE-COUNT                PIC 9(3)        VALUE ZEROS.
           Ø5  NBR-OF-ADDS               PIC 9(5)        VALUE ZEROS.
           Ø5  NBR-OF-ADD-ERRORS         PIC 9(5)        VALUE ZEROS.
           Ø5  NBR-OF-CHANGES            PIC 9(5)        VALUE ZEROS.
           Ø5  NBR-OF-CHANGE-ERRORS      PIC 9(5)        VALUE ZEROS.
           Ø5  NBR-OF-DELETES            PIC 9(5)        VALUE ZEROS.
           Ø5  NBR-OF-DELETE-ERRORS      PIC 9(5)        VALUE ZEROS.
           Ø5  NBR-OF-ORDERS-READ        PIC 9(5)        VALUE ZEROS.
           Ø5  NBR-OF-TRANS-READ         PIC 9(5)        VALUE ZEROS.
           Ø5  NBR-OF-ORDERS-WRITTEN     PIC 9(5)        VALUE ZEROS.

       Ø1  CURRENT-PROCESSING-KEY        PIC X(6).

       Ø1  MAIN-HEADING-1.
           Ø5  FILLER                    PIC X(2)        VALUE SPACES.
           Ø5  FILLER                    PIC X(6)        VALUE 'DATE:'.
           Ø5  MAIN-HDG-DATE             PIC X(8).
           Ø5  FILLER                    PIC X(38)       VALUE SPACES.
           Ø5  FILLER                    PIC X(25)       VALUE
                                         'PRODUCT DISTRIBUTION INC.'.
           Ø5  FILLER                    PIC X(43)       VALUE SPACES.
           Ø5  FILLER                    PIC X(6)        VALUE 'PAGE:'.
           Ø5  MAIN-HDG-PAGE-NBR         PIC ZZ9.
           Ø5  FILLER                    PIC X(2)        VALUE SPACES.

       Ø1  MAIN-HEADING-2.
           Ø5  FILLER                    PIC X(58)       VALUE SPACES.
           Ø5  FILLER                    PIC X(18)       VALUE
                                         'MAINTENANCE REPORT'.
           Ø5  FILLER                    PIC X(57)       VALUE SPACES.

       Ø1  COLUMN-HEADING-1.
           Ø5  FILLER                    PIC X(3)        VALUE SPACES.
           Ø5  FILLER                    PIC X(5)        VALUE 'SALES'.
           Ø5  FILLER                    PIC X(9)        VALUE SPACES.
           Ø5  FILLER                    PIC X(3)        VALUE 'SLS'.
           Ø5  FILLER                    PIC X(11)       VALUE SPACES.
           Ø5  FILLER                    PIC X(8)        VALUE 'CUSTOMER'.
           Ø5  FILLER                    PIC X(3)        VALUE SPACES.
```

FIGURE 9-53 cont.

```
           Ø5  FILLER                   PIC X(5)       VALUE 'ORDER'.
           Ø5  FILLER                   PIC X(5)       VALUE SPACES.
           Ø5  FILLER                   PIC X(4)       VALUE 'PART'.
           Ø5  FILLER                   PIC X(13)      VALUE SPACES.
           Ø5  FILLER                   PIC X(4)       VALUE 'UNIT'.
           Ø5  FILLER                   PIC X(6)       VALUE SPACES.
           Ø5  FILLER                   PIC X(3)       VALUE 'REQ'.
           Ø5  FILLER                   PIC X(5)       VALUE SPACES.
           Ø5  FILLER                   PIC X(6)       VALUE 'ACTUAL'.
           Ø5  FILLER                   PIC X(4Ø)      VALUE SPACES.

       Ø1  COLUMN-HEADING-2.
           Ø5  FILLER                   PIC X(3)       VALUE SPACES.
           Ø5  FILLER                   PIC X(5)       VALUE 'ORDER'.
           Ø5  FILLER                   PIC X(2)       VALUE SPACES.
           Ø5  FILLER                   PIC X(6)       VALUE 'BRANCH'.
           Ø5  FILLER                   PIC X(1)       VALUE SPACES.
           Ø5  FILLER                   PIC X(3)       VALUE 'REP'.
           Ø5  FILLER                   PIC X(3)       VALUE SPACES.
           Ø5  FILLER                   PIC X(5)       VALUE 'CUST#'.
           Ø5  FILLER                   PIC X(5)       VALUE SPACES.
           Ø5  FILLER                   PIC X(3)       VALUE 'PO#'.
           Ø5  FILLER                   PIC X(7)       VALUE SPACES.
           Ø5  FILLER                   PIC X(4)       VALUE 'DATE'.
           Ø5  FILLER                   PIC X(4)       VALUE SPACES.
           Ø5  FILLER                   PIC X(6)       VALUE 'NUMBER'.
           Ø5  FILLER                   PIC X(4)       VALUE SPACES.
           Ø5  FILLER                   PIC X(3)       VALUE 'QTY'.
           Ø5  FILLER                   PIC X(5)       VALUE SPACES.
           Ø5  FILLER                   PIC X(5)       VALUE 'PRICE'.
           Ø5  FILLER                   PIC X(5)       VALUE SPACES.
           Ø5  FILLER                   PIC X(4)       VALUE 'SHIP'.
           Ø5  FILLER                   PIC X(5)       VALUE SPACES.
           Ø5  FILLER                   PIC X(4)       VALUE 'SHIP'.
           Ø5  FILLER                   PIC X(9)       VALUE SPACES.
           Ø5  FILLER                   PIC X(7)       VALUE 'MESSAGE'.
           Ø5  FILLER                   PIC X(25)      VALUE SPACES.

       Ø1  DETAIL-LINE.
           Ø5  FILLER                   PIC X(2)       VALUE SPACES.
           Ø5  DET-SALES-ORD-NBR        PIC XBXXXXX.
           Ø5  FILLER                   PIC X(3)       VALUE SPACES.
           Ø5  DET-BRANCH               PIC X(2).
           Ø5  FILLER                   PIC X(3)       VALUE SPACES.
           Ø5  DET-SALES-REP            PIC X(3).
           Ø5  FILLER                   PIC X(3)       VALUE SPACES.
           Ø5  DET-CUSTOMER-NBR         PIC X(5).
           Ø5  FILLER                   PIC X(3)       VALUE SPACES.
           Ø5  DET-CUST-PO-NBR          PIC X(8).
           Ø5  FILLER                   PIC X(3)       VALUE SPACES.
           Ø5  DET-ORD-DATE             PIC X(6).
           Ø5  FILLER                   PIC X(3)       VALUE SPACES.
           Ø5  DET-PART-NBR             PIC X(6).
           Ø5  FILLER                   PIC X(3)       VALUE SPACES.
           Ø5  DET-QUANTITY             PIC X(5).
           Ø5  FILLER                   PIC X(4)       VALUE SPACES.
           Ø5  DET-UNIT-PRICE           PIC X(6).
           Ø5  FILLER                   PIC X(3)       VALUE SPACES.
           Ø5  DET-REQ-SHIP-DATE        PIC X(6).
           Ø5  FILLER                   PIC X(3)       VALUE SPACES.
           Ø5  DET-ACT-SHIP-DATE        PIC X(6).
           Ø5  FILLER                   PIC X(3)       VALUE SPACES.
           Ø5  DET-MESSAGE              PIC X(36).
           Ø5  FILLER                   PIC X(2)       VALUE SPACES.

       Ø1  ASTERISK-LINE.
           Ø5  FILLER                   PIC X(12)      VALUE SPACES.
           Ø5  AST-BRANCH               PIC X(2)       VALUE SPACES.
           Ø5  FILLER                   PIC X(3)       VALUE SPACES.
           Ø5  AST-SALES-REP            PIC X(3)       VALUE SPACES.
           Ø5  FILLER                   PIC X(3)       VALUE SPACES.
           Ø5  AST-CUSTOMER-NBR         PIC X(5)       VALUE SPACES.
           Ø5  FILLER                   PIC X(3)       VALUE SPACES.
           Ø5  AST-CUST-PO-NBR          PIC X(8)       VALUE SPACES.
           Ø5  FILLER                   PIC X(3)       VALUE SPACES.
           Ø5  AST-ORD-DATE             PIC X(6)       VALUE SPACES.
           Ø5  FILLER                   PIC X(3)       VALUE SPACES.
           Ø5  AST-PART-NBR             PIC X(6)       VALUE SPACES.
           Ø5  FILLER                   PIC X(3)       VALUE SPACES.
           Ø5  AST-QUANTITY             PIC X(5)       VALUE SPACES.
           Ø5  FILLER                   PIC X(3)       VALUE SPACES.
           Ø5  AST-UNIT-PRICE           PIC X(7)       VALUE SPACES.
```

FIGURE 9-53 cont.

```
    Ø5  FILLER                   PIC X(3)         VALUE SPACES.
    Ø5  AST-REQ-SHIP-DATE        PIC X(6)         VALUE SPACES.
    Ø5  FILLER                   PIC X(3)         VALUE SPACES.
    Ø5  AST-ACT-SHIP-DATE        PIC X(6)         VALUE SPACES.
    Ø5  FILLER                   PIC X(41)        VALUE SPACES.

PROCEDURE DIVISION.

    PERFORM 1ØØØ-INITIALIZATION.
    PERFORM 2ØØØ-PROCESS
        UNTIL END-OF-ORDER-FILE AND END-OF-TRAN-FILE.
    PERFORM 3ØØØ-EOJ.
    STOP RUN.

1ØØØ-INITIALIZATION.
    OPEN INPUT  ORDER-FILE
                TRANSACTION-FILE
         OUTPUT NEW-ORDER-FILE
                PRINT-FILE.
    MOVE CURRENT-DATE TO MAIN-HDG-DATE.
    PERFORM 91ØØ-READ-ORDER-FILE.
    PERFORM 92ØØ-READ-TRAN-FILE.
    PERFORM 93ØØ-SELECT-CURRENT-KEY.

2ØØØ-PROCESS.
    PERFORM 21ØØ-CHECK-ORDER-RECORD.
    PERFORM 22ØØ-APPLY-TRANSACTION
        UNTIL TRAN-SALES-ORD-NBR NOT = CURRENT-PROCESSING-KEY
    PERFORM 23ØØ-CHECK-FOR-WRITE.
    PERFORM 93ØØ-SELECT-CURRENT-KEY.

21ØØ-CHECK-ORDER-RECORD.
     IF ORD-SALES-ORD-NBR = CURRENT-PROCESSING-KEY
         MOVE WS-ORDER-RECORD TO WS-NEW-ORDER-RECORD
         MOVE 'YES' TO NEW-ORDER-EXISTS-FLAG
         PERFORM 91ØØ-READ-ORDER-FILE
     ELSE
         MOVE 'NO' TO NEW-ORDER-EXISTS-FLAG.

22ØØ-APPLY-TRANSACTION.
    IF ADD-TRANSACTION
        PERFORM 221Ø-ADD
    ELSE
        IF CHANGE-TRANSACTION
            PERFORM 222Ø-CHANGE
        ELSE
            IF DELETE-TRANSACTION
                PERFORM 223Ø-DELETE.
    PERFORM 92ØØ-READ-TRAN-FILE.

221Ø-ADD.
    IF NEW-ORDER-EXISTS
        PERFORM 2211-ADD-REJECTED
    ELSE
        PERFORM 2212-PROCESS-ADD.

2211-ADD-REJECTED.
    ADD 1 TO NBR-OF-ADD-ERRORS.
    MOVE 'ADD ERROR - RECORD ALREADY EXISTS' TO DET-MESSAGE.
    PERFORM 95ØØ-WRITE-DETAIL-FROM-TRAN.

2212-PROCESS-ADD.
    MOVE WS-TRANSACTION-RECORD TO WS-NEW-ORDER-RECORD.
    MOVE 'YES' TO NEW-ORDER-EXISTS-FLAG.
    MOVE 'ADDED' TO DET-MESSAGE.
    PERFORM 94ØØ-WRITE-DETAIL-FROM-NEW-ORD.
    ADD 1 TO NBR-OF-ADDS.

222Ø-CHANGE.
    IF NEW-ORDER-EXISTS
        IF NEW-ORD-ACT-SHIP-DATE = ZEROS
            PERFORM 2221-PROCESS-CHANGES
        ELSE
            ADD 1 TO NBR-OF-CHANGE-ERRORS
            MOVE 'CHANGE ERROR - ORDER IS SHIPPED' TO DET-MESSAGE
            PERFORM 95ØØ-WRITE-DETAIL-FROM-TRAN
    ELSE
        PERFORM 2222-CHANGE-REJECTED.

2221-PROCESS-CHANGES.

    ADD 1 TO NBR-OF-CHANGES.
```

FIGURE 9-53 cont.

```
           MOVE 'BEFORE CHANGES' TO DET-MESSAGE.
           PERFORM 9400-WRITE-DETAIL-FROM-NEW-ORD.

           IF TRAN-BRANCH NOT = SPACES
               MOVE TRAN-BRANCH TO NEW-ORD-BRANCH
               MOVE ALL '*' TO AST-BRANCH.

           IF TRAN-SALES-REP NOT = SPACES
               MOVE TRAN-SALES-REP TO NEW-ORD-SALES-REP
               MOVE ALL '*' TO AST-SALES-REP.

           IF TRAN-CUSTOMER-NBR NOT = SPACES
               MOVE TRAN-CUSTOMER-NBR TO NEW-ORD-CUSTOMER-NBR
               MOVE ALL '*' TO AST-CUSTOMER-NBR.

           IF TRAN-CUST-PO-NBR NOT = SPACES
               MOVE TRAN-CUST-PO-NBR TO NEW-ORD-CUST-PO-NBR
               MOVE ALL '*' TO AST-CUST-PO-NBR.

           IF TRAN-ORD-DATE NOT = SPACES
               MOVE TRAN-ORD-DATE TO NEW-ORD-DATE
               MOVE ALL '*' TO AST-ORD-DATE.

           IF TRAN-PART-NBR NOT = SPACES
               MOVE TRAN-PART-NBR TO NEW-ORD-PART-NBR
               MOVE ALL '*' TO AST-PART-NBR.

           IF TRAN-QUANTITY NOT = SPACES
               MOVE TRAN-QUANTITY TO NEW-ORD-QUANTITY
               MOVE ALL '*' TO AST-QUANTITY.

           IF TRAN-UNIT-PRICE NOT = SPACES
               MOVE TRAN-UNIT-PRICE TO NEW-ORD-UNIT-PRICE
               MOVE ALL '*' TO AST-UNIT-PRICE.

           IF TRAN-REQ-SHIP-DATE NOT = SPACES
               MOVE TRAN-REQ-SHIP-DATE TO NEW-ORD-REQ-SHIP-DATE
               MOVE ALL '*' TO AST-REQ-SHIP-DATE.

           IF TRAN-ACT-SHIP-DATE NOT = SPACES
               MOVE TRAN-ACT-SHIP-DATE TO NEW-ORD-ACT-SHIP-DATE
               MOVE ALL '*' TO AST-ACT-SHIP-DATE.

           MOVE 'AFTER CHANGES' TO DET-MESSAGE.
           PERFORM 9400-WRITE-DETAIL-FROM-NEW-ORD.
           WRITE PRINT-RECORD FROM ASTERISK-LINE
               AFTER ADVANCING 1 LINE.
           ADD 1 TO LINE-COUNT.
           MOVE SPACES TO ASTERISK-LINE.

       2222-CHANGE-REJECTED.
           ADD 1 TO NBR-OF-CHANGE-ERRORS.
           MOVE 'CHANGE ERROR - RECORD DOES NOT EXIST' TO DET-MESSAGE.
           PERFORM 9500-WRITE-DETAIL-FROM-TRAN.

       2230-DELETE.
           IF NEW-ORDER-EXISTS
               PERFORM 2231-PROCESS-DELETE
           ELSE
               PERFORM 2232-DELETE-REJECTED.

       2231-PROCESS-DELETE.
           MOVE 'NO' TO NEW-ORDER-EXISTS-FLAG.
           ADD 1 TO NBR-OF-DELETES.
           MOVE 'DELETED' TO DET-MESSAGE.
           PERFORM 9400-WRITE-DETAIL-FROM-NEW-ORD.

       2232-DELETE-REJECTED.
           ADD 1 TO NBR-OF-DELETE-ERRORS.
           MOVE 'DELETE ERROR - RECORD DOES NOT EXIST' TO DET-MESSAGE.
           PERFORM 9500-WRITE-DETAIL-FROM-TRAN.

       2300-CHECK-FOR-WRITE.
           IF NEW-ORDER-EXISTS
               WRITE NEW-ORDER-RECORD FROM WS-NEW-ORDER-RECORD
               ADD 1 TO NBR-OF-ORDERS-WRITTEN.

       3000-EOJ.
           WRITE PRINT-RECORD FROM ASTERISK-LINE AFTER ADVANCING PAGE.
           DISPLAY 'NBR-OF-ADDS              ' NBR-OF-ADDS.
           DISPLAY 'NBR-OF-ADD-ERRORS        ' NBR-OF-ADD-ERRORS.
           DISPLAY 'NBR-OF-CHANGES           ' NBR-OF-CHANGES.
```

FIGURE 9-53 cont.

```
    DISPLAY 'NBR-OF-CHANGE-ERRORS   ' NBR-OF-CHANGE-ERRORS.
    DISPLAY 'NBR-OF-DELETES         ' NBR-OF-DELETES.
    DISPLAY 'NBR-OF-DELETE-ERRORS   ' NBR-OF-DELETE-ERRORS.
    DISPLAY 'NBR-OF-ORDERS-READ     ' NBR-OF-ORDERS-READ.
    DISPLAY 'NBR-OF-TRANS-READ      ' NBR-OF-TRANS-READ.
    DISPLAY 'NBR-OF-ORDERS-WRITTEN  ' NBR-OF-ORDERS-WRITTEN.
    CLOSE ORDER-FILE
          TRANSACTION-FILE
          NEW-ORDER-FILE
          PRINT-FILE.

9100-READ-ORDER-FILE.

    IF END-OF-ORDER-FILE
        NEXT SENTENCE
    ELSE
        READ ORDER-FILE INTO WS-ORDER-RECORD
            AT END
                MOVE 'YES'       TO END-FLAG-ORDER-FILE
                MOVE HIGH-VALUES TO ORD-SALES-ORD-NBR.

    IF NOT END-OF-ORDER-FILE
        ADD 1 TO NBR-OF-ORDERS-READ.

9200-READ-TRAN-FILE.

    IF END-OF-TRAN-FILE
        NEXT SENTENCE
    ELSE
        READ TRANSACTION-FILE INTO WS-TRANSACTION-RECORD
            AT END
                MOVE 'YES'       TO END-FLAG-TRAN-FILE
                MOVE HIGH-VALUES TO TRAN-SALES-ORD-NBR.

    IF NOT END-OF-TRAN-FILE
        ADD 1 TO NBR-OF-TRANS-READ.

9300-SELECT-CURRENT-KEY.
    IF ORD-SALES-ORD-NBR < TRAN-SALES-ORD-NBR
        MOVE ORD-SALES-ORD-NBR TO CURRENT-PROCESSING-KEY
    ELSE
        MOVE TRAN-SALES-ORD-NBR TO CURRENT-PROCESSING-KEY.

9400-WRITE-DETAIL-FROM-NEW-ORD.
    MOVE NEW-ORD-SALES-ORD-NBR     TO DET-SALES-ORD-NBR.
    MOVE NEW-ORD-BRANCH            TO DET-BRANCH.
    MOVE NEW-ORD-SALES-REP         TO DET-SALES-REP.
    MOVE NEW-ORD-CUSTOMER-NBR      TO DET-CUSTOMER-NBR.
    MOVE NEW-ORD-CUST-PO-NBR       TO DET-CUST-PO-NBR.
    MOVE NEW-ORD-DATE              TO DET-ORD-DATE.
    MOVE NEW-ORD-PART-NBR          TO DET-PART-NBR.
    MOVE NEW-ORD-QUANTITY          TO DET-QUANTITY.
    MOVE NEW-ORD-UNIT-PRICE        TO DET-UNIT-PRICE.
    MOVE NEW-ORD-REQ-SHIP-DATE     TO DET-REQ-SHIP-DATE.
    MOVE NEW-ORD-ACT-SHIP-DATE     TO DET-ACT-SHIP-DATE.
    IF LINE-COUNT > 50
        PERFORM 9700-HEADINGS.
    WRITE PRINT-RECORD FROM DETAIL-LINE
        AFTER ADVANCING 2 LINES.
    ADD 2 TO LINE-COUNT.

9500-WRITE-DETAIL-FROM-TRAN.
    MOVE TRAN-SALES-ORD-NBR        TO DET-SALES-ORD-NBR.
    MOVE TRAN-BRANCH               TO DET-BRANCH.
    MOVE TRAN-SALES-REP            TO DET-SALES-REP.
    MOVE TRAN-CUSTOMER-NBR         TO DET-CUSTOMER-NBR.
    MOVE TRAN-CUST-PO-NBR          TO DET-CUST-PO-NBR.
    MOVE TRAN-ORD-DATE             TO DET-ORD-DATE.
    MOVE TRAN-PART-NBR             TO DET-PART-NBR.
    MOVE TRAN-QUANTITY             TO DET-QUANTITY.
    MOVE TRAN-UNIT-PRICE           TO DET-UNIT-PRICE.
    MOVE TRAN-REQ-SHIP-DATE        TO DET-REQ-SHIP-DATE.
    MOVE TRAN-ACT-SHIP-DATE        TO DET-ACT-SHIP-DATE.
    IF LINE-COUNT > 50
        PERFORM 9700-HEADINGS.
    WRITE PRINT-RECORD FROM DETAIL-LINE
        AFTER ADVANCING 2 LINES.
    ADD 2 TO LINE-COUNT.

9700-HEADINGS.
    ADD 1 TO PAGE-COUNT.
    MOVE PAGE-COUNT TO MAIN-HDG-PAGE-NBR.
```

FIGURE 9-53 cont.

```
            WRITE PRINT-RECORD FROM MAIN-HEADING-1
                AFTER ADVANCING PAGE.
            WRITE PRINT-RECORD FROM MAIN-HEADING-2
                AFTER ADVANCING 1 LINE.
            WRITE PRINT-RECORD FROM COLUMN-HEADING-1
                AFTER ADVANCING 2 LINES.
            WRITE PRINT-RECORD FROM COLUMN-HEADING-2
                AFTER ADVANCING 1 LINE.
            MOVE 5 TO LINE-COUNT.
```

FIGURE 9-53 cont.

SUMMARY

No new COBOL elements have been introduced in this chapter.

EXERCISES

I. Indicate whether each of the following is a valid situation (V) or an invalid situation (I) when encountered in a sequential-file maintenance program.

______ **1.** An ADD transaction with no matching master
______ **2.** A DELETE transaction with no matching master
______ **3.** A CHANGE transaction with no matching master
______ **4.** An ADD transaction with a matching master
______ **5.** A CHANGE transaction with a matching master
______ **6.** A DELETE transaction with a matching master
______ **7.** A master with no matching transaction

II. Choose the appropriate action for each comparison. Assume that file matching has been handled properly up to the point of the comparison for each question.

a. Addition
b. Change
c. Deletion
d. Addition rejected
e. Change rejected
f. Deletion rejected
g. Copy (old master to new master)

		MASTER	TRANSACTION	
______	**1.**	100	100	CHANGE
______	**2.**	500	501	ADD
______	**3.**	300	295	DELETE
______	**4.**	188	200	CHANGE
______	**5.**	200	180	CHANGE
______	**6.**	300	200	ADD
______	**7.**	400	400	ADD
______	**8.**	200	200	DELETE

III. Given the following records for the master and transaction files, list the comparisons that will be made in the order that they will be made and indicate the appropriate action. For example, the first comparison is 420–420 and it is a rejected addition.

MASTER FILE	TRANSACTION FILE	
420	420	ADD
430	430	CHANGE
450	440	DELETE
/*	/*	

PROJECTS

For each of the following specifications and input record layouts, design a print chart and code a COBOL program that satisfies the specification.

PROJECT 9–1 Payroll

PROGRAM SPECIFICATION

Program Name: PAY9

Program Function:

This program will update a PAYROLL-FILE using the hours worked from a TRANSACTION-FILE. The updated version of the file is written to NEW-PAYROLL-FILE. A report is produced listing all records written to the new file and a total of hours worked.

Input Files:

I. PAYROLL-FILE

```
INPUT DEVICE:          DISK
FILE ORGANIZATION:     SEQUENTIAL
RECORD LENGTH:         80 BYTES
FILE SEQUENCE:         ASCENDING ON DIVISION /
                                 DEPARTMENT /
                                 SOCIAL SECURITY NBR
```

II. TRANSACTION-FILE

```
INPUT DEVICE:          DISK
FILE ORGANIZATION:     SEQUENTIAL
RECORD LENGTH:         16 BYTES
FILE SEQUENCE:         ASCENDING ON DIVISION /
                                 DEPARTMENT /
                                 SOCIAL SECURITY NBR
```

Output Files:

I. NEW-PAYROLL-FILE

```
OUTPUT DEVICE:         DISK
FILE ORGANIZATION:     SEQUENTIAL
RECORD LENGTH:         80 BYTES
FILE SEQUENCE:         ASCENDING ON DIVISION /
                                 DEPARTMENT /
                                 SOCIAL SECURITY NBR
```

II. PRINT-FILE

```
OUTPUT DEVICE:         PRINTER
RECORD LENGTH:         133 BYTES
```

Processing Requirements:

The program will read the PAYROLL-FILE and the TRANSACTION-FILE and create a new version of the PAYROLL-FILE (NEW-PAYROLL-FILE). The key field is a composite of division, department, and social security number. The TRANSACTION-FILE will contain the key field and hours worked.

For records from the TRANSACTION-FILE, the matching record from the PAYROLL-FILE is to be updated with the hours worked shown on the TRANSACTION-RECORD. Then the record is to be written to the NEW-PAYROLL-FILE.

If there is no TRANSACTION-RECORD for a PAYROLL-RECORD, zeros should be moved to hours worked in the PAYROLL-RECORD and the record should be written to the NEW-PAYROLL-FILE.

A detail line should be printed for all PAYROLL-RECORDS, and a company total for hours worked should be calculated and printed. If there is no matching PAYROLL-RECORD for a TRANSACTION-RECORD, a detail line which uses the data from the TRANSACTION-RECORD should be printed with an appropriate error message.

Output Requirements:

The NEW-PAYROLL-FILE should contain every record from the PAYROLL-FILE.

The following are formatting requirements for the report:

1. Each page of the report should contain:
   (a) a main heading which includes the company name, the report name, the report date, and a page number.
   (b) column headings which describe the items printed underneath them.
2. Detail lines should include the division, department, social security number, and hours worked.
3. Detail lines should be double spaced.
4. The total for hours worked should be double spaced.
5. A message should be printed for any transactions without a master.

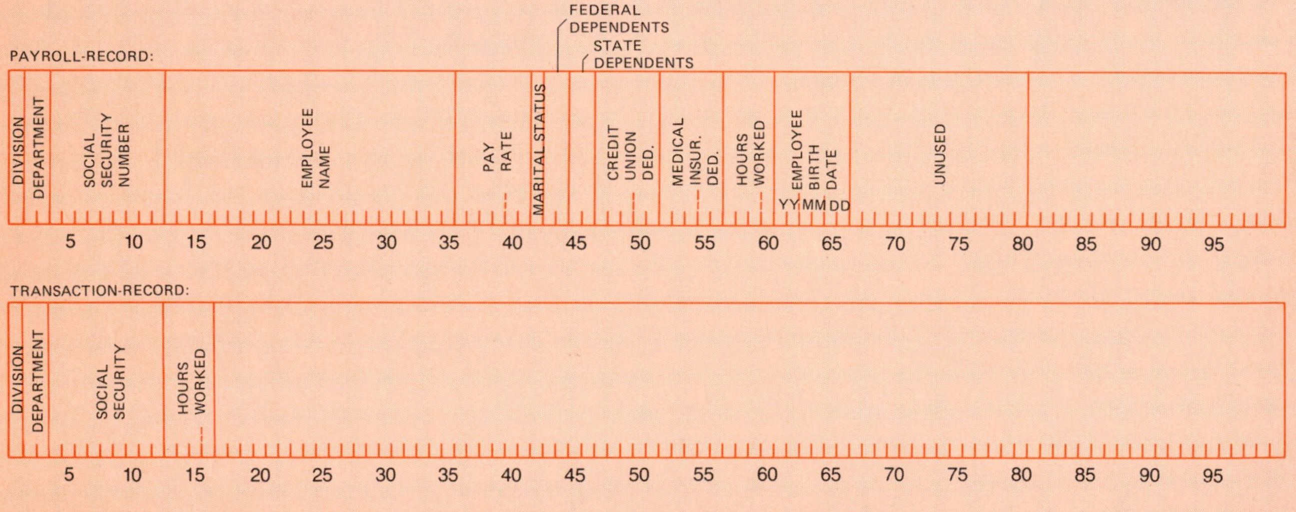

PROGRAM SPECIFICATION

Program Name: INV9

Program Function:

This program will update an INVENTORY-FILE using the quantity on hand and quantity on order from a TRANSACTION-FILE. The updated version of the file is written to NEW-INVENTORY-FILE. A report is to be produced listing only changes and erroneous records.

Input Files:

I. INVENTORY-FILE

INPUT DEVICE:	DISK
FILE ORGANIZATION:	SEQUENTIAL
RECORD LENGTH:	80 BYTES
FILE SEQUENCE:	ASCENDING ON INVENTORY STOCK NUMBER

II. TRANSACTION-FILE

INPUT DEVICE:	DISK
FILE ORGANIZATION:	SEQUENTIAL
RECORD LENGTH:	15 BYTES
FILE SEQUENCE:	ASCENDING ON INVENTORY STOCK NUMBER

Output Files:

I. NEW-INVENTORY-FILE

OUTPUT DEVICE:	DISK
FILE ORGANIZATION:	SEQUENTIAL
RECORD LENGTH:	80 BYTES
FILE SEQUENCE:	ASCENDING ON INVENTORY STOCK NUMBER

II. PRINT-FILE

OUTPUT DEVICE:	PRINTER
RECORD LENGTH:	133 BYTES

Processing Requirements:

The program will read the INVENTORY-FILE and the TRANSACTION-FILE and create a new version of the INVENTORY-FILE (NEW-INVENTORY-FILE). The key field is the stock number. The TRANSACTION-FILE will contain the key field, quantity on hand, and quantity on order. The quantity fields are signed in both records.

For records from the TRANSACTION-FILE, the matching record in the INVENTORY-FILE is to be updated by *adding* the quantity on hand and quantity on order from the TRANSACTION-RECORD to the quantity on hand and quantity on order in the INVENTORY-RECORD. The INVENTORY-RECORD should then be written to NEW-INVENTORY-FILE. A detail line should be prepared and written using the new quantities.

If there is no matching TRANSACTION-RECORD for an INVENTORY-RECORD, the unchanged INVENTORY-RECORD should be written to the NEW-INVENTORY-FILE.

If a TRANSACTION-RECORD has no matching record from the INVENTORY-FILE, a detail line containing data from the transaction record and an error message should be prepared and written.

A total for quantity on hand and quantity on order should be kept for *all* INVENTORY-RECORDS written to the new file (using the new quantities for the updated records).

Output Requirements:

All records from the INVENTORY-FILE should appear on the NEW-INVENTORY-FILE.

The following are formatting requirements for the report:

1. Each page of the report should contain:
   (a) a main heading which includes the company name, the report name, the report date, and a page number.
   (b) column headings which describe the items printed underneath them.
2. Detail lines should include the stock number, quantity on hand, and quantity on order.
3. Detail lines should be double spaced.
4. The total line for quantity on hand and quantity on order should be double spaced.
5. A message should be printed for any transaction without a matching master.

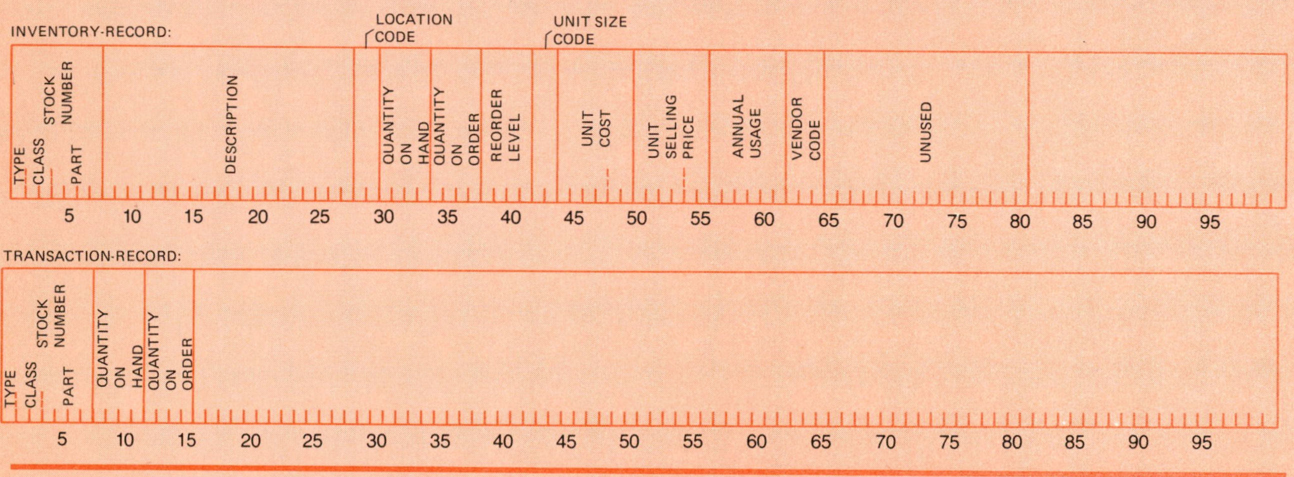

PROJECT 9–3 Accounts Payable

PROGRAM SPECIFICATION

Program Name: AP9

Program Function:

This program will perform sequential-file maintenance on an ACCOUNTS-PAYABLE-FILE using a TRANSACTION-FILE. The TRANSACTION-FILE has ADD, CHANGE, and DELETE records which represent new invoices, field changes, and paid invoices, respectively. A listing will be produced showing all additions, changes, and deletions, as well as errors.

Input Files:

I. ACCOUNTS-PAYABLE-FILE

INPUT DEVICE:	DISK
FILE ORGANIZATION:	SEQUENTIAL
RECORD LENGTH:	80 BYTES
FILE SEQUENCE:	ASCENDING ON DIVISION / CONTROL NBR

II. TRANSACTION-FILE

INPUT DEVICE:	DISK
FILE ORGANIZATION:	SEQUENTIAL
RECORD LENGTH:	81 BYTES
FILE SEQUENCE:	ASCENDING ON DIVISION / CONTROL NBR

Output Files:

I. NEW-ACCOUNTS-PAYABLE-FILE

OUTPUT DEVICE:	DISK
FILE ORGANIZATION:	SEQUENTIAL
RECORD LENGTH:	80 BYTES
FILE SEQUENCE:	ASCENDING ON DIVISION / CONTROL NBR

II. PRINT-FILE

OUTPUT DEVICE:	PRINTER
RECORD LENGTH:	133 BYTES

Processing Requirements:

The program will read the ACCOUNTS-PAYABLE-FILE and the TRANSACTION-FILE and perform file maintenance to create a new version of the ACCOUNTS-PAYABLE-FILE (NEW-ACCOUNTS-PAYABLE-FILE). The key field is a composite of the division and control number. The TRANSACTION-FILE has the same fields as the ACCOUNTS-PAYABLE-FILE, plus a TRAN-TYPE field used to indicate whether the transaction is an addition, change, or deletion.

If there is no matching TRANSACTION-RECORD for an ACCOUNTS-PAYABLE-RECORD, the unchanged ACCOUNTS-PAYABLE-RECORD should be written to the NEW-ACCOUNTS-PAYABLE-FILE.

If a record from the TRANSACTION-FILE has a matching record on the ACCOUNTS-PAYABLE FILE, the transaction must be either a change or a deletion. Changes are made to the ACCOUNTS-PAYABLE-FILE based on the presence or absence (spaces) of data in the transaction record. After changes are made, the record is written to the NEW-ACCOUNTS-PAYABLE-FILE. Two detail lines are printed, one before and one after the changes. A record to be deleted is not written to the NEW-ACCOUNTS-PAYABLE-FILE; however, a detail line is printed. Any TRANSACTION-RECORD with a matching ACCOUNTS-PAYABLE-RECORD that is not a change or a deletion is in error, and a detail line should be printed to indicate this.

If a TRANSACTION-RECORD has no matching record in the ACCOUNTS-PAYABLE-FILE, the transaction should be an addition and the TRANSACTION-RECORD should be written to the NEW-ACCOUNTS-PAYABLE-FILE. A detail line should then be printed with an appropriate error message.

Counts should be kept of the number of ACCOUNTS-PAYABLE-RECORDS read, TRANSACTION-RECORDS read, additions, changes, deletions, addition errors,change errors, deletion errors, and records written to the NEW-ACCOUNTS-PAYABLE-FILE. The counts should be printed at the end of the update listing.

Output Requirements:

The NEW-ACCOUNTS-PAYABLE-FILE should reflect all file maintenance transactions.

The following are formatting requirements for the report:

1. Each page of the report should contain:
   (a) a main heading which includes the company name, the report name, the report date, and a page number.
   (b) column headings which describe the items printed underneath them.
2. Detail lines should include all fields from the input.
3. Detail lines should be double spaced.
4. Each detail line should have a message indicating its type.
5. Changed fields should be highlighted with an asterisk underline.
6. Counts displayed should be single spaced.

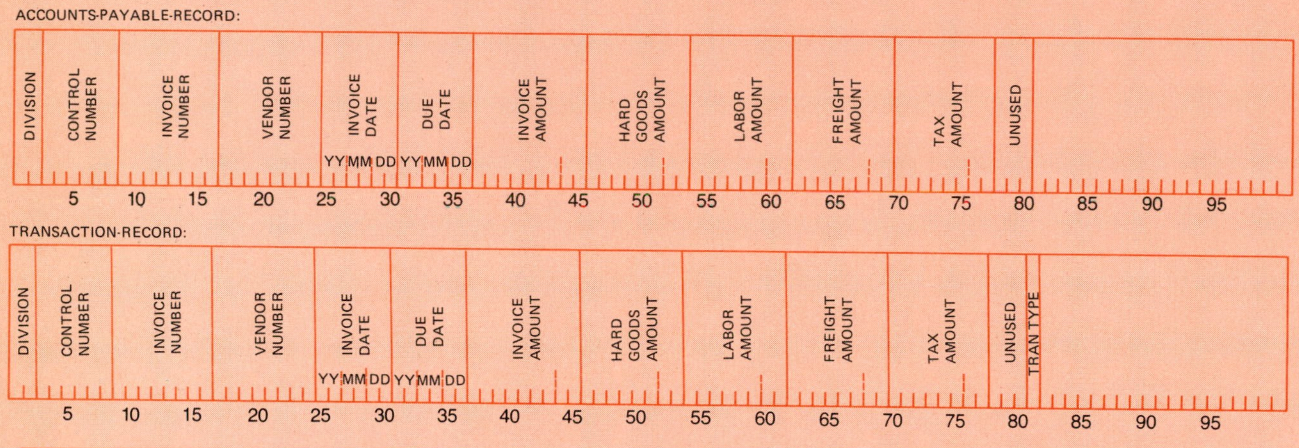

PROJECT 9–4 Pension

PROGRAM SPECIFICATION

Program Name: PEN9

Program Function:

This program will perform sequential-file maintenance on a PENSION-FILE using a TRANSACTION-FILE. The TRANSACTION-FILE has ADD, CHANGE, and DELETE records which represent new employees, field changes, and terminated employees, respectively. A listing will be produced showing all additions, changes, deletions, and errors.

Input Files:

I. PENSION-FILE

INPUT DEVICE:	DISK
FILE ORGANIZATION:	SEQUENTIAL
RECORD LENGTH:	80 BYTES

FILE SEQUENCE: ASCENDING ON DIVISION /
DEPARTMENT /
SOCIAL SECURITY NUMBER

II. TRANSACTION-FILE

INPUT DEVICE: DISK
FILE ORGANIZATION: SEQUENTIAL
RECORD LENGTH: 81 BYTES
FILE SEQUENCE: ASCENDING ON DIVISION /
DEPARTMENT /
SOCIAL SECURITY NUMBER

Output Files:

I. NEW-PENSION-FILE

OUTPUT DEVICE: DISK
FILE ORGANIZATION: SEQUENTIAL
RECORD LENGTH: 80 BYTES
FILE SEQUENCE: ASCENDING ON DIVISION /
DEPARTMENT /
SOCIAL SECURITY NUMBER

II. PRINT-FILE

OUTPUT DEVICE: PRINTER
RECORD LENGTH: 133 BYTES

Processing Requirements:

The program will read the PENSION-FILE and the TRANSACTION-FILE and create a new version of the PENSION-FILE (NEW-PENSION-FILE). The key field is a composite of the division, department, and social security number. The TRANSACTION-FILE has the same fields as the PENSION-FILE, plus a TRANS-TYPE field used to indicate whether the transaction is an addition (A), change (C), or deletion (D).

If there is no matching TRANSACTION-RECORD for a PENSION-RECORD, the unchanged PENSION-RECORD should be written to the NEW-PENSION-FILE.

If a record from the TRANSACTION-FILE has a matching record on the PENSION-FILE, the transaction record must be either a change or a deletion. Changes are made to the PENSION-FILE based on the presence or absence (spaces) of data in the transaction record. After changes are made, the record is written to the NEW-PENSION-FILE. Two detail lines are printed, one before and one after the changes. A record to be deleted is not written to the NEW-PENSION-FILE; however, a detail line is printed. Any record with a matching record on the PENSION-FILE that is not a change or a deletion is in error, and a detail line should be printed to indicate this.

If a TRANSACTION-RECORD has no matching record in the PENSION-FILE, the transaction should be an addition and the TRANSACTION-RECORD should be written to the NEW-PENSION-FILE. A detail line should then be printed indicating an addition to the file. If the transaction is not an addition, a detail line should be printed with an appropriate error message.

Counts should be kept of the number of PENSION-RECORDS read, TRANSACTION-RECORDS read, additions, changes, deletions, addition errors, change errors, deletion errors, and records written to NEW-PENSION-FILE. The counts should be printed at the end of the update listing.

Output Requirements:

The NEW-PENSION-FILE should reflect all file maintenance transactions.

The following are formatting requirements for the report:

1. Each page of the report should contain:
   (a) a main heading which includes the company name, the report name, the report date, and a page number.
   (b) column headings which describe the items printed underneath them.
2. Detail lines should include all fields from the appropriate input file.
3. Detail lines should be double spaced.
4. Detail lines should include a message indicating the action taken.
5. Changed fields should be highlighted with an asterisk underline.
6. Counts displayed should be single spaced.

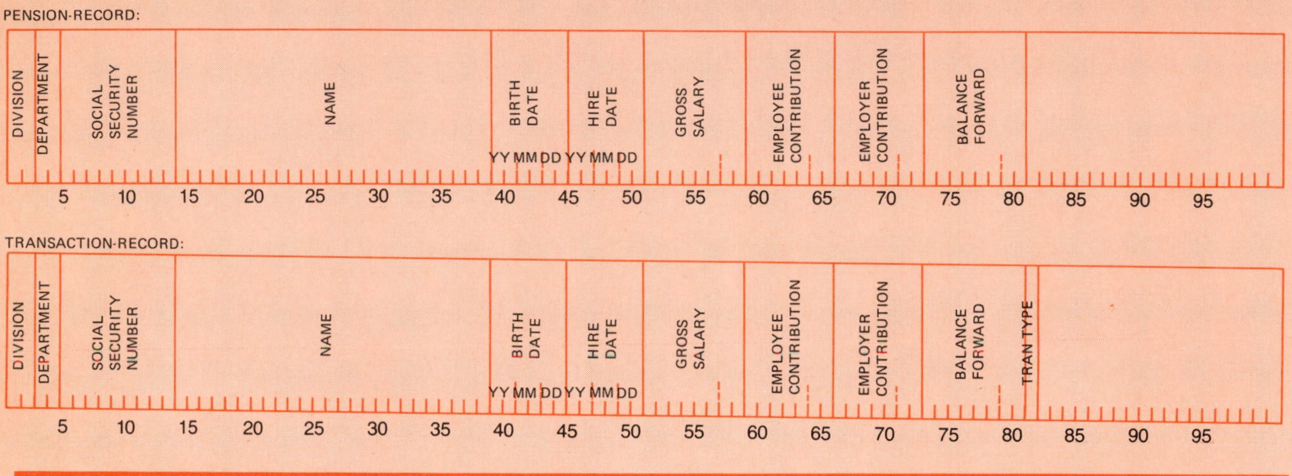

PROJECT 9–5 Bill of Materials

PROGRAM SPECIFICATION

Program Name: BOM9

Program Function:

This program will perform sequential-file maintenance on a BILL-OF-MATERIALS-FILE using a TRANSACTION-FILE. The TRANSACTION-FILE has ADD, CHANGE, and DELETE records which represent new parts, field changes, and discontinued parts, respectively. A listing will be produced showing all additions, changes, deletions, and errors.

Input Files:

I. BILL-OF-MATERIALS-FILE

INPUT DEVICE:	DISK
FILE ORGANIZATION:	SEQUENTIAL
RECORD LENGTH:	55 BYTES
FILE SEQUENCE:	ASCENDING ON MASTER PART NUMBER

II. TRANSACTION-FILE

INPUT DEVICE:	DISK
FILE ORGANIZATION:	SEQUENTIAL
RECORD LENGTH:	56 BYTES

FILE SEQUENCE:	ASCENDING ON MASTER PART NUMBER

Output Files:

I. NEW-BILL-OF-MATERIALS-FILE

OUTPUT DEVICE:	DISK
FILE ORGANIZATION:	SEQUENTIAL
RECORD LENGTH:	55 BYTES
FILE SEQUENCE:	ASCENDING ON MASTER PART NUMBER

II. PRINT-FILE

OUTPUT DEVICE:	PRINTER
RECORD LENGTH:	133 BYTES

Processing Requirements:

The program will read the BILL-OF-MATERIALS-FILE and the TRANSACTION-FILE and create a new version of the BILL-OF-MATERIALS-FILE (NEW-BILL-OF-MATERIALS-FILE). The key field is the master part number. The TRANSACTION-FILE has the same fields as the BILL-OF-MATERIALS-FILE, plus a TRANS-TYPE field used to indicate whether the transaction is an addition (A), change (C), or deletion (D).

If there is no matching TRANSACTION-RECORD for a BILL-OF-MATERIALS-RECORD, the unchanged BILL-OF-MATERIALS-RECORD should be written to the NEW-BILL-OF-MATERIALS-FILE.

If a record from the TRANSACTION-FILE has a matching record on the BILL-OF-MATERIALS-FILE, the transaction record must be either a change or a deletion. Changes are made to the BILL-OF-MATERIALS-FILE based on the presence or absence (spaces) of data in the transaction record. After changes are made, the record is written to the NEW-BILL-OF-MATERIALS-FILE. Two detail lines are printed, one before and one after the changes. A record to be deleted is not written to the NEW-BILL-OF-MATERIALS-FILE; however, a detail line is printed. Any record with a matching record on the BILL-OF-MATERIALS-FILE that is not a change or a deletion is in error, and a detail line should be printed to indicate this.

If a TRANSACTION-RECORD has no matching record in the BILL-OF-MATERIALS-FILE, the transaction should be an addition and the TRANSACTION-RECORD should be written to the NEW-BILL-OF-MATERIALS-FILE. A detail line should then be printed indicating an addition to the file. If the transaction is not an addition, a detail line should be printed with an appropriate error message.

Counts should be kept of the number of BILL-OF-MATERIALS-RECORDS read, TRANSACTION-RECORDS read, additions, changes, deletions, addition errors, change errors, deletion errors, and records written to NEW-BILL-OF-MATERIALS-FILE. The counts should be printed at the end of the update listing.

Output Requirements:

The NEW-BILL-OF-MATERIALS-FILE should reflect all file maintenance transactions.

The following are formatting requirements for the report:

1. Each page of the report should contain:
   (a) a main heading which includes the company name, the report name, the report date, and a page number.
   (b) column headings which describe the items printed underneath them.
2. Detail lines should include all fields from the input.
3. Detail lines should be double spaced.

4. Detail lines should include a message indicating the action taken.
5. Changed fields should be highlighted with an asterisk underline.
6. Counts displayed should be single spaced.

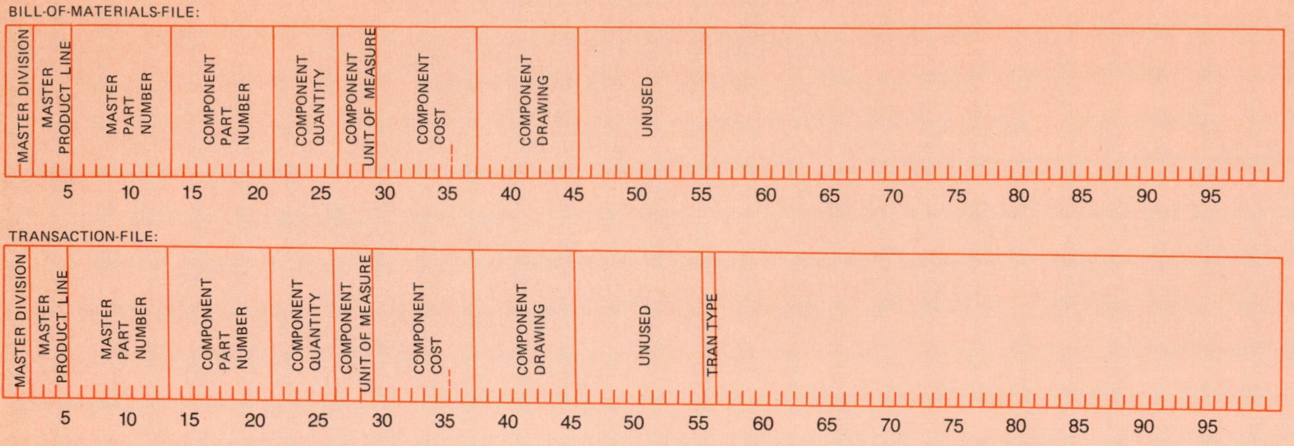

PROJECT 9–6 Cost

PROGRAM SPECIFICATION

Program Name: COST9

Program Function:

This program will perform sequential-file maintenance on a COST-FILE using a TRANSACTION-FILE. The TRANSACTION-FILE has ADD, CHANGE, and DELETE records which represent new parts, field changes, and discontinued parts, respectively. A listing will be produced showing all additions, changes, deletions, and errors.

Input Files:

I. COST-FILE

INPUT DEVICE:	DISK
FILE ORGANIZATION:	SEQUENTIAL
RECORD LENGTH:	75 BYTES
FILE SEQUENCE:	ASCENDING ON PART NUMBER

II. TRANSACTION-FILE

INPUT DEVICE:	DISK
FILE ORGANIZATION:	SEQUENTIAL
RECORD LENGTH:	76 BYTES
FILE SEQUENCE:	ASCENDING ON PART NUMBER

Output Files:

I. NEW-COST-FILE

OUTPUT DEVICE:	DISK
FILE ORGANIZATION:	SEQUENTIAL
RECORD LENGTH:	75 BYTES
FILE SEQUENCE:	ASCENDING ON PART NUMBER

II. PRINT-FILE

OUTPUT DEVICE:	PRINTER
RECORD LENGTH:	133 BYTES

Processing Requirements:

The program will read the COST-FILE and the TRANSACTION-FILE and create a new version of the COST-FILE (NEW-COST-FILE). The key field is the part number. The TRANSACTION-FILE has the same fields as the COST-FILE, plus a TRANS-TYPE field used to indicate whether the transaction is an addition (A), change (C), or deletion (D).

If there is no matching TRANSACTION-RECORD for a COST-RECORD, the unchanged COST-RECORD should be written to the NEW-COST-FILE.

If a record from the TRANSACTION-FILE has a matching record on the COST-FILE, the transaction record must be either a change or a deletion. Changes are made to the COST-FILE based on the presence or absence (spaces) of data in the transaction record. After changes are made, the record is written to the NEW-COST-FILE. Two detail lines are printed, one before and one after the changes. A record to be deleted is not written to the NEW-COST-FILE; however, a detail line is printed. Any record with a matching record on the COST-FILE that is not a change or a deletion is in error, and a detail line should be printed to indicate this.

If a TRANSACTION-RECORD has no matching record in the COST-FILE, the transaction should be an addition and the TRANSACTION-RECORD should be written to the NEW-COST-FILE. A detail line should then be printed indicating an addition to the file. If the transaction is not an addition, a detail line should be printed with an appropriate error message.

Counts should be kept of the number of COST-RECORDS read, TRANS-ACTION-RECORDS read, additions, changes, deletions, addition errors, change errors, deletion errors, and records written to NEW-COST-FILE. The counts should be printed at the end of the update listing.

Output Requirements:

The NEW-COST-FILE should reflect all file maintenance transactions.

The following are formatting requirements for the report:

1. Each page of the report should contain:
   (a) a main heading which includes the company name, the report name, the report date, and a page number.
   (b) column headings which describe the items printed underneath them.
2. Detail lines should include all fields from the input and the total for the cost factors.
3. Detail lines should be double spaced.
4. Detail lines should include a message indicating the action taken.
5. Changed fields should be highlighted with an asterisk underline.
6. Counts displayed should be single spaced.

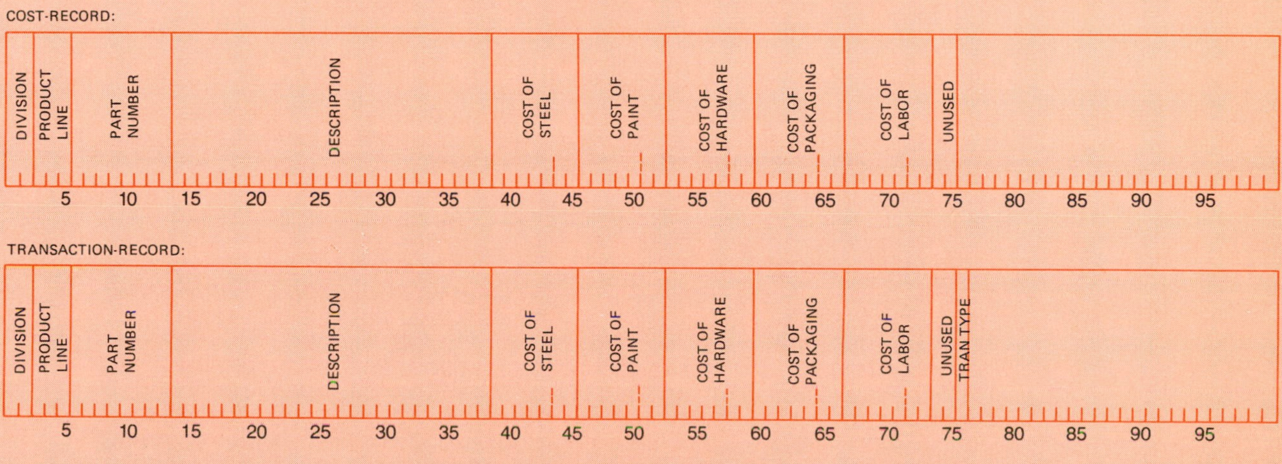

CHAPTER

10 Sorting

The programming projects of this chapter combine topics covered in previous chapters in new ways by means of a COBOL sort. The COBOL SORT verb provides a variety of methods for handling files that are to be sorted, as well as files that are the result of the sort. Four COBOL programs show the four possible sorting combinations.

The debugging section covers a group of diagnostics that might be generated as a result of using the SORT verb. The EXHIBIT verb used for debugging purposes is discussed.

SORTS

A COBOL sort is used to arrange the records of a file into a new sequence. One or more fields in the record are selected to be the key fields, and the rearrangement of the records is based on the contents of these fields. The programmer may specify

UNSORTED DATA

```
Ø12Ø1ØØ3ØØE1Ø12   B123358711Ø5WB493EØØØØ2Ø54ØØØ871122ØØØØØØ
Ø12Ø1ØØ3ØØPO173   B12383871Ø25GN4Ø2AØØØØ1Ø45ØØØ871116ØØØØØØ
Ø891521Ø78        B71Ø45871ØØ1FV782TØØØØ3ØØ28ØØ8711158711Ø9
Ø8174ØØ5Ø1        B81Ø418711Ø8JG96ØEØØØØ2Ø28Ø3587Ø214ØØØØØØ
Ø361182888P2783733B8433Ø871Ø25HL289BØØØ1ØØ234ØØ8711138711Ø9
Ø3ØØ7739897747    B892888711Ø6MF848JØØØØ5Ø2145Ø88Ø13ØØØØØØØ
Ø344Ø6948187Ø341  GØ418Ø87Ø2Ø9JGØ4ØXØØØØ1Ø525ØØ88Ø619ØØØØØØ
Ø12Ø1Ø47278372    G4838887Ø913WB7Ø2XØØØ9ØØ115ØØ8711Ø18711Ø9
Ø8174314Ø865      H4189187Ø412TK61ØLØØØ18ØØ78ØØ87Ø63Ø8711Ø9
Ø36115Ø912        H6915Ø87Ø2Ø6MF848TØØØØ3Ø36ØØØ8712Ø1ØØØØØØ
Ø3ØØ7ØØ378EBNER   H8457987Ø811VX922PØØ8ØØØØ127589112ØØØØØØØ
Ø3ØØ7473ØØ        H8477787Ø223MF4Ø3TØØØØ5Ø4ØØØØ87Ø5Ø2ØØØØØØ
Ø891562Ø54SCHUH   L5Ø6818711Ø8TK814EØØØØ6Ø565ØØ88Ø1Ø5ØØØØØØ
Ø8174Ø18Ø5R7278   T2164287Ø81ØTK497XØØØ1ØØ118ØØ87113Ø8711Ø9
Ø361128375T7838   T7829987Ø323JG563WØØØØ6Ø43ØØØ871Ø18ØØØØØØ
Ø8174Ø18Ø5R8322   Y211Ø587Ø6Ø1TN116TØØØØ1Ø3ØØØØ871221ØØØØØØ
Ø3ØØ7473ØØ        Y289Ø387Ø811VXØØ1LØØ2ØØØØ622Ø8712Ø3ØØØØØØ
```

SORTED DATA

```
Ø8174ØØ5Ø1        B81Ø418711Ø8JG96ØEØØØØ2Ø28Ø3587Ø214ØØØØØØ
Ø891562Ø54SCHUH   L5Ø6818711Ø8TK814EØØØØ6Ø565ØØ88Ø1Ø5ØØØØØØ
Ø3ØØ7739897747    B892888711Ø6MF848JØØØØ5Ø2145Ø88Ø13ØØØØØØØ
Ø12Ø1ØØ3ØØE1Ø12   B123358711Ø5WB493EØØØØ2Ø54ØØØ871122ØØØØØØ
Ø12Ø1ØØ3ØØPO173   B12383871Ø25GN4Ø2AØØØØ1Ø45ØØØ871116ØØØØØØ
Ø361182888P2783733B8433Ø871Ø25HL289BØØØ1ØØ234ØØ8711138711Ø9
Ø891521Ø78        B71Ø45871ØØ1FV782TØØØØ3ØØ28ØØ8711158711Ø9
Ø12Ø1Ø47278372    G4838887Ø913WB7Ø2XØØØ9ØØ115ØØ8711Ø18711Ø9
Ø3ØØ7ØØ378EBNER   H8457987Ø811VX922PØØ8ØØØØ127589112ØØØØØØØ
Ø3ØØ7473ØØ        Y289Ø387Ø811VXØØ1LØØ2ØØØØ622Ø8712Ø3ØØØØØØ
Ø8174Ø18Ø5R7278   T2164287Ø81ØTK497XØØØ1ØØ118ØØ87113Ø8711Ø9
Ø8174Ø18Ø5R8322   Y211Ø587Ø6Ø1TN116TØØØØ1Ø3ØØØØ871221ØØØØØØ
Ø8174314Ø865      H4189187Ø412TK61ØLØØØ18ØØ78ØØ87Ø63Ø8711Ø9
Ø361128375T7838   T7829987Ø323JG563WØØØØ6Ø43ØØØ871Ø18ØØØØØØ
Ø3ØØ7473ØØ        H8477787Ø223MF4Ø3TØØØØ5Ø4ØØØØ87Ø5Ø2ØØØØØØ
Ø344Ø6948187Ø341  GØ418Ø87Ø2Ø9JGØ4ØXØØØØ1Ø525ØØ88Ø619ØØØØØØ
Ø36115Ø912        H6915Ø87Ø2Ø6MF848TØØØØ3Ø36ØØØ8712Ø1ØØØØØØ
```

FIGURE 10–1

an ascending or descending arrangement for each of the key fields. Figure 10–1 contains two sets of data from an order file. The first set is in no particular sequence. The second set is the same data after it has been sorted in descending order on the order date field (the sixth field) and ascending order on the sales representative field (the second field) within each order date.

The arrangement of the data is dependent on the collating sequence of the data-encoding scheme being used. Two of the more popular encoding schemes are the Extended Binary Coded Decimal Interchange Code (EBCDIC) and the American Standard Code for Information Interchange (ASCII). Figure 10–2 shows

FIGURE 10–2
Partial List of ASCII and EBCDIC

DEC	HEX	BINARY	ASCII	EBCDIC	DEC	HEX	BINARY	ASCII	EBCDIC
32	20	0010 0000	SP		91	5B	0101 1011		$
33	21	0010 0001	!		92	5C	0101 1100		*
34	22	0010 0010	"		93	5D	0101 1101		)
35	23	0010 0011	#		94	5E	0101 1110		;
36	24	0010 0100	$		95	5F	0101 1111		
37	25	0010 0101	%		96	60	0110 0000		-
38	26	0010 0110	&		97	61	0110 0001		/
39	27	0010 0111	'						
40	28	0010 1000	(		108	6C	0110 1100		%
41	29	0010 1001	)		109	6D	0110 1101		-
42	2A	0010 1010	*		110	6E	0110 1110		>
43	2B	0010 1011	+		111	6F	0110 1111		?
44	2C	0010 1100	,						
45	2D	0010 1101	-		122	7A	0111 1010		:
46	2E	0010 1110	.		123	7B	0111 1011		#
47	2F	0010 1111	/		124	7C	0111 1100		@
48	30	0011 0000	0		125	7D	0111 1101		'
49	31	0011 0001	1		126	7E	0111 1110		=
50	32	0011 0010	2		127	7F	0111 1111		"
51	33	0011 0011	3						
52	34	0011 0100	4		193	C1	1100 0001		A
53	35	0011 0101	5		194	C2	1100 0010		B
54	36	0011 0110	6		195	C3	1100 0011		C
55	37	0011 0111	7		196	C4	1100 0100		D
56	38	0011 1000	8		197	C5	1100 0101		E
57	39	0011 1001	9		198	C6	1100 0110		F
58	3A	0011 1010	:		199	C7	1100 0111		G
59	3B	0011 1011	;		200	C8	1100 1000		H
60	3C	0011 1100	<		201	C9	1100 1001		I
61	3D	0011 1101	=						
62	3E	0011 1110	>		209	D1	1101 0001		J
63	3F	0011 1111	?		210	D2	1101 0010		K
64	40	0100 0000	@	SP	211	D3	1101 0011		L
65	41	0100 0001	A		212	D4	1101 0100		M
66	42	0100 0010	B		213	D5	1101 0101		N
67	43	0100 0011	C		214	D6	1101 0110		O
68	44	0100 0100	D		215	D7	1101 0111		P
69	45	0100 0101	E		216	D8	1101 1000		Q
70	46	0100 0110	F		217	D9	1101 1001		R
71	47	0100 0111	G						
72	48	0100 1000	H		226	E2	1110 0010		S
73	49	0100 1001	I		227	E3	1110 0011		T
74	4A	0100 1010	J		228	E4	1110 0100		U
75	4B	0100 1011	K	.	229	E5	1110 0101		V
76	4C	0100 1100	L	<	230	E6	1110 0110		W
77	4D	0100 1101	M	(	231	E7	1110 0111		X
78	4E	0100 1110	N	+	232	E8	1110 1000		Y
79	4F	0100 1111	O		233	E9	1110 1001		Z
80	50	0101 0000	P	&					
81	51	0101 0001	Q		240	F0	1111 0000		0
82	52	0101 0010	R		241	F1	1111 0001		1
83	53	0101 0011	S		242	F2	1111 0010		2
84	54	0101 0100	T		243	F3	1111 0011		3
85	55	0101 0101	U		244	F4	1111 0100		4
86	56	0101 0110	V		245	F5	1111 0101		5
87	57	0101 0111	W		246	F6	1111 0110		6
88	58	0101 1000	X		247	F7	1111 0111		7
89	59	0101 1001	Y		248	F8	1111 1000		8
90	5A	0101 1010	Z		249	F9	1111 1001		9

the relative positions in the collating sequence for uppercase letters and digits in each of these encoding schemes.

Rather than requiring a programmer to write a sorting code to rearrange the records, COBOL allows the programmer to request a SORT directly within the COBOL program. The programmer specifies the name of the file to be sorted, the fields to be used as sort keys, the sequence desired for each key field, the relative importance of the key fields, and the file-handling methods to be used before and after the sort.

COBOL SORT

Format

```
SORT file-name-1
        {ASCENDING }
     ON {DESCENDING}    KEY data-name-1 [data-name-2] . . .

        {ASCENDING }
   [ON  {DESCENDING}    KEY data-name-3 [data-name-4] . . .] . . .

   [COLLATING SEQUENCE IS alphabet-name]
  {USING file-name-2 [file-name-3] . . .                        }
  {INPUT PROCEDURE IS section-name-1                            }
  {                                  {THROUGH}                  }
  {                                [ {THRU   }   section-name-2]}

  {GIVING file-name-4                                           }
  {OUTPUT PROCEDURE is section-name-3                           }
  {                                [ {THROUGH}                  }
  {                                  {THRU   }   section-name-4]}
```

Sort Files

The file to be sorted must be described in an SD (sort description) entry in the DATA DIVISION. The format of an SD is similar to that of an FD. The records to be sorted must be transferred from an input file or files to the file described by the SD before the actual sort can take place. The rearrangement takes place using the disk or tape storage allocated to the sort file. The sorted data is then transferred from the sort file to an output file.

Format

```
SD file-name
   [RECORD CONTAINS [integer-1 TO] integer-2 CHARACTERS]
   [DATA {RECORD IS   } data-name-1 [data-name-2]. . . ].
         {RECORDS ARE }
```

Each file input to the sort or output from the sort must have an FD entry and record description in the FILE SECTION. Also, the file to be sorted must have an SD entry and record description in the FILE SECTION. The record description does not have to be in detail; however, it must contain at least enough detail to identify the data items which are to be used as sort keys.

In the following example, only the position of the sort key, SORT-PART-NBR, is identified in the sort record. The remainder of the record is designated as FILLER. Whether to describe the record in full or describe only the sort key(s) is a decision made by the programmer. The choice depends on what data must be referenced elsewhere in the program and whether that data is described in detail elsewhere.

```
01  SORT-RECORD.
    05  FILLER          PIC X(30).
    05  SORT-PART-NBR   PIC X(6).
    05  FILLER          PIC X(34).
```

Sort Keys

A sort key is a data item in a sort record whose contents are used to determine the arrangement of the records in a file. There may be up to 12 sort keys specified for a single sort. Each key may specify either an ASCENDING or DESCENDING arrangement of the records based on the contents of that key.

The record description for a sort file must describe the data items within the record that are to be used as sort keys. If there is more than one record described for a sort file (DATA RECORDS ARE), the sort key(s) need to be described in only one of the records. Data items used as sort keys must not have OCCURS clauses or be subordinate to a data item containing an OCCURS clause.

The names of the data items to be used as sort keys, their order of importance, and the direction of the sort (ASCENDING/DESCENDING) on each key are specified using the ON (ASCENDING/DESCENDING) KEY clause of the SORT statement.

Sort keys must be listed in the KEY clause(s) from major to minor importance. Multiple data items may be combined in one KEY clause as long as the direction of the sort remains the same. When the direction changes, another KEY clause is added. Figure 10–3 gives examples of the KEY clause, together with explanations, from the programs that appear later in this chapter.

EXAMPLE 1

```
ASCENDING KEY SORT-PART-NBR
```

The sorted file will be in ascending order by part number.

EXAMPLE 2

```
DESCENDING KEY SORT-ORD-DATE
ASCENDING KEY SORT-SALES-REP
              SORT-CUSTOMR-NBR
```

The sorted file will be in descending order by order date, starting with the largest (most recent) date and going to the smallest (least recent) date. (Remember, the dates are arranged in order of year, month, and day.) Within each date the records will be in ascending order by sales representative, and within each sales representative the records will be in ascending order by customer number.

EXAMPLE 3

```
ASCENDING KEY SORT-BRANCH
DESCENDING KEY SORT-EXTENDED-PRICE
```

The sorted file will be in ascending order by branch. Within each branch the records will be in descending order by extended price.

EXAMPLE 4

```
ASCENDING KEY SORT-SALES-REP
              SORT-CUSTOMER-NBR
              SORT-CUST-PO-NBR
```

The sorted file will be in ascending order by sales representative. Within the records for each sales representative, the records will be in ascending order by customer number, and within each customer number the records will be in ascending order by customer purchase order number.

FIGURE 10–3

File-Handling Procedures

To provide input to a sort, either INPUT PROCEDURE or USING may be used. For the output from a sort, either OUTPUT PROCEDURE or GIVING may be used. The choice between INPUT PROCEDURE or USING and OUTPUT PROCEDURE or GIVING yields four file-handling combinations that may be used for a COBOL sort. The programmer chooses either INPUT PROCEDURE or USING depending on the processing required for a file *before* it is sorted. The choice between OUTPUT PROCEDURE or GIVING is dependent upon the processing required for a file *after* it has been sorted.

INPUT PROCEDURE

The INPUT PROCEDURE clause names a section or group of sections in the PROCEDURE DIVISION which contains the processing steps to be executed before the sort occurs. This section or group of sections must be self-contained, i.e., all paragraphs to be performed as a part of the INPUT PROCEDURE must be within the section(s).

A file that requires processing before it is sorted will need an INPUT PROCEDURE. The processing might be an extraction, an edit, or simply a calculation whose result will become one of the sort keys. Contrast this with USING, where no processing takes place before the sort.

An extraction in an INPUT PROCEDURE selects records from the input file which meet the established criteria and transfers only those records to the sort file. The sorted file containing the extracted records will thus in general be smaller than the original file, reducing the amount of time needed to do the sorting. Although it is possible to sort first and then extract the records needed, this procedure is not recommended because of the extra time required to sort the unneeded records.

Like an extraction, an edit in an INPUT PROCEDURE is likely to result in fewer records to sort, and all sorted records will contain valid data.

The record description of a sort file does not have to be the same as that of the original input file. An INPUT PROCEDURE may be used to create a new record format with a different number and arrangement of data items. Because the end use of the sorted file may require only a few of the data items from the original file, time and space are saved if only the records and data items needed are transferred.

In an INPUT PROCEDURE, records are transferred from the input file(s) to the sort file. In the DATA DIVISION the input file(s) are defined with an FD, the sort file with an SD. The file(s) described in the FD and used in an INPUT PROCEDURE must be opened and closed. The sort file, however, should not be opened or closed. Data from the input file(s) is placed in the sort record through MOVE statements or calculations. When each sort record is complete, it is written to the sort file using the reserved word RELEASE.

RELEASE

Format

```
RELEASE record-name [FROM identifier]
```

RELEASE transfers a record to the sort file through the input/output area established in the associated SD entry. The word RELEASE is followed by the record-name established for the sort file. Its action is similar to the verb WRITE; however, the two verbs are not interchangeable. Figure 10–4 shows the transfer from the input/output area to the sort file caused by a RELEASE statement.

When the FROM option is used, data is moved from the identifier specified to the input/output area of the sort file and then written to the sort file. Figure 10–5 gives two examples of the FROM option. The first involves a transfer from another input/output area, the second a transfer from WORKING-STORAGE.

RELEASE must be specified in an INPUT PROCEDURE associated with a SORT statement. It may not be used elsewhere. Each INPUT PROCEDURE *must* have a RELEASE statement in order to transfer records to the sort file.

```
DATA DIVISION.
     .
     .
     .
SD   SORT-FILE
     RECORD CONTAINS 70 CHARACTERS
     DATA RECORD IS SORT-RECORD.

01   SORT-RECORD.
     .
     .
     .

PROCEDURE DIVISION.
     .
     .
     .
     RELEASE SORT-RECORD.
```

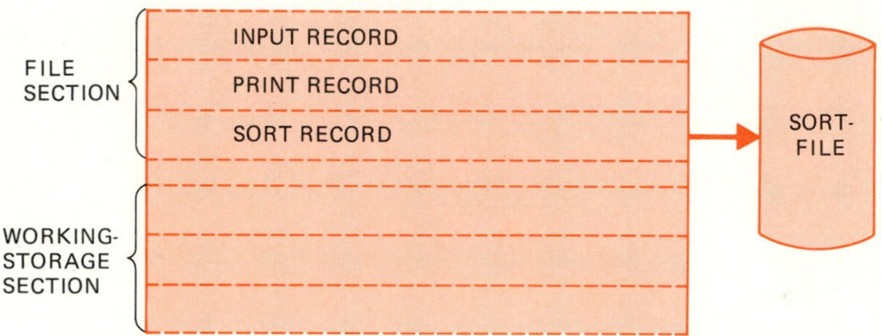

FIGURE 10–4

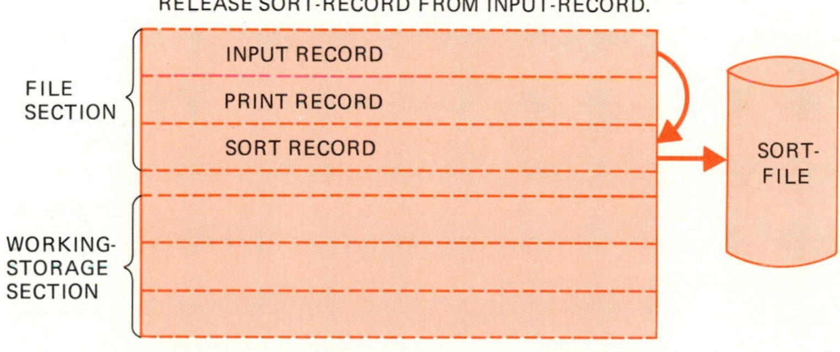

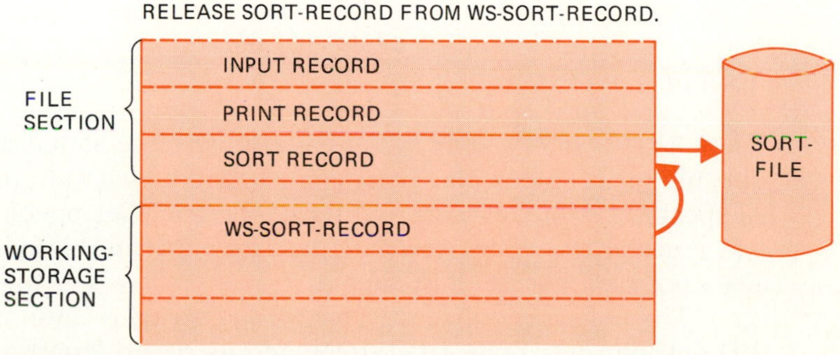

FIGURE 10–5

USING

If the records in an input file do not require any processing before they are sorted, the USING option may be used. Any records in the input file specified after the word USING are automatically transferred to the sort file. The compiler opens the input file(s), reads the records, transfers the records to the sort file, and closes the input file(s). The programmer does not code any of these steps.

There may be as many as eight input files specified in a USING statement. Each of the files must be defined with an FD entry in the DATA DIVISION. The record length of each file must be identical to that of the sort record, since there is no opportunity to modify the records before they are transferred.

OUTPUT PROCEDURE

The OUTPUT PROCEDURE clause names a section or group of sections in the PROCEDURE DIVISION which contains the processing steps to be executed after the sort occurs. As with the INPUT PROCEDURE, all paragraphs to be performed as a part of the OUTPUT PROCEDURE must be contained within the section(s). An OUTPUT PROCEDURE is used to process records *after* a sort is complete. The OUTPUT PROCEDURE transfers records from the sort file to another file or files. The records may be modified during this transfer. A common use of an OUTPUT PROCEDURE is to create a printed report of the records from the sorted file.

Each record is retrieved from the SORT-FILE using the word RETURN. There must be at least one RETURN in an OUTPUT PROCEDURE, and the word RETURN may only be used in an OUTPUT PROCEDURE for a sort.

RETURN

Format

```
RETURN file-name [INTO identifier]
    AT END imperative statement
```

RETURN transfers records from the sort file to the input/output area established in the associated SD entry. Its action is similar to the word READ; however, the two verbs may not be used interchangeably. The word RETURN is followed by the name of the sort file. Figure 10–6 shows the transfer from the sort file to the input/output area for the sort file.

When the INTO option is used, data is transferred from the sort file to the input/output area for the sort file and then moved to the identifier that follows the word INTO. Figure 10–7 gives an example of the INTO option that involves a transfer from the sort input/output area to an area in WORKING-STORAGE.

GIVING

The GIVING option may be used to transfer the sorted records directly from the sort file to an output file. The name of the file that is to receive the sorted records is specified after the word GIVING. The compiler opens this file, reads the sort file, transfers the sorted records to the output file, and closes the file. The programmer does not code any of these steps.

The output file that will receive the sorted records must be defined with an FD entry in the DATA DIVISION, and its record length must be the same as the record length of the sort file.

```
DATA DIVISION.
     .
     .
     .
SD   SORT-FILE
     RECORD CONTAINS 70 CHARACTERS
     DATA RECORD IS SORT-RECORD.
01   SORT-RECORD.
     .
     .
     .
PROCEDURE DIVISION.
     .
     .
     .
     RETURN SORT-FILE.
```

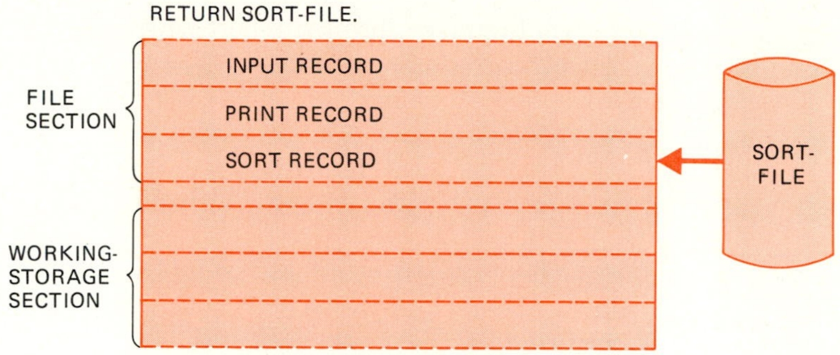

"
"
"

RETURN SORT-FILE.

FILE SECTION	INPUT RECORD
	PRINT RECORD
	SORT RECORD ← SORT-FILE
WORKING-STORAGE SECTION	

FIGURE 10–6

RETURN SORT-FILE INTO WS-SORT-RECORD.

FILE SECTION	INPUT RECORD
	PRINT RECORD
	SORT RECORD ← SORT-FILE
WORKING-STORAGE SECTION	WS-SORT-RECORD

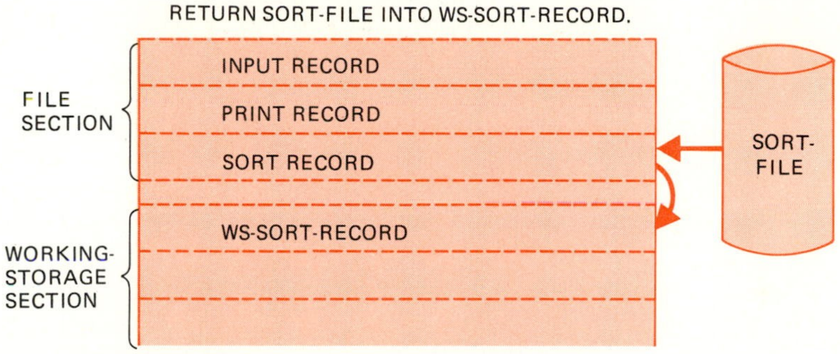

FIGURE 10–7

COMBINATIONS

There are four combinations that may be formed with the file-handling options:

INPUT PROCEDURE/OUTPUT PROCEDURE
USING/GIVING
INPUT PROCEDURE/GIVING
USING/OUTPUT PROCEDURE

A programming project is presented for each of these combinations. Each project is complete with program specification, logic tools, test data, sample output, and COBOL program. The explanation of the COBOL sort technique follows the COBOL source listing.

SAMPLE PROGRAM 1: INPUT PROCEDURE/OUTPUT PROCEDURE

In the first programming project, the manufacturing department of a firm requires a backlog report showing all unshipped orders. The orders are to be in ascending order by part number, and the report will be used to identify parts with large backlogs.

Since unshipped orders are to be listed in part number sequence, only those orders from the ORDER-FILE with zeros in the actual shipping date require sorting. An INPUT PROCEDURE to extract these records and RELEASE them to the sort is an appropriate choice. After the sort is complete, a report is to be printed. An OUTPUT PROCEDURE may be used for this purpose.

The program specification is shown in Figure 10–8. The input file is still the ORDER-FILE used in previous chapters. The input record layout is repeated in Figure 10–9 for convenience. The print chart for the report produced by the program is shown in Figure 10–10.

PROGRAM SPECIFICATION: SORT-1

PROGRAM SPECIFICATION

Program Name: SORT1

Program Function:

This program will produce a printed report which is a listing of the order backlog. All orders which have not been shipped will appear on the report in sequence by part number.

Input Files:

I. ORDER-FILE

INPUT DEVICE:	DISK
FILE ORGANIZATION:	SEQUENTIAL
RECORD LENGTH:	70 BYTES
FILE SEQUENCE:	ASCENDING ON SALES ORDER NBR

Output Files:

I. PRINT-FILE

OUTPUT DEVICE:	PRINTER
RECORD LENGTH:	133 BYTES

Processing Requirements:

The report will include only orders which have not been shipped (actual shipping date = zero). Orders appearing on the report will be listed in part number sequence.

Output Requirements:

The following are formatting requirements for the report.

1. Each page of the report should contain:
   (a) a main heading which includes the company name, the report name, the report date, and a page number.
   (b) column headings which describe the items printed underneath them.
2. Detail lines should include the part number of an item, its sales order number, requested shipping date, quantity, and unit price.
3. Detail lines should be double spaced.

FIGURE 10–8

Input Record Layout

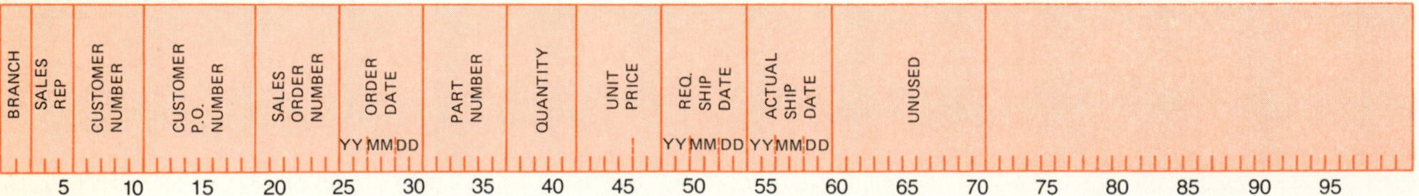

FIGURE 10–9

Print Chart

```
                         DATE: XX/XX/XX              PRODUCT DISTRIBUTION INC.                    PAGE: ZZ9
                                                           BACKLOG REPORT

                           PART          SALES ORDER        REQUESTED                                UNIT
                         NUMBER            NUMBER           SHIP DATE            QUANTITY            PRICE

                         XXXXXX            XXXXXX            99-99-99             ZZZZ9            $$$$9.99

                         XXXXXX            XXXXXX            99-99-99             ZZZZ9            $$$$9.99
```

FIGURE 10–10

LOGIC FOR INPUT PROCEDURE/OUTPUT PROCEDURE SORT

A hierarchy chart for SORT1 is shown in Figure 10–11. Pseudocode and a flowchart are shown in Figures 10–12 and 10–13, respectively.

Hierarchy Chart

The INPUT PROCEDURE was assigned the 1000 series of numbers, with its initialization 1100, processing 1200 and end of job 1300. The OUTPUT PROCEDURE was assigned the 2000 series of numbers, with its initialization 2100, processing 2200, and end of job 2300. This approach was taken because a new level is added to the hierarchy chart in utilizing INPUT PROCEDURE and OUTPUT PROCEDURE.

For routines that are performed from more than one location, the second digit is a 9 to indicate this fact and the leading digit indicates whether they are part of the INPUT PROCEDURE or the OUTPUT PROCEDURE. Routines may not be shared by the INPUT PROCEDURE and the OUTPUT PROCEDURE.

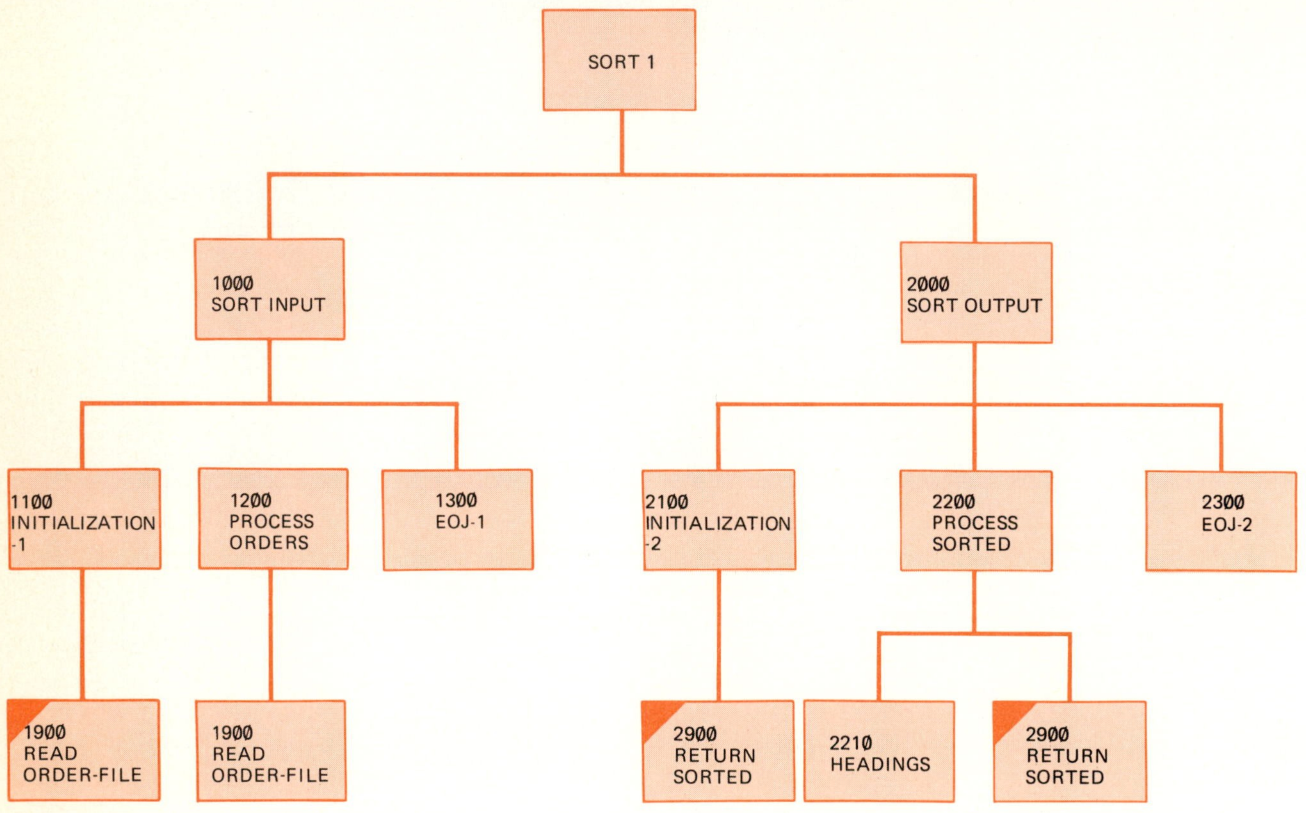

FIGURE 10–11

Pseudocode

```
MAIN LINE
     DO input main line
     SORT order file ascending, part number
     DO output main line
     END

INPUT MAIN LINE
     DO initialization-1
     DO WHILE more order records
          DO process orders
     ENDDO
     DO eoj-1
```

FIGURE 10–12

```
INITIALIZATION-1
     MOVE date to heading
     OPEN files
     DO read an order

PROCESS ORDERS
     IF actual ship date = zeros
          WRITE record to sort file
     ENDIF
     DO read an order

EOJ-1
     CLOSE files

READ AN ORDER
     READ order file

OUTPUT MAIN LINE
     DO initialization-2
     DO WHILE more sorted records
          DO process sorted orders
     ENDDO
     DO eoj-2

INITIALIZATION-2
     OPEN files
     DO read sorted order

PROCESS SORTED ORDERS
     IF line count > 50
          DO headings
     ENDIF
     MOVE input to output
     WRITE detail line
     ADD 2 to line count
     DO read a sorted order

HEADINGS
     ADD 1 to page count
     MOVE page count to output
     WRITE main heading line one
     WRITE main heading line two
     WRITE column heading line one
     WRITE column heading line two
     MOVE 5 to line count
     READ order file

EOJ-2
     CLOSE files

READ A SORTED ORDER
     READ sorted order file
```

FIGURE 10-12 cont.

Flowchart

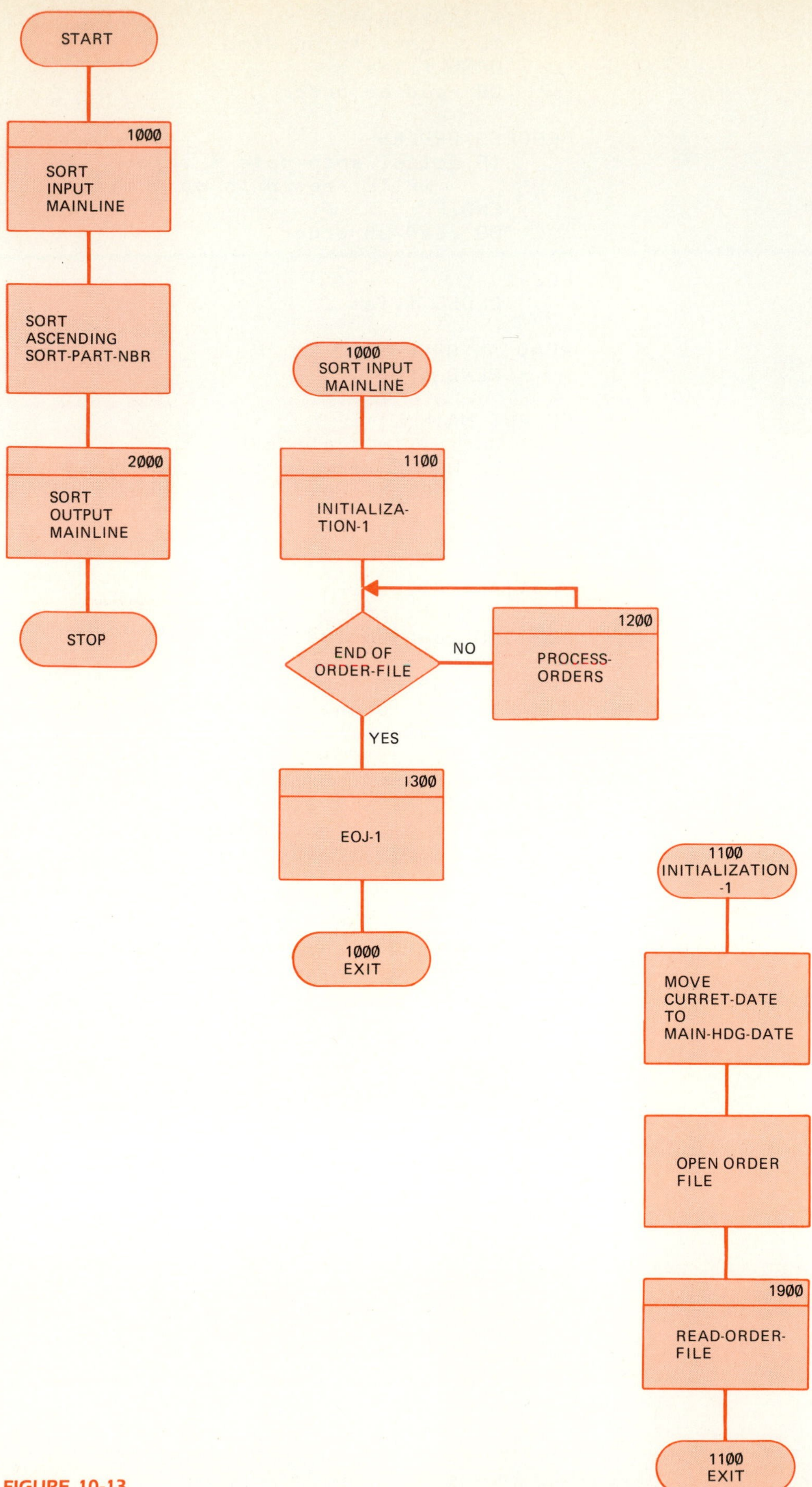

FIGURE 10-13

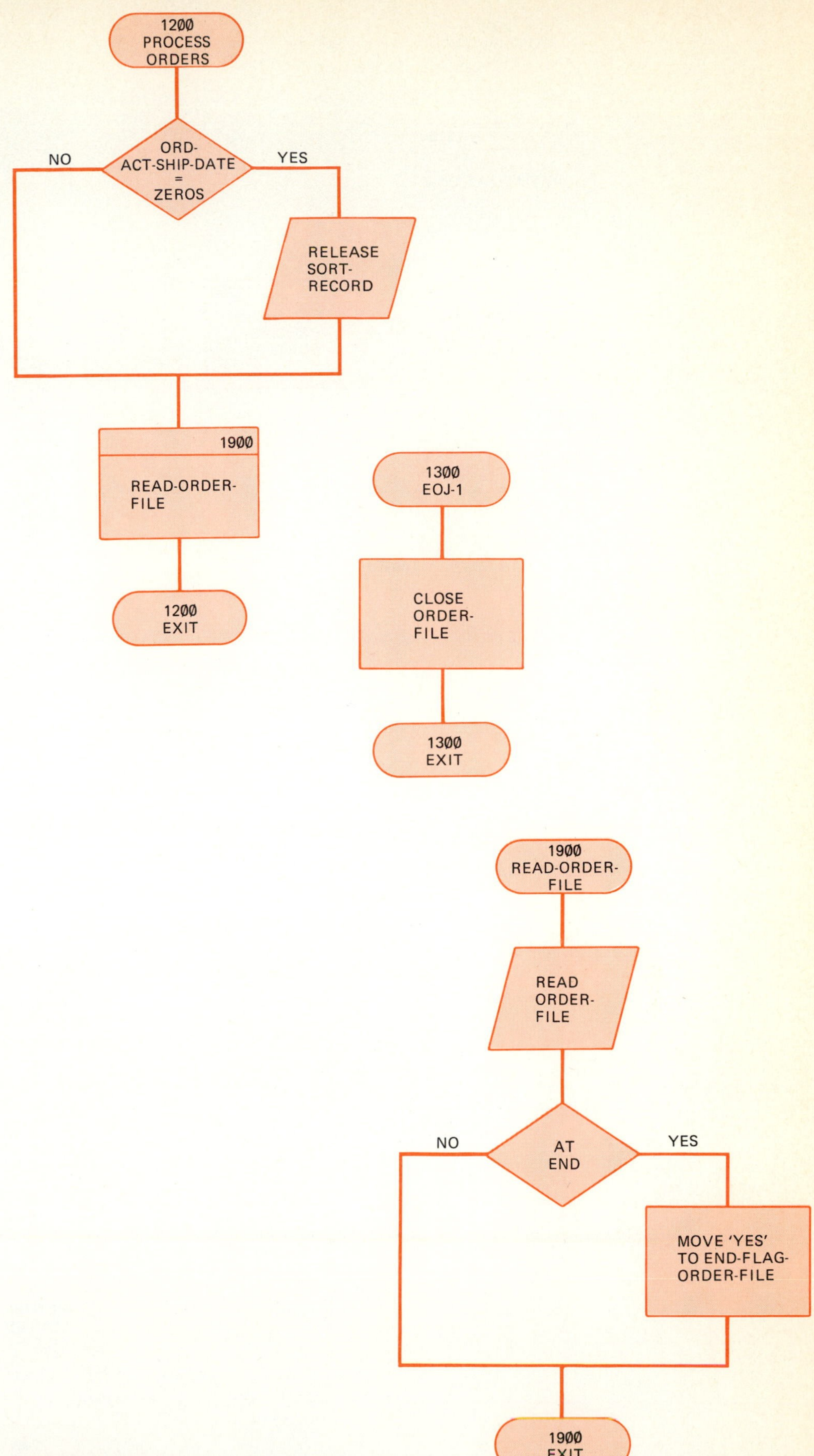

FIGURE 10-13 cont.

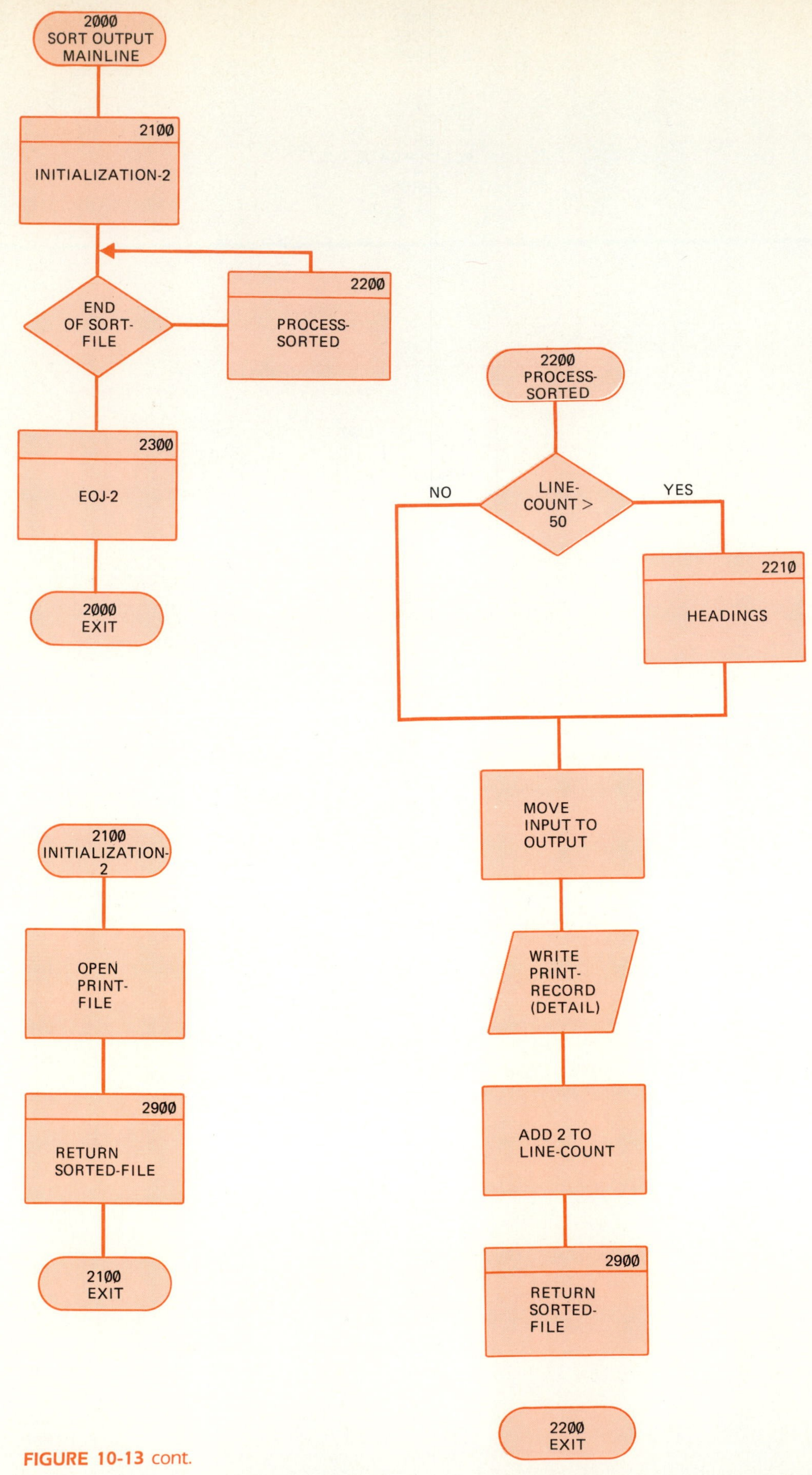

FIGURE 10-13 cont.

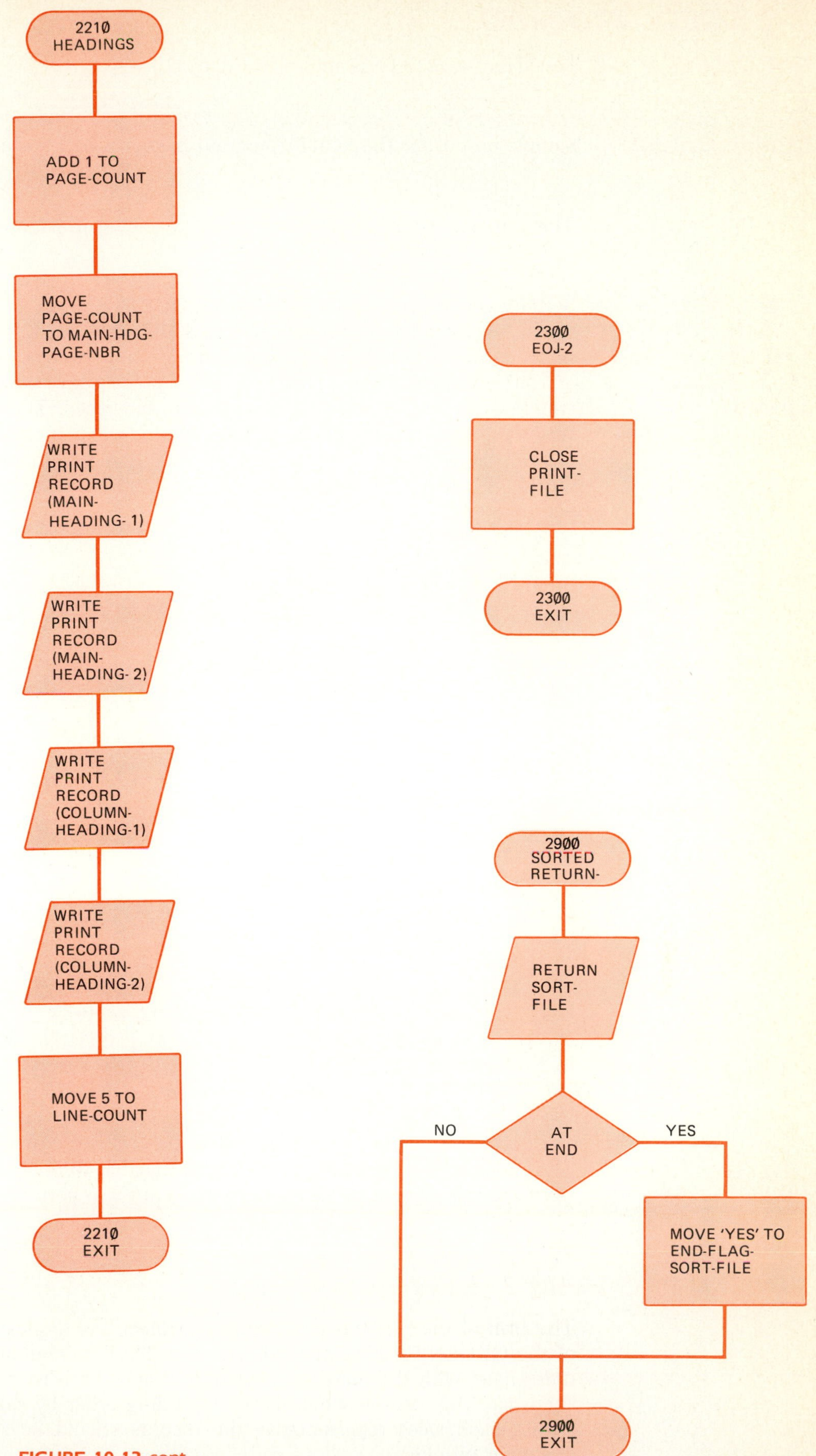

FIGURE 10-13 cont.

Logic for Input Procedure/Output Procedure Sort

THE COBOL PROGRAM

Test Data

Test data for SORT1 is shown in Figure 10–14.

Sample Output

Sample output for the SORT1 program is shown in Figure 10–15.

The Program

The complete COBOL SORT1 program is shown in Figure 10–16.

Explanation of COBOL Sort (INPUT PROCEDURE/ OUTPUT PROCEDURE)

SORT1 consists of an INPUT PROCEDURE and an OUTPUT PROCEDURE whose execution is controlled by the SORT statement. The important thing to notice is how COBOL passes control from one part of the program to another.

The INPUT PROCEDURE does not present any new logic concepts; it is a simple extraction which selects records to be sorted. The basis for selecting the records is the contents of the actual shipping date. If this data item has a value of zero, the order has not been shipped and should be included on the report. The OUTPUT PROCEDURE produces a listing of the order records after they have been sorted.

The statement

```
SORT SORT-FILE
        ASCENDING KEY SORT-PART-NUMBER
```

is used to set up the parameters for the sort. However, no sort takes place at this point, as there are no records in the SORT-FILE. Instead, the statement

```
INPUT PROCEDURE 1000-SORT-INPUT
```

transfers control to section 1000-SORT-INPUT. In order to structure the section as much as possible, a main line is used to perform the routines within it. When the main line is completed, a GO TO is used to reach 1000-SECTION-EXIT, transferring control to the statement

```
OUTPUT PROCEDURE 2000-SORT-OUTPUT.
```

This statement transfers control to section 2000-SORT-OUTPUT. 2000-SORT-OUTPUT also has a main line to control the routines in it. When the main line is completed, a GO TO is used to reach 2000-SECTION-EXIT, transferring control to STOP RUN.

Figure 10–17 is a summary of the flow of data through the SORT1 program. INPUT PROCEDURE is used to read records from the input file and transfer (RELEASE) them to the sort file. When this transfer is complete, the sort occurs. The program then uses OUTPUT PROCEDURE to read (RETURN) the records from the sort file and transfer them to a printed report.

SAMPLE PROGRAM 2: USING/GIVING

The firm of the previous programming project has requested that a new version of the ORDER-FILE be created. The new file is to contain the order records by order date, with the most recent date first and the least recent date last. Within each date the records should be in ascending order by sales representative, and within each sales representative the records should be in ascending order by customer number.

(text continued on page 481)

```
Ø1201ØØ3ØØE1Ø12  B123358711Ø5WB493EØØØØ2Ø54ØØØ871122ØØØØØØ
Ø1201ØØ3ØØPO173  B12383871Ø25GN4Ø2AØØØØ1Ø45ØØØ871116ØØØØØØ
Ø891521Ø78       B71Ø45871ØØ1FV782TØØØØ3ØØ28ØØ8711158711Ø9
Ø8174ØØ5Ø1       B81Ø418711Ø8JG96ØEØØØØ2Ø28Ø3587Ø214ØØØØØØ
Ø361182888P2783733B8433Ø871Ø25HL289BØØØ1ØØ234ØØ8711138711Ø9
Ø3ØØ7739897747   B892888711Ø6MF848JØØØØ5Ø2145Ø88Ø13ØØØØØØØ
Ø344Ø6948187Ø341 GØ418Ø87Ø2Ø9JGØ4ØXØØØØ1Ø525ØØ88Ø619ØØØØØØ
Ø1201Ø47278372   G4838887Ø913WB7Ø2XØØØ9ØØ115ØØ8711Ø1871109
Ø817431408 65    H4189187Ø412TK61ØLØØØ18ØØ78ØØ87Ø63Ø871109
Ø36115Ø912       H69150 87Ø2Ø6MF848TØØØØ3Ø36ØØØ8712Ø1ØØØØØØ
Ø3ØØ7ØØ378EBNER  H8457987Ø811VX922PØØ8ØØØØ127589112ØØØØØØØ
Ø3ØØ747300       H8477787Ø223MF4Ø3TØØØØ5Ø4ØØØØ87Ø5Ø2ØØØØØØ
Ø891562Ø54SCHUH  L5Ø681871108TK814EØØØØ6Ø565ØØ88Ø1Ø5ØØØØØØ
Ø8174Ø18Ø5R7278  T2164287Ø81ØTK497XØØØ1ØØ118ØØ87113Ø871109
Ø361128375T7838  T7829987Ø323JG563WØØØØ6Ø43ØØØ871Ø18ØØØØØØ
Ø8174Ø18Ø5R8322  Y211Ø587Ø6Ø1TN116TØØØØ1Ø3ØØØØ871221ØØØØØØ
Ø3ØØ747300       Y289Ø387Ø811VXØØ1LØØ2ØØØØ622Ø8712Ø3ØØØØØØ
```

FIGURE 10–14

DATE: 11/09/87 PRODUCT DISTRIBUTION INC. PAGE: 1

BACKLOG REPORT

PART NUMBER	SALES ORDER NUMBER	REQUESTED SHIP DATE	QUANTITY	UNIT PRICE
GN402A	B12383	11-16-87	1	$450.00
JG040X	G04180	06-19-88	1	$525.00
JG563W	T78299	10-18-87	6	$430.00
JG960E	B81041	02-14-87	2	$280.35
MF403T	H84777	05-02-87	5	$400.00
MF848J	B89288	01-30-88	5	$214.50
MF848T	H69150	12-01-87	3	$360.00
TK814E	L50681	01-05-88	6	$565.00
TN116T	Y21105	12-21-87	1	$300.00
VX001L	Y28903	12-03-87	200	$62.20
VX922P	H84579	11-20-89	800	$12.75
WB493E	B12335	11-22-87	2	$540.00

FIGURE 10–15

```
       IDENTIFICATION DIVISION.

       PROGRAM-ID.    SORT1.

       AUTHOR.        HELEN HUMPHREYS.

       INSTALLATION.  PRODUCT DISTRIBUTION INC.

       DATE-WRITTEN.  1Ø/Ø1/87.

       DATE-COMPILED. 1Ø/Ø5/87.

      *****************************************************************
      *                                                               *
      *    THIS PROGRAM WILL PRODUCE A PRINTED REPORT WHICH IS A      *
      *    LISTING OF THE ORDER BACKLOG.  ALL ORDERS WHICH HAVE NOT   *
      *    BEEN SHIPPED WILL APPEAR ON THE REPORT IN SEQUENCE BY      *
      *    PART NUMBER.                                               *
      *                                                               *
      *****************************************************************

       ENVIRONMENT DIVISION.
```

FIGURE 10–16

FIGURE 10-16 cont.

```
       CONFIGURATION SECTION.

       SOURCE-COMPUTER.
           IBM-37Ø.
       OBJECT-COMPUTER.
           IBM-37Ø.

       INPUT-OUTPUT SECTION.
       FILE-CONTROL.
           SELECT ORDER-FILE  ASSIGN TO DISK.
           SELECT PRINT-FILE  ASSIGN TO PRINTER.
           SELECT SORT-FILE   ASSIGN TO DISK.

       DATA DIVISION.
       FILE SECTION.

       FD  ORDER-FILE
           LABEL RECORDS ARE STANDARD
           RECORD CONTAINS 7Ø CHARACTERS
           DATA RECORD IS ORDER-RECORD.

       Ø1  ORDER-RECORD                 PIC X(7Ø).

       FD  PRINT-FILE
           LABEL RECORDS ARE OMITTED
           RECORD CONTAINS 133 CHARACTERS
           DATA RECORD IS PRINT-RECORD.

       Ø1  PRINT-RECORD                 PIC X(133).

       SD  SORT-FILE
           RECORD CONTAINS 7Ø CHARACTERS
           DATA RECORD IS SORT-RECORD.

       Ø1  SORT-RECORD.
           Ø5  FILLER                   PIC X(3Ø).
           Ø5  SORT-PART-NBR            PIC X(6).
           Ø5  FILLER                   PIC X(34).

       WORKING-STORAGE SECTION.

       Ø1  WS-COUNTERS.
           Ø5  LINE-COUNT                PIC 9(2)        VALUE 99.
           Ø5  PAGE-COUNT                PIC 9(3)        VALUE ZEROS.

       Ø1  WS-SWITCHES.
           Ø5  END-FLAG-ORDER-FILE       PIC X(3)        VALUE 'NO'.
               88  END-OF-ORDER-FILE                     VALUE 'YES'.
           Ø5  END-FLAG-SORT-FILE        PIC X(3)        VALUE 'NO'.
               88  END-OF-SORT-FILE                      VALUE 'YES'.

       Ø1  WS-ORDER-RECORD.
           Ø5  ORD-BRANCH                PIC 9(2).
           Ø5  ORD-SALES-REP             PIC 9(3).
           Ø5  ORD-CUSTOMER-NBR          PIC 9(5).
           Ø5  ORD-CUST-PO-NBR           PIC X(8).
           Ø5  ORD-SALES-ORD-NBR         PIC X(6).
           Ø5  ORD-DATE.
               1Ø  ORD-YY                PIC 9(2).
               1Ø  ORD-MM                PIC 9(2).
               1Ø  ORD-DD                PIC 9(2).
           Ø5  ORD-PART-NBR              PIC X(6).
           Ø5  ORD-QUANTITY              PIC 9(5).
           Ø5  ORD-UNIT-PRICE            PIC 9(4)V9(2).
           Ø5  ORD-REQ-SHIP-DATE.
               1Ø  ORD-REQ-SHIP-YY       PIC 9(2).
               1Ø  ORD-REQ-SHIP-MM       PIC 9(2).
               1Ø  ORD-REQ-SHIP-DD       PIC 9(2).
           Ø5  ORD-ACT-SHIP-DATE.
               1Ø  ORD-ACT-SHIP-YY       PIC 9(2).
               1Ø  ORD-ACT-SHIP-MM       PIC 9(2).
               1Ø  ORD-ACT-SHIP-DD       PIC 9(2).
           Ø5  FILLER                    PIC X(11).

       Ø1  MAIN-HEADING-1.
           Ø5  FILLER                    PIC X(26)       VALUE SPACES.
           Ø5  FILLER                    PIC X(6)        VALUE 'DATE:'.
           Ø5  MAIN-HDG-DATE             PIC X(8).
           Ø5  FILLER                    PIC X(14)       VALUE SPACES.
           Ø5  FILLER                    PIC X(25)       VALUE
                                         'PRODUCT DISTRIBUTION INC.'.
           Ø5  FILLER                    PIC X(19)       VALUE SPACES.
```

FIGURE 10-16 cont.

```
           Ø5  FILLER                  PIC X(6)        VALUE 'PAGE:'.
           Ø5  MAIN-HDG-PAGE-NBR       PIC ZZ9.
           Ø5  FILLER                  PIC X(26)       VALUE SPACES.

       Ø1  MAIN-HEADING-2.
           Ø5  FILLER                  PIC X(6Ø)       VALUE SPACES.
           Ø5  FILLER                  PIC X(14)       VALUE
                                       'BACKLOG REPORT'.
           Ø5  FILLER                  PIC X(59)       VALUE SPACES.

       Ø1  COLUMN-HEADING-1.
           Ø5  FILLER                  PIC X(27)       VALUE SPACES.
           Ø5  FILLER                  PIC X(4)        VALUE 'PART'.
           Ø5  FILLER                  PIC X(11)       VALUE SPACES.
           Ø5  FILLER                  PIC X(11)       VALUE
                                                       'SALES ORDER'.
           Ø5  FILLER                  PIC X(8)        VALUE SPACES.
           Ø5  FILLER                  PIC X(9)        VALUE
                                                       'REQUESTED'.
           Ø5  FILLER                  PIC X(31)       VALUE SPACES.
           Ø5  FILLER                  PIC X(4)        VALUE 'UNIT'.
           Ø5  FILLER                  PIC X(28)       VALUE SPACES.

       Ø1  COLUMN-HEADING-2.
           Ø5  FILLER                  PIC X(26)       VALUE SPACES.
           Ø5  FILLER                  PIC X(6)        VALUE 'NUMBER'.
           Ø5  FILLER                  PIC X(12)       VALUE SPACES.
           Ø5  FILLER                  PIC X(6)        VALUE 'NUMBER'.
           Ø5  FILLER                  PIC X(11)       VALUE SPACES.
           Ø5  FILLER                  PIC X(9)        VALUE
                                                       'SHIP DATE'.
           Ø5  FILLER                  PIC X(11)       VALUE SPACES.
           Ø5  FILLER                  PIC X(8)        VALUE 'QUANTITY'.
           Ø5  FILLER                  PIC X(12)       VALUE SPACES.
           Ø5  FILLER                  PIC X(5)        VALUE 'PRICE'.
           Ø5  FILLER                  PIC X(27)       VALUE SPACES.

       Ø1  DETAIL-LINE.
           Ø5  FILLER                  PIC X(26)       VALUE SPACES.
           Ø5  DET-PART-NBR            PIC X(6).
           Ø5  FILLER                  PIC X(12)       VALUE SPACES.
           Ø5  DET-SALES-ORD-NBR       PIC X(6).
           Ø5  FILLER                  PIC X(12)       VALUE SPACES.
           Ø5  DET-REQ-SHIP-MM         PIC X(2).
           Ø5  FILLER                  PIC X(1)        VALUE '-'.
           Ø5  DET-REQ-SHIP-DD         PIC X(2).
           Ø5  FILLER                  PIC X(1)        VALUE '-'.
           Ø5  DET-REQ-SHIP-YY         PIC X(2).
           Ø5  FILLER                  PIC X(12)       VALUE SPACES.
           Ø5  DET-QUANTITY            PIC ZZZZ9.
           Ø5  FILLER                  PIC X(12)       VALUE SPACES.
           Ø5  DET-UNIT-PRICE          PIC $$$$9.99.
           Ø5  FILLER                  PIC X(26)       VALUE SPACES.

       PROCEDURE DIVISION.

           SORT SORT-FILE
               ASCENDING KEY SORT-PART-NBR
                   INPUT PROCEDURE 1ØØØ-SORT-INPUT
                   OUTPUT PROCEDURE 2ØØØ-SORT-OUTPUT.
           STOP RUN.

       1ØØØ-SORT-INPUT SECTION.
       1ØØØ-SORT-INPUT-MAINLINE.
           PERFORM 11ØØ-INITIALIZATION-1.
           PERFORM 12ØØ-PROCESS-ORDERS
               UNTIL END-OF-ORDER-FILE.
           PERFORM 13ØØ-EOJ-1.
           GO TO 1ØØØ-SECTION-EXIT.

       11ØØ-INITIALIZATION-1.
           MOVE CURRENT-DATE TO MAIN-HDG-DATE.
           OPEN INPUT ORDER-FILE.
           PERFORM 19ØØ-READ-ORDER-FILE.

       12ØØ-PROCESS-ORDERS.
           IF ORD-ACT-SHIP-DATE = ZEROS
               RELEASE SORT-RECORD FROM WS-ORDER-RECORD.
           PERFORM 19ØØ-READ-ORDER-FILE.

       13ØØ-EOJ-1.
           CLOSE ORDER-FILE.

       19ØØ-READ-ORDER-FILE.
```

```
           READ ORDER-FILE INTO WS-ORDER-RECORD
               AT END
                   MOVE 'YES' TO END-FLAG-ORDER-FILE.

       1000-SECTION-EXIT.
           EXIT.


       2000-SORT-OUTPUT SECTION.
       2000-SORT-OUTPUT-MAINLINE.
           PERFORM 2100-INITIALIZATION-2.
           PERFORM 2200-PROCESS-SORTED
               UNTIL END-OF-SORT-FILE.
           PERFORM 2300-EOJ-2.
           GO TO 2000-SECTION-EXIT.

       2100-INITIALIZATION-2.
           OPEN OUTPUT PRINT-FILE.
           PERFORM 2900-RETURN-SORTED.

       2200-PROCESS-SORTED.
           IF LINE-COUNT > 50
               PERFORM 2210-HEADINGS.
           MOVE ORD-PART-NBR          TO DET-PART-NBR.
           MOVE ORD-SALES-ORD-NBR     TO DET-SALES-ORD-NBR.
           MOVE ORD-REQ-SHIP-YY       TO DET-REQ-SHIP-YY.
           MOVE ORD-REQ-SHIP-MM       TO DET-REQ-SHIP-MM.
           MOVE ORD-REQ-SHIP-DD       TO DET-REQ-SHIP-DD.
           MOVE ORD-QUANTITY          TO DET-QUANTITY.
           MOVE ORD-UNIT-PRICE        TO DET-UNIT-PRICE.
           WRITE PRINT-RECORD FROM DETAIL-LINE
               AFTER ADVANCING 2 LINES.
           ADD 2 TO LINE-COUNT.
           PERFORM 2900-RETURN-SORTED.

       2210-HEADINGS.
           ADD 1 TO PAGE-COUNT.
           MOVE PAGE-COUNT TO MAIN-HDG-PAGE-NBR.
           WRITE PRINT-RECORD FROM MAIN-HEADING-1
               AFTER ADVANCING PAGE.
           WRITE PRINT-RECORD FROM MAIN-HEADING-2
               AFTER ADVANCING 1 LINE.
           WRITE PRINT-RECORD FROM COLUMN-HEADING-1
               AFTER ADVANCING 2 LINES.
           WRITE PRINT-RECORD FROM COLUMN-HEADING-2
               AFTER ADVANCING 1 LINE.
           MOVE 5 TO LINE-COUNT.

       2300-EOJ-2.
           CLOSE PRINT-FILE.

       2900-RETURN-SORTED.
           RETURN SORT-FILE INTO WS-ORDER-RECORD
               AT END
                   MOVE 'YES' TO END-FLAG-SORT-FILE.

       2000-SECTION-EXIT.
           EXIT.
```

FIGURE 10-16 cont.

INPUT PROCEDURE / OUTPUT PROCEDURE

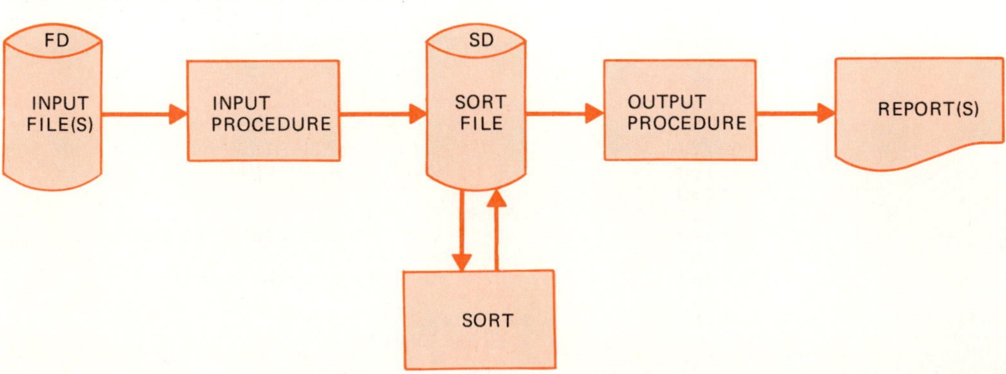

FIGURE 10–17

No reports have been requested from this new file. However, the new file would lend itself to future reports showing sales productivity over a period of time.

The program specification is shown in Figure 10–18. The input file is again the ORDER-FILE, whose record layout is shown in Figure 10–19. There is no printed output from the program. The output is simply a file recorded on disk with the same record layout as the input file. The program requires only a rearrangement of records in the file, making it suitable for the USING/GIVING combination.

LOGIC FOR USING/GIVING SORT

The hierarchy chart for the SORT-2 program consists of a single box and is shown in Figure 10–20. The pseudocode and flowchart contain only a main line and are shown in Figures 10–21 and 10–22, respectively. The main line gives some details of the sort, such as the name of the sort file and the sort keys. With the USING/GIVING option, this is all that is required in the PROCEDURE DIVISION.

PROGRAM SPECIFICATION: SORT-2

PROGRAM SPECIFICATION

Program Name: SORT2

Program Function:

The program will create a new file whose records are all those from the ORDER-FILE and whose record format is the same as the format for the ORDER-FILE. The new file will be in sequence by customer number (ascending), within sales representative (ascending), within order date (descending).

Input Files:

I. ORDER-FILE

```
INPUT DEVICE:          DISK
FILE ORGANIZATION:     SEQUENTIAL
RECORD LENGTH:         70 BYTES
FILE SEQUENCE:         ASCENDING ON SALES ORDER NBR
```

Output Files:

I. SORTED-ORDER-FILE

```
OUTPUT DEVICE:         DISK
FILE ORGANIZATION:     SEQUENTIAL
RECORD LENGTH:         70 BYTES
FILE SEQUENCE:         DESCENDING ON ORDER DATE
                       ASCENDING ON  SALES REP
                                     CUSTOMER NBR
```

Processing and Output Requirements:

All records from the input are to be included on the output in the same record format. The sequence of the new file is to be descending on order date, and ascending on sales representative and customer number.

FIGURE 10–18

Input Record Layout

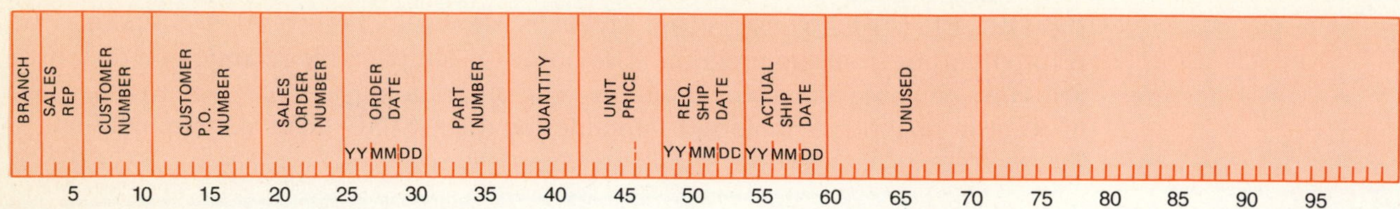

FIGURE 10–19

Hierarchy Chart

SORT 2

FIGURE 10–20

Pseudocode

```
MAIN LINE
     SORT order file
          descending order date
          ascending sales representative
                    customer number
```

FIGURE 10–21

Flowchart

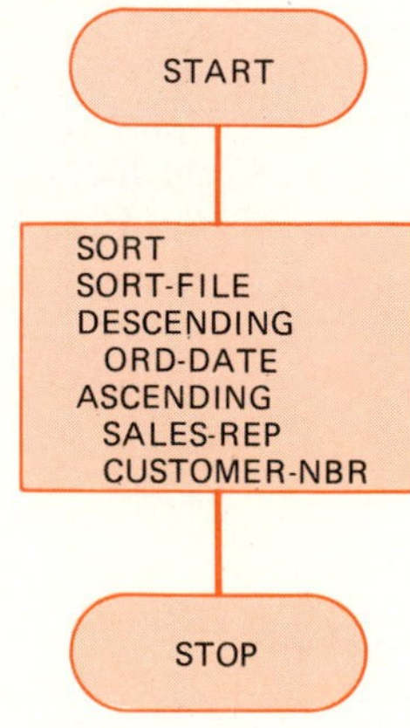

FIGURE 10–22

THE COBOL PROGRAM

Test Data

Figure 10–23 shows test data for the SORT-2 program. The data is the same for all the programs in this chapter and is repeated for convenience.

Sample Output

The program does not produce any printed output; it does produce a disk file whose record layout is the same as the input record layout. Figure 10–24 shows how the records on the disk would look *if* an output listing were made of them.

The Program

The complete COBOL SORT-2 program is shown in Figure 10–25.

Explanation of COBOL SORT (USING/GIVING)

The PROCEDURE DIVISION for the USING/GIVING sort combination is composed of a SORT statement and STOP RUN. COBOL statements like OPEN, CLOSE, READ, WRITE, and MOVE are noticeably absent. The SORT statement controls the opening and closing of files and the transfer of data from one file to another,

```
Ø1201ØØ3ØØE1Ø12   B12335871105WB493EØØØØ2Ø54ØØØ871122ØØØØØØ
Ø1201ØØ3ØØPO173   B12383871Ø25GN4Ø2AØØØØ1Ø45ØØØ871116ØØØØØØ
Ø891521Ø78        B71Ø45871ØØ1FV782TØØØØ3ØØ28ØØ8711158711Ø9
Ø8174ØØ5Ø1        B81Ø41871108JG96ØEØØØØ2Ø28Ø3587Ø214ØØØØØØ
Ø361182888P2783733B8433Ø871Ø25HL289BØØØ1ØØ234ØØ8711138711Ø9
Ø3ØØ7739897747    B89288871106MF848JØØØØ5Ø2145Ø88Ø13ØØØØØØØ
Ø344Ø6948187Ø341  GØ418Ø87Ø2Ø9JGØ4ØXØØØØ1Ø525ØØ88Ø619ØØØØØØ
Ø1201Ø47278372    G4838887Ø913WB7Ø2XØØØ9ØØ115ØØ8711Ø1871109
Ø81743140865      H4189187Ø412TK61ØLØØØ18ØØ78ØØ87Ø63Ø871109
Ø36115Ø912        H6915Ø87Ø2Ø6MF848TØØØØ3Ø36ØØØ8712Ø1ØØØØØØ
Ø3ØØ7ØØ378EBNER   H8457987Ø811VX922PØØ8ØØØØ1275891120ØØØØØØ
Ø3ØØ7473ØØ        H8477787Ø223MF4Ø3TØØØØ5Ø4ØØØØ87Ø5Ø2ØØØØØØ
Ø891562Ø54SCHUH   L5Ø681871108TK814EØØØØ6Ø565ØØ88Ø1Ø5ØØØØØØ
Ø8174Ø18Ø5R7278   T2164287Ø81ØTK497XØØØ1ØØ118ØØ87113Ø871109
Ø361128375T7838   T7829987Ø323JG563WØØØØ6Ø43ØØØ871Ø18ØØØØØØ
Ø8174Ø18Ø5R8322   Y211Ø587Ø6Ø1TN116TØØØØ1Ø3ØØØØ871221ØØØØØØ
Ø3ØØ7473ØØ        Y289Ø387Ø811VXØØ1LØØ2ØØØØ622Ø8712Ø3ØØØØØØ
```

FIGURE 10–23

```
Ø8174ØØ5Ø1        B81Ø41871108JG96ØEØØØØ2Ø28Ø3587Ø214ØØØØØØ
Ø891562Ø54SCHUH   L5Ø681871108TK814EØØØØ6Ø565ØØ88Ø1Ø5ØØØØØØ
Ø3ØØ7739897747    B89288871106MF848JØØØØ5Ø2145Ø88Ø13ØØØØØØØ
Ø1201ØØ3ØØE1Ø12   B12335871105WB493EØØØØ2Ø54ØØØ871122ØØØØØØ
Ø1201ØØ3ØØPO173   B12383871Ø25GN4Ø2AØØØØ1Ø45ØØØ871116ØØØØØØ
Ø361182888P2783733B8433Ø871Ø25HL289BØØØ1ØØ234ØØ8711138711Ø9
Ø891521Ø78        B71Ø45871ØØ1FV782TØØØØ3ØØ28ØØ8711158711Ø9
Ø1201Ø47278372    G4838887Ø913WB7Ø2XØØØ9ØØ115ØØ8711Ø1871109
Ø3ØØ7ØØ378EBNER   H8457987Ø811VX922PØØ8ØØØØ1275891120ØØØØØØ
Ø3ØØ7473ØØ        Y289Ø387Ø811VXØØ1LØØ2ØØØØ622Ø8712Ø3ØØØØØØ
Ø8174Ø18Ø5R7278   T2164287Ø81ØTK497XØØØ1ØØ118ØØ87113Ø871109
Ø8174Ø18Ø5R8322   Y211Ø587Ø6Ø1TN116TØØØØ1Ø3ØØØØ871221ØØØØØØ
Ø81743140865      H4189187Ø412TK61ØLØØØ18ØØ78ØØ87Ø63Ø871109
Ø361128375T7838   T7829987Ø323JG563WØØØØ6Ø43ØØØ871Ø18ØØØØØØ
Ø3ØØ7473ØØ        H8477787Ø223MF4Ø3TØØØØ5Ø4ØØØØ87Ø5Ø2ØØØØØØ
Ø344Ø6948187Ø341  GØ418Ø87Ø2Ø9JGØ4ØXØØØØ1Ø525ØØ88Ø619ØØØØØØ
Ø36115Ø912        H6915Ø87Ø2Ø6MF848TØØØØ3Ø36ØØØ8712Ø1ØØØØØØ
```

FIGURE 10–24

as well as the sorting of the data. First, the statement

```
SORT SORT-FILE
     DESCENDING KEY SORT-ORD-DATE
     ASCENDING  KEY SORT-SALES-REP
                    SORT-CUSTOMER-NBR
```

identifies the file whose contents are to be sorted, the sort keys, the order of importance of the sort keys, and the direction of the sort for each sort key. Then the clause

```
USING ORDER-FILE
```

opens the ORDER-FILE, transfers each record from the ORDER-FILE to the SORT-FILE, and closes the ORDER-FILE. At this point, the rearrangement of the data occurs in the SORT-FILE.

Finally, the clause

```
GIVING SORTED-ORDER-FILE.
```

opens the SORTED-ORDER-FILE. Records which have been rearranged in the SORT-FILE are then transferred in their new sequence to the SORTED-ORDER-FILE, and the SORTED-ORDER-FILE is closed. If the programmer elected to make further use of the SORTED-ORDER-FILE in this program, it would be necessary to OPEN the SORTED-ORDER-FILE as INPUT and READ from it.

```
       IDENTIFICATION DIVISION.

       PROGRAM-ID.    SORT2.

       AUTHOR.        HELEN HUMPHREYS.

       INSTALLATION.  PRODUCT DISTRIBUTION INC.

       DATE-WRITTEN.  1Ø/Ø8/87.

       DATE-COMPILED. 1Ø/14/87.

      ******************************************************************
      *                                                                *
      *    THIS PROGRAM WILL CREATE A NEW FILE.  ALL RECORDS FROM     *
      *    THE ORDER-FILE WILL BE INCLUDED ON THE NEW FILE AND THE    *
      *    RECORD FORMAT WILL BE THE SAME AS THE FORMAT FOR THE       *
      *    ORDER-FILE.  THE NEW FILE WILL BE IN SEQUENCE BY CUSTOMER  *
      *    NUMBER (ASCENDING), WITHIN SALES REPRESENTATIVE            *
      *    (ASCENDING), WITHIN ORDER DATE (DESCENDING).               *
      *                                                                *
      ******************************************************************

       ENVIRONMENT DIVISION.

       CONFIGURATION SECTION.

       SOURCE-COMPUTER.
           IBM-37Ø.
       OBJECT-COMPUTER.
           IBM-37Ø.

       INPUT-OUTPUT SECTION.
       FILE-CONTROL.
           SELECT ORDER-FILE           ASSIGN TO DISK.
           SELECT SORTED-ORDER-FILE    ASSIGN TO DISK.
           SELECT SORT-FILE            ASSIGN TO DISK.

       DATA DIVISION.
       FILE SECTION.

       FD  ORDER-FILE
           LABEL RECORDS ARE STANDARD
           RECORD CONTAINS 7Ø CHARACTERS
           DATA RECORD IS ORDER-RECORD.

       Ø1  ORDER-RECORD                    PIC X(7Ø).

       FD  SORTED-ORDER-FILE
           LABEL RECORDS ARE STANDARD
           RECORD CONTAINS 7Ø CHARACTERS
           DATA RECORD IS SORTED-ORDER-RECORD.

       Ø1  SORTED-ORDER-RECORD             PIC X(7Ø).

       SD  SORT-FILE
           RECORD CONTAINS 7Ø CHARACTERS
           DATA RECORD IS SORT-RECORD.

       Ø1  SORT-RECORD.
           Ø5  FILLER                     PIC X(2).
           Ø5  SORT-SALES-REP             PIC 9(3).
           Ø5  SORT-CUSTOMER-NBR          PIC 9(5).
           Ø5  FILLER                     PIC X(14).
           Ø5  SORT-ORD-DATE              PIC X(6).
           Ø5  FILLER                     PIC X(4Ø).

       PROCEDURE DIVISION.

           SORT SORT-FILE
               DESCENDING KEY  SORT-ORD-DATE
               ASCENDING KEY   SORT-SALES-REP
                               SORT-CUSTOMER-NBR
                   USING ORDER-FILE
                   GIVING SORTED-ORDER-FILE.
           STOP RUN.
```

FIGURE 10–25

The movement of the data in a SORT with the USING/GIVING option is summarized in the system flowchart segment shown in Figure 10–26.

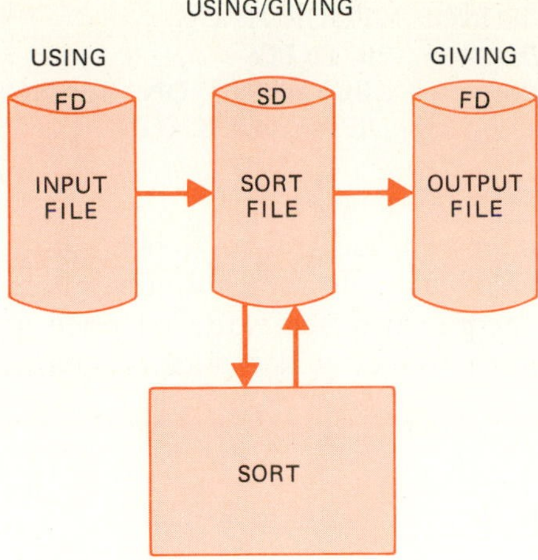

FIGURE 10–26

SAMPLE PROGRAM 3: INPUT PROCEDURE/GIVING

SORT-3 creates a new file with a different record layout from the original. Only records from branches 1 through 5 are included on the new file; this file is used to sort the records in descending order by extended price (within a branch). The resulting file could be used to prepare a report highlighting the largest orders for these branches.

The program specification for the third programming project is shown in Figure 10–27. The input file is still the ORDER-FILE which has been used since the beginning of the text. The input record layout is shown in Figure 10–28.

PROGRAM SPECIFICATION: SORT-3

PROGRAM SPECIFICATION

Program Name: SORT3

Program Function:

This program will create a new file from the input ORDER-FILE. However, the new file will not contain every record from the ORDER-FILE, and its records will not have the same layout as the order record. The new file will be in sequence by extended price (descending) within branch (ascending).

Input Files:

I. ORDER-FILE

INPUT DEVICE:	DISK
FILE ORGANIZATION:	SEQUENTIAL
RECORD LENGTH:	70 BYTES
FILE SEQUENCE:	ASCENDING ON SALES ORDER NBR

FIGURE 10–27

Output Files:

I. MARKETING-FILE

OUTPUT DEVICE:	DISK
FILE ORGANIZATION:	SEQUENTIAL
RECORD LENGTH:	30 BYTES
FILE SEQUENCE:	ASCENDING ON BRANCH DESCENDING ON EXTENDED PRICE

Processing and Output Requirements:

Only records from Branches 1 through 5 are to be included in the output file. The branch, customer number, and sales order number fields from the input are to appear on the output record. Also, the extended price should be calculated and included on the output record. (Extended price = quantity × unit price.)

FIGURE 10–27 cont.

Input Record Layout

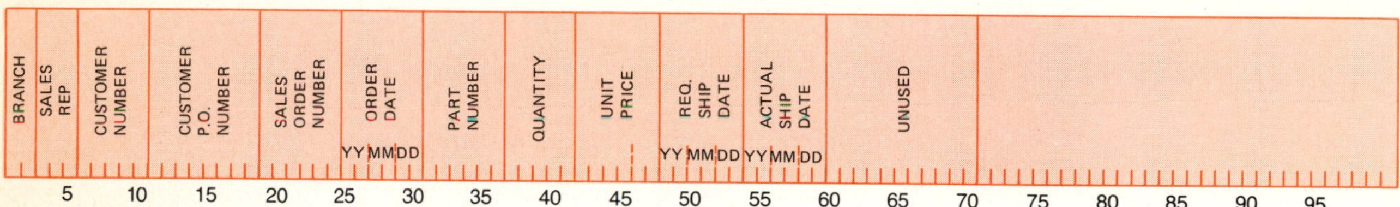

FIGURE 10–28

Output Record Layout

The output produced by SORT3 is a disk file, each record of which contains only some of the original fields and one additional field (extended price). (See Figure 10–29.)

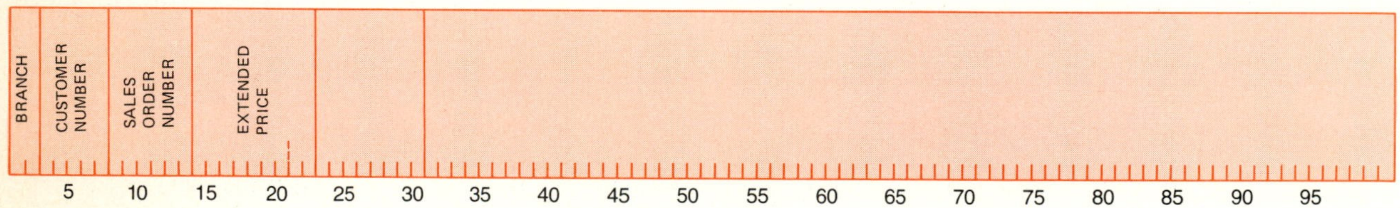

FIGURE 10–29

LOGIC FOR INPUT PROCEDURE/GIVING SORT

A hierarchy chart for SORT3 is shown in Figure 10–30. Pseudocode and a flowchart are shown in Figures 10–31 and 10–32, respectively.

Explanation of Logic

With the exception of the main routine, the routines shown are a part of the INPUT PROCEDURE. The output is transferred from the SORT-FILE to the MARKETING-FILE by the GIVING instruction. This transfer is handled by COBOL and does not require detailed logic on the part of the programmer.

Hierarchy Chart

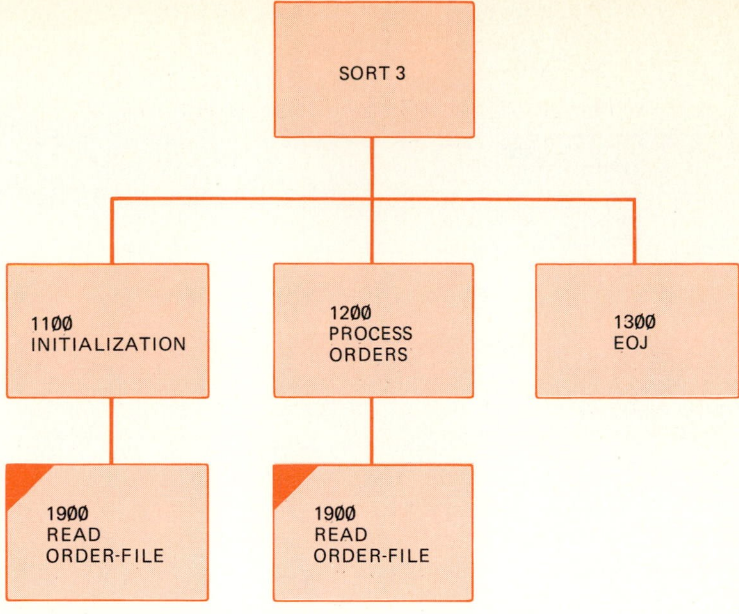

FIGURE 10–30

Pseudocode

```
MAIN LINE
     DO input main line
     SORT order file ascending branch
                     descending extended price

INPUT MAIN LINE
     DO initialization
     DO WHILE more orders
          DO process orders
     ENDDO
     DO eoj

INITIALIZATION
     OPEN files
     DO read an order

PROCESS ORDERS
     CALCULATE extended price
     IF branch < 6
          MOVE branch, customer number, sales order
            number, and extended price to sort record
          WRITE sort record
     ENDIF
     DO read an order

READ AN ORDER
     READ order file
```

FIGURE 10–31

THE COBOL PROGRAM

Test Data

Test data for the SORT3 program is shown in Figure 10–33.

Sample Output

The output is recorded on a disk file. The listing in Figure 10–34 depicts what the data on the disk file would look like it if were printed out.

Flowchart

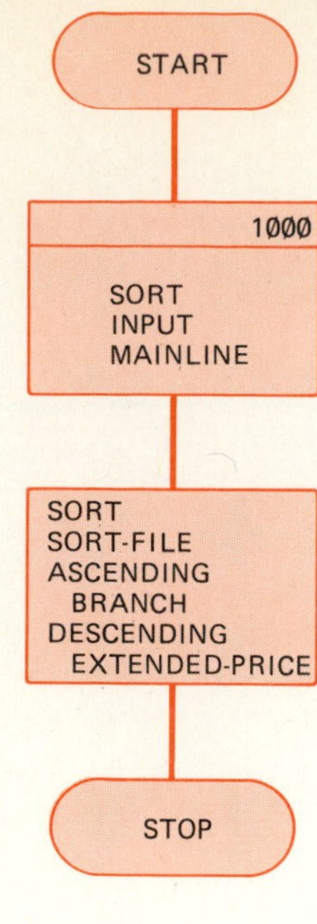

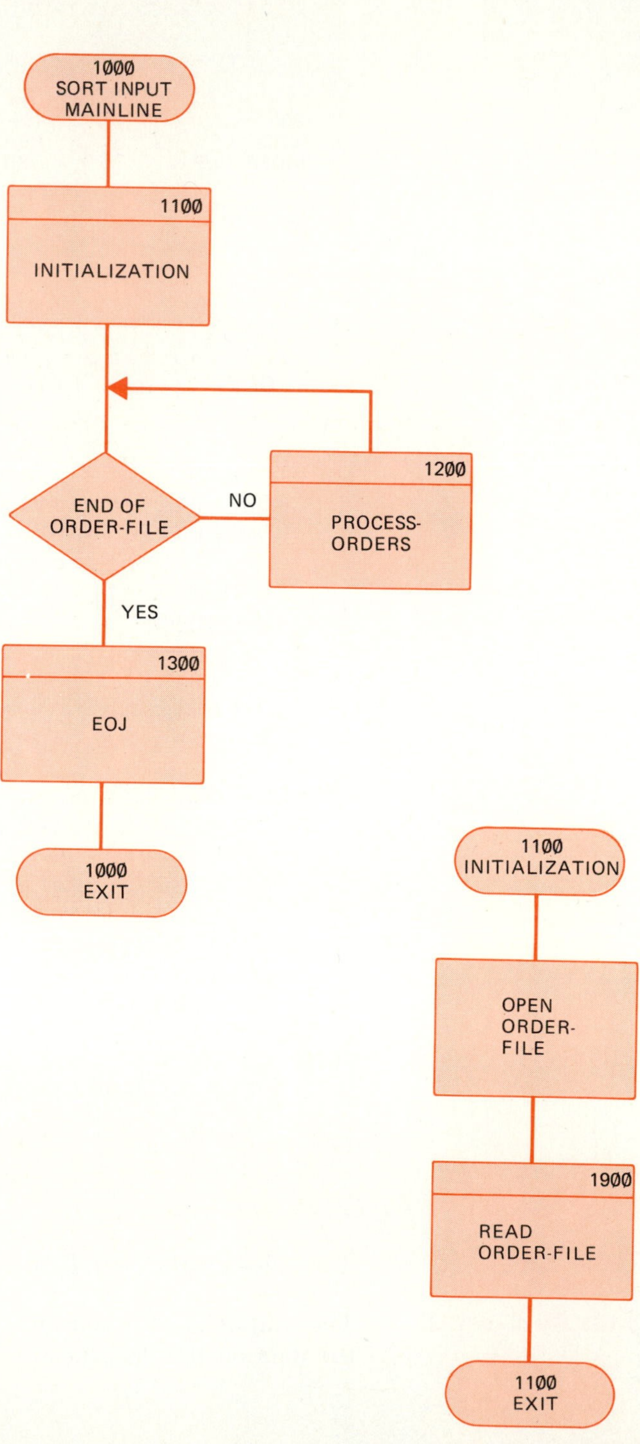

FIGURE 10–32

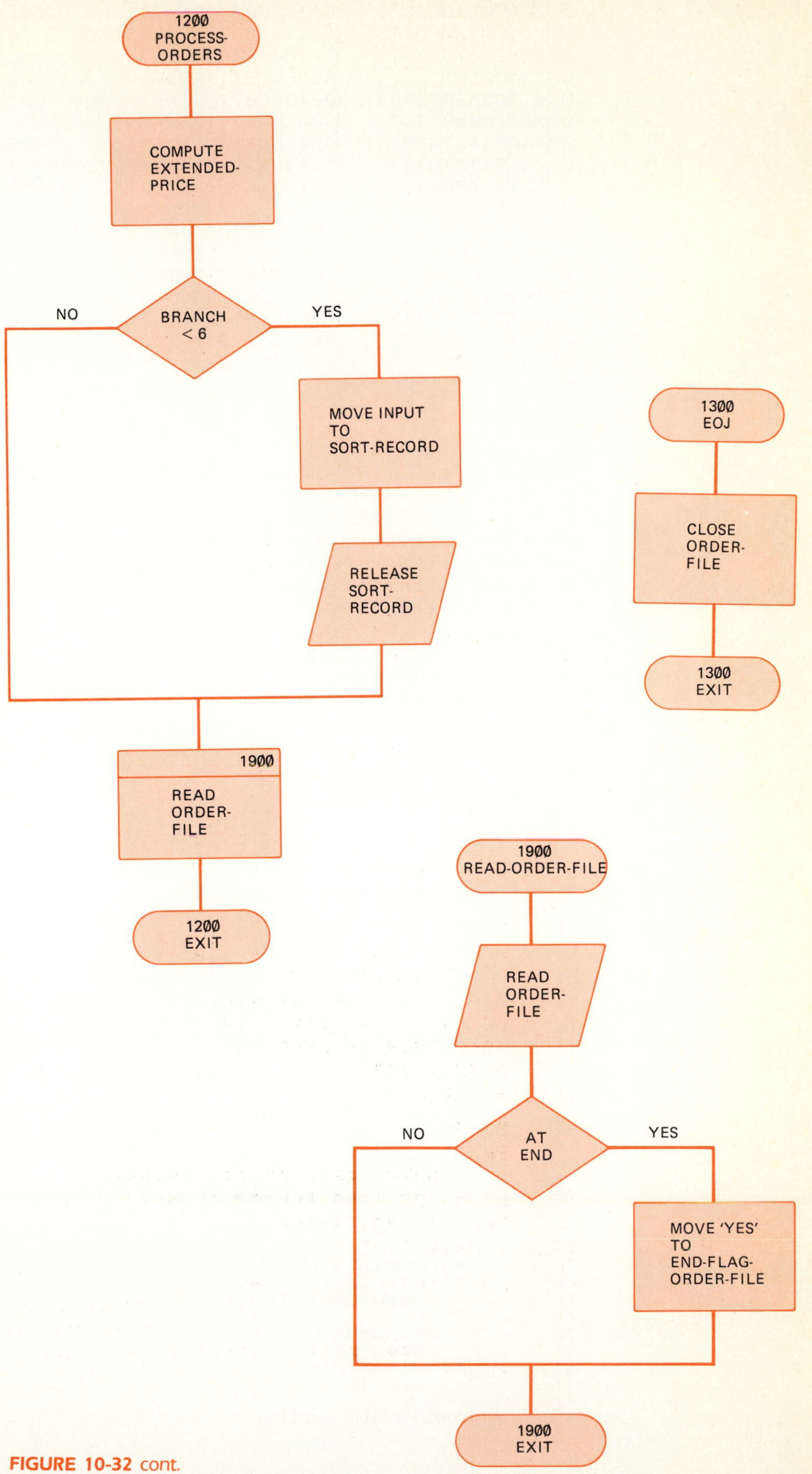

FIGURE 10-32 cont.

```
Ø12Ø1ØØ3ØØE1Ø12   B12335871105WB493EØØØØ2Ø54ØØØ871122ØØØØØØ
Ø12Ø1ØØ3ØØPO173   B12383871Ø25GN4Ø2AØØØØ1Ø45ØØØ871116ØØØØØØ
Ø891521Ø78        B71Ø45871ØØ1FV782TØØØØ3ØØ28ØØ8711158711Ø9
Ø8174ØØ5Ø1        B81Ø41871108JG96ØEØØØØ2Ø28Ø3587Ø214ØØØØØØ
Ø361182888P2783733B8433Ø871Ø25HL289BØØØ1ØØ234ØØ8711138711Ø9
Ø3ØØ7739897747    B89288871106MF848JØØØØ5Ø2145Ø88Ø13ØØØØØØØ
Ø344Ø6948187Ø341  GØ418Ø87Ø2Ø9JGØ4ØXØØØØ1Ø525ØØ88Ø619ØØØØØØ
Ø12Ø1Ø47278372    G4838887Ø913WB7Ø2XØØØ9ØØ115ØØ8711Ø1871109
Ø817431408 65     H4189187Ø412TK61ØLØØØ18ØØ78ØØ87Ø63Ø871109
Ø36115Ø912        H6915Ø87Ø2Ø6MF848TØØØØ3Ø36ØØØ8712Ø1ØØØØØØ
Ø3ØØ7ØØ378EBNER   H8457987Ø811VX922PØØ8ØØØØ127589112ØØØØØØØ
Ø3ØØ7473ØØ        H8477787Ø223MF4Ø3TØØØØ5Ø4ØØØØ87Ø5Ø2ØØØØØØ
Ø891562Ø54SCHUH   L5Ø681871108TK814EØØØØ6Ø565ØØ88Ø1Ø5ØØØØØØ
Ø8174Ø18Ø5R7278   T2164287Ø81ØTK497XØØØ1ØØ118ØØ87113Ø871109
Ø361128375T7838   T7829987Ø323JG563WØØØØ6Ø43ØØØ871Ø18ØØØØØØ
Ø8174Ø18Ø5R8322   Y211Ø587Ø6Ø1TN116TØØØØ1Ø3ØØØØ871221ØØØØØØ
Ø3ØØ7473ØØ        Y289Ø387Ø811VXØØ1LØØ2ØØØØ622Ø8712Ø3ØØØØØØ
```

FIGURE 10–33

```
Ø1Ø4727G48388ØØ1Ø35ØØØ
Ø1ØØ3ØØB12335ØØØ1Ø8ØØØ
Ø1ØØ3ØØB12383ØØØØ45ØØØ
Ø347300Y289Ø3ØØ1244ØØØ
Ø3ØØ378H84579ØØ1Ø2ØØØØ
Ø328375T78299ØØØ258ØØØ
Ø382888B8433ØØØØ234ØØØ
Ø347300H84777ØØØ2ØØØØØ
Ø35Ø912H6915ØØØØ1Ø8ØØØ
Ø373989B89288ØØØ1Ø725Ø
Ø369481GØ418ØØØØØ525ØØ
```

FIGURE 10–34

The Program

The complete COBOL SORT3 program is shown in Figure 10–35.

```
       IDENTIFICATION DIVISION.

       PROGRAM-ID.    SORT3.

       AUTHOR.        HELEN HUMPHREYS.

       INSTALLATION.  PRODUCT DISTRIBUTION INC.

       DATE-WRITTEN.  1Ø/17/87.

       DATE-COMPILED. 1Ø/21/87.

      *****************************************************************
      *                                                               *
      *    THIS PROGRAM CREATES A NEW FILE.  THE NEW FILE WILL BE     *
      *    CREATED FROM THE ORDER-FILE.  HOWEVER, THE NEW FILE WILL   *
      *    NOT CONTAIN EVERY RECORD FROM THE ORDER-FILE AND THE NEW   *
      *    RECORD WILL NOT HAVE THE SAME LAYOUT AS THE ORDER RECORD.  *
      *    THE NEW FILE WILL BE IN SEQUENCE BY EXTENDED PRICE         *
      *    (DESCENDING) WITHIN BRANCH (ASCENDING).                    *
      *                                                               *
      *****************************************************************

       ENVIRONMENT DIVISION.

       CONFIGURATION SECTION.

       SOURCE-COMPUTER.
           IBM-37Ø.
       OBJECT-COMPUTER.
           IBM-37Ø.

       INPUT-OUTPUT SECTION.
```

FIGURE 10–35

```
       FILE-CONTROL.
           SELECT ORDER-FILE     ASSIGN TO DISK.
           SELECT MARKETING-FILE ASSIGN TO DISK.
           SELECT SORT-FILE      ASSIGN TO DISK.

       DATA DIVISION.
       FILE SECTION.

       FD  ORDER-FILE
           LABEL RECORDS ARE STANDARD
           RECORD CONTAINS 7Ø CHARACTERS
           DATA RECORD IS ORDER-RECORD.

       Ø1  ORDER-RECORD                   PIC X(7Ø).

       FD  MARKETING-FILE
           LABEL RECORDS ARE STANDARD
           RECORD CONTAINS 3Ø CHARACTERS
           DATA RECORD IS MARKETING-RECORD.

       Ø1  MARKETING-RECORD               PIC X(3Ø).

       SD  SORT-FILE
           RECORD CONTAINS 3Ø CHARACTERS
           DATA RECORD IS SORT-RECORD.

       Ø1  SORT-RECORD.
           Ø5  SORT-BRANCH               PIC 9(2).
           Ø5  FILLER                    PIC X(11).
           Ø5  SORT-EXTENDED-PRICE       PIC 9(7)V9(2).
           Ø5  FILLER                    PIC X(Ø8).

       WORKING-STORAGE SECTION.

       Ø1  WS-SWITCHES.
           Ø5  END-FLAG-ORDER-FILE        PIC X(3)        VALUE 'NO'.
               88  END-OF-ORDER-FILE                      VALUE 'YES'.

       Ø1  CALCULATED-FIELDS.
           Ø5  EXTENDED-PRICE             PIC 9(7)V9(2).

       Ø1  WS-ORDER-RECORD.
           Ø5  ORD-BRANCH                 PIC 9(2).
           Ø5  ORD-SALES-REP              PIC 9(3).
           Ø5  ORD-CUSTOMER-NBR           PIC 9(5).
           Ø5  ORD-CUST-PO-NBR            PIC X(8).
           Ø5  ORD-SALES-ORD-NBR          PIC X(6).
           Ø5  ORD-DATE.
               1Ø  ORD-YY                 PIC 9(2).
               1Ø  ORD-MM                 PIC 9(2).
               1Ø  ORD-DD                 PIC 9(2).
           Ø5  ORD-PART-NBR               PIC X(6).
           Ø5  ORD-QUANTITY               PIC 9(5).
           Ø5  ORD-UNIT-PRICE             PIC 9(4)V9(2).
           Ø5  ORD-REQ-SHIP-DATE.
               1Ø  ORD-REQ-SHIP-YY        PIC 9(2).
               1Ø  ORD-REQ-SHIP-MM        PIC 9(2).
               1Ø  ORD-REQ-SHIP-DD        PIC 9(2).
           Ø5  ORD-ACT-SHIP-DATE.
               1Ø  ORD-ACT-SHIP-YY        PIC 9(2).
               1Ø  ORD-ACT-SHIP-MM        PIC 9(2).
               1Ø  ORD-ACT-SHIP-DD        PIC 9(2).
           Ø5  FILLER                     PIC X(11).

       Ø1  WS-MARKETING-RECORD.
           Ø5  MKTG-BRANCH                PIC 9(2).
           Ø5  MKTG-CUSTOMER-NBR          PIC 9(5).
           Ø5  MKTG-SALES-ORD-NBR         PIC X(6).
           Ø5  MKTG-EXTENDED-PRICE        PIC 9(7)V9(2).
           Ø5  FILLER                     PIC X(Ø8).

       PROCEDURE DIVISION.

           SORT SORT-FILE
               ASCENDING  KEY SORT-BRANCH
               DESCENDING KEY SORT-EXTENDED-PRICE
                   INPUT PROCEDURE 1ØØØ-SORT-INPUT
                   GIVING MARKETING-FILE.
           STOP RUN.

       1ØØØ-SORT-INPUT SECTION.
       1ØØØ-SORT-INPUT-MAINLINE.
```

FIGURE 10-35 cont.

```
           PERFORM 1100-INITIALIZATION.
           PERFORM 1200-PROCESS-ORDERS
               UNTIL END-OF-ORDER-FILE.
           PERFORM 1300-EOJ.
           GO TO 1000-SECTION-EXIT.

       1100-INITIALIZATION.
           OPEN INPUT ORDER-FILE.
           PERFORM 1900-READ-ORDER-FILE.

       1200-PROCESS-ORDERS.
           COMPUTE EXTENDED-PRICE = ORD-QUANTITY * ORD-UNIT-PRICE.
           IF ORD-BRANCH < 6
               MOVE SPACES              TO WS-MARKETING-RECORD
               MOVE ORD-BRANCH          TO MKTG-BRANCH
               MOVE ORD-CUSTOMER-NBR    TO MKTG-CUSTOMER-NBR
               MOVE ORD-SALES-ORD-NBR   TO MKTG-SALES-ORD-NBR
               MOVE EXTENDED-PRICE      TO MKTG-EXTENDED-PRICE
               RELEASE SORT-RECORD FROM WS-MARKETING-RECORD.
           PERFORM 1900-READ-ORDER-FILE.

       1300-EOJ.
           CLOSE ORDER-FILE.

       1900-READ-ORDER-FILE.
           READ ORDER-FILE INTO WS-ORDER-RECORD
               AT END
                   MOVE 'YES' TO END-FLAG-ORDER-FILE.

       1000-SECTION-EXIT.
           EXIT.
```

FIGURE 10-35 cont.

Explanation of COBOL Sort (INPUT PROCEDURE/GIVING)

The combination of INPUT PROCEDURE and GIVING allows the input file (ORDER-FILE) to be manipulated before the records are sorted. In this particular case, records from Branches 1 to 5 were selected and a calculation was made so that the extended price could be included in the records of the file to be sorted. After the sort is complete, GIVING causes a transfer of the contents of the SORT-FILE to the output file (MARKETING-FILE).

First, the statement

```
SORT SORT-FILE
    ASCENDING KEY SORT-BRANCH
    DESCENDING KEY SORT-EXTENDED-PRICE
```

identifies the file to be sorted and the key fields to be used for the rearrangement of the records. The sort, however, does not take place until the records have been transferred to the SORT-FILE. Notice that one of the fields represents data that will be transferred from the input record. The second field (SORT-EXTENDED-PRICE) does not exist on the input record; it will be calculated in the INPUT PROCEDURE and then moved to the SORT-RECORD.

The statement

```
INPUT PROCEDURE 1000-SORT-INPUT
```

transfers control to the INPUT PROCEDURE, which is named 1000-SORT-INPUT. The INPUT PROCEDURE has a main line which controls it entirely.

In 1000-SORT-INPUT, each record from the ORDER-FILE is read and an extended price is computed. Then control passes to 1200-PROCESS-ORDERS, where the record is tested to determine whether ORD-BRANCH < 6. If it is, data is transferred to the SORT-RECORD area and the record is RELEASEd to the SORT-FILE. This continues until the end of the ORDER-FILE is reached, whereupon 1300-EOJ is performed out of 1000-SORT-INPUT. Instead of a STOP RUN statement, 1000-SORT-INPUT has a GO TO 1000-SECTION-EXIT. This statement is used to transfer control to the end of the INPUT PROCEDURE. After control reaches the end of the INPUT PROCEDURE, the records are rearranged in the SORT-FILE and control moves to

```
GIVING MARKETING-FILE
```

which causes the transfer of the rearranged records from the SORT-FILE to the MARKETING-FILE. There is no opportunity for the programmer to intervene in this transfer.

Notice that the ORDER-FILE used in the INPUT PROCEDURE was both opened and closed. Records were read from ORDER-FILE and RELEASEd to SORT-FILE. SORT-FILE must never be opened or closed. MARKETING-FILE was neither opened nor closed, since it was created by using the GIVING statement. The flow of data through the INPUT PROCEDURE/GIVING type of sort program is shown in Figure 10–36.

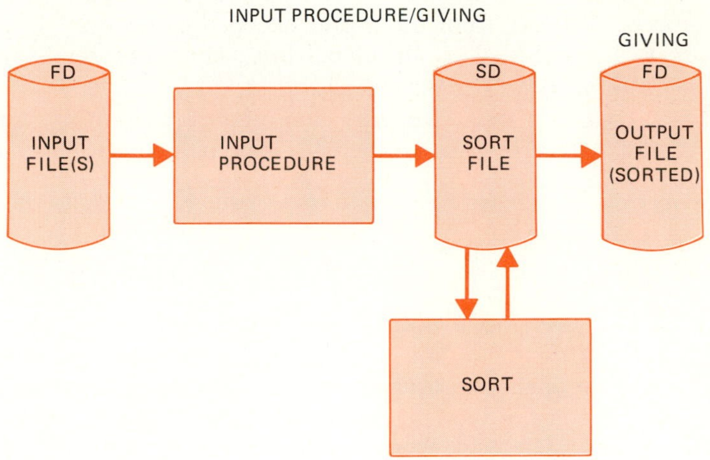

FIGURE 10–36

SAMPLE PROGRAM 4: USING/OUTPUT PROCEDURE

The program specification for the last programming project of the chapter is shown in Figure 10–37. The input file is again ORDER-FILE. The program is to produce a listing which contains all of the records from ORDER-FILE. Since the format and the number of records are to remain the same, the records may be sorted without any processing prior to the sort. This makes a USING clause the appropriate choice. The major sort key is the sales representative (ascending), the intermediate sort key is the customer number (ascending), and the minor sort key is the customer purchase order number (ascending).

PROGRAM SPECIFICATION: SORT-4

PROGRAM SPECIFICATION

Program Name: SORT4

Program Function:

The program will produce a printed report listing orders by sales representative. Within each sales representative, orders will be sequenced by customer number and customer purchase order number. For each sales representative, an average unit price will be calculated and printed.

Input Files:

I. ORDER-FILE

INPUT DEVICE:	DISK
FILE ORGANIZATION:	SEQUENTIAL

FIGURE 10–37

RECORD LENGTH:	70 BYTES
FILE SEQUENCE:	ASCENDING ON SALES ORDER NBR

Output Files:

I. PRINT-FILE

OUTPUT DEVICE:	PRINTER
RECORD LENGTH:	133 BYTES

Processing Requirements:

Each record from the sorted order file should be printed on one line of the output report. All fields from the input, except for the branch and sales representative, are to be included on the detail line. The sales representative number is to be included in the main heading.

Totals for extended price and quantity are to be accumulated for each sales representative so that an average unit price may be calculated and printed for each.

Output Requirements:

The following are formatting requirements for the report:

1. Each page of the report should contain:
   (a) a main heading which includes the company name, the report name, the report date, a page number, and the sales representative number.
   (b) column headings which describe the items printed underneath them.
2. Each new sales representative should begin on a new page.
3. Detail lines should be double spaced. A blank line should be left between different customers.
4. Average unit price for each sales representative should be double spaced.

FIGURE 10-37 cont.

Input Record Layout

The input record layout is shown in Figure 10–38.

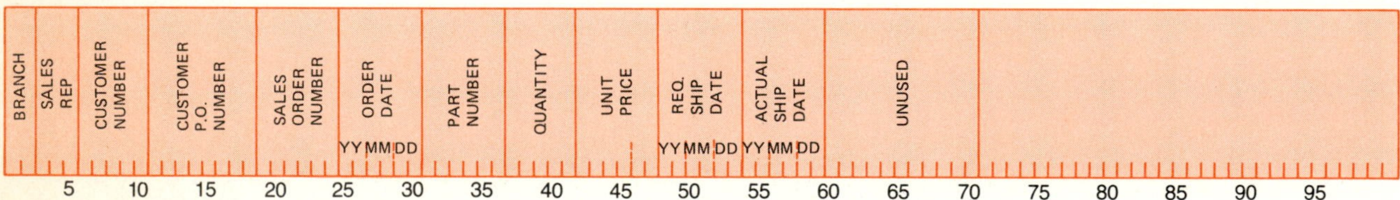

FIGURE 10–38

Print Chart

The print chart is shown in Figure 10–39.

LOGIC FOR USING/OUTPUT PROCEDURE SORT

A hierarchy chart for the SORT4 program is shown in Figure 10–40. Pseudocode and a flowchart are shown in Figures 10–41 and 10–42, respectively.

Explanation of Logic

With the exception of the main routine, the logic routines shown are part of the OUTPUT PROCEDURE. The transfer of the ORDER-FILE to the SORT-FILE is handled by the COBOL sort.

```
           DATE: XX/XX/XX                            PRODUCT DISTRIBUTION INC.                                  PAGE: ZZ9
                                                  ORDERS BY SALES REPRESENTATIVE

           SALES REPRESENTATIVE: XXX

           CUSTOMER    PURCHASE     SALES         ORDER       REQUESTED     ACTUAL        PART                     UNIT
            NUMBER      ORDER       ORDER         DATE        SHIP DATE     SHIP DATE    NUMBER     QUANTITY      PRICE

            99999      XXXXXXXX     XXXXXX       99-99-99     99-99-99      99-99-99     XXXXXX      ZZZZ9      $$$$9.99

            99999      XXXXXXXX     XXXXXX       99-99-99     99-99-99      99-99-99     XXXXXX      ZZZZ9      $$$$9.99


           AVERAGE UNIT PRICE: $$$$9.99
```

FIGURE 10–39

Hierarchy Chart

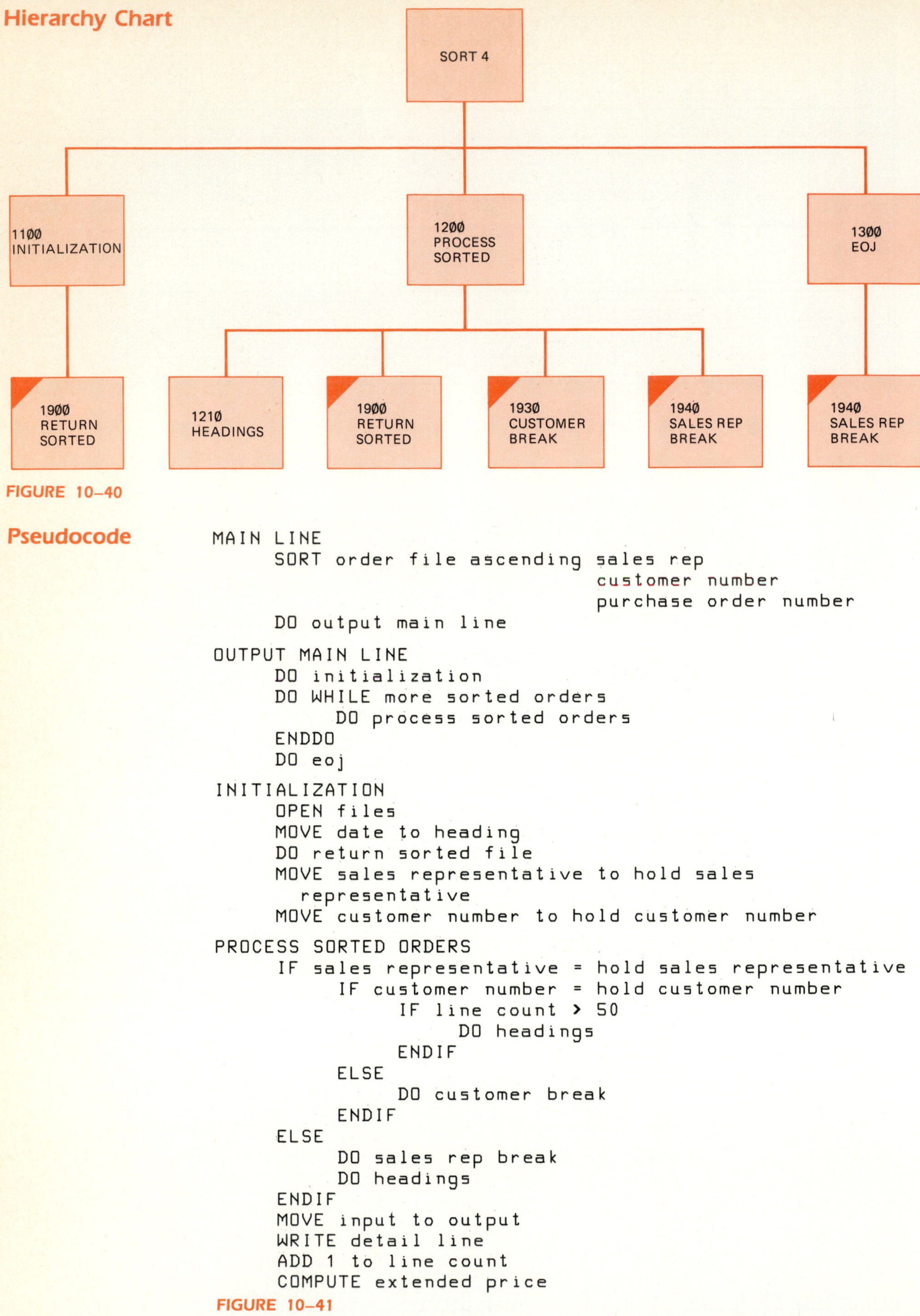

FIGURE 10–40

Pseudocode

```
MAIN LINE
     SORT order file ascending sales rep
                               customer number
                               purchase order number
     DO output main line
OUTPUT MAIN LINE
     DO initialization
     DO WHILE more sorted orders
          DO process sorted orders
     ENDDO
     DO eoj
INITIALIZATION
     OPEN files
     MOVE date to heading
     DO return sorted file
     MOVE sales representative to hold sales
       representative
     MOVE customer number to hold customer number
PROCESS SORTED ORDERS
     IF sales representative = hold sales representative
          IF customer number = hold customer number
               IF line count > 50
                    DO headings
               ENDIF
          ELSE
               DO customer break
          ENDIF
     ELSE
          DO sales rep break
          DO headings
     ENDIF
     MOVE input to output
     WRITE detail line
     ADD 1 to line count
     COMPUTE extended price
```

FIGURE 10–41

```
        ADD extended price to sales rep extended price
        ADD quantity to sales rep quantity
        DO return sorted file
HEADINGS
        ADD 1 to page count
        WRITE main heading one
        WRITE main heading two
        WRITE main heading three
        WRITE column heading one
        WRITE column heading two
        MOVE 7 to line count
EOJ
        DO sales rep break
        CLOSE print file
RETURN SORTED FILE
        RETURN sort file
CUSTOMER BREAK
        WRITE blank line
        ADD 1 to line count
        MOVE customer number to customer number hold
SALES REP BREAK
        IF sales representative quantity = zeros
            MOVE zeros to average unit price
        ELSE
            CALCULATE average unit price = sales rep
              extended price / sales rep quantity
        ENDIF
        MOVE average unit price to output
        WRITE sales rep footing
        MOVE zeros to sales rep quantity, sales rep
          extended price
        MOVE sales rep to hold sales rep
```

FIGURE 10-41 cont.

THE COBOL PROGRAM

Test Data

Test data for the SORT4 PROGRAM is shown in Figure 10–43.

Sample Output

Sample output generated by the SORT4 program is shown in Figure 10–44.

The Program

The complete COBOL SORT4 program is shown in Figure 10–45.

Explanation of COBOL Sort (USING/OUTPUT PROCEDURE)

SORT-4 produces a report that is separated by sales representative. Accordingly, its input ORDER-FILE is sorted by sales representative, and then within each sales representative the records are sorted by customer number and within each customer number they are sorted by customer purchase order number. The SORT statement

```
SORT SORT-FILE
    ASCENDING KEY SORT-SALES-REP
                  SORT-CUSTOMER-NBR
                  SORT-CUST-PO-NBR
```

sets up the parameters for the sort by identifying the name of the sort file, the names of the sort keys, and the direction of the sort. The clause

```
USING ORDER-FILE
```

causes the transfer of the records from the ORDER-FILE to the SORT-FILE. The programmer does not open or close either file or perform any reads or writes. After the transfer is complete, SORT-FILE is sorted.
(*text continued on page 507*)

Flowchart

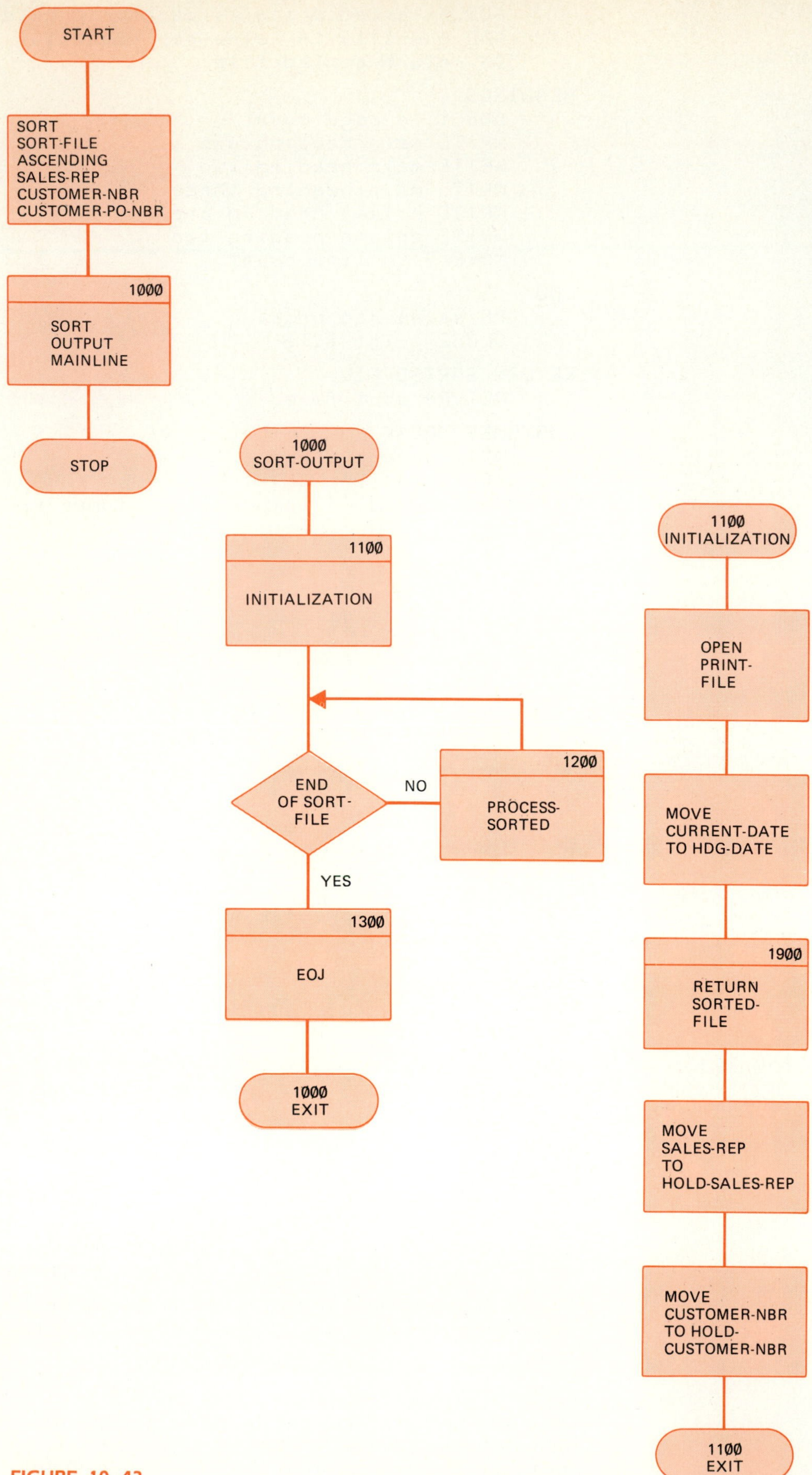

FIGURE 10–42

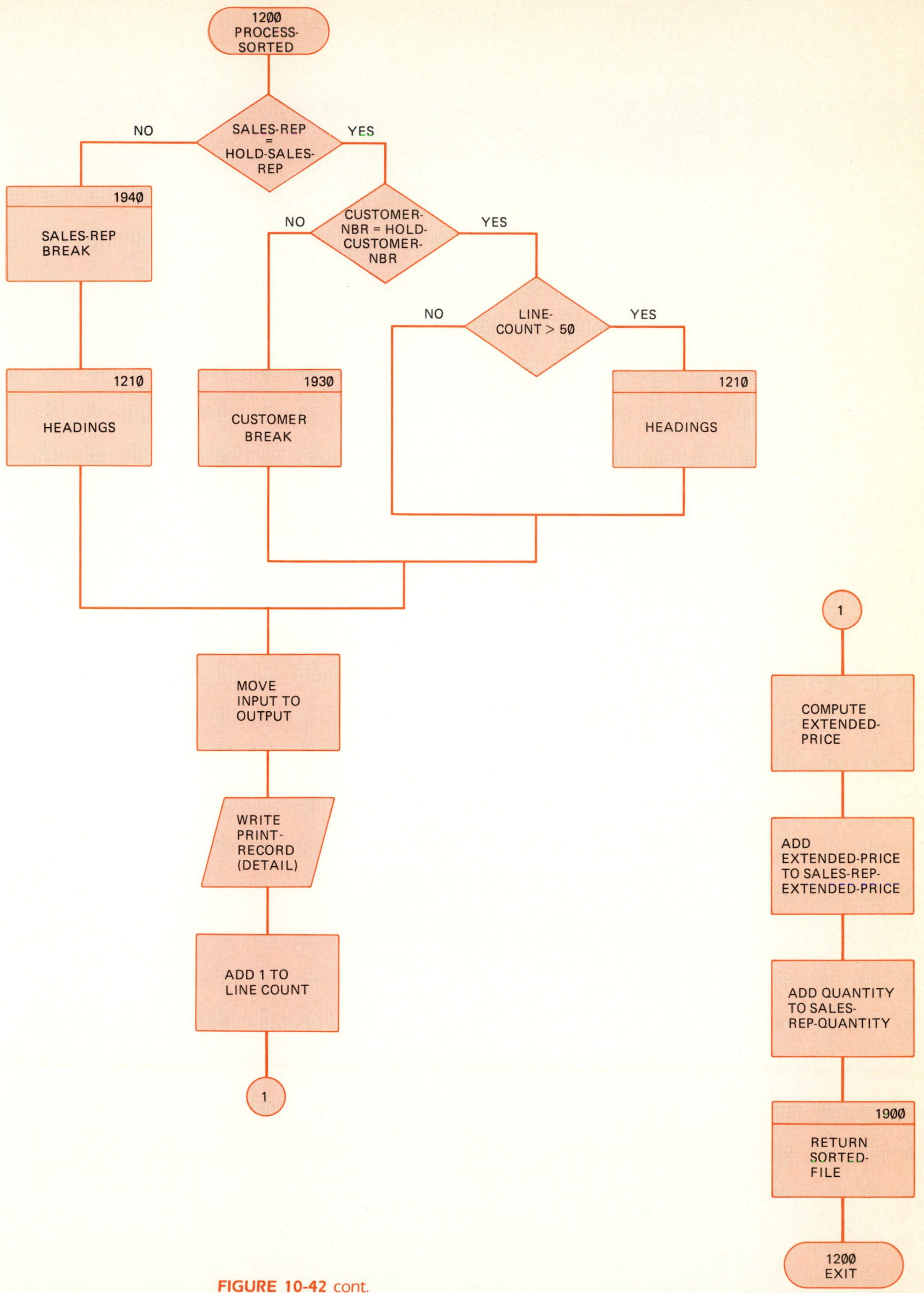

FIGURE 10-42 cont.

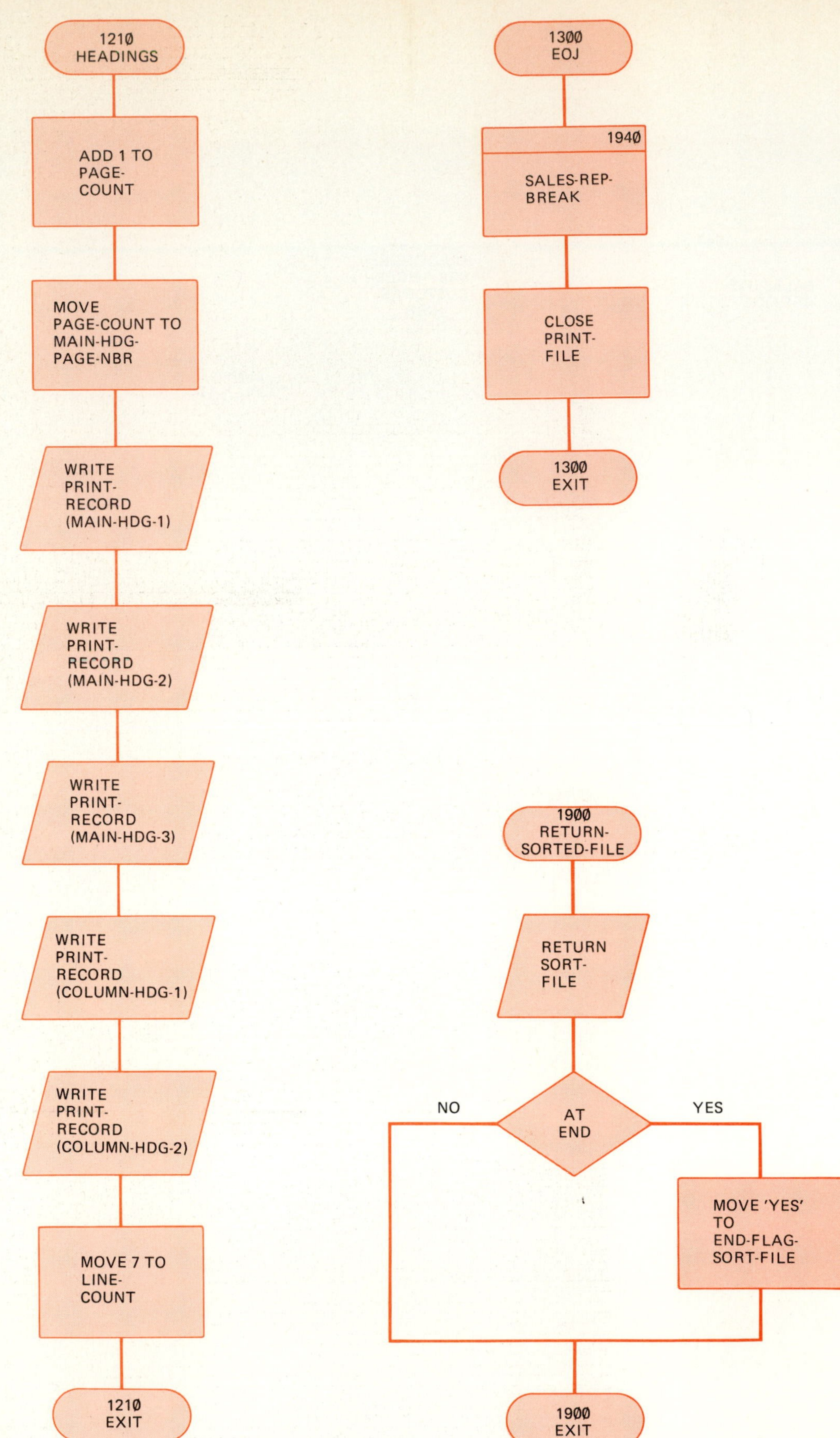

FIGURE 10-42 cont.

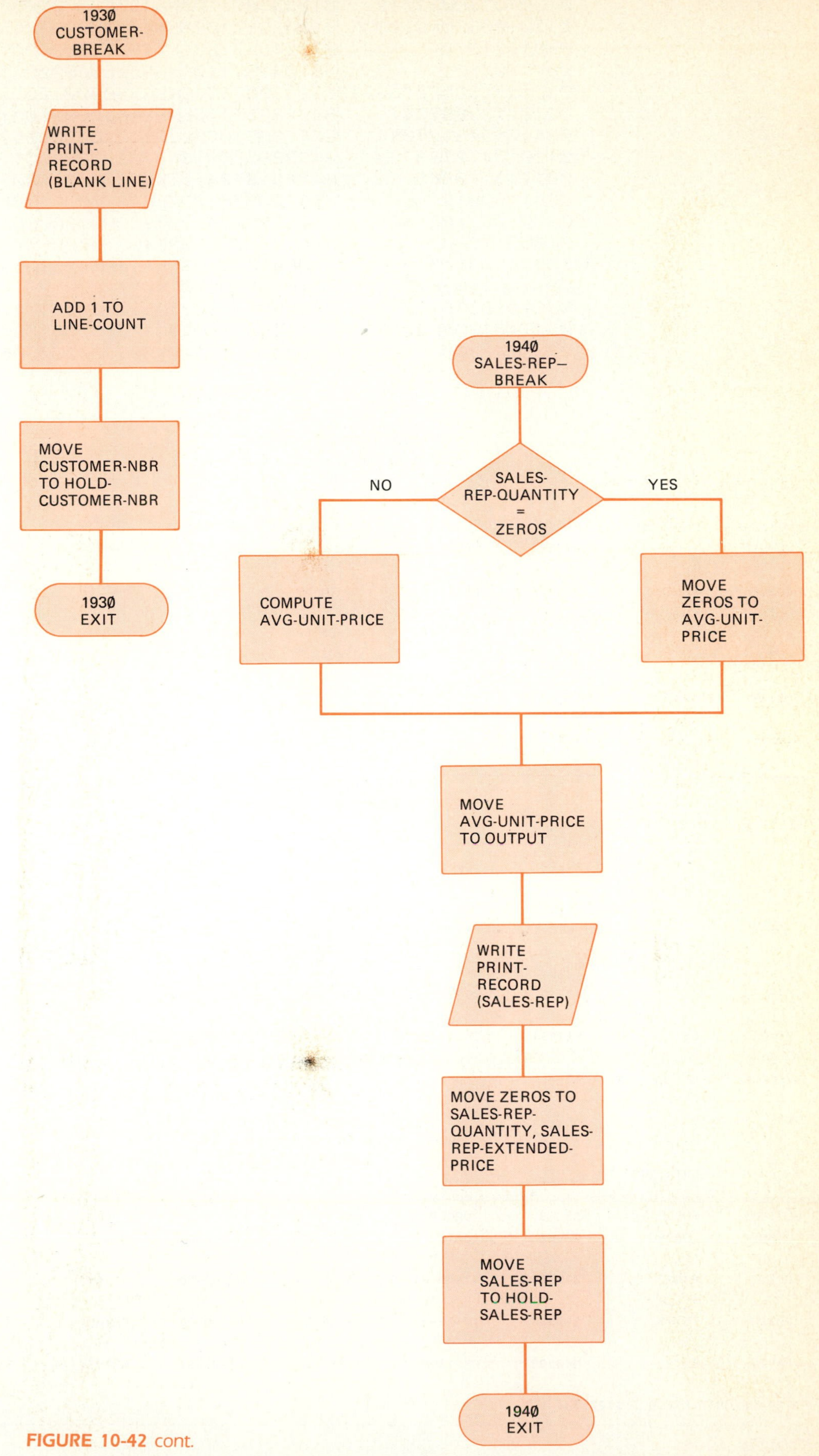

FIGURE 10-42 cont.

```
Ø1201ØØ3ØØE1Ø12   B12335871105WB493EØØØØ2Ø54ØØØ871122ØØØØØØ
Ø1201ØØ3ØØPO173   B12383871Ø25GN4Ø2AØØØØ1Ø45ØØØ871116ØØØØØØ
Ø891521Ø78        B71Ø45871ØØ1FV782TØØØØ3ØØ28ØØ871115871109
Ø8174ØØ5Ø1        B81Ø41871108JG96ØEØØØØ2Ø28Ø35870214ØØØØØØ
Ø361182888P2783733B8433Ø871Ø25HL289BØØØ1ØØ234ØØ871113871109
Ø3ØØ7739897747    B89288871106MF848JØØØØ5Ø2145Ø88Ø13ØØØØØØ
Ø344Ø69481870341  GØ418Ø870209JGØ4ØXØØØØ1Ø525ØØ880619ØØØØØØ
Ø12Ø1Ø47278372    G48388870913WB7Ø2XØØØ9ØØ115ØØ8711Ø1871109
Ø817431408 65     H41891870412TK61ØLØØØ18ØØ78ØØ87Ø63Ø871109
Ø36115Ø912        H6915Ø870206MF848TØØØØ3Ø36ØØØ8712Ø1ØØØØØØ
Ø3ØØ7ØØ378EBNER   H84579870811VX922PØØ8ØØØØ1275891120ØØØØØØ
Ø3ØØ747300        H84777870223MF4Ø3TØØØØ5Ø4ØØØØ87Ø5Ø2ØØØØØØ
Ø891562Ø54SCHUH   L5Ø681871108TK814EØØØØ6Ø565ØØ88Ø1Ø5ØØØØØØ
Ø8174Ø18Ø5R7278   T2164287Ø81ØTK497XØØØ1ØØ118ØØ87113Ø871109
Ø36112837 5T7838  T78299870323JG563WØØØØ6Ø43ØØØ871Ø18ØØØØØØ
Ø8174Ø18Ø5R8322   Y2110587Ø6Ø1TN116TØØØØ1Ø3ØØØØ871221ØØØØØØ
Ø3ØØ747300        Y289Ø387Ø811VXØØ1LØØ2ØØØØ622Ø8712Ø3ØØØØØØ
```

FIGURE 10–43

DATE: 11/09/87 PRODUCT DISTRIBUTION INC. PAGE: 1

ORDERS BY SALES REPRESENTATIVE

SALES REPRESENTATIVE: 007

CUSTOMER NUMBER	PURCHASE ORDER	SALES ORDER	ORDER DATE	REQUESTED SHIP DATE	ACTUAL SHIP DATE	PART NUMBER	QUANTITY	UNIT PRICE
00378	EBNER	H84579	08-11-87	11-20-89	00-00-00	VX922P	800	$12.75
47300		Y28903	08-11-87	12-03-87	00-00-00	VX001L	200	$62.20
47300		H84777	02-23-87	05-02-87	00-00-00	MF403T	5	$400.00
73989	7747	B89288	11-06-87	01-30-88	00-00-00	MF848J	5	$214.50

AVERAGE UNIT PRICE: $25.45

DATE: 11/09/87 PRODUCT DISTRIBUTION INC. PAGE: 2

ORDERS BY SALES REPRESENTATIVE

SALES REPRESENTATIVE: 174

CUSTOMER NUMBER	PURCHASE ORDER	SALES ORDER	ORDER DATE	REQUESTED SHIP DATE	ACTUAL SHIP DATE	PART NUMBER	QUANTITY	UNIT PRICE
00501		B81041	11-08-87	02-14-87	00-00-00	JG960E	2	$280.35
01805	R7278	T21642	08-10-87	11-30-87	11-09-87	TK497X	10	$118.00
01805	R8322	Y21105	06-01-87	12-21-87	00-00-00	TN116T	1	$300.00
31408	65	H41891	04-12-87	06-30-87	11-09-87	TK610L	18	$78.00

AVERAGE UNIT PRICE: $111.11

DATE: 11/09/87 PRODUCT DISTRIBUTION INC. PAGE: 3

ORDERS BY SALES REPRESENTATIVE

SALES REPRESENTATIVE: 201

CUSTOMER NUMBER	PURCHASE ORDER	SALES ORDER	ORDER DATE	REQUESTED SHIP DATE	ACTUAL SHIP DATE	PART NUMBER	QUANTITY	UNIT PRICE
00300	E1012	B12335	11-05-87	11-22-87	00-00-00	WB493E	2	$540.00
00300	PO173	B12383	10-25-87	11-16-87	00-00-00	GN402A	1	$450.00
04727	8372	G48388	09-13-87	11-01-87	11-09-87	WB702X	90	$115.00

AVERAGE UNIT PRICE: $127.74

FIGURE 10–44

DATE: 11/09/87 PRODUCT DISTRIBUTION INC. PAGE: 4

ORDERS BY SALES REPRESENTATIVE

SALES REPRESENTATIVE: 440

CUSTOMER NUMBER	PURCHASE ORDER	SALES ORDER	ORDER DATE	REQUESTED SHIP DATE	ACTUAL SHIP DATE	PART NUMBER	QUANTITY	UNIT PRICE
69481	870341	G04180	02-09-87	06-19-88	00-00-00	JG040X	1	$525.00

AVERAGE UNIT PRICE: $525.00

DATE: 11/09/87 PRODUCT DISTRIBUTION INC. PAGE: 5

ORDERS BY SALES REPRESENTATIVE

SALES REPRESENTATIVE: 611

CUSTOMER NUMBER	PURCHASE ORDER	SALES ORDER	ORDER DATE	REQUESTED SHIP DATE	ACTUAL SHIP DATE	PART NUMBER	QUANTITY	UNIT PRICE
28375	T7838	T78299	03-23-87	10-18-87	00-00-00	JG563W	6	$430.00
50912		H69150	02-06-87	12-01-87	00-00-00	MF848T	3	$360.00
82888	P2783733	B84330	10-25-87	11-13-87	11-09-87	HL289B	10	$234.00

AVERAGE UNIT PRICE: $315.78

DATE: 11/09/87 PRODUCT DISTRIBUTION INC. PAGE: 6

ORDERS BY SALES REPRESENTATIVE

SALES REPRESENTATIVE: 915

CUSTOMER NUMBER	PURCHASE ORDER	SALES ORDER	ORDER DATE	REQUESTED SHIP DATE	ACTUAL SHIP DATE	PART NUMBER	QUANTITY	UNIT PRICE
21078		B71045	10-01-87	11-15-87	11-09-87	FV782T	3	$28.00
62054	SCHUH	L50681	11-08-87	01-05-88	00-00-00	TK814E	6	$565.00

AVERAGE UNIT PRICE: $386.00

FIGURE 10-44 cont.

```
IDENTIFICATION DIVISION.

PROGRAM-ID.    SORT4.

AUTHOR.        HELEN HUMPHREYS.

INSTALLATION.  PRODUCT DISTRIBUTION INC.

DATE-WRITTEN.  1Ø/22/87.

DATE-COMPILED. 1Ø/25/87.

****************************************************************
*                                                              *
*    THIS PROGRAM WILL PRODUCE A PRINTED REPORT LISTING ORDERS *
*    BY SALES REPRESENTATIVE.  WITHIN SALES REPRESENTATIVE,    *
*    ORDERS WILL BE SEQUENCED BY CUSTOMER.  FOR EACH SALES     *
*    REPRESENTATIVE, AN AVERAGE UNIT PRICE WILL BE CALCULATED  *
*    AND PRINTED.                                              *
*                                                              *
****************************************************************

ENVIRONMENT DIVISION.

CONFIGURATION SECTION.
```

FIGURE 10–45

```
       SOURCE-COMPUTER.
           IBM-37Ø.
       OBJECT-COMPUTER.
           IBM-37Ø.
       INPUT-OUTPUT SECTION.
       FILE-CONTROL.
           SELECT ORDER-FILE  ASSIGN TO DISK.
           SELECT PRINT-FILE  ASSIGN TO PRINTER.
           SELECT SORT-FILE   ASSIGN TO DISK.
       DATA DIVISION.
       FILE SECTION.
       FD  ORDER-FILE
           LABEL RECORDS ARE STANDARD
           RECORD CONTAINS 7Ø CHARACTERS
           DATA RECORD IS ORDER-RECORD.
       Ø1  ORDER-RECORD                PIC X(7Ø).
       FD  PRINT-FILE
           LABEL RECORDS ARE OMITTED
           RECORD CONTAINS 133 CHARACTERS
           DATA RECORD IS PRINT-RECORD.
       Ø1  PRINT-RECORD               PIC X(133).
       SD  SORT-FILE
           RECORD CONTAINS 7Ø CHARACTERS
           DATA RECORD IS SORT-RECORD.
       Ø1  SORT-RECORD.
           Ø5  FILLER                 PIC X(2).
           Ø5  SORT-SALES-REP         PIC 9(3).
           Ø5  SORT-CUSTOMER-NBR      PIC 9(5).
           Ø5  SORT-CUST-PO-NBR       PIC X(8).
           Ø5  FILLER                 PIC X(52).
       WORKING-STORAGE SECTION.
       Ø1  WS-COUNTERS.
           Ø5  LINE-COUNT              PIC 9(2)        VALUE 99.
           Ø5  PAGE-COUNT              PIC 9(3)        VALUE ZEROS.
       Ø1  WS-SWITCHES.
           Ø5  END-FLAG-SORT-FILE      PIC X(3)        VALUE 'NO'.
               88  END-OF-SORT-FILE                    VALUE 'YES'.
       Ø1  WS-HOLDS.
           Ø5  HOLD-SALES-REP          PIC 9(3).
           Ø5  HOLD-CUSTOMER-NBR       PIC 9(5).
       Ø1  CALCULATED-FIELDS.
           Ø5  EXTENDED-PRICE          PIC 9(7)V9(2).
           Ø5  AVG-UNIT-PRICE          PIC 9(4)V9(2).
       Ø1  SALES-REP-TOTAL-FIELDS.
           Ø5  SALES-REP-QUANTITY      PIC 9(8)        VALUE ZERO.
           Ø5  SALES-REP-EXTENDED-PRICE    PIC 9(8)V9(2)   VALUE ZERO.
       Ø1  WS-ORDER-RECORD.
           Ø5  ORD-BRANCH              PIC 9(2).
           Ø5  ORD-SALES-REP           PIC 9(3).
           Ø5  ORD-CUSTOMER-NBR        PIC 9(5).
           Ø5  ORD-CUST-PO-NBR         PIC X(8).
           Ø5  ORD-SALES-ORD-NBR       PIC X(6).
           Ø5  ORD-DATE.
               1Ø  ORD-YY              PIC 9(2).
               1Ø  ORD-MM              PIC 9(2).
               1Ø  ORD-DD              PIC 9(2).
           Ø5  ORD-PART-NBR            PIC X(6).
           Ø5  ORD-QUANTITY            PIC 9(5).
           Ø5  ORD-UNIT-PRICE          PIC 9(4)V9(2).
           Ø5  ORD-REQ-SHIP-DATE.
               1Ø  ORD-REQ-SHIP-YY     PIC 9(2).
               1Ø  ORD-REQ-SHIP-MM     PIC 9(2).
               1Ø  ORD-REQ-SHIP-DD     PIC 9(2).
           Ø5  ORD-ACT-SHIP-DATE.
               1Ø  ORD-ACT-SHIP-YY     PIC 9(2).
               1Ø  ORD-ACT-SHIP-MM     PIC 9(2).
               1Ø  ORD-ACT-SHIP-DD     PIC 9(2).
           Ø5  FILLER                  PIC X(11).
```

FIGURE 10-45 cont.

```
       Ø1  MAIN-HEADING-1.
           Ø5  FILLER                  PIC X(11)       VALUE SPACES.
           Ø5  FILLER                  PIC X(6)        VALUE 'DATE:'.
           Ø5  MAIN-HDG-DATE           PIC X(8).
           Ø5  FILLER                  PIC X(29)       VALUE SPACES.
           Ø5  FILLER                  PIC X(25)       VALUE
                                       'PRODUCT DISTRIBUTION INC.'.
           Ø5  FILLER                  PIC X(34)       VALUE SPACES.
           Ø5  FILLER                  PIC X(6)        VALUE 'PAGE:'.
           Ø5  MAIN-HDG-PAGE-NBR       PIC ZZ9.
           Ø5  FILLER                  PIC X(11)       VALUE SPACES.

       Ø1  MAIN-HEADING-2.
           Ø5  FILLER                  PIC X(51)       VALUE SPACES.
           Ø5  FILLER                  PIC X(3Ø)       VALUE
                                       'ORDERS BY SALES REPRESENTATIVE'.
           Ø5  FILLER                  PIC X(52)       VALUE SPACES.

       Ø1  MAIN-HEADING-3.
           Ø5  FILLER                  PIC X(11)       VALUE SPACES.
           Ø5  FILLER                  PIC X(22)       VALUE
                                       'SALES REPRESENTATIVE:'.
           Ø5  MAIN-HDG-SALES-REP      PIC 9(3).
           Ø5  FILLER                  PIC X(97)       VALUE SPACES.

       Ø1  COLUMN-HEADING-1.
           Ø5  FILLER                  PIC X(11)       VALUE SPACES.
           Ø5  FILLER                  PIC X(8)        VALUE 'CUSTOMER'.
           Ø5  FILLER                  PIC X(4)        VALUE SPACES.
           Ø5  FILLER                  PIC X(8)        VALUE 'PURCHASE'.
           Ø5  FILLER                  PIC X(6)        VALUE SPACES.
           Ø5  FILLER                  PIC X(5)        VALUE 'SALES'.
           Ø5  FILLER                  PIC X(8)        VALUE SPACES.
           Ø5  FILLER                  PIC X(5)        VALUE 'ORDER'.
           Ø5  FILLER                  PIC X(8)        VALUE SPACES.
           Ø5  FILLER                  PIC X(9)        VALUE
                                                       'REQUESTED'.
           Ø5  FILLER                  PIC X(6)        VALUE SPACES.
           Ø5  FILLER                  PIC X(6)        VALUE 'ACTUAL'.
           Ø5  FILLER                  PIC X(8)        VALUE SPACES.
           Ø5  FILLER                  PIC X(4)        VALUE 'PART'.
           Ø5  FILLER                  PIC X(21)       VALUE SPACES.
           Ø5  FILLER                  PIC X(4)        VALUE 'UNIT'.
           Ø5  FILLER                  PIC X(12)       VALUE SPACES.

       Ø1  COLUMN-HEADING-2.
           Ø5  FILLER                  PIC X(12)       VALUE SPACES.
           Ø5  FILLER                  PIC X(6)        VALUE 'NUMBER'.
           Ø5  FILLER                  PIC X(6)        VALUE SPACES.
           Ø5  FILLER                  PIC X(5)        VALUE 'ORDER'.
           Ø5  FILLER                  PIC X(8)        VALUE SPACES.
           Ø5  FILLER                  PIC X(5)        VALUE 'ORDER'.
           Ø5  FILLER                  PIC X(8)        VALUE SPACES.
           Ø5  FILLER                  PIC X(4)        VALUE 'DATE'.
           Ø5  FILLER                  PIC X(9)        VALUE SPACES.
           Ø5  FILLER                  PIC X(9)        VALUE
                                                       'SHIP DATE'.
           Ø5  FILLER                  PIC X(5)        VALUE SPACES.
           Ø5  FILLER                  PIC X(9)        VALUE
                                                       'SHIP DATE'.
           Ø5  FILLER                  PIC X(5)        VALUE SPACES.
           Ø5  FILLER                  PIC X(6)        VALUE 'NUMBER'.
           Ø5  FILLER                  PIC X(5)        VALUE SPACES.
           Ø5  FILLER                  PIC X(8)        VALUE 'QUANTITY'.
           Ø5  FILLER                  PIC X(6)        VALUE SPACES.
           Ø5  FILLER                  PIC X(5)        VALUE 'PRICE'.
           Ø5  FILLER                  PIC X(12)       VALUE SPACES.

       Ø1  DETAIL-LINE.
           Ø5  FILLER                  PIC X(12)       VALUE SPACES.
           Ø5  DET-CUSTOMER-NBR        PIC 9(5).
           Ø5  FILLER                  PIC X(6)        VALUE SPACES.
           Ø5  DET-CUST-PO-NBR         PIC X(8).
           Ø5  FILLER                  PIC X(6)        VALUE SPACES.
           Ø5  DET-SALES-ORD-NBR       PIC X(6).
           Ø5  FILLER                  PIC X(6)        VALUE SPACES.
           Ø5  DET-ORD-MM              PIC 9(2).
           Ø5  FILLER                  PIC X(1)        VALUE '-'.
           Ø5  DET-ORD-DD              PIC 9(2).
           Ø5  FILLER                  PIC X(1)        VALUE '-'.
           Ø5  DET-ORD-YY              PIC 9(2).
           Ø5  FILLER                  PIC X(6)        VALUE SPACES.
           Ø5  DET-REQ-SHIP-MM         PIC 9(2).
           Ø5  FILLER                  PIC X(1)        VALUE '-'.
```

FIGURE 10-45 cont.

```
    Ø5  DET-REQ-SHIP-DD         PIC 9(2).
    Ø5  FILLER                  PIC X(1)        VALUE '-'.
    Ø5  DET-REQ-SHIP-YY         PIC 9(2).
    Ø5  FILLER                  PIC X(6)        VALUE SPACES.
    Ø5  DET-ACT-SHIP-MM         PIC 9(2).
    Ø5  FILLER                  PIC X(1)        VALUE '-'.
    Ø5  DET-ACT-SHIP-DD         PIC 9(2).
    Ø5  FILLER                  PIC X(1)        VALUE '-'.
    Ø5  DET-ACT-SHIP-YY         PIC 9(2).
    Ø5  FILLER                  PIC X(6)        VALUE SPACES.
    Ø5  DET-PART-NBR            PIC X(6).
    Ø5  FILLER                  PIC X(6)        VALUE SPACES.
    Ø5  DET-QUANTITY            PIC ZZZZ9.
    Ø5  FILLER                  PIC X(6)        VALUE SPACES.
    Ø5  DET-UNIT-PRICE          PIC $$$$9.99.
    Ø5  FILLER                  PIC X(11)       VALUE SPACES.

Ø1  BLANK-LINE                  PIC X(133)      VALUE SPACES.

Ø1  SALES-REP-FOOTING.
    Ø5  FILLER                  PIC X(11)       VALUE SPACES.
    Ø5  FILLER                  PIC X(2Ø)       VALUE
                                 'AVERAGE UNIT PRICE:'.
    Ø5  AVG-UNIT-PRICE-OUT      PIC $$$$9.99.
    Ø5  FILLER                  PIC X(94)       VALUE SPACES.

PROCEDURE DIVISION.

    SORT SORT-FILE
        ASCENDING KEY SORT-SALES-REP
                      SORT-CUSTOMER-NBR
                      SORT-CUST-PO-NBR
            USING ORDER-FILE
            OUTPUT PROCEDURE 1ØØØ-SORT-OUTPUT.
    STOP RUN.


1ØØØ-SORT-OUTPUT SECTION.
1ØØØ-SORT-OUTPUT-MAINLINE.
    PERFORM 11ØØ-INITIALIZATION.
    PERFORM 12ØØ-PROCESS-SORTED
        UNTIL END-OF-SORT-FILE.
    PERFORM 13ØØ-EOJ.
    GO TO 1ØØØ-SECTION-EXIT.

11ØØ-INITIALIZATION.
    OPEN OUTPUT PRINT-FILE.
    MOVE CURRENT-DATE TO MAIN-HDG-DATE.
    PERFORM 19ØØ-RETURN-SORTED.
    MOVE ORD-SALES-REP TO HOLD-SALES-REP.
    MOVE ORD-CUSTOMER-NBR TO HOLD-CUSTOMER-NBR.

12ØØ-PROCESS-SORTED.

    IF ORD-SALES-REP = HOLD-SALES-REP
        IF ORD-CUSTOMER-NBR = HOLD-CUSTOMER-NBR
            IF LINE-COUNT > 5Ø
                PERFORM 121Ø-HEADINGS
            ELSE
                NEXT SENTENCE
        ELSE
            PERFORM 193Ø-CUSTOMER-BREAK
    ELSE
        PERFORM 194Ø-SALES-REP-BREAK
        PERFORM 121Ø-HEADINGS.

    MOVE ORD-CUSTOMER-NBR      TO DET-CUSTOMER-NBR.
    MOVE ORD-CUST-PO-NBR       TO DET-CUST-PO-NBR.
    MOVE ORD-SALES-ORD-NBR     TO DET-SALES-ORD-NBR.
    MOVE ORD-YY                TO DET-ORD-YY.
    MOVE ORD-MM                TO DET-ORD-MM.
    MOVE ORD-DD                TO DET-ORD-DD.
    MOVE ORD-REQ-SHIP-YY       TO DET-REQ-SHIP-YY.
    MOVE ORD-REQ-SHIP-MM       TO DET-REQ-SHIP-MM.
    MOVE ORD-REQ-SHIP-DD       TO DET-REQ-SHIP-DD.
    MOVE ORD-ACT-SHIP-YY       TO DET-ACT-SHIP-YY.
    MOVE ORD-ACT-SHIP-MM       TO DET-ACT-SHIP-MM.
    MOVE ORD-ACT-SHIP-DD       TO DET-ACT-SHIP-DD.
    MOVE ORD-PART-NBR          TO DET-PART-NBR.
    MOVE ORD-QUANTITY          TO DET-QUANTITY.
    MOVE ORD-UNIT-PRICE        TO DET-UNIT-PRICE.
    WRITE PRINT-RECORD FROM DETAIL-LINE
        AFTER ADVANCING 1 LINE.
    ADD 1 TO LINE-COUNT.
```

FIGURE 10-45 cont.

```
           COMPUTE EXTENDED-PRICE = ORD-QUANTITY * ORD-UNIT-PRICE.
           ADD EXTENDED-PRICE TO SALES-REP-EXTENDED-PRICE.
           ADD ORD-QUANTITY   TO SALES-REP-QUANTITY.
           PERFORM 1900-RETURN-SORTED.

       1210-HEADINGS.
           ADD 1 TO PAGE-COUNT.
           MOVE PAGE-COUNT TO MAIN-HDG-PAGE-NBR.
           MOVE ORD-SALES-REP TO MAIN-HDG-SALES-REP.
           WRITE PRINT-RECORD FROM MAIN-HEADING-1
               AFTER ADVANCING PAGE.
           WRITE PRINT-RECORD FROM MAIN-HEADING-2
               AFTER ADVANCING 1 LINE.
           WRITE PRINT-RECORD FROM MAIN-HEADING-3
               AFTER ADVANCING 2 LINES.
           WRITE PRINT-RECORD FROM COLUMN-HEADING-1
               AFTER ADVANCING 2 LINES.
           WRITE PRINT-RECORD FROM COLUMN-HEADING-2
               AFTER ADVANCING 1 LINE.
           WRITE PRINT-RECORD FROM BLANK-LINE
               AFTER ADVANCING 1 LINE.
           MOVE 7 TO LINE-COUNT.

       1300-EOJ.
           PERFORM 1940-SALES-REP-BREAK.
           CLOSE PRINT-FILE.

       1900-RETURN-SORTED.
           RETURN SORT-FILE INTO WS-ORDER-RECORD
               AT END
                   MOVE 'YES' TO END-FLAG-SORT-FILE.

       1930-CUSTOMER-BREAK.
           WRITE PRINT-RECORD FROM BLANK-LINE
               AFTER ADVANCING 1 LINE.
           ADD 1 TO LINE-COUNT.
           MOVE ORD-CUSTOMER-NBR TO HOLD-CUSTOMER-NBR.

       1940-SALES-REP-BREAK.
           IF SALES-REP-QUANTITY = ZEROS
               MOVE ZEROS TO AVG-UNIT-PRICE
           ELSE
               COMPUTE AVG-UNIT-PRICE =
                     SALES-REP-EXTENDED-PRICE / SALES-REP-QUANTITY.
           MOVE AVG-UNIT-PRICE TO AVG-UNIT-PRICE-OUT.
           WRITE PRINT-RECORD FROM SALES-REP-FOOTING
               AFTER ADVANCING 2 LINES.
           MOVE ZEROS TO SALES-REP-QUANTITY
                         SALES-REP-EXTENDED-PRICE.
           MOVE ORD-SALES-REP TO HOLD-SALES-REP.

       1000-SECTION-EXIT.
           EXIT.
```

FIGURE 10-45 cont.

The clause

```
OUTPUT PROCEDURE 1000-SORT-OUTPUT.
```

names section 1000-SORT-OUTPUT, which contains the code necessary to transfer the rearranged records from the SORT-FILE to a printed report. The section has a main line in it which controls its paragraphs. Both an INPUT PROCEDURE and an OUTPUT PROCEDURE require that once control is in the procedure the programmer execute only paragraphs within that procedure. When all records have been processed, the main line of the section uses a GO TO to transfer control to the end of the section. From there, control passes to the STOP RUN statement that follows the SORT statement.

The OUTPUT PROCEDURE contains logic for a control-break program which produces a report based on breaks in the control variables, sales representative and customer number. The records for each new sales representative are started on a new page, and extra spacing is used to separate the customers listed for a given sales representative.

Notice in particular how the records are retrieved from the SORT-FILE. RETURN is used in place of READ to access these records. As each record is returned, it is moved to a detail line and written to the PRINT-FILE. The PRINT-FILE must be opened and closed, since it is described in an FD and used in an

OUTPUT PROCEDURE. The flow of data through the USING/OUTPUT PROCEDURE combination is shown in Figure 10–46.

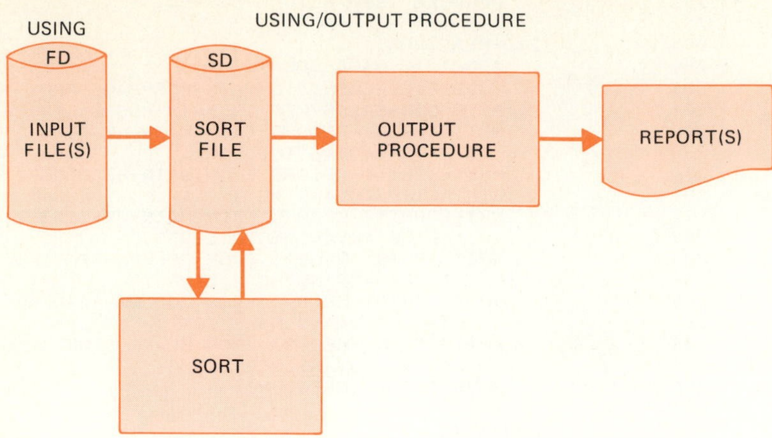

FIGURE 10–46

DEBUGGING

Diagnostics

```
SYNTAX REQUIRES 01 LEVEL SD DATA NAME IN RELEASE
  STATEMENT
```

RELEASE is used to transfer (write) data to a sort file. Consequently, just as the verb WRITE must be followed by a record-name from a file described in an FD, the verb RELEASE must be followed by a record-name from a file described in an SD.

To correct the problem, the programmer should

1. Make sure that the objective is to transfer data to a sort file. This must be done in an INPUT PROCEDURE.
2. Locate the SD in the FILE SECTION and use the 01 level record-name after the word RELEASE.

```
SYNTAX REQUIRES 'USING' ('GIVING') TO BE FOLLOWED BY
 SEQUENTIAL FILE DEFINED UNDER AN FD
```

USING is used to transfer records from a file described in an FD to a sort file described in an SD. GIVING is used to transfer records from a sort file described in an SD to a file described in an FD.

To correct the problem, the programmer should

1. In the case of USING, locate and use the name of the sequential file described in an FD whose contents require sorting. Place the file-name after the word USING.
2. In the case of GIVING, locate and use the name of the sequential file described in an FD that is to receive the sorted records from the sort file.

EXHIBIT

Format

```
EXHIBIT {NAMED        }  {identifier-1}  [identifier-2]
        {CHANGED NAMED}  {literal-1   }  [literal-2   ]  . . .
        {CHANGED      }
```

EXHIBIT is used to display the contents of data items to assist in the debugging of programs. Since it is not a part of standard COBOL, the programmer must make sure that it is available on his or her system. EXHIBIT allows the programmer three choices of style for displaying data items. The following are examples of the three formats and the output they produce:

1. ```
   EXHIBIT NAMED QUANTITY.
   QUANTITY = 999
   ```

   In this format, EXHIBIT provides the name of the data item, the spaces, the equals sign, and the current value of the data item.

2. ```
   EXHIBIT CHANGED NAMED BR-HOLD.
   BR-HOLD = 0
   ```

   This format of the EXHIBIT statement produces output the first time it is executed, and thereafter only when the contents of BR-HOLD have changed. The format is particularly useful for checking for a change in a control field. If a literal is used in the statement, it will be displayed each time the statement is executed.

3. ```
   EXHIBIT CHANGED BR-HOLD DIV-HOLD
   0          0
   1
   ```

   This format produces output only when at least one of the data items has a new value. Both are considered to have a new value the first time the statement is executed. The values are printed in a columnar format in the order in which they are listed in the EXHIBIT statement.

SUMMARY

COBOL Sort

Format

```
SORT file-name-1
      {ASCENDING  }
   ON {DESCENDING }    KEY data-name-1 [data-name-2] . . .

      {ASCENDING  }
  [ON {DESCENDING }    KEY data-name-3 [data-name-4] . . .] . . .

  [COLLATING SEQUENCE IS alphabet-name]
 {USING file-name-2 [file-name-3] . . .                       }
 {INPUT PROCEDURE IS section-name-1                           }
 {                                {THROUGH}                   }
 {                              [ {THRU   }   section-name-2] }

 {GIVING file-name-4                                          }
 {OUTPUT PROCEDURE is section-name-3                          }
 {                                {THROUGH}                   }
 {                              [ {THRU   }   section-name-4] }
```

SD

Format

```
SD file-name
   [RECORD CONTAINS [integer-1 TO] integer-2 CHARACTERS]
   [DATA {RECORD IS   } data-name-1 [data-name-2]. . . ].
         {RECORDS ARE }
```
```

RELEASE

Format

```
RELEASE record-name [FROM identifier]
```

RETURN

Format

```
RETURN file-name [INTO identifier]
    AT END imperative statement
```

EXHIBIT

Format

```
EXHIBIT {NAMED          } {identifier-1} [identifier-2] . . .
        {CHANGED NAMED  } {literal-1   } [literal-2   ]
        {CHANGED        }
```

EXERCISES

I. The following are eight data records from a personnel file that have been transferred to a sort file. The record layout of the sort file is shown following the data. Each question is in the form of a KEY clause from a SORT statement. Rearrange the records as they would be rearranged by a sort with the key clause(s) as specified.

```
1. ASCENDING KEY SORT-DIVISION
                 SORT-LAST-NAME
2. DESCENDING KEY SORT-HIRE-DATE
3. ASCENDING KEY SORT-BIRTH-DATE
4. ASCENDING KEY SORT-LAST-NAME
                 SORT-FIRST-INITIAL
```

```
Ø8JOHNSON              K45Ø617730300
14SMYTHE               B6Ø1226841115
Ø5RIVERSIDE            T38Ø118670822
Ø9CARSON               P58Ø611820227
Ø9SMYTHE                53Ø408841114
14HILL                 N6Ø113Ø86Ø7Ø1
Ø5JOHNSTONE            L55Ø32Ø791212
Ø9HOOVER               W32Ø9Ø564Ø63Ø
```

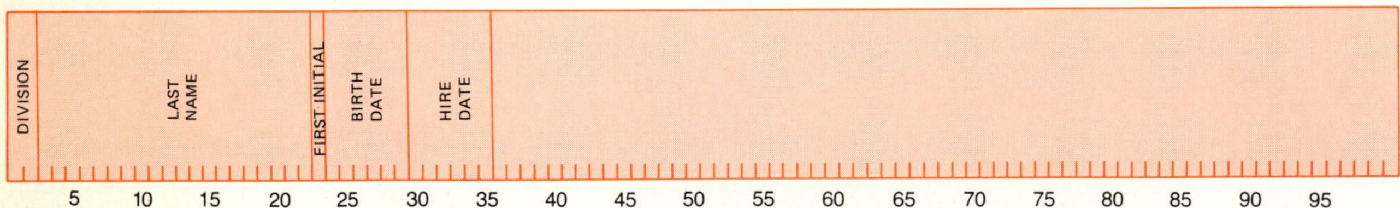

II. Each of the following specifies a file-handling combination for a COBOL sort. Each associated program will have only three files: a disk input file, a sort file, and a disk or print output file. Mark all answers that represent instructions which are likely to appear in the program.

1. INPUT PROCEDURE/OUTPUT PROCEDURE
   (a) OPEN input disk file
   (b) OPEN sort file
   (c) RELEASE sort record

(d) RETURN input disk record
(e) WRITE output print record

2. USING/GIVING
(a) OPEN input disk file
(b) OPEN sort file
(c) RELEASE sort record
(d) RETURN sort file
(e) WRITE output disk record

3. USING/OUTPUT PROCEDURE
(a) OPEN input disk file
(b) OPEN sort file
(c) RELEASE sort record
(d) RETURN sort file
(e) CLOSE sort file

4. INPUT PROCEDURE/GIVING
(a) OPEN sort file
(b) READ input disk file
(c) RELEASE sort record
(d) CLOSE input disk file
(e) RETURN sort file

III. Each of the following is a general description of a program requiring a sort. Choose the most likely *combination* of file-handling procedures for each program.

1. A disk input file is to be sorted in part number sequence. A report containing all of the data from the input file should be printed in the new sequence.
(a) INPUT PROCEDURE/GIVING
(b) USING/GIVING
(c) INPUT PROCEDURE/OUTPUT PROCEDURE
(d) USING/OUTPUT PROCEDURE

2. A disk input file is to be sorted in ascending order on the requested shipping date within each branch office. The objective is to produce a new disk file for use in another program.
(a) INPUT PROCEDURE/GIVING
(b) USING/GIVING
(c) INPUT PROCEDURE/OUTPUT PROCEDURE
(d) USING/OUTPUT PROCEDURE

3. A disk input file contains inventory data. All items of inventory whose quantity is below its reorder level should be sorted by vendor code. A printed report of these selected items should be produced.
(a) INPUT PROCEDURE/GIVING
(b) USING/GIVING
(c) INPUT PROCEDURE/OUTPUT PROCEDURE
(d) USING/OUTPUT PROCEDURE

4. A new disk file is to be created from an existing inventory file. The new file should contain the data for Branch 1 only. There are five branches on the original file.
(a) INPUT PROCEDURE/GIVING
(b) USING/GIVING
(c) INPUT PROCEDURE/OUTPUT PROCEDURE
(d) USING/OUTPUT PROCEDURE

PROJECTS

For each of the following specifications and input record layouts, design a print chart and code a COBOL program that satisfies the specification.

PROJECT 10–1 Payroll

PROGRAM SPECIFICATION

Program Name: PAY10

Program Function:

This program will produce a disk file which is in sequence by employee name.

Input Files:

I. PAYROLL-FILE

INPUT DEVICE:	DISK
FILE ORGANIZATION:	SEQUENTIAL
RECORD LENGTH:	80 BYTES
FILE SEQUENCE:	ASCENDING ON DIVISION / DEPARTMENT

Output Files:

I. NAME-FILE

OUTPUT DEVICE:	DISK
FILE ORGANIZATION:	SEQUENTIAL
RECORD LENGTH:	40 BYTES
FILE SEQUENCE:	ASCENDING ON EMPLOYEE NAME

Processing and Output Requirements:

Only the employee name and social security number from each record in the input file are to be included in the output file.

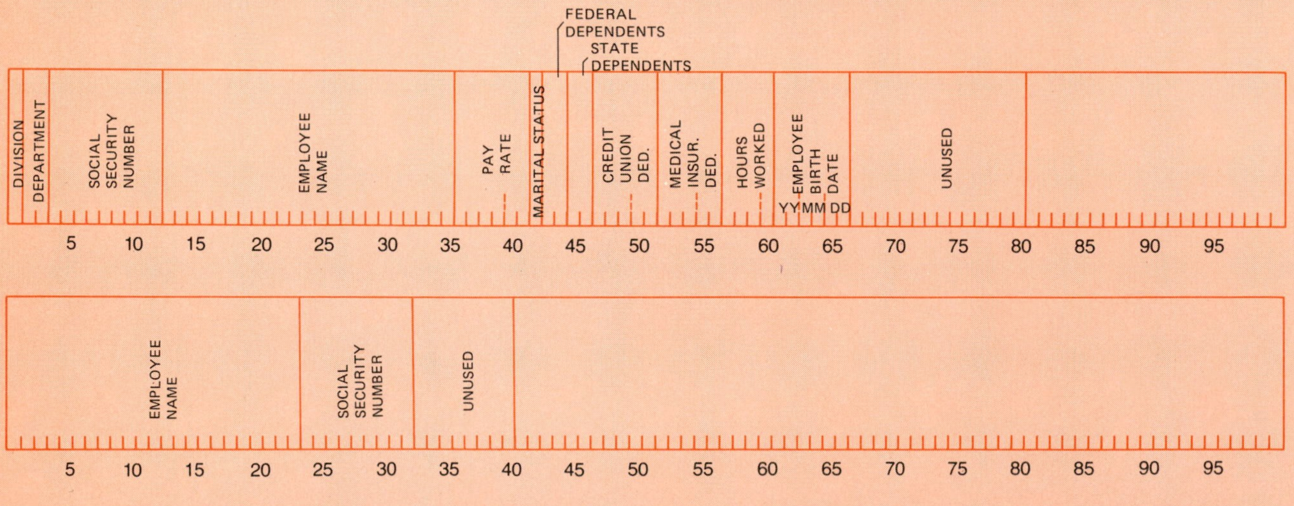

PROGRAM SPECIFICATION

Program Name: INV10

Program Function:

This program will produce a printed report which lists all items whose quantity on hand is at or below the reorder level. Items will appear in order by annual usage (descending) within vendor code (ascending).

Input Files:

I. INVENTORY-FILE

INPUT DEVICE:	DISK
FILE ORGANIZATION:	SEQUENTIAL
RECORD LENGTH:	80 BYTES
FILE SEQUENCE:	ASCENDING ON INVENTORY / STOCK NUMBER

Output Files:

I. PRINT-FILE

OUTPUT DEVICE:	PRINTER
RECORD LENGTH:	133 BYTES

Processing Requirements:

Only records for which the reorder level is greater than or equal to the quantity on hand should be printed. All fields from the input are to be included in the output.

Output Requirements:

The following are formatting requirements for the report:

1. Each page of the report should include:
   (a) a main heading which includes the company name, the report name, and the report date.
   (b) column headings which describe the items printed underneath them.
2. Detail lines are to be double spaced.

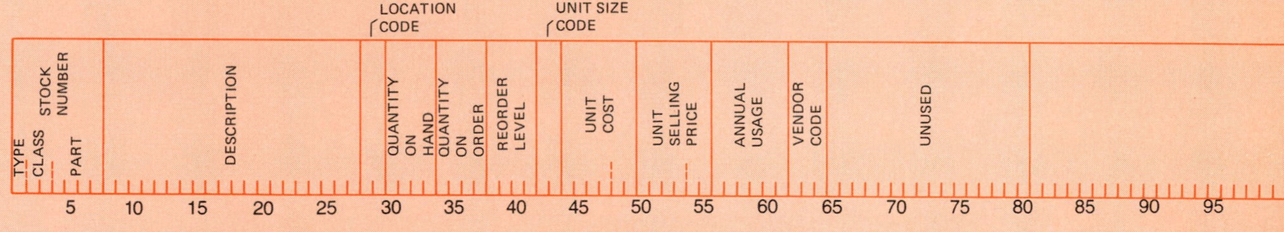

PROGRAM SPECIFICATION

Program Name: AP10

Program Function:

This program will produce a disk file which contains all records from the input file. The new file will maintain the same record format. The records in the new file will be arranged in ascending order by vendor number and in ascending order by invoice date within each vendor number.

Input Files:

I. ACCOUNTS-PAYABLE-FILE

INPUT DEVICE:	DISK
FILE ORGANIZATION:	SEQUENTIAL
RECORD LENGTH:	80 BYTES
FILE SEQUENCE:	ASCENDING ON DIVISION / CONTROL NBR

Output Files:

I. VENDOR-FILE

OUTPUT DEVICE:	DISK
FILE ORGANIZATION:	SEQUENTIAL
RECORD LENGTH:	80 BYTES
FILE SEQUENCE:	ASCENDING VENDOR-NBR / INVOICE-DATE

Processing and Output Requirements:

All records from the ORDER-FILE are to appear in the VENDOR-FILE. The record format for the two files will be identical. The ORDER-FILE is to be sorted by INVOICE-DATE (ascending) within VENDOR-NUMBER (ascending).

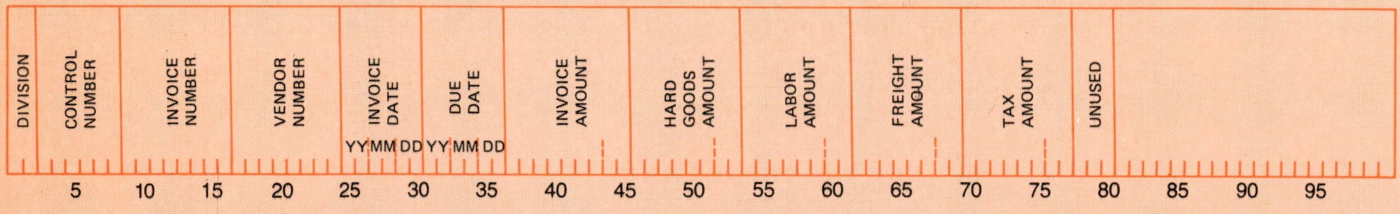

PROJECT 10–4 Pension

PROGRAM SPECIFICATION

Program Name: PEN10

Program Function:

This program will produce a printed report of employees in ascending order by birth date. The listing will include all fields from the input record.

Input Files:

I. PENSION-FILE

INPUT DEVICE:	DISK
FILE ORGANIZATION:	SEQUENTIAL
RECORD LENGTH:	80 BYTES
FILE SEQUENCE:	ASCENDING ON DIVISION / DEPARTMENT

Output Files:

I. PRINT-FILE

OUTPUT DEVICE:	PRINTER
RECORD LENGTH:	133 BYTES

Processing Requirements:

All records from the ORDER-FILE are to be sorted in ascending order by birth date. A printed report made from the sorted file should include all fields that appear on the input record.

Output Requirements:

The following are formatting requirements for the report:

1. Each page of the report should contain:
   (a) a main heading which includes the company name, the report name, the report date, and a page number.
   (b) column headings which describe the items printed underneath them.
2. Detail lines should include all fields from the input.
3. Detail lines should be double spaced.

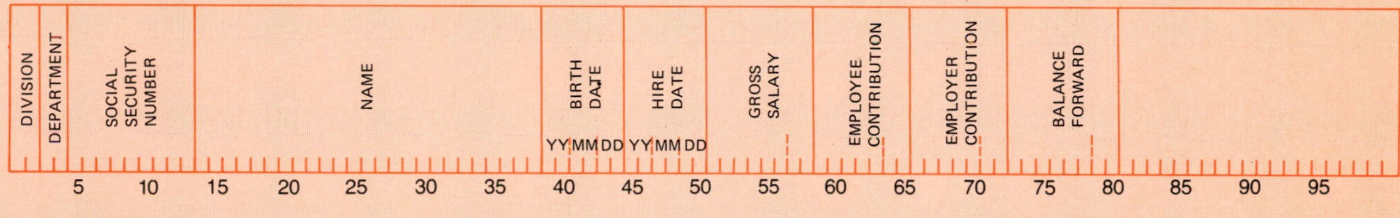

PROJECT 10–5 Bill of Materials

PROGRAM SPECIFICATION

Program Name: BOM10

Program Function:

This program will produce a printed report of a bill-of-materials file which will include the extended cost. The report will be in sequence by master part number.

Input Files:

I.

BILL-OF-MATERIALS-FILE

INPUT DEVICE:	DISK
FILE ORGANIZATION:	SEQUENTIAL

RECORD LENGTH: 55 BYTES
FILE SEQUENCE: ASCENDING ON DIVISION / PRODUCT LINE

Output Files:

I. PRINT-FILE

OUTPUT DEVICE: PRINTER
RECORD LENGTH: 133 BYTES

Processing Requirements:

Each record from the bill-of-materials file should be printed on one line of the output report. Extended cost (quantity times cost) is to be calculated for each record. Records are to be in sequence by master part number.

Output Requirements:

The following are formatting requirements for the report:

1. Each page of the report should contain:
   (a) a main heading which includes the company name, the report name, the report date, and a page number.
   (b) column headings which describe the items printed underneath them.
2. Detail lines should include all fields from the input and the extended cost.
3. Detail lines should be double spaced.

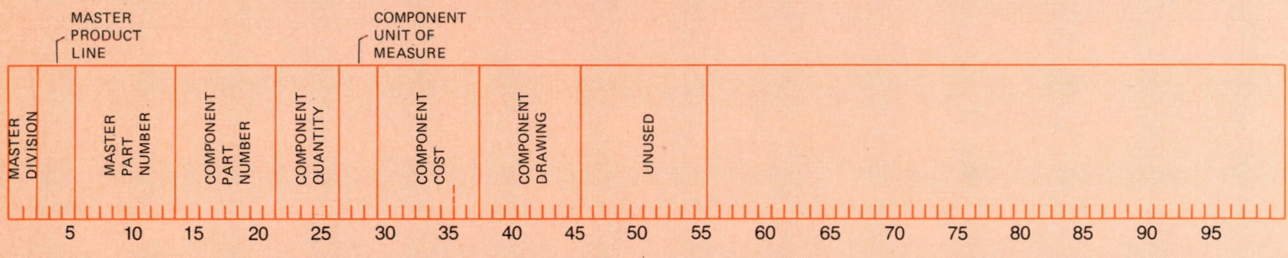

PROJECT 10–6 Cost

PROGRAM SPECIFICATION

Program Name: COST10

Program Function:

The program will product a printed report in sequence by description. The report will include only those records from product lines less than 100.

Input Files:

I. COST-FILE

INPUT DEVICE: DISK
FILE ORGANIZATION: SEQUENTIAL
RECORD LENGTH: 75 BYTES
FILE SEQUENCE: ASCENDING ON DIVISION / PRODUCT LINE

Output Files:

I. PRINT-FILE

OUTPUT DEVICE: PRINTER
RECORD LENGTH: 133 BYTES

Processing Requirements:

Each record from the cost file should be printed on one line of the output report. The report is to include only those records whose product line is less than 100. All input fields should appear on the output.

Output Requirements:

The following are formatting requirements for the report:

1. Each page of the report should contain:
   (a) a main heading which includes the company name, the report name, the report date, and a page number.
   (b) column headings which describe the items printed underneath them.
2. Detail lines should include all fields from the input.
3. Detail lines should be double spaced.

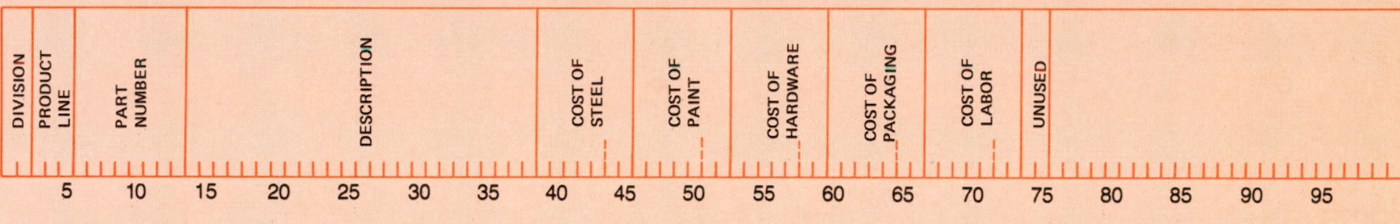

APPENDIX A: Reserved Words

ACCEPT
ACCESS
ADD
ADVANCING
AFTER
ALL
ALPHABET
ALPHABETIC
ALPHABETIC-LOWER
ALPHABETIC-UPPER
ALPHANUMERIC
ALPHANUMERIC-EDITED
ALSO
ALTER
ALTERNATE
AND
ANY
ARE
AREA
AREAS
ASCENDING
ASSIGN
AT
AUTHOR

BEFORE
BINARY
BLANK
BLOCK
BOTTOM
BY

CALL
CANCEL
CD
CF
CH
CHARACTER
CHARACTERS
CLASS
CLOSE
CODE
CODE-SET
COLLATING
COLUMN
COMMA
COMMON
COMMUNICATION
COMP
COMPUTATIONAL
COMPUTE
CONFIGURATION
CONTAINS
CONTENT
CONTINUE
CONTROL
CONTROLS
CONVERTING
COPY
CORR
CORRESPONDING
COUNT
CURRENCY

DATA
DATE
DATE-COMPILED
DATE-WRITTEN
DAY
DAY-OF-WEEK
DE
DEBUG-CONTENTS
DEBUG-ITEM
DEBUG-LINE
DEBUG-NAME
DEBUG-SUB-1
DEBUG-SUB-2
DEBUG-SUB-3
DEBUGGING
DECIMAL-POINT
DECLARATIVES
DELETE
DELIMITED
DELIMITER
DEPENDING
DESCENDING
DESTINATION
DETAIL
DISABLE
DISPLAY
DIVIDE
DIVISION
DOWN
DUPLICATES
DYNAMIC

EGI
ELSE
EMI
ENABLE
END
END-ADD
END-CALL
END-COMPUTE
END-DELETE
END-DIVIDE
END-EVALUATE
END-IF
END-MULTIPLY
END-OF-PAGE
END-PERFORM
END-READ
END-RECEIVE
END-RETURN
END-REWRITE
END-SEARCH
END-START
END-STRING
END-SUBTRACT
END-UNSTRING
END-WRITE
ENVIRONMENT
EOP
EQUAL
ERROR
ESI
EVALUATE
EXCEPTION
EXIT
EXTEND
EXTERNAL

FALSE
FD
FILE
FILE-CONTROL
FILLER
FINAL
FIRST
FOOTING
FOR
FROM

GENERATE
GIVING
GLOBAL
GO
GREATER
GROUP

HEADING
HIGH-VALUE
HIGH-VALUES

I-O
I-O-CONTROL
IDENTIFICATION
IF
IN
INDEX
INDEXED
INDICATE
INITIAL
INITIALIZE
INITIATE
INPUT
INPUT-OUTPUT
INSPECT
INSTALLATION
INTO
INVALID
IS

JUST
JUSTIFIED

KEY

LABEL
LAST
LEADING
LEFT
LENGTH
LESS
LIMIT
LIMITS
LINAGE
LINAGE-COUNTER
LINE
LINE-COUNTER
LINES
LINKAGE

LOCK
LOW-VALUE
LOW-VALUES

MERGE
MESSAGE
MODE
MOVE
MULTIPLE
MULTIPLY

NATIVE
NEGATIVE
NEXT
NO
NOT
NUMBER
NUMERIC
NUMERIC-EDITED

OBJECT-COMPUTER
OCCURS
OF
OFF
OMITTED
ON
OPEN
OPTIONAL
OR
ORDER
ORGANIZATION
OTHER
OUTPUT
OVERFLOW

PACKED-DECIMAL
PADDING
PAGE
PAGE-COUNTER
PERFORM
PF
PH
PIC
PICTURE
PLUS
POINTER
POSITION
POSITIVE
PRINTING
PROCEDURE
PROCEDURES
PROCEED
PROGRAM
PROGRAM-ID
PURGE

QUEUE
QUOTE
QUOTES

RANDOM
RD
READ
RECEIVE
RECORD
RECORDS
REDEFINES
REEL
REFERENCE
REFERENCES
RELATIVE
RELEASE
REMAINDER
REMOVAL
RENAMES
REPLACE
REPLACING
REPORT
REPORTING
REPORTS
RESERVE
RESET
RETURN
REWIND
REWRITE
RF
RH
RIGHT
ROUNDED
RUN

SAME
SD
SEARCH
SECTION
SECURITY
SEGMENT
SEGMENT-LIMIT
SELECT
SEND
SENTENCE
SEPARATE
SEQUENCE
SEQUENTIAL
SET
SIGN
SIZE
SORT
SORT-MERGE
SOURCE
SOURCE-COMPUTER
SPACE
SPACES
SPECIAL-NAMES
STANDARD
STANDARD-1
STANDARD-2
START
STATUS
STOP
STRING
SUB-QUEUE-1
SUB-QUEUE-2
SUB-QUEUE-3
SUBTRACT
SUM
SUPPRESS
SYMBOLIC
SYNC
SYNCHRONIZED

TABLE
TALLYING
TAPE
TERMINAL
TERMINATE
TEST
TEXT
THAN
THEN
THROUGH
THRU
TIME
TIMES
TO
TOP
TRAILING
TRUE
TYPE

UNIT
UNSTRING
UNTIL
UP
UPON
USAGE
USE
USING

VALUE
VALUES
VARYING

WHEN
WITH
WORKING-STORAGE
WRITE

ZERO
ZEROES
ZEROS

+
−
*
/
**
>
<
=
>=
<=

APPENDIX B: COBOL Formats*

GENERAL FORMAT FOR IDENTIFICATION DIVISION

IDENTIFICATION DIVISION.

PROGRAM-ID. program-name [IS {COMMON | INITIAL} PROGRAM]

[AUTHOR. [comment-entry] . . .]

[INSTALLATION. [comment-entry] . . .]

[DATE-WRITTEN. [comment-entry] . . .]

[DATE-COMPILED. [comment-entry] . . .]

[SECURITY. [comment-entry] . . .]

GENERAL FORMAT FOR ENVIRONMENT DIVISION

[ENVIRONMENT DIVISION.

[CONFIGURATION SECTION.

[SOURCE-COMPUTER. [computer-name]]

[OBJECT-COMPUTER. [computer-name]]]

[INPUT-OUTPUT SECTION.

FILE-CONTROL.

SELECT [OPTIONAL] file-name-1

ASSIGN TO {implementor-name-1 | literal-1} . . .]]

GENERAL FORMAT FOR DATA DIVISION

[DATA DIVISION.

[FILE SECTION.

[file-description-entry

{record-description-entry} . . .] . . .

[sort-merge-file-description-entry

{record-description-entry} . . .] . . .

[report-file-description-entry] . . .]

[WORKING-STORAGE SECTION.

[77-level-description-entry | record-description-entry] . . .]

[LINKAGE SECTION.

[77-level-description-entry | record-description-entry] . . .]

[COMMUNICATION SECTION.

[communication-description-entry

[record-description-entry] . . .] . . .]

***Based on 1985 Standard.**

[REPORT SECTION.
[report-description-entry
{report-group-description-entry} . . .] . . .]]

GENERAL FORMAT FOR FILE DESCRIPTION ENTRY

Sequential File:

FD file-name-1
[IS EXTERNAL]
[IS GLOBAL]

[BLOCK CONTAINS [integer-1 TO] integer-2 {RECORDS | CHARACTERS}]

[RECORD {CONTAINS integer-3 CHARACTERS | IS VARYING IN SIZE [[FROM integer-4] [TO integer-5] CHARACTERS] [DEPENDING ON data-name-1] | CONTAINS integer-6 *TO* integer-7 CHARACTERS}]

[LABEL {RECORD IS | RECORDS ARE} {STANDARD | OMITTED}]

[VALUE OF {implementor-name-1 IS {data-name-2 | literal-1}} . . .]

[*DATA* {RECORD IS | RECORDS ARE} {data-name-3} . . .]

GENERAL FORMAT FOR DATA DESCRIPTION ENTRY

Format 1:

level-number [data-name-1 | FILLER]
[REDEFINES data-name-2]
[IS EXTERNAL]
[IS GLOBAL]

[{PICTURE | PIC} IS character-string]

[[USAGE IS] {BINARY | COMPUTATIONAL | COMP | DISPLAY | INDEX | PACKED-DECIMAL}]

[[SIGN IS] {LEADING | TRAILING} [SEPARATE CHARACTER]]

[OCCURS integer-2 TIMES
[{ASCENDING | DESCENDING} KEY IS {data-name-3} . . .] . . .
[INDEXED BY {index-name-1} . . .]
| OCCURS integer-1 TO integer-2 TIMES DEPENDING ON data-name-4
[{ASCENDING | DESCENDING} KEY IS {data-name-3} . . .] . . .
[INDEXED BY {index-name-1} . . .]]

[{SYNCHRONIZED | SYNC} [LEFT | RIGHT]]

$\left[\begin{Bmatrix}\underline{\text{JUSTIFIED}}\\\underline{\text{JUST}}\end{Bmatrix}\text{ RIGHT}\right]$

[BLANK WHEN ZERO]

[VALUE IS literal-1].

Format 2:

66 data-name-1 RENAMES data-name-2 $\left[\begin{Bmatrix}\underline{\text{THROUGH}}\\\underline{\text{THRU}}\end{Bmatrix}\text{ data-name-3}\right]$

Format 3:

88 condition-name-1 $\begin{Bmatrix}\underline{\text{VALUE}}\text{ IS}\\\underline{\text{VALUES}}\text{ ARE}\end{Bmatrix}\left\{\text{literal-1 }\left[\begin{Bmatrix}\underline{\text{THROUGH}}\\\underline{\text{THRU}}\end{Bmatrix}\text{ literal-2}\right]\right\}\ldots$

GENERAL FORMAT FOR PROCEDURE DIVISION

Format 1:

[PROCEDURE DIVISION [USING {data-name-1} . . .].

[DECLARATIVES.

{section-name SECTION [segment-number].

USE statement.

[paragraph-name.

[sentence] . . .] . . . } . . .

END DECLARATIVES.]

{section-name SECTION [segment-number].

[paragraph-name.

[sentence] . . .] . . . } . . .]

Format 2:

[PROCEDURE DIVISION [USING {data-name-1} . . .].

{paragraph-name.

[sentence] . . . } . . .]

GENERAL FORMAT FOR COBOL VERBS

ACCEPT identifier-1 [FROM mnemonic-name-1]

ACCEPT identifier-2 FROM $\begin{Bmatrix}\underline{\text{DATE}}\\\underline{\text{DAY}}\\\underline{\text{DAY-OF-WEEK}}\\\underline{\text{TIME}}\end{Bmatrix}$

ACCEPT cd-name-1 MESSAGE COUNT

ADD $\begin{Bmatrix}\text{identifier-1}\\\text{literal-1}\end{Bmatrix}\ldots$ TO {identifier-2 [ROUNDED]} . . .

[ON SIZE ERROR imperative-statement-1]

[NOT ON SIZE ERROR imperative-statement-2]

[END-ADD]

ADD $\begin{Bmatrix}\text{identifier-1}\\\text{literal-1}\end{Bmatrix}\ldots$ TO $\begin{Bmatrix}\text{identifier-2}\\\text{literal-2}\end{Bmatrix}$

GIVING {identifier-3 [ROUNDED]} . . .

[ON SIZE ERROR imperative-statement-1]

[NOT ON SIZE ERROR imperative-statement-2]

[END-ADD]

```
ADD {CORRESPONDING} identifier-1 TO identifier-2 [ROUNDED]
    {CORR         }
   [ON SIZE ERROR imperative-statement-1]
   [NOT ON SIZE ERROR imperative-statement-2]
   [END-ADD]

ALTER {procedure-name-1 TO [PROCEED TO] procedure-name-2} . . .

CALL {identifier-1} [USING {[BY REFERENCE] {identifier-2} . . .} . . .]
     {literal-1   }        {BY CONTENT {identifier-2} . . .    }
   [ON OVERFLOW imperative-statement-1 [END-CALL]]

CALL {identifier-1} [USING {[BY REFERENCE] {identifier-2} . . .} . . .]
     {literal-1   }        {BY CONTENT {identifier-2} . . .    }
   [ON EXCEPTION imperative-statement-1]
   [NOT ON EXCEPTION imperative-statement-2]
   [END-CALL]

CANCEL {identifier-1} . . .
       {literal-1   }

CLOSE {file-name-1 [ {REEL} [FOR REMOVAL]         ]} . . .
                   [ {UNIT}                       ]
                   [                              ]
                   [ WITH {NO REWIND}             ]
                   [      {LOCK     }             ]

CLOSE {file-name-1 [WITH LOCK]} . . .

COMPUTE{identifier-1 [ROUNDED]} . . . = arithmetic-expression-1
   [ON SIZE ERROR imperative-statement-1]
   [NOT ON SIZE ERROR imperative-statement-2]
   [END-COMPUTE]

CONTINUE

DELETE file-name-1 RECORD
   [INVALID KEY improvement-statement-1]
   [NOT INVALID KEY imperative-statement-2]
   [END-DELETE]

DISABLE {INPUT [TERMINAL]} cd-name-1
        {I-O TERMINAL    }
        {OUTPUT          }

DISPLAY {identifier-1} . . . [UPON mnemonic-name-1] [WITH NO ADVANCING]
        {literal-1   }

DIVIDE {identifer-1} INTO {identifier-2 [ROUNDED]} . . .
       {literal-1  }

   [ON SIZE ERROR imperative-statement-1]

   [NOT ON SIZE ERROR imperative-statement-2]

   [END-DIVIDE]

DIVIDE {identifier-1} INTO {identifier-2}
       {literal-1   }      {literal-2   }
```

GIVING {identifier-3 [ROUNDED]} . . .

[ON SIZE ERROR imperative-statement-1]

[NOT ON SIZE ERROR imperative-statement-2]

[END-DIVIDE

DIVIDE {identifier 1 | literal-1} BY {identifier-2 | literal-2}

GIVING {identifier-3 [ROUNDED]} . . .

[ON SIZE ERROR imperative-statement-1]

[NOT ON SIZE ERROR imperative-statement-2]

[END-DIVIDE]

DIVIDE {identifier 1 | literal-1} INTO {identifier-2 | literal-2} GIVING identifier-3 [ROUNDED]

REMAINDER identifier-4

[ON SIZE ERROR imperative-statement-1]

[NOT ON SIZE ERROR imperative-statement-2]

[END-DIVIDE]

DIVIDE {identifier 1 | literal-1} BY {identifier-2 | literal-2} GIVING identifier-3 [ROUNDED]

REMAINDER identifier-4

[ON SIZE ERROR imperative-statement-1]

[NOT ON SIZE ERROR imperative-statement-2]

[END-DIVIDE]

ENABLE {INPUT [TERMINAL] | I-O TERMINAL | OUTPUT} cd-name-1

EVALUATE {identifier-1 | literal-1 | expression-1 | TRUE | FALSE} [ALSO {identifier-2 | literal-2 | expression-2 | TRUE | FALSE}] . . .

((WHEN

{ANY | condition-1 | TRUE | FALSE | [NOT] {identifier-3 | literal-3 | arithmetic-expression-1} [{THROUGH | THRU} {identifier-4 | literal-4 | arithmetic-expression-2}]}

(ALSO

```
  ⎧ANY                                                                          ⎫⎤  ⎫
  ⎪condition-2                                                                  ⎪⎥  ⎪
  ⎪TRUE                                                                         ⎪⎥  ⎪
  ⎨FALSE                                                                        ⎬⎥  ⎬
  ⎪      ⎧⎧identifier-5          ⎫ ⎡⎧THROUGH⎫ ⎧identifier-6          ⎫⎤⎫        ⎪⎥  ⎪
  ⎪[NOT] ⎨⎨literal-5             ⎬ ⎢⎨       ⎬ ⎨literal-6             ⎬⎥⎬        ⎪⎥ ...⎪ ...
  ⎩      ⎩⎩arithmetic-expression-3⎭ ⎣⎩THRU   ⎭ ⎩arithmetic-expression-4⎭⎦⎭       ⎭⎦  ⎭

  imperative-statement-1} ...

  [WHEN OTHER imperative-statement-2]

  [END-EVALUATE]

EXIT

EXIT PROGRAM

GENERATE {data-name-1  }
         {report-name-1}

GO TO [procedure-name-1]

GO TO {procedure-name-1} ... DEPENDING ON identifier-1

IF condition-1 THEN {{statement-1} ...} {ELSE {statement-2} ... [END-IF]}
                    {NEXT SENTENCE    } {ELSE NEXT SENTENCE              }
                                        {END-IF                          }
INITIALIZE {identifier-1} ...

  ⎡          ⎧⎧ALPHABETIC          ⎫                              ⎫    ⎤
  ⎢          ⎪⎪ALPHANUMERIC        ⎪                              ⎪    ⎥
  ⎢REPLACING ⎨⎨NUMERIC             ⎬ DATA BY {identifier-2}       ⎬ ...⎥
  ⎢          ⎪⎪ALPHANUMERIC-EDITED ⎪         {literal-1   }       ⎪    ⎥
  ⎣          ⎩⎩NUMERIC-EDITED      ⎭                              ⎭    ⎦

INITIATE {report-name-1} ...

INSPECT identifier-1 TALLYING

  ⎧                  ⎧CHARACTERS [{BEFORE} INITIAL {identifier-4}] ...                                 ⎫    ⎫
  ⎪                  ⎪            {AFTER }         {literal-2   }                                      ⎪    ⎪
  ⎨identifier-2 FOR  ⎨                                                                                 ⎬ ...⎬ ...
  ⎪                  ⎪{ALL    } {{identifier-3} [{BEFORE} INITIAL {identifier-4}] ... } ...            ⎪    ⎪
  ⎩                  ⎩{LEADING} {{literal-1   } [{AFTER }         {literal-2   }]     }                ⎭    ⎭

INSPECT identifier-1 REPLACING

  ⎧CHARACTERS BY {identifier-5} [{BEFORE} INITIAL {identifier-4}] ...                                  ⎫
  ⎪              {literal-3   } [{AFTER }         {literal-2   }]                                      ⎪
  ⎨{ALL    }                                                                                           ⎬ ...
  ⎪{LEADING} {{identifier-3} BY {identifier-5} [{BEFORE} INITIAL {identifier-4}] ... } ...             ⎪
  ⎩{FIRST  } {{literal-1   }    {literal-3   } [{AFTER }         {literal-2   }]     }                 ⎭

INSPECT identifier-1 TALLYING

  ⎧                  ⎧CHARACTERS [{BEFORE} INITIAL {identifier-4}] ...                                 ⎫    ⎫
  ⎪                  ⎪            {AFTER }         {literal-2   }                                      ⎪    ⎪
  ⎨identifier-2 FOR  ⎨                                                                                 ⎬ ...⎬ ...
  ⎪                  ⎪{ALL    } {{identifier-3} [{BEFORE} INITIAL {identifier-4}] ... } ...            ⎪    ⎪
  ⎩                  ⎩{LEADING} {{literal-1   } [{AFTER }         {literal-2   }]     }                ⎭    ⎭
```

```
   REPLACING
   { CHARACTERS BY {identifier-5} [ {BEFORE} INITIAL {identifier-4} ] . . .                                      }
   {               {literal-3   } [ {AFTER }         {literal-2   } ]                                          }
   {                                                                                                           }
   { {ALL    } { {identifier-3} BY {identifier-5} [ {BEFORE} INITIAL {identifier-4} ] . . . } . . .            } . . .
   { {LEADING} { {literal-1   }    {literal-3   } [ {AFTER }         {literal-2   } ]       }                  }
   { {FIRST  }                                                                                                 }

INSPECT identifier-1 CONVERTING {identifier-6} TO {identifier-7}
                                {literal-4   }    {literal-5   }
   [ {BEFORE} INITIAL {identifier-4} ] . . .
   [ {AFTER }         {literal-2   } ]

MERGE file-name-1 { ON {ASCENDING } KEY {data-name-1} . . . } . . .
                  {    {DESCENDING}                         }
   [COLLATING SEQUENCE IS alphabet-name-1]
   USING file-name-2 {file-name-3} . . .
   { OUTPUT PROCEDURE IS procedure-name-1 [ {THROUGH} procedure-name-2 ] }
   { GIVING {file-name-4} . . .           [ {THRU   }                  ] }

MOVE {identifier-1} TO {identifier-2} . . .
     {literal-1   }

MOVE {CORRESPONDING} identifier-1 TO identifier-2
     {CORR         }

MULTIPLY {identifier-1} BY {identifier-2 [ROUNDED]} . . .
         {literal-1   }
   [ON SIZE ERROR imperative-statement-1]
   [NOT ON SIZE ERROR imperative-statement-2]
   [END-MULTIPLY]

MULTIPLY {identifier-1} BY {identifier-2}
         {literal-1   }    {literal-2   }
   GIVING {identifier-3 [ROUNDED]} . . .
   [ON SIZE ERROR imperative-statement-1]
   [NOT ON SIZE ERROR imperative-statement-2]
   [END-MULTIPLY]

     { INPUT {file-name-1 [WITH NO REWIND]} . . .      }
OPEN { OUTPUT {file-name-2 [WITH NO REWIND]} . . .     } . . .
     { I-O {file-name-3} . . .                         }
     { EXTEND {file-name-4} . . .                      }

     { INPUT {file-name-1} . . .   }
OPEN { OUTPUT {file-name-2} . . .  } . . .
     { I-O {file-name-3} . . .     }
     { EXTEND {file-name-4} . . .  }

OPEN { OUTPUT {file-name-1 [WITH NO REWIND]} . . . } . . .
     { EXTEND {file-name-2} . . .                  }

PERFORM [ procedure-name-1 [ {THROUGH} procedure-name-2 ] ]
        [                  [ {THRU   }                  ] ]
   [imperative-statement-1 END-PERFORM]
```

```
PERFORM [procedure-name-1 [{THROUGH | THRU} procedure-name-2]]
    {identifier-1 | integer-1} TIMES [imperative-statement-1 END-PERFORM]

PERFORM [procedure-name-1 [{THROUGH | THRU} procedure-name-2]]
    [WITH TEST {BEFORE | AFTER}] UNTIL condition-1
    [imperative-statement-1 END-PERFORM]

PERFORM [procedure-name-1 [{THROUGH | THRU} procedure-name-2]]
    [WITH TEST {BEFORE | AFTER}]
    VARYING {identifier-2 | index-name-1} FROM {identifier-3 | index-name-2 | literal-1}
        BY {identifier-4 | literal-2} UNTIL condition-1
      [AFTER {identifier-5 | literal-3} FROM {identifier-6 | index-name-4 | literal-3}
          BY {identifier-7 | literal-4} UNTIL condition-2] . . .
    [imperative-statement-1 END-PERFORM]

PURGE cd-name-1

READ file-name-1 [NEXT] RECORD [INTO identifier-1]
    [AT END imperative-statement-1]
    [NOT AT END imperative-statement-2]
    [END-READ]

READ file-name-1 RECORD [INTO identifier-1]
    [INVALID KEY imperative-statement-3]
    [NOT INVALID KEY imperative-statement-4]
    [END-READ]

READ file-name-1 RECORD [INTO identifier-1]
    [KEY IS data-name-1]
    [INVALID KEY imperative-statement-3]
    [NOT INVALID KEY imperative-statement-4]
    [END-READ]

RECEIVE cd-name-1 {MESSAGE | SEGMENT} INTO identifier-1
    [NO DATA imperative-statement-1]
    [WITH DATA imperative-statement-2]
    [END-RECEIVE]

RELEASE record-name-1 [FROM identifier-1]
```

```
RETURN file-name-1 RECORD [INTO identifier-1]
   AT END imperative-statement-1
   [NOT AT END imperative-statement-2]
   [END-RETURN]
```

```
REWRITE record-name-1 [FROM identifier-1]
```

```
REWRITE record-name-1 [FROM identifier-1]
   [INVALID KEY imperative-statement-1]
   [NOT INVALID KEY imperative-statement-2]
   [END-REWRITE]
```

```
SEARCH identifier-1 [VARYING {identifier-2  }]
                             {index-name-1  }
   [AT END imperative-statement-1]
   {WHEN condition-1 {imperative-statement-2}} ...
                     {NEXT SENTENCE         }
   [END-SEARCH]
```

```
SEARCH ALL identifier-1 [AT END imperative-statement-1]
   WHEN {data-name-1 {IS EQUAL TO} {identifier-3             }}
        {            {IS =       } {literal-1                }}
        {                          {arithmetic-expression-1  }}
        {condition-name-1                                     }
    [AND {data-name-2 {IS EQUAL TO} {identifier-4             }}] ...
    [    {            {IS =       } {literal-2                }}]
    [    {                          {arithmetic-expression-2  }}]
    [    {condition-name-2                                     }]
   {imperative-statement-2}
   {NEXT SENTENCE         }
   [END-SEARCH]
```

```
SEND cd-name-1 FROM identifier-1
```

```
                                        {WITH identifier-2}
SEND cd-name-1 [FROM identifier-1]      {WITH ESI         }
                                        {WITH EMI         }
                                        {WITH EGI         }

   [{BEFORE} ADVANCING {{identifier-3} [LINE ] }]
   [{AFTER }           {{integer-1   } [LINES] }]
   [                   {{mnemonic-name-1}      }]
   [                   {{PAGE           }      }]
   [REPLACING LINE]
```

```
SET {index-name-1} ... TO {index-name-2}
    {identifier-1}        {identifier-2}
                          {integer-1   }
```

```
SET {index-name-3} ... {UP BY  } {identifier-3}
                       {DOWN BY} {integer-2   }
```

```
SET {{mnemonic-name-1} ... TO {ON }} ...
                              {OFF}
```

```
SET {condition-name-1} ... TO TRUE
```

```
SORT file-name-1 {ON {ASCENDING } KEY {data-name-1} . . . } . . .
                     {DESCENDING}
    [WITH DUPLICATES IN ORDER]
    [COLLATING SEQUENCE IS alphabet-name-1]
    {INPUT PROCEDURE IS procedure-name-1 [{THROUGH} procedure-name-2]}
    {                                     {THRU   }                  }
    {USING {file-name-2} . . .                                       }
    {OUTPUT PROCEDURE IS procedure-name-3 [{THROUGH} procedure-name-4]}
    {                                      {THRU   }                  }
    {GIVING {file-name-3} . . .                                       }

                        { IS EQUAL TO                      }
                        { IS =                             }
                        { IS GREATER THAN                  }
START file-name-1 [ KEY { IS >                             } data-name-1 ]
                        { IS NOT LESS THAN                 }
                        { IS NOT <                         }
                        { IS GREATER THAN NOR EQUAL TO     }
                        { IS >=                            }
    [INVALID KEY imperative-statement-1]
    [NOT INVALID KEY imperative-statement-2]
    [END-START]

STOP {RUN      }
     {literal-1}

                                                 {identifier-2}
STRING {{identifier-1} . . . DELIMITED BY {literal-2   }} . . . .
        {literal-1   }                           {SIZE        }
    INTO identifier-3
    [WITH POINTER identifier-4]
    [ON OVERFLOW imperative-statement-1]
    [NOT ON OVERFLOW imperative-statement-2]
    [END-STRING]

SUBTRACT {identifier-1} . . . FROM {identifier-3 [ROUNDED]} . . .
         {literal-1   }
    [ON SIZE ERROR imperative-statement-1]
    [NOT ON SIZE ERROR imperative-statement-2]
    [END-SUBTRACT]

SUBTRACT {identifier-1} . . . FROM {identifier-2}
         {literal-1   }            {literal-2   }
    GIVING {identifier-3 [ROUNDED]} . . .
    [ON SIZE ERROR imperative-statement-1]
    [NOT ON SIZE ERROR imperative-statement-2]
    [END-SUBTRACT]

SUBTRACT {CORRESPONDING} identifier-1 FROM identifier-2 [ROUNDED]
         {CORR         }
    [ON SIZE ERROR imperative-statement-1]
    [NOT ON SIZE ERROR imperative-statement-2]
    [END-SUBTRACT]
```

```
SUPPRESS PRINTING

TERMINATE {REPORT-NAME-1} . . .

UNSTRING identifier-1
   [DELIMITED BY [ALL] {identifier-2} [OR [ALL] {identifier-3}] . . . ]
                       {literal-1   }           {literal-2   }
   INTO {identifier-4 [DELIMITER IN identifier-5] [COUNT IN identifier-6]} . . .
   [WITH POINTER identifier-7]
   [TALLYING IN identifier-8]
   [ON OVERFLOW imperative-statement-1]
   [NOT ON OVERFLOW imperative-statement-2]
   [END-UNSTRING]
                                                             {{file-name-1} . . .}
                                                             {INPUT              }
USE [GLOBAL] AFTER STANDARD {EXCEPTION} PROCEDURE ON {OUTPUT             }
                            {ERROR    }                      {I-O                }
                                                             {EXTEND             }

USE [GLOBAL] BEFORE REPORTING identifier-1

                         {cd-name-1                             }
                         {[ALL REFERENCES OF] identifier-1      }
USE FOR DEBUGGING ON {file-name-1                           } . . .
                         {procedure-name-1                      }
                         {ALL PROCEDURES                        }

WRITE record-name-1 [FROM identifier-1]
   [                          {{identifier-2} [LINE ]}]
   [{BEFORE} ADVANCING        {{integer-1   } [LINES]}]
   [{AFTER }                  {                       }]
   [                          {{mnemonic-name-1}      }]
   [                          {{PAGE           }      }]
   [AT {END-OF-PAGE} imperative-statement-1]
   [   {EOP        }                       ]
   [NOT AT {END-OF-PAGE} imperative-statement-2]
   [       {EOP        }                       ]
   [END-WRITE]

WRITE record-name-1 [FROM identifier-1]
   [INVALID KEY imperative-statement-1]
   [NOT INVALID KEY imperative-statement-2]
   [END-WRITE]
```

Index

A

B

C

D

E

F

G

H

I

J

K

L

M

N

O

S

T

U

V

W

Z